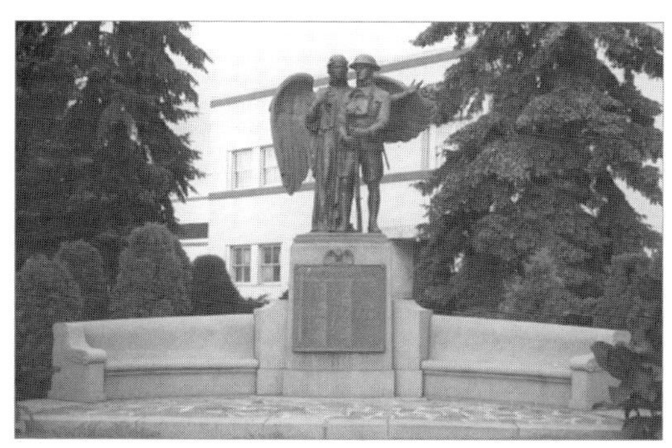

Public Sculpture in Wisconsin

An Atlas of Outdoor Monuments, Memorials & Masterpieces in the Badger State

Anton Rajer
Christine Style

1999
SOS! Save Outdoor Sculpture, Wisconsin

PUBLIC SCULPTURE IN WISCONSIN
An Atlas of Outdoor Monuments, Memorials & Masterpieces
in the Badger State

A collection of essays and an atlas of outdoor monuments, memorials, and masterpieces in Wisconsin, including traditional statuary, veterans monuments, church grotto art, self-taught visionary environments, chainsaw carving, fiberglass creations, Native American effigy mounds, government and corporate public sculpture, and the commissioning, maintenance and conservation of outdoor public sculpture.

© 1999 Anton Rajer, Christine Style

Publisher: *SOS! Wisconsin, Save Outdoor Sculpture* and
Fine Arts Conservation Services, Madison, Wisconsin

Though all attempts were made to include accurate information in this book, some errors probably crept in over a seven year period. The authors accept responsibility for this and apologize for any errors. Please contact us to correct or update the information.

This book commemorates the centennial of the Spanish-American War, 1898-1998.

ISBN: 0-9664180-2-6

Library of Congress: 98-090939

Editing: Michele Gale-Sinex, David Eagan, and Victoria Goff.
Index Editor: Althea A. Reetz

Art Director: Christine Style with graphic design and production assistance from University of Wisconsin-Green Bay students, Jenny Anderson, Heidi Barta, Chad Peters, Kevin Snell, Jamie Schmit, Laurie Voeltz (lead assistant), and Allissa Wied.

Photograph credits: We thank the many people who sent us photographs with their SOS! reports. In addition, particular thanks to Zane Williams, Ron Byers, the State Historical Society of Wisconsin, and Green Bay's Neville Public Museum for their unique photographs.

Printing: Van Lanen Inc., Green Bay, Wisconsin

Distribution: The University of Wisconsin Press, Madison, Wisconsin

Cover Images:

Wisconsin by Daniel Chester French, located in Madison, Dane County

Kau by Deborah Butterfield, located in Wausau, Marathon County

Kit Carson by Fred Smith, located in Phillips, Price County

Indian Chief by Carl Schels, located in Eagle River, Vilas County

G.A.R. Monument located in Beloit, Rock County

Immigrant Mother by Ivan Mestrovic, located in downtown Milwaukee, Milwaukee County

Anidonts by Luis Arata, located in LaCrosse, LaCrosse County

The First Northern Loggers by Lyndon Fayne Pomeroy, located in Green Bay, Brown County

Giant Muskie by F.A.S.T., located in Hayward, Sawyer County

End of the Trail by James Earl Fraser, located in Waupun, Dodge County

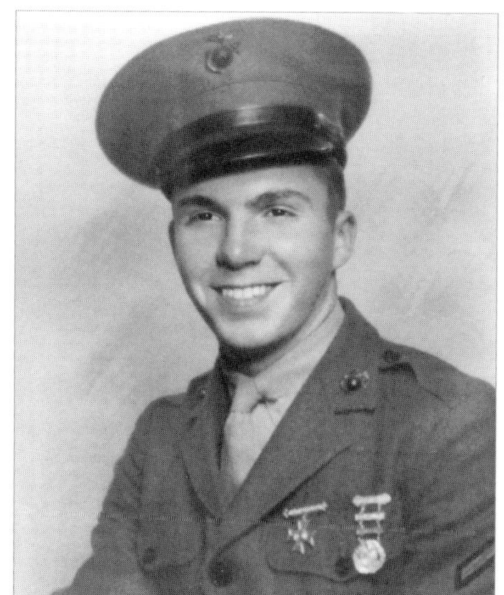

Private Courtenay Style Muehlmeier, 1944

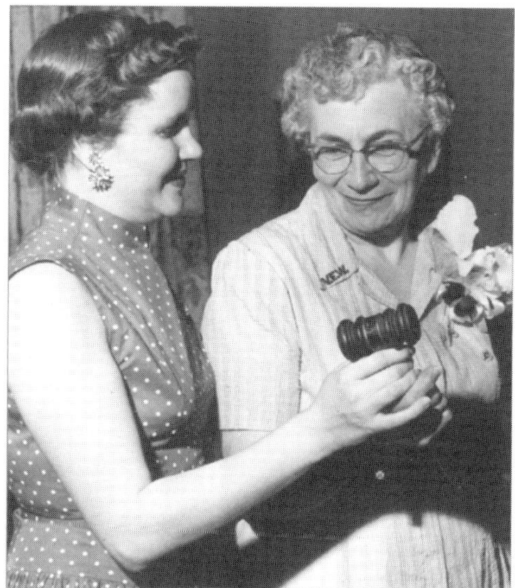

Mildred Johnson (right) receiving the VFW World War I Ladies Auxiliary President's gavel, 1967

DEDICATION

The authors dedicate this book to family members who served in patriotic duty as soldiers and auxiliary personnel.

Courtenay Style Muehlmeier (1924-1945), Christine Style's uncle, gave his life for America in World War II. He served in the 3rd Marines, 1st Division and was killed in action on Iwo Jima.

This book is also dedicated to Alfred (1899-1952) and Mildred (1903-1978) Johnson, Anton Rajer's grandparents. Alfred served in World War I in France as a doughboy, and Mildred was a life-long member of the VFW World War I Ladies Auxiliary and served as treasurer/secretary and president on many occasions.

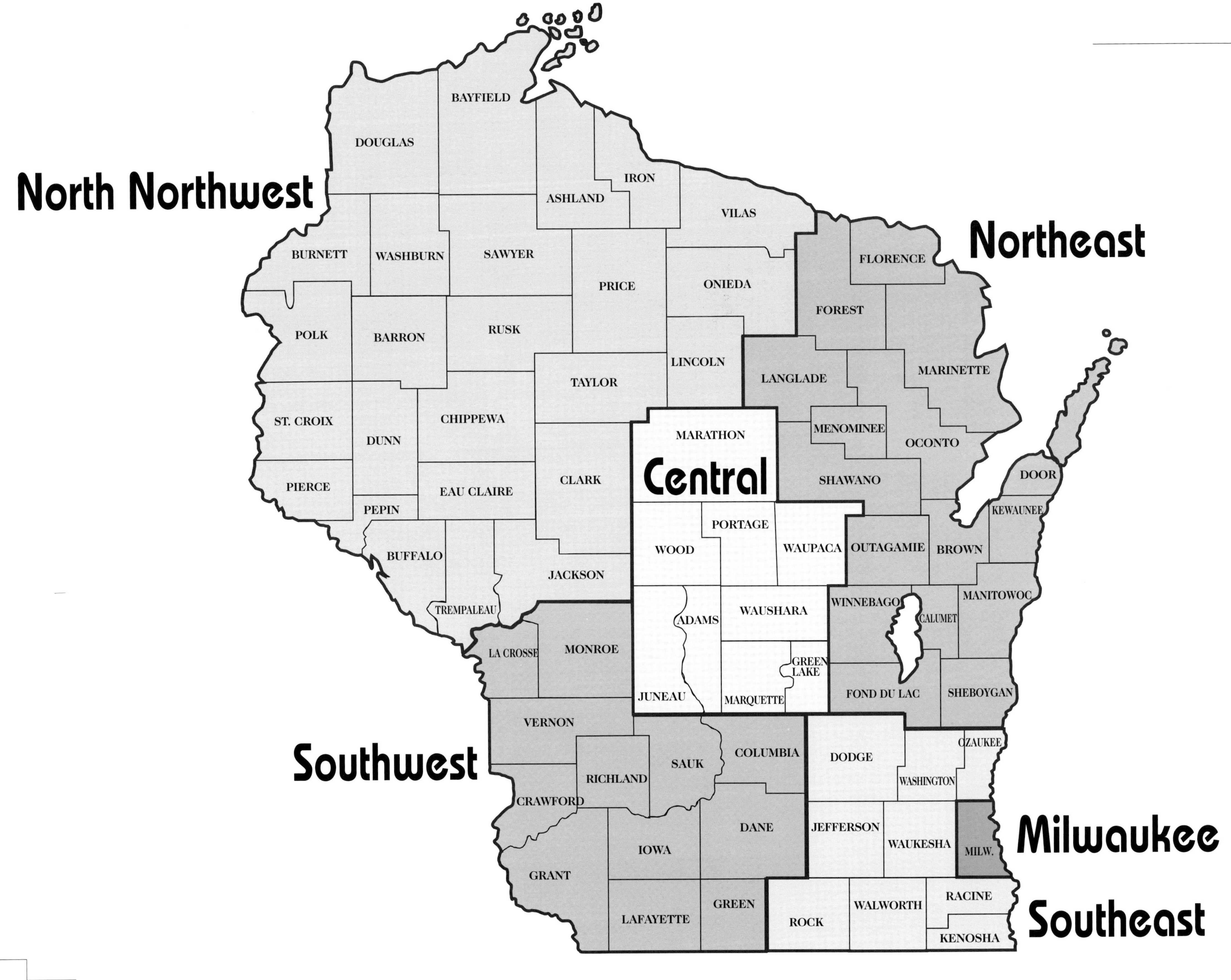

North Northwest
Northeast
Central
Southwest
Milwaukee
Southeast
BAYFIELD
DOUGLAS
IRON
ASHLAND
VILAS
BURNETT
WASHBURN
SAWYER
FLORENCE
FOREST
PRICE
ONIEDA
MARINETTE
POLK
BARRON
RUSK
LINCOLN
LANGLADE
MENOMINEE
OCONTO
ST. CROIX
TAYLOR
MARATHON
DUNN
CHIPPEWA
SHAWANO
DOOR
PIERCE
CLARK
KEWAUNEE
EAU CLAIRE
PEPIN
PORTAGE
BUFFALO
WOOD
WAUPACA
OUTAGAMIE
BROWN
JACKSON
WINNEBAGO
MANITOWOC
TREMPALEAU
WAUSHARA
CALUMET
ADAMS
LA CROSSE
MONROE
GREEN LAKE
JUNEAU
MARQUETTE
FOND DU LAC
SHEBOYGAN
VERNON
OZAUKEE
COLUMBIA
DODGE
SAUK
WASHINGTON
RICHLAND
CRAWFORD
JEFFERSON
WAUKESHA
MILW.
DANE
GRANT
IOWA
RACINE
GREEN
LAFAYETTE
ROCK
WALWORTH
KENOSHA

Public Sculpture in Wisconsin   Contents

SOS! Save Outdoor Sculpture

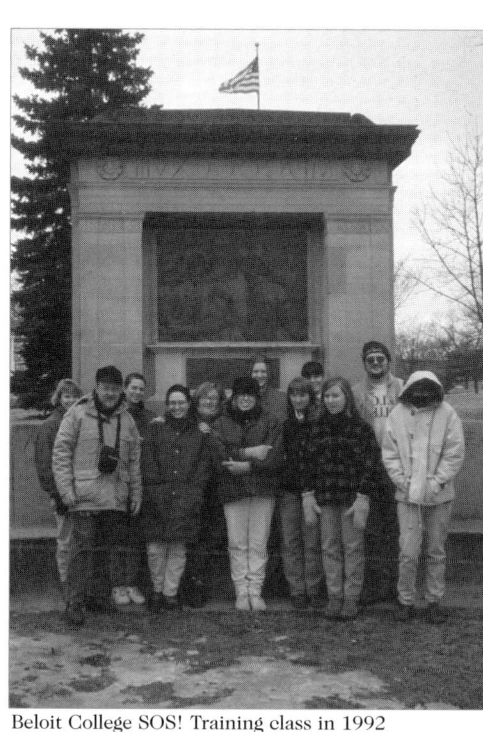

Beloit College SOS! Training class in 1992

The story you are about to read is the summary of an amazing journey of exploration and discovery. It tells of Wisconsin's contribution to the history of public sculpture, not only in our state but throughout America. It is the result of nearly seven years of effort to document public sculpture in Wisconsin.

It started out with a simple question. A noted historian in Madison asked whether public sculpture could be found outside Wisconsin's metropolitan areas. Indeed it could.

The Save Outdoor Sculpture (SOS!) project goal was to locate, identify, and document as many public sculptures as possible in America, including Wisconsin. To this end we worked in Wisconsin with nearly 300 volunteers throughout the state and more than 185 different organizations statewide over the past seven years. In the course of the SOS! survey, volunteers found hundreds of public sculptures—one or more pieces in each of the state's seventy-two counties. The project turned into a truly monumental effort: the inventory currently contains more than seven hundred individual works.

THE HISTORY OF SOS! IN WISCONSIN

The initiative for this project came from Washington, D.C., and the National SOS! Save Outdoor Sculpture Project to locate, document, and inventory all public sculpture in America. To date, SOS!, a program of Heritage Preservation Inc. in cooperation with the Smithsonian Institution's National Museum of American Art, has located more than 32,000 sculptures in the United States, Puerto Rico, and Guam.

In 1991, the State Historical Society of Wisconsin, Division of Historic Preservation, received a grant from SOS! Save Outdoor Sculpture, to locate, document, and inventory the public sculpture in Wisconsin—excluding Milwaukee, which had its own SOS! project.

By 1993, the State Historical Society of Wisconsin determined it could not finish the project. The national SOS! headquarters contacted conservator Anton (Tony) Rajer to see if he would continue working with this project. He was already familiar with the national project since its creation in 1988 by art conservator Arthur Beale of Harvard University. Tony consented to stay with the project and to report its findings and later write a book. The Wisconsin Arts Board then became the fiscal receiver for completion of the project with Tony as project director.

Within five years, more than seven hundred sculptures had been found and documented, far more than anyone expected. The project completion coincided with Wisconsin's Sesquicentennial. A grant from the Wisconsin Humanities Council and the Sesquicentennial Commission allowed SOS! Wisconsin to turn the mountains of data and documentation of this grassroots effort into the publication you are now holding, under the guidance and support of the Wisconsin Veterans Museum.

Welcome, then, to this unprecedented look at outdoor public sculpture in the Badger State. Our hope is that you will not only enjoy browsing these pages but will use it as a field guide for your own explorations and art adventures around Wisconsin, a state of the arts.

WHAT IS INCLUDED IN THIS GUIDEBOOK?

As a part of the SOS! project, we inventoried and chose monuments with more artistic value over those with purely historical or sentimental value. National SOS! guidelines primarily requested an inventory of the state's principal 19th and 20th Century sculptural monuments. This book depicts a much broader range, including 1) Native American effigy mounds, a form of pre-historic art particular to Wisconsin, 2) art environments by primarily self-taught artists, 3) chainsaw art, born from the northwoods lumber industry, 4) sculptural memorials, for individuals and the armed services, and 5) traditional and modern sculptures. In some cases we had to be quite flexible with the definition of public sculpture.

For the purposes of this guidebook, sculpture that is generally accessible to the public at convenient times is considered public sculpture. Anything mounted indoors was excluded, except sculpture that was formerly outdoors, but moved indoors because it required protection for preservation. One example is the statue *Forward* in Madison, Wisconsin, which originally stood in front of the State Capitol but now is located at the headquarters of the State Historical Society of Wisconsin. A replica of *Forward* was made and is located on the Capitol Square.

We have included sculptures which have been lost, removed and in storage, or part of temporary outdoor sculpture exhibits as a record of what we had. Also included are privately owned but publicly accessible sculpture such as one might find in front of a business, museum, hospital, college, church, clinic, or even a home. Often these private institutions commissioned outdoor sculpture for the public's benefit.

Anton (Tony) Rajer
Christine Style

Foreword

SOS!

Save Outdoor Sculpture

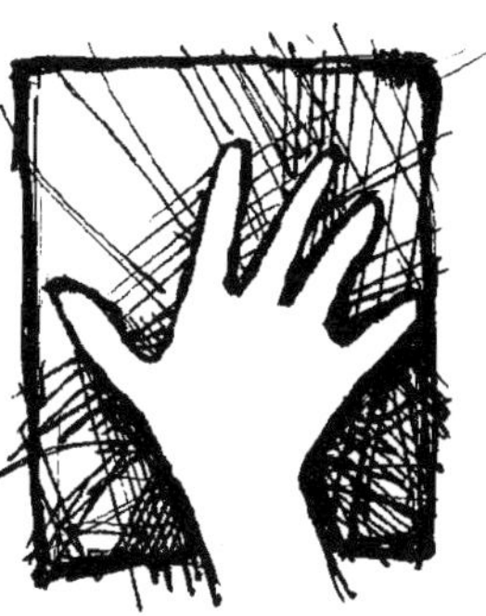

Congratulations on the completion of the survey of outdoor sculpture in Wisconsin. Since 1991, when SOS! was formally launched, more than four hundred organizations and more than seven thousand volunteers have identified and assessed the condition of more than 32,000 sculptures nationwide, while raising public awareness of the need to care for them. The survey has shown that 45 percent of public sculptures are in critical need of attention while 9 percent require urgent conservation treatment to survive the coming century.

Your interest in producing a book about the Badger State collection is commendable and is one of several ways in which people who care for and care about outdoor sculpture can become aware of the value of public sculpture and its precarious state. Related examples are symposia, web sites, videotapes, and articles in the press. We encourage all SOS! projects to continue to press for local action on behalf of local sculpture. I wish you well in your continuing efforts to save Wisconsin's sculpture and again, congratulations on the book, *Public Sculpture in Wisconsin*.

Susan Nichols

Director, National SOS!, Save Outdoor Sculpture, Washington, D.C.
Heritage Preservation, Inc., Washington, D.C.

Acknowledgments

National SOS! is supported by Target Stores, National Endowment for the Arts, the Pew Charitable Trusts, the Getty Grant Program, and the Henry Luce Foundation, among others.

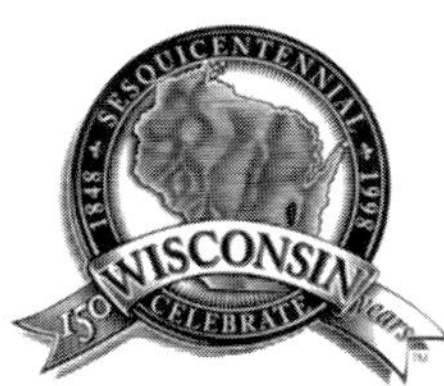

This project has been funded in part by the Wisconsin Sesquicentennial Commission, with a grant from the Wisconsin Humanities Council, including funds from the State of Wisconsin, and individuals and corporate contributors. We'd like to express our appreciation for the generosity of these corporations and recognize them below.

Wisconsin Sesquicentennial Corporate Sponsors, including S.C. Johnson & Sons, Credit Unions of Wisconsin, and AT&T

Other Sponsors include Van Lanen Printing and Wisconsin Veterans Museum

INSTITUTIONS that assisted in the Wisconsin SOS!

Bay View Public Library
Beloit College
Brown County Library
Citi-Arts Madison
City of Oshkosh
City of Waupun
Council for Local History
Crandon Public Library
Frank Lloyd Wright Foundation
John Michael Kohler Arts Center
Kaukauna Public Library
Lawrence University
Leigh Yawkey Woodson Art Museum
Madison Art Center
Milwaukee Art Museum
Milwaukee Public Library
National Museum of American Art, Smithsonian Institution
Neville Public Museum
Olbrich Botanical Gardens
Olsen Family Foundation
Oshkosh Volunteers for Preservation
Richland Center Chamber of Commerce
State Historical Society of Wisconsin
Taliesin Preservation Commission
Two Rivers Parks Department
University of Wisconsin-Eau Claire
University of Wisconsin-Fond du Lac
University of Wisconsin-Green Bay
University of Wisconsin-LaCrosse
University of Wisconsin-Madison
University of Wisconsin-Milwaukee
University of Wisconsin-Stout
University of Wisconsin-Whitewater
Wisconsin Chambers of Commerce
Wisconsin Painters and Sculptors
Wisconsin Veterans Museum
Wriston Art Center
Wisconsin Arts Board

Individuals

Dean Amhaus
Tom Atwood
Arthur Beale
Dawn Belleau
Robert Birmingham
Judy Borke
Steve Boyum
Lorenzo Burton
Peter Calderwood
Amy Chung
Dr. Leslie Crocker
Cait Dallas
Sarah Davitt
Mary DiNovo
Cynthia Dobson
Larry Donoval
Mike Duvall
David Eagan
Carol Emmons

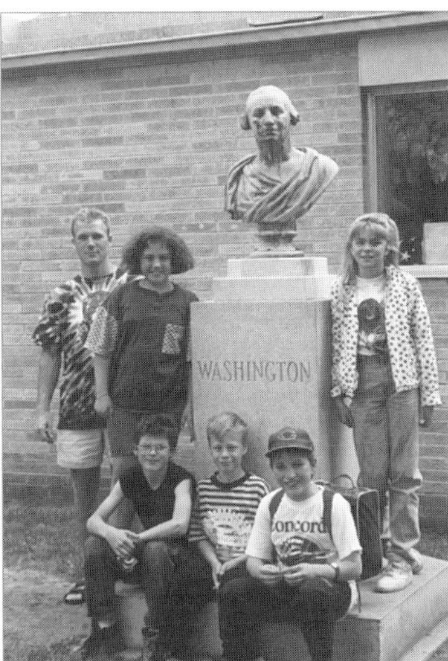

SOS! volunteers in Oshkosh

Lenore Farrell
Beth Fisher
Mary Fletcher
Rick Fletcher
Elizabeth Frechette
William Griffith
Chris and Janet Graff
Stephannie Hammes
Jill Haycock
Tim Holland
Rebecca Jones
Brenda Jordon
Norman Keats
Jane Ketchum
Jim Kivela
Susannah Koerber
Robert Kret
Terry Laib
Emile Mathis
Tom McKay
Jessica Moore
Ruth Muehlmeier
Leslie Nelson
Jeremy Olmsted
Delores Olsen
Lori O'Neil
Dee and Lyle Peacock
Lynette Penewell
Jeanne Peters
Karen Powers
Larry Powers
Jeff Prust
Keith and Carol Raddatz
Janet and Kurt Sailor
Art Schnur
Pat Schroeder
O.V. Shaffer
Claudia Smith
Dianne Steinbach
Susan Sulterman
Lynn Thiele
Elizabeth Walsh
Dave Watson
Wade Weber
Jane Weinke
Robin White
David Wied
Lynnette Wolfe
Paul Wolter
Virginia Woods
Bruce Zellner
Fred and Jan Zimmerer

Local Historical Societies that helped in the SOS! project

Note: Regions are based upon the State Historical Society list.

Capital Region

Albany Historical Society
Albion Academy Historical Society
Belleville Area Historical Society
Beloit Historical Society
Black Earth Historical Society
Brodhead Historical Society
Clinton Community Historical Society
Cottage Grove Area Historical Society
Cross Plains-Berry Historical Society
Dane County Historical Society
DeForest Area Historical Society
Fitchburg Historical Society
Green County Historical Society
Historic Blooming Grove Historical Society
Koshkonong Prairie Historical Society
Luther Valley Historical Society
McFarland Historical Society
Marshall Area Historical Society
Mazomanie Historical Society
Middleton Area Historical Society
Milton Historical Society
Monticello Area Historical Society
Mount Horeb Area Historical Society
New Glarus Historical Society
Oregon Area Historical Society
Rock County Historical Society
Stoughton Historical Society
Sun Prairie Historical Society
Wisconsin Archaeological Survey
Wisconsin Pottery Association
Wisconsin State Genealogical Society

Central Region

Adams County Historical Society
Almond Historical Society
Cambria-Friesland Historical Society
Clintonville Area Historical Society
Columbia County Historical Society
Dells County Historical Society
Elroy Area Historical Society
Historic Point Basse, Inc.
Iola Historical Society
Juneau County Historical Society
Lodi Valley Historical Society
Marion Area Historical Society
Marquette County Historical Society
New London Heritage Historical Society
North Wood County Historical Society
Portage Historical Society
Portage County Historical Society
Poynette Area Historical Society
South Wood County Historical Corporation
Waupaca Historical Society
Waupaca County Historical Society
Waushara County Historical Society
Wild Rose Historical Society

East Central Region

Berlin Historical Society
Brandon Historical Society
Cedarburg Cultural Center
Dartford Historical Society
Dodge County Historical Society

Fond du Lac County Historical Society
Fox Lake Historical Museum
Germantown Historical Society
Horicon Historical Society
Hustisford Historical Society
Jackson Historical Society
Kewaskum Historical Society
Lebanon Historical Society
Markesan Historical Society
Marquette Historical Society
Mayville Historical Society
Mequon Historical Society
Neosho Historical Society
Omro Area Historical Society
Ozaukee County Historical Society
Plymouth Historical Society
Port Washington Historical Society
Princeton Historical Society
Richfield Historical Society
Ripon Historical Society
Saukville Area Historical Society
Sheboygan County Historical Research Center
Sheboygan County Historical Society
Theresa Historical Society
Washington County Historical Society
Waupun Historical Society
Winnebago County Historical and Archeological Society
Winneconne Historical Society

Metropolitan Milwaukee Region

Bay View Historical Society
Brown Deer Historical Society
Cudahy Historical Society
Franklin Historical Society
Greendale Historical Society
Greenfield Historical Society
Hales Corners Historical Society
Historic Milwaukee, Inc.
Milwaukee County Historical Society
St. Francis Historical Society
Wisconsin Black Historical Society & Museum
Wisconsin State Old Cemetery Society

Northeastern Region

Ashwaubenon Historical Society
Brillion Historical Society
Brown County Historical Society
Calumet County Historical Society

De Pere Historical Society
Door County Historical Society
High Cliff Historical Society
Kewaunee County Historical Society
Kiel Area Historical Society
Manitowoc County Historical Society
Menasha Historical Society
Neenah Historical Society
New Holstein Historical Society
Oconto County Historical Society
Outagamie County Historical Society
Pulaski Area Historical Society
St. Nazainz Area Historical Society
Seymour Community Historical Society
Two Rivers Historical Society
Winchester Area Historical Society

Northwestern Region

Ashland Historical Society
Barron County Historical Society
Bayfield County Historical Society
Bayfield Heritage Association
Washburn Area Historical Society
Birchwood Area Historical Society
Bruce Area Historical Society
Burnett County Historical Society
Clear Lake Historical Society
Douglas County Historical Society
Gordon-Wascott Historical Society
Grantsburg Area Historical Society
Iron County Historical Society
Jump River Valley Historical Society
Knox Creek Heritage Center
Mellen Area Historical Society
Moquah Heritage Society
Northern Wisconsin History Center
Osceola Historical Society
Polk County Historical Society
Price County Historical Society
Rusk County Historical Society
Sawyer County Historical Society
Solon Springs Historical Society
Stone Lake Area Historical Society
Washburn County Historical Society

Northwoods Region

Bonduel Community Archives
Boulder Junction Area Historical Society

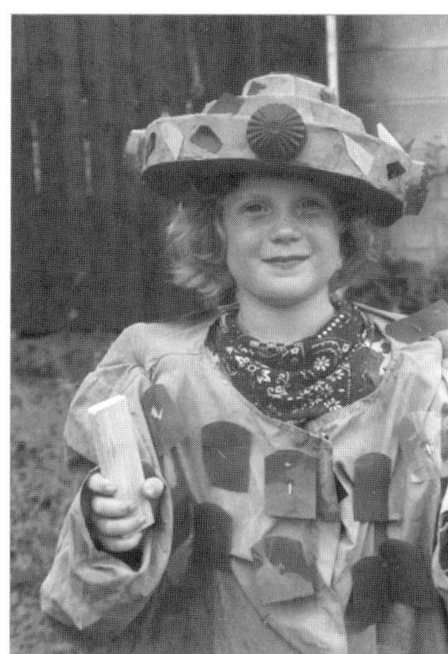

Girl dressed as one of Fred Smith's outdoor sculptures in a parade at *Wisconsin Concrete Park*, Phillips, Price County

Crivitz-Stephenson Historical Society
Woodruff Historical Society & Library
Eagle River Historical Society
Florence County Historical Society
Forest County Historical and Genealogical Society
Lac du Flambeau Historical & Cultural Society
Land O'Lakes Historical Society
Langlade County Historical Society
Marathon County Historical Society
Marinette County Historical Society
Merrill Historical Society
Niagara Historical Society
Northland Historical Society
Peshtigo Historical Society
Rhinelander Historical Society
Shawano County Historical Society
Stratford Area Historical Society
Three Lakes Historical Society
Tigerton Area Historical Society
White Lake Area Historical Society
Wittenberg Area Historical Society

Southeastern Region

Bark River Woods Historical Society

Big Bend-Vernon Historical Society
Burlington Historical Society
Concord Historical Society
East Troy Area Historical Society
Elmbrook Historical Society
Fort Atkinson Historical Society
Genesee Heritage Society
Geneva Lake History Buffs
Hartland Historical Society
Hawks Inn Historical Society
Heritage Military Music Foundation, 1st Brigade Band
Jefferson Historical Society
Kenosha County Historical Society
Lake Mills-Aztalan Historical Society
Menomonee Falls Historical Society
Muskego Historical Society
New Berlin Historical Society
Norway Historical Society
Oconomowoc Historical Society
Palmyra Historical Society
Pewaukee Area Historical Society
Racine Heritage Museum
Sharon Historical Preservation Society
Walworth County Historical Society
Watertown Historical Society
Waukesha County Historical Society
Western Kenosha County Historical Society
Whitewater Historical Society
Wisconsin Postal History Society

Southwestern Region

Bangor and Area Historical Society
Boscobel Area Heritage Museum
Cassville Historical Society
Crawford County Historical Society
Friendship Rural School Historical Society
Grant County Historical Society
Hillsboro Area Historical Society
Historical Society of the Upper Baraboo Valley
Holmen Area Historical Society
Iowa County Historical Society
La Crosse County Historical Society
Lafayette County Historical Society
Mineral Point Historical Society
Monroe County Historical Society
Onalaska Area Historical Society

Prairie du Chien Historical Society
Reedsburg Area Historical Society
Richland County Historical Society
Sauk County Historical Society
Sauk-Prairie Area Historical Society
Tomah Area Historical Society
Vernon County Historical Society
West Salem Historical Society
Westby Area Historical Society

West Central Region

Alma Historical Society
Buffalo County Historical Society
Cadott Area Historical Society
Chippewa County Historical Society
Chippewa Valley Museum
Clark County Historical Society
Dunn County Historical Society
Fountain City Area Historical Society
Gilman Area Historical Society
Jackson County Historical Society
Laura Ingalls Wilder Memorial Society
Mondovi Area Historical Society
New Richmond Preservation Society
Osseo Historical Society
Pepin County Historical Society
Pierce County Historical Association
St. Croix County Historical Society
Stanley Area Historical Society
Taylor County Historical Society
Thorp Area Historical Society
Trempealeau County Historical Society

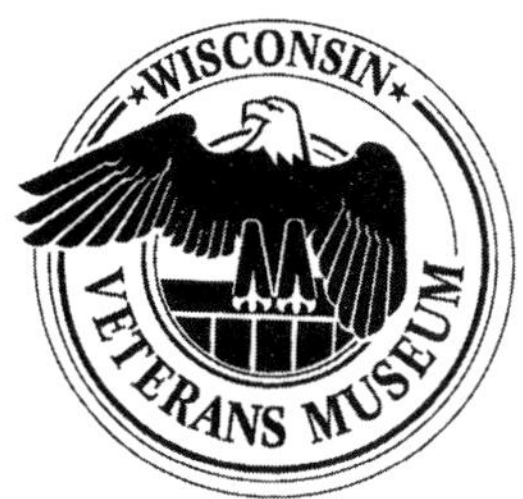

INTRODUCTION

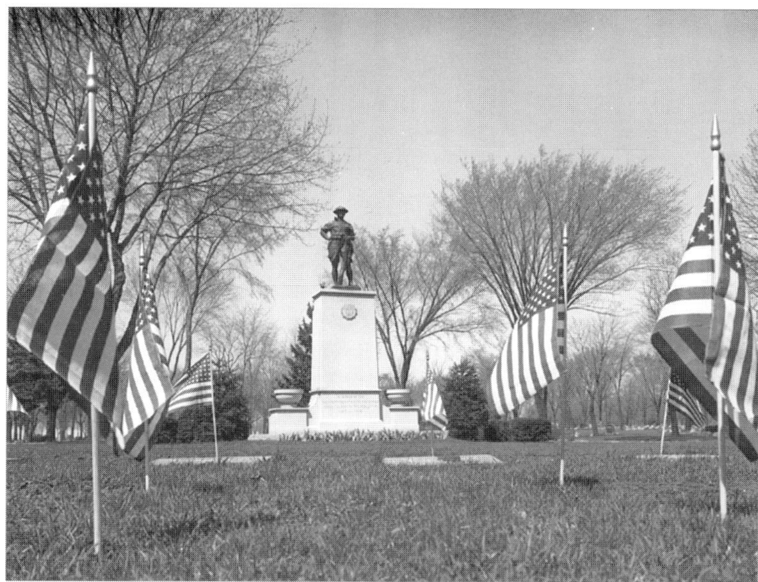

Veterans Monument at Graceland Cemetery in Racine

It is a pleasure to introduce *Public Sculpture in Wisconsin: An Atlas of Outdoor Monuments, Memorials and masterpieces in the Badger State* by Anton Rajer and Christine Style. *Public Sculpture in Wisconsin* is both informative as well as utilitarian. It can be used as a guidebook for touring interesting sites around Wisconsin. And, as the state celebrates the first 150 years of its existence, the book documents variety and vitality in Wisconsin's public sculpture. A work of this type promises to have a long shelf life because of its comprehensive nature. It will undoubtedly contribute to helping the public appreciate the artistic resources of local communities throughout the state.

There are more than seven hundred statues and memorials in Wisconsin. Nearly 35 percent are associated with the services and contributions of state veterans. In an age when the present tense seems able to obliterate any sense of a shared past, overwhelming the memory of ties that bind people together, encouraging, in its place, feelings of isolation, veterans monuments and memorials remind us of shared community values. Monuments and memorials are important societal markers because they represent attempts of one generation to communicate to the next.

This work represents a part of a national effort to inventory public sculpture. The Smithsonian Institution and Heritage Preservation, Inc. began the Save Outdoor Sculpture (SOS!) program eight years ago. For seven years, Anton Rajer has been involved in inventorying outdoor public sculpture on behalf of the SOS! program in Wisconsin. The state's Sesquicentennial became the occasion for transforming the inventory data into an illustrated guidebook.

The Wisconsin Veterans Museum collaborated with Anton Rajer and Christine Style on this worthy project for several reasons. The Wisconsin Veterans Museum has collected information about the location of veteran memorials in the state since 1987. We now take satisfaction in knowing that the information will be made readily accessible to the public. In addition, *Public Sculpture in Wisconsin* represents a contribution to the understanding of veterans affairs since so many of the public sculptures in the state relate to the experiences of citizens who have served in the nation's military during times of peril. Finally, the Wisconsin Veteran Museum is pleased to take part in educational projects since its mission is one of promoting an understanding and appreciation of history. The fact that the book approaches the presentation of educational information through an arts focus simply increases the uniqueness of the project insofar as the Wisconsin Veterans Museum is concerned. We trust that the public will enjoy this book.

Richard H. Zeitlin

Director, Wisconsin Veterans Museum
Madison, Wisconsin

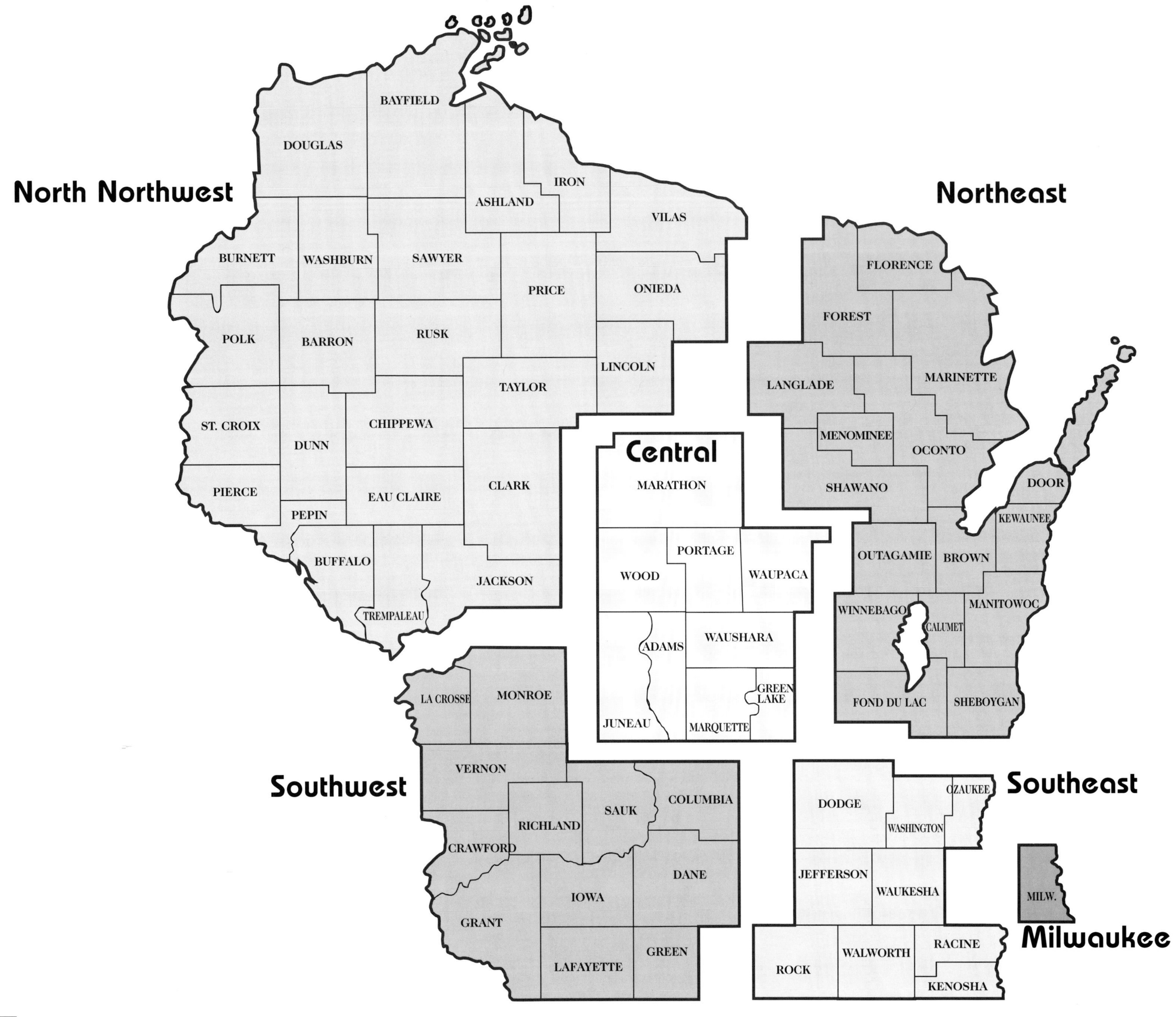
North Northwest
Northeast
Central
Southwest
Southeast
Milwaukee
BAYFIELD
DOUGLAS
IRON
ASHLAND
VILAS
BURNETT
WASHBURN
SAWYER
FLORENCE
PRICE
ONIEDA
FOREST
POLK
BARRON
RUSK
MARINETTE
LANGLADE
LINCOLN
ST. CROIX
CHIPPEWA
TAYLOR
MENOMINEE
OCONTO
DUNN
SHAWANO
DOOR
PIERCE
CLARK
MARATHON
KEWAUNEE
PEPIN
EAU CLAIRE
PORTAGE
OUTAGAMIE
BROWN
BUFFALO
WOOD
WAUPACA
WINNEBAGO
MANITOWOC
JACKSON
CALUMET
TREMPALEAU
ADAMS
WAUSHARA
LA CROSSE
MONROE
GREEN
LAKE
FOND DU LAC
SHEBOYGAN
JUNEAU
MARQUETTE
VERNON
OZAUKEE
DODGE
SAUK
COLUMBIA
WASHINGTON
RICHLAND
CRAWFORD
JEFFERSON
WAUKESHA
DANE
MILW.
GRANT
IOWA
GREEN
ROCK
WALWORTH
RACINE
LAFAYETTE
KENOSHA

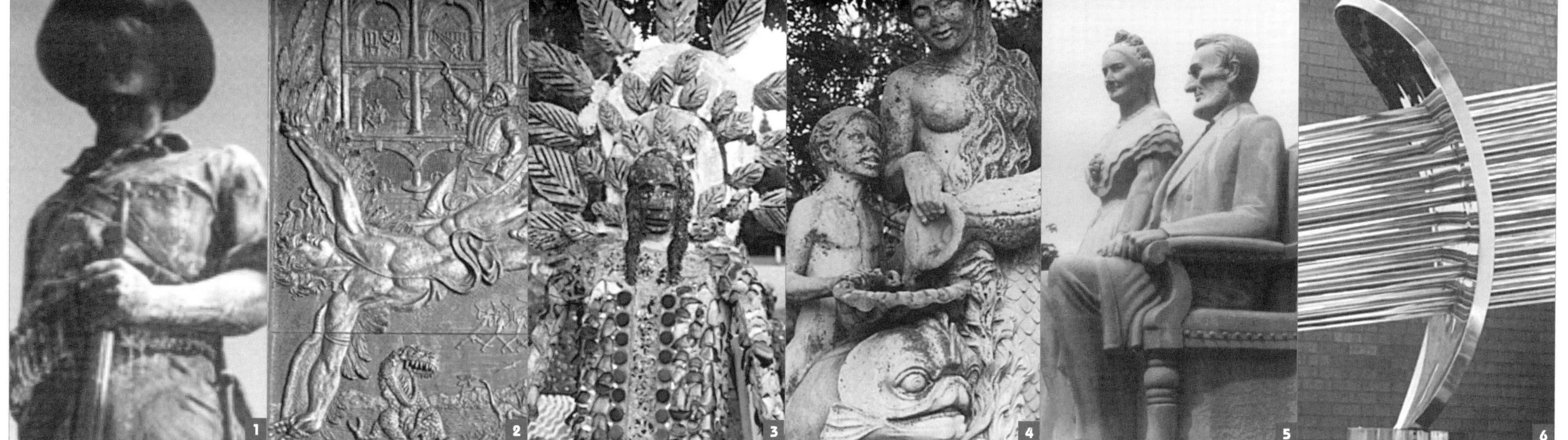

1) *Spanish American War Monument* in Oakwood Cemetery, Beloit, Rock County. 2) *Clocktower* relief detail at Mead Public Library in Sheboygan, Sheboygan County. 3) *Native American* in Wisconsin Concrete Park, Phillips, Price County. 4) *Annie C. Stewart Memorial Fountain* in Madison, Dane County. 5) *Abraham and Mary Todd Lincoln Monument* in Racine, Racine County. 6) *Deflected Jets* in Milwaukee, Milwaukee County.

AN OVERVIEW OF WISCONSIN'S PUBLIC SCULPTURE

Public sculpture in Wisconsin is a diverse cultural resource found in every county throughout the state. Hundreds of monuments enliven the landscape in our cities and towns. They stand in parks and in front of churches, libraries, courthouses, and other civic and private structures. The variety is endless as is the diversity of our people and those who created these works.

Native Americans produced Wisconsin's first public sculpture in the form of effigy mounds. These well-known works took many forms, including oval and conical shapes and animals like deer, turtles, birds, and bears.

The European settlers of Wisconsin began to erect public sculpture in the mid-nineteenth century, following the growth of cities and conclusion of the American Civil War. Milwaukee, Lancaster, Sheboygan, and Paris are homes to some of the state's oldest outdoor statues and monuments. Many are war memorials, commemorating those who fought in the Civil War as well as the Spanish American War. Stone and metal became popular materials for these monuments, particularly marble and bronze.

Early in the twentieth century, the City Beautiful movement, in conjunction with the Beaux Arts school, encouraged urban planning, sanitation, and civic pride. Public statuary was one piece of this vision in Wisconsin as elsewhere. And while public sculptures were being erected in urban areas for civic edification, some Wisconsinites in rural areas began building folk art environments. Many were religious in nature—some built by churches, such as the Holy Ghost Grotto at Dickeyville, and others by private individuals driven to create in glass and concrete as Wisconsin Concrete Park at Phillips.

In addition, there is an active and growing movement in chainsaw carving throughout the state, with many chainsaw artists located in the northern part of the state. This is part of a larger movement nationwide.

Between the first and second World Wars some sculpture was placed around the state, but because of the Great Depression many projects were abandoned. Nonetheless, there are a few examples of the Art Deco movement as well as interesting examples built built during the New Deal era by groups such as the Works Progress Administration (WPA).

In the last quarter of this century various programs have been started by Milwaukee, West Bend and other cities to promote the Arts. At the state level, the Wisconsin Arts Board's Percent for Art Program has commissioned dozens of works for state facilities throughout Wisconsin. Milwaukee and Madison also have their own percent for art programs.

Finally, there is the question of preservation. Frequently, public art projects in the past had no maintenance programs. Once the work of art was put up, people promptly forgot about it. We now know that in order to preserve these cultural resources, funds must be set aside for their care. The harsh Wisconsin climate wreaks havoc on not only our homes and cars, but also our public art. Sculpture contributes to a national, state, and local community identity. Efforts like SOS! can help focus attention on these resources that make the Badger State unique. This heritage of 150 years of public sculpture is our legacy to the new century.

A History of Wisconsin's Public Sculpture & Veterans Memorials

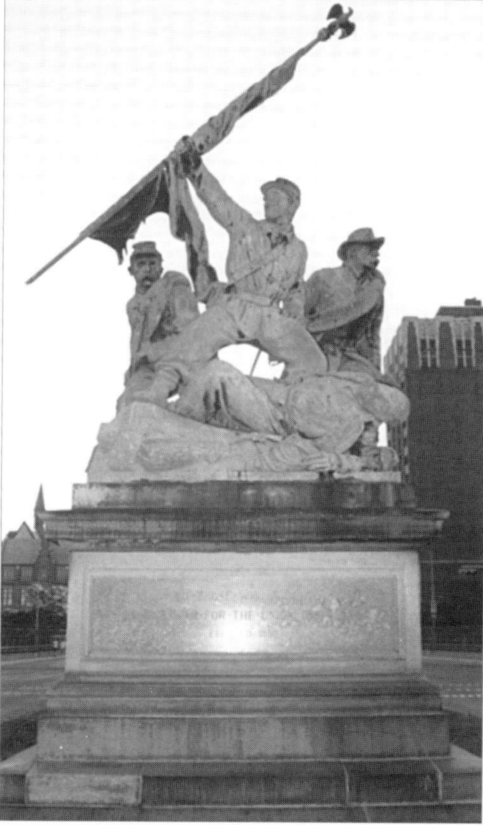

What is public sculpture? Years ago the concept was more narrowly defined than today. Made of bronze or stone, a sculpture stood on its own and served to reflect some lofty ideal. The American sculptor Paul Manship said in 1933 that public sculpture should be a permanent monument, beautiful and fit for high moral and devotional purposes Many monuments throughout Wisconsin meet these criteria. However, there is now a broader definition of sculpture that evolved in the late twentieth century. It includes both traditional statuary and folk art environments around our state as well as the burgeoning interest in chainsaw art and a reflection on our own pre-historic past by a new viewing of Native American effigy mounds as works of art.

The Earliest Sculptures

The first public sculptures in Wisconsin were the carved headstones in cemeteries. These were generally simple, but occasionally featured elaborate carvings to decorate tombs. Although it may seem odd from today's perspective, the early graveyards had multiple functions in this era before the advent of public parks. They served not only as burial grounds but also as places to gather and converse and to stroll and relax.

European immigrants to America brought with them the tradition of stone funerary monuments, many taking the form of obelisks. The obelisk has a long history of use as a commemorative and mortuary monument. Its widespread use in the early days of the American Republic is associated with the 18th century neo-classical revival in Europe that utilized Greek and Roman models. The prime example of this is the Washington Monument obelisk in Washington, D.C.

After the Revolutionary War and the War of 1812, a few public monuments were created, mostly as memorials to commemorate specific battles that took place on the East Coast or soldiers who had lost their lives in the conflicts.

When Wisconsin became a state in 1848, the only public sculptures were Native American effigy mounds and decorated cemetery gravestones. Examples are found in Oak Hill Burying Ground in Milwaukee, Fort Howard Cemetery in the Town of Howard, and West Koshkonong Church Cemetery in Pleasant Springs Township, Dane County. All of these sites have monuments with the inscribed date of 1848.

After the Civil War, both Northern and Southern states began erecting monuments at battlefields and in towns across America. Hundreds of Civil War monuments were erected. In the beginning, many were as simple as an obelisk, such as the ones in Lancaster and Paris, Wisconsin. Later, more elaborate statues were erected. A good example is the *Hans Christian Heg* statue at the Wisconsin State Capitol. Time and time again, Grand Army of the Republic (G.A.R). veterans raised funds to honor the war dead and remember past victories and losses. The G.A.R. was composed of veterans of the Civil War Union army. Today, G.A.R. memorials are the most prevalent monument type in the northern states. Most of the Civil War Monuments listed in the book's inventory are G.A.R.

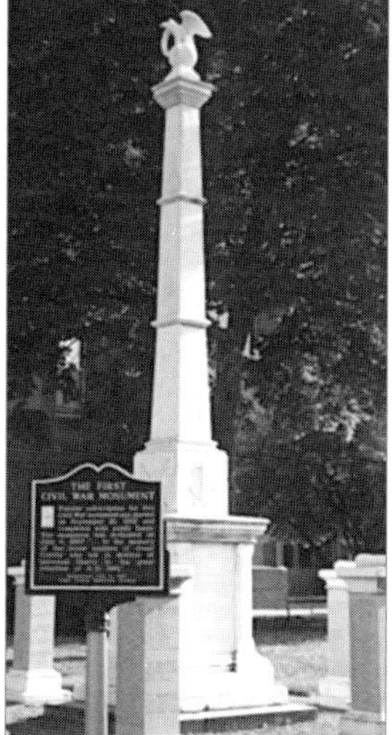

Early G.A.R. obelisk with eagle dated 1867, located in Lancaster, Grant County

Above: *Victorious Charge* in the Court of Honor, Milwaukee

Top right: *Midsummer Carnival Shaft* located in the Court of Honor, Milwaukee. When erected In 1900, it had an eagle on top.

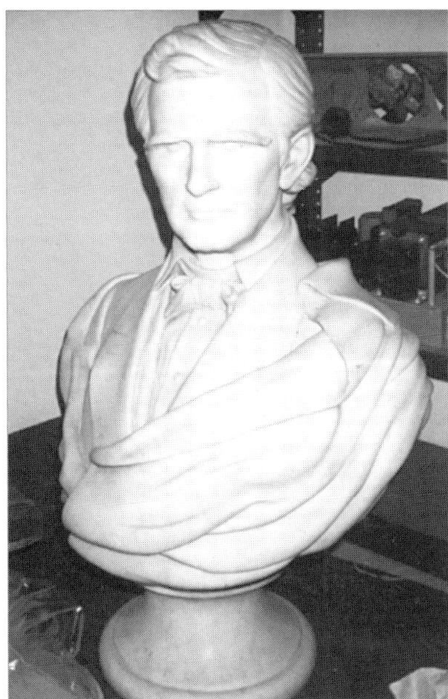
Bust of *Governor Dodge*

Marble Portrait Bust of Governor Dodge

In 1870, the Wisconsin Legislature authorized creation of a memorial portrait bust of Wisconsin's first territorial governor, Henry Dodge. This portrait is the first work of art commissioned by the state. Elisha Knowles carved the life-sized bust using photos and Dodge family interviews. He chose white Carrara marble in imitation of ancient Roman portraits. The commission cost $2,000—which was quite an investment for its time.

By state statute, chapter 57, section 1 (March 19, 1870), the portrait of Governor Dodge was supposed to be displayed "in some fit and conspicuous place within the Capitol." The bust miraculously survived the Capitol fire in 1904 and made its way into the new Capitol, where it was exhibited in the Governor's Conference Room for many years. Unfortunately it was removed from the conference room in 1968 and put in storage.

In 1992, it was conserved and put back in its rightful place in the Governor's Conference room where it had stood for nearly half a century.

Late Nineteenth-Early Twentieth Century Examples

Some of Wisconsin's earliest documented public sculptures were located in Madison, Milwaukee and Sheboygan.

Milwaukee's *Spirit of Commerce* Statue. The female statue *Spirit of Commerce* in Jackson Park, Milwaukee, is the earliest figurative piece known in the state (see photo, page 146). It was designed for the Chamber of Commerce Building and stood at 225 East Michigan, home of the Grain Exchange. Townsend Mix, the building's architect, commissioned the work. Mix had German-American artist Gustav Haug carve a wooden version that was then cast in zinc in New York. The cost in 1881 was $1,500. *Spirit of Commerce* is a classically inspired figure bearing symbols associated with business, such as a quill pen and bags of grain at her feet. She was vandalized repeatedly over the years. In 1991, she was finally restored and returned to her early beauty. Haug also executed the gilded statue of *Justice* which stood atop the old Milwaukee Courthouse as well as other ornamental works in Milwaukee *(Buck and Palmer, 107-109)*.

Sheboygan's Missing *Hope*. In Sheboygan another female statue came to be much admired by the community but has since disappeared. Her name was *Hope*, and for nearly nine decades, from 1886 to 1973, she stood atop the Henry Scheele Monument Company at 712 N. 8th Street. It is believed that the statue was carved of white Italian marble. The artist is unknown. She was clothed in robes and supported an anchor in one hand and held a laurel leaf in the other. The building where she stood was razed in 1973 to make way for the new Mead Public Library. *Hope* was placed in front of the new library but became the focus of repeated acts of vandalism. Eventually Sheboygan removed the statue with the intent of restoration. Since that time, the statue has not been found.

Madison's *Annie C. Stewart Fountain*. Another unfortunate saga in Wisconsin's sculptural history is that of the *Annie C. Stewart Memorial Fountain* in Madison. In 1906 Mary C. Stewart, the wife of the U.S. District Court clerk, left $2,000 in her will for a memorial fountain in memory of her daughter, Annie. Cincinnati artist Frederic J. Clasgens sculpted three groups: a central figure of a child riding a dolphin with a companion mermaid and two smaller figures that would serve as drinking fountains. An elaborate circular base supported the fountain. The work was dedicated in 1925 at a cost, by then, of $5,700. It was placed strategically at the entrance to the much-visited Vilas Zoo. Today, the fountain's elaborate carving and ornate decoration have suffered from repeated vandalism. In addition, the entrance to the zoo was moved. The fountain is now isolated in the park and no longer works. Vandals broke off the shells, stole one water fountain figure, and broke off other pieces. The city removed the other water fountain figure, which is in storage, and in 1994, put money toward resurfacing and cleaning the ensemble. Today it looks better, but it is far from its original intent as a place for people to gather, enjoy a drink of water, and stroll into the zoo in memory of Annie. Neighbors have continued to express concern about the *Annie C. Stewart Fountain* though no preservation project has emerged to return this sculpture to its former beauty *(F. Hurst, 24)*.

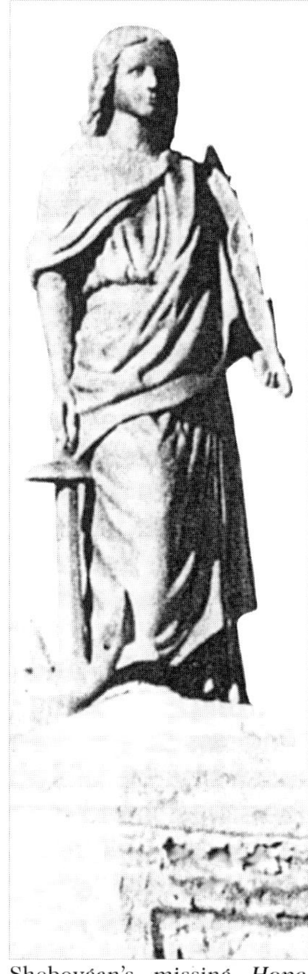

Sheboygan's missing *Hope*, 1886

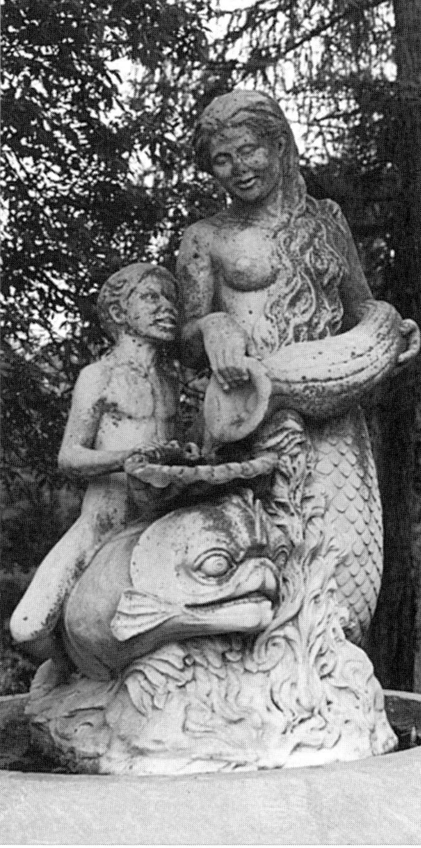

Annie C. Stewart Fountain, 1925, located at old entrance to Vilas Park, Madison

Modernist Sculpture in the Twentieth Century

The whole idea of public sculpture began to change radically with art movements of the twentieth century. Cubism, Abstract Expressionism, Surrealism, Art Deco, and other art movements changed forever the prevailing concept of public sculpture, expanding what was seen as public art. Wisconsin has a few examples of public sculpture representing these various artistic styles. The finest example is the Bradley Sculpture Garden in Milwaukee which has an exceptional collection representing the major art movements of the twentieth century including Minimalism, Hard Edge, and Modernist Abstraction.

Art Deco-Inspired Public Sculpture

Several fine examples of Art Deco-inspired public sculpture are found in Green Bay and Milwaukee.

The Spirit of the Northwest. This monument on the grounds of the Brown County Courthouse in Green Bay has qualities that characterize sculpture from this era, such as solid geometric monumental proportions, clean descriptive lines, and suppression of detail in favor of overall volume. Three figures—a citizen of the Fox Indian Nation and two French explorers (Father Claude Allouez and Nicholas Perrot)—are linked together in a solid block of carved Bedford limestone. Sidney Bedore (1883-1955) created the sculpture in 1931. It is one of Wisconsin's earliest monuments to be inspired by the simplified naturalism of the 1920s and the burgeoning Art Deco style.

The story of the commission is an interesting one and highlights the tremendous patience needed by artists to have their dreams realized. Sidney Bedore's mother was from Green Bay though he was born in Michigan where the family lived until his father's death. When he was 12, around 1900, his mother and stepfather moved the family to Green Bay. As a young man, Bedore worked for years in the Finnagan brickyard. It was at this time that he visited the Art Institute of Chicago and started to show an interest in art. Enthused by the possibility of becoming an artist, Bedore saved his money and eventually moved to Chicago where he was admitted to the Art Institute as a student. Later he did additional coursework in New York and with his artist wife, Margaret Lou, studied at the Ecole des Beaux Arts in Paris.

His first important commission was to sculpt a portrait of Teddy Roosevelt for Benton, Michigan, which he completed in 1922.

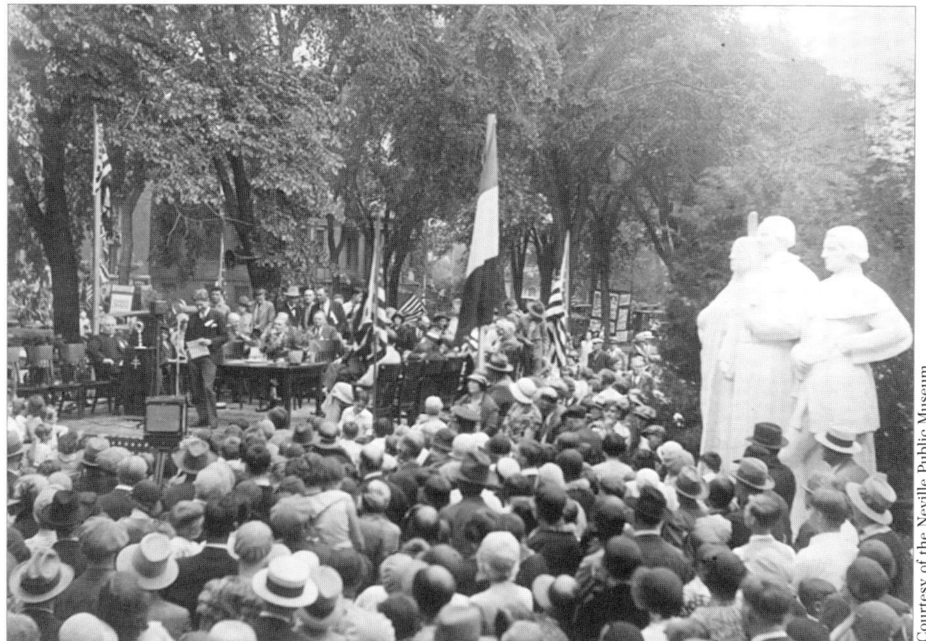

Above: 1931 dedication of *Spirit of the Northwest* statue carved by Sidney Bedore in Green Bay

Below: *Jean Nicolet* in Green Bay, 1951

He maintained his family ties with Green Bay, and around 1921 began modeling in plaster a group of figures symbolizing the *Spirit of the Northwest*. Deborah Martin, Mr. and Mrs. Arthur Courtney Neville, and R. C. Buchanan became interested in Bedore's art project and supported the work. They became the nucleus of the committee that promoted the idea for the sculpture. A public fund was established after a small model was exhibited in Green Bay. Bedore agreed to do the work for $7,500, of which $3,750 was an appropriation from the Brown County Board around 1929.

It is worth noting that Bedore's proposal was economical for its time: monumental sculptures of this type cost substantially more than the commission he was asking. The beginning of the Great Depression, combined with Bedore's love of Green Bay, may have prompted him to reduce the fee. The statue was dedicated on June 10, 1931, with huge crowds on hand at the courthouse grounds. It has stood there ever since, admired by the thousands who pass by it every day.

Bedore went on to sculpt the bronze portrait of Frenchman Jean Nicolet, located near Red Banks on Highway 57, north of Green Bay. It was commissioned by the state of Wisconsin in 1939, but only completed in 1951 because of World War II and other setbacks in procuring the necessary funds . . . and the bronze. This project was funded in part by pennies donated by Wisconsin children. The statue is situated near the place where

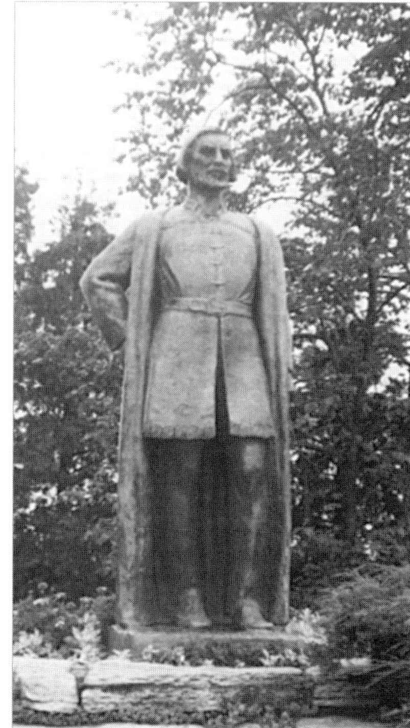

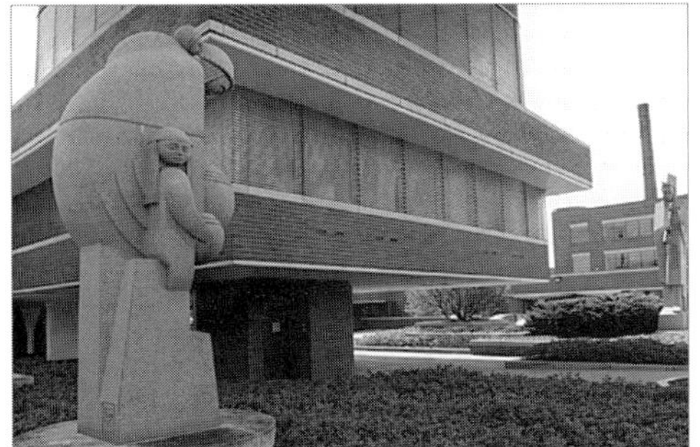
Nakomis in foreground and *Nakoma* designed by Frank Lloyd Wright are located at S.C. Johnson & Son Company in Racine

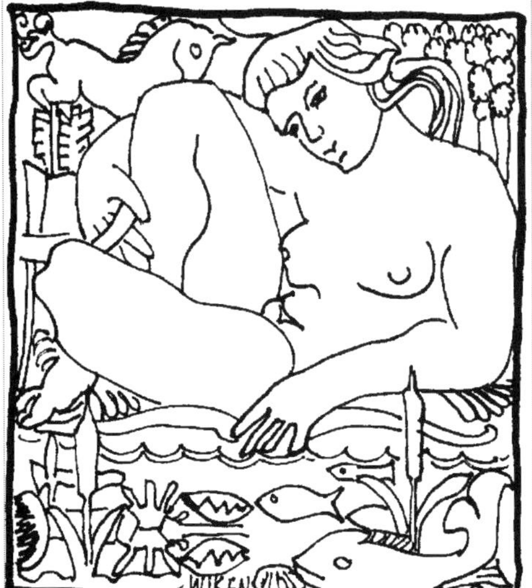
Drawing of the *Diana* bas-relief carved in 1954 and located on the facade of the Milwaukee Athletic Club

it is believed that Nicolet first landed in 1634 while exploring for a Northwest Passage to China. Little did he realize that he missed the mark by some nine thousand miles, but in doing so was the first European to set foot upon the beautiful land that became Wisconsin.

Frank Lloyd Wright's contributions. While traditional statuary was being erected in many Wisconsin cities, architect Frank Lloyd Wright (1867-1959) visited the Orient on business. He acquired works of art on these visits, including many sculptures that he placed within the gardens at Taliesin, his home near Spring Green. Examples include a seated *Quan-yin* and other fascinating figures that enhanced the environment of his home, studio, and school. Wright was inspired by oriental art, in particular Japanese art introduced at the 1893 Columbian World's Fair. Years later, in 1924, Wright designed the sculptures known as *Nakomis* and *Nakoma*, located at the S.C. Johnson & Son Corporation in Racine. These large scale works meld the diverse influence of streamlined modernism with a Native American theme. They are Wright's contribution to the simplified artistic forms of the period known as Art Deco.

Milwaukee's *Diana* bas-relief. The Milwaukee Athletic Club at 758 Broadway has a beautiful Bedford limestone bas-relief of the mythological Diana, seated next to a body of water as she fishes with her bow. The work is by Dick Wiken (1913-1985) in collaboration with Adolph Roegner. Carved in 1954, it strongly exhibits the vocabulary of the Art Deco period. A clear sense of design is inherent in this work: strong curvilinear lines, smooth surfaces, and compact composition (Buck and Palmer, 32).

Veterans Memorials and Monuments in Wisconsin

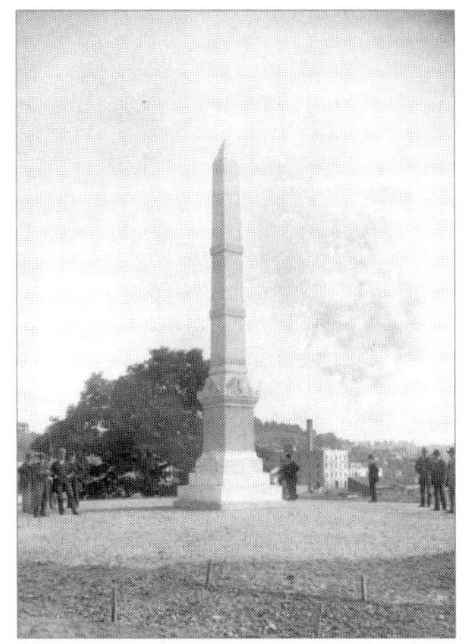
Veterans Monument, circa 1900

As Wisconsin's Native Americans honored their dead with hundreds of effigy mounds, so have Wisconsin's war dead been honored through numerous public monuments found in almost every county throughout the state. Nearly a fourth of the estimated seven hundred public outdoor sculptures in Wisconsin are dedicated to veterans.

Civil War Memorials

Wisconsin's first public monuments were erected after the Civil War to memorialize the war dead. These sculptures were dedicated to the Grand Army of the Republic, or G.A.R. Organizations composed of Union veterans, including the G.A.R., actively promoted efforts to build monuments. There are three types of G.A.R. monuments in the state.

The first and earliest monuments, erected between 1867 and 1875, were mostly small marble or limestone obelisks with inscriptions. Examples include Lancaster's obelisk monument which was dedicated in 1867 to the Civil War, or Sheboygan County's Rhine Center obelisk, dated 1868. Another in Paris, Kenosha County—was completed in 1868. These early monuments were frequently ordered from cemetery monument companies, hence the generic obelisk form was often used.

The second and most prevalent monument type began to be erected after 1875. Civil War veterans raised money to commission more ambitious monuments, including stone figures and bronze statuary. This trend continued until around World War I. These monuments were paid for by private donations. Large granite monuments in the form of columns or obelisks topped with bronze or stone statues became the norm, and generic statues of an individual uniformed Union soldier became popular. A single G.A.R. figure typically honors an entire regiment whose names are frequently inscribed below. The figure was essentially a common soldier standing with his rifle on guard duty, frequently referred to as Lone Sentry figures. The design conveys G.A.R. values of vigilance and virtue. Such statues were

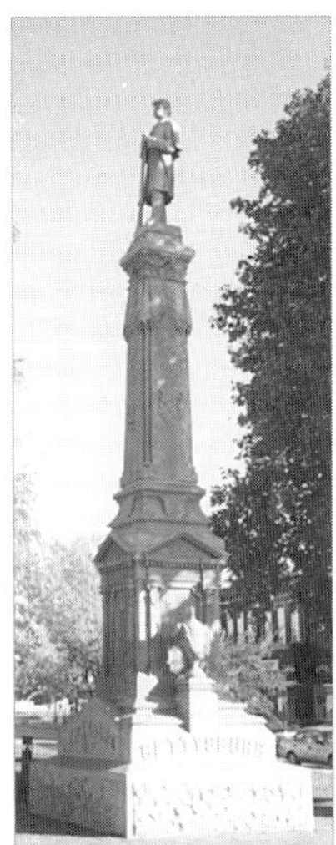
G.A.R. in Fond du Lac

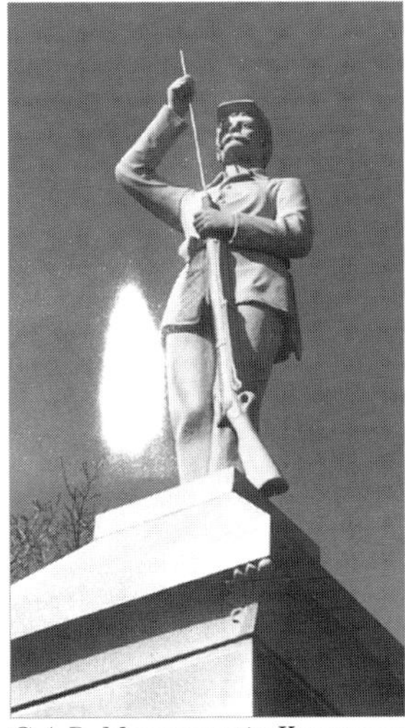
G.A.R. Monument in Kewaunee

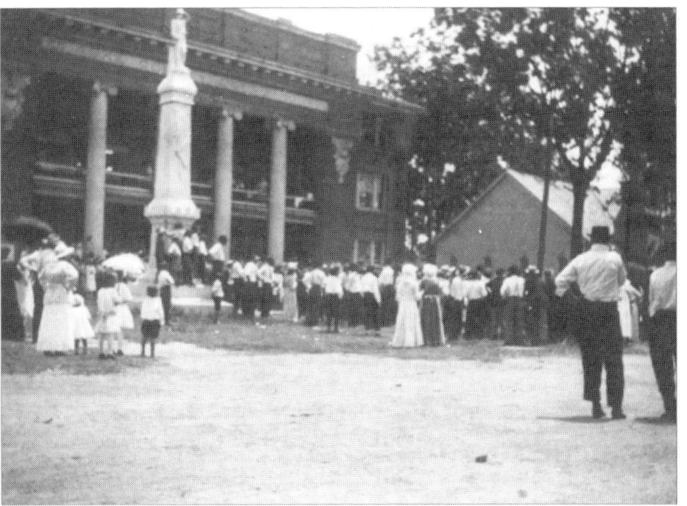
Dedication of Clark County *G.A.R. Monument*, circa 1900, in Neillsville

manufactured and sold in great numbers by commercial statuary firms in New York, Chicago and other cities to meet the demand from veterans and civic organizations. They came in stone, like Sheboygan's G.A.R. monument, sheet metal, like Two Rivers' G.A.R. soldier, or Fond du Lac's cast metal G.A.R. obelisk. Many were cast in American foundries such as Ames company in Massachusetts, Henry-Bonnard Bronze Co., New York, and Bureau Brothers in Philadelphia. Some also came from France, Germany and Italy.

Commercially produced generic statues, of which Wisconsin has a few, cost around $400 apiece, excluding the base. On the other hand, large monumental portraits cast in bronze with single or multiple figures cost many thousands of dollars. This was the case with the *Soldier's Square Monument* in Oshkosh, which cost $10,000 in 1907 and was mostly paid for by local citizen John Hicks (1847 1917). Three larger-than-life figures charge forward with rifles fitted with bayonets. A similar statue is located in Appleton. It was unusual for small communities such as Oshkosh to receive such large and important monuments. This was made possible by the philanthropic efforts of individuals like Hicks, who donated monumental bronzes to his city throughout his life. Hicks became acquainted with outdoor statuary while visiting the 1893 Columbian World's Fair in Chicago. Over a period of twenty-five years, he purchased at least eleven bronze statues and donated them to Oshkosh. This was the largest gift of public sculpture made by one individual in the early twentieth century in Wisconsin.

Before 1860, most war monuments in America were erected near battlefields. After the Civil War, most, though not all, memorials erected nationwide stood in communities that had contributed citizens and arms to the war effort. Approximately two thousand monuments to Union soldiers are found in the states that comprised the Union. Wisconsin has about thirty-one large G.A.R. monuments, many with standing figures. Three excellent examples of these G.A.R. memorials are the monumental obelisks in Beloit, Stevens Point and Wausau. In addition, there are literally hundreds of smaller G.A.R. memorials.

Madison's *Camp Randall Arch*. The third form of G.A.R. monument is the Camp Randall memorial arch, the only

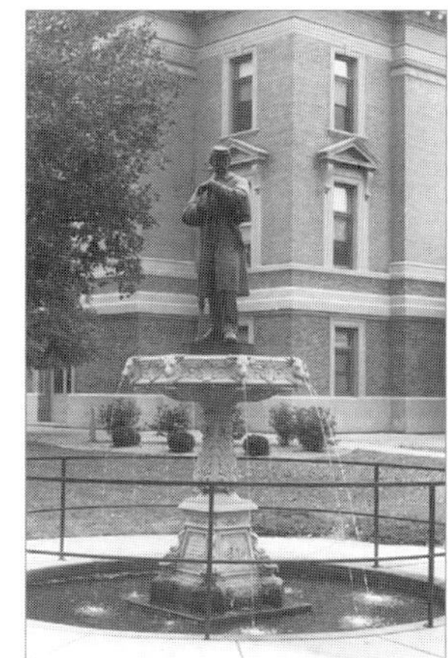

1906 cast iron *Civil War Soldiers Fountain* located in Lancaster, Grant County

permanent triumphal arch in Wisconsin. Paid for by the state of Wisconsin, it was erected to commemorate Wisconsin's participation in the Civil War and is one of Wisconsin's most distinguished monuments. Camp Randall, southwest of the University of Wisconsin campus in Madison, was used as a training station for more than 70,000 citizens in preparation for war service. The G.A.R. lobby felt some grand public monument was needed to commemorate the site and exerted pressure on the State Legislature to have a fitting structure erected.

A formal request for funds was introduced in 1910, and the Legislature made an appropriation of $25,000 in 1911 for a "fit and permanent monument." Construction began almost immediately, as the plans were already in hand, having been drawn up by Lew Porter, supervising architect for the construction of the new Capitol. He may have been assisted by artist Karl Bitter, then working at the Capitol on the pediments. Bitter was acquainted with triumphal arches in Europe and New York. One of these was the Grand Army Plaza in Prospect Park, Brooklyn, built to commemorate G.A.R. victories. The triumphal arch came to America with the 1893 World's Fair: several arched entryways welcomed fairgoers to the grounds. Bitter planned some of the decorations for the 1893 Columbian World's Fair in Chicago.

Fortuitously, Porter was able to obtain the same granite stone and employ the same contractor for both the Capitol and the arch. Within a year it was completed—on time and on budget. Committee members for Wisconsin's G.A.R. arch project included Josea Rood, who served as the "patriotic instructor" for the Twelfth Regiment and later became the first curator of the G.A.R. Room in the Capitol.

The arch takes its form from the ancient Roman structures of the same type. The first triumphal arches in the ancient world were built for victory celebrations but were impermanent—made of wood and cloth. Over time, the Romans in particular found that the architectural form of a city gate provided a suitable structure for ceremonial passages, including the display of trophies and statuary. Some ancient arches had one, two, or three openings to accommodate the parades. The most famous are the arches of Constantine and Titus in Rome. These structures are made of stone and were surmounted by bronze statuary, none of which has survived.

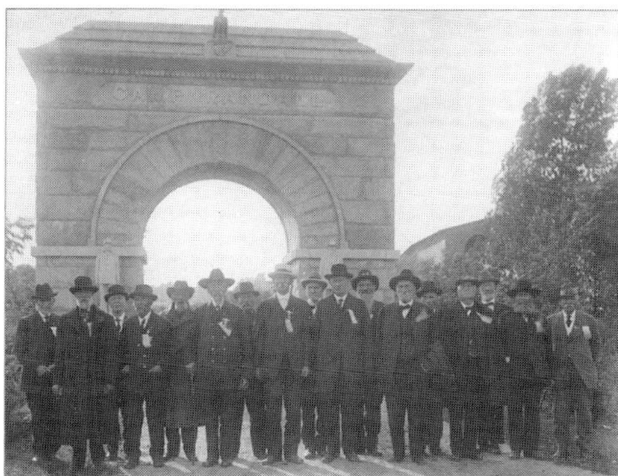

Camp Randall Arch dedication held in 1912 in Madison

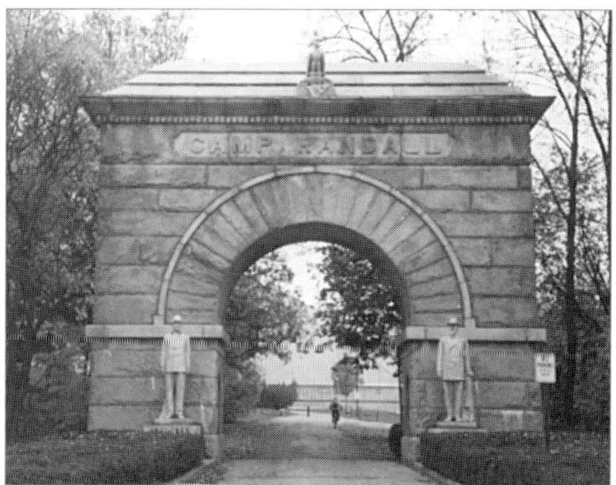

Camp Randall Arch in 1998, Madison

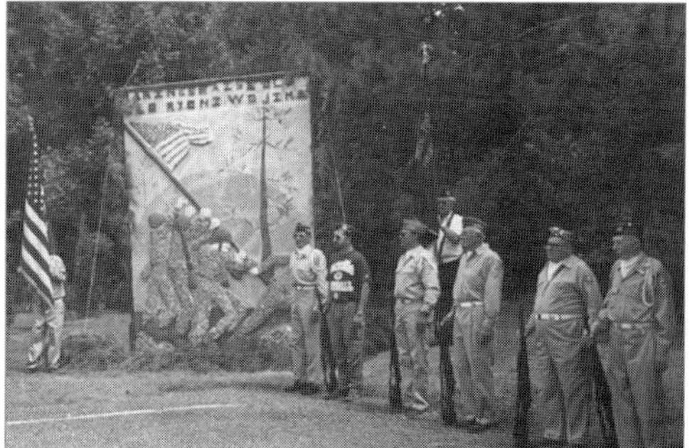

Veterans celebration at Wisconsin Concrete Park in front of the *Iwo Jima Monument* created by Fred Smith

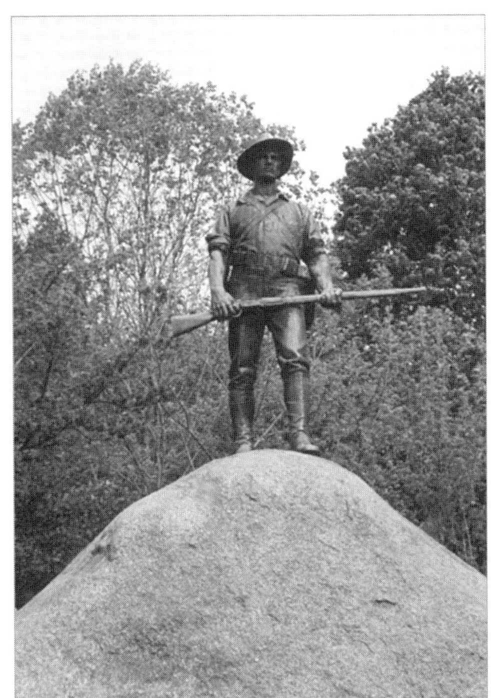

1939 bronze *Hiker Monument* by Theo Ruggles Kitson in Oshkosh

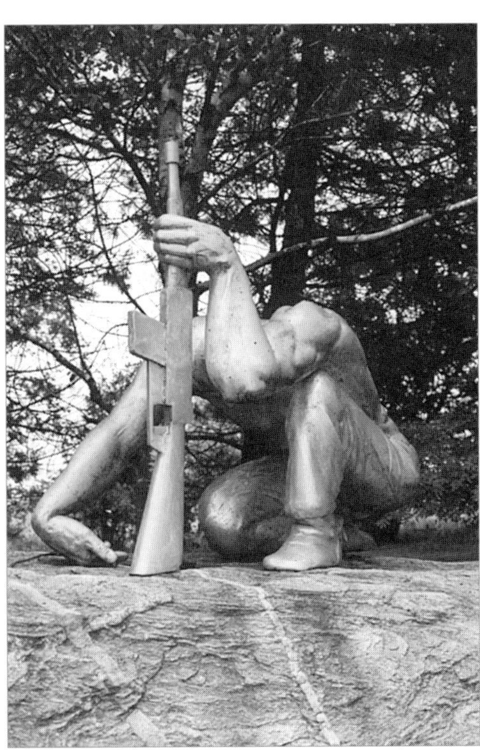

Cast aluminum *Weary Veteran* by Harry Whitehorse made in 1960, located in Fitchburg

Porter's arch is interesting from several points of view. The structure's large, solid mass is punctuated by one large opening that leads from the street to the camp. Unlike the granite he used at the Capitol, he chose to rusticate the arch's stone; that is, give it an aged, weathered appearance. At the apex of the arch is a statue of Old Abe, the legendary eagle mascot of the Wisconsin Eighth Regiment. Below it, proudly announcing the location, is the inscription "Camp Randall." Later differences in aesthetic opinion between the G.A.R. and the University of Wisconsin prompted the addition of two figures—one a young soldier with the inscription "1861-65" and the other a mature veteran in double-breasted greatcoat with a service medal with the date 1912. The arch was dedicated in June 1912 with a huge ceremony attended by thousands of people, including many G.A.R. veterans (F. Hurst, 14).

Twentieth Century War Memorials

Spanish-American War. Another impetus for veterans monuments came from the Spanish American War in 1898. Following the war, monuments of all types were built. The most popular was the *Hiker Monument*, an archetype of Spanish-American War veteran, standing with rifle in hand, looking off into the distance. Many Hikers are found throughout the country. Good examples are found in Oshkosh and in Fond du Lac. The practice of attaching inscribed plaques to existing memorials, rather than commissioning new ones, began with the Spanish American War. These became known as "all-wars" memorials.

The *Hiker Monument* in Oshkosh is the work of Theo Alice Ruggles Kitson and was cast by the Gorham Bronze Foundry in Providence, Rhode Island. It was purchased by the John Hicks fund for $6,458 in 1939. About forty copies of this statue are known throughout the United States. Most of them are in New England.

World War I. Following World War I, there was another burst of building activity in veterans memorials with the doughboy soldier the most common theme. A doughboy is an idealized World War I American infantry soldier. Beautiful examples abound throughout the state. One of the most noteworthy is in Wausau. An angel of winged victory embraces a doughboy attired in uniform with a gas-mask (see photo on title page of book). Below the figures is a bronze tablet inscribed with the names of those who died in World War I from the Wausau area. C.A. Heber created this work of art in 1923. It is located in a small elevated

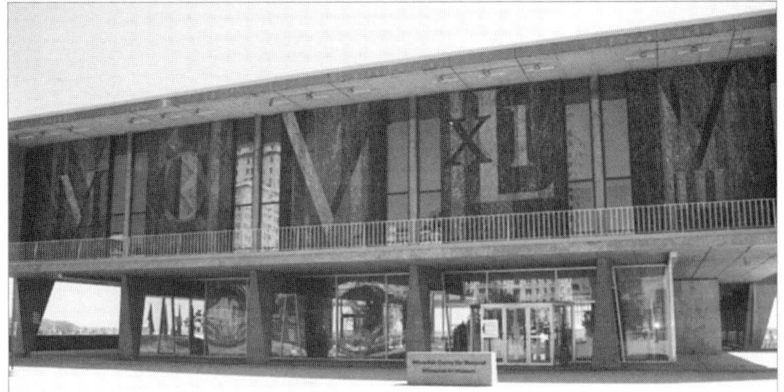

War Memorial building with facade mosaic by Edmund Lewandowski, 1954, located in Milwaukee

plaza, approached by a low granite step with curved seating. This ensemble is known as an *exedra* and harks back to ancient Greek models. The red granite stone used for the base beautifully complements the plantings in the park. A sense of idealized naturalism prevails in this work as a result of the academic tradition which Heber was following. An identical doughboy statue is located in New York City in Monsignor McGolrick Park.

Many of these monuments were paid for by subscription, and sometimes it took years to acquire the necessary funds to commission the memorial. Veterans groups, including the ladies auxiliary associations, held innumerable fundraisers to gather funds for purchasing a monument. In addition, veterans groups lobbied other civic organizations for support. These veterans monuments and memorials provide a permanent remembrance to those patriots who died in service to the nation.

Changes In Sculptural Style. The stock market crash of 1929, the subsequent Great Depression, and changes in art style brought about the demise of the statuary tradition. Most of the

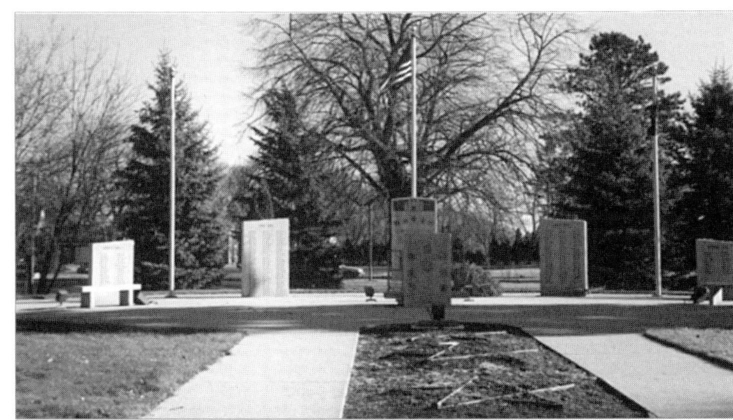

All Wars Veterans Memorial in Manitowoc circa 1997

war memorials that followed were nonrepresentational; that is, shafts or blocks of stone inscribed with names and memorial verses. A contributing factor to this change was the dramatic rise in production costs for bronze statuary. In the late nineteenth century, bronze casting in America was cheaper than carving stone statues. This accounts in part for the number of bronze monuments, even in Wisconsin.

Following World War II, many people in Milwaukee lobbied to erect a modern veterans monument. The result is a stunning War Memorial complex, completed in 1954. Strategically situated at the east end of Wisconsin Avenue, the building overlooks the lake. The War Memorial was designed by famed architect Aero Saarinen and includes a multicolored mosaic on the facade by Edmund Lewandowski. This was the first time in decades that an entire structure was dedicated to Wisconsin veterans.

Revival Of Realism At Late Century. The late twentieth century has seen something of a revival of figurative themes for veterans memorials. The most noteworthy examples are the Veterans Park in Trempealeau County, the *Vietnam War Memorial Park* in Arcadia and the *Vietnam Veterans Memorial Park* in Neillsville. In the wake of recent military engagements such as the Vietnam War and Desert Storm in Iraq, a whole new wave of veterans memorials are being erected, not all of them figurative. One of the largest and most inspiring is the *Sheboygan County Veterans Memorial* by architect Erik Jensen. Art and architecture combine to convey a sense of reverence. Individual plaques list the veterans' names, and the architecture conveys the solemn nature of the theme. These memorials influence our attitude toward the past and add depth to our understanding of them. In the best of these memorials, like the *National Vietnam Veterans Memorial* in Washington, D.C., the viewer is engaged in a journey from armed conflict to serenity. As author Jan Scruggs has said, "We do not seek to make any statement about the correctness of war, rather by honoring those who sacrificed, we hope to provide a symbol of unity and reconciliation." Many of our fine veterans monuments in Wisconsin do just that.

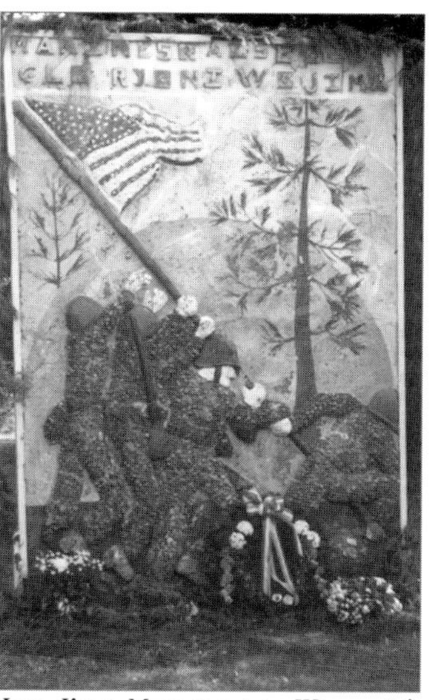

Iwo Jima Monument in Wisconsin's Concrete Park, Phillips, Price County

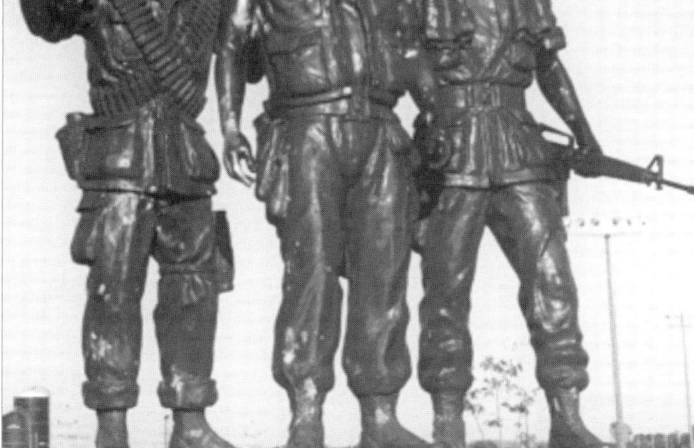

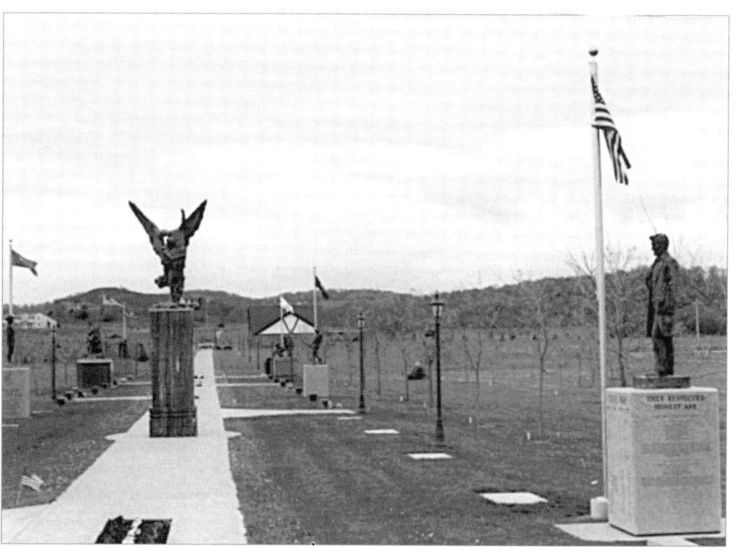

Above right: Arcadia Memorial Park with the *Angel of Mercy* surrounded by many other sculptures in Arcadia, Trempealeau County

Left: ***Arcadia Memorial Veterans Monument*** in Acadia Memorial Park, Trempealeau County

Further Reading

Diane Buck and Virginia A. Palmer. *Outdoor Sculpture in Milwaukee, A Cultural and Historical Guidebook*. Madison: State Historical Society of Wisconsin, 1995.

Frances W. Hurst and Fran Rall. *Common Joy II: Outdoor Art in Madison with Celebratory Verse*. Madison: Self-published, 1991, 1994.

Mead Public Library. *Sheboygan's Hope*. Sheboygan: 1978 (brochure).

Marilyn Crews-Nelson, Laura Exner, Michael Gallagher, Zoltan Grossman, Amelia Janes, and Jerry Maas. *Historical Atlas of Wisconsin*. Madison: Wisconsin Cartographers' Guild, 1998.

Donald Martin Reynolds. *Monuments and Masterpieces*. New York: Macmillan, 1988.

State of Wisconsin. *Blue Book*, 1997-1998, sesquicentennial edition. Madison: State of Wisconsin, 1998.

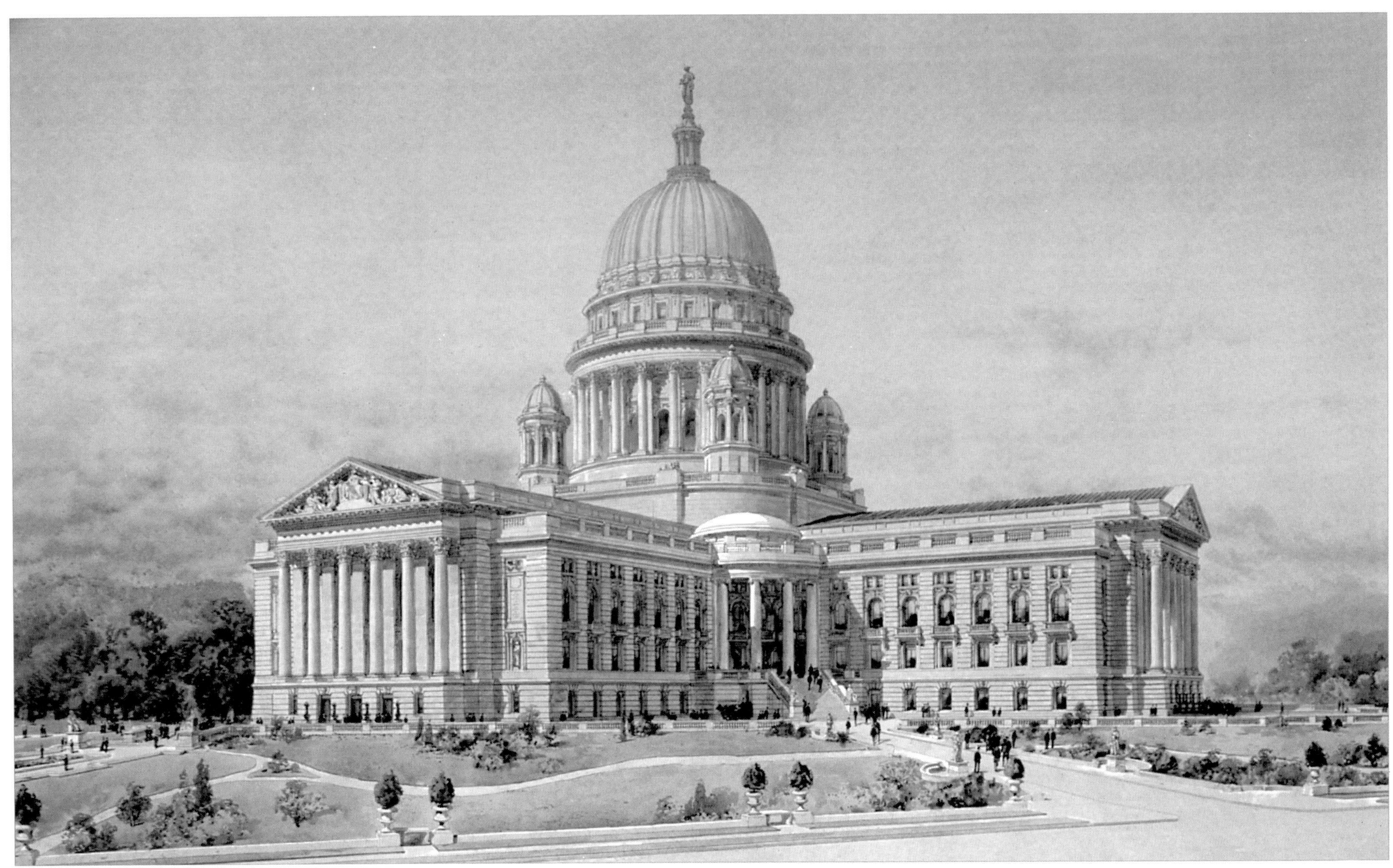

Architectural drawing of the Capitol by George Post

Beaux Arts & City Beautiful Monuments and Sculptures

Two of the most important artistic movements of the nineteenth century arose from efforts to transform cities into places of enlightenment and civic pride. Cities of the era were, by today's standards, incredibly filthy places. Raw sewage, garbage, mud roads, crowding, and millions of horses contributed to an unhealthy urban environment. Architects, engineers, and social thinkers began to discuss the problems of urban life and concluded that radical changes were needed to make cities cleaner and healthier. Many planners in Europe as well as in the United States recognized the importance of green space within the urban fabric. The American landscape architect Frederick Law Olmsted (1822-1903), working on the East Coast, laid out Central Park in New York in the late nineteenth century and proposed many changes to improve cities. Green spaces like parks could serve not only as places of relaxation and enjoyment but also enlightenment. Public sculpture placed in parks, along boulevards, or integrated into architecture, was an integral part of this vision.

The City Beautiful Movement

This movement to improve cities became known as the City Beautiful Movement. One of several sources of inspiration for this wide-ranging development was the 1893 Columbian World's Fair held in Chicago along the shore of Lake Michigan on a site that had formerly been a swamp. The fair lasted less than a year, but its impact was felt all over the United States as well as in Wisconsin for years to come. Several Wisconsin cities, including Milwaukee, Madison, and Oshkosh, reflect the fair's impact in their urban planning and architecture. These cities have green urban spaces that exemplify both the City Beautiful Movement and a later development called City Functional.

In Milwaukee, Wisconsin Avenue and the extensive interconnected system of parks echo the 1893 fair's parkways. In addition, many of Milwaukee's fine parks have statuary. In Madison, urban green spaces along the lakes and boulevards that radiate out from the state capitol are classic the City Beautiful themes. Landscape architect John Nolen (1869-1937) was responsible for many of Madison's best urban features, including the first city master plan to advocate limiting building heights around the Capitol, expanding the University of Wisconsin campus, and developing a city park system. Nolen also created city plans for Milwaukee, LaCrosse, Janesville, and Kenosha. In Oshkosh, similar developments in Menominee Park and along city streets like Algoma Boulevard helped make Oshkosh a miniature City Beautiful, studded with public sculpture.

The Beaux Arts Movement

The Beaux Arts Movement, along with the City Beautiful movement endeavored to develop a monumental style of art and architecture to fit the grand new urban spaces. We use the French term Beaux Arts (pronounced "bows arts") because of its close association with the National Art and Architecture Academy in France that so fervently promoted this system of architecture and helped spread it throughout the world, from Paris to New York to Buenos Aires and cities such as Madison.

Based on classical designs and motifs, Beaux Arts architecture became the standard for civic edifices around the world for decades. Many Wisconsinites became acquainted with this

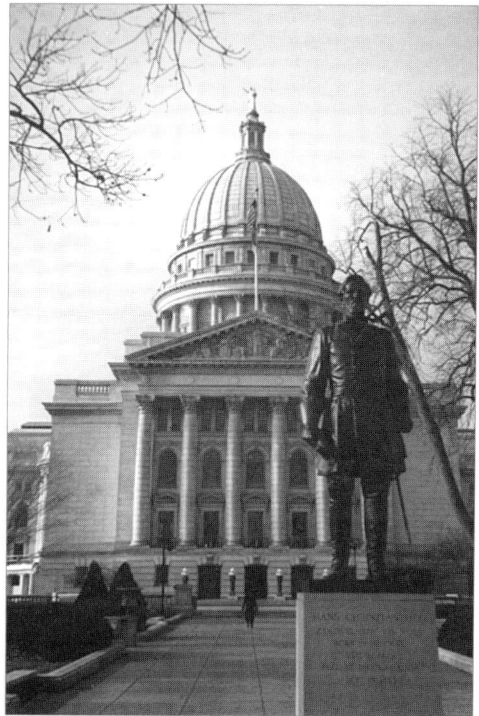

View of Capitol Square in Madison with *Hans Christian Heg* statue in foreground

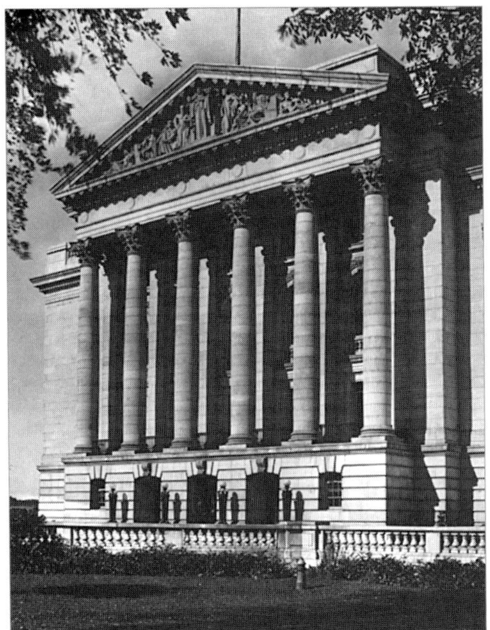

View of Capitol building with South pediment in Madison.   WHi (A61)6224

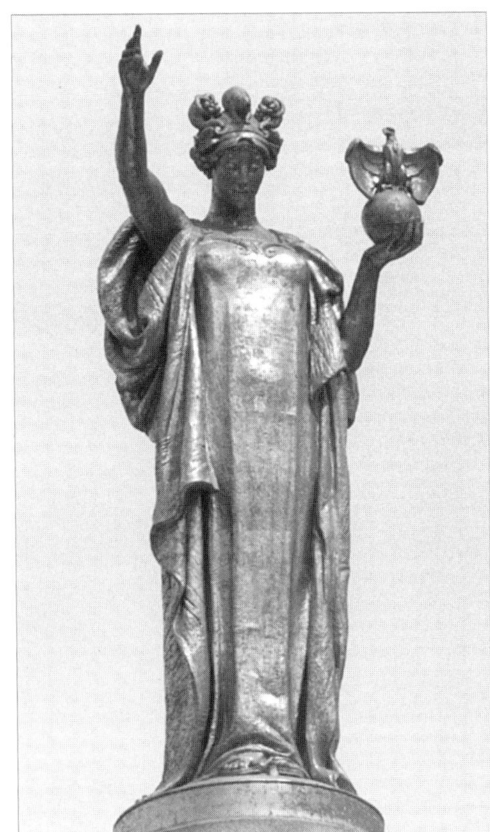

Wisconsin statue on top of the State Capitol dome in Madison

style of architecture at the 1893 Columbian World's Fair. Most of the fair's architecture was inspired by the Beaux Arts movement. The huge buildings at the fair had classical columns, domes, and grand entrances and were brimming with allegorical and mytho- logical sculptures of heroes and heroines from the ancient to the modern world. All were based upon ancient Greek and Roman models, reinterpreted through the Beaux Arts tradition.

Some Wisconsin buildings were directly influenced by the fair. The most prominent are the State Capitol in Madison, the old Milwaukee Public Museum (today the Milwaukee Public Library) and the Oshkosh Public Library, and the Brown County Courthouse. Each sports the characteristic dome, pediment, and columns. They include elements of classical Roman and Greek architecture and closely integrate sculpture into the whole, yielding a harmonious ensemble. Greek architecture was thought to be a good choice for public buildings, since it was seen to symbolize the democracy of ancient Athens. In fact, the present Wisconsin State Capitol was conceived as a temple to democracy.

Madison: The State Capitol's Exterior Sculpture

The State Capitol in Madison is one of the most spectacular and stunning Beaux Arts buildings ever built in America. The capitol's architect, George Post (1837-1913), designed many other prominent buildings in America, including the New York Stock Exchange and the Arts and Industry building at the 1893 Chicago World's Fair. Post was trained in Paris at the Beaux Arts school and knew the importance of integrating art and archi- tecture to make a unified impression. He accomplished this to perfection in the Wisconsin State Capitol, the last great Beaux Arts building completed in America before the advent of the styles known as Art Deco and Functional Modernism.

Working with prominent artists Daniel Chester French (1850-1931), Karl Bitter (1867-1915), Adolph Weinman (1870- 1952), Attilio Piccirilli (1866-1945) and others, Post was able to create a building to house state government that was uplifting, functional, and beautiful at the same time. An entire program of decoration was envisioned, including exterior sculpture atop the dome, at the dome's base, on the four wing ends, and in Capitol Park. It is no exaggeration to say this building is a museum of classically inspired academic Beaux Arts sculpture.

Rarely have art and architecture been so beautifully joined as in the Wisconsin State Capitol. The numerous sculptural groups throughout the building are testimony to the ability of artist and

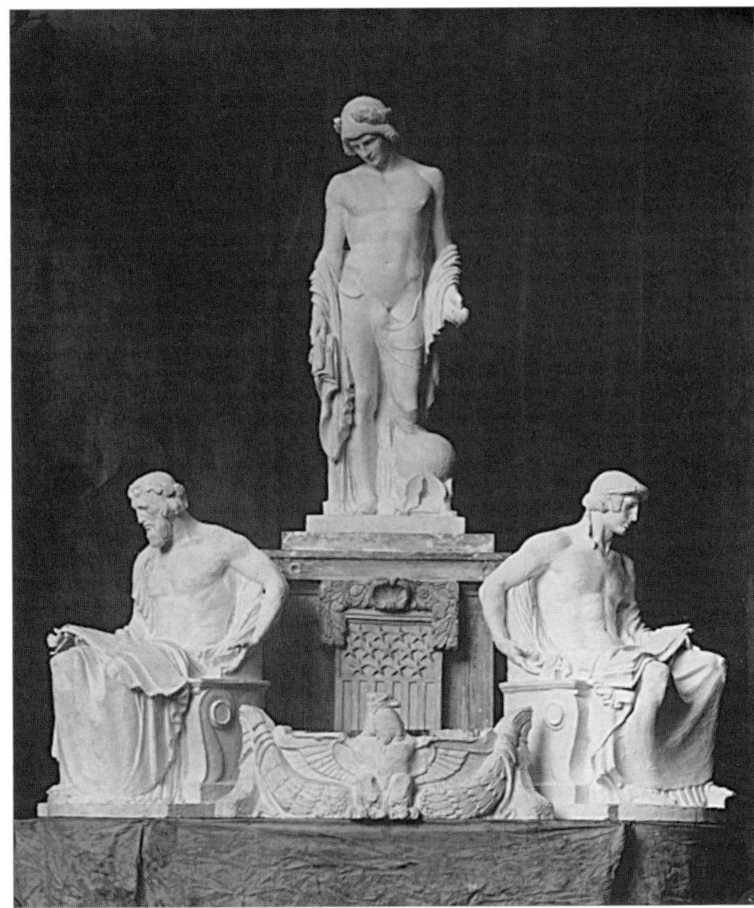

Plaster models representing knowledge by Karl Bitter (1911-1915). The carved sculp- tures are located on the base of the Capitol dome facing East Washington Street in Madison.   WHi (W6) 6204

architect to work together to create a unified artistic statement that is both beautiful and functional. The exterior sculptural program at the Capitol is one of the most extensive for any building in America, comparable to the U.S. Congress in Washington, D.C., or the Minnesota State Capitol. This is an extraordinary legacy for the Badger State. What follows are descriptions of a few of the most notable works.

The Golden Lady. The most spectacular sculpture at the State Capitol is without question the golden lady on the dome (see photos on pages 52-58). It is the work of American artist Daniel Chester French, who also made the seated statue of Abraham Lincoln at the *Lincoln Memorial* in Washington, D.C. The dome statue was cast at New York's Roman Bronze Foundry and transported to Madison by rail. The three-ton statue was hoisted onto the dome and bolted in place in 1914.

It is a common misperception that the statue's name is *Forward* or *Miss Forward*. In fact, while she does symbolize the state motto, her name is *Wisconsin*. She faces southeast, toward the nation's capital of Washington, D.C., and the coming dawn, thus representing the dawn of a new age. Her outstretched right arm welcomes people forward, and she holds in her left hand a globe surmounted by an eagle, symbol of the American republic.

Located atop the dome, more than 280 feet above the ground, the statue is difficult to see. But *Wisconsin* is rich in detail. She wears on her head a Greek warrior's helmet, same as the ancient statues of Athena after whom she is modeled. Athena was the goddess of the arts, and also the crafts, mercy, wisdom, and war (only as a last resort). Surmounting her helmet is Wisconsin's state animal, the badger, whose back is the highest architectural point in Madison. Fruits and corncobs decorate either side of her helmet. On the front of her dress, decorating her bust line, is a large W for Wisconsin.

This stunning bronze statue was conserved in 1990 when more than 18,000 small sheets of gold were used to regild the monumental state icon. She is truly one of the most spectacular cultural and artistic resources we have and an outstanding example of public sculpture at its best and brightest.

The Dome Base Sculptures. When George Post designed the Capitol, he envisioned four small domes at the base of the great dome. These were never built, but in their place we have four groups of sculpture. At the base of the dome over the pavilion doorways are four sets of granite sculpture, each consisting of three sculptural figures—one standing, the other two seated (see photos, page 110). These are by Karl Bitter, who executed the monumental sculptures on the Administration Building at the 1893 World's Fair. The themes are *Faith* (located above the Dr. Martin Luther King Jr. Boulevard entrance), *Strength* (above the West Washington Avenue entrance), *Prosperity and Abundance* (above the Wisconsin Avenue entrance), and *Knowledge* (above the East Washington Avenue entrance). The four groups were completed between 1911 and 1915 and set in place as the

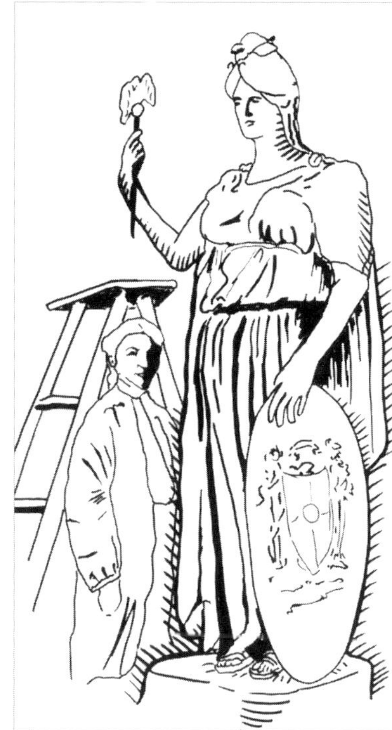

Drawing of Helen Farnsworth Mears and her version of *Wisconsin*

Helen Farnsworth Mears was one of Wisconsin's most talented artists. An example of her work appears at the first floor southeast entrance to the Capitol: a marble statue entitled *The Genius of Wisconsin*. Born in 1871 in Oshkosh, Mears studied at the Art Institute of Chicago with the prominent sculptor Lorado Taft. She and Jean Pond Miner Coburn shared the artist-in-residence appointment at the Wisconsin Pavilion of the 1893 World's Columbian Exposition.

The story of her involvement with the Capitol dome statue illustrates the difficulty that women artists have faced in having their work recognized and their contributions appreciated. Capitol architect George Post had originally suggested to sculptor Daniel Chester French that he might design a statue for the new Capitol dome. But French said he was too busy.

Architect Post then recommended Helen Mears to the Capitol Commission. She was well trained, had experience, and was from Wisconsin. She was then led to believe that the contract for designing the Capitol dome statue was hers even though she had received no written contract. So she worked on refining her sketches and even visited Daniel Chester French in New York to seek his advice.

Shortly after Mears' visit to French, architect Post received a letter from French indicating that he was interested in the project. Post immediately wrote to the Capitol Commission, recommending that the project be given to him and that Mears be paid something for her efforts before being removed from the project. He then wrote to Mears, informing her of the news.

Thus, a talented Wisconsin artist lost an important commission to an easterner who never visited the state. The contract might have made her a famous sculptor. Instead, we have a beautiful statue at the expense of her career: it was Helen Farnsworth Mears who originated the ideas of a helmeted goddess with a badger on her head. Her early sketches clearly indicate that French took her ideas and used them for the statue he created.

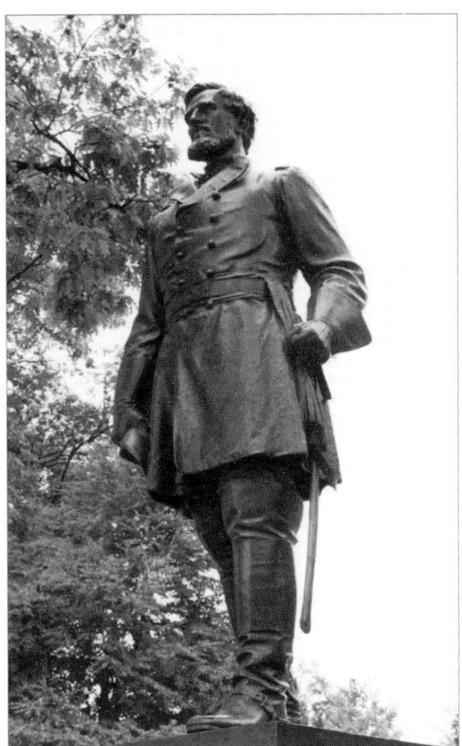

Hans Christian Heg statue by Paul Fjelde (1925) on Capitol grounds in Madison

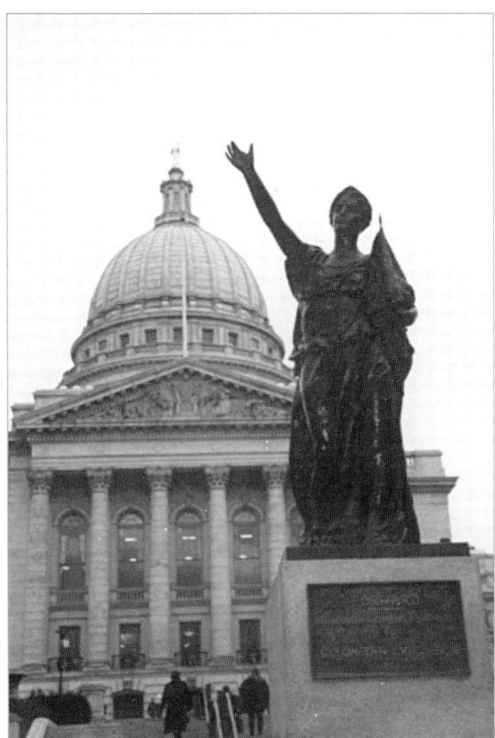

Forward statue cast in bronze in 1995 by Jean P. Miner (copper version completed in 1893) on Capitol grounds in Madison

Nearly a dozen figures of men, women, and children crowd into this north pediment in which wisdom, enlightenment and maternity are allegorically shown. This last Capitol pediment group was installed in 1917 and marked the end of the Capitol's exterior decoration program. Scores of workmen had labored for years to create these masterpieces in hard Bethel Vermont granite, the same material used for the exterior of the building.

Sculptures on the Capitol Grounds

On the Capitol grounds, additional sculptures were envisioned but only two were actually positioned there. At the King Street entrance is the *Hans Christian Heg Monument*, commemorating this Grand Army of the Republic (G.A.R.) civil war hero who fought in the 15th Wisconsin Regiment and died in the Battle of Chickamauga in 1863. The Norwegian Society of America commissioned Paul Fjelde of Norway to create this standing monument. Identical castings are found in Norway Township, near Waterford, Wisconsin and in Oslo, Norway.

On the west side of the State Capitol, at the State Street entrance, is the statue called *Forward*, the work of Jean P. Miner (1865-1967), a Madison artist. The statue was originally sculpted in clay at the 1893 World's Fair, where Miner was artist-in-residence along with Helen Farnsworth (see previous page). Miner had intended the statue to be cast in bronze, but budgetary limits only allowed it to be made of thin copper sheets, similar in technique to the *Statue of Liberty* in New York. *Forward* was brought to Wisconsin and eventually placed in State Capitol Park. Because of the fragile nature of the material, the thin copper sheets badly corroded over time due to the weather, neglect, and vandalism. In 1995, a campaign spearheaded by several Wisconsin women's groups, raised funds to cast the statue in bronze. After more than one hundred years, Miner's dream of a bronze version of her statue, dedicated to our state motto "Forward," became a reality. The original copper statue is now located in the lobby of the State Historical Society at the University of Wisconsin end of State Street. Thus the State of Wisconsin owns two similar Forward statues.

In 1998 a new low circular granite monument was placed at the north end of Capitol Park at Mifflin and Pinckney streets. The monument's title is *Law Enforcement Officers Memorial* and it honors officers killed in the line of duty. In keeping with the Beaux Arts tradition of the Capitol, a bronze statue could be added to lend additional dignity.

building was completed. Because of their location, they are difficult to appreciate, but with a little extra effort—and a good pair of field glasses—these wonderful works can be seen clearly. The sculptures have a rigid archaic quality that reflects Bitter's interest in early Greek sculpture. Each group exhibits a keen sense of design based upon solid geometric forms. A play of light and shadow defines the forms and gives them a strong three-dimensional quality, resulting in a simple yet classical ensemble.

The Wing-ends Sculptures. On the wing ends of the Capitol are sculptures that fit the triangular shapes called pediments, which lie above the giant Corinthian columns. Each pediment tells a different story. On the east, *Liberty* is supported by the Law. This sculpture was executed by Karl Bitter and completed in place in 1910. The subject is fitting as the Supreme Court is located in the building's east wing. The subject of the south pediment is *Virtues and Traits of Character*, befitting the wing that houses the State Senate. It is the work of Adolph Wienman, dated 1913. The west pediment theme is *Agriculture of Wisconsin*. It was conceived by Karl Bitter and completed in 1909. The north pediment is the work of Attilio Piccirilli. Its theme is *Wisdom and Learning of the World*.

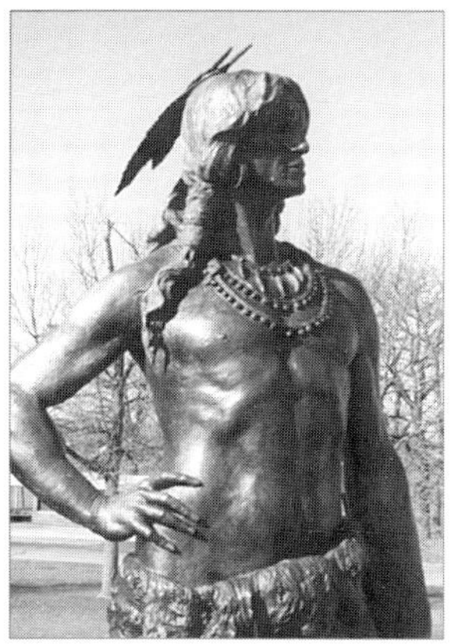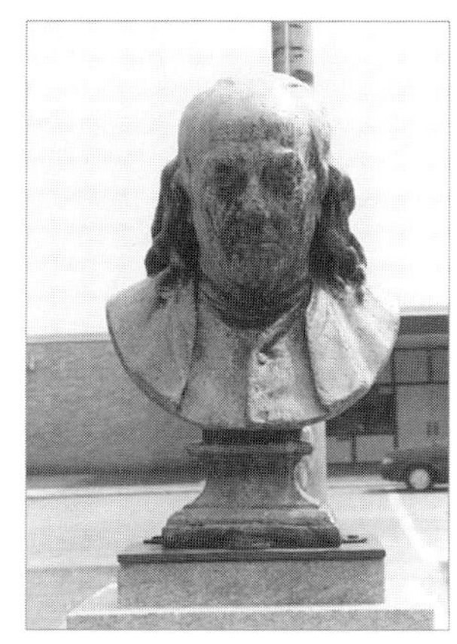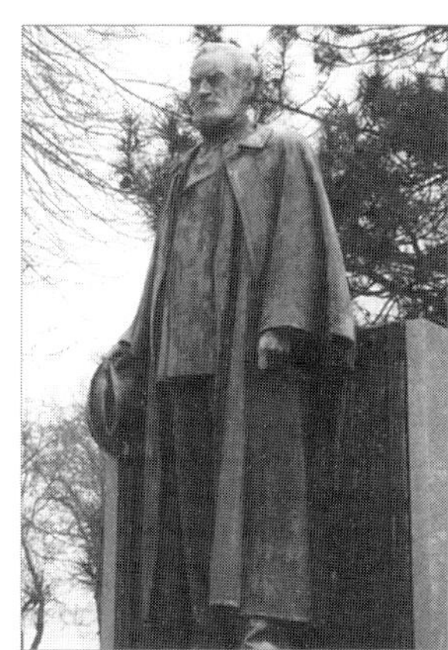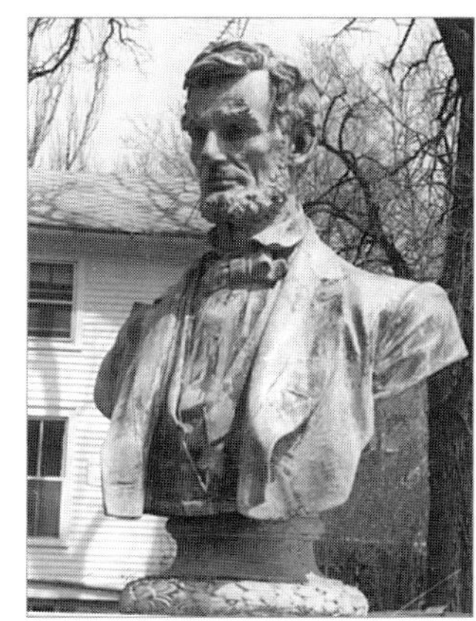

Oshkosh sculptures left to right:

Chief Oshkosh (1911) detail

Ben Franklin bust, after Houdon (1911)

Carl Schurz (1914)

Abraham Lincoln (1909) bust

Oshkosh, City of Beautiful Monuments

Because of the generosity of John Hicks (1847-1917), Oshkosh can be proud of its numerous public and Beaux Arts monuments. Hicks was a prominent newspaper businessman and diplomat who, along with 28 million others, visited the Colombian World's Fair in Chicago in 1893. He fell in love with public sculpture and continued to buy it out of his personal fortune, donating it to the city of Oshkosh throughout his lifetime. His gifts include monuments to *Carl Schurz* (1914), the statue of *Chief Oshkosh* (1911) and the statue of *Washington*, many near or in Menominee Park.

The story of the statue titled *George Washington* captures the tastes of the times. Through Thomas Jefferson's intervention, the state of Virginia commissioned the foremost sculptor of 18th century France, Jean Antoine Houdon (1741-1828), to carve a life-size portrait of George Washington for the Virginia State House. The completed statue in white marble was placed in the State House Rotunda in 1792, where it remains today. The sculpture embodies many ideals of the French Enlightenment and ancient Roman Republican portraits, which Houdon used as models and successfully merged into a single work of art

Washington is shown standing with a gentleman's cane in his right hand. He rests his left arm on his cape, which covers a bundle of rods, called Fasces in Latin which symbolizes union, and his sword is also shown. Behind him and at his feet is a plow, a symbol of his profession as citizen-planter. The statue portrays Washington as the statesman who defends and leads the nation. His restrained attire includes a military dresscoat, vest, and leggings. He looks off proudly into space with his hair pulled back in the style of the period. These symbols of restrained and dignified attire were considered appropriate to a young democratic republic and embody ideals of simplicity, not royal ostentation.

The bronze copy in Oshkosh is identical in size to the original and was cast at the Gorham Foundry, Providence, Rhode Island. John Hicks purchased it in 1911 for $5,000. Hicks admired Washington as the father of the republic. The portrait does not idealize Washington but captures his features in an honest straightforward way.

Unfortunately, the Oshkosh statue has been much abused over the years and suffered repeated acts of vandalism and neglect. This beautiful statue is repeatedly defaced with pumpkins by local youths around Halloween. In addition, aggressive cleaners have damaged the granite base and the metal suffers from bronze disease.

Identical statues are found in several cities in the United States and there is a beautifully maintained example in front of the National Gallery of Art in London, where it holds a prominent position on Trafalagar Square.

Additional portrait sculptures donated by Hicks are located in front of elementary schools and are of Benjamin Franklin and presidents Lincoln, Jefferson, and Washington. Hicks' contribution to Oshkosh is truly noteworthy for its goal of promoting public monuments for the pleasure, enlightenment, and education of its citizens. That tradition continues today in Oshkosh, thanks to the endowment Hicks established to acquire and preserve public sculpture.

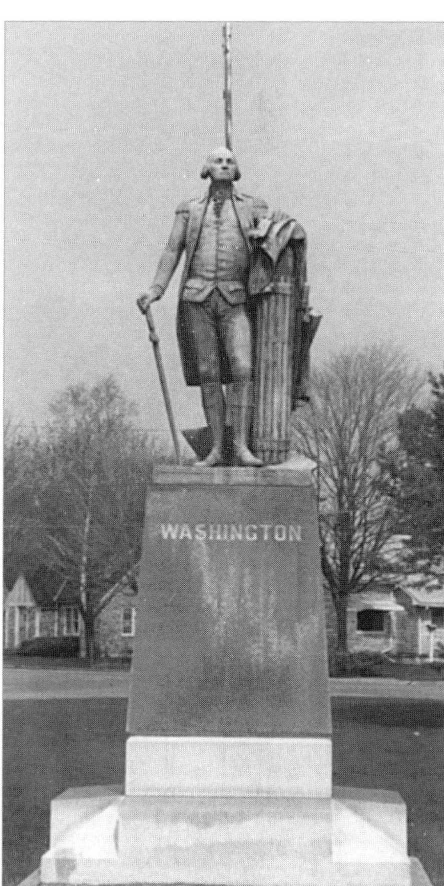

The bronze copy of Houdon's *Monument to George Washington* in Menominee Park, Oshkosh

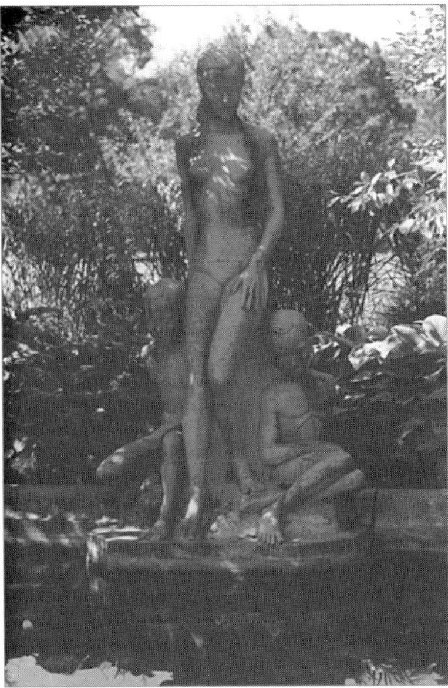

Reflecting Pool Statuary by Jefferson Greer located at Boerner Botanical Gardens, Hales Corners, Milwaukee County

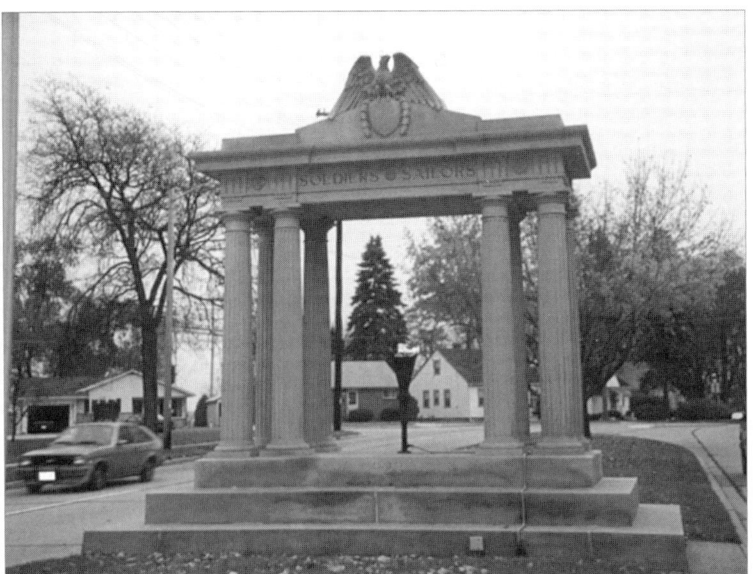

Soldiers and Sailors Monument with eternal flame in Manitowoc, built in 1923

Public Sculpture After World War I

The grand era of figurative sculpture in Wisconsin started in the late nineteenth century and extended until about 1930. Dozens of the state's finest public sculptures were added to Wisconsin's heritage during this period as an outgrowth of the City Beautiful Movement and the tradition of Beaux Arts art and architecture. But after World War I, changing styles and tastes led to fewer and fewer figurative monuments being erected in Wisconsin. In their place several different types of public monuments evolved. One relied upon artistic developments in the fine arts, such as streamlined modernism and abstraction. The other was dedicatory in nature, listing on tablets events and people associated with the commemorated event.

Depression and New Deal ERA Public Sculpture

The hard times of the Great Depression led to few public sculptures being erected in Wisconsin. The 1929 stock market crash abruptly cancelled many projects. The era of grand monuments had come nearly to an end, with the exception of a few war memorials and other statuary. In its place arose a new type of functional art born out of the federal government's massive intervention in the national economy. The New Deal programs of Franklin Delano Roosevelt's administration had an important impact on Wisconsin's public sculpture heritage.

Fond du Lac's Stone Wildlife. One of the few New Deal Art Programs outside major Wisconsin metropolitan areas was in Fond du Lac. The city received a New Deal outdoor public sculpture program with the construction of a post office at South Macy and West First Streets in 1935. Artist Boris Gilbertson was commissioned in 1937 to decorate the exterior of the new building with stone bas-reliefs of Wisconsin fauna. He had always been fond of wildlife and found this a unique chance to represent it in permanent form. His *Wild Birds* and *Animals of Wisconsin (Fauna of Wisconsin)* sculptures serve as wonderful visual documents of Wisconsin's larger wildlife. Eleven limestone sculptures are still in place today at the building which is no longer a post office. Located high on the building's exterior, however, the work is hard to appreciate. These were the only exterior sculptural decorations commissioned by the U.S. Postal Service in Wisconsin in the 1930s.

Milwaukee's New Deal Sculpture. Milwaukee was the recipient of many New Deal programs to employ artists. Between 1932 and 1941, work was provided by the Civilian Conservation

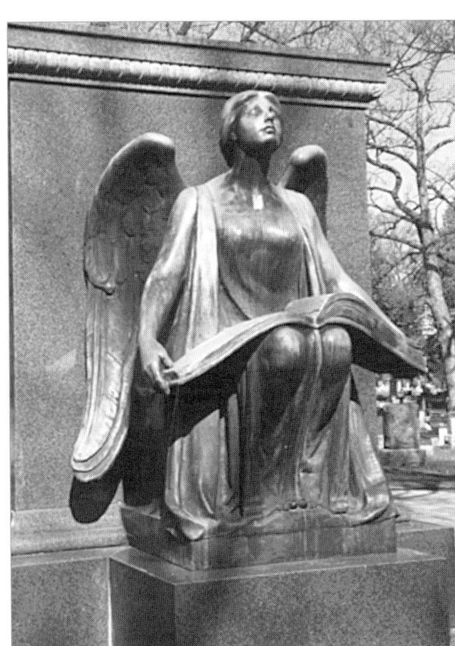

The Recording Angel by Lorado Taft (1923) in Waupun

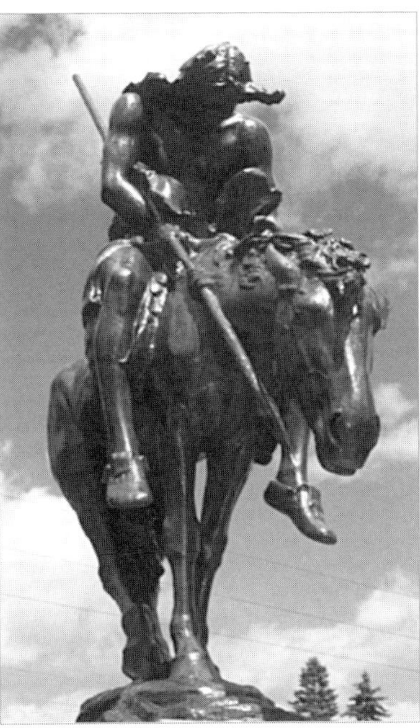

Bronze *End of the Trail* by James Earl Fraser (1928) in Waupun

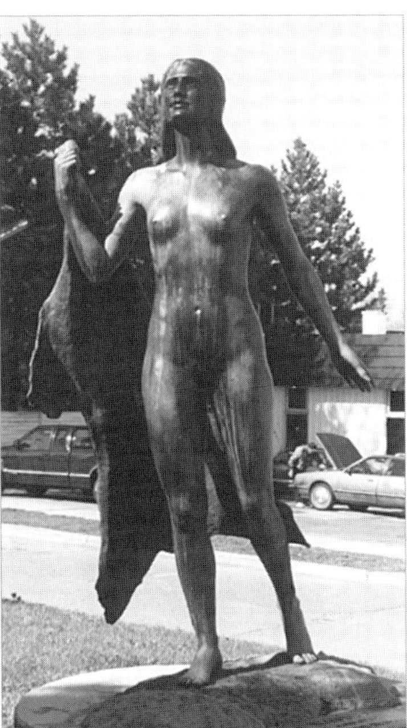

Bronze *Dawn of Day* by Clarence Shaler (1931) in Waupun

Corps (CCC), the Works Progress Administration (WPA), the National Youth Administration (NYA), and Milwaukee County relief labor. One notable project was the embellishment of Boerner Botanical Gardens in Hales Corners. The gardens were established out of the philosophies of Alfred Boerner (1900-1955) and Charles Whitnall (1859-1949) who believed that city life could be enhanced by having parks available to the populace. In the 1920s, Whitnall purchased farmland which was later named in his honor and this helped establish the Milwaukee County Park System. Boerner designed the botanical garden in Whitnall Park.

The WPA's *Public Works of Art Project (PWAP)* is responsible for the Boerner Garden's sculpture and was the largest WPA-sponsored outdoor sculpture project in Wisconsin. Artist George Adams Dietrich directed the program, which included his *Reflecting Pool Statuary*, depicting a mother and two boys. Jefferson Greer (1905-1958) created other garden statuary, including children, animals, and birds. James Gehr carved the turtle, sea crab and birds. Richard Wilken and Karl Kahlich contributed wooden carvings in the administration building. The park's sundial was the work of Evelyn Sindel (Buck, 171-121).

Though many of the New Deal projects, such as the WPA, came to an abrupt end with World War II, the legacy of government funded art still lives on in the public monuments created during this period.

Waupun, City of Sculpture. Despite the harsh economic realities of the Great Depression, Clarence Shaler (1860-1941) of Waupun first purchased and later created monumental bronze statuary. He donated many of these sculptures to his hometown. The story is a fascinating one of self-determination, luck, and love of the arts. Shaler made his fortune early in life by successfully marketing automobile tire patches, golf clubs, and umbrellas. By the late 1920s, he was already a self-made millionaire and had begun buying sculpture. His first major purchase was *The Recording Angel* by Lorado Taft (1923), which decorates his wife's grave. Next he negotiated with James Earl Fraser for a full scale monumental bronze version of the *End of the Trail*, which arrived in Waupun in 1929, months before the stock market crash. By this time Shaler was residing part of the year in Pasadena, California, where he came in contact with the Nelli Art Foundry. Soon after, he began making his own art.

Throughout the 1930s, Shaler gave Waupun *Dawn of Day* (1931), and *The Pioneers* (1938, dedicated 1940), and he gave the Waupun Country Club, *Group of Deer* (1933). After the death of Shaler's sister he created *Morning of Life,* a bronze statue of her for the grave site, which he completed in 1936. In addition, he donated to the University of Wisconsin-Madison *He Who Sows Believes in God*, also known as *Who Sows* (1937), which later was given to Waupun. He gave Ripon College *Genesis* (1936) and *Lincoln the Dreamer* (1939). His last work of art before his death, the powerful *Citadel* (1939), he gave to the University of Southern California which later gave it to the city of Waupun. The *Citadel* is an unusual work of art that embodies Shaler's fear about the death of civilization and the rise of Fascism, which he believed might conquer the free world. His extraordinary gifts of public sculpture to small Wisconsin communities is unprecedented in our state's history, except perhaps the Hicks bequest a generation earlier in Oshkosh. Both Shaler and Hicks left an amazing legacy of outdoor public sculptures for our enjoyment.

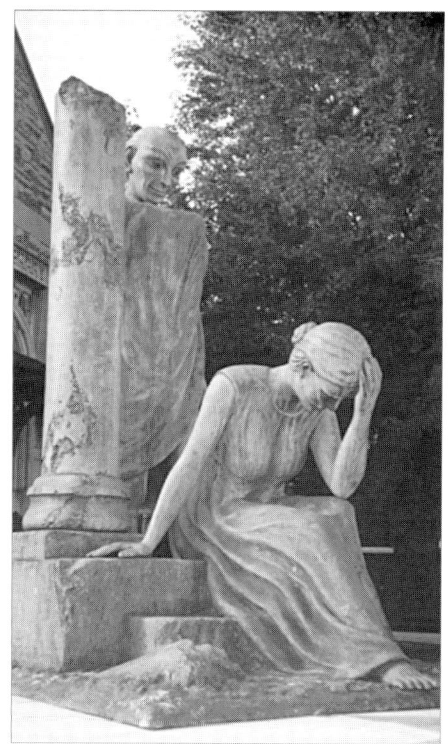

Citadel (1939) by Clarence Shaler in Waupun

Further Reading

Diane Buck and Virginia A. Palmer. *Outdoor Sculpture in Milwaukee, a Cultural and Historical Guidebook*. Madison: State Historical Society of Wisconsin, 1995.

Frances W. Hurst and Fran Rall. *Common Joy II: Outdoor Art in Madison*. Self-published, 1991, 1994.

June Kelly, *Public Sculpture in Waupun, the Gift of Clarence Shaler*. Waupun: Waupun Printing, 1964.

David Mollenhoff. *Madison: A History of the Formative Years*. Dubuque: Kendall-Hunt, 1982.

Wisconsin State Capitol Guide and History. Madison: State of Wisconsin, 1991.

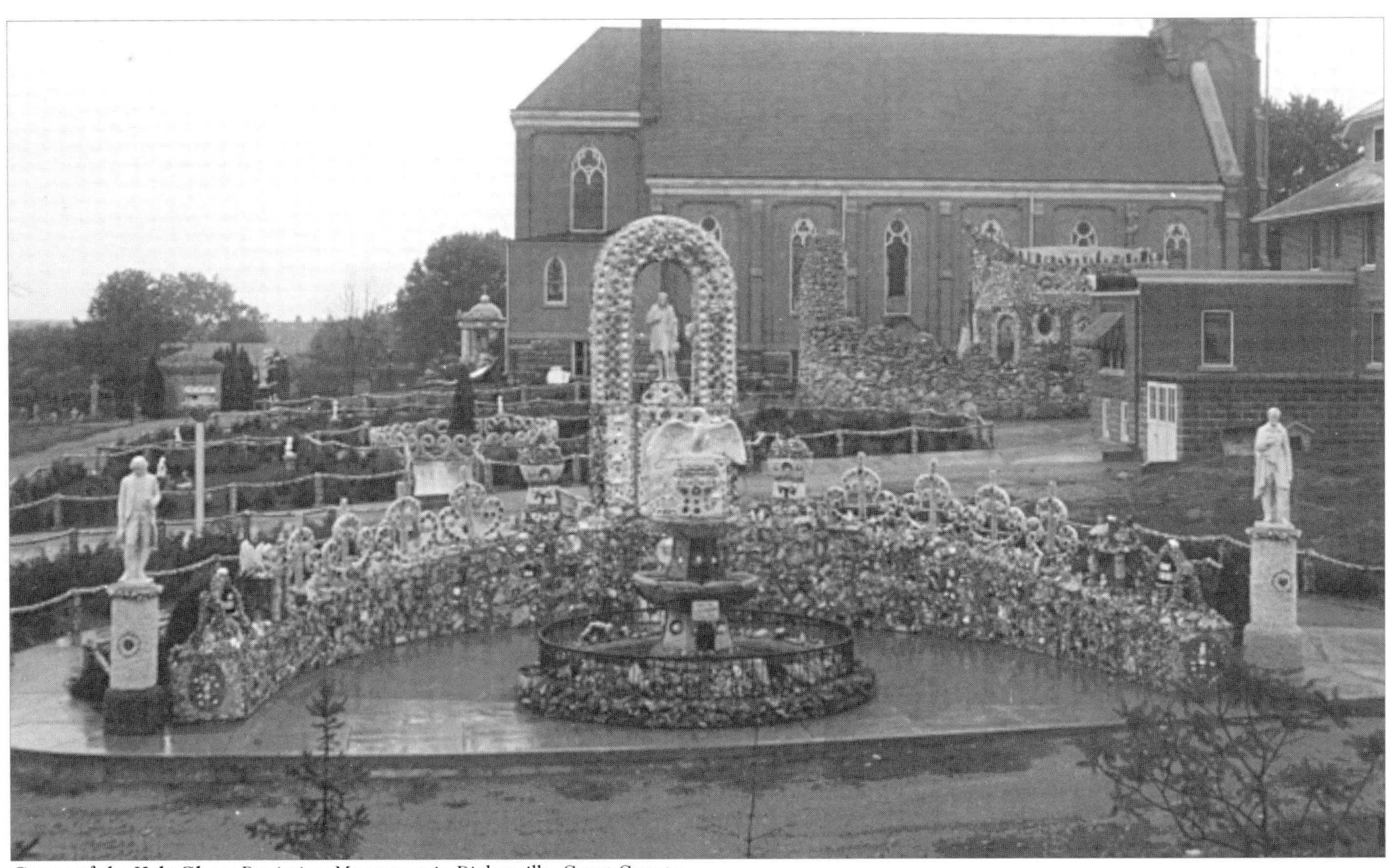

Grotto of the Holy Ghost, Patriotism Monument in Dickeyville, Grant County

Nontraditional Public Sculpture

Church Grottoes, Visionary Environments, Chainsaw Carvings, Fiberglass, and Native American Effigy Mounds as Art

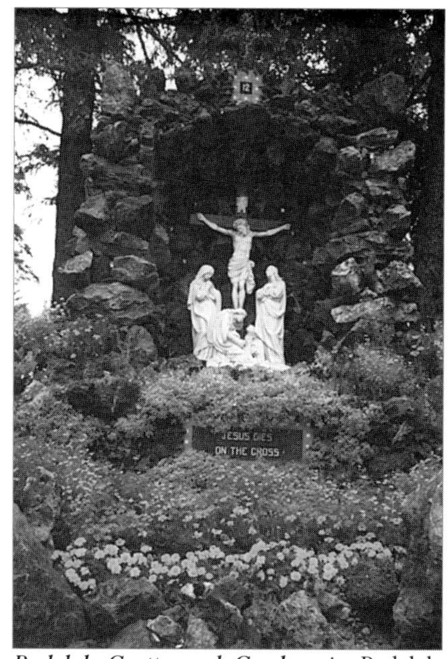

Rudolph Grotto and Gardens in Rudolph, Wood County

Wisconsin is rich in nontraditional public sculptures that do not fit into any of the usual art categories. Examples include the Dickeyville Grotto, Wisconsin Concrete Park, Bill Vinneaux's Gallery of Chainsaw Art, and Sparta's fiberglass art factory. Another nontraditional public sculpture category is our Native American heritage in the form of effigy mounds—which are artistic in nature, outdoors, and accessible to the viewing public. And so we include these varied works in this discussion of public outdoor sculpture in Wisconsin. In their own way, non-traditional artists have responded to the Wisconsin landscape, constructing art forms surrounded by nature and enriching the cultural fabric of the state.

Many of these nontraditional sculptures were the works of individuals who created art because of some inner need to express themselves in visual form. And notably, the artists described in this section are all self-taught. That is, they had no formal art training before embarking upon their artistic careers. All of them were individuals of strong character. These artists, in one way or another, felt inspired to give material form to their imaginations and often transformed everyday objects into art. Inspired by religion, patriotism, civic pride, or simply the urge to create, these people have labored to make something lasting and a permanent witness to their vision.

Many terms have been used to describe these artistic creations set within a landscape: folk art environments, folk art sites, self-taught art environments, and grotto art. In this section we consider some of Wisconsin's most widespread forms of the folk art environment: church grottoes, visionary art environments, chainsaw art, fiberglass art, and Native American effigy mounds.

Concrete Faith: Church Grottoes and Outdoor Religious Shrines

> "Images of the Lord are
> abundantly represented
> throughout the state."
> SOS! volunteer

Gardens, grottoes, and parks have been a source of inspiration and contemplation for centuries. The Western world has long been fascinated with caves and grottoes as places of revelation, mystery, fear, revulsion, and inspiration. Caves evoke alternating emotions of repulsion and attraction, dread and curiosity, and the practices of speleolatry, or cave worship, come from the Latin, *speleum*, meaning cave.

In ancient mythology, caves were believed to have healing and curative powers, particularly if associated with a water source or sacred springs. One characteristic of grottoes is the disparity between their interior and exterior: the mundane exterior both hides and beckons to an interior that opens onto the unknown. The cave is a place of passage.

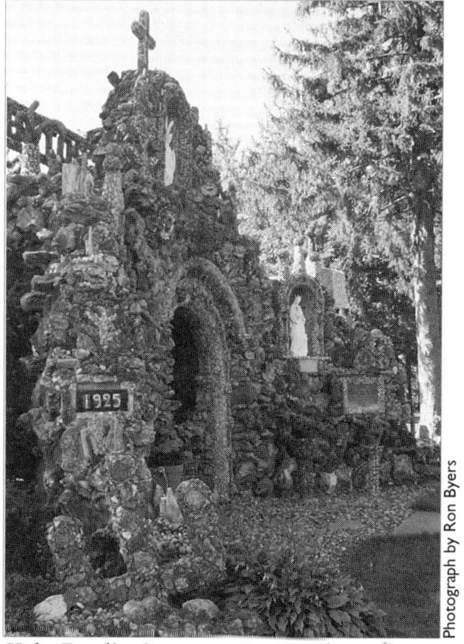

Holy Famliy Grotto in St. Joseph, LaCrosse County

Photograph by Ron Byers

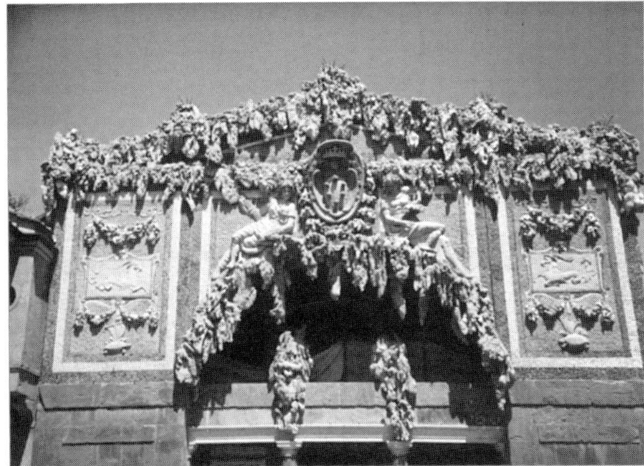

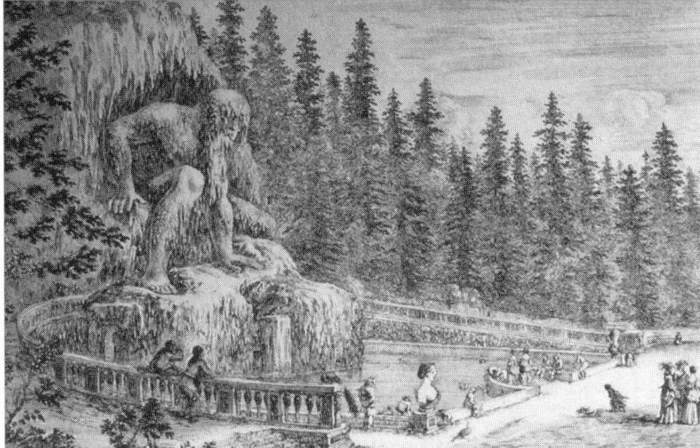

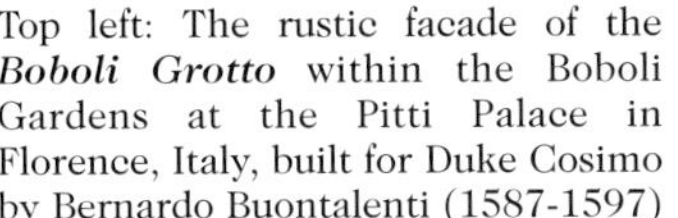

Top left: The rustic façade of the *Boboli Grotto* within the Boboli Gardens at the Pitti Palace in Florence, Italy, built for Duke Cosimo by Bernardo Buontalenti (1587-1597)

Top right: *The Appennine Giant* at the Gardens of Pratolino in Italy

Below: *Organ Fountain* at Villa d'Este (Tivoli Garden), Tivoli, Italy

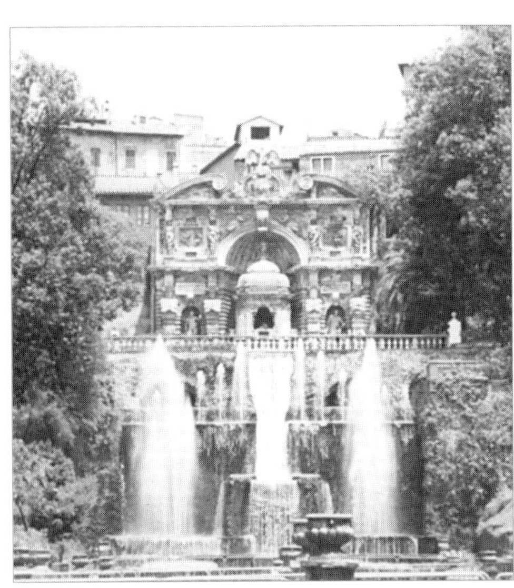

Beginning in the ancient Mediterranean world and spreading across Europe, church and garden grottoes were plentiful long before they came with European settlers to North America. Many were built, especially in Upper Midwest churchyards. Grottoes are caves fashioned by humans, a frozen architecture of rock, crystal, porcelain, shells, and other *wunderkummer*. Nature was always the starting point for these contrivances of artful arrangements of rocks and stones. Many of the more elaborate grotto constructions, such as the Rudolph Grotto, were endowed with cosmic and divine significance. Grottoes were above all sacred places where apparitions revealed themselves and acts of healing were performed.

In ancient Greece and Rome, fountains and watersources were consecrated to the nymphs, hence the Greek name *nymphaea*, place of the nymphs. Over the centuries, this meaning and the association with divine or supernatural forces were radically transformed with the growth of Christianity and the church's need for alternate sites of worship. The rustic grotto came to be an informal location where the church sanctioned worship and encouraged the faith as it did in the much more formal structure of churches. So grottoes came to be both religious and utilitarian at once: places of inspiration and a cover from the elements. They also had a theatrical role as rustic stage and backdrop for church plays and ceremonies invoking the pastoral, the sacred, the idyllic and the dramatic.

Christianity and Judaism initiated the association of caves and grottoes as resting places of the elders of the faith. Grottoes and caves in the Holy Land were frequently places of revelation. The sanctity of caves is also associated with hermits and wilderness saints, such as St. Jerome or St. Anthony, serving as places of seclusion and inspiration for their divine writings.

Finally, in the Judaeo-Christian tradition, caves served as places of refuge during times of persecution. The catacombs in Rome can be seen as a type of human-made cave, fashioned to protect early Christians from their persecutors.

One of Europe's most spectacular grotto complexes is the famed Boboli Gardens which is attached to the Pitti Palace in Florence. Built for Duke Cosimo by Bernardo Buontalenti between 1587 and 1597, the *Boboli Grotto*, within the Garden is built of rough-hewn rock and encrusted with rustic aggregate, artificial stalactites, odd creatures, lava, shells, and unusual stones. This artificial environment is convincingly built to appear as a natural product of time. The grotto houses three chambers, each deeper and more mysterious than the last. The immediate impetus for creation of this grotto was to house the four unfinished statues of slaves by Michelangelo, which the Duke had acquired. The unfinished state of the statues harmonized with the grotto's rustic tableaux. In the second of three chambers stood Vincenzo Rossi's sculptures of Theseus and Helena. In the third chamber, lit from above by a hole in the ceiling, was Giambologna's white marble nude Venus rising from her bath. The overall impression is that of an ancient ruin with a blend of art, architecture, nature, and plantings interspersed to create a theatrical effect of beauty, inspiration, and wonder. The grotto has recently undergone major sensitive restoration, which recaptures much of its previously lost beauty and mystery.

By the Italian Renaissance, many noble families commissioned parks and gardens to adjoin their city or country homes. During this revival in classical villas, families of great means built stunning garden environments that enhanced and transformed the landscape, often using water, fountains, and unusual materials to produce an otherworldly effect. A frequently cited example is the *Tivoli Garden* at Villa d'Este near Rome, built for a cardinal in the 16th century. The architectural follies, waterfalls, topiary, and fantastic sculptures, and a splendid union of art and nature are unprecedented and never since matched. There are gravity-driven waterworks of every imaginable type, providing sound, motion, and even music: the gardens even included a hydro-powered organ.

The *Tivoli Gardens* are enhanced by their setting in the foothills of the Apennine Mountains, with some of the grotto caves carved into the mountain forming a curtain of flowing water.

Equally powerful, though much altered by time, is the Fantasy Garden at Pratolino near Florence with its stone giants and water pond plantings. A seventeenth century visitor described it as "a cave three miles long with many fountains of water, from whence by many pipes the waters are brought to serve the works in the gardens." The French traveler Michel de Montaigne visited the garden and described it as a "marvel of a grotto with many niches and rooms, formed of all crusted matter enriched by water." Numerous other grottoes, both secular and religious, abound in Italy with sculptures of giants, monsters, madonnas, masks, and fantasy creations. Many of these sites incorporate grottoes or underground shrines for meditation and prayer.

Grotto building came to Germany, as it had in France, as an outgrowth of landscape architecture efforts beginning in the seventeenth century, with religious, royal, and ducal patrons interested in reviving classical themes. One of the earliest German garden grottoes was built for Duke William of Bavaria for the Residenz in Munich around 1616. Today it is referred to as the court grotto. It consisted of fountains, rustic walls, and grotto-like figures, juxtaposed with classically themed statues. Many of the German grottoes take their inspiration from Italian models, including the use of hydraulic machines, the presence of classical statues, and the use of rustic materials. Wilhelmshohe and Schwetzingen, both in Southern Germany, have extensive gardens and grotto structures.

For years, the Catholic Church was closely associated with the political structure of Southern Germany, particularly in Bavaria. Many bishops served both as temporal and spiritual leaders and because of their position were required to have stately residences. To this day, Catholic churches, especially in rural Southern Germany, abound with grotto-like structures. Several of these have fantastic garden grottoes that may have served as inspiration for the later grotto efforts in the United States. Publications, reproductions, and the close association of German Catholic priests with many Upper Midwest rural churches in the early twentieth century were likely vectors for the movement of the grotto idea.

The palace at Mainz in Germany was noted for its garden grotto, arbors, and pavilions. Prince Bishop of Bamberg, who became Elector-Archbishop in Mainz in 1695, ordered their construction. In nearby Bamberg, at Pommersfelden, another splendid garden with grotto was added by Johann Lucas von Hildebrandt. Its most unique feature is the unusually large interior room with fountains and a fireplace for the winter. It became in essence a rustic house with plasterwork, statuary, and

frosted glass and walls encrusted with quartz, mica, colored gems, and ceramics. It is Baroque in all its aspects and delights all the senses throughout the year. Additional grotto gardens of note in Germany include the Hermitage in Bayreuth, Hellbrun's Rock Theater, and Veitschochheim's Grotto-Belevedere.

The exact extent of influence from these and other garden grottoes in England, France, and Italy to the creations in Wisconsin will probably never be known. We do know that many educated Germans settled in the Upper Midwest and of course these immigrants would be familiar with their own religious and cultural heritage. Also, many of the Catholic priests who served in Wisconsin were of German descent. They brought with them to the New World a familiarity with religious art in Germany and Europe, and they knew the power of popular images to instruct the faithful.

Technological advances such as the automobile, truck, railroads, and mass availability of concrete combined with religious fervor in the early twentieth century, inspired parish priests and others to construct religious grotto art environments in the vicinity of their churches. The largest site in the Upper Midwest, created by the Catholic parish priest Father Dobberstein, is located in the most unlikely of places, attesting to the power of faith to build monuments. The West Bend, Iowa, *Grotto of the Redemption* is in Central Northwest Iowa and covers several acres and includes shrines, pathways, and a lake. Father Dobberstein galvanized his congregation to help build this monument to faith between 1915 and 1945. It was used for religious ceremonies such as confirmations and holy communions as well as other parish events.

In Wisconsin, notable grotto examples are in Dickeyville, Rudolph, and Brussels.

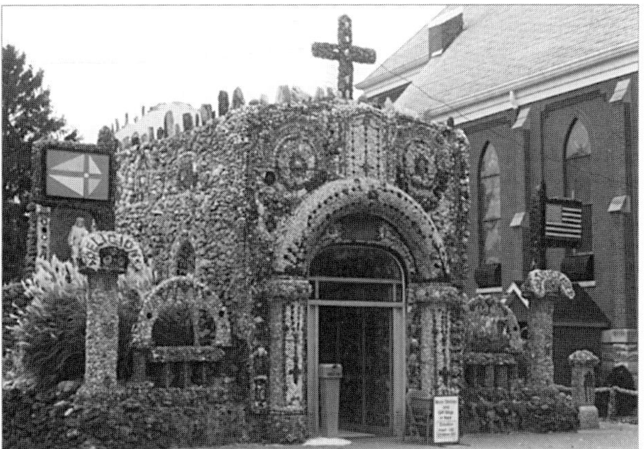

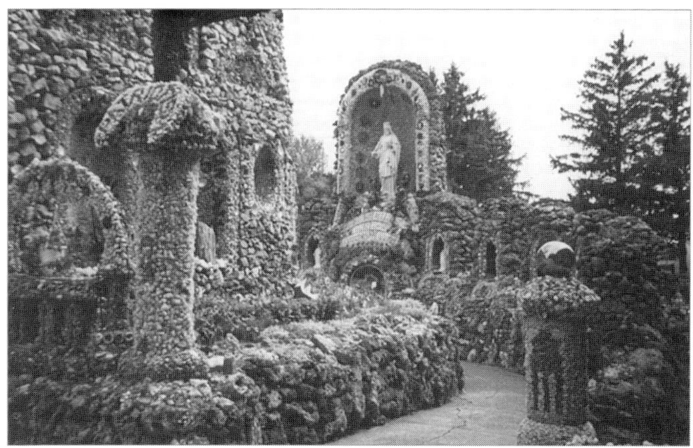

Top left: Front of the *Grotto of the Holy Ghost* in Dickeyville, Grant County

Top right: The open walkway behind the *Grotto of the Holy Ghost* in Dickeyville

Below: Christopher Columbus Monument at the *Grotto of the Holy Ghost* in Dickeyville

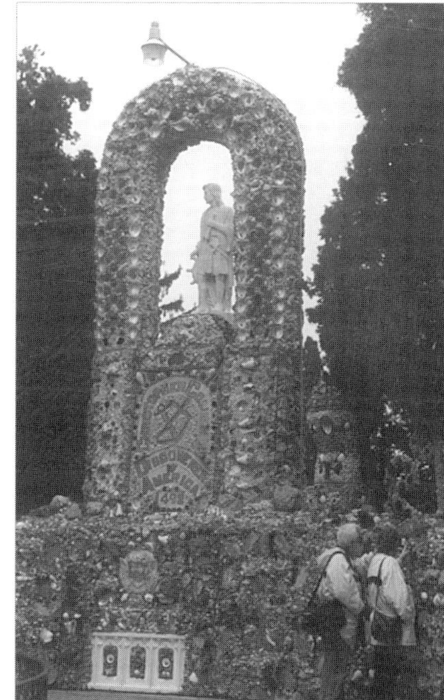

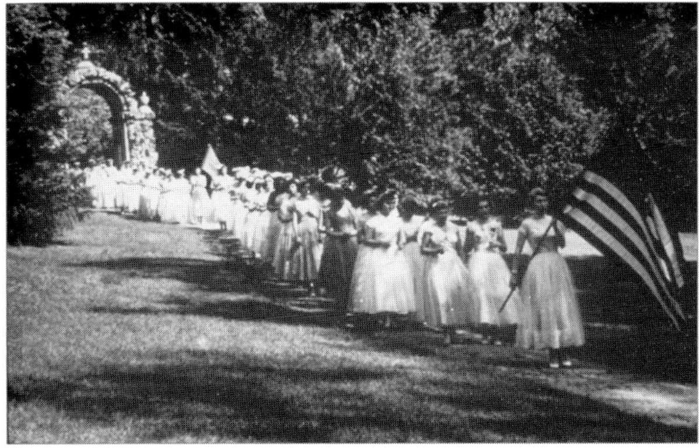

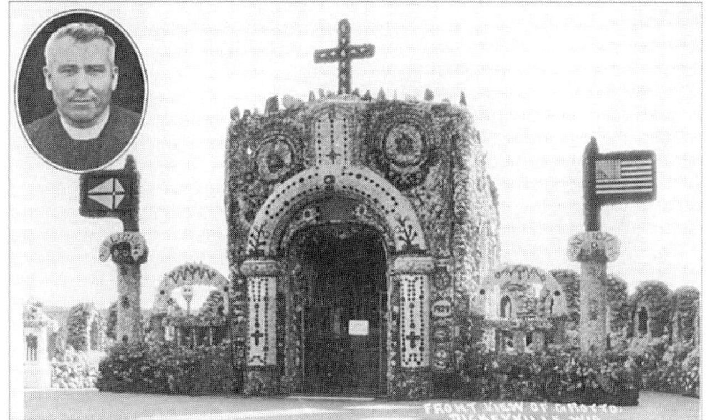

Left: Grotto May Crowning procession with patriotic display, circa 1930

Right: Dickeyville's *Grotto of the Holy Ghost* postcard with inset of the priest/artist Father Mathias Wernerus

Dickeyville's Grotto of the Holy Ghost

The largest and most unusual religious grotto art site in Wisconsin is Dickeyville's *Grotto of the Holy Ghost*.

The effort to build it was led by Father Mathias Wernerus. Born in Kettenis, in Eastern Belgium in 1873, he was admitted to the Salesian religious school in Liege, Belgium, at 24. It was in Liege that he may have seen his first grotto at the Benedictine Abbey of Peace. The Liege grotto is in ruins today and may have inspired him in later life. In addition, the rich altarpieces of St. Hubert's Church and others in Liege may have had a permanent effect on his understanding of the power of images in the spiritual and temporal lives of the faithful.

In 1904, Wernerus embarked for Milwaukee, where he was admitted to the St. Francis Seminary and where another small grotto existed. He was ordained in 1907 and shortly thereafter served several small Wisconsin parishes before coming to Dickeyville in April 1910. The Holy Ghost Parish would be his greatest challenge and triumph, a place where he demonstrated that faith could indeed move mountains—in this case the human-made mountains of rock and stone that formed his *Grotto of the Holy Ghost*.

Upon his arrival, he immediately set out to improve his small rural German-American parish. In quick succession, a new school, convent, and other enhancements were built. He began the first of his many commemorative works in 1918—the cruci-fixion group in the parish cemetery. The cemetery statues were purchased from the Munich Statue and Altar Company in Milwaukee.

By 1924, Fr. Wernerus had another project underway, a eucharistic altar in the form of a grotto, with domed room, columns, gilded tiles, semiprecious stones, and other embellish-ments. This was followed by an even more ambitious project dedicated to Christ the King and the Virgin Mary. It was to become the largest freestanding grotto structure in the state. Flags of the Vatican and the United States, in concrete, embellish the front of the grotto. Composed of two parts, the roofed grotto holds a beautiful statue of Mary and the Christ Child, with an open walkway behind it dedicated to Christ the King. Surfaces are elaborately decorated with niches, unusual stones, semiprecious materials, marble, and ceramics and other statues. Fr. Wernerus went on to construct several other embellished groupings in the churchyard, including the monumental shrine to patriotism, a shrine to the Sacred Heart of Jesus, and others, completed between 1928 and 1930. Assisting him in these projects were his devoted congregation, modern means of transport, and access to building materials, including concrete and heavy stones.

The shrine complex was formally dedicated on September 14, 1930, with an outdoor mass followed by a speech by Governor Kohler. Thousands attended the celebration, and the local press covered it in detail. It is possible that Fr. Wernerus had plans for additional grotto work, but ill health and the loss of several key collaborators curtailed these plans, and he died in 1931.

Rudolph's Grotto to Our Lady of Lourdes

One of the largest garden grotto complexes in Wisconsin is in the small town of Rudolph. It covers nearly twelve acres and is the creation of another artist-priest, Father Philip Wagner. Born in Iowa in 1882 and trained as a priest in Innsbruck, Austria, Fr. Wagner suffered from poor health due to overwork and exhaustion. He made a pilgrimage to the holy grotto at Lourdes, known for its curative properties and pledged that, if cured, he would someday undertake a project devoted to the Lady. He was indeed cured, received his ordination in Austria, and returned to the United States, where he was assigned to the small parish in Rudolph in 1917.

Father Wagner proved to be a capable, energetic, and devoted parish priest, and he set about establishing gardens and an ambitious grotto building project in 1927. The first grotto would be dedicated to Our Lady of Lourdes. It took three years to complete. He was assisted by Edmund Rybicki, who helped him with this project and with those that followed. Shrines to Christ the King, the Stations of the Cross, and Our Lady of Fatima rose from the soil, embellished with plantings, readymade Italian marble statues, a beautiful local red stone, mosaics, and other decorations.

By 1935, Fr. Wagner and many or his parishioners undertook their most ambitious work: a mountain of rock with meandering interior caverns and walkways revealing a tableaux of the life of Christ and the saints. It came to be known as the *Wonder Cave*. The rugged man-made exterior hides an impressive array of rustic art and architecture that appears to be made by nature. Nearby, the log cabin chapel of St. Jude, patron saint of the impossible, stands as a worthy patron to this monumental project. Fr. Wagner and his assistants continued their building projects for decades. He died in 1959, and Rybicki remained involved with the site until his death in 1991.

Our Lady of Lourdes Grotto in Brussels

The Door County peninsula has a beautiful Catholic church grotto at St. Francis Xavier Church in Brussels. Immigrants from Belgium prompted the local archdiocese in Green Bay to establish a mission in 1878, which became the site of a Neo-Gothic brick church in 1909. Further growth led to the establishment of a full parish in 1919. Father J.J. Gloudemans, who spoke several languages, was the first fulltime priest. He approached the job with great energy and like other priests in the region sought to make the church a place of refuge and inspiration for his parishioners.

It is not known if Father Gloudemans visited Dickeyville or other Midwest church grotto sites, but without a doubt he would have been familiar with them through postcards and other publications. In addition, several other churches in the region had grotto shrines, including St. Nazianz, Mount Calvary, Holy Hill, and Holy Name Catholic Church in Sheboygan.

The local Belgian-American community also brought with them the long and active tradition of roadside chapels, some of which still survive today. The close-knit community of farmers were acquainted with building bees in which everyone joined to build barns and houses. It seemed natural, when Father Gloudemans sought their help in building a grotto in the church cemetery in the early 1930s, that they would help. Father Gloudeman's initial reason was to erect his own tomb, strategically located beneath the grotto in the center of the complex. Whether it was ill health or prudent preparation for the future we will never know. The tomb was never used, though the granite grave stone remains with his name. He left the parish in 1946 and never returned.

The grotto is a composite of several popular Catholic images of the time. The devotional following to the Blessed Virgin at Lourdes had been gaining numbers since the 1858 apparition in Lourdes, France, by the young Bernadette. Gradually the Catholic Church recognized this as a genuine miracle and sanctioned its devotion. The Belgians had a particular fondness for Lourdes as Bernadette came from a farming family, not unlike them. By the 1930s, the apparition at Lourdes had a great following and seemed an appropriate theme for the Brussels church. Because of budgetary restrictions, Father Gloudemans created a grotto with several themes in one structure. This novel solution placed the image of Christ at Calvary on top, attended by St. John and the Virgin Mary. Immediately below is the apparition at Lourdes scene, and along the sides and back are various saints, including St. Francis of Assissi, St. Anthony of Padua, and others. The grotto incorporates many aspects of Catholic iconography in a simple outdoor structure. Along either side are dedicatory plaques with the date 1935. Many parishioners assisted in the project and several are named on the plaques, including Alphonse Gerondale and J.A. Stoneman. Carl Manthey and sons contributed building materials and labor.

Hundreds of people gathered on October 29, 1935 for the dedication of the completed grotto, as they had at Dickeyville, Rudolph and other outdoor grotto devotional sites during this period. The Catholic Church was in a period of tremendous growth in America and the outdoor grottoes helped to spread the faith.

By the 1950s, Wisconsin churches had at least ten grottoes devoted to Our Lady at Lourdes. The theme remains one of the most ubiquitous in grotto art today. The story of the lonely farm girl who witnessed a vision of the Holy Lady is told over and over again in churchyards throughout the state.

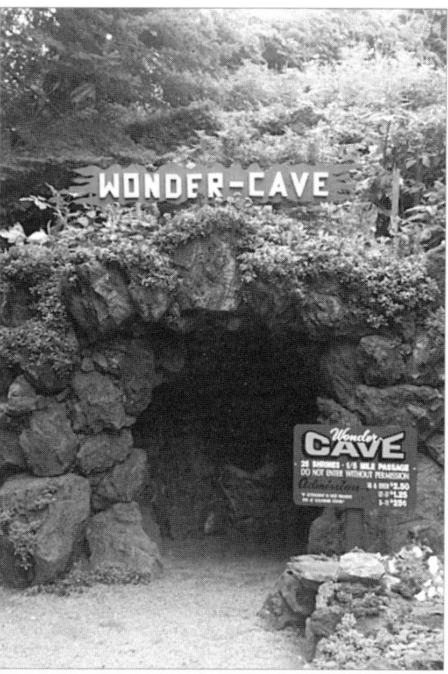

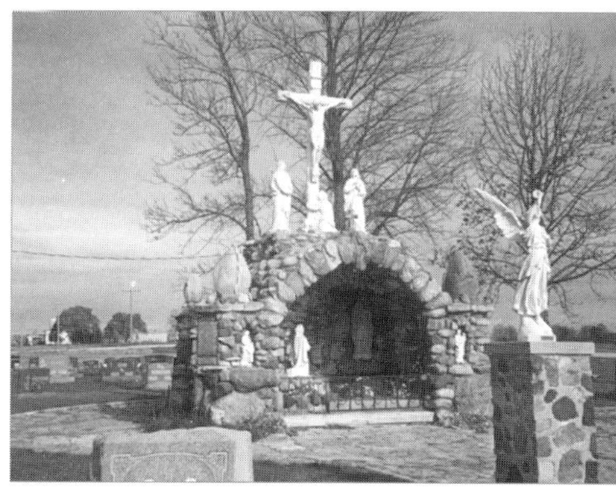

Top: *Wonder Cave* at the Rudolph Grotto, Wood County

Above: *Our Lady of Lourdes Grotto* in Brussels, Door County

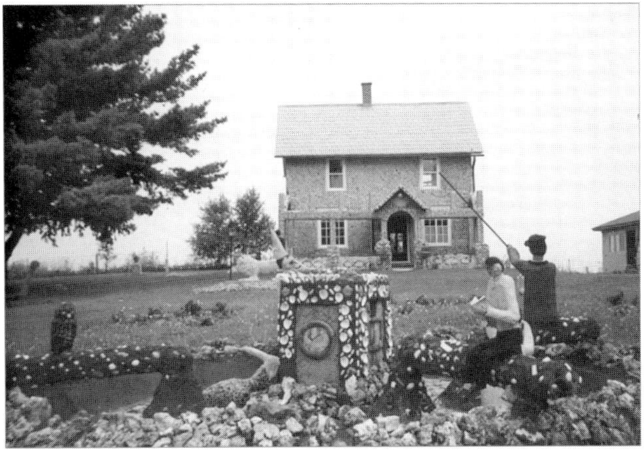

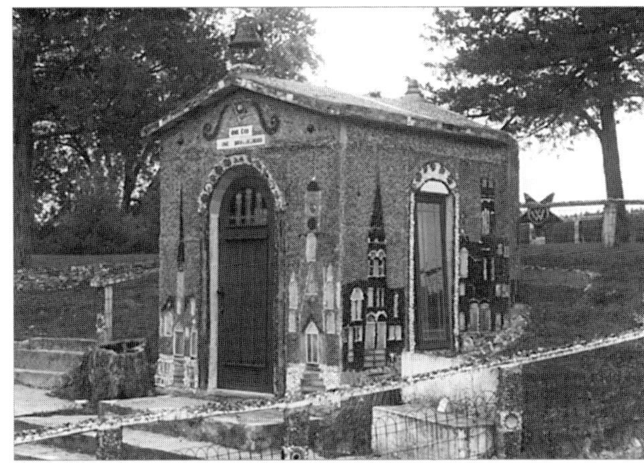

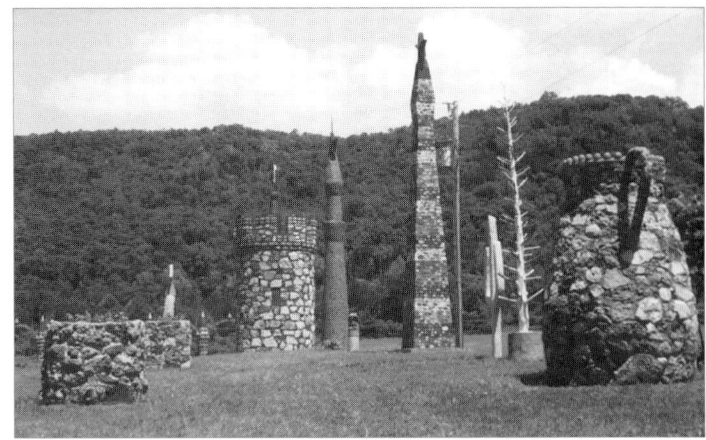

Top left: *Grandview* near Hollandale, Iowa County

Top center: *Wegner Grotto* near Sparta, Monroe County

Top right: *The Herman Rusch, Prairie Moon Site* near Cochrane, Buffalo County

Below right: *Native American Indian* at *Wisconsin Concrete Park* near Phillips, Price County

Below: *Wisconsin Concrete Park* entrance, Phillips, Price County

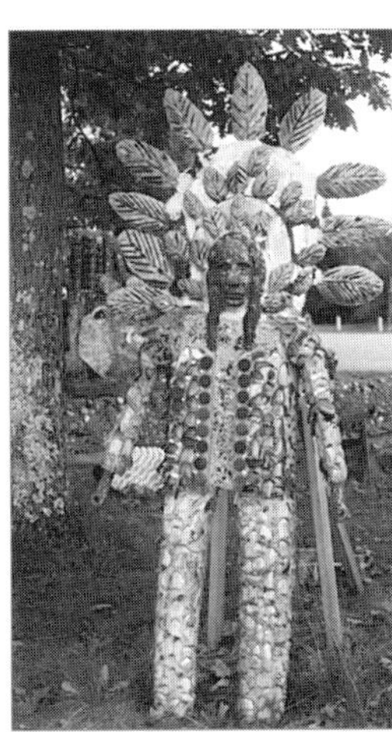

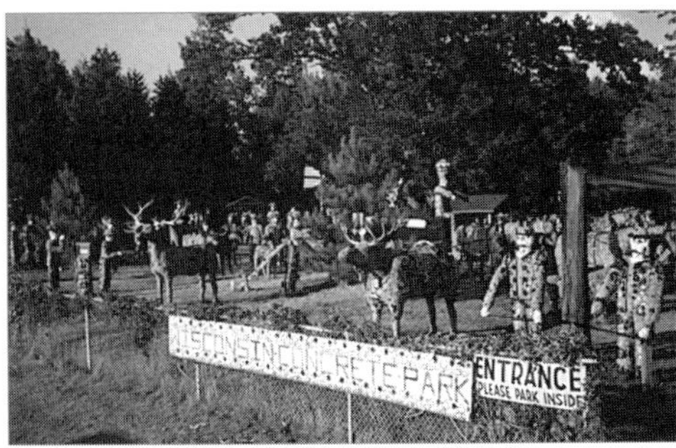

Art Environments By Self-Taught Visionaries

Distinct from the religious art environments are the numerous folk art environments around the state, created by individuals with a strong will and desire to build, who often worked alone and with modest means.

Wisconsin Concrete Park. One of the largest, best-known, and best-preserved art environments is *Wisconsin Concrete Park* in the central part of North-Northwest Wisconsin, just south of Phillips in Price County. Fred Smith (1886-1976), the artist who created the site, worked as a lumberjack and tavern owner. He created the park by decorating his yard as a hobby over a 30-year period after retiring from the lumber industry. More than two hundred larger-than-life pieces of concrete sculpture, embellished with broken glass, create a spectacular and unique park dedicated to the American people. Among the more notable pieces: the *Double Wedding, Ben Hur, Kerosene Wagon, Paul Bunyan, Sun-Yat Sen,* and *Budweiser's Clydesdale Team.* Phillips is a small town with the distinction of being the community with the highest percentage of public sculpture per capita of any other city in the state, outranking even Milwaukee and Madison. The *Wisconsin Concrete Park* is operated by Price County and is open year round.

The Wegner Grotto. Wegner Grotto, near Sparta, started out as a retirement project by Paul (1864-1937) and Matilda (1867-1942) Wegner. After visiting the Dickeyville Grotto in 1929, they decided to decorate the family yard. Years later their work encompassed the entire yard and included sculptures such as an elaborate peace monument, glass chapel, glass wedding cake, miniature steamship, and other unique creations. The Wegners are perhaps best remembered as being insatiable in their interests in glass and mosaic constructions. Even in their resting place in a nearby cemetery, they lie under decorated tombstones of their own creation.

Grandview. One of the most interesting characters to create a rural art environment in Wisconsin was Nick Engelbert (1881-1962). Born in what was the Austro-Hungarian Empire, he traveled the world before settling in Southwestern Wisconsin in 1913 with his new American bride, Katherine Thoni. Beginning in 1937, he filled the family yard near Hollandale with dozens of flower beds, concrete sculpture, and picnic tables. He completely embellished the family home with concrete, glass, and other materials. Around 1951, he retired from making sculpture and turned to oil painting. The site, which he called *Grandview,* was later abandoned but has recently been restored and renovated. Many of the original sculptures are now in the Kohler Arts Center and replicas have been created and placed in the art environment.

The Herman Rusch, Prairie Moon Site. Herman Rusch (1885-1985) was another individual accustomed to hard work and not afraid to experiment. He created dozens of outdoor sculptures—including sun catchers, a medieval tower, and a long decorated fence—at a beautiful site on the Mississippi River near Cochrane that also included a dance hall and small museum of idiosyncratic items. Rusch worked at the site nearly 35 years. He found inspiration in magazines and other popular literature. To enliven his art garden he later added four concrete sculptures made by Halvor Landsverk. The *Prairie Moon Site* is a public park today though all the sculptures have been repainted.

The James Tellen Site. James Tellen (1880-1957) of Sheboygan had a love of nature, community, and church. He was a devout Catholic and life-long member of St. Peter Claver Catholic Church and parish societies. He and his wife and children lived in Sheboygan but spent their summers south of Sheboygan in the family's rustic log cabin, located a few blocks from the shores of Lake Michigan.

The rustic setting in the woods, combined with his interest in art and encouragement from family and friends, prompted him to begin making sculpture in 1942, a hobby he maintained until his death in 1957.

Tellen built his sculptures from concrete with interior wire mesh to make it light but strong. During the winter, he modeled his figures, particularly the heads, at his home in Sheboygan. During the summer, he completed the work by creating realistic tableaux that blended into the woods and enhanced the landscape. He also enjoyed painting, wood carving, and metal work.

His first major project was a long concrete rustic fence at the front of the lot along the road. It is several hundred feet in length and punctuated by several animated tableaux. Two life-size figures of Native Americans, a man and woman, are positioned near fallen concrete trees. The man wears a large headdress, and the woman looks on with interest as he steps across a fallen log. Toward the north end of the fence is the entrance driveway to the site. Here Tellen created a large tree trunk with a standing mother bear and her cubs.

Turning his attention to the front yard along the driveway, he began a whole series of sculptures, including a wishing well, equestrian figure, and woman at a well with dogs. One of his most animated groups, *The Little People*, is a miniature tableaux of men and women at a picnic enjoying themselves with drink and merriment of the type that Tellen himself would have enjoyed at the nearby Black River Advancement Hall down the road. Leading the visitor along the driveway is a youthful Abe Lincoln, splitting logs with Bible, coat, and hat nearby.

Whether it was Walt Disney or another source of inspiration, Tellen's *We Whistle While We Work* is his most colorful and amusing scene. Originally it was painted to imitate the green of the forest, embellished with concrete fruits. There is a band of elves playing musical instruments and other elves making wine. It is a joyful work of art that Tellen and friends had fun playing with, as they occasionally posed for photographs in front of it.

Beyond the garage, in the back half of the wooded property, Tellen continued his project with more scenes from life, including a miniature basilica that Tellen decorated for Easter Sundays when he invited fellow St. Peter Claver parishioners, including Tony Rajer's family.

Along the winding path toward the distant river are additional sculptures. They include the prehistoric world in miniature, raft with survivor, a life-size portrait of Christ, and the standing Blessed Virgin in prayer. This was one of Tellen's last sculptures.

The Catholic church and prayer were an important part of Tellen's life. The family, along with other parish members, came to the Blessed Virgin statue and would pray the rosary. Church members several decades later recalled these gatherings in the mid-1950s at the Tellen site. Many of them remembered the kind, generous, and thoughtful nature of the man they called Jim Tellen, the statue artist. For friends nearby, he also created a small grotto to St. Francis, a statue of St. Peter, and other sculptures. He is buried in Holy Cross cemetery in Sheboygan.

The Tellen site, like so many others around the state, was repeatedly vandalized after the artist's death though the family tried to keep it up. Finally, a local preservation organization, the Kohler Foundation, Inc., purchased the site and plans to open it as a park.

The *James Tellen Site*, like others such as *Rudolph Grotto*, inform us about the way Wisconsinites, inspired by the love of nature, used landscape to enhance their artistic statements. They created works of art that appear as natural as an outgrowth of nature. Each site has a magical quality that is revealed by the changing seasons of the year.

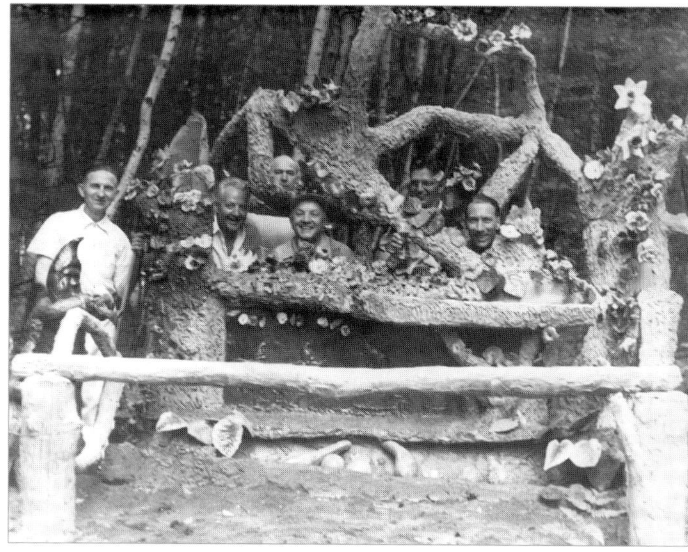

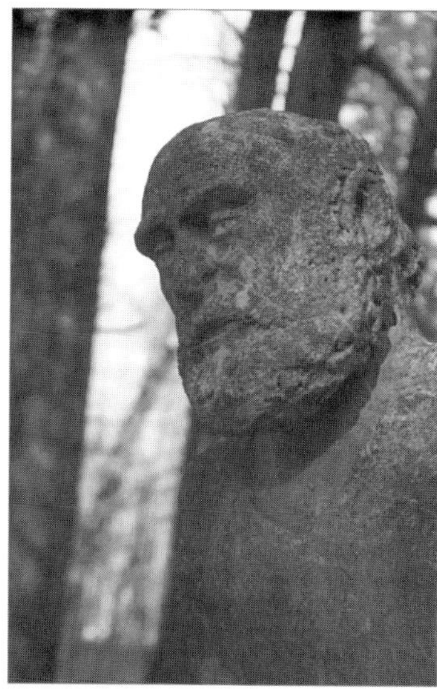

Top left: James Tellen and friends with *We Whistle While We Work* in Sheboygan County

Top right: *St. Peter, the Fisherman* by James Tellen, Sheboygan County

Below: James Tellen's decorated concrete fence with Native Americans

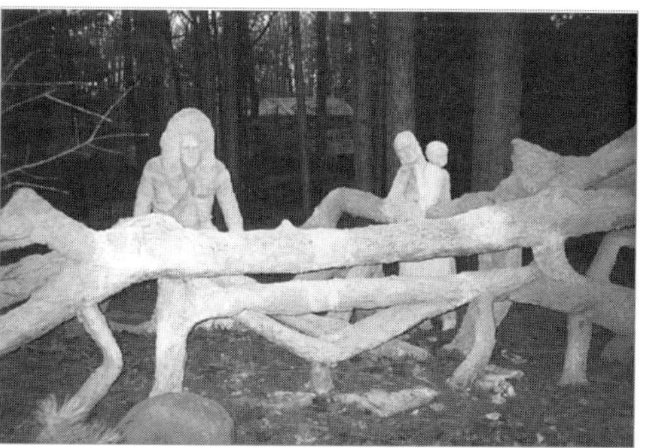

The Tom Every Site. Another large art environment by a self-taught, living artist in Wisconsin is Tom Every's site across the road from the soon-to-be-decommissioned Badger Army Ammunition Plant near Baraboo. Hundreds of sculptures cover the site, which comprises several acres. The largest is the *Forevertron*, a machine built for imaginary time and inter-galactic travel. Every uses huge quantities of recycled industrial material to create his art. He operated a scrap salvage company for many years and is a constant recycler. It is one of the most extraordinary art sites in the region.

Numerous other visionary artists in Wisconsin have created environments: Mona Webb (Madison), Mary Nohl (Milwaukee), Frank Oebser (Menomonie), and Sid Boyum (Madison) to name a few.

What do these examples of public sculpture tell us about the people of Wisconsin? They affirm the human need to embellish our environment; to create worlds that reflect our sense of beauty, duty, aspirations, hopes and fears, and to give material form to abstract concepts. Each satisfies some deep inner need to create something permanent. In the above-mentioned cases, with the exception of Tom Every and Mary Nohl, all the artists are now deceased. What we have left is their testimony in art for current and future generations to enjoy. They mark our passing through this world and expand the boundaries of art and public sculpture in Wisconsin.

Further Reading

For further information on the Kohler Foundation Folk Art sites, call 920-458-1972

Robert Bishop and Jacqueline M. Atkins. *Folk Art in American Life.* New York: Viking/Penguin, 1995.

Dickeyville Grotto: The Vision of Father Mathias Wernerus. Oxford: University of Mississippi Press, 1997.

John Maizels. *Raw Creation: Outsider Art and Beyond.* London: Phaidon, 1996.

Roger Manley and Mark Sloan. *Visionary Folk Art Environments.* New York: Aperture, 1997.

The Rudolph Grotto. Rudolph, Wis.: Rudolph Church Parish publi-cation, Rudolph, WI, undated.

Lisa Stone and Jim Zanzi. *Sacred Spaces and Other Places.* Chicago: School of the Art Institute of Chicago, 1993.

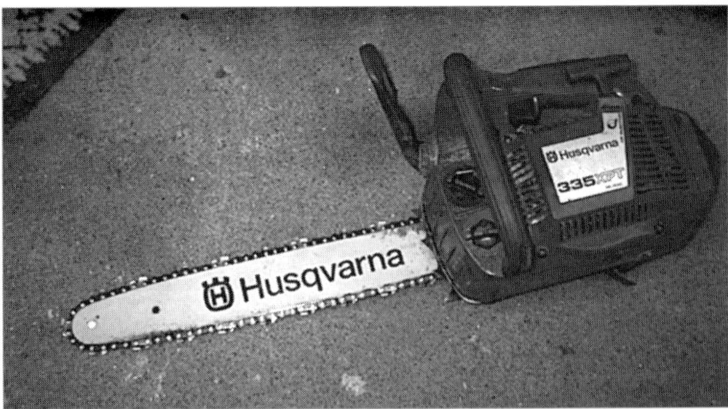

Husqvarna chainsaw

The Cutting Edge: Chainsaw Art in Wisconsin

"There's something in every log, you just gotta take the right pieces off." Jim Kivela, chainsaw artist

There is an artistic revolution going on in Wisconsin, not in museums or art schools, but in people's backyards and garages. Dozens of self-taught artists have learned to transform stumps and blocks of wood into bears, eagles, wolves, dragons, lumber-jacks, sailors, totem poles, and trolls. The choice of subjects reflects the artists' strong interests in wildlife, nature and history. Chainsaw carving has come into its own as an art form, and is an example of non-traditional public sculpture that is springing up around the state in parks, businesses, homes, and elsewhere.

What is chainsaw art? Unlike most art, it is defined by the tool used to produce it. Most chainsaw artists are self-taught and came to the art through their trade skills such as carpentry, lumbering, or traditional wood carving. Most see it as a part-time hobby or hidden talent. Some, however, because of the strength and originality of their art, are able to earn a living through chainsaw carving.

During the Wisconsin SOS! project, we inventoried dozens of wood sculptures made by chainsaw and woodcarver artists throughout the state. Wisconsin has an active tradition of sculpture made by chainsaw artists. It is not unique to this state, but because of the high number of creative artists and abundant wood resources, Wisconsin—along with Minnesota, California, New York, Oregon, and Washington—is a leader in the field. Canada also has an active chainsaw carving tradition. Contrary to popular belief, chainsaw artists are located in all areas of the state, not just up north.

An early successful chainsaw artist in the 1960s was Don Colp from Canada. He began producing pieces for sale from his garage. Today the family tradition is carried on by his son. In Scandinavia, chainsaw carving has also recently become popular, especially in Finland.

Invented in Germany around 1926, early chainsaws were large and cumbersome and required two men to operate. The machine was invented to provide the lumber industry a mechanical method to cut trees more rapidly for the ever-expanding demand for wood products. By the 1960s, substantial improvements had been made by European and American saw manufacturers. Hand held saws with gasoline operated engines soon became popular. Further improvements in the 1970s led to the chainsaws in use today. A chainsaw has a linked chain with sharp blades that rotates around a part known as the bar. The bar comes in different sizes, with a large bar ideal for rough cuts and a small bar preferred for detail carving. One of the most respected chainsaws for art carving is Husqvarna. It comes in several bar sizes perfect for the carver. Other popular brands are Craftsman, Poulan, Echo, and Homelite. Because chainsaw artists tend to prefer one manufacturer's tool over another, many chainsaw distributors hire sculptors to demonstrate their products. In this way artists also receive commissions for further work.

In the 1970s, chainsaw carving spread to the upper Midwest, including Minnesota and Wisconsin. Chainsaw carvers began demonstrating their talents at craft fairs and later in competitive shows, such as the 1991 Tall Timber Days celebration in Grand Rapids, Minnesota, where they vied for the title of International Grand Champion. At the show the carvers wore protective headgear, goggles, and steel-toed boots for safety, as well as gear to protect their hearing. Each artist was given a log and six hours to carve it, with judges awarding prizes. Once the figure is carved, it can be painted, stained, or varnished. If the sculpture remains outside, annual care is needed, but many artists prefer to varnish their work and let nature create a patina of age. Oak, pine, ash, and elm have been popular woods for chainsaw carving.

Notable Chainsaw Artists

Dave Watson, who lives near Wisconsin Dells, is one of the most creative and original chainsaw artists working in Wisconsin today. He came to the art through a career as a pastry chef, also a creative profession. Watson's work is characterized by the usual production of items such as eagles, bears, and snakes, but he imbues his art with a dynamic quality that sets it apart from others. He also adds color to his sculptures and works in close artistic collaboration with his wife Annette. Watson has been nationally recognized for his talent and in 1992 won the National Grand Championship for chainsaw carving in Minnesota. Watson continues to do trade shows across the nation where he demonstrates his craft to the gratification of thousands of admirers.

William (Bill) Vienneaux, who lives near Washburn in northern Wisconsin, operates what might be called a chainsaw art colony. His Wayward Wind Studio and Gallery houses nearly a dozen individual studios where various artists from the region gather to make art. Vienneaux's work is characterized by its monumental scale. Large ambitious sculptures dot his studio yard. His passion for carving is obvious when he says, "I make it all, I make what I want, and I have fun doing it. I love this work." Bill's chainsaw themes reflect his northern locale: bears, eagles, sailors, and lumberjacks. His son works as a chainsaw carver in his own studio nearby.

Another artist of unusual talent who is not afraid to experiment is Brian Johnson, near Hayward. Johnson has a large repertoire of art that includes the usual eagles, bears, deer, and wildlife, but his innovative work has been in portraiture. He captures a bold sense of the person portrayed and imbues the work with a remarkable lifelike quality. Johnson uses not only chainsaws to carve, but also other fine tools to do detail work, as is the practice with many other chainsaw artists. Johnson's best work has a realistic quality that sets it apart from others, especially his attention to detail and surface treatment.

Jim Kivela, who lives near Rosendale, has been carving for years, but he started cautiously by first sculpting mushrooms and later working on more complex bears and eagles. "I learned through my mistakes," he explains. Today he has pieces throughout Wisconsin, including a larger-than-life figure of a Native American near Minocqua. Like many chainsaw artists, Kivela will travel to a tree stump and carve on site but prefers to work at his studio where supplies and tools are on hand.

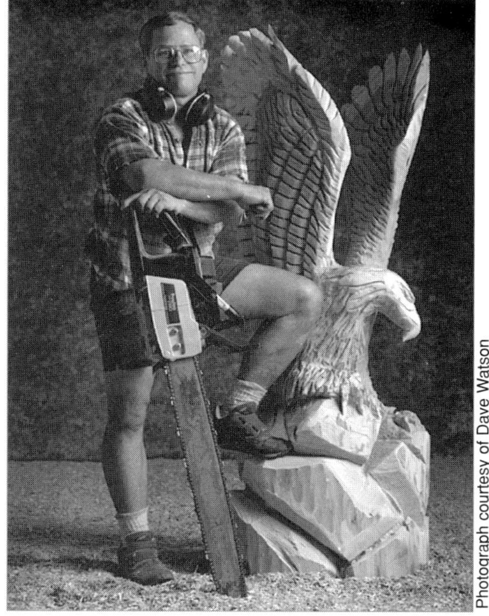

Above: Dave Watson, chainsaw artist from Wisconsin Dells, Columbia County

Below left: *Bear, Fish and Eagle* by Dave Watson in Mauston, Juneau County

Below right: *Totems and Bears* by Willis Lewan in Westboro, Taylor County

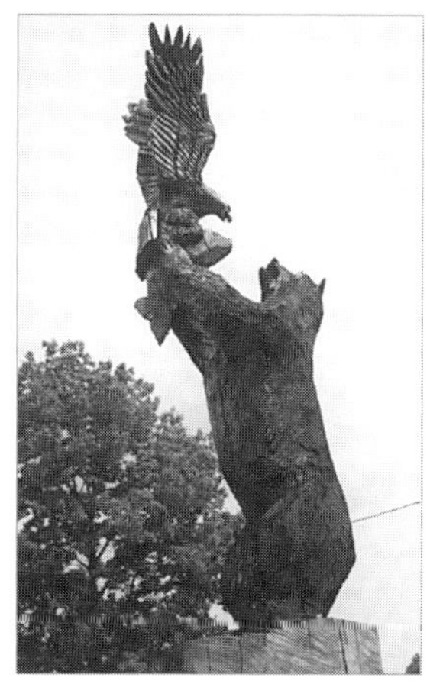

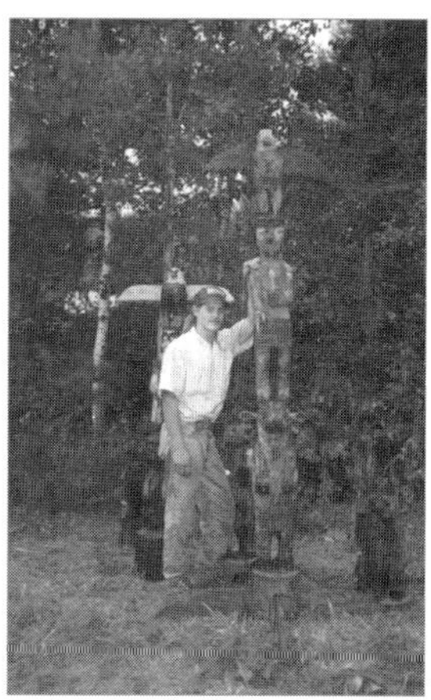

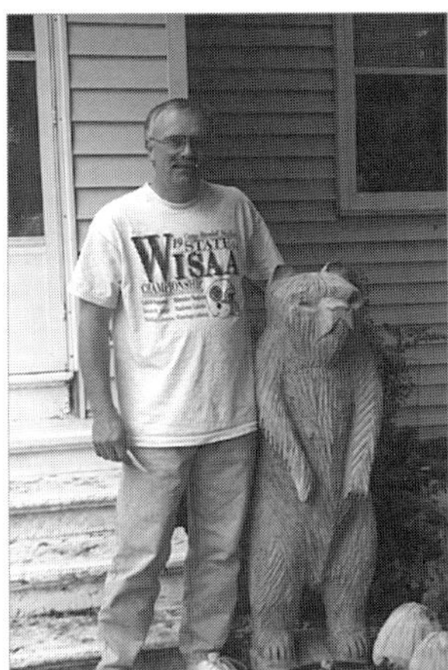

Jim Kivela in Rosendale, Fond du Lac County, with bear

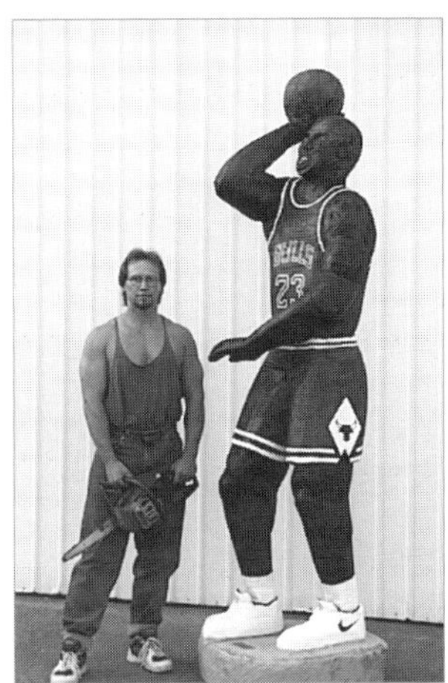

James Barber with his painted chainsaw basketball figure

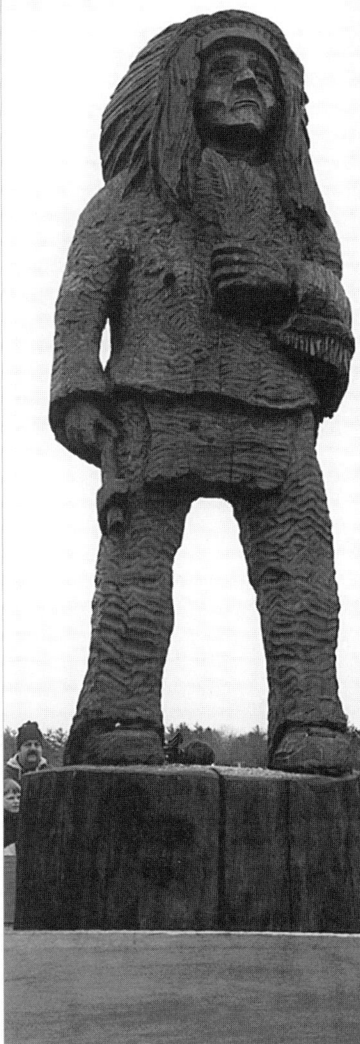

Giant Indian chainsaw figure located at Carl's Wood Art Museum in Eagle River, Vilas County

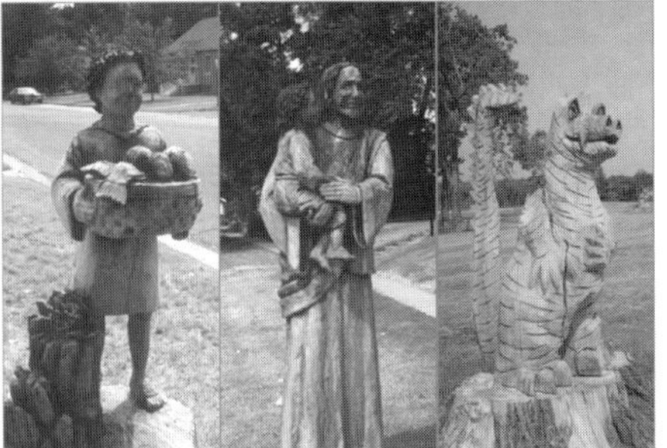

Chainsaw art in Iowa, including religious figures and a dragon

Wisconsin's only chainsaw art carving museum is located in Eagle River. Called Carl's Wood Art Museum, it is the brainchild of Carl Schels, Sr., his wife Martha, and son Ken, who is also an accomplished chainsaw carver. Established around 1985, the museum houses a large and diverse collection of wood carvings, wood veneers, an old trapper's cabin, lumbering history, and other items related to life in the north woods. Chainsaw carving is also demonstrated on the grounds of the museum.

Many communities have embraced chainsaw carving for its tourist appeal. One such community is Mount Horeb, the self-proclaimed troll capital of the state. More than a dozen chainsaw carved trolls inhabit Main Street in this small town just off Highway 18/151 in southwestern Wisconsin (see photos, page 112). Most of these whimsical trolls are the work of Mike Feeney, a local carver who also has a few carved trolls in nearby Little Norway Heritage Center. A similar public display can be seen in Hope, British Columbia, Canada, where local artist Pete Ryan has carved more than 20 large chainsaw sculptures throughout the city. He was commissioned by the community to do the carving. His work has sparked an increase in tourism for this small western city.

Most chainsaw artists rely on a standard repertoire of wildlife subjects, including north woods characters such as the lumberjack or Native Americans. A few venture into more ambitious themes such as religious figures and abstract art. Religious themes are rare with chainsaw artists though a few examples exist. In Southeastern Iowa the trunks of several trees near a church were transformed into a *Christ Holding a Child* and an *Apostle with Fish* and *Loaves of Bread*. In Lake Elmo, Minnesota, Dennis Weimar carved a figure of Jesus from a tree trunk at St. John's Lutheran Church. In this instance the artist came to the site and transformed the tree, seeking divine guidance in his creation.

The scope of chainsaw carving is limited by the size of the log, its location, whether it is attached to the ground or freestanding, and the carver's imagination and skill. The type of wood—hardwood or softwood of various species—also influences the art being produced. Chainsaw carving is a subtractive art form in which the artist removes material to create the work, rather than adding material, as in ceramics. Many of the chainsaw artists interviewed during the SOS! project have the ability to see the sculpture within the log, freeing it by carefully carving with the chainsaw and other tools.

The weather also plays a role in creating opportunities for chainsaw carving. This was the case several years ago when a horrific wind storm damaged dozens of trees on the state fair grounds in Des Moines, Iowa. Rather than clear-cut the site, fair officials commissioned carvers to transform the tree trunks into art. Today the Iowa State Fair has more than a dozen fascinating and novel chainsaw carvings. This same story was repeated in Auld Park in Knoxville, Iowa, where storm-damaged trees were later transformed into art by chainsaw carver Harold Clark. The artist went on to complete additional tree stump carvings at the VA Medical Center in Knoxville. As Harold says, "I work days at the Maytag factory and come home and grab the saw to work on a new sculpture. I enjoy carving."

State fairs and public trade shows throughout the nation have been instrumental in promoting chainsaw carving. Each year, at fairs across the nation, chainsaw carvers can be seen demonstrating and producing art. Thousands of visitors see the work at the fairs, stimulating added interest in the craft and further promoting developments in the field, such as increased attention to detail, varied subject matter, and improved carving techniques. More exciting innovations are appearing on the horizon as books, videos, and internet information bring this art form to millions of people. Wisconsin is at the cutting edge of this artistic movement.

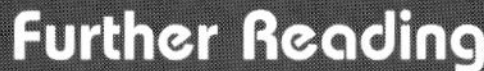

Further Reading

Sharon R. Armstrong and Skip Armstrong. *Chainsaw Sculpture: The Art of J. Chester 'Skip' Armstrong*. Oxford: University of Mississippi Press, 1995.

Mark Lindquist. *Sculpting Wood: Contemporary Tools and Techniques*. Worcester, Massachusetts: Davis Publications, 1986.

William Westhaven. *Fun and Profitable Chainsaw Carving*. 1978.

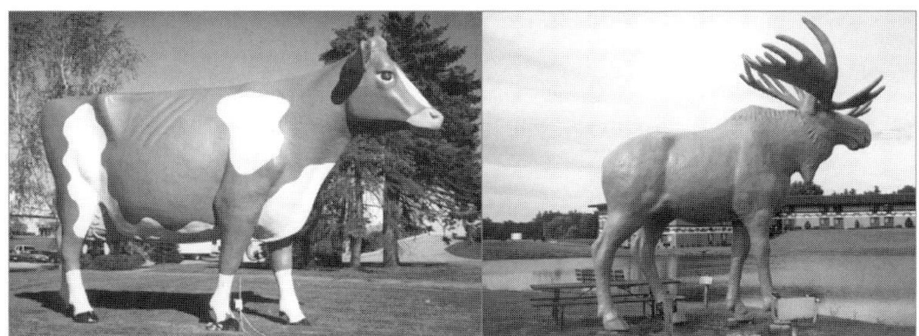

Left: *Bessie*, a fiberglass cow in Waukesha County

Right: *Orange Moose* in Black River Falls, Jackson County

Fiberglass Art

Another form of public statuary well-represented in Wisconsin is fiberglass sculpture. Sparta is home to one of America's largest fiberglass sculpture studios, the Fiberglass, Animals, Shapes, and Trademarks (F.A.S.T.). Here Jerry Veterrus and his many assistants produce an amazing variety of forms from fiberglass and polyester resin, including giant gorillas, bears, chickens, animals of all kinds, the Statue of Liberty, and even E.T. Much of this art would fall under the category of advertising art or popular culture, but because of the sheer quantity and uniqueness, they can be called public sculpture. And some fiberglass art blurs the line between the promotional arts and the fine arts. For instance, Veterrus' largest piece—the largest piece of public sculpture in the state—is the *Giant Muskie* in Hayward. Rising several stories and hundreds of feet in length, this monumental sculpture of a fish exemplifies Wisconsin's love of its outdoor resources as well as the artist's love for the unique and the desire to call attention to what Wisconsinites believe in.

Effigy Mounds as Public Sculpture

To the Native Americans who thousands of years ago settled in what is now Wisconsin, the land must have appeared as paradise. Waterways, forests, and prairies no doubt inspired them in their daily lives as much as these features inspire us today. Those early inhabitants of Wisconsin produced our first public earthen sculptures in the form of effigy mounds. Throughout the lower two-thirds of the state, Wisconsin's early inhabitants created an estimated 15,000 mounds roughly between the years of 400 and 1300 A.D. Their culture is referred to as the Late Woodland or Effigy Mound Culture.

The distribution of effigy mounds is primarily in Wisconsin, but the mound-building culture extends a few miles into northern Illinois, eastern Iowa, and eastern Minnesota. Especially in the days of the open prairie landscape, earth mounds must have been dramatic and prominent statements of the culture's beliefs. The size of these structures—a few of which spanned up to an acre—astonished early European settlers.

The exact function of the mounds will never be fully known, but based on artifacts found in and near them, we can surmise that they played a vital public role in social practices, including religion and clan organization. Their large number indicates a wide dissemination of shared beliefs among the peoples of the region at the time. Many of the mounds served a mortuary function as revealed by burial remains discovered in numerous cases.

The largest number of mounds are simple in shape: conical or linear. Yet many are zoomorphic or animal-shaped: birds, bears, deer, turtles, and other woodland creatures. The early inhabitants typically placed their mounds in strategic locations, taking advantage of serene natural settings such as high bluffs, along lakes, or next to waterways. The mounds are frequently grouped into arrangements that appear random, but upon close examination they follow the land's topography or some other orderly system. It is believed that they may represent a cosmic view of the universe, in material form, much as a church building or grotto does today. And it is believed the builders intended the mounds to draw added significance from the landscape, much as a modern landscape architect might enhance a structure's statement by taking advantage of a particular setting.

One fascinating aspect of the mounds is that they are constructed as if to be viewed from above. Their outlines depict abstract forms, described as naturalistic or geometric in shape. Large animals, like bears, deer, and panthers, are depicted in standing silhouette. Birds appear to be flying, with wings stretched wide. And for some mounds, it is uncertain which animal a zoomorphic mound is meant to represent. Different labels—turtles, bears, and such—have been attached to mounds, depending on different researchers' views, but the truth is, nobody really knows. They may represent spirit animals, important to different religious or clan groups. Or they may represent something else entirely.

Huge numbers of mounds are clustered in certain locations. On the shores of Lake Koshkonong near Fort Atkinson, Jefferson County, early European settlers found more than five hundred diverse mounds. Most were destroyed by agriculture and urbanization. But others have been preserved as a cultural resource

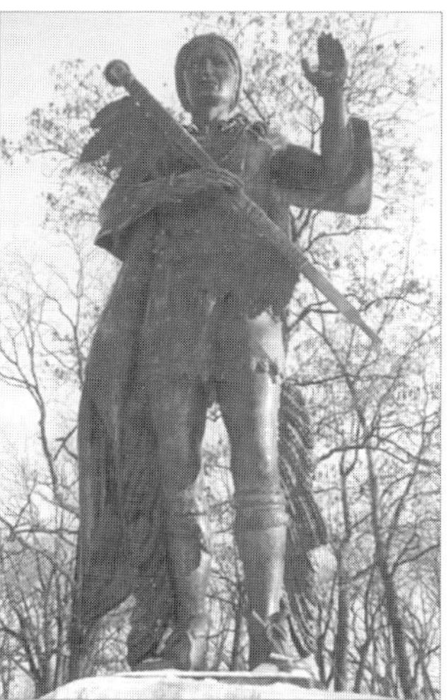

Chief Red Bird statue in High Cliff State Park, Calumet County

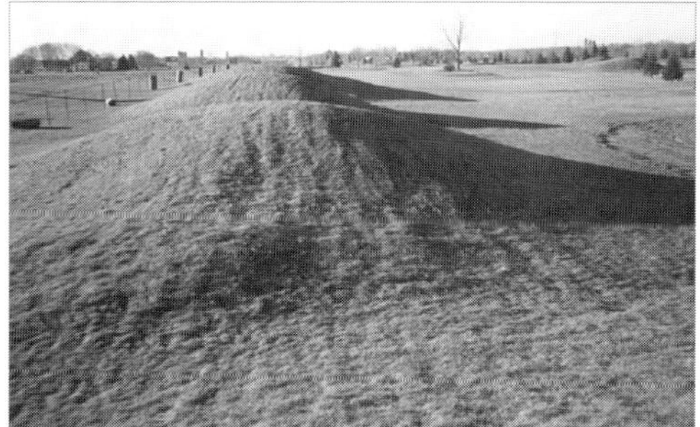

Effigy Mound in High Cliff State Park, Calumet County

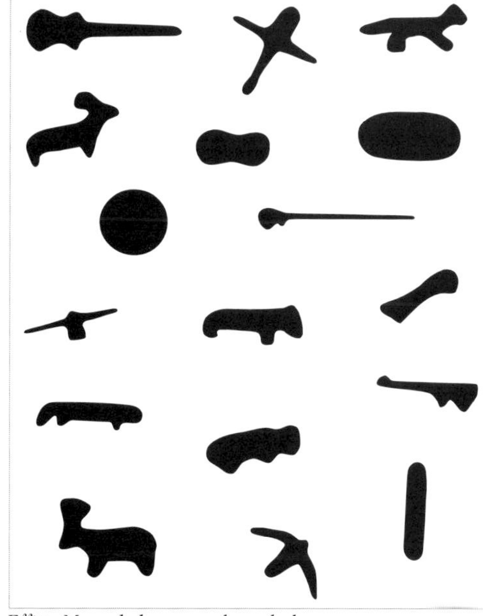

Effigy Mound shapes and symbols

under Wisconsin's burial protection law. Today in the Lake Koshkonong area, there are seventy effigy mounds remaining, the highest concentration of mounds in the state.

Some contemporary art forms have drawn inspiration from these mounds. One of these, Earth Art, was an aesthetic movement in the 1960s and 1970s that used earth as a medium of expression. It was aligned with the emerging ecological movement, with its back-to-the-land philosophy and spiritual attitude toward the planet. Landscapes were enhanced by sculpting them with depressions, mounds, berms, and plantings. Notable artists of this movement were Robert Smithson, and Michael Heizer who created massive earthworks in the deserts of the American Southwest. Native American artist Truman Lowe, now living near Madison, continues this tradition in some of his work. Wisconsin artist Amy Cropper showed effigy mound influences in her work *Embedded Bookcase*, which uses earth as an important component. It is located at the UW-Waukesha field station in Waterville.

Native Wisconsinites from a millennium ago modified the landscape by sculpting it, adding forms that were visual representations of their belief systems that combined religious faith with aesthetic expression. Carefully constructed and situated at scenic locations, these ancient earthworks were obviously well-planned. Perhaps no mound group better exemplifies this than the extensive complexes at Wyalusing State Park in Grant County. Located along the beautiful river bluff at the confluence of the Mississippi and Wisconsin Rivers, the groups contain examples of all types of mounds—conical, linear, and animal.

Fourteen counties in the state have important effigy mound groups that are open to the public and can be visited year-round: Calumet, Dane, Grant, Jefferson, Juneau, LaCrosse, Pierce, Rock, Sauk, Sheboygan, Walworth, Washington, Waushara, and Winnebago. These mounds are the oldest continuous artform practiced in Wisconsin, and though we will always be faced with mysteries as to their use and creation, we can admire and revere them, and view them as sacred sites.

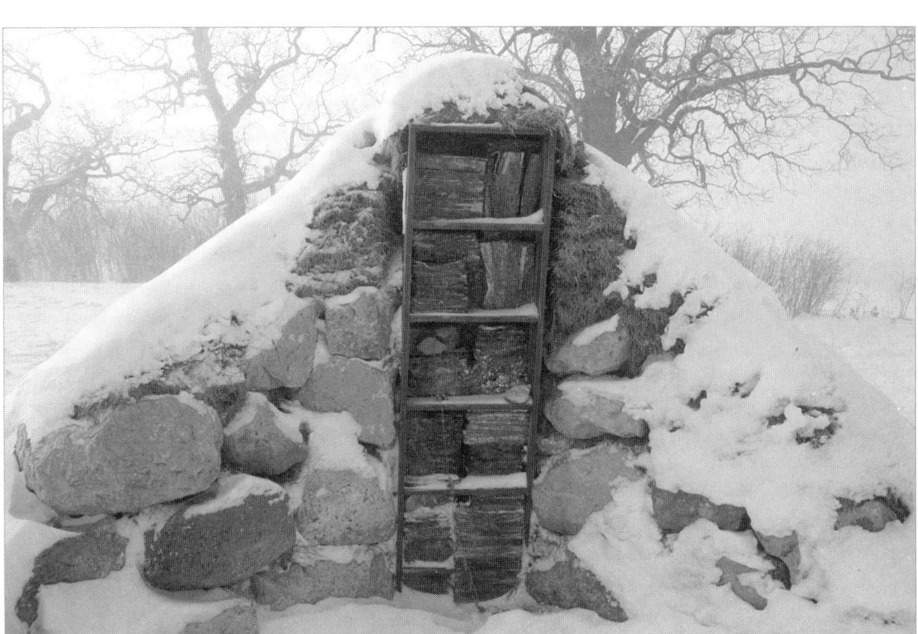

Embedded Bookcase by Amy Cropper (1997) in Waukesha County

Further Reading

Robert Birmingham, Carol Mason, and James Stoltman, eds. *The Wisconsin Archeologist*. (78:1,2), January-February, 1997.

Robert Birmingham and Katherine Rankin. *Native American Mounds in Madison and Dane County*. Madison: Madison Heritage Publication, 1996.

Hugh Highsmith. *The Mounds of Koshkonong and Rock River*. Fort Atkinson, Wis.: Highsmith Press, 1997.

Further information on Wisconsin's effigy mounds is available from the State Historical Society of Wisconsin's Division of Historic Preservation: (608) 264-6500.

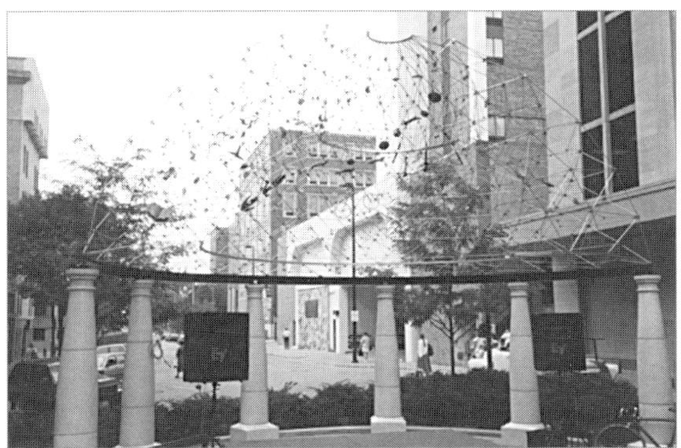

Amphitheater in the Plaza, the Forum of Origin is located on Capitol Square and was commissioned through Madison CitiArts. This 1993 work by Brower Hatcher is 23 feet high and made of stone columns, stainless steel mesh, and bronze, aluminum and iron castings of representational forms.

Projects, Proposals, and Partnerships:

Recent Government, Corporate, and Community Public Sculpture

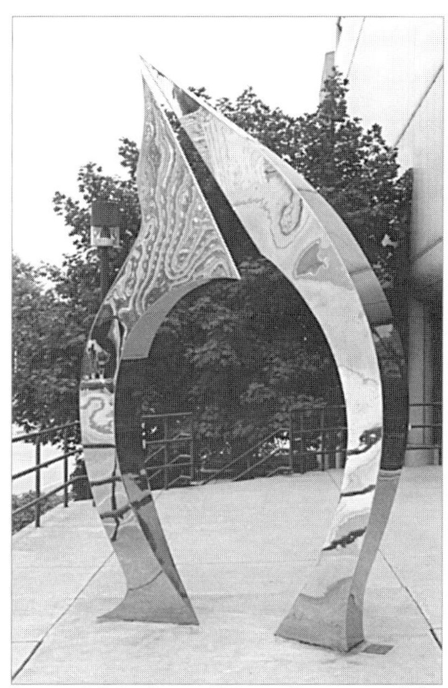

Interspirit by James T. Russell was one of the first works commissioned through the Wisconsin Arts Board Percent For Art Program in 1983. The polished stainless steel sculpture is 13 feet high and is located at the entrance to the SERF building on the University of Wisconsin-Madison campus.

A number of innovative programs in the last quarter of the twentieth century have sought to encourage new public sculpture in Wisconsin. A variety of corporate, private, and foundation initiatives have supported sculpture through outdoor gardens and other venues. This section provides a brief introduction to these and other trends, including geometric abstraction, representational, and environmental sculpture.

Wisconsin's Percent for Art

A statewide program under the auspices of the Wisconsin Arts Board, *Percent For Art,* aims to put contemporary art into new state-funded facilities, either through commissions or purchases. Initiated in 1980 by the Wisconsin Legislature, the program follows models in other states. The Wisconsin Arts Board can use two-tenths of one percent of the total budget of any project costing $250,000 or more to acquire art or support commissions.

There are several ways in which the Percent For Art Program can acquire works of art. One method is through competitions which are open to state, regional, and national artists, though preference is given to Wisconsin residents. Another method is through the Art and Architecture Design Team, which provides artists with the opportunity to collaborate directly with architects and other allied professionals. Lastly, open only to Wisconsin artists, the Arts Board can acquire art through direct purchase.

Preference is given to Wisconsin artists though work from outside the state is sometimes supported. Most of the projects created have been situated indoors, but some fall into the category of outdoor public sculpture. They include:

- *Interspirit* by James Russell, located at the University of Wisconsin-Madison SERF building.
- *Wisconsiana* by Lloyd Hamrol, 1988, located at the GEF 3 State Office Building in Madison.
- *Woodland Spire* by Robert Gehrke, located at the University of Wisconsin-Stout campus in Menomonie.
- *Gathering Place* by Kinji Akagawa, located at the University of Wisconsin-Eau Claire Technology Center.
- *Abstract Figure and Hands* by Guido Brink, located at the University of Wisconsin-Whitewater auditorium.
- *Happy-Go-Luckies of Technologies* by Guido Brink, located at the University of Wisconsin-Milwaukee School of Business.
- *White etched glass lights* by Cliff Garten, located at the University of Wisconsin-Madison biotechnology building.
- *Endless Fence* by Peter Flanary, located at the University of Wisconsin-Green Bay Student Union.
- *The terrazzo floor mosaics* by Nori Sato in the new University of Wisconsin-Madison biochemistry

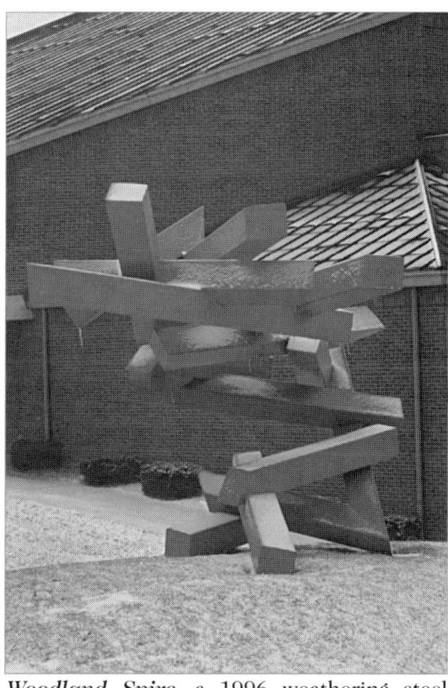

Woodland Spire, a 1996 weathering steel work by Robert Gehrke located at the University of Wisconsin-Stout campus in Menomonie, Dunn County.

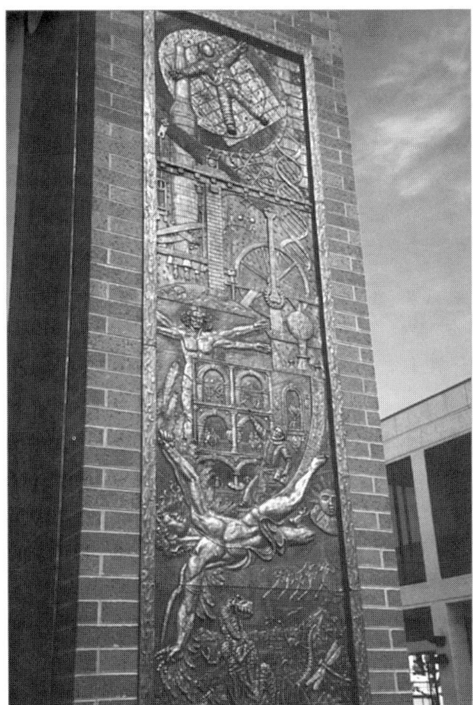

The *Clocktower* bronze reliefs by Sharon Quasius at the Mead Public Library in Sheboygan.

THE WORK OF SHARRON QUASIUS

In 1997, Sheboygan artist Sharron Quasius completed a monumental series of four bronze bas-reliefs for the new clocktower at the Mead Public Library in Sheboygan. Quasius' work was sponsored by the Weill Charitable Fund, with the casting done at the Kohler Company with support from several private contributors. The results are impressive. The art work tells the story of literature, the arts, world history and science and technology in bold, beautiful clear images, comprehensible to everyone. Quasius says of the work, "Having a major work of art in my own hometown is quite thrilling. I feel so good about it. It's quite an honor."

Quasius has also undertaken another project, the *Gates of Venus*. Her starting point has been Rodin's *Gates of Hell*, reinterpreted with a feminist theme that focuses on life and joy rather than suffering. It is hoped that, when complete, this monumental work will be placed outdoors for the enjoyment of the public.

building, though not located outdoors, are worth noting as a fine example of the marriage of modern art and architecture.

- Another site-specific work which is integrated throughout the interior four-story central glassed corridor of the School of Architecture and Urban Planning on the University of Wisconsin-Milwaukee campus is *Mneme XXXI: Dwelling in the Plan* by Carol Emmons and Paul Emmons. This 1993-1995 Percent For Art commission included an outdoor component of a cast iron manhole cover with text which reads "LANDSCAPES ARE TRANSCRIPTIONS OF OURSELVES."

Other Sculpture Programs

Madison CitiArts Commission. In 1979, Madison started its own public art program. In 1983, *Timekeeper* by Robert Curtis was the first commissioned piece by the Madison Committee for the Arts. The program was designed so that 1 percent of the total cost of a new or renovated building project could be used for art. In 1995, the organization was renamed the Madison CitiArts Commission for Art in Public Places, now administered through the Department of Planning and Development.

Several major pieces have been added to the city's art collection thanks to this program. They include Frank Brown's *Living the Dream*, a 1993 monument to Dr. Martin Luther King, Jr., Brower Hatcher's *Amphitheater in the Plaza* (1993), and Mary Michie's *Sunbathers* (1994).

The program will probably be reorganized in 1999 so that the city will commission works of art, rather than providing grants. In this way, the city will design artworks around selected sites, with more community input per project.

Arts in Industry Partnerships in Sheboygan. Another innovative program with an international perspective is the Arts in Industry program in Sheboygan County. Under the aegis of the John Michael Kohler Arts Center but based in the Kohler Company, this unique corporate art program has brought dozens of artists into the factory to work in an industrial setting. Some of the many artists that have participated in this program are Martha Glowacki, Ann Agee, Gerhard Hahn, Tom Bevan, Yoshiko Kanai, Sarah Peters, Javier Brewster Brockman, and Aldwyth. It is the only program of its kind in America, and since its inception in 1974, it has been a leader in supporting artists who are given the opportunity to use industrial technology in their work. The results have been amazing: innovative ceramics, fabulous metal

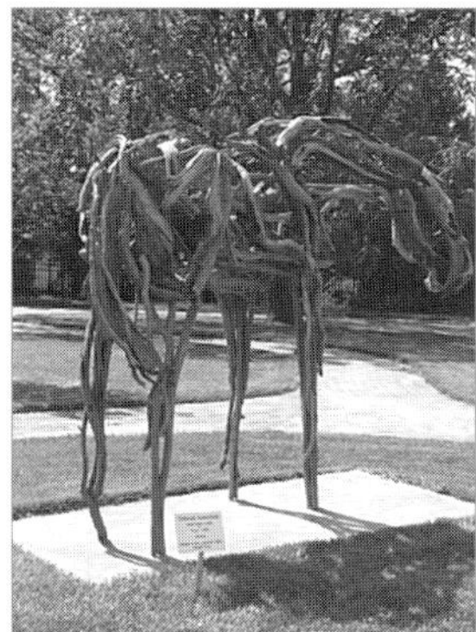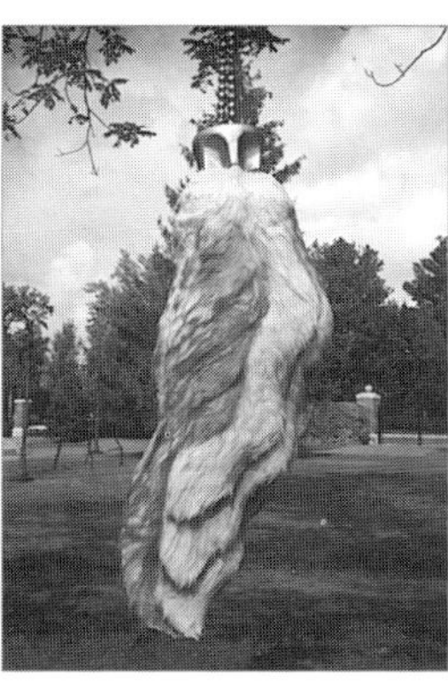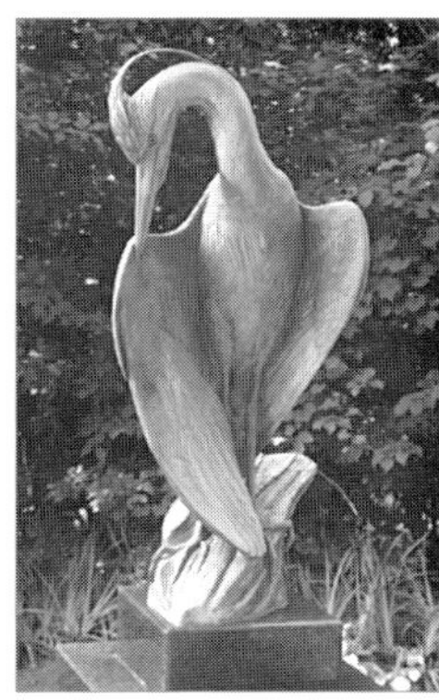

Left: *Kua*, a 1995 cast bronze sculpture by Deborah Butterfield, is part of the permanent outdoor sculpture collection in the Leigh Yawkey Woodson Art Museum in Wausau.

Center: ***Bon Chance Bébé***, a 1998 playful work by Karin Giusti is part of the inaugural temporary, two-year exhibit, ***Just The Thing: Contemporary Outdoor Sculpture and the Object,*** at the Margaret Woodson Fisher Sculpture Gallery in Wausau.

Right: *Great Blue Heron*, a 1988 bronze by Kent Ullberg is part of the permanent outdoor sculpture collection in the Leigh Yawkey Woodson Art Museum in Wausau.

castings, and extraordinary sculpture, some of which has been placed outside around Sheboygan County, most notably in the village of Kohler and city of Sheboygan.

In addition, the Kohler Arts Center's new wing will have a public sculpture garden where many new pieces will be placed in the next century. The Kohler Company's corporate sponsorship of the arts, in conjunction with the Arts Center in Sheboygan, is one of the best programs of its kind in America today, recognized nationwide by the arts and industry community.

Wausau's Leigh Yawkey Woodson Art Museum. Created in 1995, this is one of the few sculpture gardens in the nation with a program of rotating outdoor exhibits as well as a permanent outdoor collection. The inaugural exhibition included many large contemporary sculptures in diverse materials and themes. Included in the show were works by Fletcher Benton, Gwynn Murrill, David Anderson, and Deborah Butterfield. The success of this first show has led to the mounting of a second, which includes twelve works by nationally known artists working in a variety of media and exploring themes such as time, nature, love, luck, life, death, history, and popular culture. Works in the second exhibit are by Meredith Bergman, Niki Ketchman, Tony Stanzione, and others. The museum was able to mount this exhibit through a unique partnership with community sponsors who could adopt a sculpture, thereby making its installation or inclusion in the garden possible.

Milwaukee's Bradley Sculpture Garden. The largest publicly accessible sculpture garden in the state, the Bradley Sculpture Garden, is an amazing collection of sculpture from the major art movements of the 1960s and 1970s. Pieces are beauti-

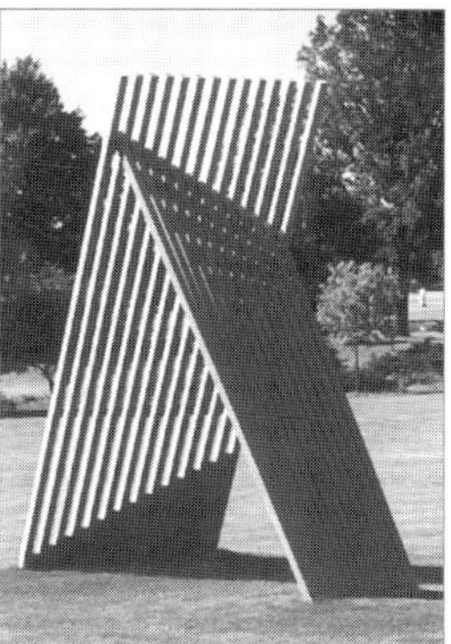
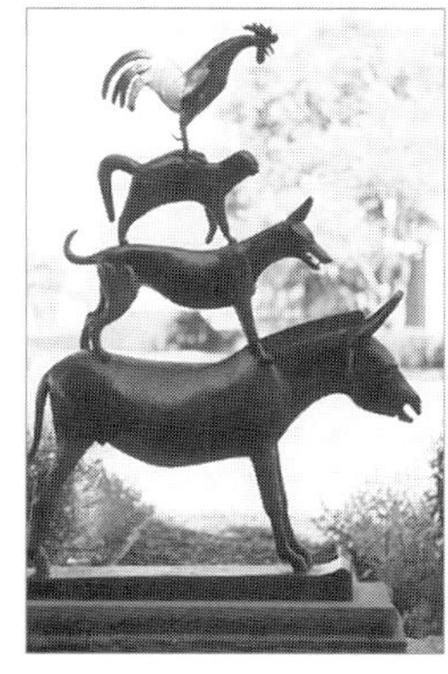
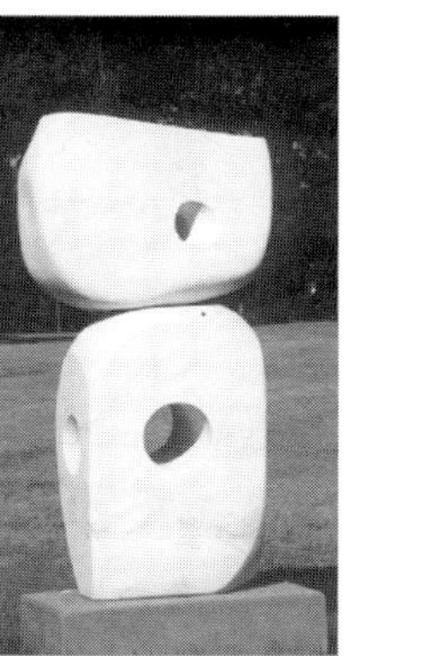

At The Bradley Sculpture Garden, northwest Milwaukee left to right:

Sky Fence by Linda Howard is a 1976 aluminum work

Bremen Town Musicians by Gerhard Marcks, a 1951 cast bronze

Sea Form (Atlantic) by Barbara Hepworth, 1964

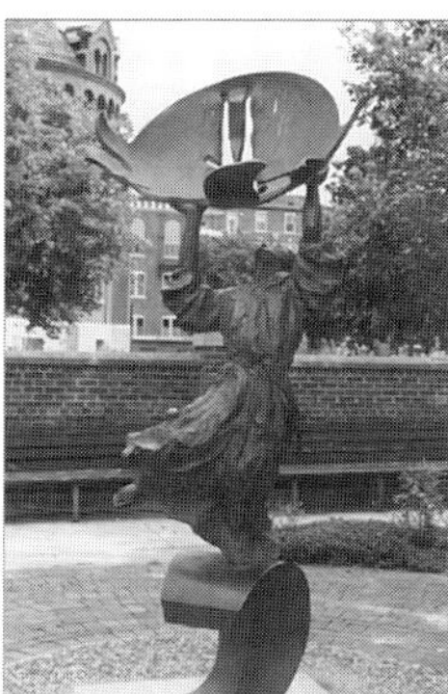
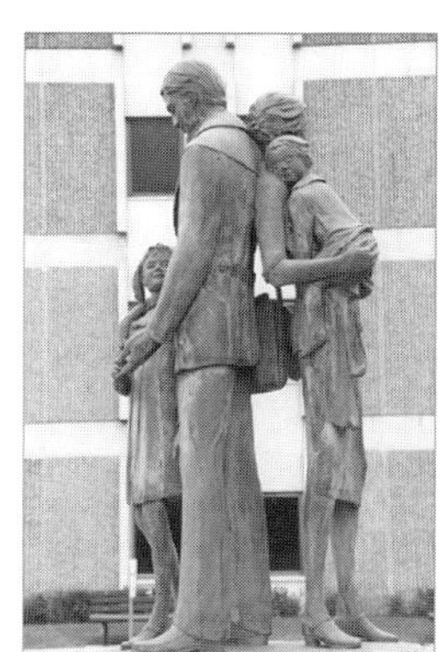
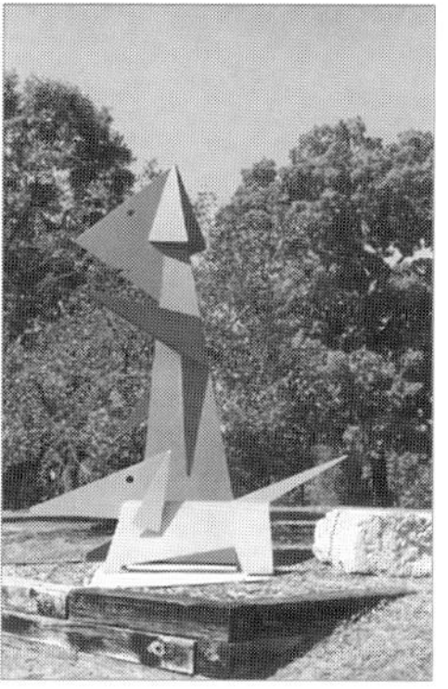
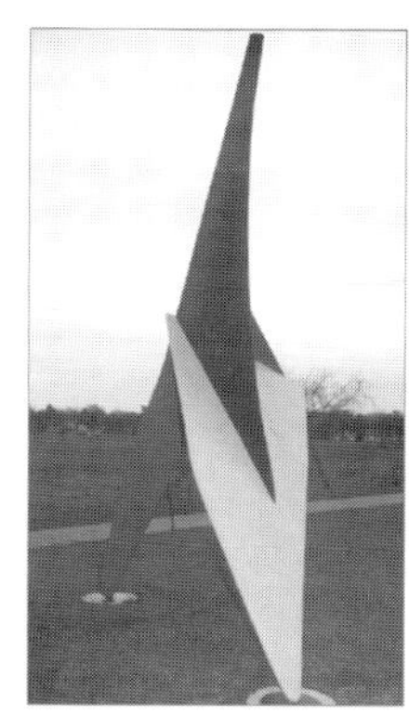

Left to right:

Dancing St. Francis, a 1987 bronze by Paul Granlund, at Viterbo College in LaCrosse

Family, a 1982 bronze by Elmer Peterson, in LaCrosse

Anidonts by Luis Arata, 1982. A painted aluminum piece in LaCrosse's Myrick Park

Paradisedae by Narendra Patel. A painted steel work at Riverfront Parkway in West Bend, Washington County

fully displayed in a setting where nature harmonizes with the works and highlights them.

The garden was established by Harry and Peg Bradley, who in 1928 acquired forty acres of land on West Brown Deer Road in Milwaukee County. By 1935, the Bradleys had hired a gardener from Germany, Carl Urban, who brought a certain order and plan to the farmland. The Bradleys began buying sculpture in 1962, and after Mr. Bradley's death in 1965, Mrs. Bradley continued to acquire important works. At the time of her death in 1978, the gardens had more than sixty pieces representing more than forty artists. Some of the artists represented in the Bradley Collection include Barbara Hepworth, Linda Howard, Ellsworth Kelly, Alexander Liberman, Henry Moore, Isamu Noguchi, Ernest Shaw, and George Sugarman (Buck and Palmer, 167).

The Bradley Family Foundation administers and preserves the garden, and visits are by reservation only. Call (414) 276-6840.

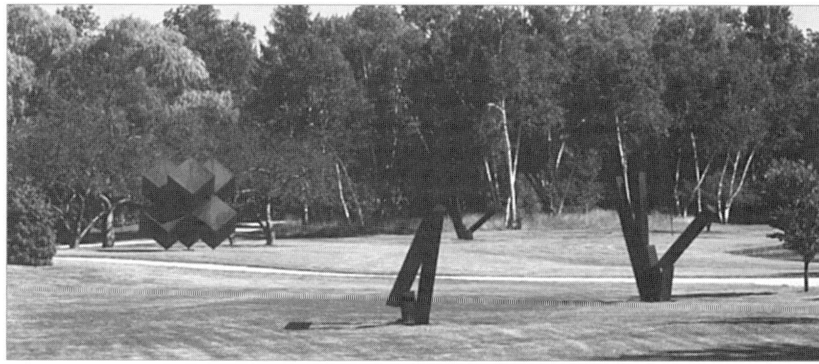

The Bradley Sculpture Garden, northwest Milwaukee

LaCrosse's Museum Without Walls. One of the most remarkable communities in terms of its extensive support for the arts, LaCrosse has begun a fairly recent tradition of public patronage of sculpture. This is another example of the marriage of public and private funding to give opportunities to artists for the creation of outdoor sculpture. The effort has been spearheaded by artist Elmer Peterson, a LaCrosse resident since 1978. He has worked with various private sponsors, including D.B. Reinhart and Charles D. Gelatt, to enrich the community with public sculptures. Along with other members of the LaCrosse Committee for Public Sculpture, formalized in 1993, Peterson has continued to lobby for public art, including the city's newest piece, *Scroll* by Dale Kendrick.

The result is a museum without walls for citizens and visitors to LaCrosse, with public sculpture ranging from popular traditional pieces to pure abstraction. At present, Peterson is busy on yet another commission for nearby Galesville—a welded Corten steel monument of *The Reverend Van Slyke*, which will be installed in 1999.

In addition, there is a Folk Art site in the city: Paul Hefti's decorated house and yard. Unfortunately, another important Folk Art site, St. Rose Grotto, was demolished several years ago.

West Bend's Public Art Program. Although West Bend has some fine examples of traditional outdoor sculpture, it recently embarked upon an ambitious program to bring contemporary sculpture to its citizens. Through grass-roots efforts, sculptures have been situated in Regner Park, including a large Corten steel wall with life-size human cut-outs, *Tableau in Steel* by David Genszler (1993).

One of the highlights of this ambitious new program is the Riverside Parkway. Sculpture is placed throughout a natural

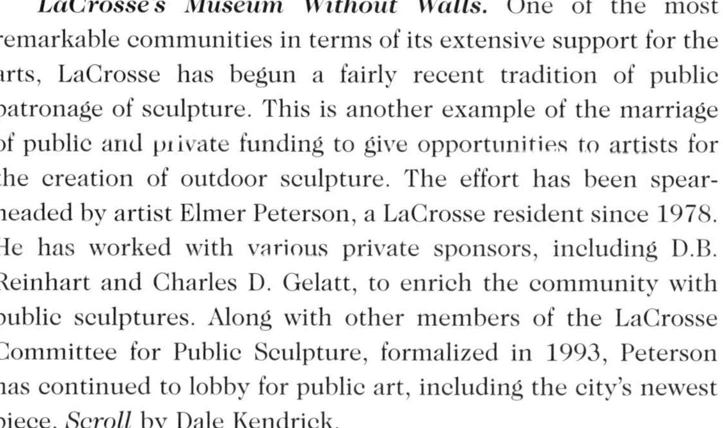

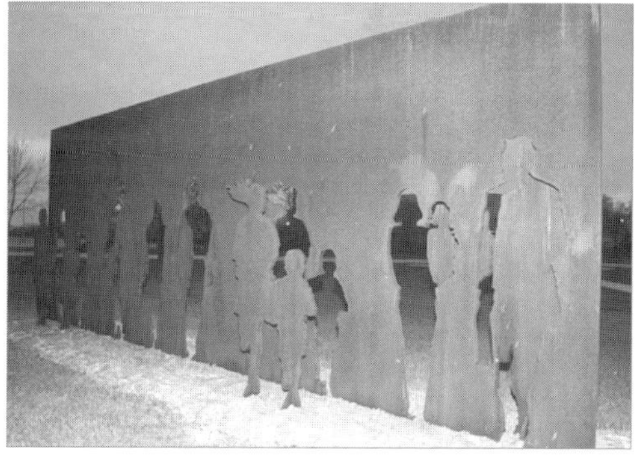

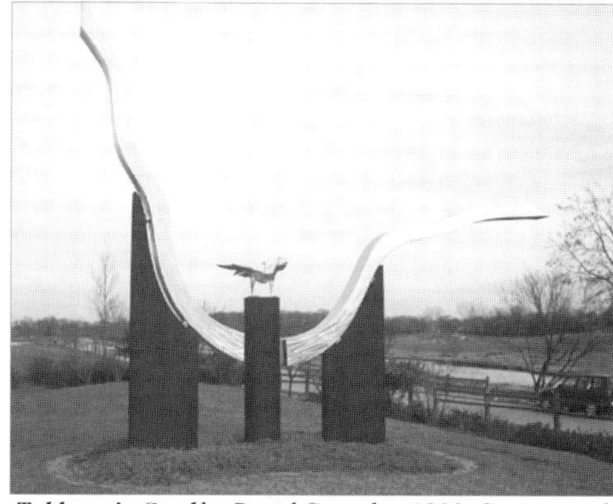

Tableau in Steel by David Genszler, 1993. Corten steel piece located in Regner Park, LaCrosse

West Bend Resolve by O.V. Shaffer, 1995. Corten steel, stainless steel and gold leaf over bronze, located at Riverfront Parkway in West Bend, Washington County

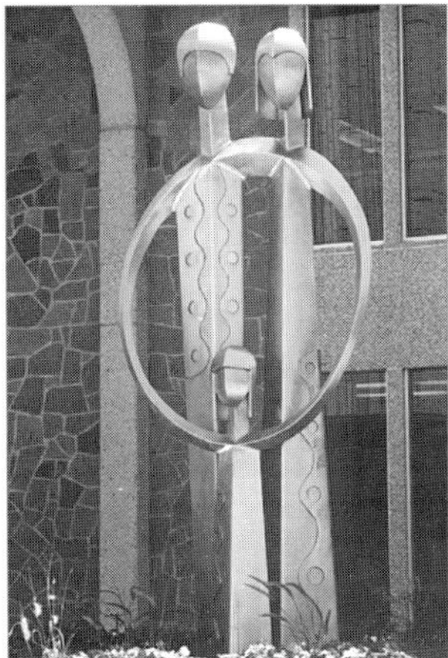

The Family by Joseph Puccetti in Milwaukee

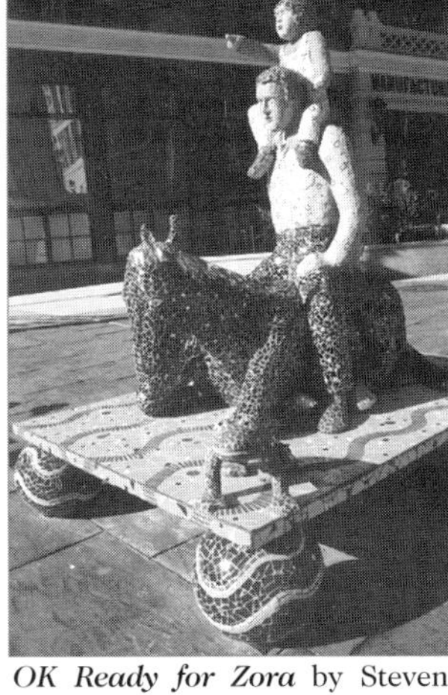

OK Ready for Zora by Steven Feren in Milwaukee

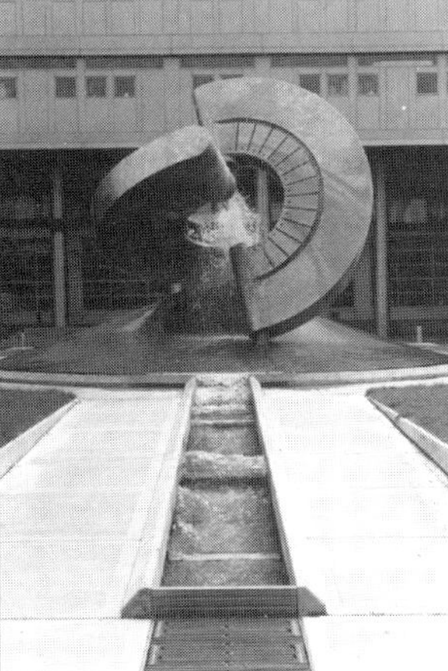

Máquina, The Descendant's Fountain, at UW-Madison

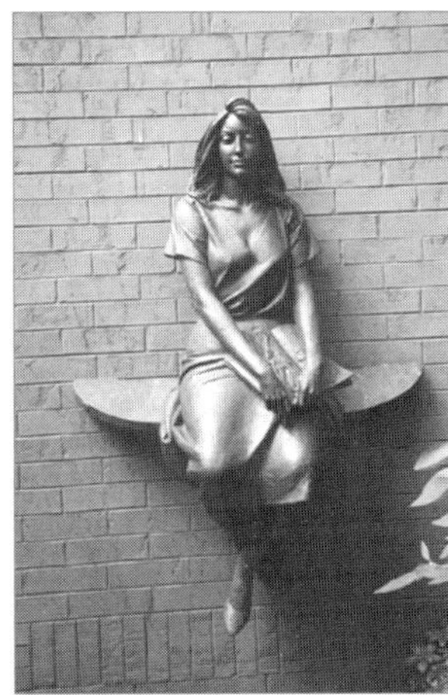

Seated Woman by B. Lucchesi in Manitowoc

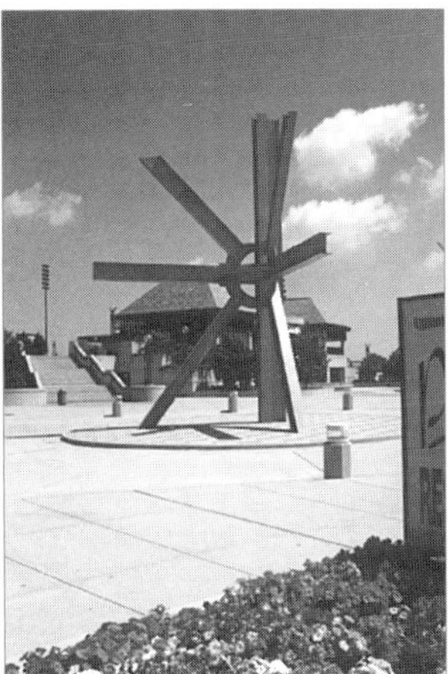

The Calling by Mark Di Suvero, in Milwaukee near the Milwaukee Art Museum

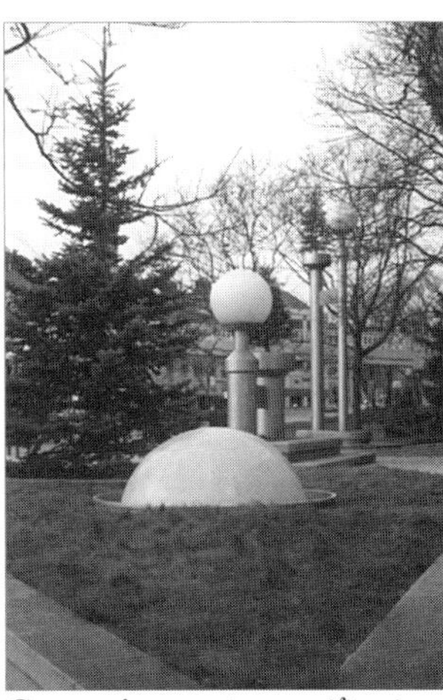

Generations, a site-specific piece by Richard Artschwager, at the Elvehjem Art Museum, UW-Madison

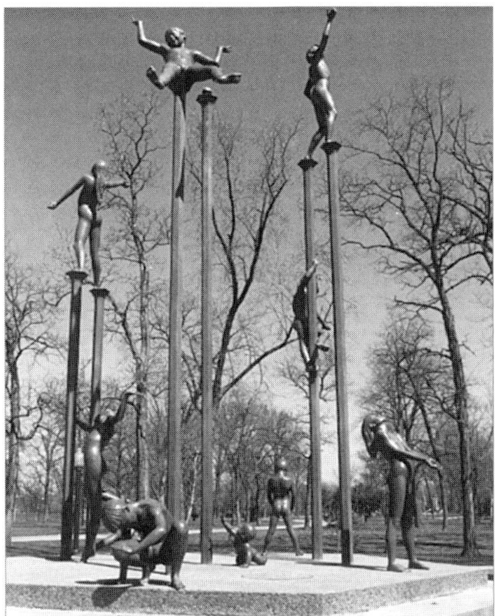

Playing in the Rain by Dallas Anderson in Neenah

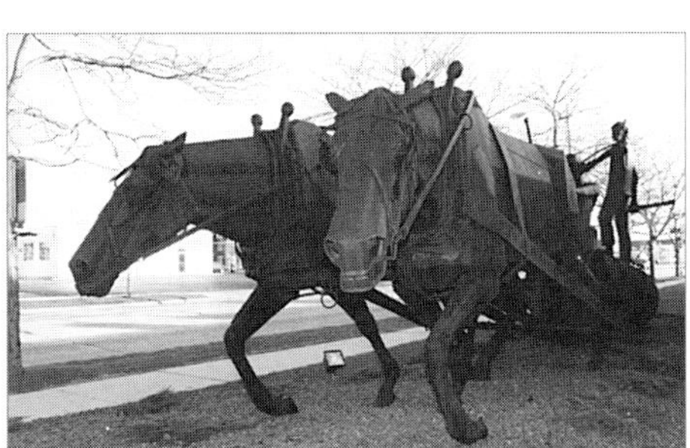

The First Northern Loggers by Lyndon Fayne Pomeroy in Green Bay

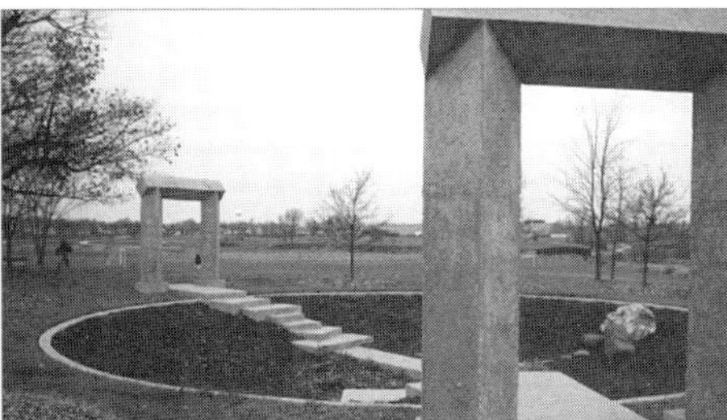

Ajuga Daydream, a site-specific piece by Thomas Lidtke, in West Bend

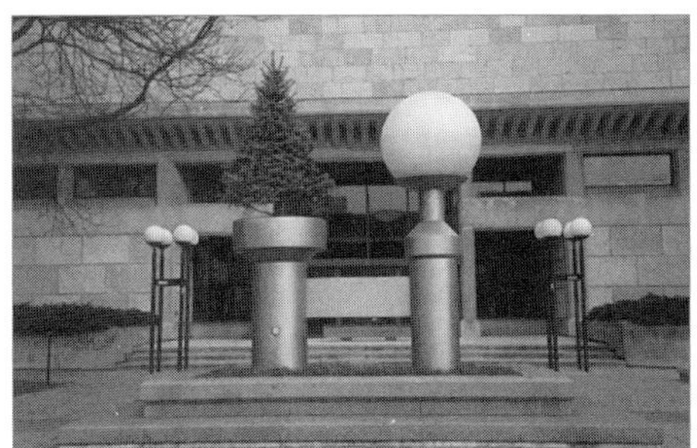

Generations, a 1991 site-specific piece by Richard Artschwager, at the Elvehjem Art Museum, UW-Madison

prairie environment with wandering paths and bridges. Several major works have already been sited, including *West Bend Resolve* by O.V. Shaffer, *Ajuga Daydream* by Thomas Lidtke, *Paradisedae* by Narendra Patel, and *Fluvio* by Paul Trappe.

Noteworthy Trends in Public Sculpture

Following national trends, several different types of public sculpture have emerged in the 1990s. They are abstraction (figurative and geometric), realistic, and site-specific environmental works.

Figurative abstraction is seen in works such as *Anidonts* by Luis Arata (LaCrosse), *Kua* by Deborah Butterfield (Wausau), and *Referee* by Tom Queoff (Milwaukee). These works use representational forms of a dog, horse, or man as a source of reference and point of departure for abstraction. *Anidonts* (see photo, page 114) is a painted steel piece with large-scale dog forms made as if they are folded origami. *Kua* (see photo, page 100) is a work which asserts the naturalistic form of the horse but is actually a careful arrangement of wood sticks, cast in bronze. Works that exemplify geometric or organic abstraction include *Máquina* by William Conrad Severson (Madison), *The Great Double* by Alicia Penalba (Milwaukee, see photo, page 140)), *The Calling* by Mark DiSuvero (Milwaukee), and *Alexa* by Susan Walsh (Madison, see photo, page 106). In these works there are less apparent representational points of reference, or the forms may be symbolic representations using the elements (line, shape, texture, value, color, or mass) and principles (contrast, balance, scale, orientation, or spatial relationships) of art as the idea.

Recent representational sculpture in realistic or naturalistic forms are located throughout the state. These include many works that are located at various firehouses in Milwaukee County, including *On Watch* by David M. Wanner (see photo, page 144). On Barkers Island, near Superior, is the *Seamen of the Great Lakes* Monument by William Bradford Frost and Debra Anunti (see photo, page 63). *The First Northern Loggers* in Green Bay by Lyndon Fayne Pomeroy is a figurative construction of Corten steel. *Seated Woman* by B. Lucchesi (Manitowoc) is a cast bronze naturalistic portrait of a woman waiting, and *Challenge* by Mike Casper (Wausau, 1998, see photo, page 99) is a cast bronze man in a kayak.

Site-specific environmental works frequently utilize a complex interplay of materials and spatial relationships. The prime example is Artschwager's *Generations* at the Elvehjem Art

Museum at the University of Wisconsin-Madison. The artwork encompasses the entire entrance plaza on University Avenue in Madison and places live Colorado blue spruce trees on top of stainless steel poles. Illuminated globes, partially buried in the ground (visually playing with the contemporary light-post form), are interspersed with architectural forms and nature. Russell Panczenko, Director of the Elvehjem Museum of Art, notes, "The work and the site are inseparable, both visually and conceptually. In fact, the concept of site predominates over what is usually understood by the term 'work of art.' In the final analysis, the sculpture belongs more to the public than it does to the artist." Also in Madison there are *Earth Flight* by Beth Sahagian and *Timekeeper* by Robert Curtis. *Ajuga Daydream* by Thomas Lidtke (West Bend) is another site-specific sculpture that integrates architectural forms and nature.

Other Notable Collections and Efforts

Many other institutions and corporations throughout the state have art collections, including Heritage Insurance (Sheboygan), the Marshfield Clinic (Marshfield), and S.C. Johnson & Son (Racine). Some have even begun building corporate sculpture collections.

The Milwaukee Art Museum's new wing and grounds will probably sponsor a wonderful array of public sculptures in years to come and will bring back some old favorites to the museum grounds including the *Walking Man* (1905) by Rodin, *Monumental Holistic III* (1979) by Betty Gold, and *Bullfinch* (1968) by Lyman Kipp.

In addition, Milwaukee will continue to play a role in promoting outdoor sculpture creation and preservation. Its most recent endeavor has been *Milwaukee's River Sculpture*. This temporary outdoor exhibit, which ran from June until October 1998, included twelve sculptures by noted American artists such as Steven Feren, Claire Lieberman, and Tom Uebelherr. The works were sited along the Milwaukee River between Third and Water streets. This program also highlighted permanent sculpture near the river, including works such as *Laureate* by Seymour Lipton and *Trigon* by Allen Ditson. This project has brought the creative spirit of contemporary art to an outdoor public venue. It is hoped that future events will continue to enrich, inspire, and entertain everyone. This project was made possible through a partnership of the City of Milwaukee, the River Walk District, and Nextel Communications.

University and college art programs throughout the state have also contributed many sculptures. Many works were sponsored through the Wisconsin Arts Board *Percent for Art Program* but many more are by faculty, students, and community donations.

The variety of public sculpture throughout the Badger State is nearly endless. We have examples of almost anything imaginable in any size, shape, or color. Outdoor monuments are found in many of the cities, towns, and villages in the state. Each was erected for a reason, and all but a few were intended to last forever in recognition of some individual, event, or ideal. Many of our sculptural monuments are war memorials or related to faith. Some were built by self-taught visionaries, and others by professional artists. Still others were created as part of a larger building program. In other words, we have it all here in Wisconsin. Like many of the other Sesquicentennial celebrations in 1998, *Public Sculpture in Wisconsin* is a celebration of what makes our state unique within the union. Outdoor public sculpture is for all of us to enjoy and admire.

As we head into the next century, we can be proud of our artistic accomplishments. Hundreds of monuments enliven cities and towns. By preserving these monuments, we leave a legacy to the future about our hopes, values, and creative spirit, recognizing all types of people who made a difference.

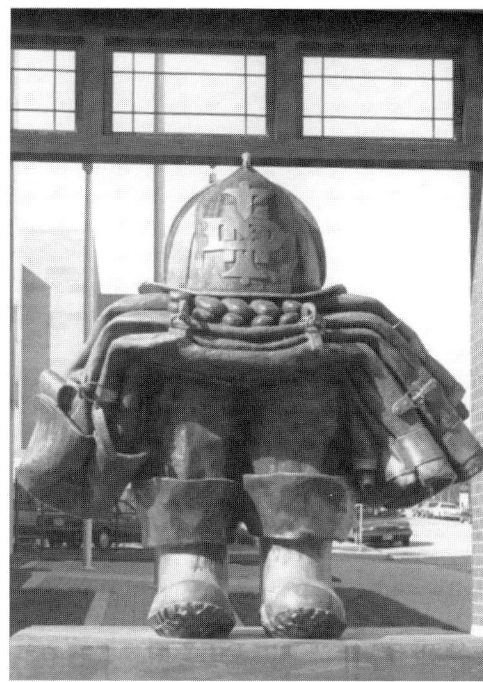

Last Alarm at Engine No. 2 firehouse in Milwaukee

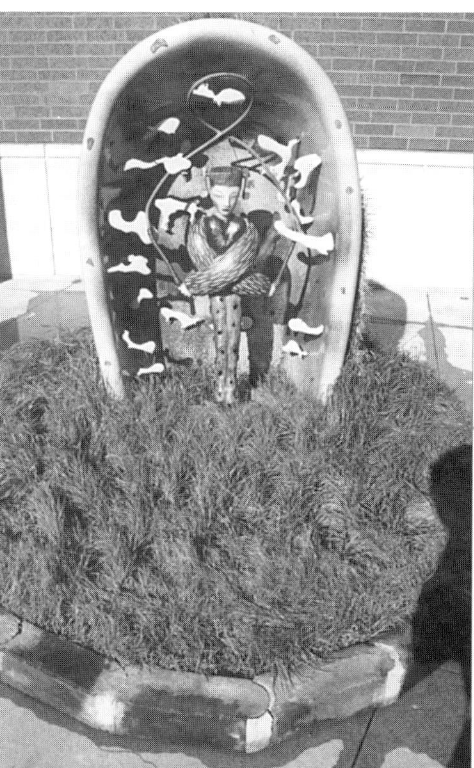

Bathtub Madonna by Tom Uebelherr was part of the Riverwalk Temporary Outdoor Sculpture exhibit located in downtown Milwaukee, Kohler Arts and Industry project.

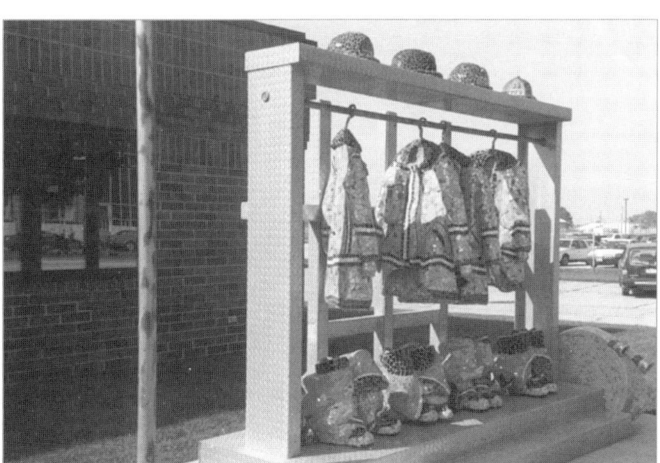

Gear, 23 sculpture by Steven Feren in Milwaukee is one of many outdoor sculptures commissioned by the city for various firehouses in Milwaukee County

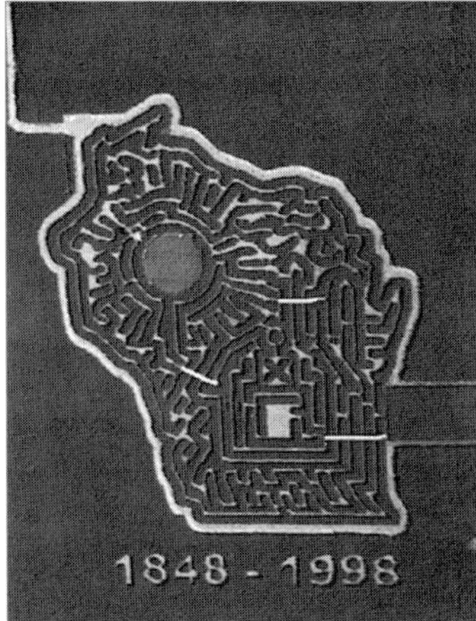

Corn Maze near Janesville

THE CORN MAZE
A Living Sesquicentennial Outdoor Sculpture

The most unusual and novel outdoor sculpture created for the state's 150th birthday was the giant 10-acre corn maze in Janesville. The maze was designed as a tribute to Wisconsin farmers and their contribution to the growth of our state. Long before Wisconsin was known as the dairy state we were the wheat state, known for our grains, including corn.

The Whilden Randall Hughes family of Rock County sponsored this gigantic living earth sculpture on their family farm. The 10-acre maze was carved out of a corn field by Adrian Fisher, a renowned maze maker from England. The huge maze was the shape of Wisconsin. It had many passages and trails to intrigue the visitor into getting lost, and many received guidance from mazemaster helpers. Fortunately, a victory bridge exit was provided for those still lost at the end of a day, though many made it out of the maze on their own. There were moonlight maze tours, maze dinners, and square dances. Thousands of people visited this unique artistic creation between July 25 and October 31, 1998. A combination of high technology, hard work, community spirit, and fun made this giant puzzle come to life. Many sponsors contributed to making this a successful project of people, businesses, civic organizations, and devoted individuals working in partnership to celebrate the state's Sesquicentennial.

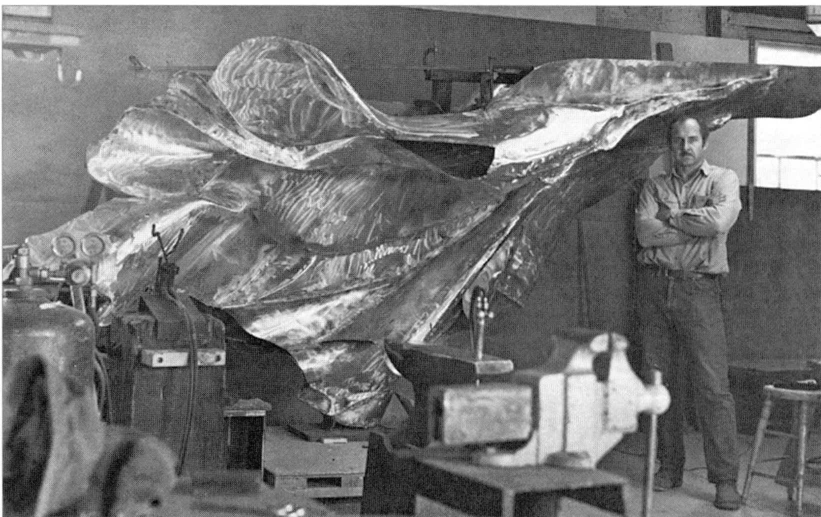

O.V. Shaffer with *Voyageur* in his studio in 1968

Shaffer's Organic Sculpture

Owen Vernon (Verne) Shaffer (b.1928 in Princeton, Illinois) currently lives in Mineral Point and did maintain a studio in Clinton for 25 years. He has been quietly and diligently producing public sculpture since 1961 without government support or grants. Shaffer has degrees from Beloit College and Michigan State University. He taught at Olivet College in Michigan, and then was the director of Wright Art Museum at Beloit College for 25 years. He has placed his works in more than twenty locations throughout the state, including Madison, Beloit, Janesville, Green Bay, and Fond du Lac. His work is abstract in nature, utilizing organic forms. On many occasions he has worked in conjunction with architectural projects around Wisconsin and in other states. Shaffer's success can be attributed to his close working relationship with architects and engineers. He is not interested in art as a competitive endeavor, but prefers to work one-on-one with site-specific projects. His large-scale welded brass and steel sculptures enliven plazas, building entrances and parks. Shaffer says, "I never let anyone tell me what to do. If people would just get down and get to work, you can do a lot."

Further Reading

Elvehjem Museum of Art and Russell Panczenko. *Richard Artschwager, Public (public)*. Madison: Regents of the University of Wisconsin System, 1991

Frances W. Hurst and Fran Rall. *Common Joy II: Outdoor Art in Madison*. Madison: Self-published, 1991, 1994.

Leigh Yawkey Woodson Art Museum. Public sculpture catalogs. Wausau, WI: Leigh Yawkey Woodson Art Museum, 1995, 1998.

WHO CARES FOR PUBLIC SCULPTURE?

Issues in Creating and Maintaining Outdoor Sculpture

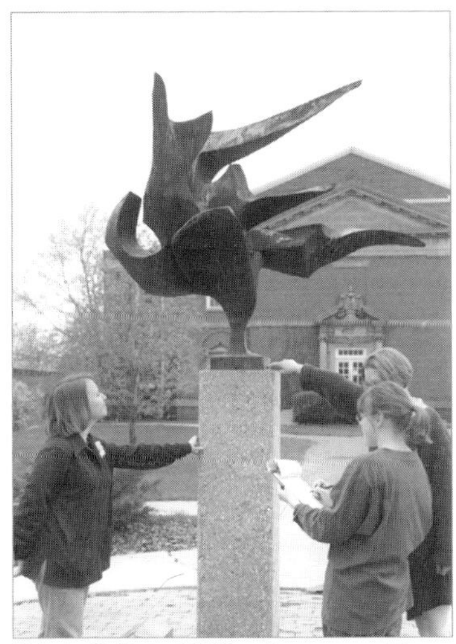

Beloit College SOS! volunteers with an O.V. Shaffer sculpture, *The Wings of Change*, at Beloit College, Rock County

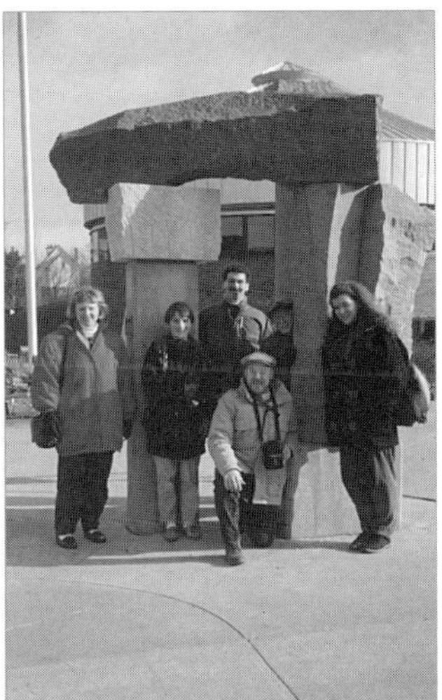

UW-Stout SOS! volunteers in 1991 in Menomonie, Dunn County

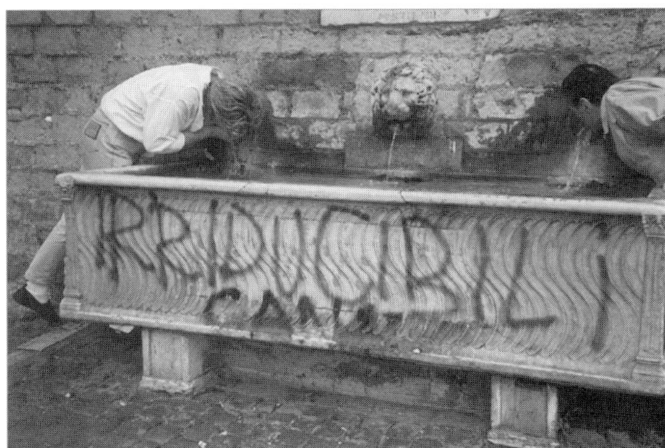

This ancient Roman marble carving has been damaged by graffiti. This type of vandalism is difficult to remove because the marble is porous and the paint has sunk into the surface. Rome, Italy.

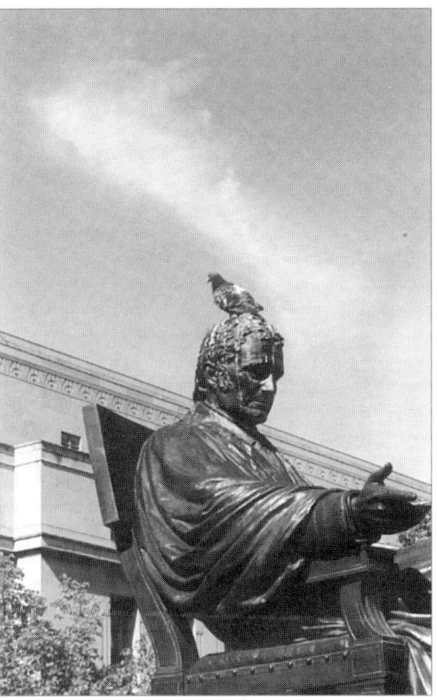

Bird guano droppings frequently disfigure outdoor statuary. Regular maintenance eliminates this problem.

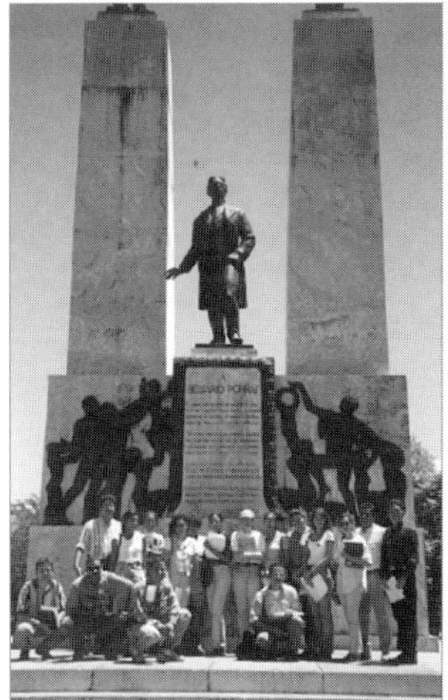

SOS! has gone international with similar efforts in Argentina, Panama, and Australia. SOS! volunteers in Panama above.

The question of value and worth

"So, what's this piece worth?"

This question was frequently asked by people during Wisconsin's SOS! project. Worth or value can carry many meanings—economic, cultural, political, historical or artistic. And like any other art form, public sculpture is open to many different interpretations of value often linked to personal taste and perspectives.

The question of worth and value associated with art was tackled in two pioneering exhibits about the value of folk art at the State Museum in Columbia, South Carolina, in 1981 and 1997. The first exhibit, "Worth Keeping," explored with photos, documents, and objects the work of Carolina folk artists. A decade and a half later, scholars revisited the theme with a show called "Still Worth Keeping." They explored what had happened to the artists in the 1981 show to learn whether their communities had recognized the value of their work. In some instances worth had been recognized; in others the artistic heritage was deemed worthless and was lost. For those forgotten works or devalued artists, the only record of their art was the exhibit and a community memory of what had been.

The South Carolina exhibits are a good introduction to the complex relationship among knowledge, memory, and appreciation—and the perceived worth of artistic heritage. Examples of

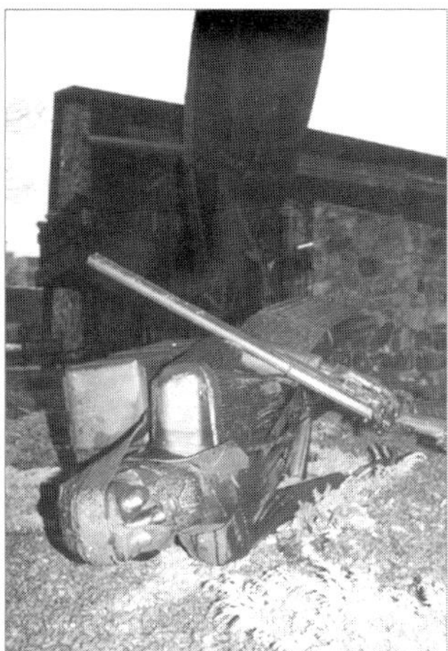

1998 wind damage to one of the *First Northern Voyageurs* figures, Green Bay, Brown County.

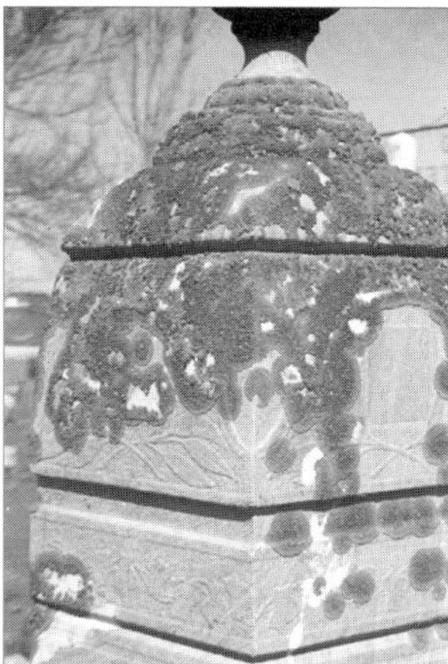

Lichen and other biological growth can disfigure and damage sculptural surfaces.

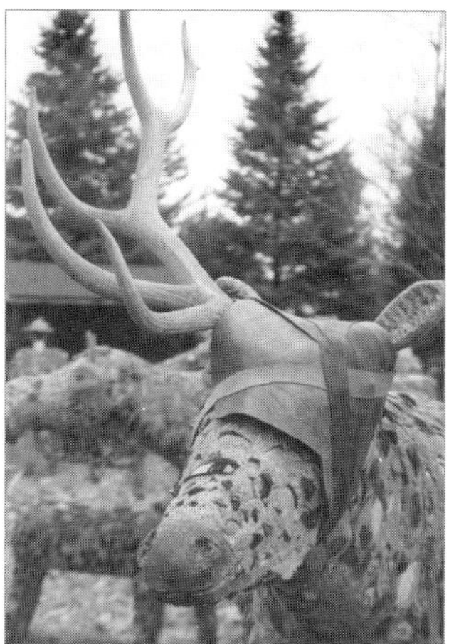

Preventive conservation can include coverings such as rubber membranes until full conservation can be undertaken. *Wisconsin Concrete Park* in Phillips, Price County.

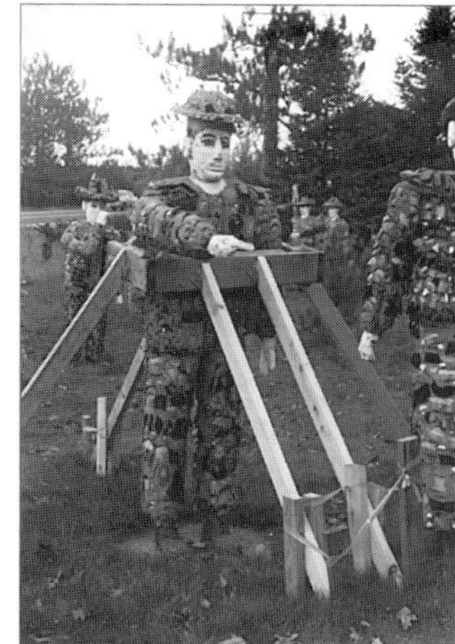

Preventive conservation can include construction of wooden supports until full conservation occurs. *Wisconsin Concrete Park*, Phillips in Price County

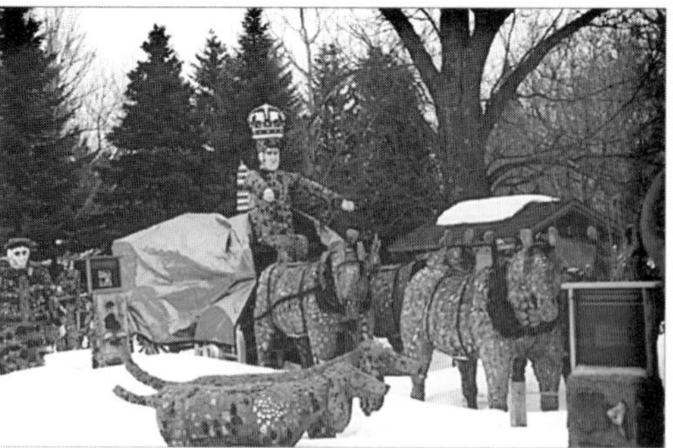

Winter covering such as tarps can help reduce the detrimental effects of a harsh climate. *Wisconsin Concrete Park* in winter.

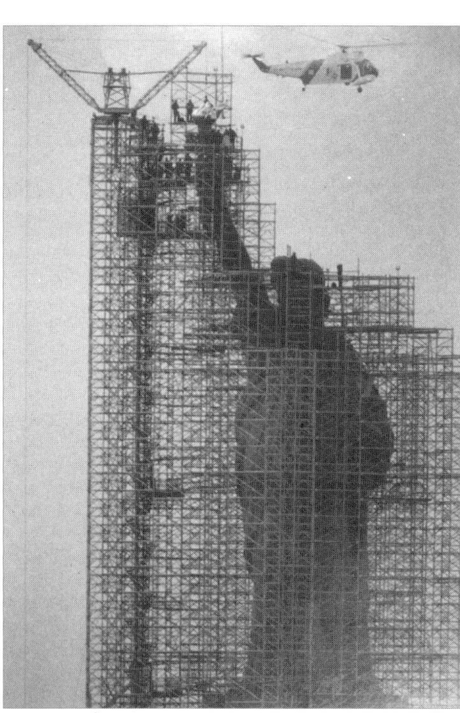

Statue of Liberty in New York City during its restoration in 1986

this phenomenon abound in Wisconsin as elsewhere. *Wisconsin Concrete Park* in Phillips is an excellent example of the preservation of one man's artistic creations as a county park open for new generations of admirers. However, the work of the state's most prolific artist and cultural resource, Dr. Rudy Rotter, in Manitowoc, needs to be preserved.

Why is this important? Appreciation provides the seeds of support for preservation, particularly funds for conservation projects. Outdoor sculpture is particularly fragile, and like any object of worth—a home or a car—needs to be maintained regularly to ensure that future generations can enjoy it. Public sculpture quickly degrades when neglected and frequently is the target for vandalism and theft.

This was the case several years ago when youth gangs repeatedly vandalized the famous Orange Show in Houston, Texas. A series of meetings with the gangs led to creating the opportunity for them to express themselves by painting their own mural. After that, vandalism ceased at the site, and the gangs now not only take pride in the Orange Show, but they help on clean-up days.

The Cycle of Attention and Neglect for Public Sculpture

"Elected officials have an enormous interest in how their city looks. Nothing looks worse, frankly, than an outdoor sculpture that is starting to crack, has lost color, is falling apart. It doesn't take a lot of money to repair and maintain it."

John Bryan, CEO
Sara Lee Corporation, Chicago, Illinois

Most sculptures in Wisconsin oscillate somewhere between the two poles of attention and neglect. In Wisconsin, constructing monuments is a popular activity, as the SOS! inventory revealed. But frequently after a statue or memorial is put up, it is forgotten.

The cycle is familiar. Huge crowds gather for the dedication of a new work and give it lots of attention. As time passes, interest fades and the place gets fewer visitors and decreasing attention. The event for which the monument was constructed is forgotten, and the artwork is taken for granted, even if it isn't actively vandalized.

But the forces of nature—wind, rain, snow, heat, and cold—don't forget sculptures. Nature, the great artist, starts to transform the materials. Metal corrodes, stone cracks, plastic and glass grow brittle. In addition, today's outdoor sculpture faces threats other than nature. In pre-industrial Europe and America, there was no acid rain, no chemical industrial pollution, and lower levels of ultraviolet light. Today these are real threats.

While the forces of deterioration—natural or industrial—are often not quickly or easily noticed until the damage becomes severe, they are constantly at work on outdoor sculpture. For example, marble, which is an ideal sculptural material for the mild climate of the Mediterranean, suffers from thermal shocks in the extreme weather conditions of Wisconsin. Acid corrodes marble and stone as well as metal. Stone monuments, particularly gravestones, exhibit a type of slow meltdown described as sugaring. Little can be done to stop it, short of covering the stone or moving it indoors. Wind also deteriorates outdoor sculpture. For instance, harsh winds can pound statues and make them sway, undermining their structure.

There is only one way to offset this deterioration—through careful and regular maintenance, appropriate to the artwork. This won't stop the deterioration entirely, but it will dramatically slow it down.

Graffiti, vandalism, and other intentional acts of destruction destroy portions of Wisconsin's artistic heritage. One example is the *Belle Austin Jacobs Memorial* in Kosciuzko Park in Milwaukee. Artist Sylvia Shaw Judson (1897-1978) created the work in 1932 as a memorial to Belle Austin, a woman pioneer in social work who helped Milwaukee's poor. The bronze statue weighed several hundred pounds. It was stolen from its black granite base in 1975 and has never been recovered (Buck, 97).

Offsetting the Deterioration of Public Sculpture

As a result of the accelerating destruction of outdoor monuments worldwide, the late twentieth century has seen a dramatic rise in efforts to provide care for them. For instance, much interest focused on the conservation and restoration of the Statue of Liberty, re-dedicated in 1986 (originally dedicated in 1886). This multi-million dollar project taught people the need to care for outdoor sculpture of any size. This project, along with the restoration of Ellis Island, was spearheaded by Lee Iacocca when the Statue of Liberty-Ellis Island Foundation was established as a partnership with private and public funds.

At the same time, across the Atlantic, the great gilded bronze horse of Emperor Marcus Aurelius that dates to 161 A.D. and stood for centuries in Rome's Campidoglio, was deteriorating from the heavily polluted air of Rome. It was moved indoors to a museum in 1989 to better preserve it, and a bronze replica has replaced it outdoors.

Wisconsin offers a similar example. Deterioration of Jean Miner's 1893 *Forward* statue at the State Capitol led it to be brought indoors to the State Historical Society of Wisconsin. A new bronze replica is now out of doors.

Few projects in the past were designed to have a permanent maintenance program associated with them. Where public sculpture is located, staff generally are not instructed in how to care for them. So the works receive the usual once-per-year hosing down to remove dust and bird droppings.

Fortunately, we do not have to accept decay and damage as inevitable. The modern profession of art conservation can help preserve endangered works of art. Responsible stewardship can lead to better care of our outdoor sculptural heritage.

The Field of Art Conservation

Art conservators are highly trained individuals with backgrounds in art history, studio arts, and chemistry. They have both theoretical knowledge and practical experience in conservation treatments. Academic training in the field is critical to the theoretical basis for conservation of cultural property. Today most conservators are university-trained, in contrast to those who were apprentice-trained in the past. A broad view of the field is necessary to understand all aspects of heritage, including the causes of deterioration and how to correct it.

Conservators are guided by high ethical standards in the care of cultural property, whether generalists or specialists in statuary, murals, paper, or other categories of art object. The American Institute for the Conservation of Historic and Artistic Works (AIC) is the national membership association for professional conservators. Its *Guide to the Maintenance of Outdoor Sculpture* (1993) describes in detail the role that conservators can play in helping save outdoor sculpture. SOS! policy was guided by the principles set forth by this national organization.

Conservators can consult on the needed treatment for a piece, perform that work themselves, or help art stewards find qualified professionals who have the training and experience required. They can help owners prepare a Request For Proposal (RFP) for conservation services and determine pre-bid qualifications and acceptable standards of practice. Frequently, before a project begins, a technical survey with an on-site examination will take place to ascertain condition and problems.

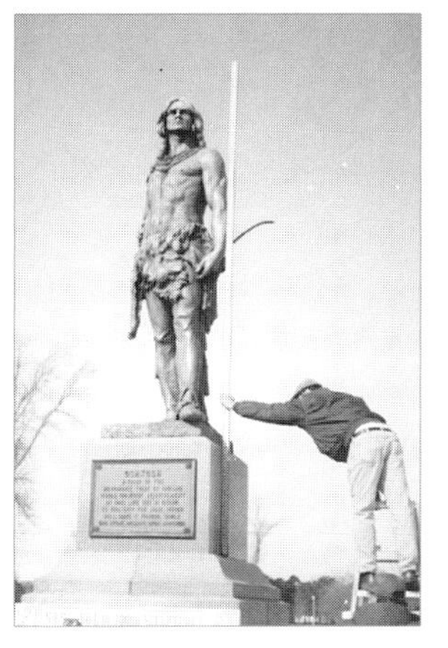

Top left: Measuring *Chief Oshkosh* as part of the SOS! inventory. Oshkosh, Winnebago County.

Top right: Metallic staining disfigures the base of this untitled sculptural group of three figures and fountain by Dennis Bauer (1971) at UW-Marathon County in Wausau.

Below: *Gateway Project*, Madison, Dane County. This statue is made of bronze powder and resin and requires periodic maintenance.

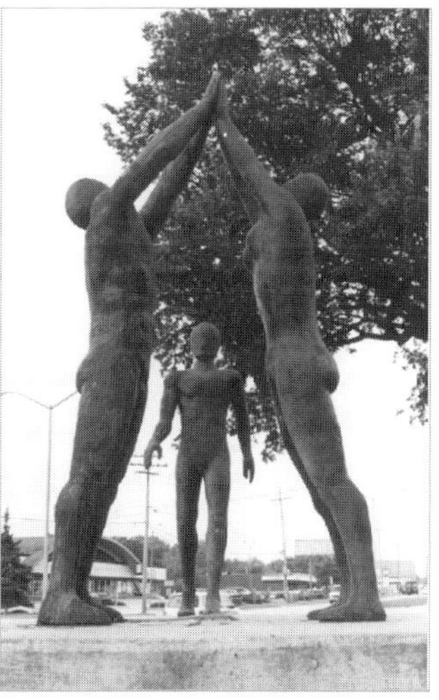

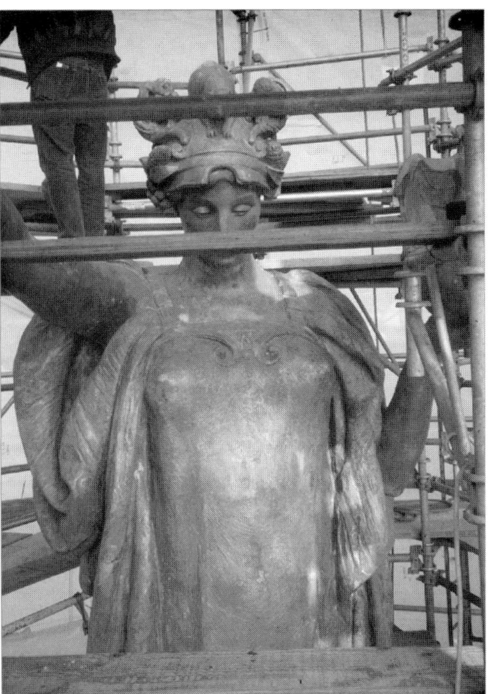

Wisconsin statue in Madison after high pressure water cleaning in preparation for regilding

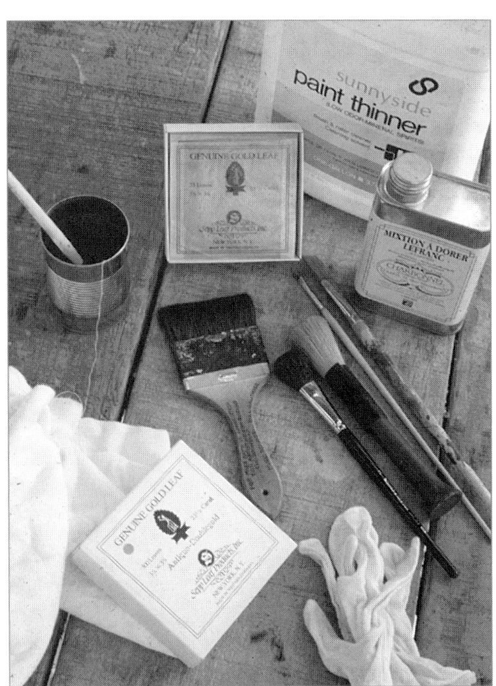

Gilding supplies including gold leaf, sizing, solvents, and brushes

The Role of Citizen-Steward

Not only professional conservators, but all of us have a role to play in preserving this heritage. Administrators who act as stewards of outdoor sculpture are the owner's representative in many cases, representing a city, private organization, state, or nation. Ultimately someone owns the work of art that stands in a park. It may take some research to ascertain who that owner is. When located, that person may be surprised to learn that they have sculpture under their care. This was the case with many of the objects catalogued by SOS! Wisconsin.

Many people can participate in conservation projects, including volunteers, artists, art historians, conservators, administrators, reporters, and allied professionals. An open discourse is best when beginning a project because outdoor sculpture has a tendency to take a high profile, with everyone having an opinion. Conscientiousness and communication are the keys to getting everyone on board before a project begins. Open public forums are a good way to start, where guest speakers are invited to talk on the subject and the public can voice its concerns.

Some Guidelines in Commissioning New Outdoor Sculpture

"The Inventory of American Sculpture is a unique catalog of our country's creative breadth and diversity. We heartily encourage owners, administrators, and sculptors to register new commissions so that the rich legacy of outdoor sculpture in the United States will be known to present and future generations."

Dr. Elizabeth Broun, Director,
National Museum of American Art,
Smithsonian Institution, Washington, D.C.

Parallel to the need to care for existing sculptural heritage is the need to better plan a proposed public sculpture project. Up until a few years ago, few new public sculpture projects had any preservation component attached to them. This comes from the illusion that outdoor sculpture is permanent and immune to deterioration or damage. This section is designed to help people who are involved with creating new outdoor public works of art, including artists, administrators, committees, landscape architects, fabricators, engineers, conservators, and concerned citizens.

Selection of Materials. The selection of materials in the beginning stages of a commission is critical. Today we have a broad range from which to choose, and some endure better than others. For example, durable, time-tested materials like granite hold up much better then enameled steel or plastics. This is particularly true in the harsh climate of Wisconsin with its hot, humid summers and bitter cold winters. Temperatures can vary by as much as 100 degrees in a typical year.

Relative humidity plays a major factor in moss and lichen growth on surfaces. Water in other forms can severely damage a surface not designed to withstand moisture or not cared for. Fountains and pipes need to be drained in winter. The sun plays a role because of the damaging effects of ultraviolet rays on statuary coatings and materials.

Site and Sculpture Maintenance. Site and sculpture maintenance are critical to preservation. A rundown site with statues marred by graffiti reflects poorly on stewardship and citizen concern. Attractive plantings, enhanced by a low maintenance but beautiful landscape, indicate a community that cares. This is the case in LaCrosse, where private-public partnerships have created and maintained a wide selection of public sculpture through an active citizens committee advocating public sculpture. Plantings can also serve a preservation function. Using shrubs as a physical barrier can help cut down on vandalism.

Creating new outdoor sculpture is a complicated process involving many people and factors. Only when all of these factors are understood can informed decisions be made about present and future needs. Several major outdoor sculpture projects to be created in Wisconsin early in the next century are already in the design phase. It is prudent to learn from our past successes and mistakes how to best proceed. The end product will be a finer, better and more durable outdoor sculpture legacy for future generations.

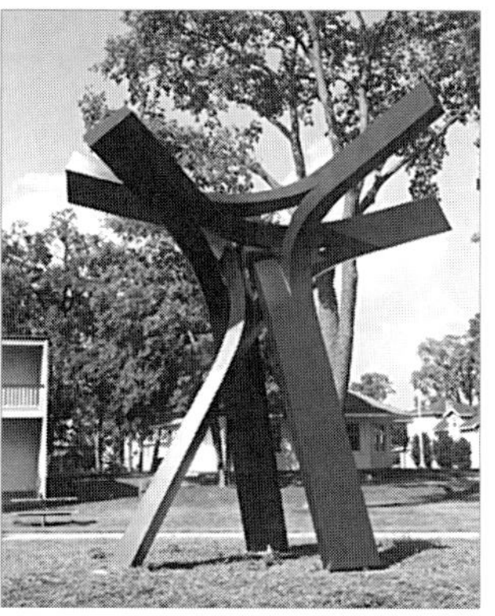

Painted sculptures require periodic repainting to maintain the surface and prevent corrosion. It is critical to have the artist's opinion regarding this issue of repainting and the technical data about the paint product in order to respect artistic intent. *Lycra* in LaCrosse, LaCrosse County.

Further Readings

Jeffrey Cruikshank and Pam Korza. *Going Public: A Field Guide to Developments in Art in Public Places.* Amherst: University of Massachusetts-Amherst, 1988.

Dennis Montagna, Susan Nichols and Rebecca Shiffer, eds. *"Public Monuments and Outdoor Sculpture, Cultural Resource Management."* Washington, D.C.: U.S. Department of the Interior (18:1), 1994.

Virginia Naude and Glenn Wharton. *Guide to the Maintenance of Outdoor Sculpture.* Washington, D.C.: American Institute for the Conservation of Historic and Artistic Works, 1993.

Save Outdoor Sculpture, SOS! *Designing Outdoor Sculpture for Today and Tomorrow.* Washington, D.C.: Heritage Preservation, 1996.

Save Outdoor Sculpture, SOS! *Selecting and Contracting with a Conservator, Informed Decision-Making Eases the Process.* Washington, D.C.: SOS! Heritage Preservation, (5:2) 1994.

Other Resources

American Institute for the Conservation of Historic and Artistic Works (AIC), 1717 K Street NW, Suite 301, Washington, D.C. 20006. Phone: 202-452-9545. The AIC can provide a referral list of conservators in your area. The AIC World Wide Web site is:

http://sul-server-2.stanford.edu/aic/

Inventory of Public Sculpture in America, National Museum of American Art, Smithsonian Institution, Washington, D.C. 20560. Find this on-line at http://www.siris.si.edu/ Scroll down until you come to "Art Inventories Catalog."

The National SOS! office at Heritage Preservation has a vast array of published materials and videos about outdoor sculpture. Write to them at: Heritage Preservation, 1730 K Street NW, Suite 566, Washington, D.C. 20006-3836.
Phone: 888-SOS-SCULP, 888-767-7285 or 202-634-1422, or 800-422-4612.

The Heritage Preservation World Wide Web site is: http://www.heritagepreservation.org/PROGRAMS/SOS/sosmain.htm or e-mail at SOS!2000@heritagepreservation.org

COMMISSIONING A NEW WORK OF ART:
What are the steps?

Commissioning a new artwork is a complex process that usually involves one or more decision-making committees. Each step along the way is crucial to the success of the project. A high degree of patience and collaboration is necessary for all factors to be considered and the best decisions to be made. This is only possible when all members of the team can participate. Everyone has a responsibility in this process.

Some of the initial steps are:

- Selecting the best qualified artist. The artist should be forward-thinking and have preservation in mind. The artist needs to submit a written statement regarding his or her feelings about future preservation needs such as conservation. Understanding an artist's intent is crucial in this process. Will the work of art be played-on in a park or simply admired? This will affect wear and artist intent considerations. Each sculpture is a separate case. Remember this is ART, not a parking lot or road you are commissioning.

- Selecting the site. Consider such factors as security, drainage, and exposure to water and the elements.

- Designing the work of art.

- Recognizing preservation factors such as long-term maintenance considerations and costs.

- Establishing a realistic project budget with maintenance as a line item.

- Presenting the proposed project before the public. Remember that by law, all new publicly accessible monuments must meet ADA requirements.

- Preparing contracts and details of work.

- Fabrication of the piece.

- Installing the piece with durable materials.

- Documenting the project and preparing an archive of photographs, reports, and press clippings.

Every step along the way needs input by concerned, informed individuals. This whole process might take years, but the result will be a lasting, maintainable monument that everyone can enjoy. Shortcuts can result in a poorly conceived work of art that requires costly repairs in the future. Some city and state agencies now require artists to use durable materials that can be maintained at low cost in the future. Maintenance contracts can also help serve to define special needs for the work of art and how best to preserve it.

1911	Daniel Chester French receives Capitol dome statue commission.
August 1912	French writes to the Capitol Building Commission from his studio in Chesterwood, Massachusetts to inform them that the half-size model of the *Wisconsin* statue is ready.
December 1912	The state of Wisconsin sends signed contract to French for the *Wisconsin* statue.
1913	The full-scale model of *Wisconsin* is shipped from Chesterwood, Massachusetts, to Brooklyn, New York, to the Roman Bronze Foundry where she is cast in bronze. The L. Marcotte & Company gild the statue at the request of the Capitol Building Commission.
February 25, 1914	*Wisconsin* is finished. She is placed in a large wooden crate in Brooklyn, New York and travels by train to Madison, Wisconsin, her new home.
March 1914	*Wisconsin* arrives in Madison at the train depot. She is 15 feet 5 inches tall and weighs 3 tons.
July 20, 1914	After much public discussion in the press as to the direction the statue is to face, French suggests southeast towards the dawn. The Capitol Building Commission favors southeast as the principle entrance to the building. *Wisconsin* is raised to the Capitol roof, then hoisted to the Capitol dome and set in place on the granite pedestal of the dome, facing southeast.
1932	A.E. Olsen Steeplejack Company of Janesville, Wisconsin, regilds the statue.
July 1957	Wallace JaKa of Milwaukee cleans and regilds *Wisconsin*.
September 3, 1990	Safeway Company of Milwaukee begins to assemble scaffolding on top of the Capitol dome.
September 24, 1990	Work begins on the water pressure-washing of *Wisconsin*.
October 8, 1990	*Wisconsin* regilding begins.
October 22, 1990	The fourth gilding of *Wisconsin* is complete.
November 30, 1990	The last of the scaffolding is removed from atop the Capitol dome.

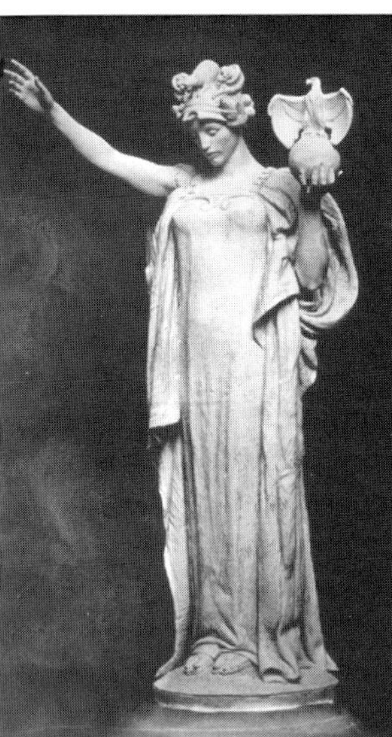

Study for *Wisconsin* by Daniel Chester French in 1912

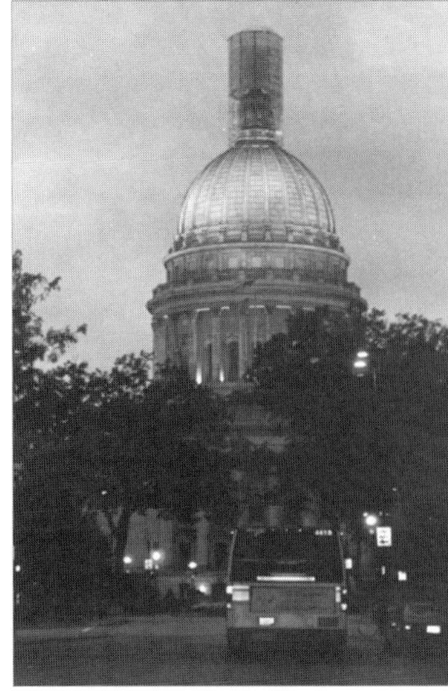

The Capitol in Madison dome with scaffolding around *Wisconsin* in 1990

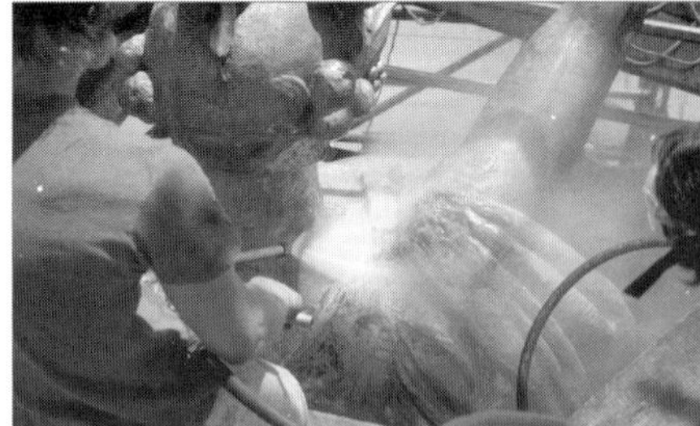

Power washing *Wisconsin* in 1990

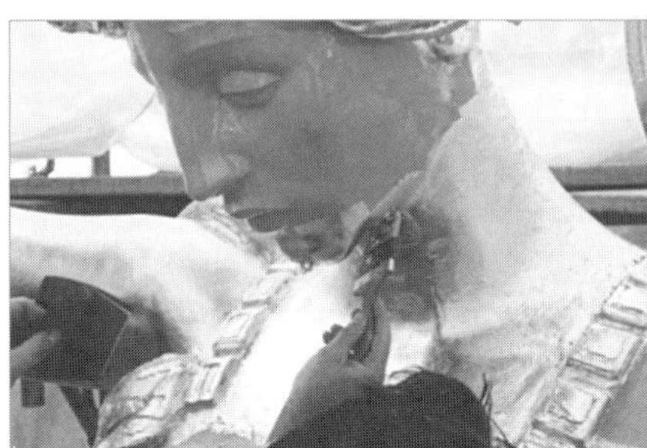

Applying a sheet of gold leaf on the *Wisconsin* statue in 1990

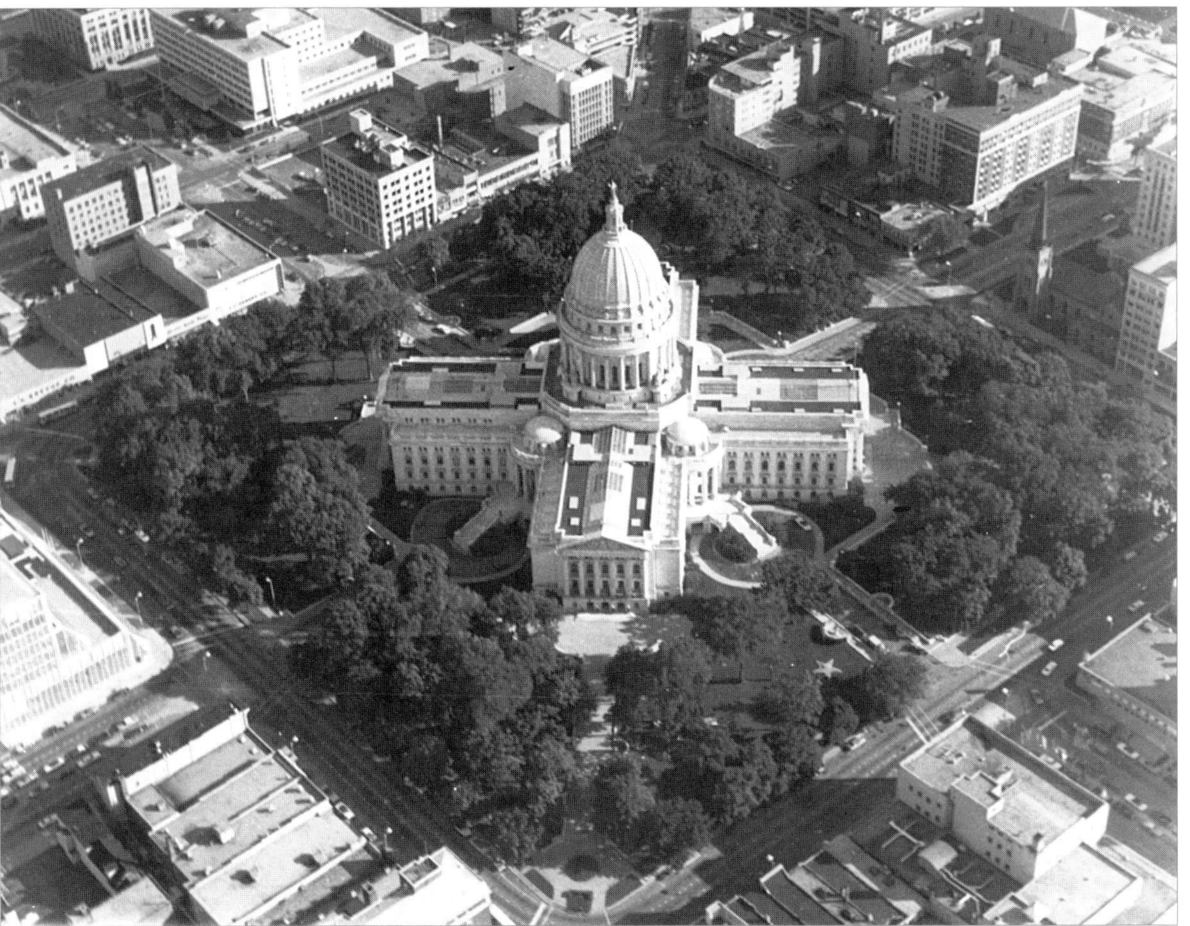

Aerial view of Wisconsin's Capitol in Madison

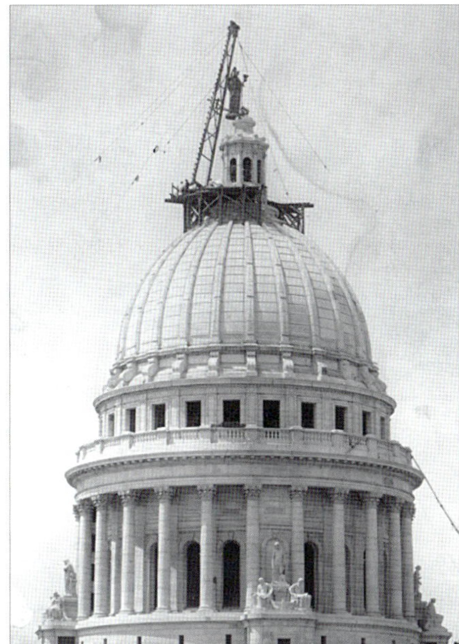

State Capitol dome in 1914 as *Wisconsin* is lowered into place

Wisconsin Statue Arrives

"Guided by a crew of men who looked like so many scrambling mannequins, *Forward*, the bronze statue typifying the Wisconsin spirit, was slowly raised to the topmost point of the capitol dome this morning. Before thousands of gaping pedestrians who lined the streets on the four sides of the capitol, the massive figure was hoisted, inch by inch, to the position it will occupy for the span of many life-times. When it was finally settled on the pedestal, an audible sigh of relief went up from those who watched the delicate operation. The awful possibilities which were presented to the mind by the imaginary snapping of a cable, were relieved by the shout from the capitol dome, 'All set.'

With the placing of the statue in position the end has come to what has been one of the most interesting expressions of popular sentiment. Thousands of State Journal readers voted their choice of the direction in which the figure should face. The capitol commission decided it by selecting Monona Avenue."

Wisconsin State Journal
July 20, 1914

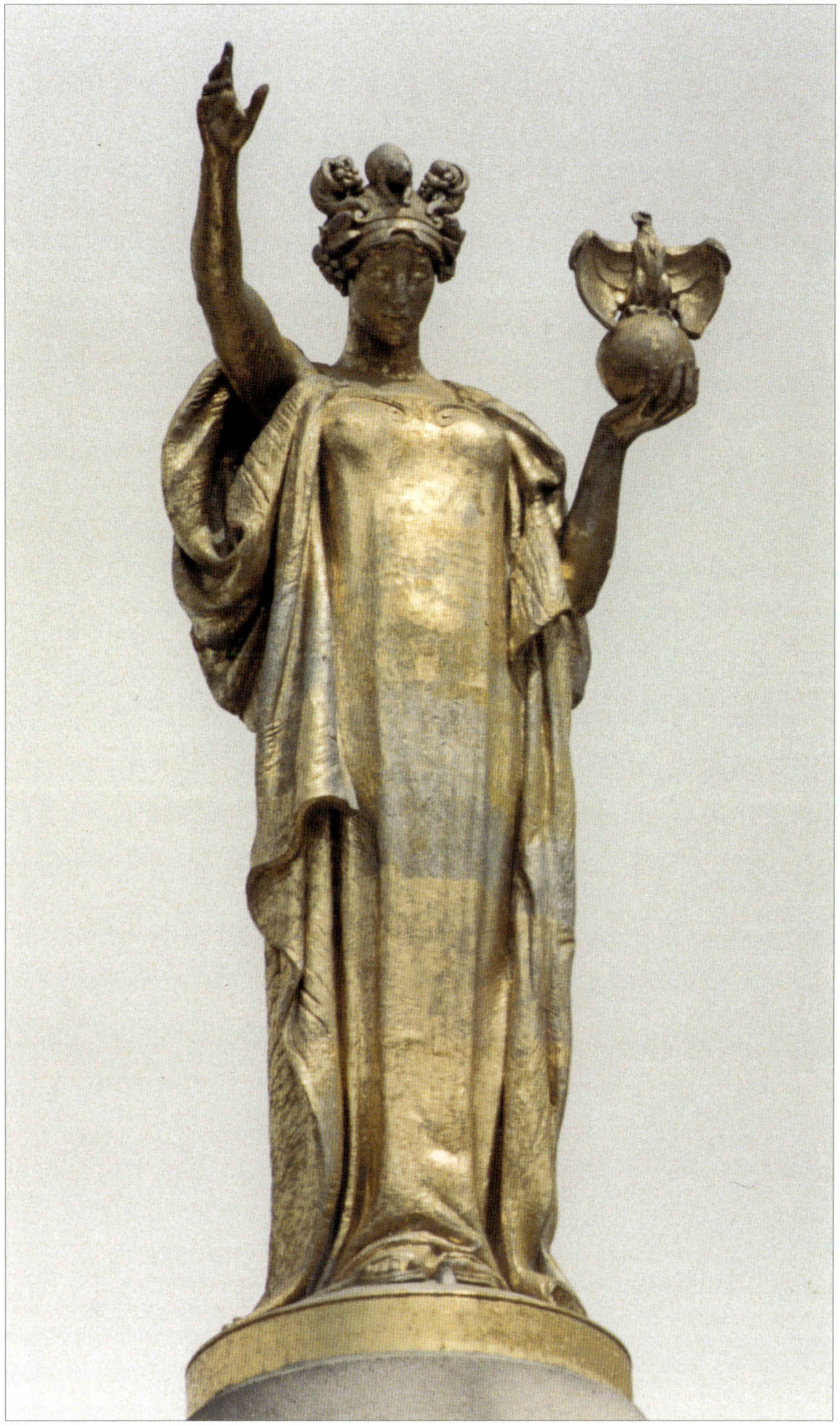

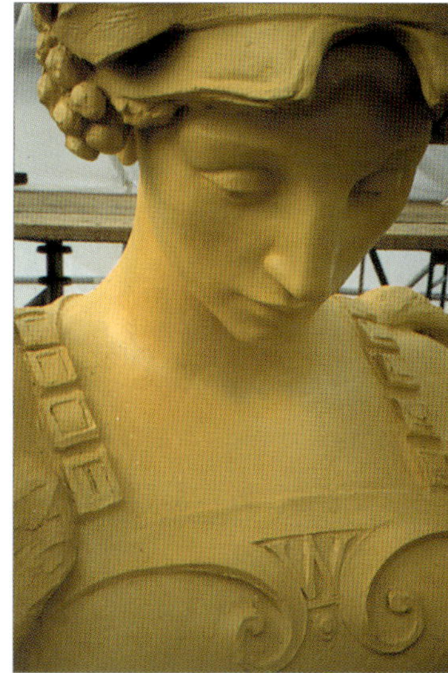

Wisconsin with underpaint primer in preparation for regilding in 1990

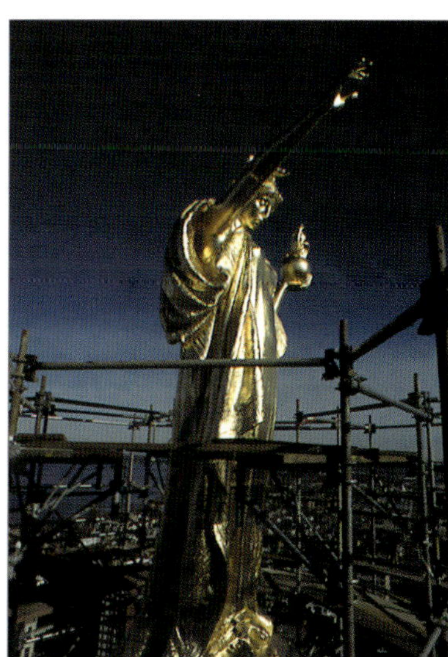

Wisconsin

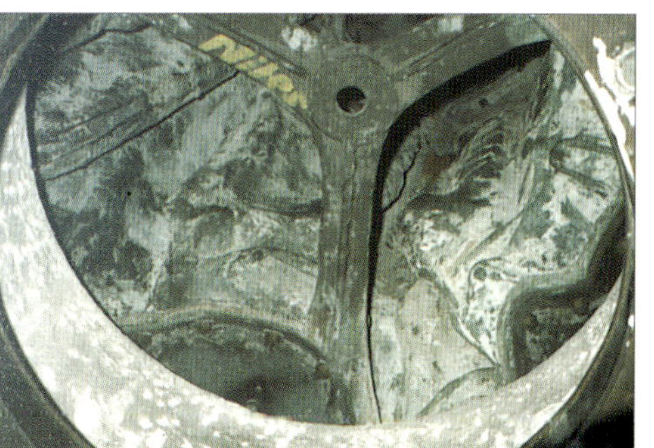

Interior view of *Wisconsin* statue before 1990 cleaning

Wisconsin statue in 1990 before regilding

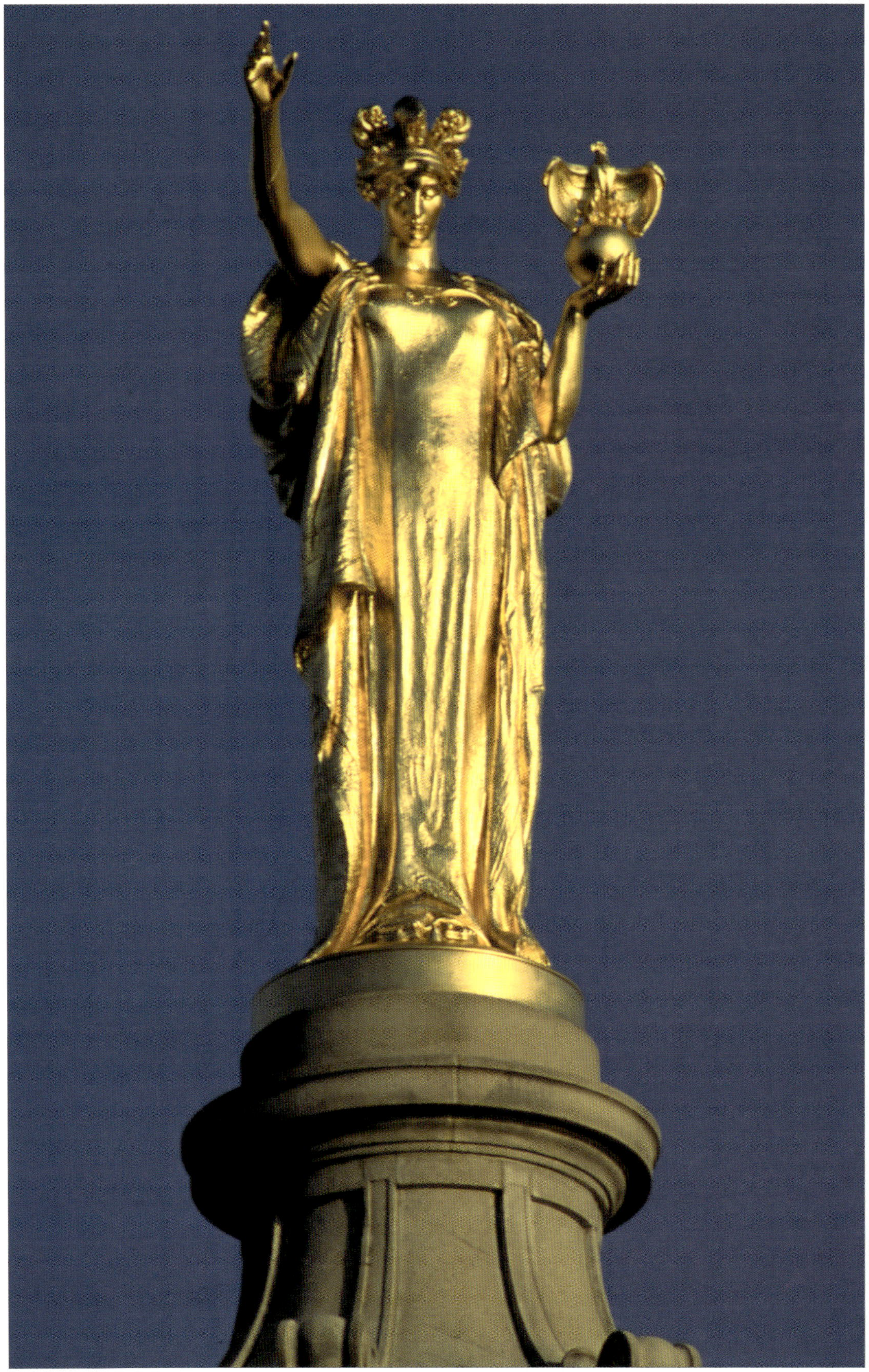

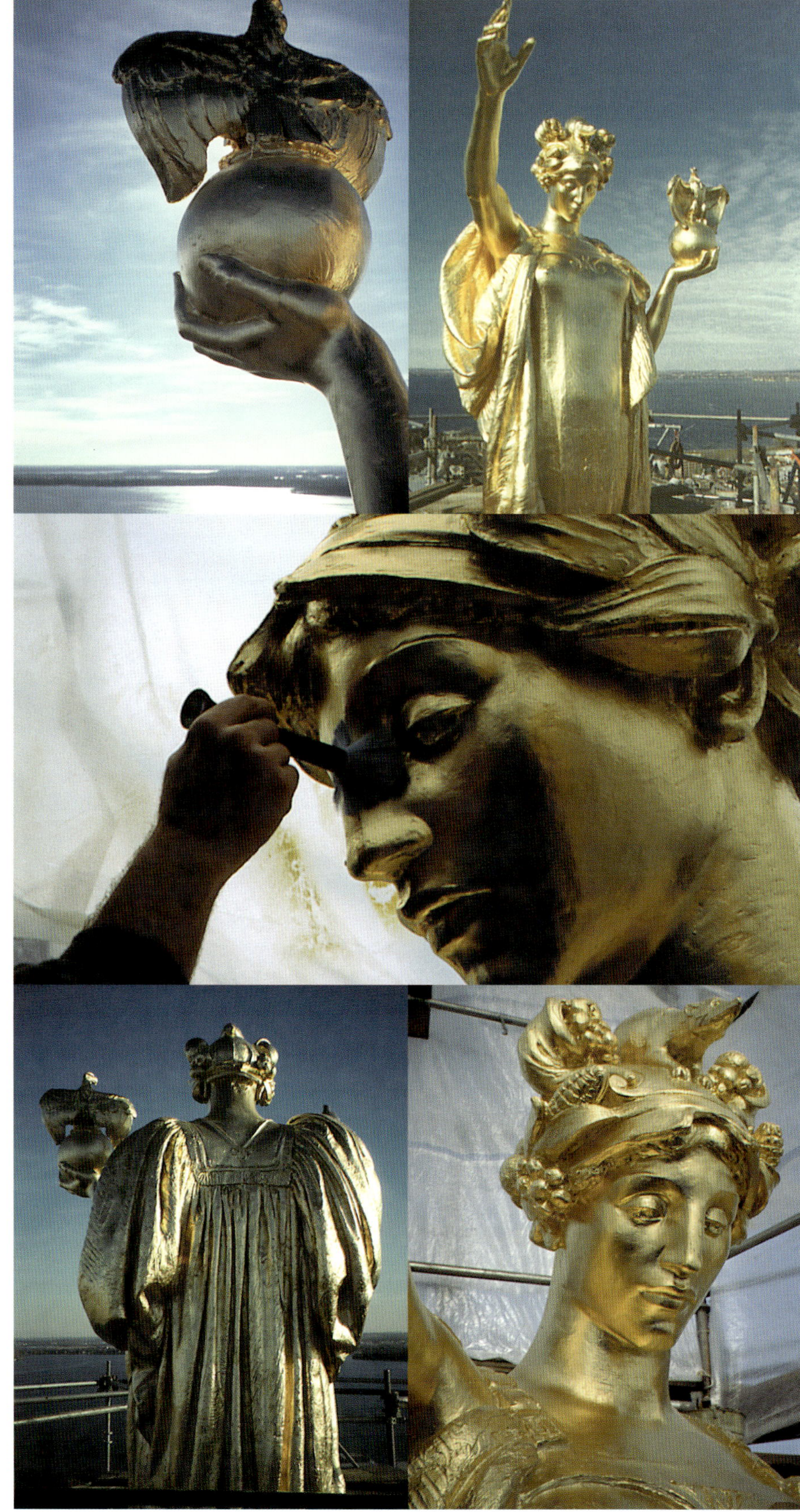

A Tribute to Wisconsin

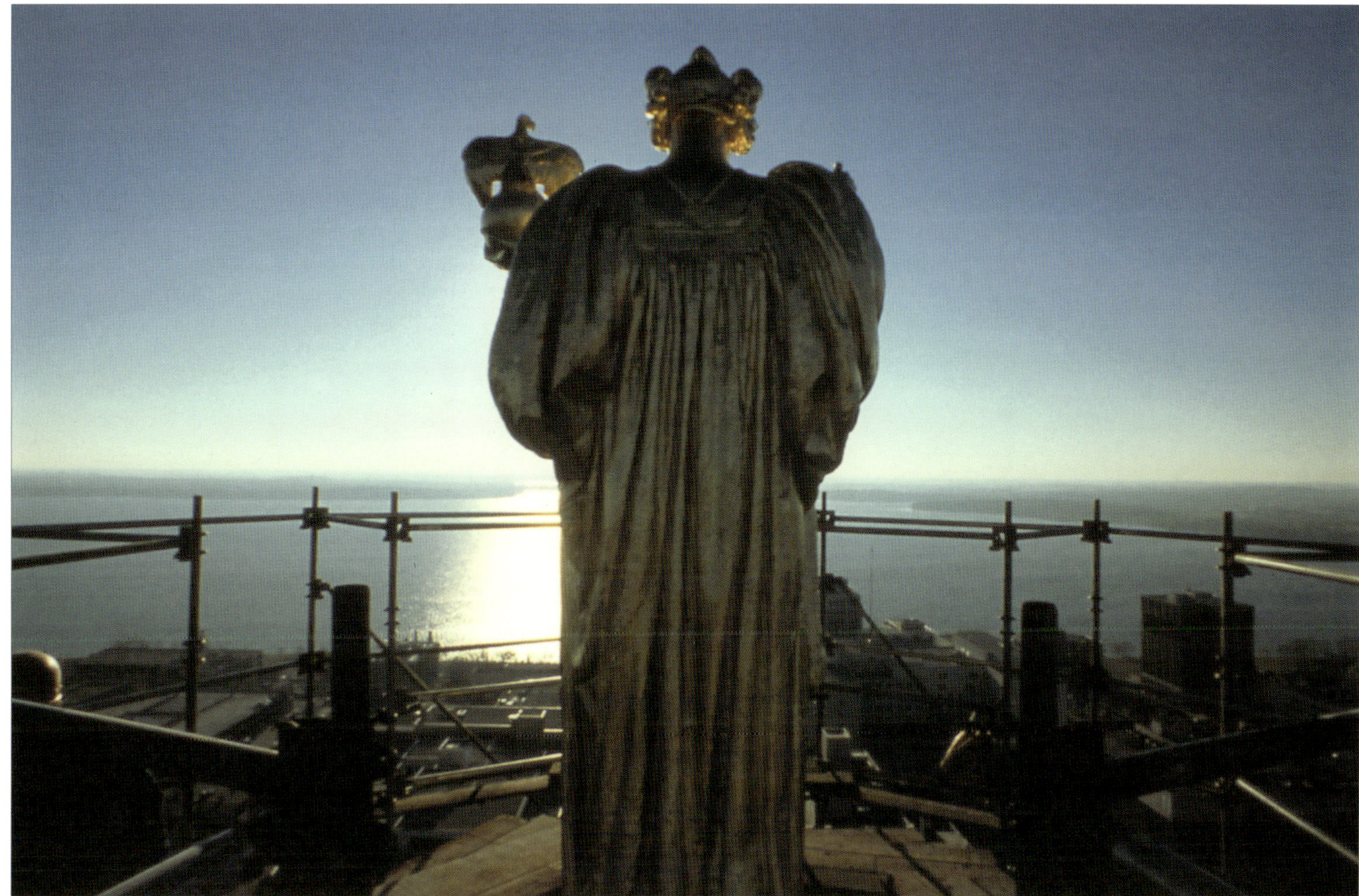

All photographs shown here are of *Wisconsin* after gilding in 1990. Above is *Wisconsin* facing the rising sun in the east over Lake Monona. *Wisconsin's* highest point reaches to a height of 284 feet above the ground, making her the highest statue in Wisconsin.

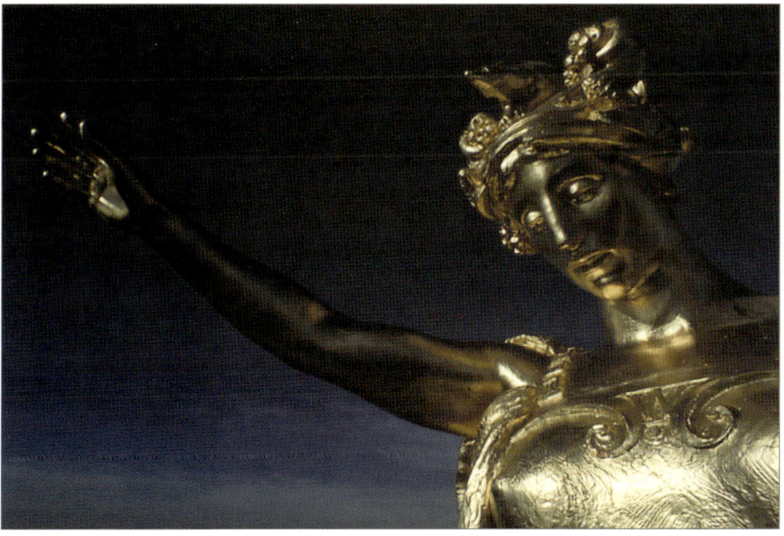

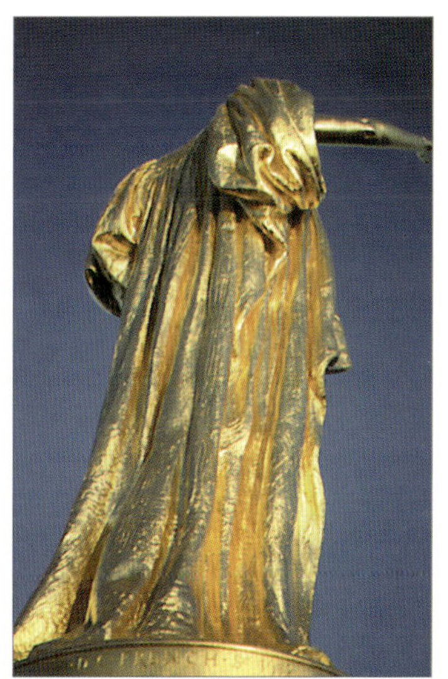

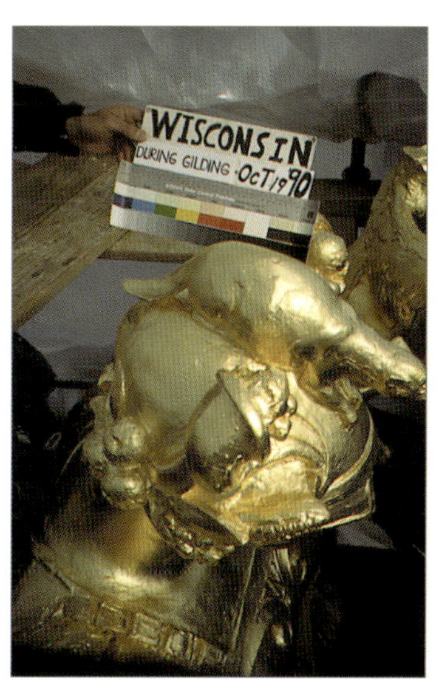

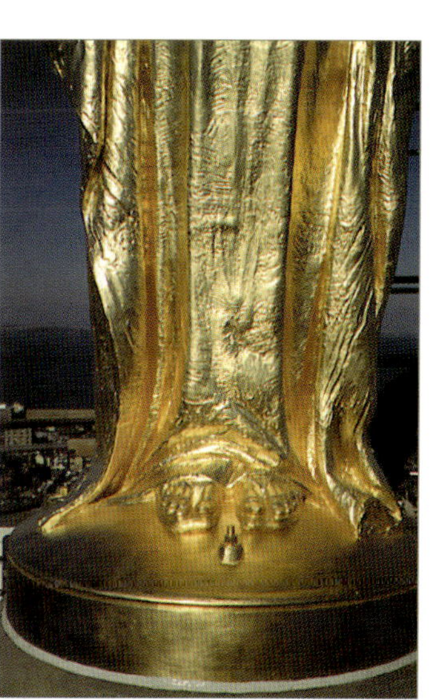

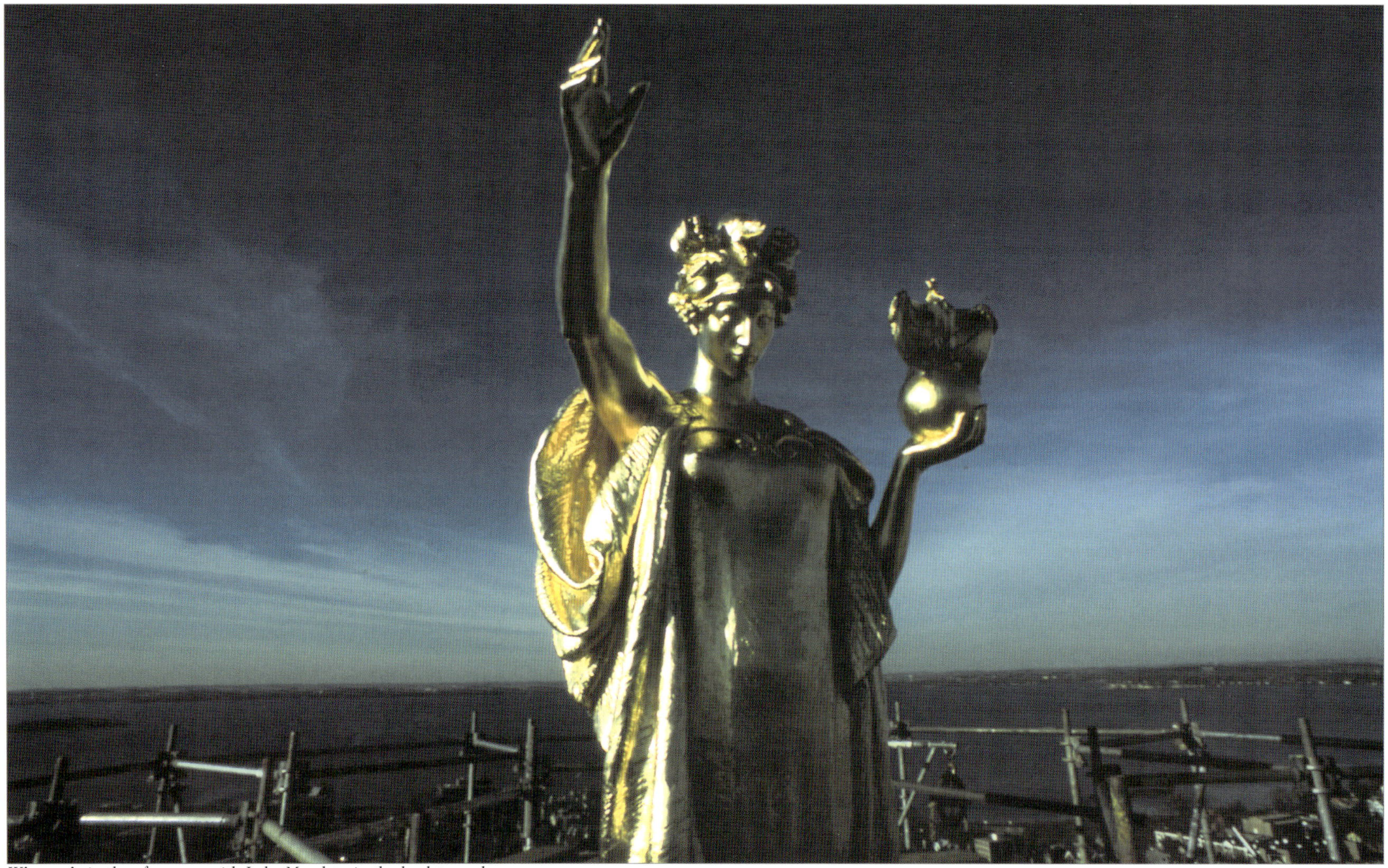

Wisconsin in the afternoon with Lake Mendota in the background.

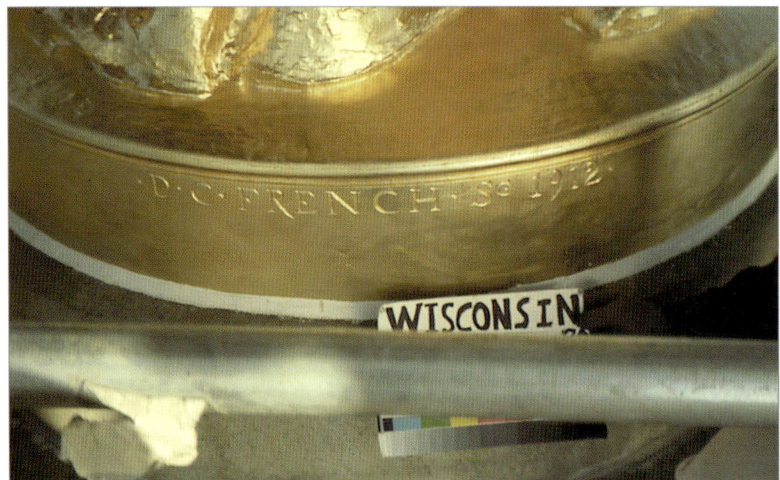

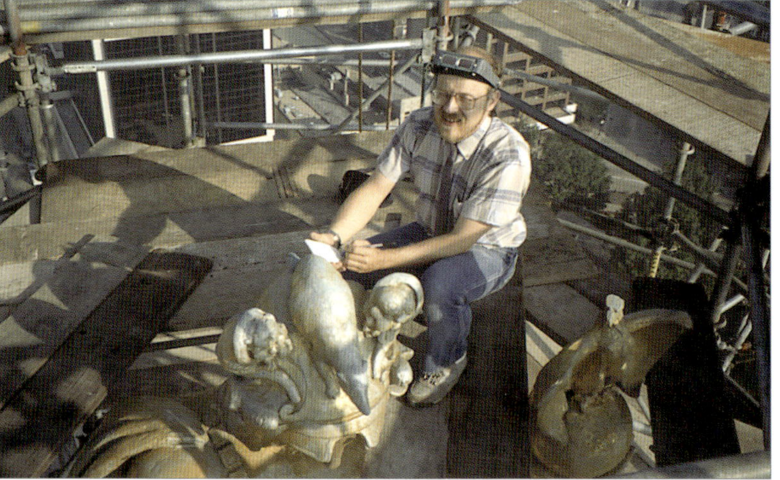

Tony Rajer examining *Wisconsin* in 1990

How To Select A Qualified Art Conservator

Caroline Keck, founding member of the AIC

☐ Education, training, and experience are the keys to making an informed decision about hiring a conservator.

☐ What is the conservator's previous experience in treating outdoor sculpture?

☐ Request a list of similar projects and treatments, with an explanation of the work performed.

☐ Bear in mind that a low bid may be in conflict with selecting the most qualified and best conservator for your project.

☐ Is the conservator affiliated with any professional organization such as AIC, and at what level? The IIC, International Institute of Conservation, is also an important international professional organization with varying membership levels. Remember that there are different levels of affiliation. For instance, AIC associate affiliation means the person pays dues to the AIC. Professional associate indicates the person meets national professional membership standards. A fellow is a senior expert in the field, and an honorary fellow is the highest and most respected level of expertise for this organization.

☐ Does the conservator abide by the AIC Code of Ethics? Is she or he familiar with the Code and Standards of Practice?

☐ Is the conservator insured? At what level and with what type of insurance?

☐ Does the conservator have employees, and what are their qualifications? Will there be subcontractors to the project such as welders, art historians, and metal experts?

☐ Who will supervise the work?

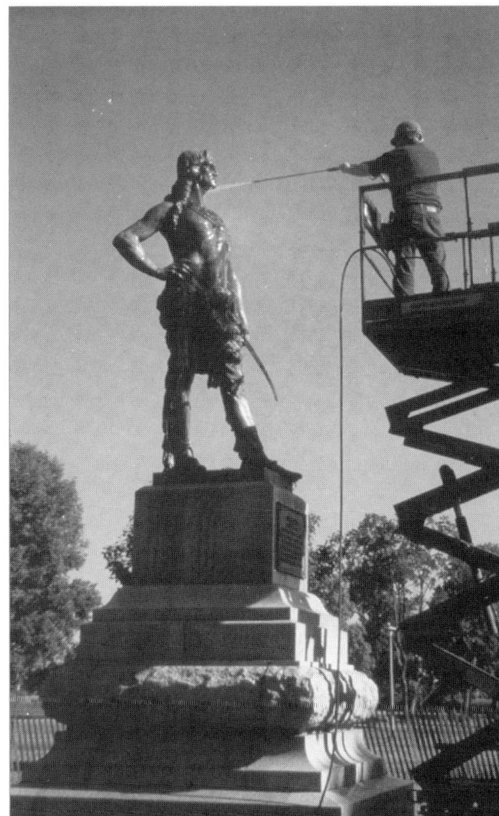

1993 high pressure water washing of *Chief Oshkosh*, created by Chevalier Gaetano Trentanove in 1911 and located in Menominee Park, Oshkosh, Winnebago County.

☐ Written and photographic documentation is critical and must be included in any project. It must include examination and treatment reports and other technical data as necessary. The treatment proposal should outline this, and you should ascertain up front where these records will be kept.

☐ What is the estimated project time frame?

☐ What will the client's involvement be in the project, in terms of permits, parking, safety, security, and insurance?

☐ Will there be a maintenance schedule for the work? Who will perform that maintenance and when?

☐ Is the artist still alive? How does he or she feel about the planned conservation?

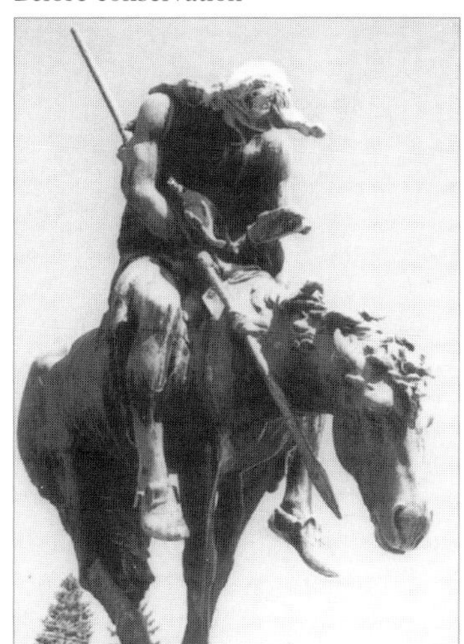

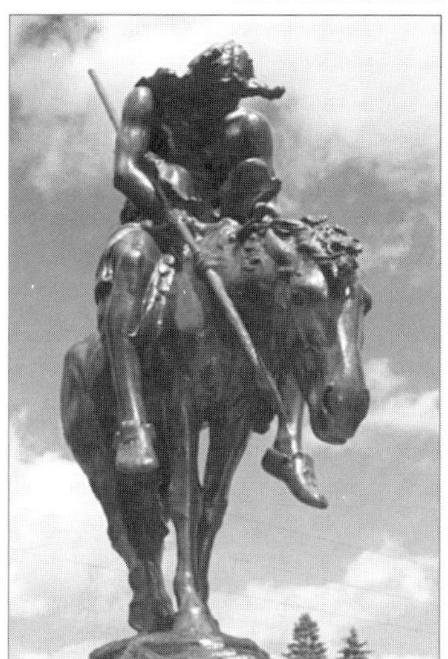

End of the Trail, cast in 1928 and installed in 1929, by James Earl Fraser. Located in Shaler Park, Waupun, Dodge County

What Does Conservation Cost?

Conservation projects are costly endeavors but, done properly, can ensure continued life of the work of art. Regular upkeep may prevent or stretch out the time before major restoration efforts and expenses are needed. Listed below are a few examples of project costs:

- Conservation of a small bronze statue, *With the Wind*, $5,000, Dallas, Texas, completed in 1992.

- Conservation of the *Fish Fountain*, $10,000, Dallas, Texas

- Conservation of a major Civil War statue and base, $50,000, Texas.

- Complete repatination of a major large bronze monument, $60,000, Chicago.

- Regilding of the *Wisconsin*, state capitol dome statue in Madison, $90,000 total ($10,000 in gold, $40,000 in conservation fees, and $40,000 in scaffolding), completed in 1990.

- Conservation of *Hans Christian Heg* bronze statue in Madison, $20,000 in 1989.

- Conservation of *General Kociuszko* statue in Washington, D.C., $28,000 in 1988.

- Conservation of a small bronze statue, single figure, $7,000, in Wisconsin in 1993.

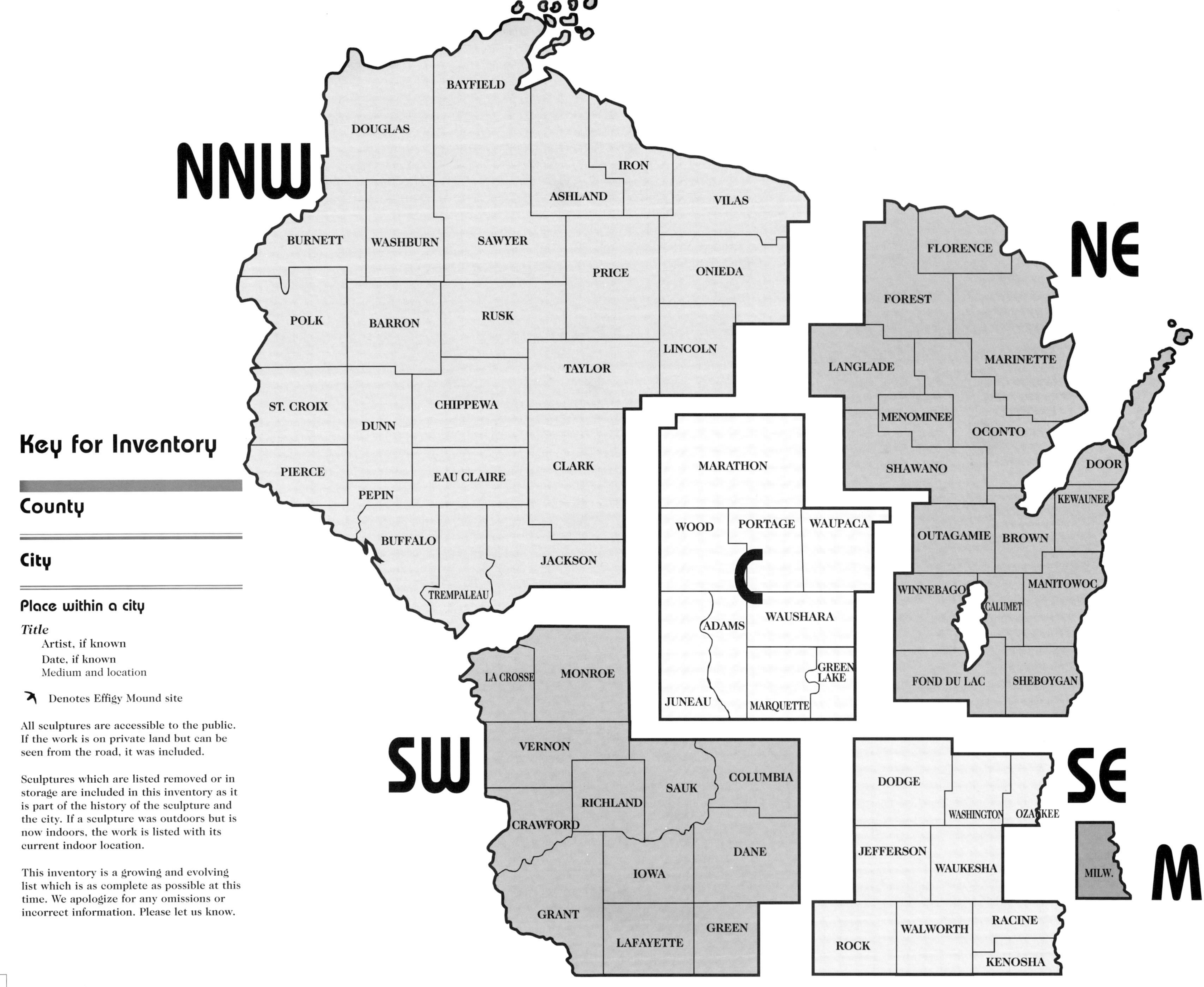

Key for Inventory

County

City

Place within a city

Title
> Artist, if known
> Date, if known
> Medium and location

↗ Denotes Effigy Mound site

All sculptures are accessible to the public. If the work is on private land but can be seen from the road, it was included.

Sculptures which are listed removed or in storage are included in this inventory as it is part of the history of the sculpture and the city. If a sculpture was outdoors but is now indoors, the work is listed with its current indoor location.

This inventory is a growing and evolving list which is as complete as possible at this time. We apologize for any omissions or incorrect information. Please let us know.

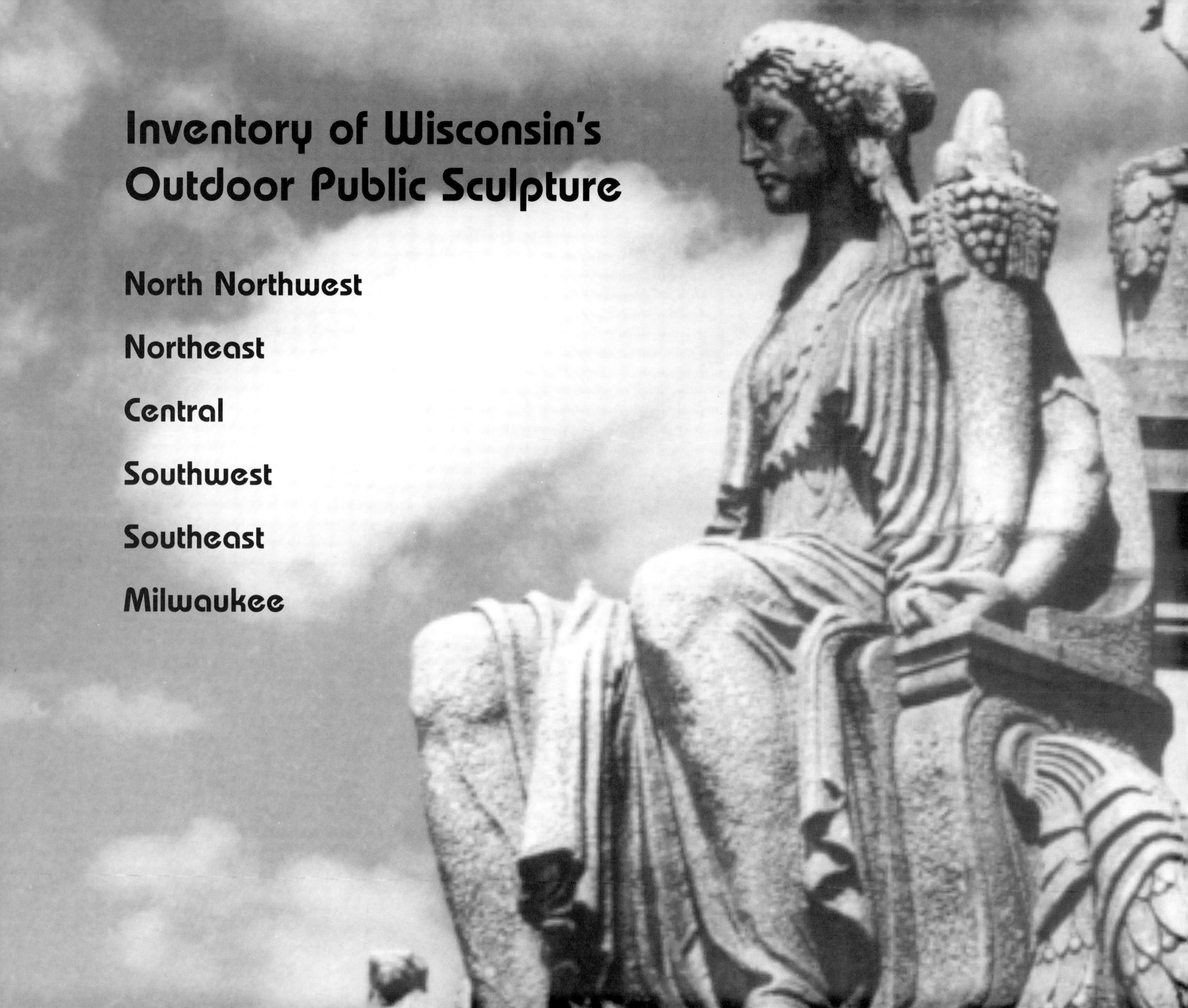
Inventory of Wisconsin's Outdoor Public Sculpture

North Northwest

Northeast

Central

Southwest

Southeast

Milwaukee

North Northwest Wisconsin Counties

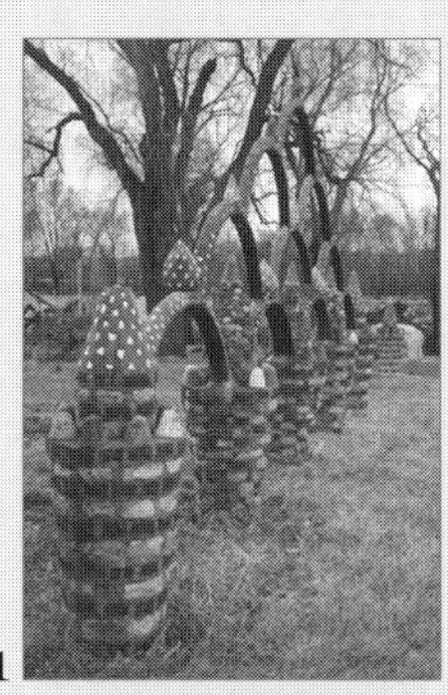

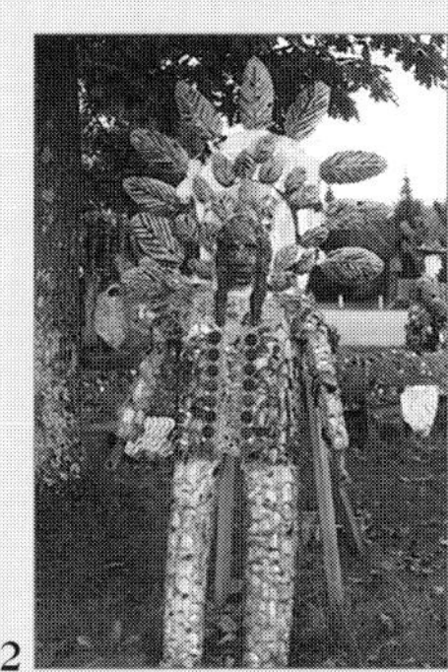

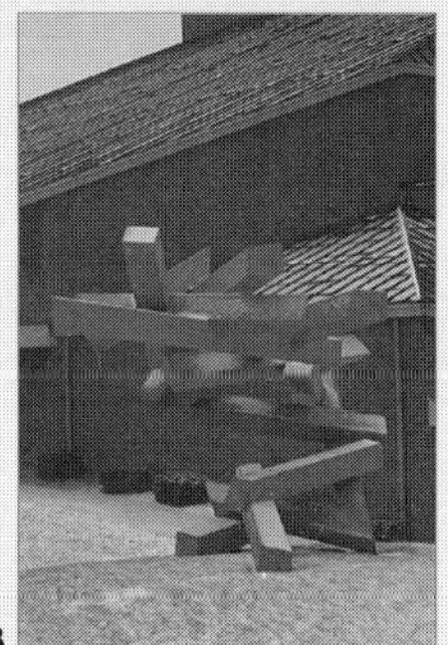

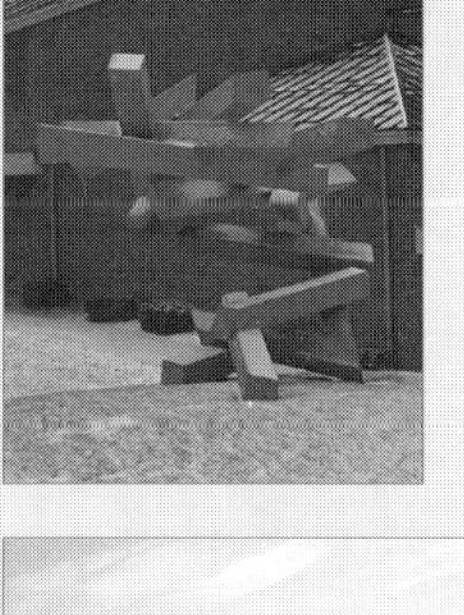

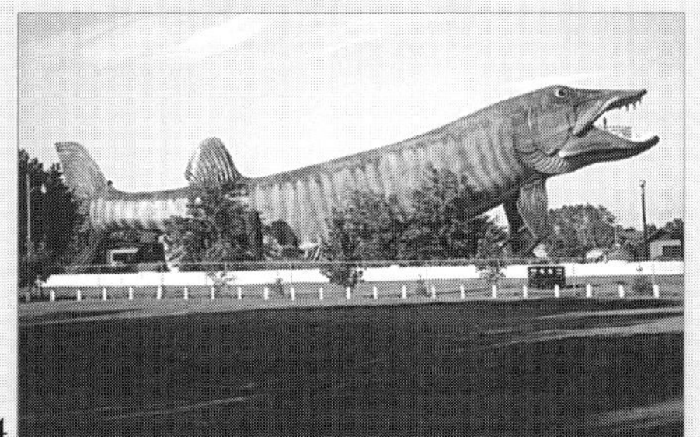

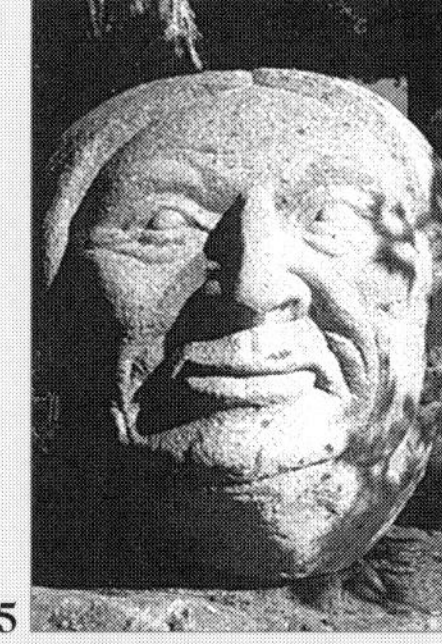

Ashland
Barron
Bayfield
Buffalo
Burnett
Chippewa
Clark
Douglas
Dunn
Eau Claire
Iron
Jackson
Lincoln
Oneida
Pepin
Pierce
Polk
Price
Rusk
Sawyer
St. Croix
Taylor
Trempealeau
Vilas
Washburn

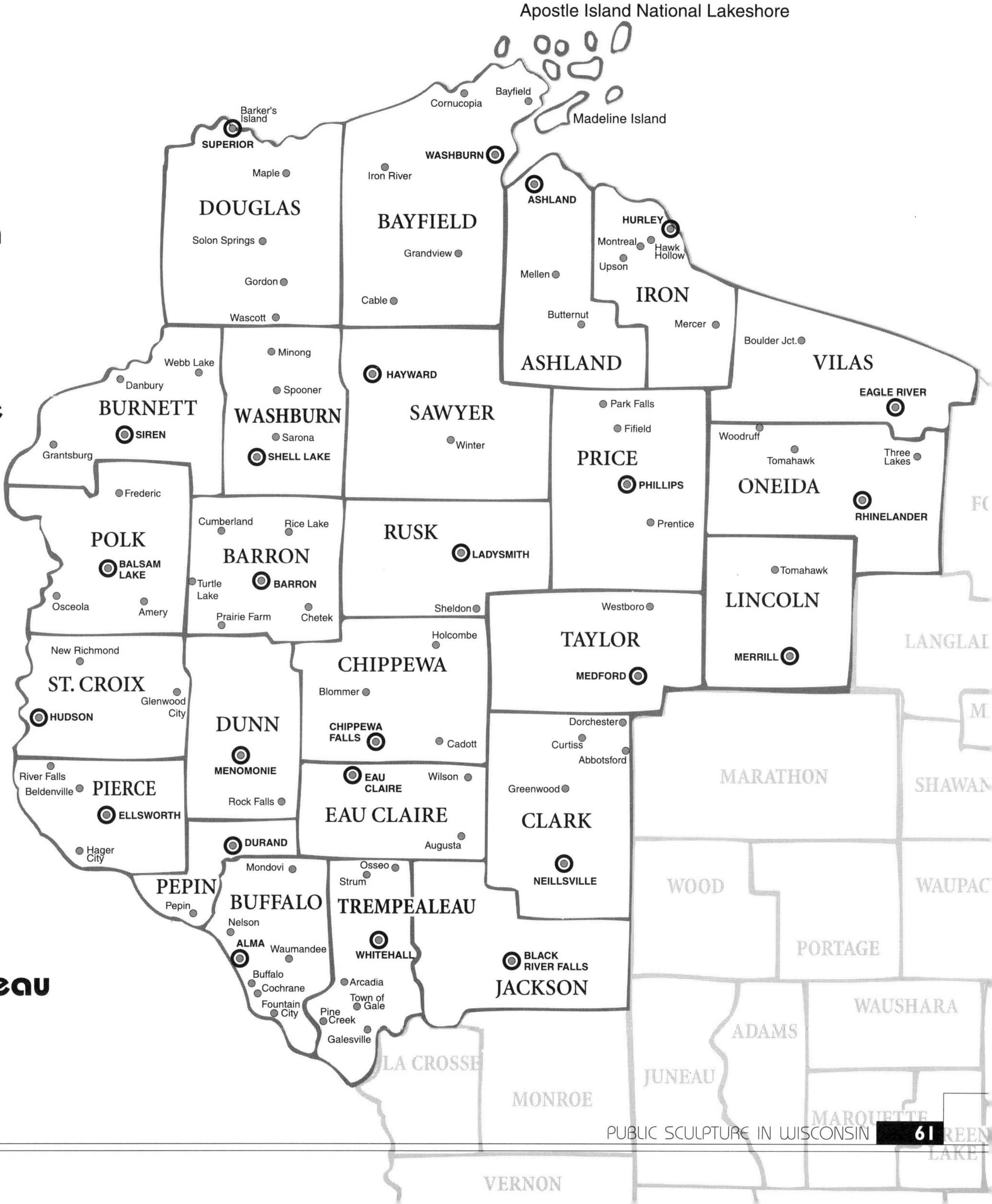

1   *Herman Rusch Site: Prairie Moon Museum and Sculpture Garden* in Cochrane, Buffalo County

2   *Native American* at Wisconsin Concrete Park, Phillips, Price County

3   *Woodland Spire* at UW-Stout, Menomonie, Dunn County

4   *The Shrine to Anglers* in Hayward, Sawyer County

5   *Indian Head, Sitting Bull* in Eagle River, Vilas County

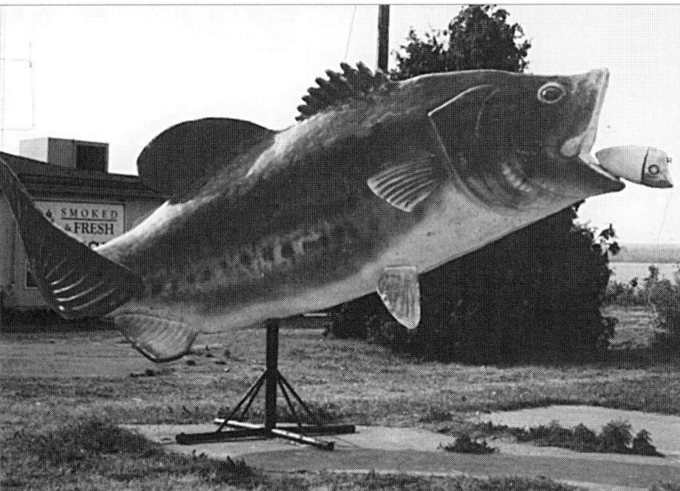

Big-ol-Fish in Ashland

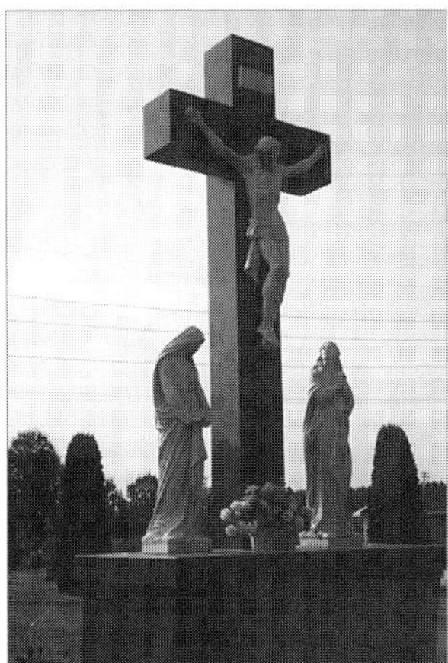

Crucifixion in Rice Lake

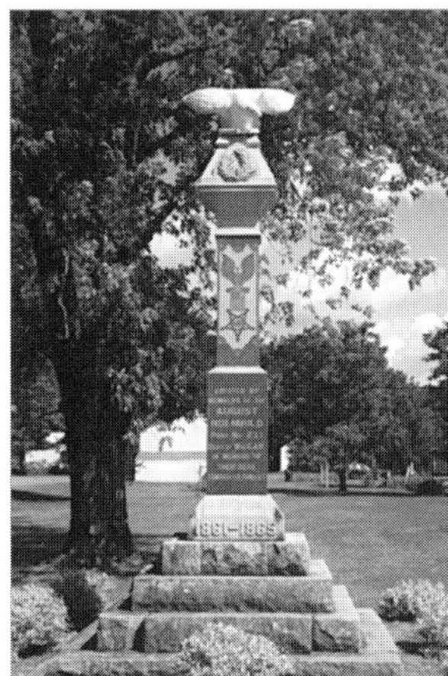

Veterans Memorial in Prairie Farm

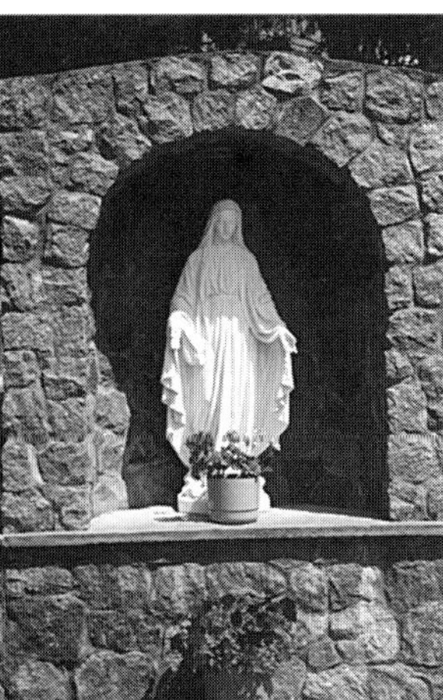

Virgin Mary in Butternut

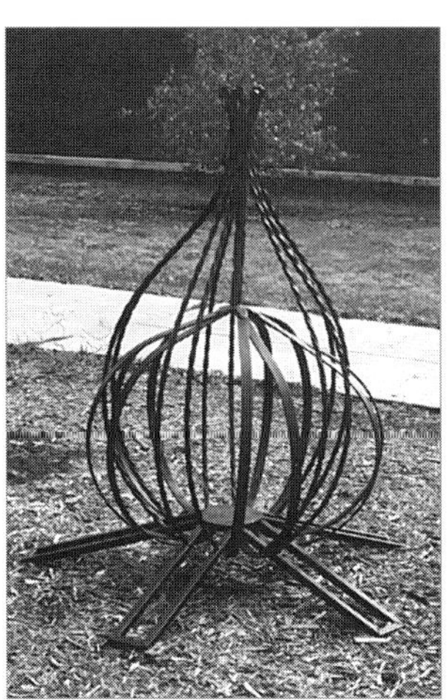

Abstract Onion at Northland College, Ashland

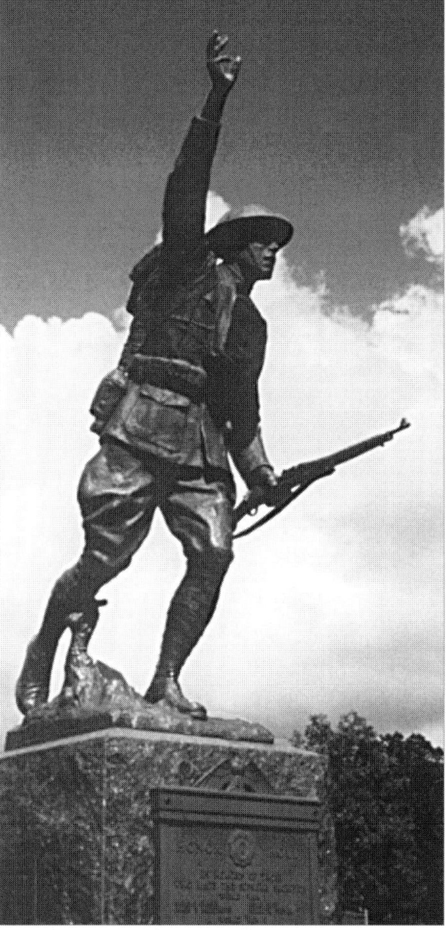

World War I Soldier in Mellen

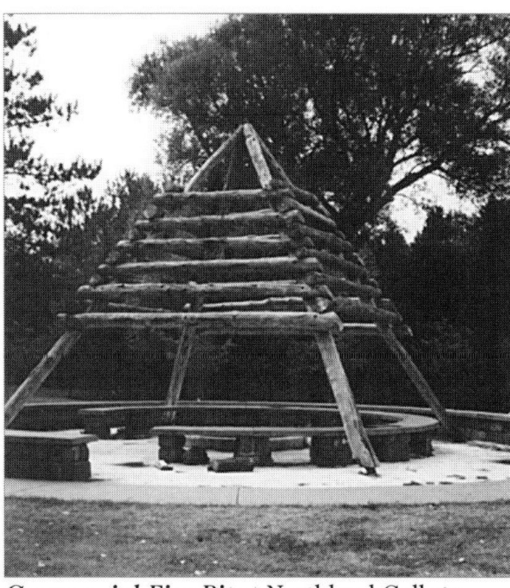

Ceremonial Fire Pit at Northland College, Ashland

North Northwest Counties

ASHLAND

Ashland

Big-ol-Fish
F.A.S.T.
Fiberglass, located on Highway 2

The Gulls
Brian Kerr
1990
Steel, located at Gene and Laura Halker Residence

Northland College

Abstract Onion
Metal, located at Wheeler Hall

Ceremonial Fire Pit
Wood, stone, concrete, located at Union

Untitled Abstract Human Form
Painted cement, located at Sports Center

Butternut

Virgin Mary
White Marble, located at Catholic Church

Mellen

World War I Soldier
Dedicated August 29, 1920
Bronze, located in Memorial Park, Fayette Street and S. Main Street

WWII Memorial
Dedicated May 27, 1945
Red Granite, located in Memorial City Park, Highway 13

BARRON

Barron

Veterans Memorial
Granite pillar with relief and eagle on top, located in Cemetery

Chetek

Veterans Memorial
Granite pillar, located in Lakeview Cemetery

Friendship Garden
Three artists from Miharu, Japan
1998
Japanese garden with traditional architectural sculptures, structures, and plantings. Carved stone, rock, wood, located on the UW-Barron County Campus, 1800 College Drive

Memorial Fountain
19th century
Painted cast iron, located at Rice Lake City Park

Prairie Farm

Veterans Memorial
Granite, located off County Highway F near Lutheran Church

Rice Lake

Crucifixion
Cast iron and granite, located at St. Joseph's Catholic Cemetery

Fountain
Painted cast iron, located in Park on Lake Street

BAYFIELD

Apostle Islands
LaPointe
Madeline Island
Islands under separate governance

Gull
Brian Kerr
1992
Steel, located on Nebraska Row

Tom Nelson Environment
Bar Tent
Steel, located on Main Street

Bayfield

Veterans Memorial
1889
Stone pillar, located in Memorial Park

Memorial to Commercial Fishermen
Harold and Brian Kerr
1980
Metal and wood, located on the Bayfield Waterfront, S3901 Highway 12

Lineage
Brian Kerr
1995
Wood, located at Trek and Trail Patio, Highway 13

Washburn

Lumberjack
Bear
Mushroom
Bill Vienneau
Wood, chain saw art, located on Highway 13

Art Colony with Outdoor Sculpture
Bill Vienneau
Wood, including chain saw art and a complex of artist studios, located on Highway 13

BUFFALO

Alma

Virgin Mary and Bernadette at Lourdes
Circa 1940
Concrete, located at Catholic Church, 203 S. 2nd Street

Buffalo

Viking
Sparta Advertising
Dedicated 1963
Fiberglass, located at Viking Motel, 675 North River Road

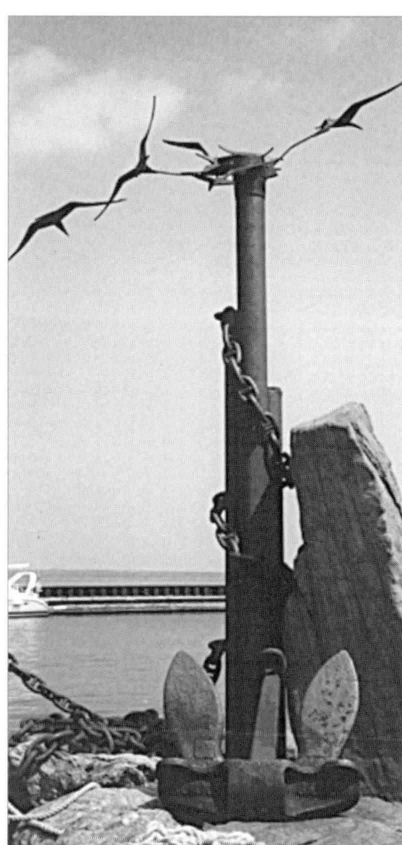
Memorial to Commercial Fishermen in Bayfield

Cochrane

Herman Rusch Site: Prairie Moon Museum and Sculpture Garden
Herman Rusch
1950s onward
Embellished painted concrete, located on Highway 35, over two dozen sculptures at this fascinating Folk Art site

Fountain City

Crucifixion
Virgin Mary
Dedicated 1926
Concrete, located at Immaculate Conception Catholic Church Cemetery on Jefferson Street

Fountain City Rock Garden
John Mehringer
1930s
Concrete, stone, and glass, located at Eagle Bluff, off Highway 95

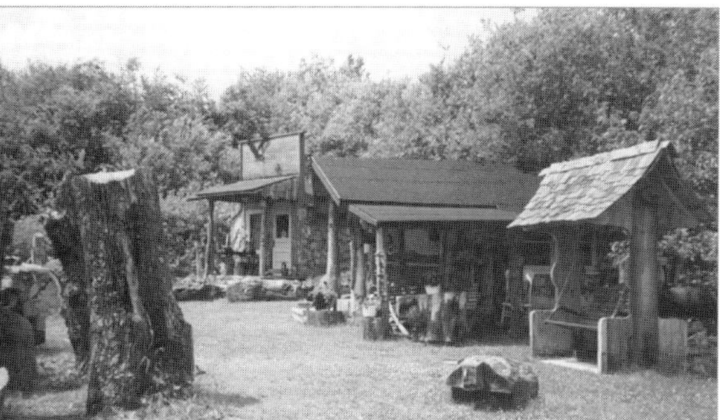
Art Colony with Outdoor Sculpture in Washburn

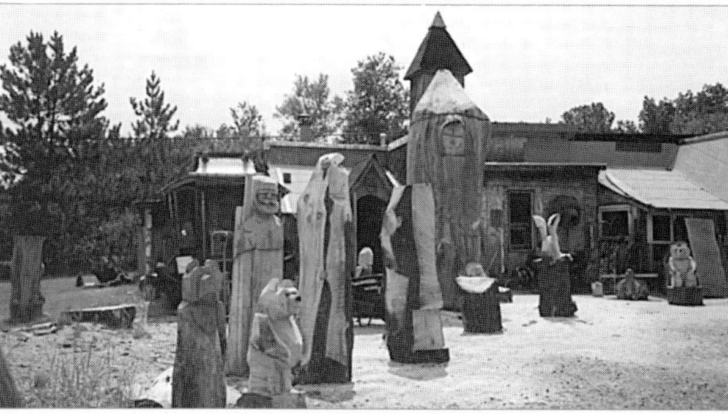
Art Colony with Outdoor Sculpture in Washburn

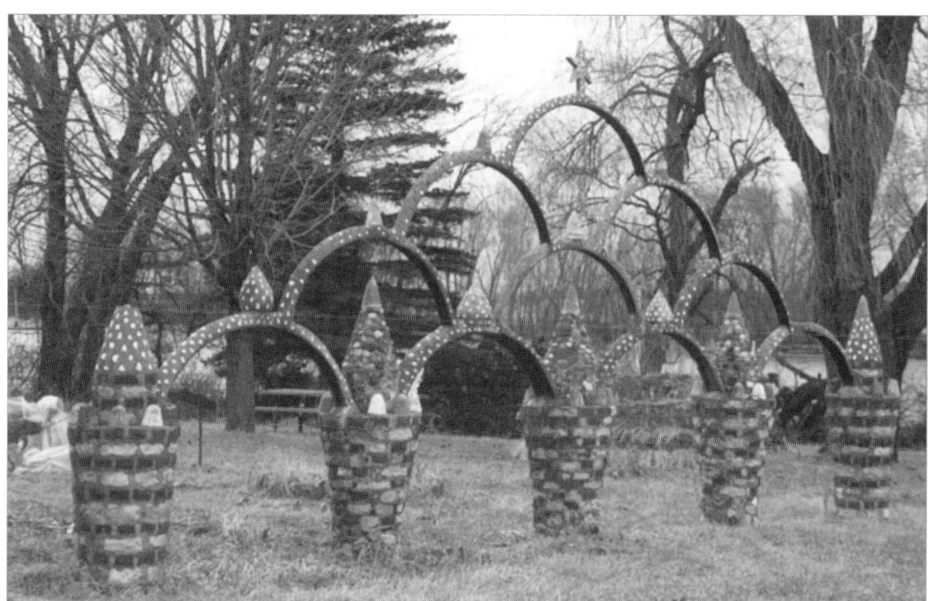
Herman Rusch Site: Prairie Moon Museum and Sculpture Garden in Cochrane

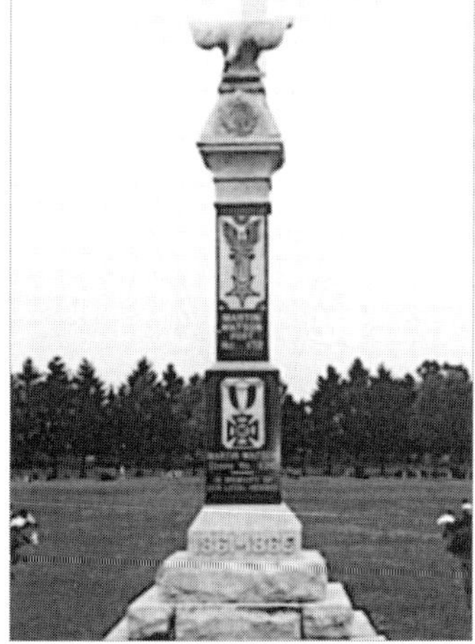
Veterans Memorial in Bayfield

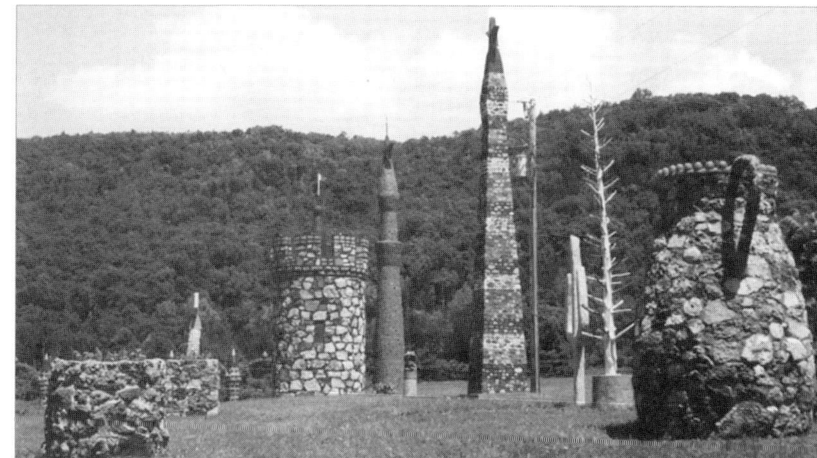
Herman Rusch Site: Prairie Moon Museum and Sculpture Garden in Cochrane

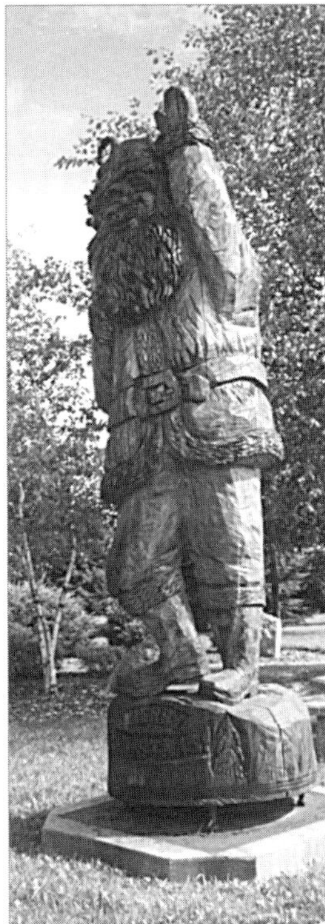

Santa Claus in Holcombe

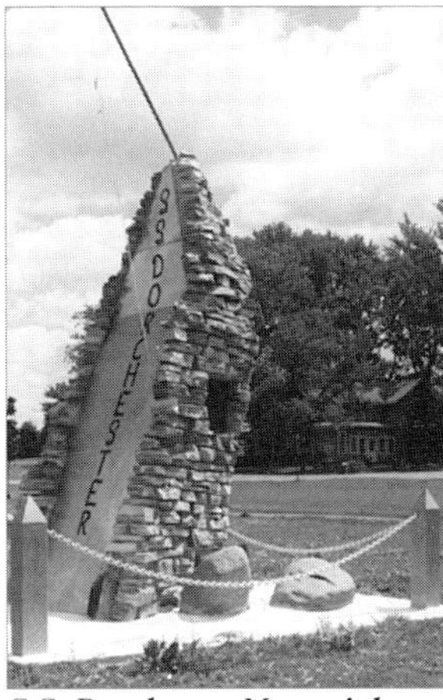

S.S. Dorchester Memorial
in Dorchester

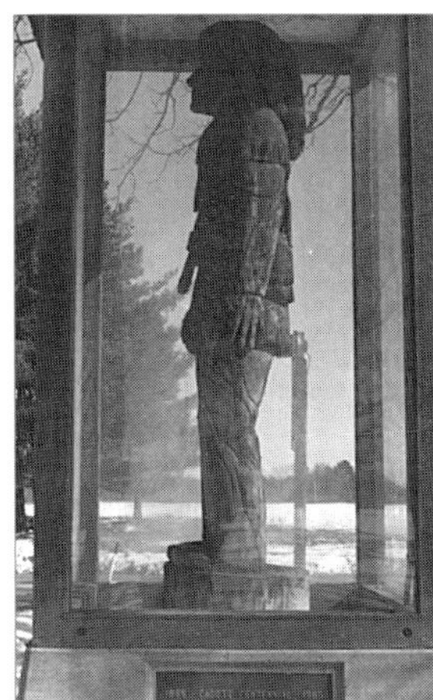

Cadotte Fur Traders in
Cadott

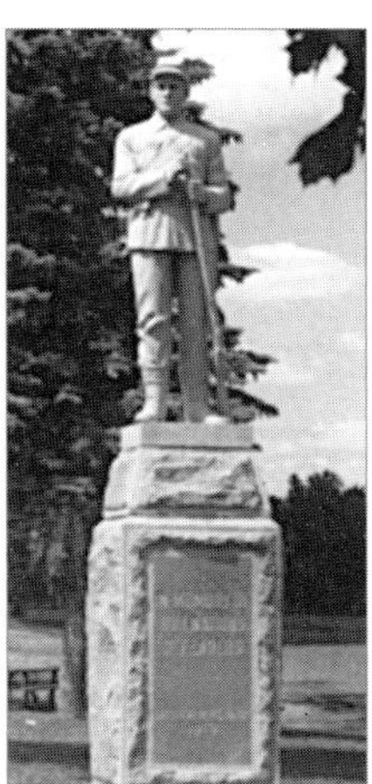

Veterans Monument
G.A.R. in Mondovi

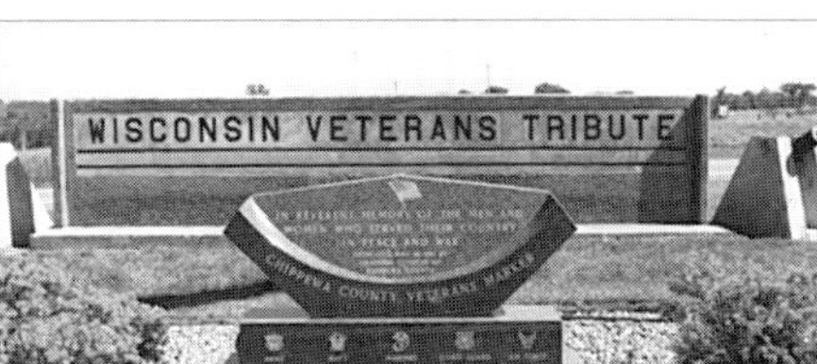

Chippewa County Veterans Memorial
in Chippewa Falls

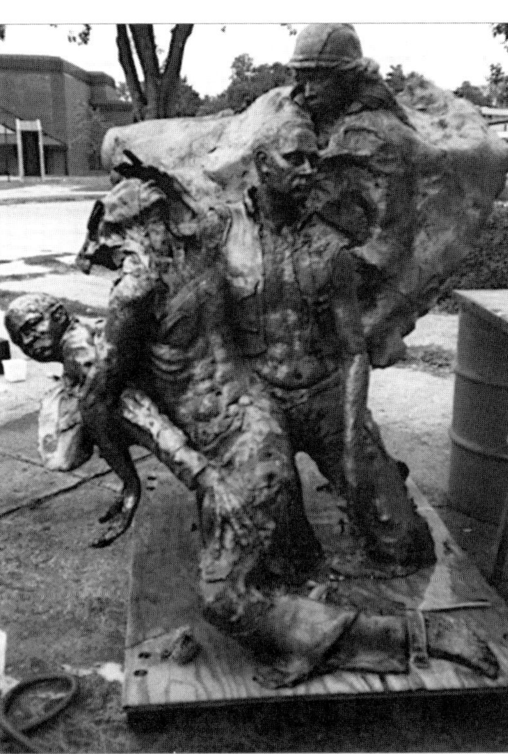

The Highground (pre-installation) in Neillsville

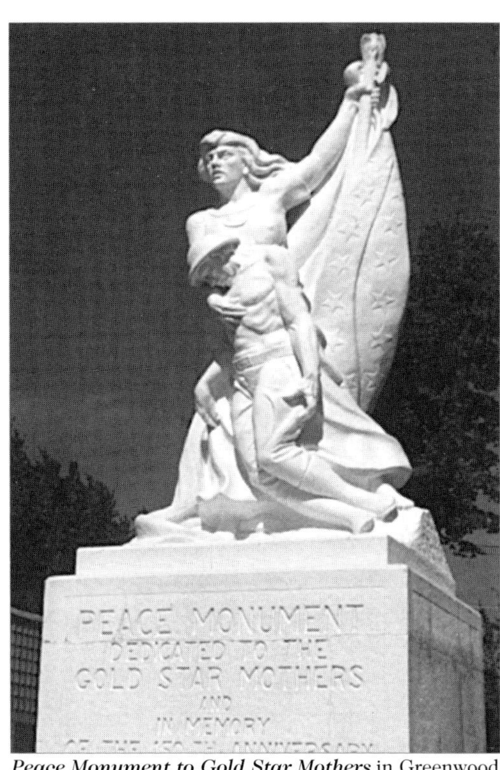

Peace Monument to Gold Star Mothers in Greenwood

Mondovi

Folk Art Environment, Park
R. Winters
Circa 1922, demolished

High School Buffalo
(F.A.S.T) Sparta Fiberglass Plant
Circa 1979
Fiberglass, located at Mondovi Public
High School, Jackson Street

The Sacred Heart
Circa 1935
Concrete, located at Sacred Heart
Catholic Church, W. Hudson Street

Veterans Monument, G.A.R.
Dedicated October 15, 1914
Granite, located in Mirror Lake Park

Nelson

The Readers
James Smit
1986
Basswood, chain saw art, located at
238 E. Cleveland

Folk Art Sculpture Garden
*Indian With Flag, Cowboy/Sheriff,
Indian on Horse, Indian Mother and
Child, Indian and Boy with Bow
and Arrow, Bugs Bunny, and Little
Red Riding Hood and Big Bad Wolf*
Richard Hanson
1986-1992
Concrete, located at S1059 Mill Road

Waumandee

Miniature Church House
Blessed Virgin in Niche
Louis Zeller
1930s
Stone, located at private residence on
County Highway U

BURNETT

Grantsburg

Big Gust
Alf Olson
Dedicated September 20, 1980
Wood, located at 416 S. Pine Street

CHIPPEWA

Cadott

Cadotte Fur Traders
Jerry Holter
Dedicated July 14, 1974
Wood chain saw art, located in Upper
Riverview Park, State Highway 27

Chippewa Falls

Chippewa County Veterans Memorial
Granite, located at intersection of
Highways 29 and 27

Our Lady of the Falls, Lourdes Grotto
Circa 1952
Mixed media, located at Notre Dame
Parish, 117 Allen Street

Holcombe

Santa Claus
Dave Clark
1988
Wood chain saw art, located on
Highway 27

CLARK

Abbotsford

Deer
Fred Smith
Concrete and glass, located on
Highway 13

Dorchester

S.S. Dorchester Memorial
Stone and concrete, located south of
Park Village

Greenwood

Peace Monument Memorial to Gold Star Mothers
Ernest Durig from Switzerland
Unveiling October 3, 1939
White sand and white cement, located
in Greenwood City Park, 102 North
Main Street

Neillsville

The Highground (Group of Wounded Soldiers)
Cast bronze, located at Wisconsin
Vietnam Veterans Memorial Park,
4 miles west of Neillsville

DOUGLAS

Barkers Island Superior

Seamen of the Great lakes Monument
William Bradford Frost and Debra
Anunti
1978
Cast bronze sailor facing north
towards Lake Superior on Barkers
Island

Maple

Indian Chief, Bears and Wolves
Justin Howland
Wood, chain saw art, located at
1147 E. Highway 2

Solon Springs

Pope Pius IX
Carved White marble, located at
Catholic Church

Silhouette Statue
Tony D. Jelich
1996
Steel plate, 16 feet high, located at
Overlook Wayside, across from the
airport and overlooking Great Street,
Croix Lake and river

Superior

Abstract
Welded steel, located at Superior
Public Library

All Wars Veterans Memorial
Granite and concrete, located at intersection of Highway 53 and Highway 2

Chain Saw Art display
Dean Nelson
Wood, chain saw art, located
on Highway 53

Crucifixion
Painted metal, located at Superior
Cemetery, 35 S. 10th

Daphne, The Cup Bearer
Late 19th Century
Cast metal, located at Fairlawn
Mansion and Museum on corner of
9th Avenue East and Harbor View
Parkway

Folding Fountain
Welded steel, located at the Superior
Public Library

James J. Hill Portrait
Bronze, located at Douglas High
School

Soldier's Circle, G.A.R.
Granite, located at 8402 Tower
Avenue

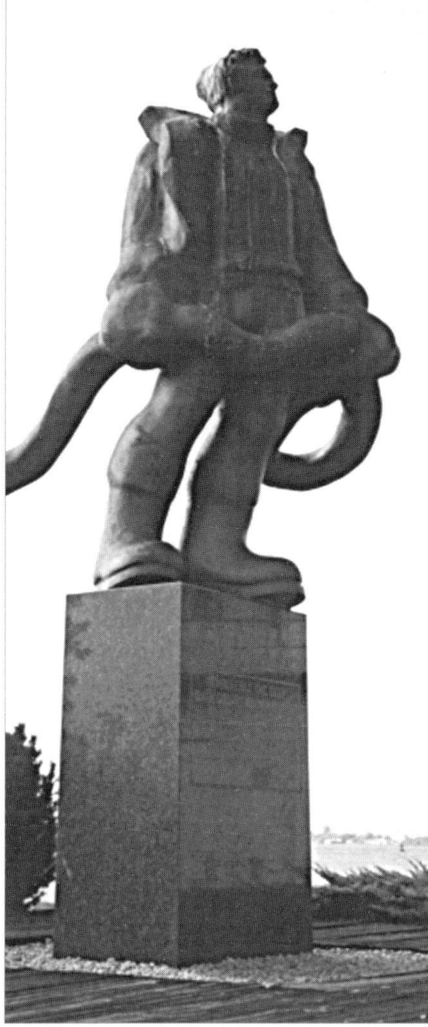

Seamen of the Great Lakes Monument on
Barkers Island

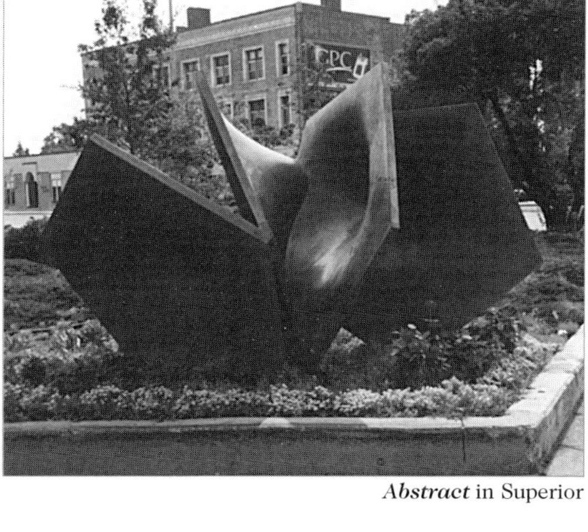

Abstract in Superior

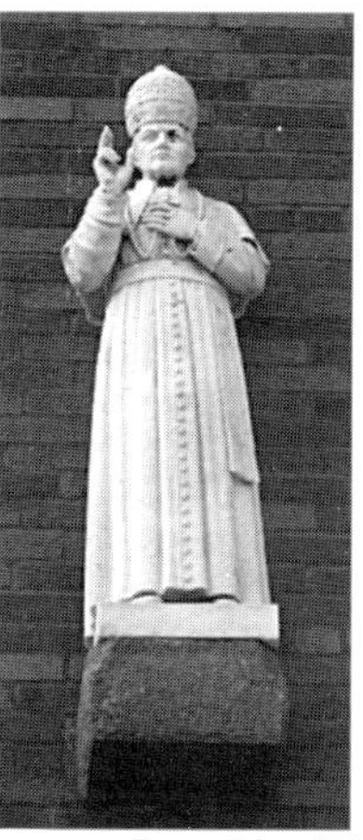

Pope Pius IV
in Solon Springs

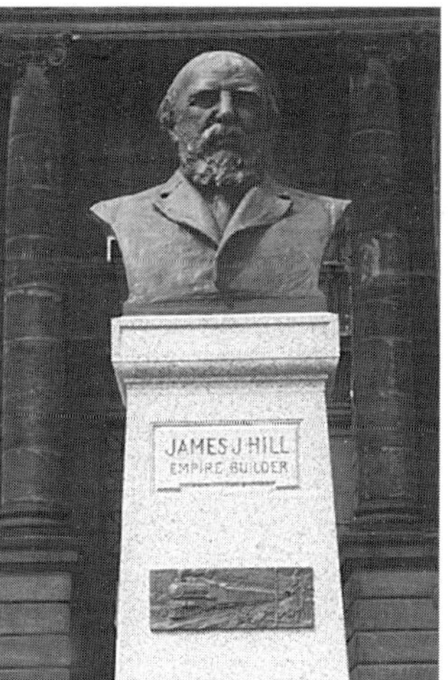

James J. Hill Portrait in Superior

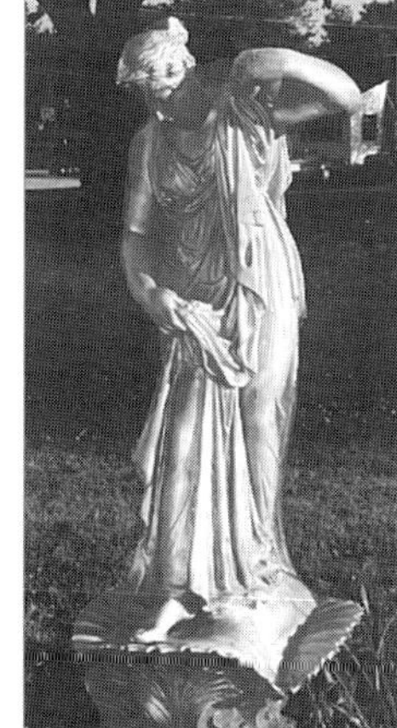

*Daphne, The Cup
Bearer* in Superior

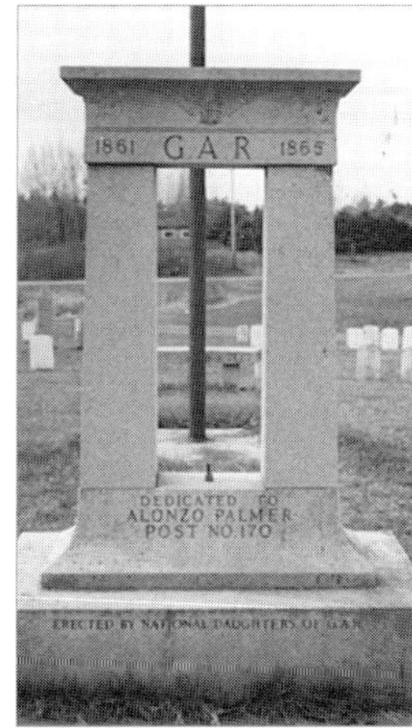

Soldiers' Circle in Superior

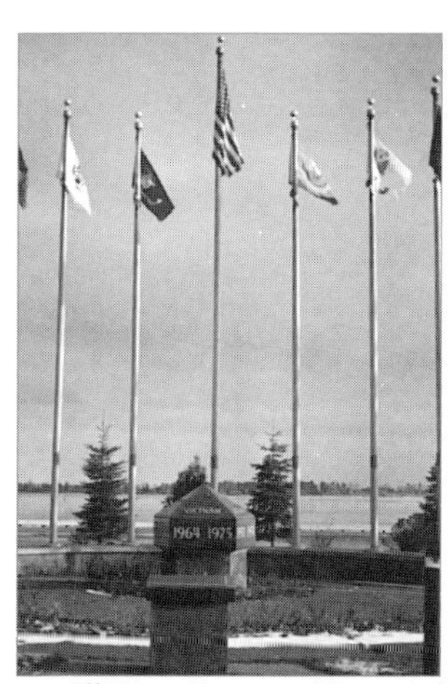

All Wars Veterans Memorial
in Superior

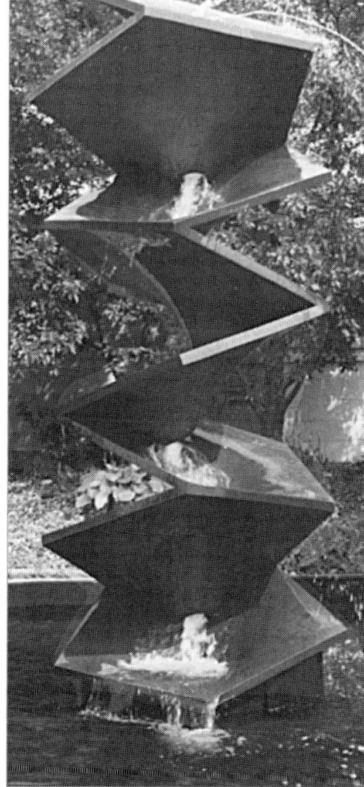

Folding Fountain in Superior

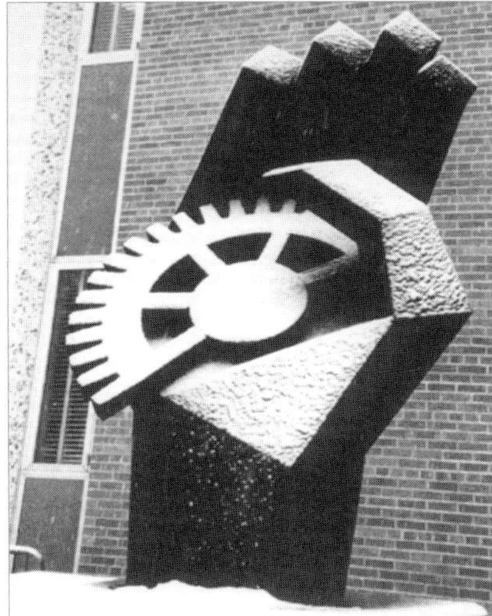

The Search for Knowledge in Eau Claire

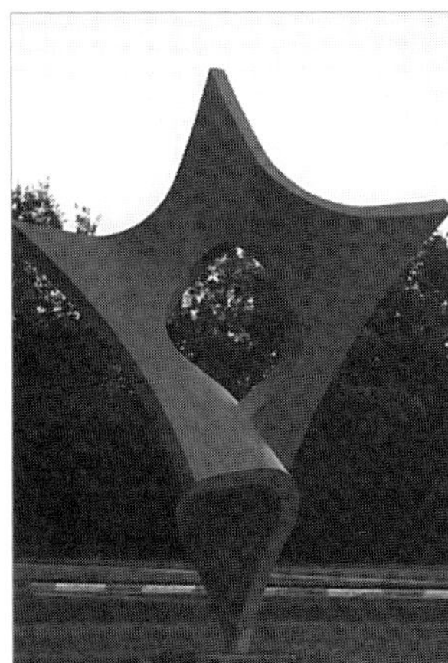

Orange Fold at UW-Eau Claire

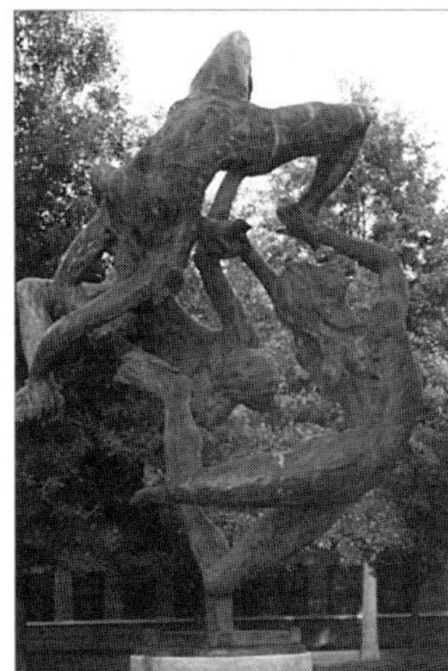

Sprites at UW-Eau Claire

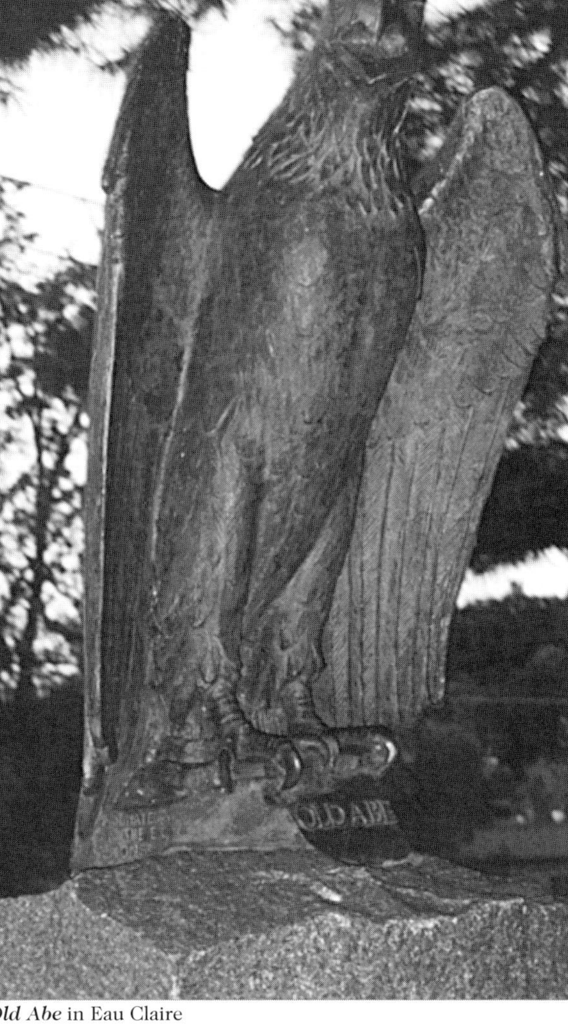

Old Abe in Eau Claire

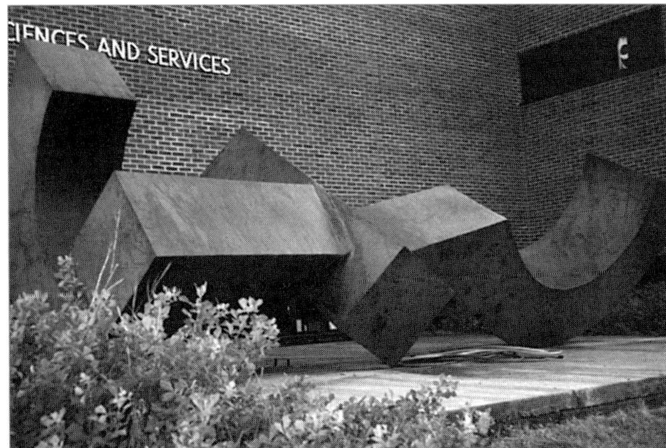

Blue Cubes at UW-Eau Claire

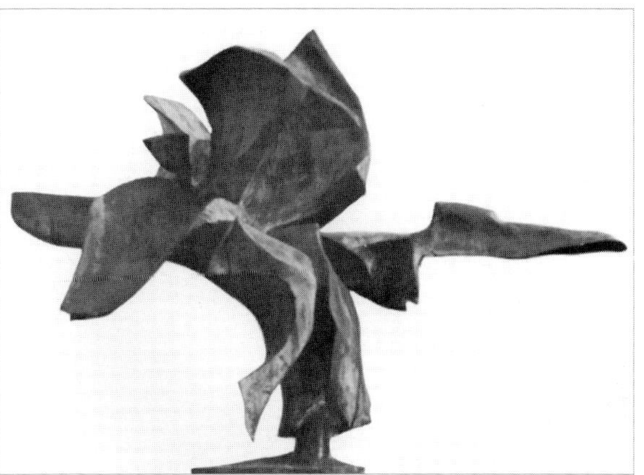

Encounter at UW-Eau Claire

DUNN

Menomonie

Folk Art Environment
Frank Oebser
Circa 1970-1990
Mixed Media, currently in storage with the Historical Society in Menomonie

UW-Stout

Borderline
Gateway
Portal
Sentinel
Robert Curtis
1987
Granite, located on grounds near Memorial Student Center, 10th Avenue and 3rd Street

F-Stop
Carl Reed
1987
Steel and redwood, located at northwest corner of Graphics and Photography Laboratory

Untitled
Scott Wallace
1989
Painted steel, located on the west outside wall of the Physical Education Building

Woodland Spire
Robert Gehrke
1996
Weathering steel, located in front of Jarvis Hall of Applied Arts. Percent for Art commission

WYSIWYG
Anne Allardyce
1998
Stainless steel, located on southern wall of Fryklund Hall, 3rd Street

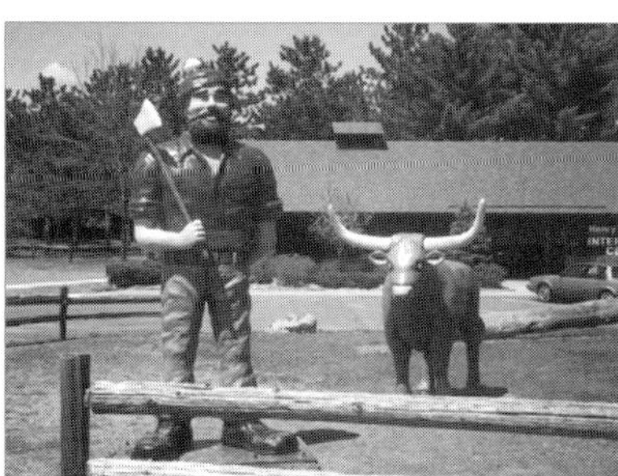

Paul Bunyan and Babe in Eau Claire

EAU CLAIRE

Eau Claire

Hank Aaron Tribute
Kenneth E. Campbell
Dedicated August 17, 1994
Bronze, located in Carson Park

Old Abe
Cast bronze, located in City Park

Paul Bunyan and Babe
Circa 1982
Fiberglass, located in front of the Interpretive Center at The Paul Bunyan Logging Camp, 1110 Carson Park Drive

The Search For Knowledge
Brian Kerr
1978
Steel, located at Chippewa Valley Technical Institute

UW-Eau Claire

Blue Cubes
Painted steel, located at upper campus, Sciences and Services building

Encounter
O.V. Shaffer
1973
Forged and welded brass, located on Art Center grounds

Orange Fold
Painted steel, located at upper campus, behind the Fine Arts building

Sprites
Cast bronze, located at lower campus Commons area

IRON

Hurley

Cowboy
Jeff Prust
Wood, chain saw art, located at Branding Iron Restaurant

Willie Nelson
Jeff Prust
Wood, chain saw art, located at Hawk Hollow, on Highway 77

Mercer

Giant Loon
Creative Displays, F.A.S.T.
1981
Painted fiberglass, 16 feet tall, located in mini-park south of town on Highway 51

Montreal

Veterans Monument
Mixed media, located at 53 Wisconsin Avenue

Morzenti Memorial
Larry De Groot
1958
Ceramic and brick, located at Morzenti Memorial Park

JACKSON

Black River Falls

Orange Moose
Jerry Vetterus, F.A.S.T.
Circa 1985
Fiberglass, located at Best Western Motel, Black River Crossing Oasis on Interstate 90/94

LINCOLN

Merrill

Blue Jay
Jeff Prust
Wood, chain saw art, located at Merrill High School

Cenotaph, WWI Memorial
H. J. Mitbauer and the Merrill Marble and Granite Works
Dedication August 18, 1923
White marble, located at the intersection of Grand Avenue and Prospect Street

Lincoln County Centennial Totem Pole
Marshal 'Red' Hayden
1974
Wood, 20 feet tall, located on the southeast corner of the Lincoln County Court House, 1104 East Main Street

Pere Rene Menard Monument
Merrill Marble and Granite Works
1923
Red granite, located at the top of Nine Mile Hill in the wayside on State Highway 107, nine miles northwest of Merrill

River Rafter
Jeff Prust
1997
Wood, chainsaw art, nine feet tall, located in Stanges Park near the Prairie River

Veterans of Foreign Wars Monument
1998
Red granite, located on the northeast corner of the Lincoln County Courthouse

Tomahawk

Folk Art Environment
Dave Siedler
1990s
Painted wood and concrete, located on Deer Trail Road, near Highway 51. Various wonderful artistic creations including Aliens and UFOs

ONEIDA

Woodruff

Basketball Player
James Barber
Painted wood, chain saw art, located at Packerland Store, 535 Flambeau Street

Girl with Doves
Dave Wynne
1969, installed 1971
Bronze, located on grounds of Howard Young Medical Center

PEPIN

Durand

Civil War Soldier
Dedicated 1926-1930
Granite, located at the Old Courthouse Museum, Washington Square, on 3rd Avenue between Madison and Wells streets

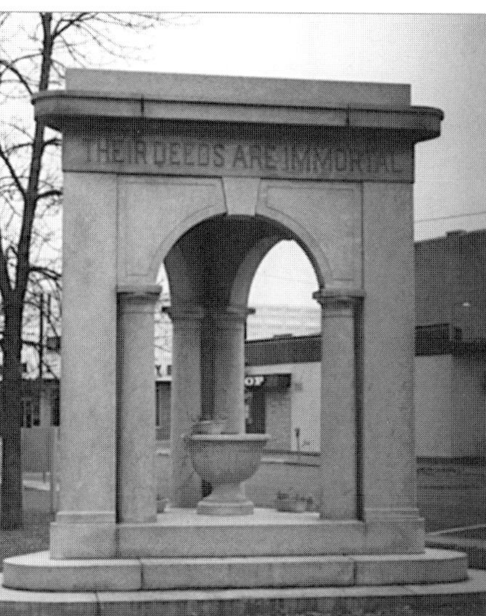

Cenotaph, WWI Memorial in Merrill

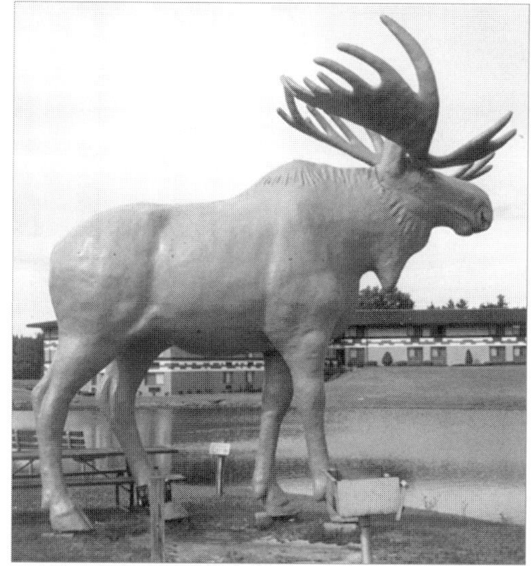

Orange Moose in Black River Falls

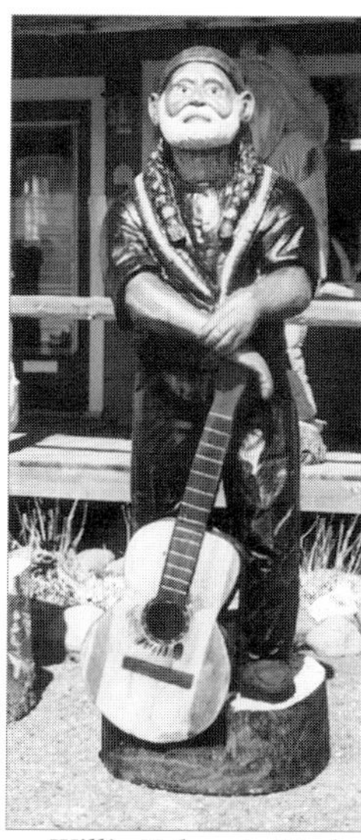

Willie Nelson in Hurley

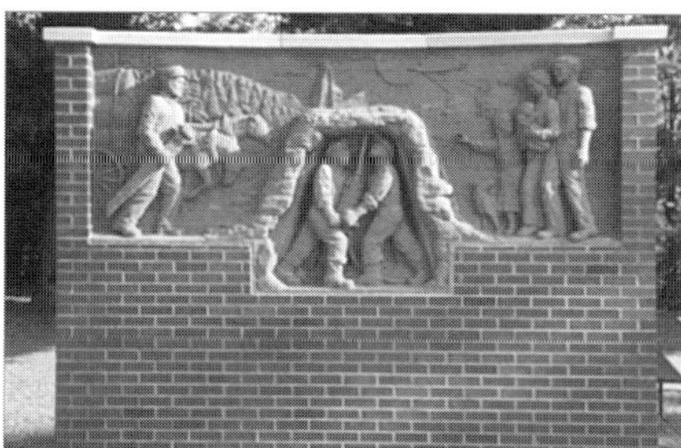

Morzenti Memorial in Merrill

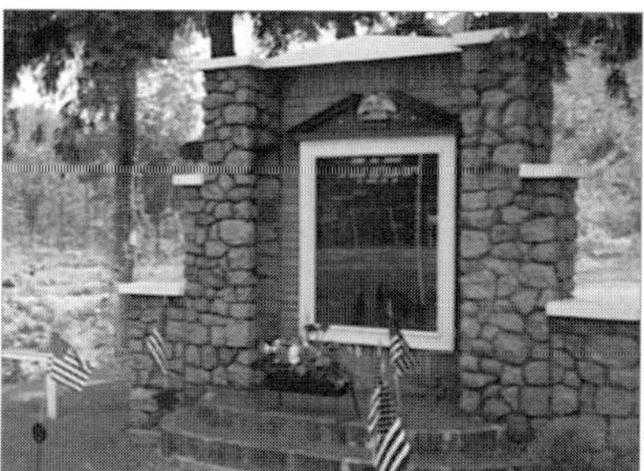

Veterans Monument in Montreal

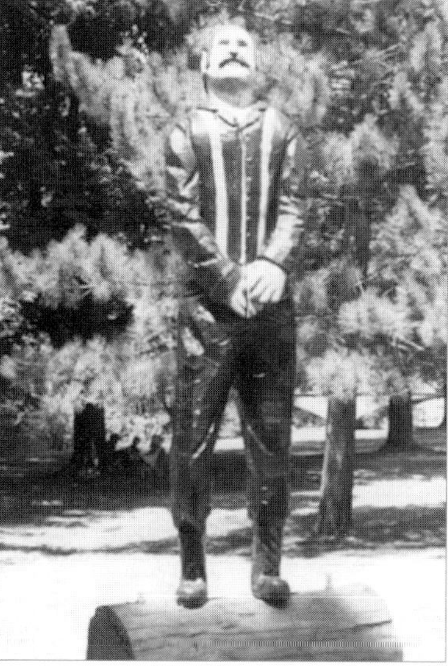

The River Rafter in Merrill

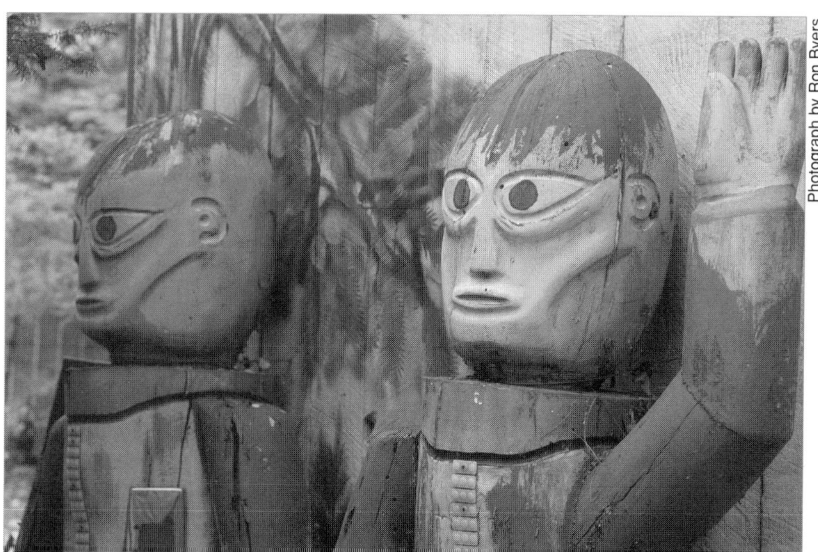

Photograph by Ron Byers

Folk Art Environment in Tomahawk

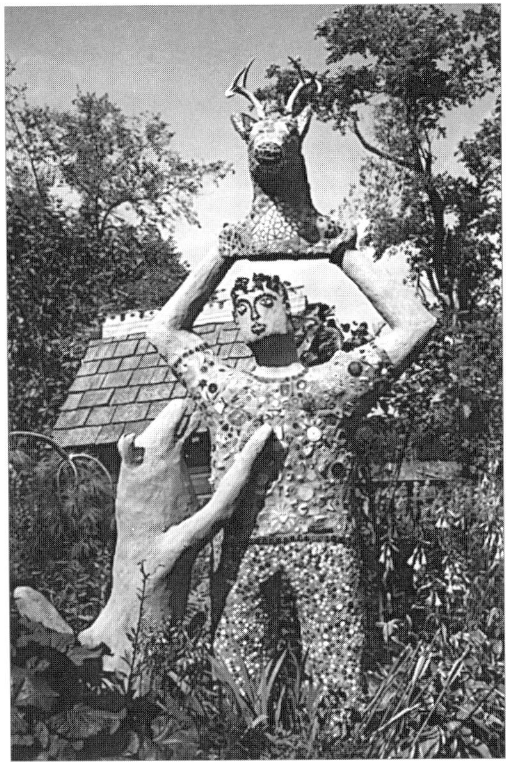

Sculpture Garden in Beldenville

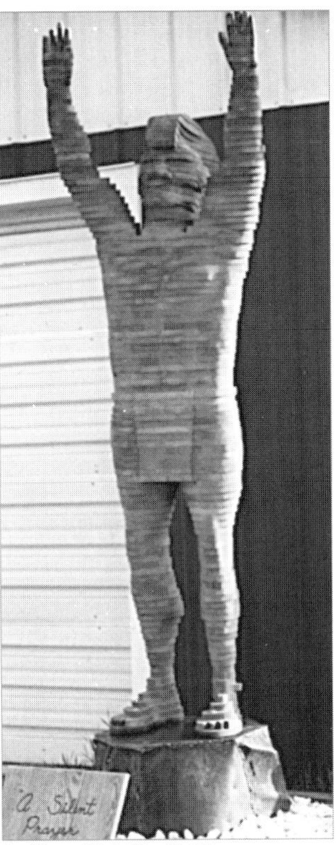

Indian Chief in Phillips

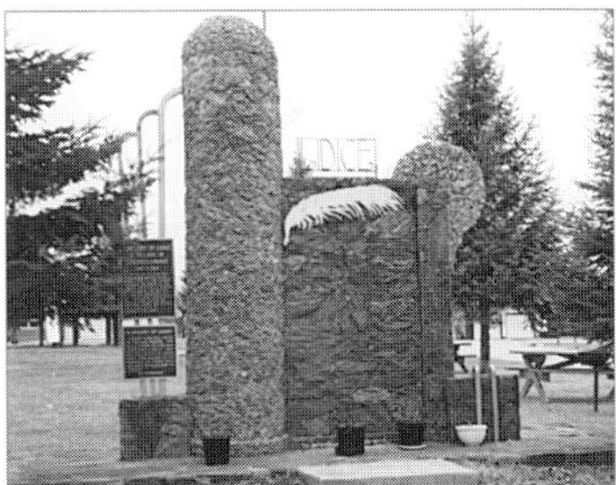

Lidice Monument in Phillips

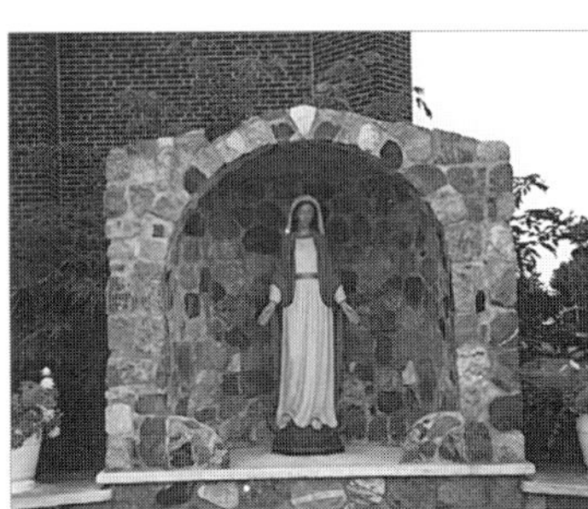

Virgin Mary in Phillips

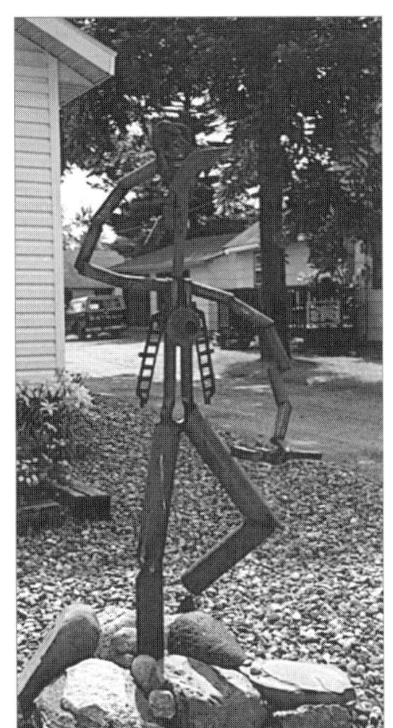

The Plumber in Phillips

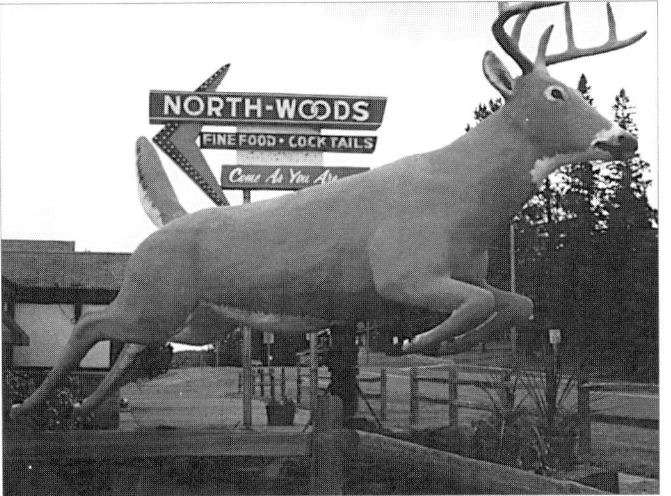

Whitetail Deer in Fifield

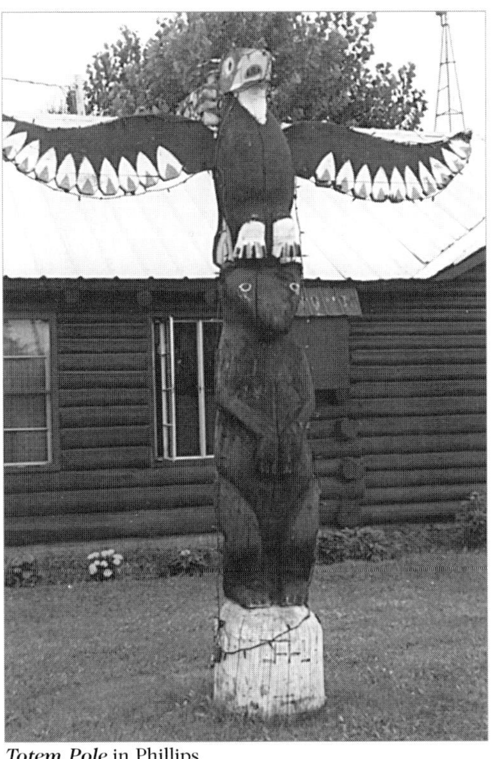

Totem Pole in Phillips

The American Eagle Veterans Memorial
in Park Falls

PIERCE

Hager City

Boulder Effigy Mound

This effigy mound consists of a line
of boulders shaped like an animal or
object, located along Highway 35,
1 mile south of the junction of
Highway 35 and Highway 63

River Falls

Art Environment
Mollie Jenson
Starting around 1938
Mixed media, included the Dutch
Mill, Fireplace, Horseshoe, and Small
Zoo. Mostly demolished in the 1970s,
located on County Highway M,
private property, view from road

Whirling Man
Riana de Raad
1997
Concrete with tile, located at
Earth Works Landscape Company

Beldenville

Sculpture Garden
Riana de Raad
Six concrete and tile sculptures,
call (715)273-5959

POLK

Osceola

Eagle and Nest
Andy Lutter
Wood, chain saw art, located at
605 River Street

Indian Chief
Andy Lutter
Wood, chain saw art, located at
103 N. Cascade Street

Native American Chief
Painted concrete, located on Main
Street

Osceola Indian
Darrell Wirrkula
Wood, located at 107 N. Cascade
Street

PRICE

Fifield

Jumping Deer
F.A.S.T. Jerry Vetterus
Fiberglass, located on Highway 13
at North Woods Supper Club

Park Falls

The American Eagle Veterans Memorial
F.A.S.T.
1987 dedication
Fiberglass, located on Highway 13 at
Park Falls High School

Phillips

Eagle
James Barber
Wood, chain saw art, located on South
Fork of Flambeau River, view from
river

Indian Chief
James Barber
Wood, chain saw art, located on South
Fork of Flambeau River

Lidice Monument
Joe Skomaroske
1944
Stone, metal, and concrete, located at
City Park

The Plumber
Corroded steel, located at a private
residence on Highway 13 in town

Totem Pole
Painted wood, located at the
Museum Bar, north on Highway 13

Virgin Mary
Painted concrete, located at Our Lady
of the Northwoods Catholic Church
corner of Argyle and Chestnut streets

Whitetail Deer
Fiberglass, located at Northwoods
Restaurant, Highway 13 and
Highway 70

Wisconsin Concrete Park Folk Art Environment
Fred Smith (1886-1976)
Circa 1950-67
One of the largest folk art environments in North America with over
200 concrete and glass embellished
sculptures dedicated to the American
people, located south of Phillips on
Highway 13

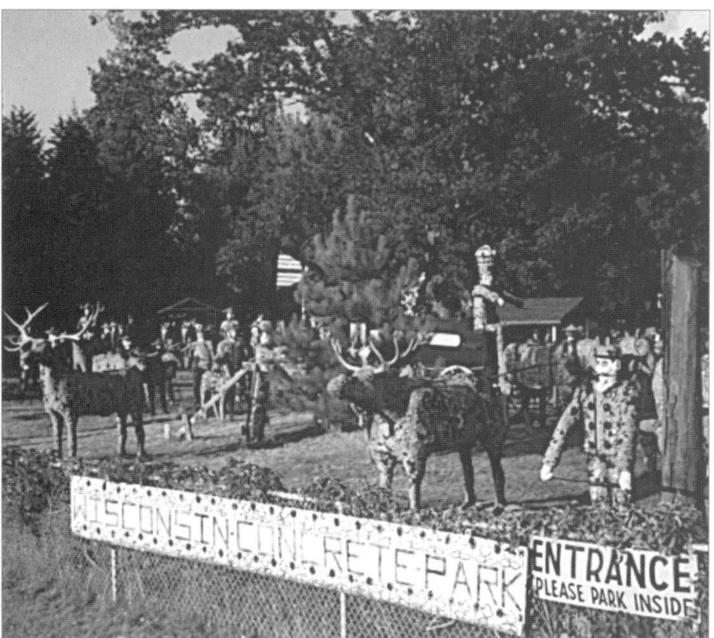

Wisconsin Concrete Park Entrance to Park in Phillips

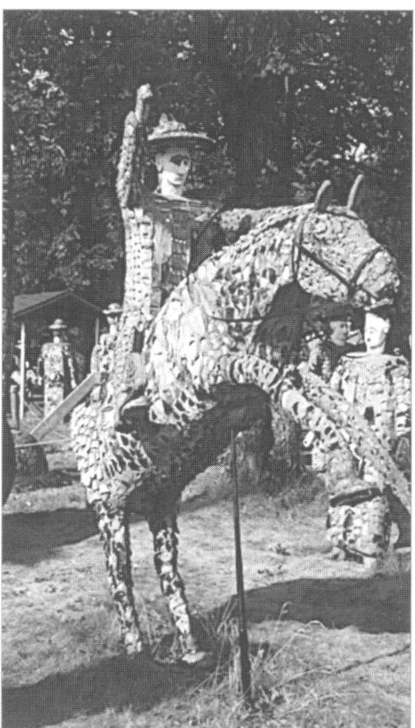
Wisconsin Concrete Park Kit Carson in Phillips

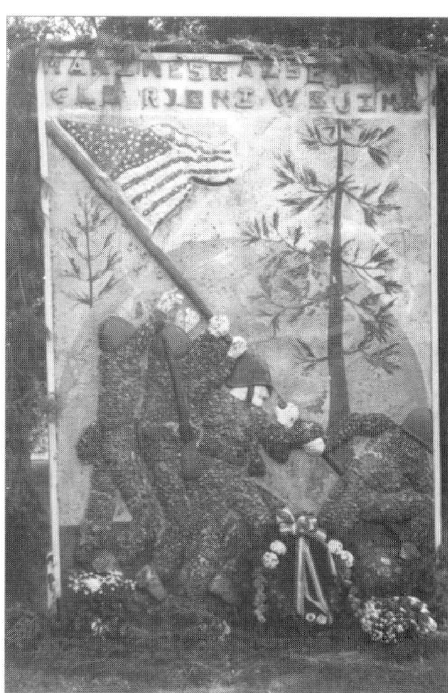
Wisconsin Concrete Park Iwo Jima Memorial in Phillips

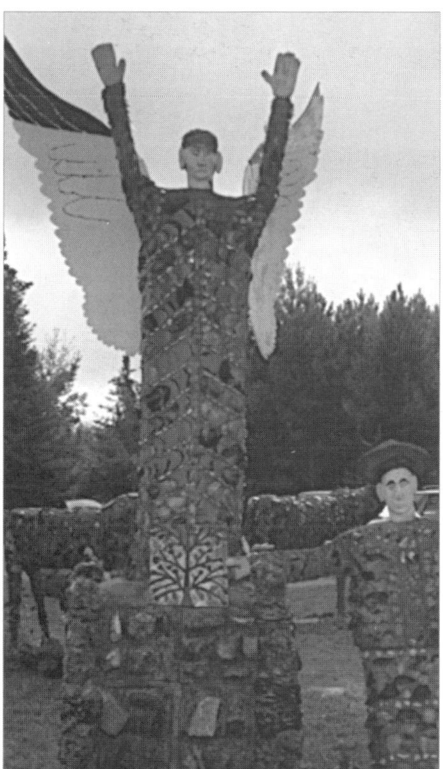
Wisconsin Concrete Park Angel and Woman in Phillips

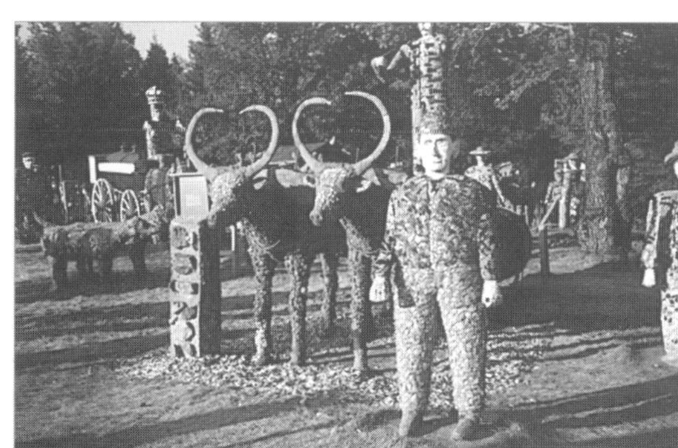
Mr. Knox and Oxen at Wisconsin Concrete Park, Phillips

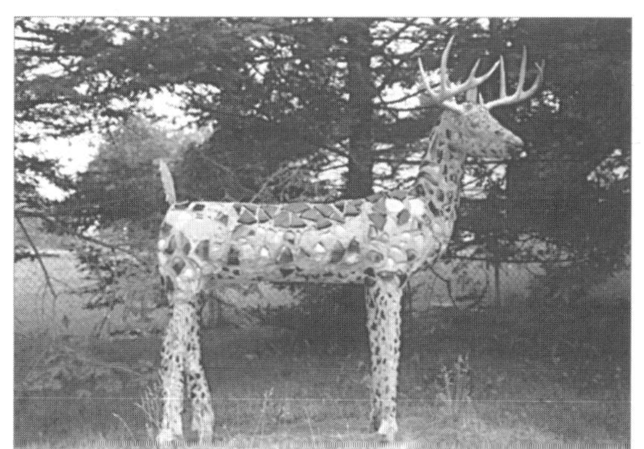
Wisconsin Concrete Park Deer in Phillips

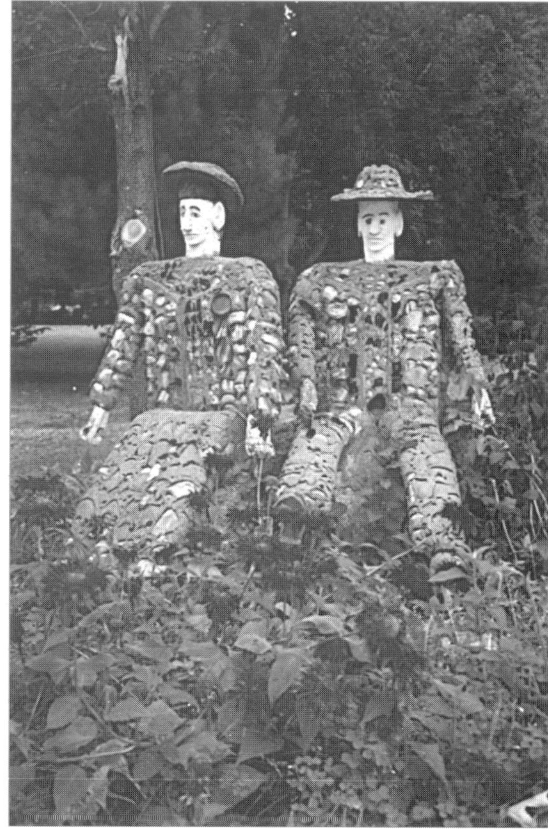
Wisconsin Concrete Park Man and Woman in Phillips

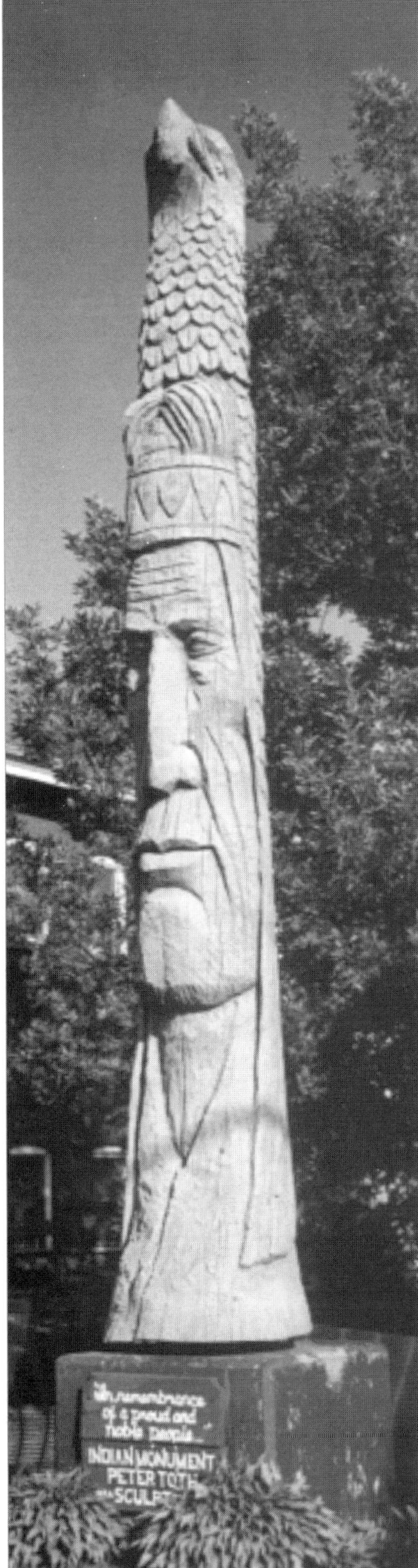

Tribute to the Ojibwe in Hayward

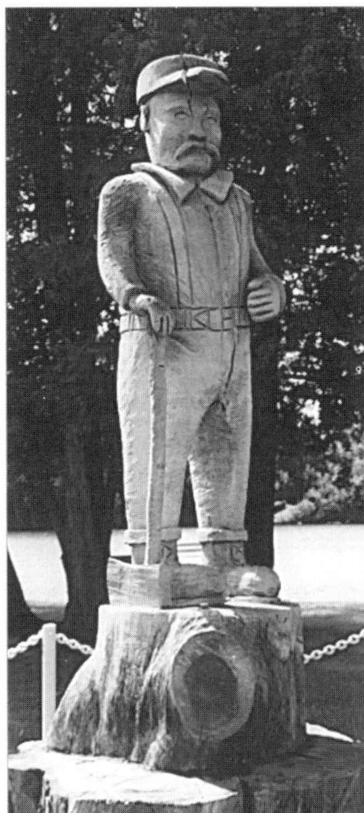

Lumberjack in Ladysmith

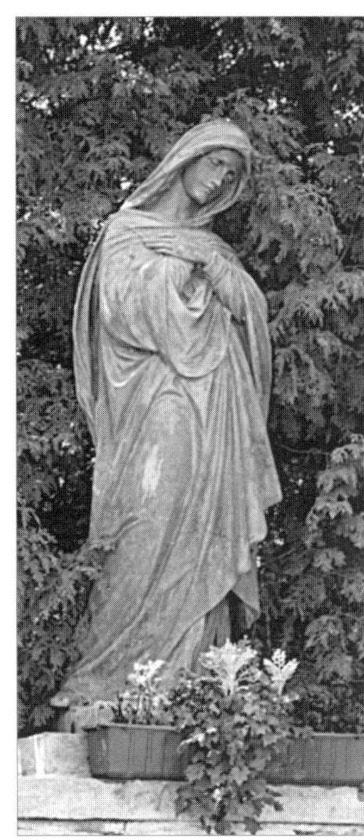

Our Lady of Sorrows in Ladysmith

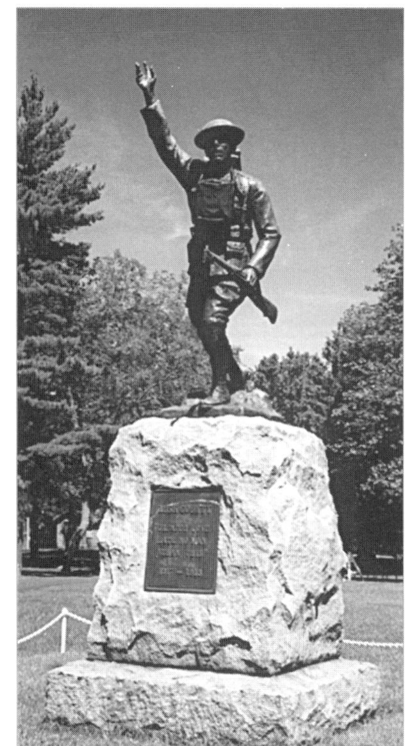

World War I Doughboy in Ladysmith

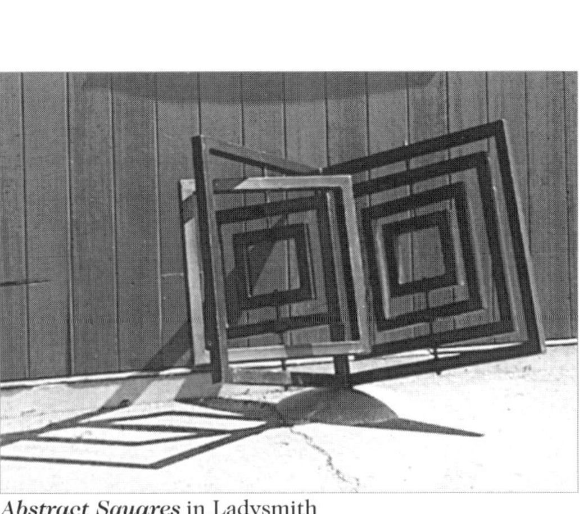

Abstract Squares in Ladysmith

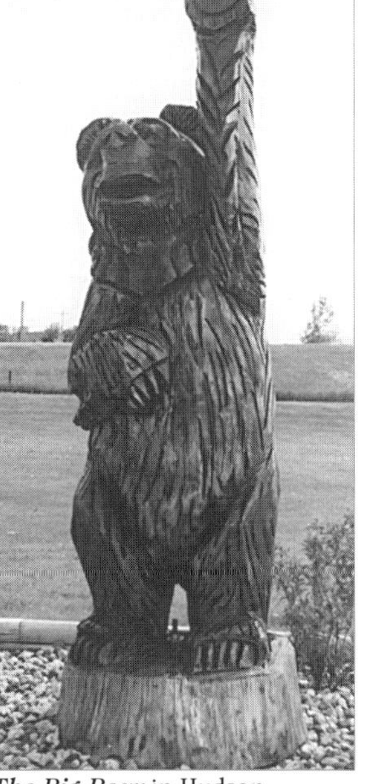

The Big Bear in Hudson

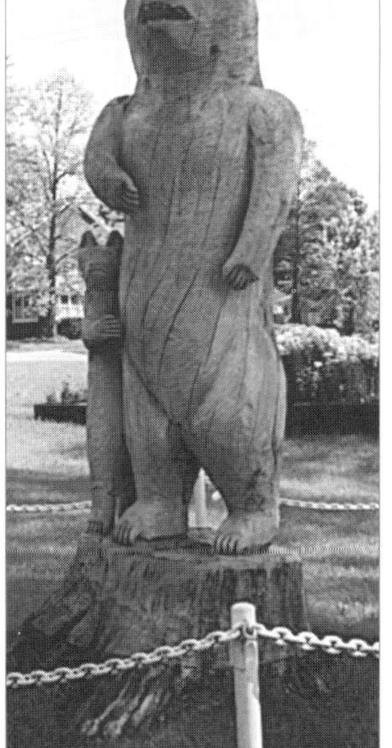

Bear and Her Cub in Ladysmith

RUSK

Ladysmith

Abstract of Geometric Squares
Circa 1970
Steel, located at Mt. Senario College,
Fine Arts Center

Bear and Her Cub
Signed F.N.
1991
Wood, chain saw art, located in
City Park

Lumberjack
1991
Wood, chain saw art, located in
City Park

Our Lady of Sorrows
Daprato Statuary Company
Circa 1935
Metal, located at Mt. Senario College,
Servants of Mary Covenant, 1000
College Avenue West

World War I Doughboy
Jay Paulding
1929
Bronze, American Art Bronze
Foundry, located in City Park near
the Flambeau River

ST. CROIX

Hudson

Lewis Massey (first settler)
Bronze, located on 1st Street

Ship's Captain
Larry Hensen
Wood, chain saw art, located at the
Twin City East 76 Truck Stop,
I-94 and Highway 12

**St. Croix County Veterans
Memorial**
New Richmond Granite Works
Dedicated May 19, 1984
Granite, located at Government
Center, St. Croix County Courthouse

The Big Bear
Larry Jensen
Wood, chain saw art, located at the
Twin City East 76 Truck Stop,
I-94 and Highway 12

Three Eagles
Dave Watson and Joe Moudry
Dedicated September 1991
Wood, chain saw art, located in
Lakefront Park

Voyageur
Joe Moudry
Dedicated July 5, 1991
Wood, chain saw art, located in
Lakefront Park

SAWYER

Hayward

Chain Saw Artist Studio
Brian Johnson
Circa 1980-90s
Wood, located east on Highway 77,
including bears, eagles, birds, fish
and more

The Shrine to Anglers, the Giant Muskie
Jerry Vetterus, F.A.S.T.
1978
Fiberglass, located at the
Fishing Hall of Fame
*The Giant Muskie is the largest
outdoor sculpture in the state*

Totem Pole
Painted wood, located on Brandt Road
at Lost Land Lake

Tribute to the Ojibwe
Peter Toth
October 8, 1977
Wood, 15 feet tall, located near the
Carnegie Library, Highway 63 North
and S. Main Street
*Peter Toth achieved his goal of
carving a totem pole in every state
by 1988*

Winter

Black Bear
Sculptured Advertising
1964
Fiberglass, located at Big Bear Lodge,
W1614 County Highway W

TAYLOR

Medford

Sacred Heart of Jesus
Carved stone, located at Wayside
on Highway 13

World War I Infantry Soldier
Dedicated 1921
Gray limestone, located at
224 S. 2nd Street

Westburo

Totems and Bears grouping
Willis Lewan
Wood, chainsaw art display, located
on Highway 13 includes the grouping
of totems, bears and other critters

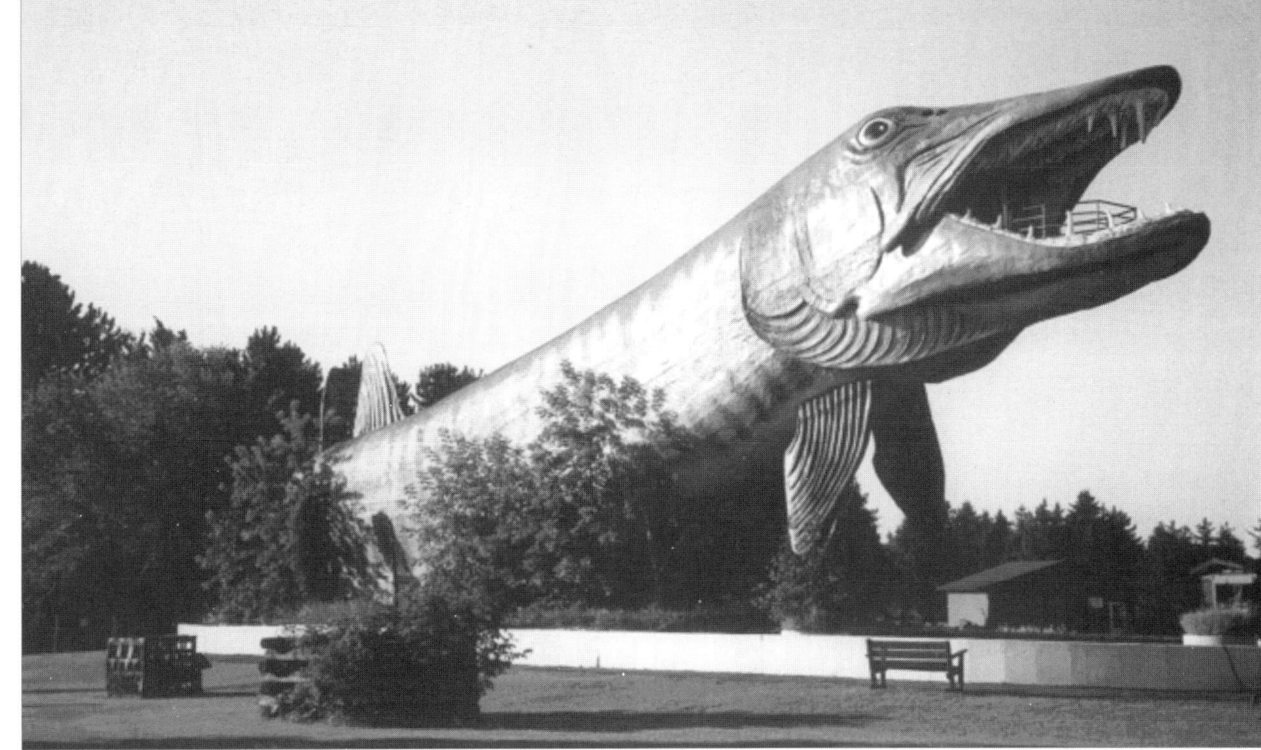
The Shrine to Anglers in Hayward

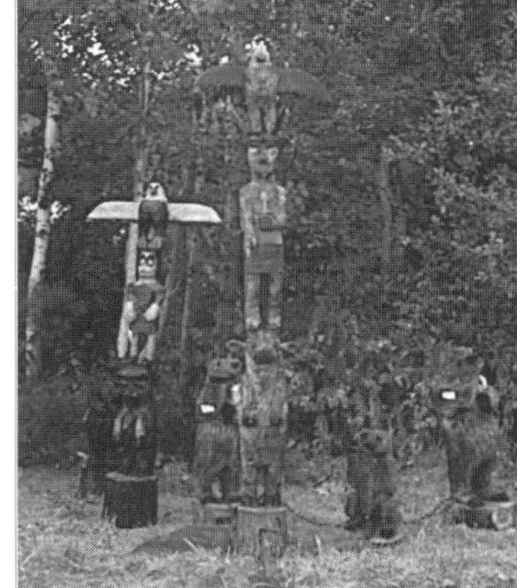
Totem and Bears grouping
in Westboro

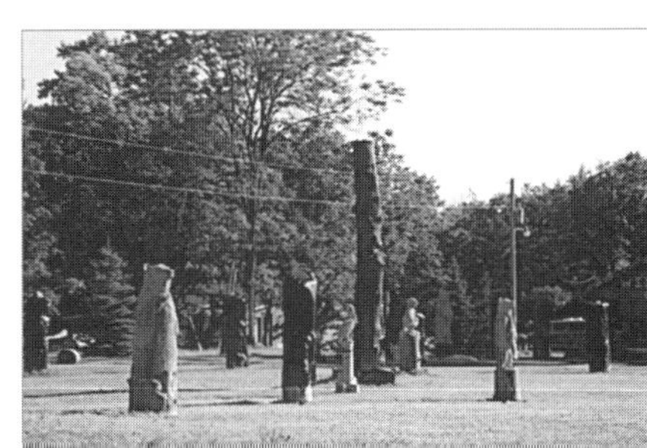
Chainsaw Art Display at Wildlife Gallery
in Hayward

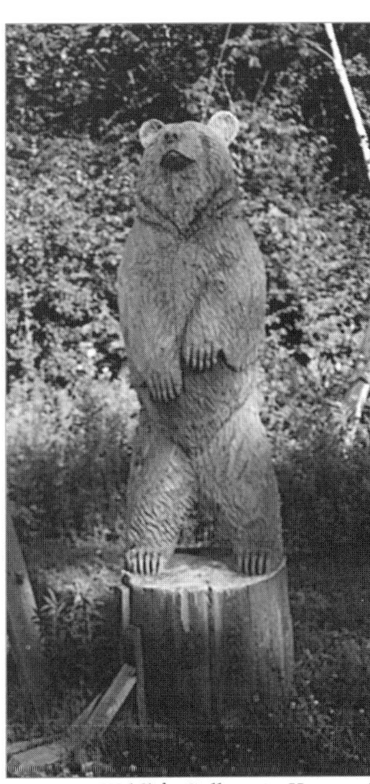
Bear at Wildlife Gallery in Hayward

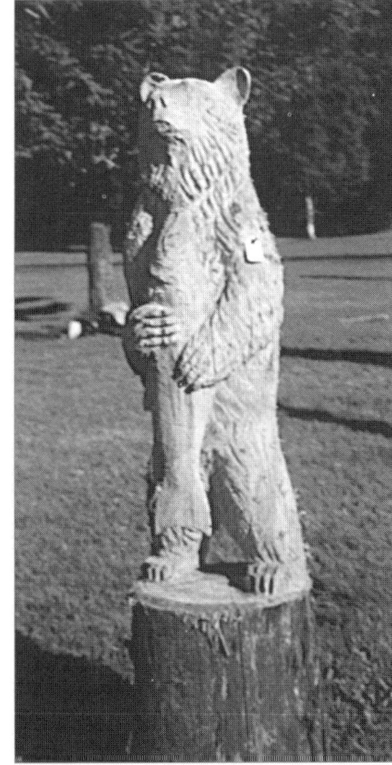
Bear with Fish at Wildlife Gallery in
Hayward

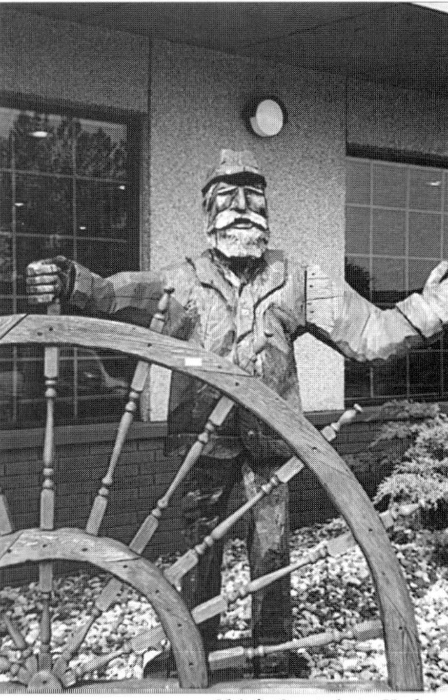
Ship's Captain in Hudson

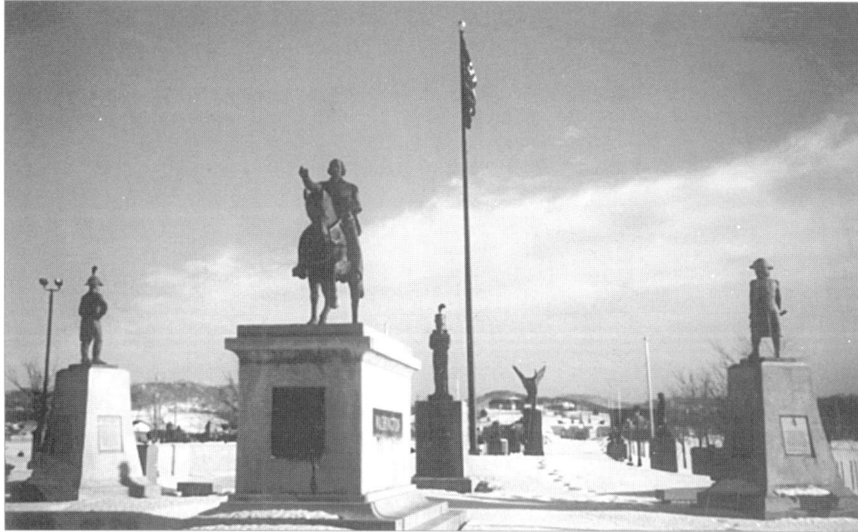

Washington and overall view at Arcadia Memorial Park in Arcadia

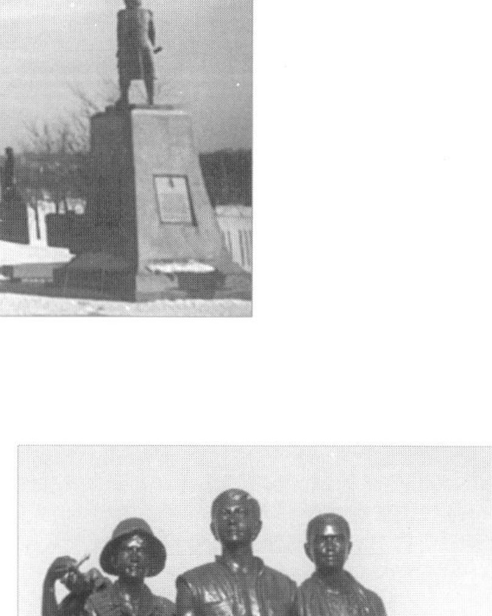

World War II Monument at Arcadia Memorial Park in Arcadia

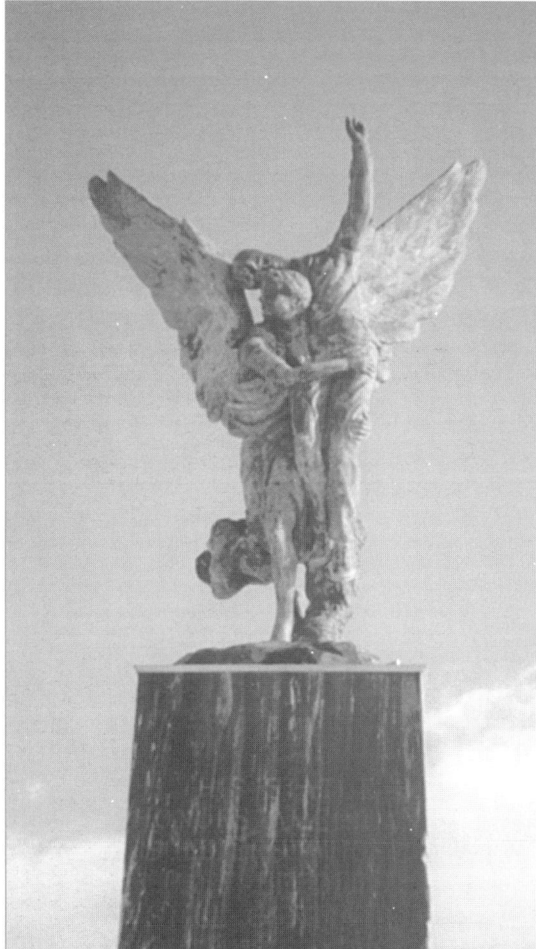

Angel of Mercy in Arcadia Memorial Park in Arcadia

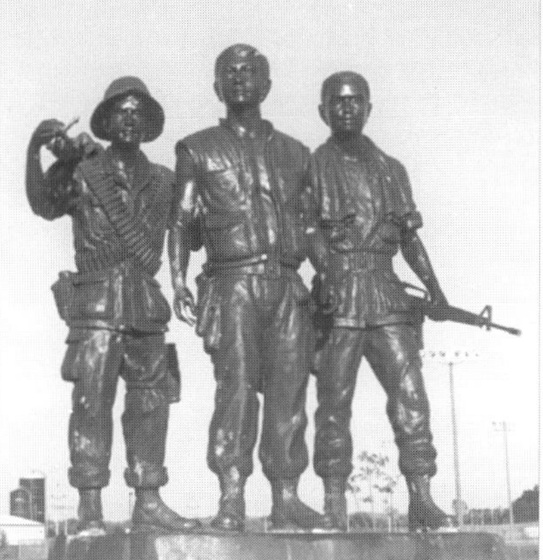

Vietnam War Monument in Arcadia Memorial Park in Arcadia

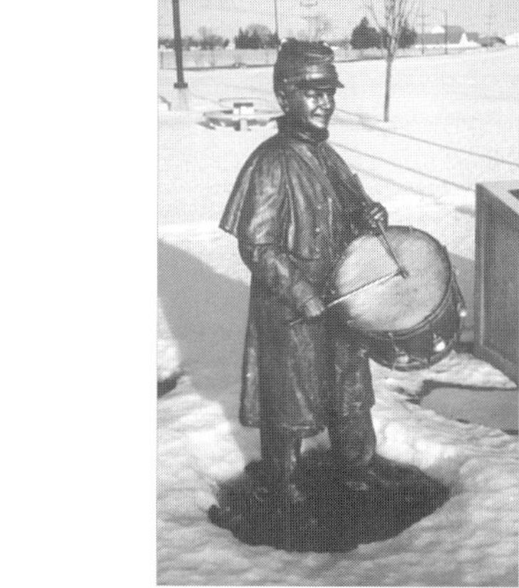

Civil War Monument detail of *Drummerboy* in Arcadia Memorial Park in Arcadia

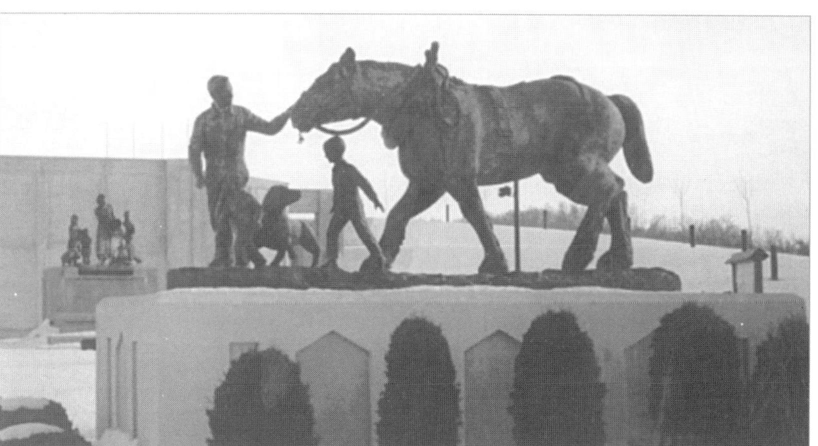

Pioneers at Arcadia Memorial Park in Arcadia

TREMPEALEAU

Arcadia

African Lions
Metal, located at Ashley Furniture Company, 1 Ashley Way

Our Lady of Perpetual Help
Circa 1950
Concrete, located at Our Lady's Catholic Church, Washington Street

The Virgin of Fatima grouping
Concrete, located at St. Stanislaus Catholic Church, 223 Maple Street. Other pieces include urns, girls, boy, sheep, and lamb

Arcadia Memorial Park
County Highway J and Gavney Road

Angel of Mercy
Designed by Ronald G. Wanek
Dedicated May 24, 1992
Bronze

Civil War Monument, G.A.R., C.S.A.
Bronze

Korean War Monument
Designed by Ronald G. Wanek
Dedicated May 30, 1993
Bronze

Millennium Amphitheater
To be dedicated August 20, 2000

Pioneer Monument
Dedicated May 30, 1993
Bronze horse, dog, and boy grouping

Vietnam War Monument
Designed by Ron and Todd Wanek
Dedicated May 27, 1991
Bronze

Washington Monument
Bronze

World War I Monument, Dough Boy
Designed by Ronald G. Wanek
Dedicated May 30, 1993
Bronze

World War II Monument, Iwo Jima
Original by Felix de Weldon, 1953
Dedicated May 24, 1992
Bronze

St. Joseph Hospital grounds
464 S. Street Joseph Avenue

Blessed Virgin Mary in Grotto
Dedicated 1952
Painted Concrete

Saint Bernadette
Concrete

Saint Francis
Concrete

Christ the King
Dedicated 1952
Concrete

Town of Gale

Princess Marinouka Memorial
Circa 1930
Painted concrete, located near
Artie Springs Restaurant, French
Road on the way to Galesville

Galesville

Marynook Retreat Center
500 S. 12th Street

Our Lady of Confidence
Dedicated May 1940
Concrete

St. Joseph
Dedicated May 1940
Concrete

*The Virgin Mary, St. John and
Christ on the Cross*
Mel Meyer
1961
Concrete

Osseo

*Pipe Sculpture
Triangular Spike and Curved
Forms
Rectangular and Curved Forms
Airplane
Triangular and Pyramid Forms*
Carl Bong
Circa late 1960s, early 1970s
Sheet metal and piping grouping of
sculptures, located on Route 1

Pine Creek

Christ at Calvary
Circa 1940
Metal, located at Pine Creek
Cemetery, County Highway G

Virgin Mary
Circa 1930
Concrete, located at Pine Creek
Cemetery, County Highway G

Strum

Red Cardinal
Sparta Fiberglass Plant, F.A.S.T.
Jerry Vetterus
Dedicated 1985
Fiberglass, located at Eleva-Strum
Central High School, Highway 10

Totem Pole
Circa 1960
Wood, located at Strum Rod and
Gun Park, 5th Avenue North

VILAS

Eagle River

Carl's Wood Art Museum
Ken and Carl Schels
Wood, chain saw art, located on
Highway 51 north and Highway M,
1230 Sundstein Road including
monumental *Indian Chief*

Indian Head (Sitting Bull)
Charles P. Reed
1936
Granite, located on Highway 45 north
of Eagle River in front of Bonsons Mall
(formerly located in Conover, WI)

Eagles
Jeff Prust
Wood, chain saw art, located at
Eagle River High School

Mountain Man
*The Indian Princess
Two Loggers With a Sawbuck
The Musher With His Dog
Bears With Their Eagle*
Jeff Prust
Wood, chainsaw art, located in
Klondike Park

St. Peter the Fisherman,
Catholic Church Fatima Shrine
Mixed media, located at 509 Wall
Street

WASHBURN

Minong

Chittoamo Cemetery Monument
Mixed media, located at County G
and Culton Road

Sarona

Uncle Sam
1976
Painted carved wood, chainsaw art,
located at N1408 Highway 53

Shell Lake

Museum of Woodcarving
Joseph Barta
1930s–1970s
Wood sculptures on the life of Christ
and the Saints, some of which were
outside and now all are inside, located
in town of Shell Lake

Spooner

Giant Cowboy
F.A.S.T. Jerry Vetterus
Circa 1985
Fiberglass, located at the Spooner
Amusement Park

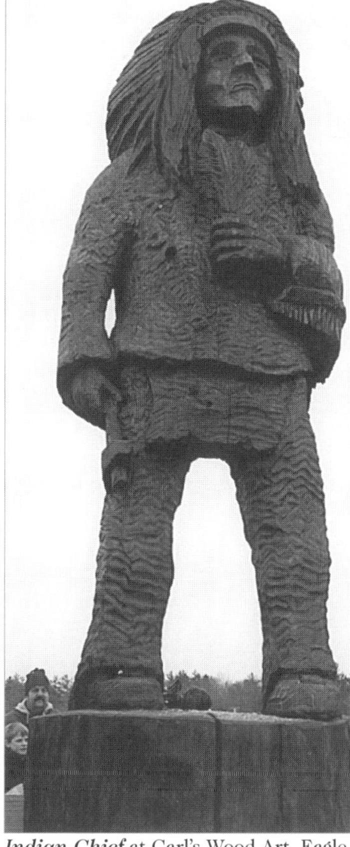

Indian Chief at Carl's Wood Art, Eagle
River

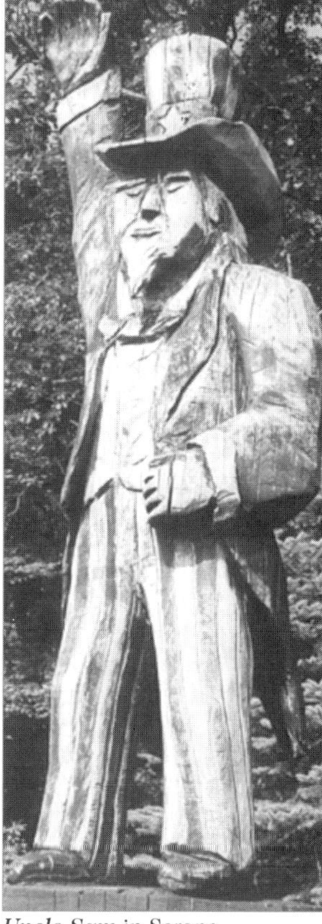

Uncle Sam in Sarona

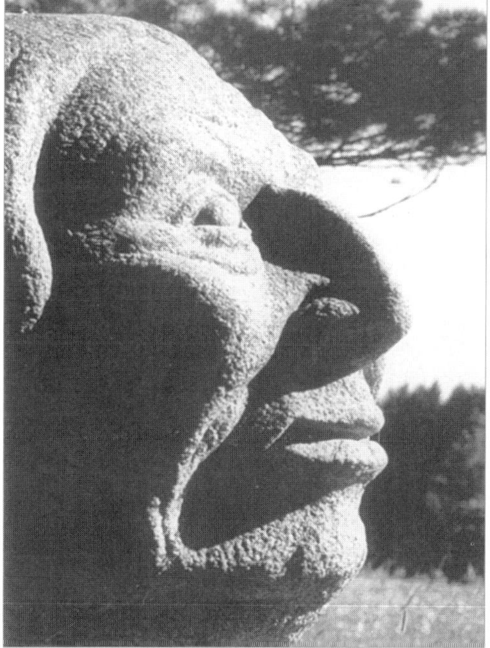

Indian Head, Sitting Bull in Eagle River

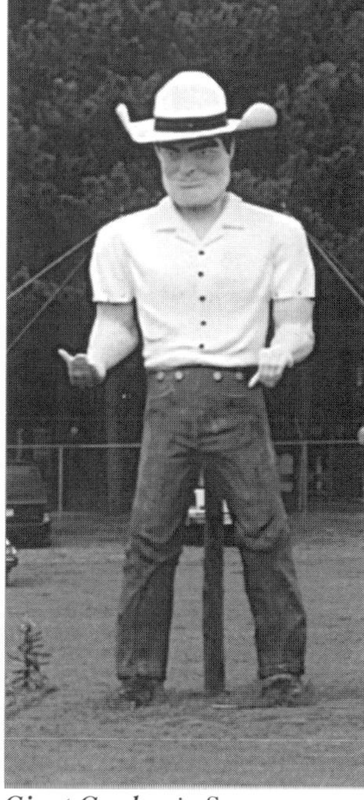

Giant Cowboy in Spooner

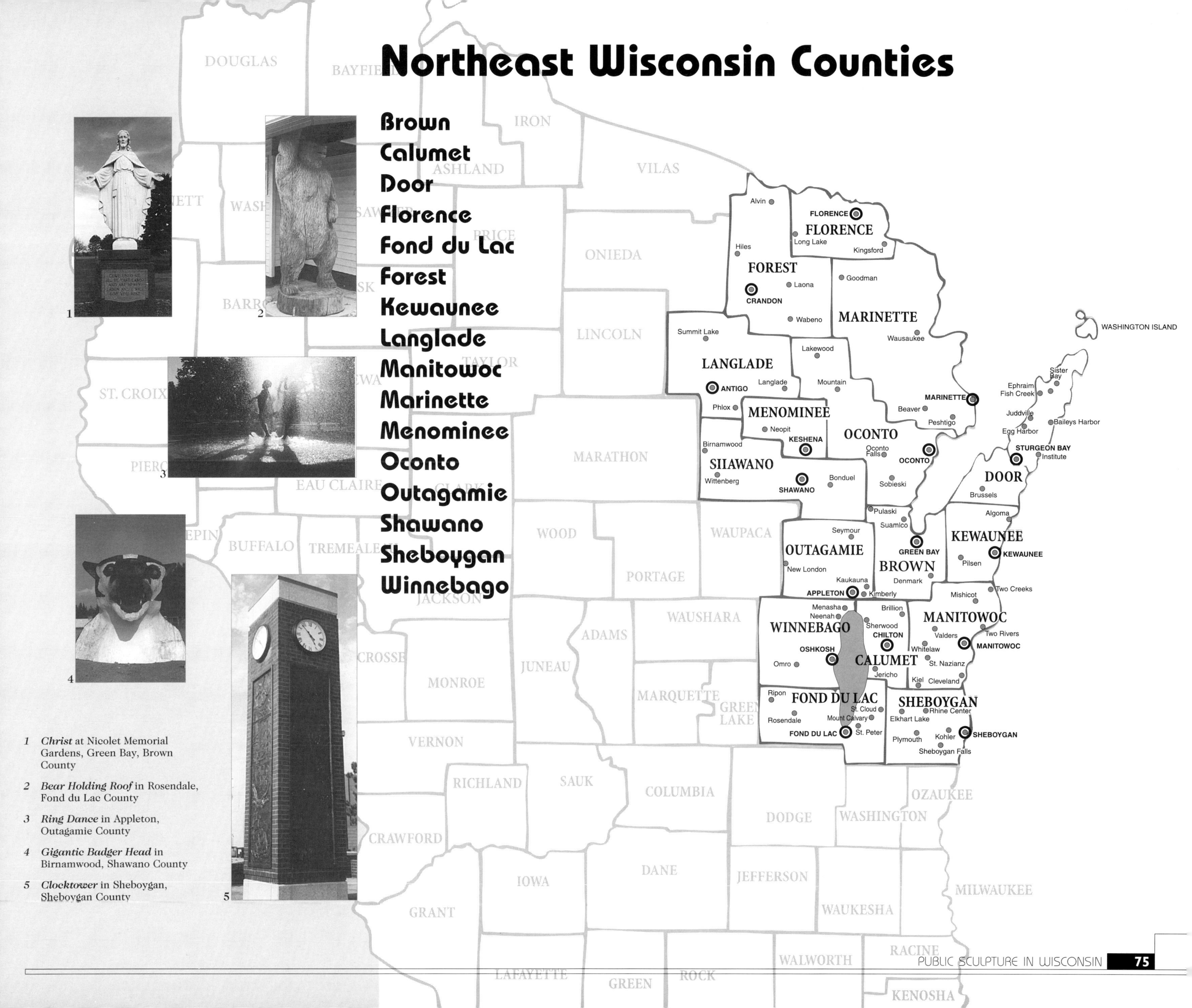

1   *Christ* at Nicolet Memorial Gardens, Green Bay, Brown County

2   *Bear Holding Roof* in Rosendale, Fond du Lac County

3   *Ring Dance* in Appleton, Outagamie County

4   *Gigantic Badger Head* in Birnamwood, Shawano County

5   *Clocktower* in Sheboygan, Sheboygan County

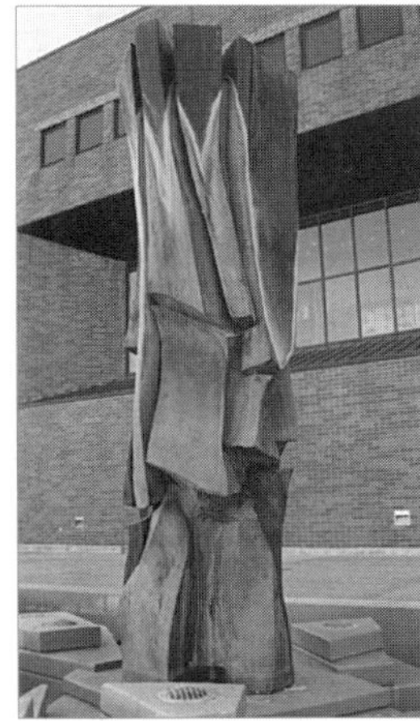

Glacial Edge in Green Bay

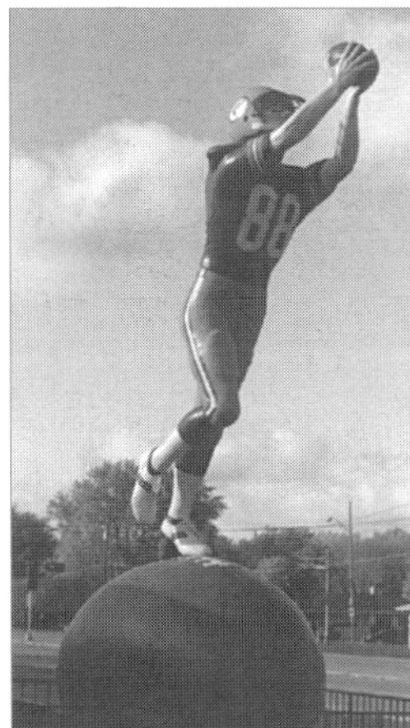

Packer Hall of Fame Player in Green Bay

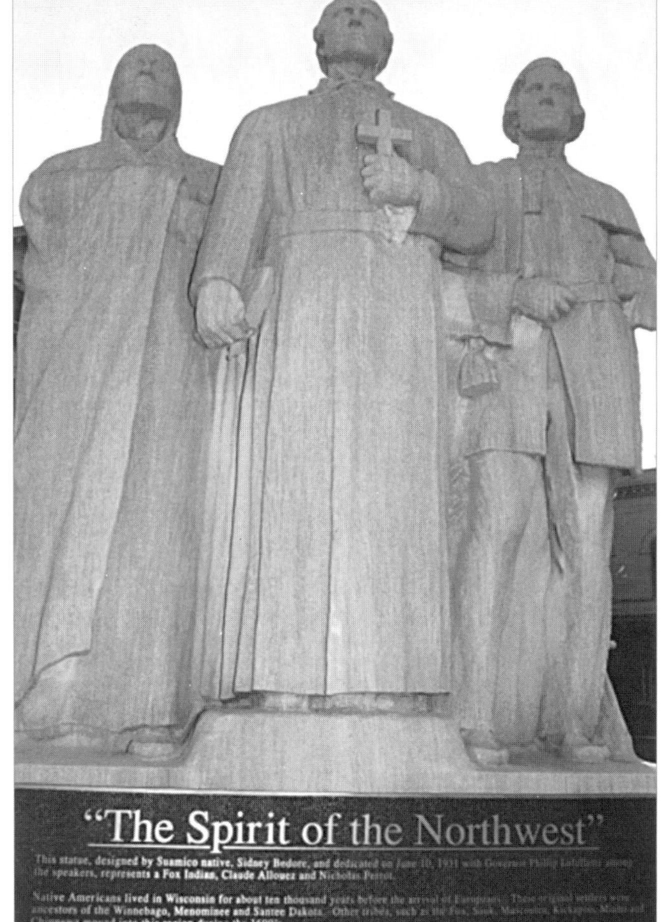

Spirit of the Northwest in Green Bay

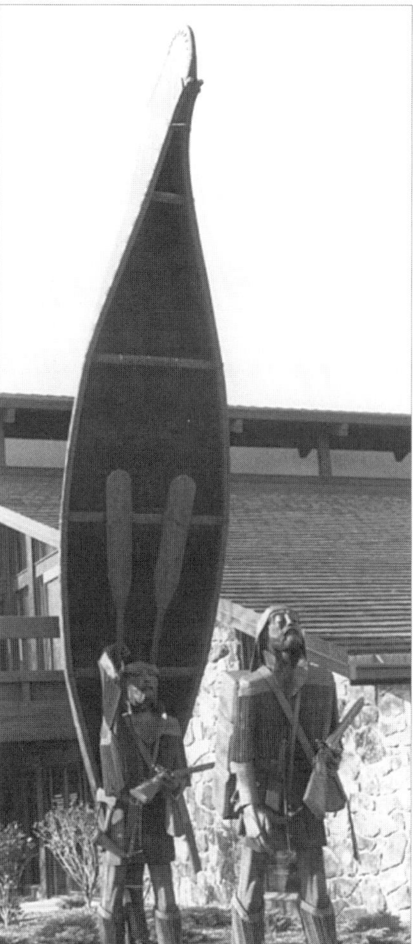

The First Northern Voyageurs in Green Bay

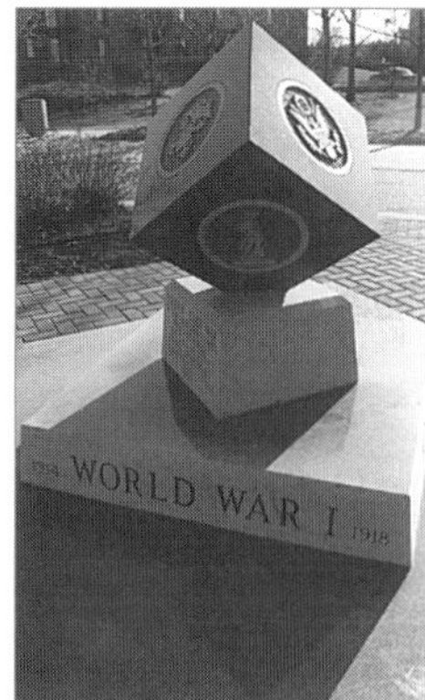

Veterans Memorial Cube in Green Bay

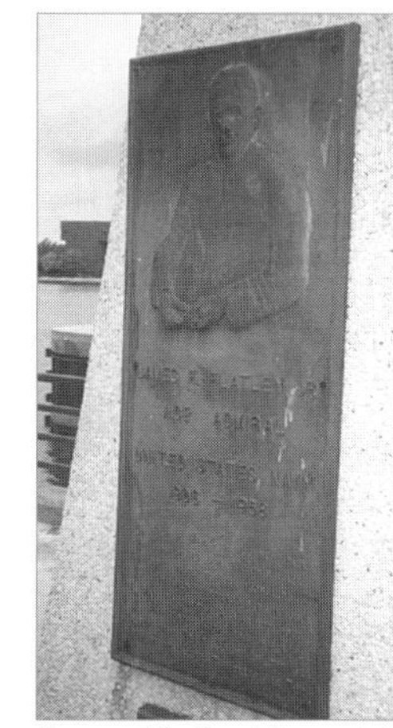

James Flatley Memorial in Green Bay

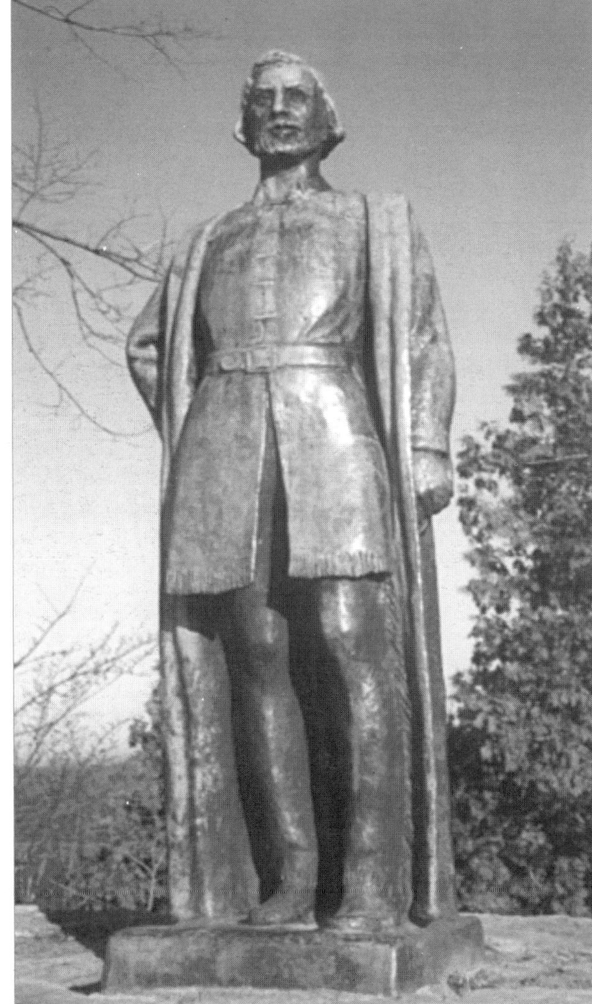

Memorial to Jean Nicolet in Green Bay

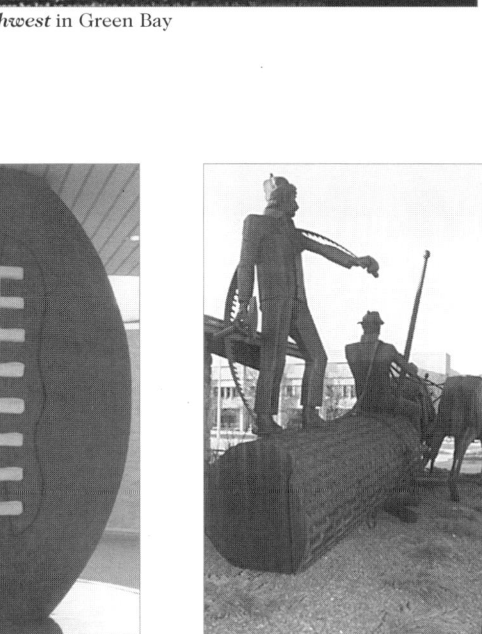

Football at Packer Hall of Fame, Green Bay

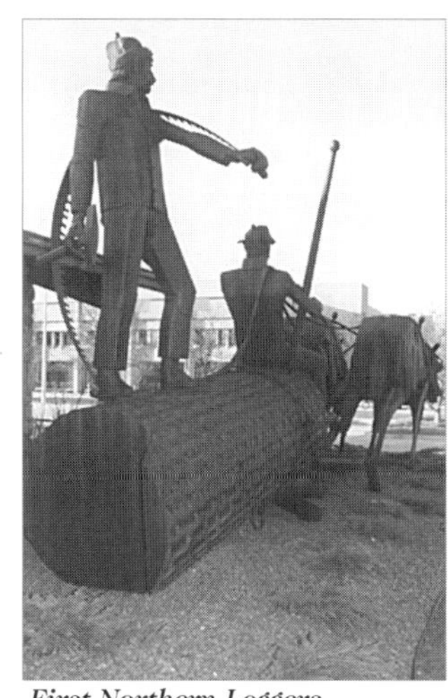

First Northern Loggers in Green Bay

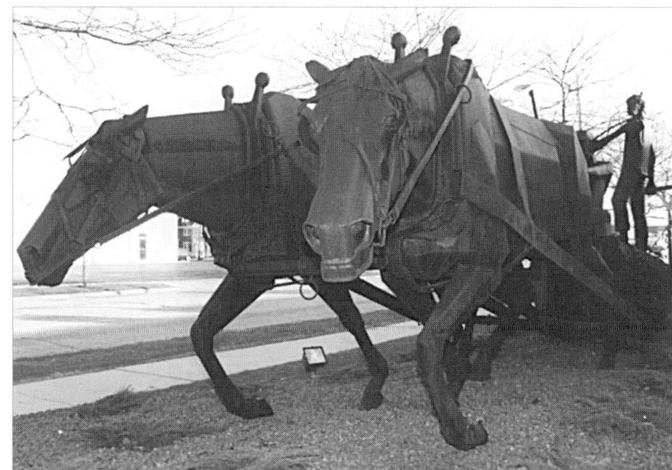

The First Northern Loggers in Green Bay

Northeast Counties

BROWN

Green Bay

Abstraction of the Sun
Donald Noel
1994
Metal, was located on E. Main Street
Removed from site

Dilemma
Rick Penterman
1998
Stainless steel, located at 2731 Bay
Settlement Road. Private, view from
road

Glacial Edge
O.V. Shaffer
1983
Forged and welded brass fountain,
located in front of the Neville Public
Museum

Grazing
Tim Kussow
1997
Painted steel, located at 2731 Bay
Settlement Road. Private, view from
road

James Flatley Jr. Memorial
Cast bronze, located in park near
Fox River, E. Main Street

Memorial to Jean Nicolet
Sidney Bedore
Commissioned 1939, dedicated 1951
Bronze, located north of Green Bay
along Highway 57 at the Historical
Marker site

**Packer Hall of Fame Player
Giant Football**
Painted concrete, located in front
of the Packer Hall of Fame on
Lombardi Drive

Spirit of the Northwest
Sidney Bedore
1931, June 10 dedication
Bedford limestone, located in front
of the Brown County Courthouse,
Walnut Street

The First Northern Loggers
Lyndon Fayne Pomeroy
1980
Steel, located in front of the
First Northern Savings Bank,
Monroe Street

The First Northern Voyageurs
Lyndon Fayne Pomeroy
1975
Steel, 30 feet tall, located in front
of the First Northern Saving Bank,
Monroe Street

Veterans Memorial Cube
Red granite, located south of the
Neville Public Museum along the
Fox River

St. Francis
White marble, located in front of
Holy Cross Sisters of St. Francis,
3009 Bay Settlement Road

Trees
Donald Noel
1994
Aluminum and steel, was located on
E. Main Street. Removed from site

UW-Green Bay
2420 Nicolet Drive

Abstract Circles
Bill Little
Painted steel, located at the entrance
of the Phoenix Sport Center

Abstract Gazelle
Steve Ebben
Steel, located at lower south entrance
to Theater Hall and Studio Arts

Abstract Notes
Bill Little
Steel, located at lower south entrance
to Theater Hall and Studio Arts

Abstract Construction
Bill Little
Steel, located outside the concourse
walkway between Student Services
and the Cofrin Library

Abstract Towers
Tim Kussow
Corten steel, located south of the
Theater Hall lobby upper entrance

Doe with Fawns
David H. Turner
Cast bronze, located at the south
entrance

Endless Fence
Peter Flanary
1996
Steel and stone, located north of the
University Union. Percent for Art
Project

**Heini Hagemeister Jr. Memorial
Sculpture**
Designed by Hagemeister before
his death in 1970, created by
Daniel Bresnashan
Dedicated 1984
Stainless steel rods located in front of
the Theater Hall lobby

Red Abstraction
Jeff Benzow
Painted steel, located near Studio Arts

Two Abstract Forms
Bill Little
Steel, located near Studio Arts

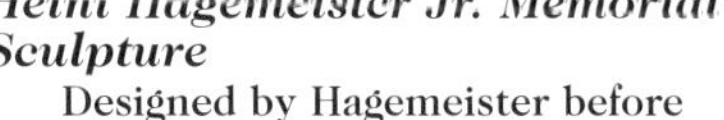

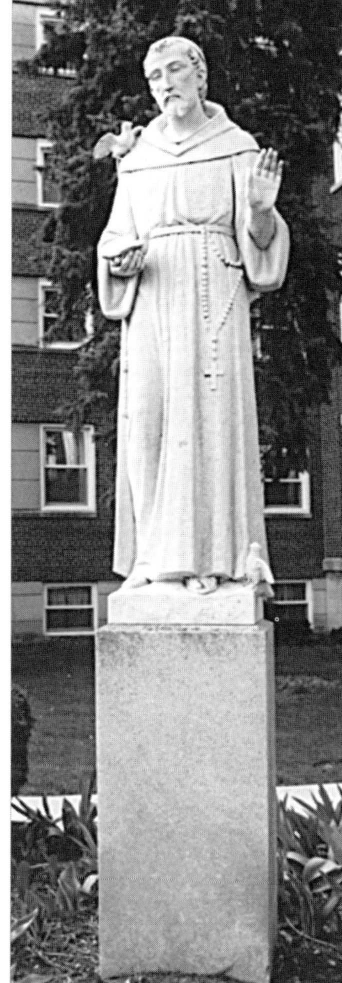

Heini Hagemeister Jr. Memorial Sculpture
at UW-Green Bay

St. Francis in Green Bay

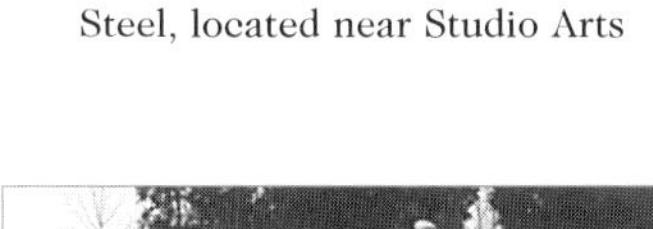

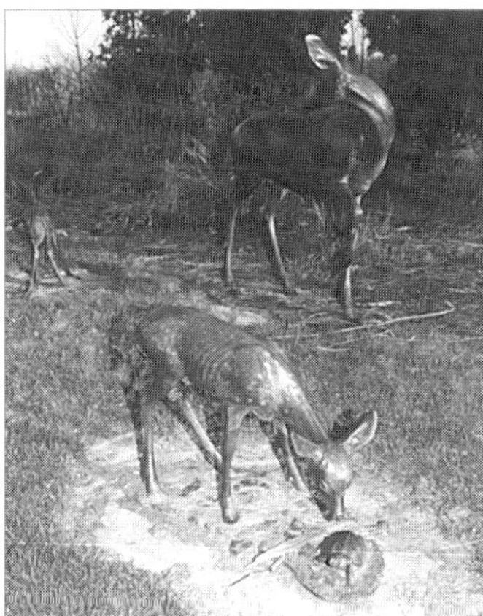

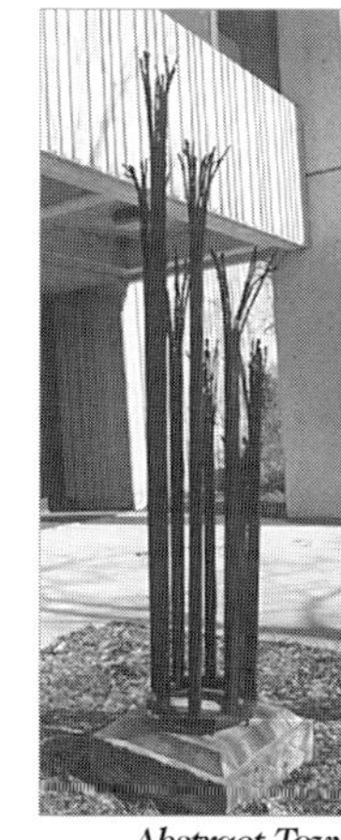

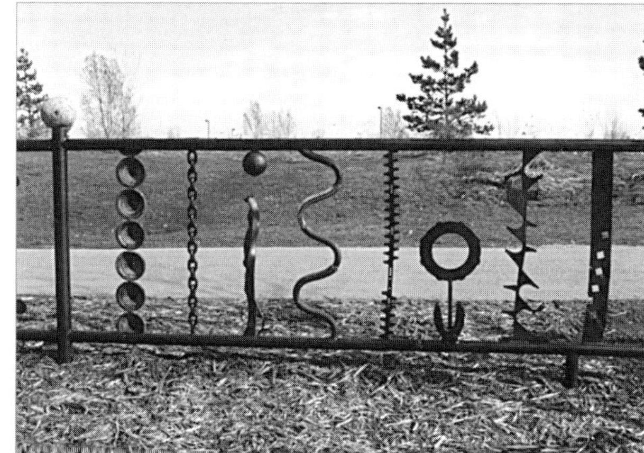

Doe With Fawns at UW-Green Bay

Abstract Towers
at UW-Green Bay

Endless Fence at UW-Green Bay

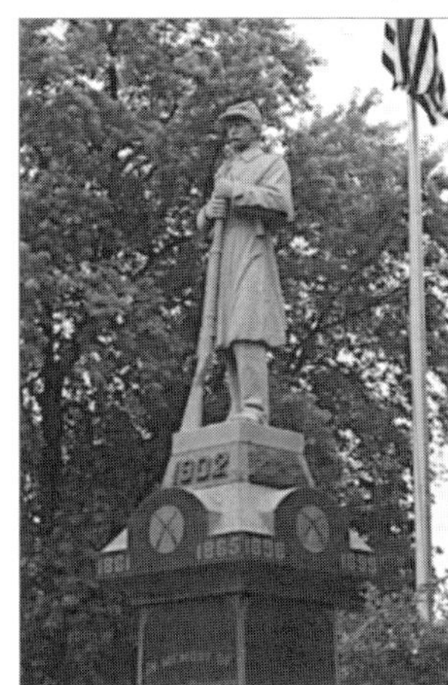

Civil War Monument
in Chilton

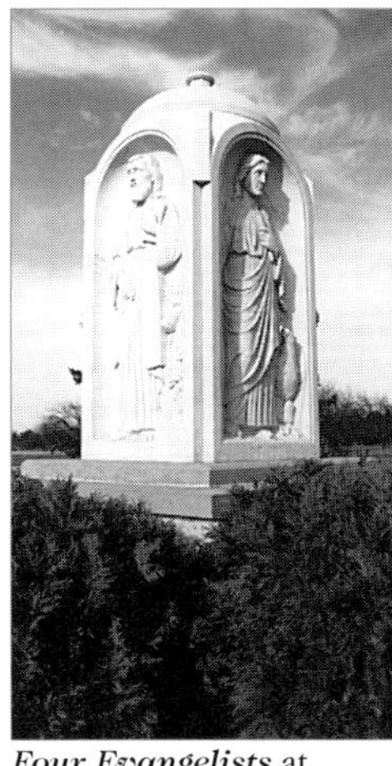

Four Evangelists at
Nicolet Memorial
Gardens, Green Bay

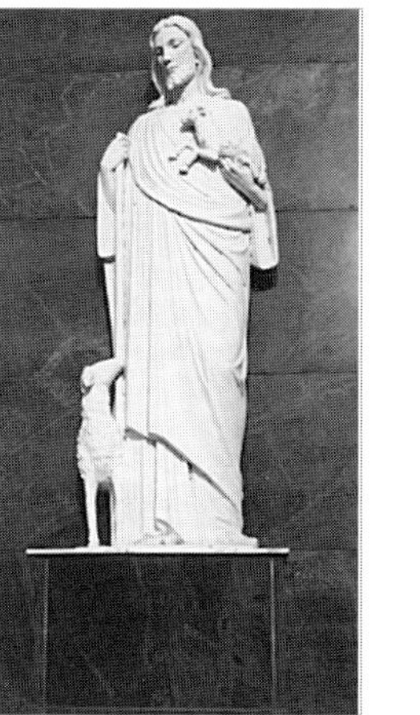

Good Shepherd at
Nicolet Memorial
Gardens, Green Bay

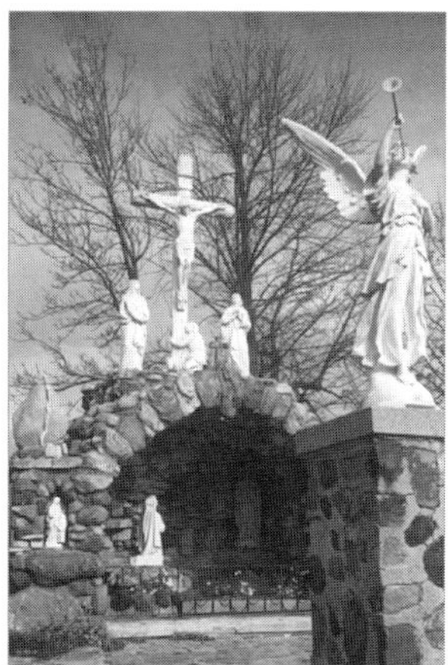

Saint Francis Xavier Grotto
in Brussels

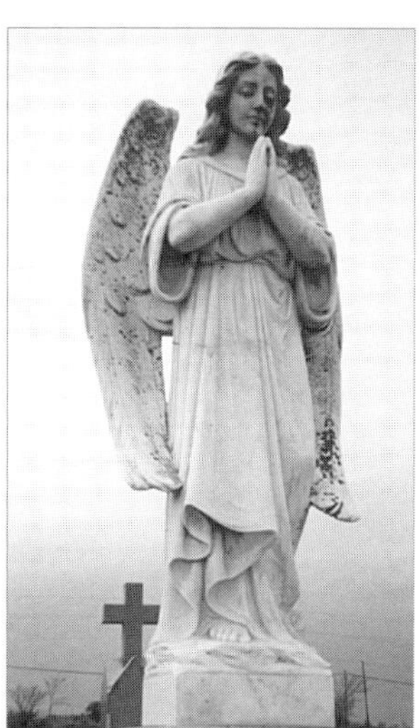

Nicolet Memorial Gardens

2800 Bay Settlement Road

Christ

White marble, located in center garden

Four Evangelists

White marble, located in south garden

Good Shepherd

White marble, located on front
building facade

Good Shepherd

White marble, located on back
building facade

Pulaski

Jankowski Angel Memorial

Circa 1949
Stone, located at Polish National
Cemetery, Chase Road and Highway 32

CALUMET

Brillion

Spirit of Life

Fiore de Henriquez
Dedicated 1984
Bronze, located in front of the
Airens Company Office, Highway 10

Chilton

Civil War Monument

1902
Granite, 16 feet high, located at the
County Courthouse, 206 Court Street

Jericho

Madonna

Richard Groh
1985
Indiana limestone, located at
Holy Trinity Church, on County H

Sherwood

↗ High Cliffs Effigy Mounds

High Cliffs State Park, located on the
eastern shoreline of Lake Winnebago,
contains animal and geometric
shaped effigy mounds

Religious Father

Al Deber
Circa 1985
Found objects attached to metal,
located at The Highcliff Studio,
398 N. Military Road

DOOR

Baileys Harbor

Blessed Virgin in Prayer

Stone, located at St. Mary of the Lake
Catholic Church, Highway 42 and
Main Street

Brussels

Saint Francis Xavier Grotto

Father Gloudemans
Dedicated October 29, 1935
Mixed media, located at Church of
St. Francis Xavier, off Highway 57

Ephraim

Collection of Animals

Fiberglass, 15-foot fiberglass animals,
located in the Metro One Gallery
outdoor courtyard

Paul Bunyan and Babe

Elmer Winter
1986
Painted car bumpers, located on
Orchard Road

Fish Creek

Peninsula Art School

County F, north of Fish Creek

Jumping Angel

Cast bronze

Hay Claw

Elmer Winter
1986
Painted and mounted farm implement

Shield

Bill Little
1991
Painted steel

A Saint

Ranier Sturgis
Cast bronze

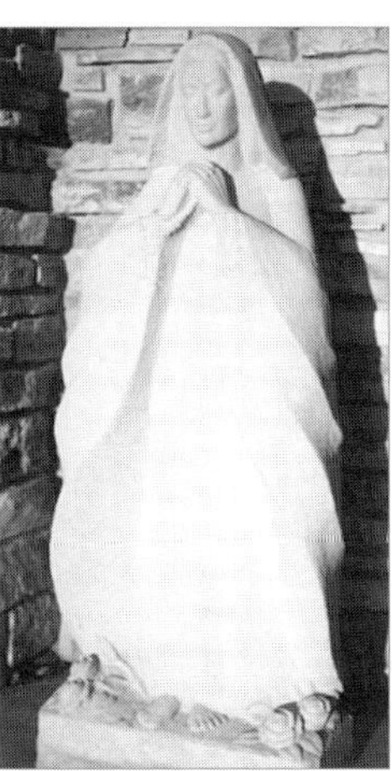

Spirit of Life in Brillion

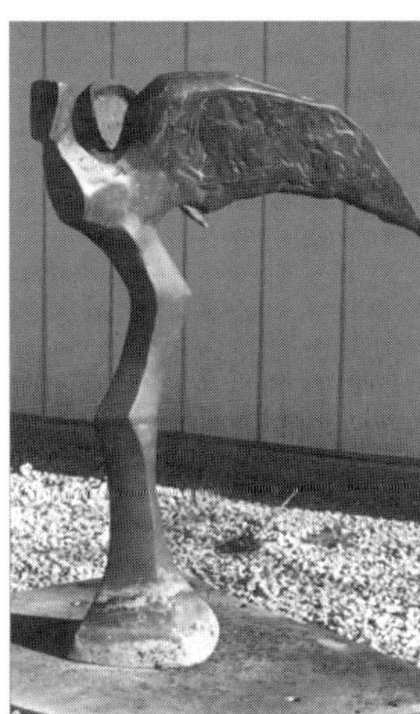

Jankowski Angel Memorial
in Pulaski

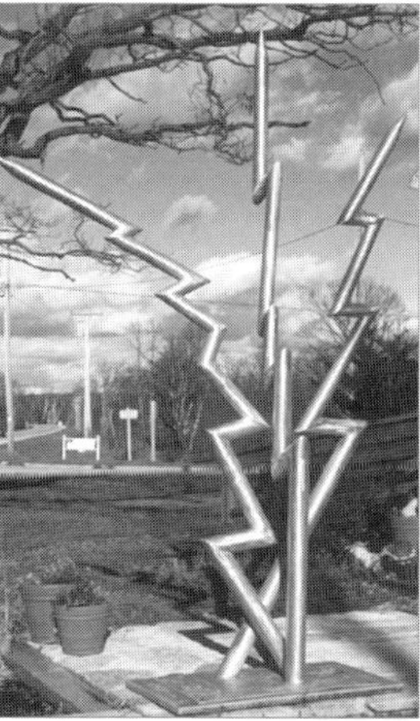

Madonna in Jericho

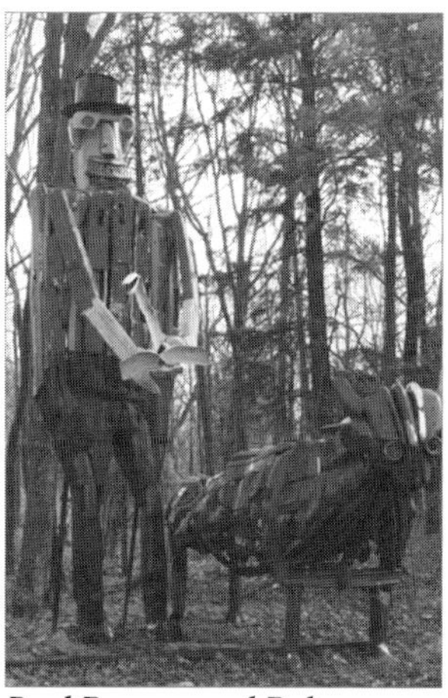

Jumping Angel at Peninsula
Art School, Fish Creek

You're Out. . .You're In
in Juddville

Paul Bunyan and Babe
in Ephraim

Institute

The Sacred Heart of Jesus
Circa 1931
Concrete, located at St. Peter and
St. Paul Catholic Church, corner of
Highway 57 and Dunn Road

Juddville

You're Out. . .You're In
John Slavik
1997
Polished aluminum, 12 feet high
located at Woodwalk Gallery,
Highway 42

Sister Bay

Sister Bay Memorial
Stone, located in Sister Bay
Village Park

Two Vikings
Jeff Prust
Wood, chain saw art, located at
the Scandinavian Lodge

Washington Island

Washington Island Memorial
Limestone, located in front of
courthouse

FLORENCE

Florence

State Basketball / Track Statue
1986 Basketball, 1998 Track
Wood and fiberglass, located at
junction of Highways 141 and 70

Statue of St. Mary
Circa 1946
Cement, located at St. Mary's Church,
308 Florence Avenue

Peterson Memorial
1891
Granite, located at Woodlawn
Cemetery

FOND DU LAC

Fond du Lac

Civil War Monument
Cast iron obelisk, located in City Park
on S. Main Street

Fauna of Wisconsin
Boris Gilbertson
1935 building date, 1937 artwork date
11 limestone bas-reliefs, sponsored by
the WPA, located at S. Macy and
W. 1st Street

Grotesques
Richard Groh
1991
Bedford limestone, two reliefs located
at The Goldsmith's Shop, 177 S. Main

Guardian Angel with Child
Painted cast iron, located at
St. Mary's Academy on Highway 23

Sacred Heart of Jesus
Cast iron, located at St. Mary's
Academy on Highway 23

Spanish American War Monument
American Art Bronze Foundry,
Chicago
1936
Bronze, located at the corner of
W. Scott Street and Main Street

St. Joseph
Circa 1920
White stone, located at St. Joseph
Catholic Church, S. Marr and E. 2nd

UW-Fond du Lac

Abstract in Red
Jon Humleker
Circa 1990
Painted steel

Blue Abstract Shapes
Jon Humleker
Circa 1990
Painted steel

Canadian Geese
Welded copper

Linear Abstraction
Jon Humleker
Circa 1990
Steel

Migration
O.V. Shaffer
1968
Forged and welded brass

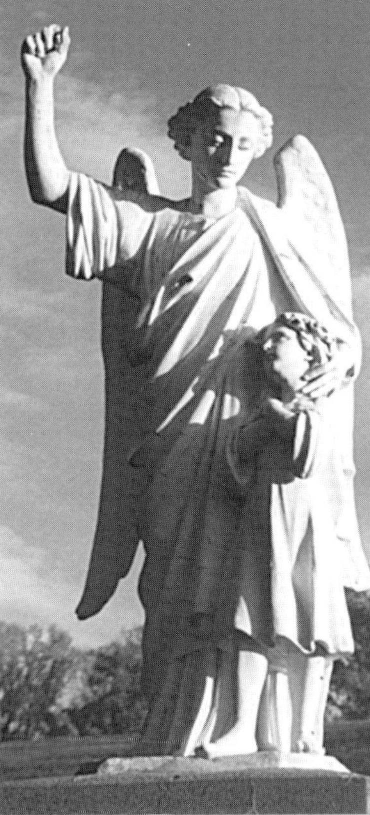

Guardian Angel with Child in Fond du Lac

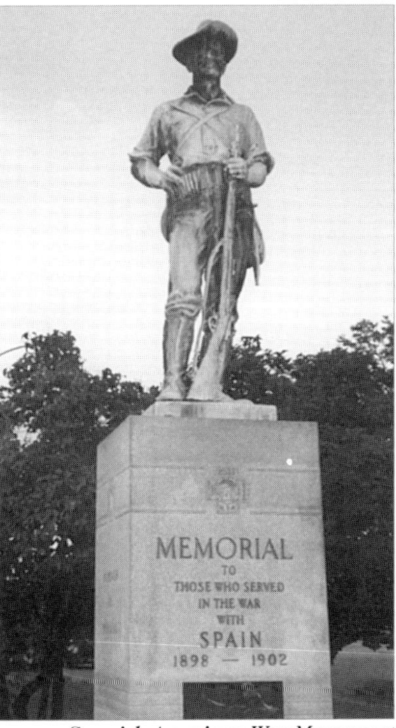

Spanish American War Monument
in Fond du Lac

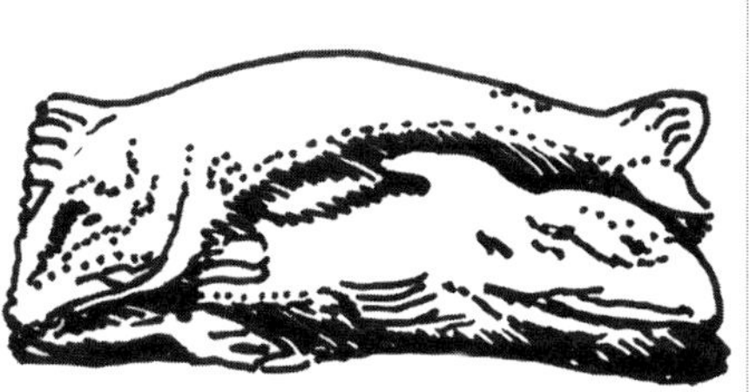

Fauna of Wisconsin sketch from Post Office
in Fond du Lac

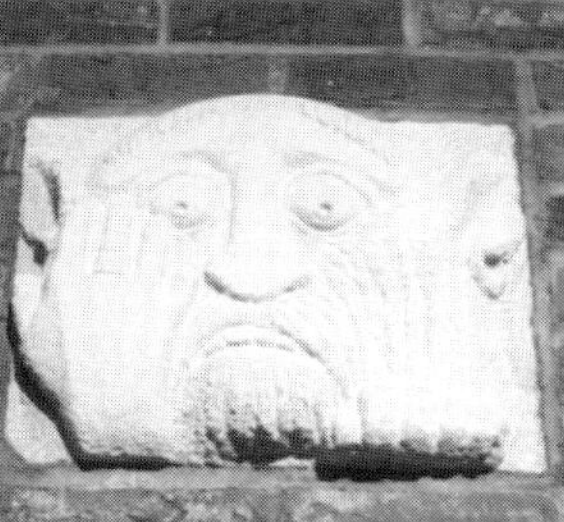

Grotesque in Fond du Lac

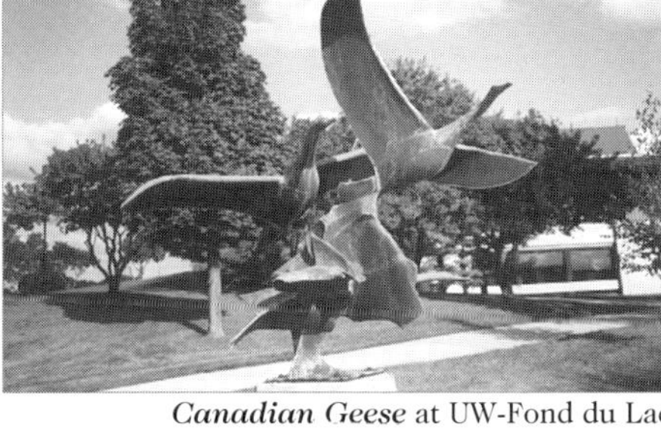

Canadian Geese at UW-Fond du Lac

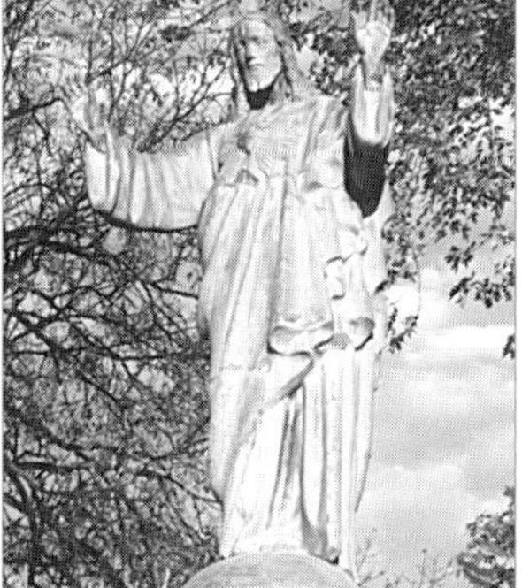

Sacred Heart of Jesus
in Fond du Lac

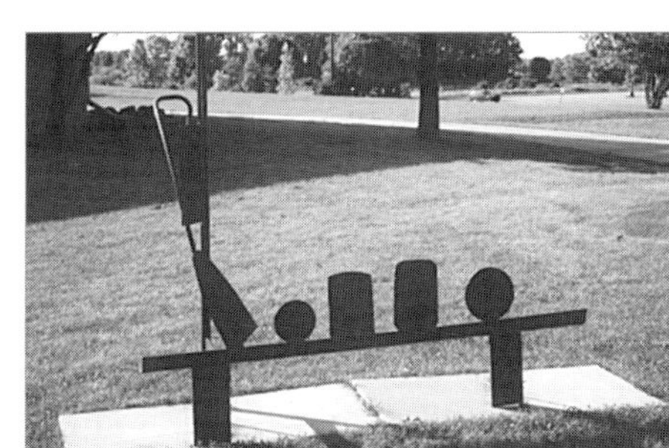

Linear Abstract at UW-Fond du Lac

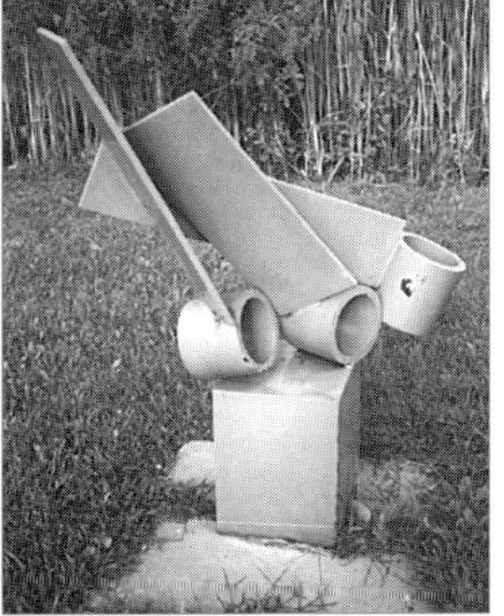

Blue Abstract Shapes
at UW-Fond du Lac

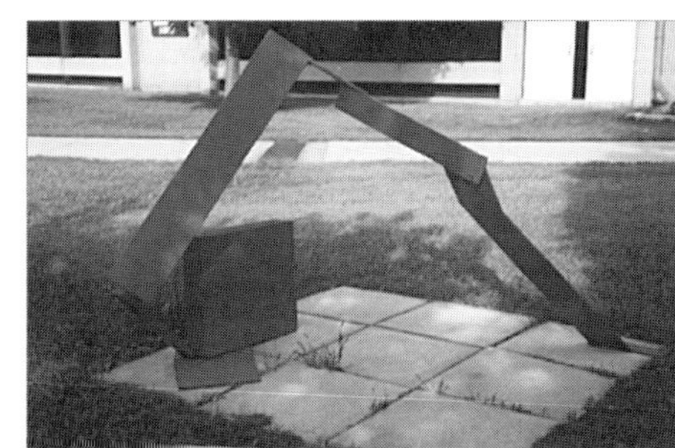

Abstract in Red at UW-Fond du Lac

Also, the Civil War Monument image:

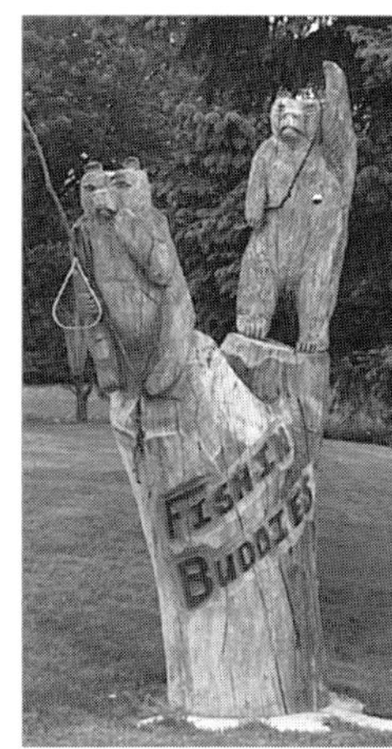

Fishin' Buddies
in Rosendale

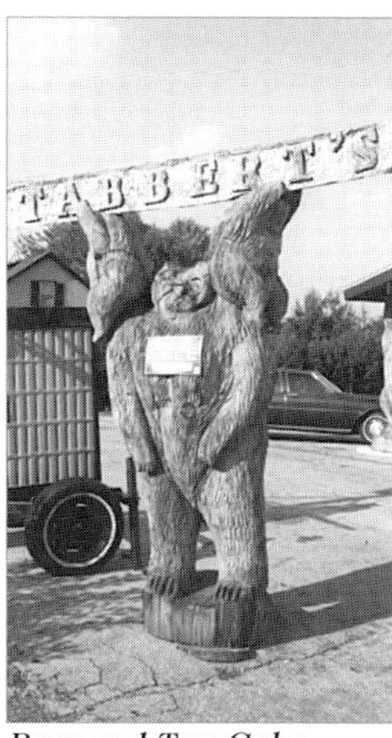

Bear and Two Cubs
in Rosendale

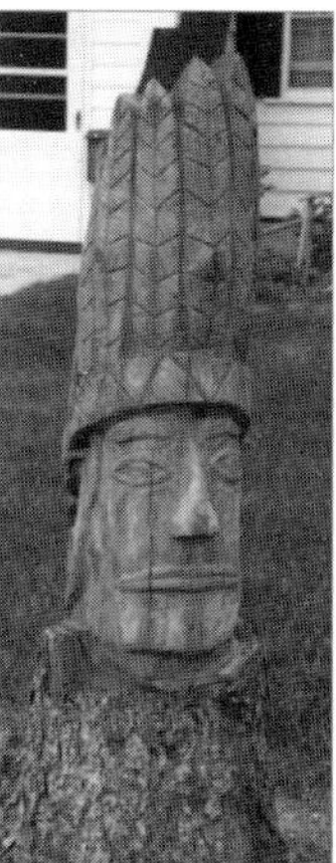

*Portrait of a
Native American*
in Kewaunee

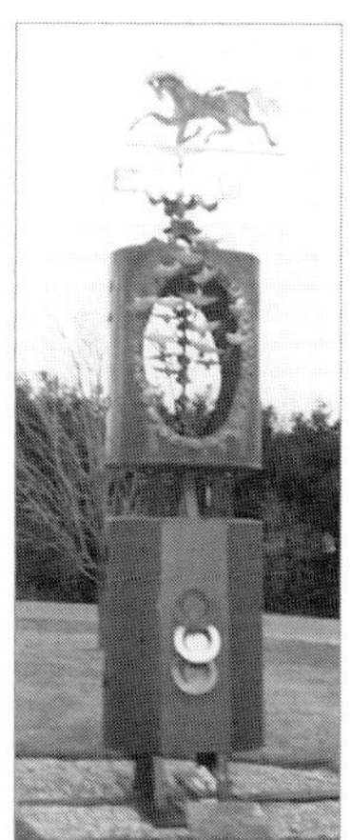

*Bird Haven
(Memorial to Ross
Spirgler)* in Ripon

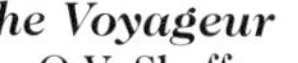

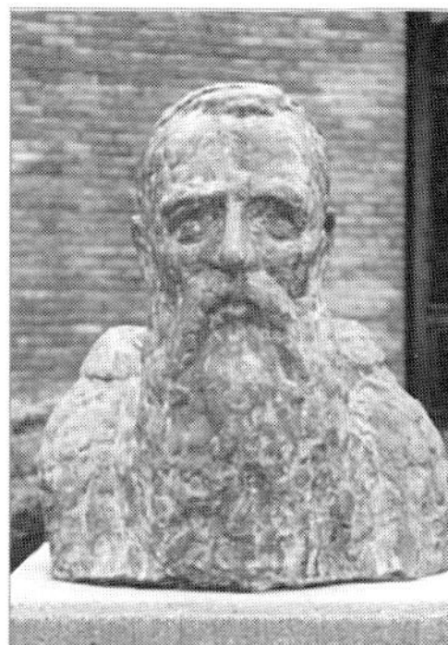

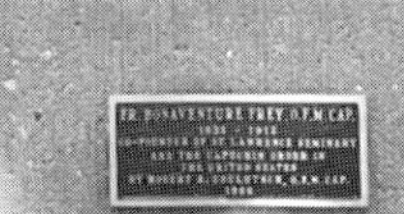

Father Frey at
St. Lawrence Seminary,
Mount Calvery

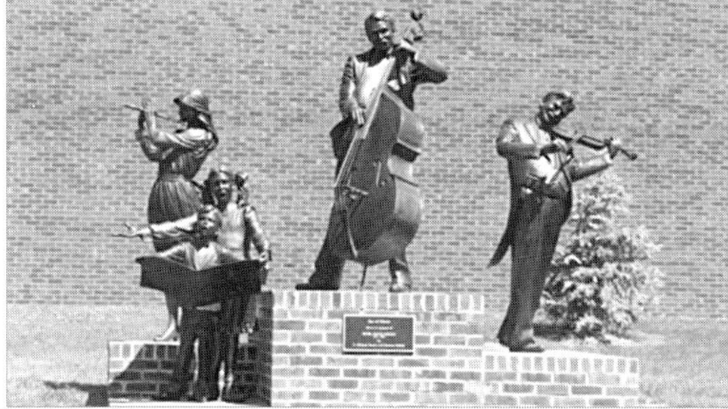

Joy of Music at Ripon College

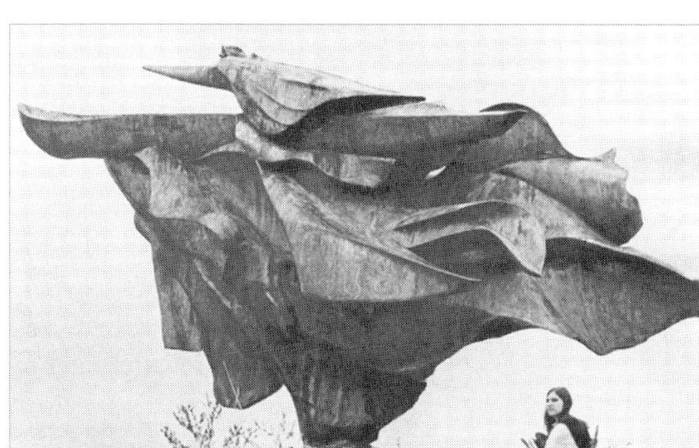

The Voyageur at UW-Fond du Lac

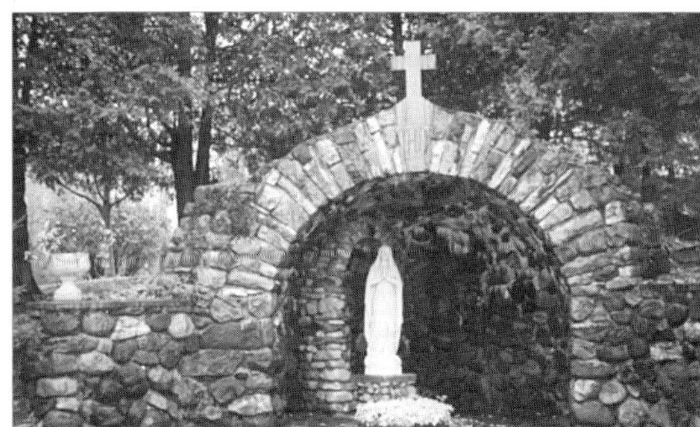

Grotto of the Virgin Mary in St. Cloud

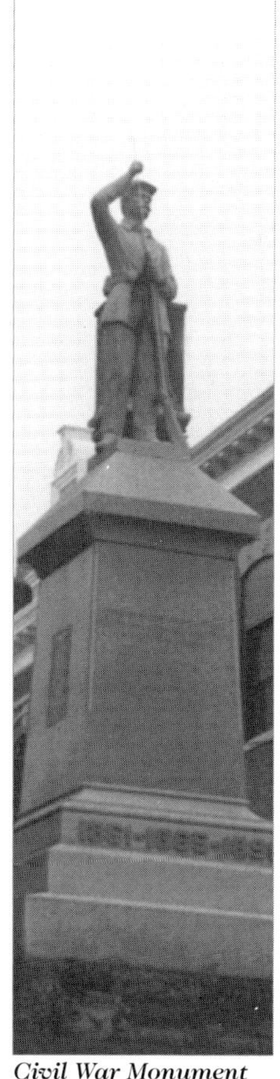

Civil War Monument
in Kewaunee

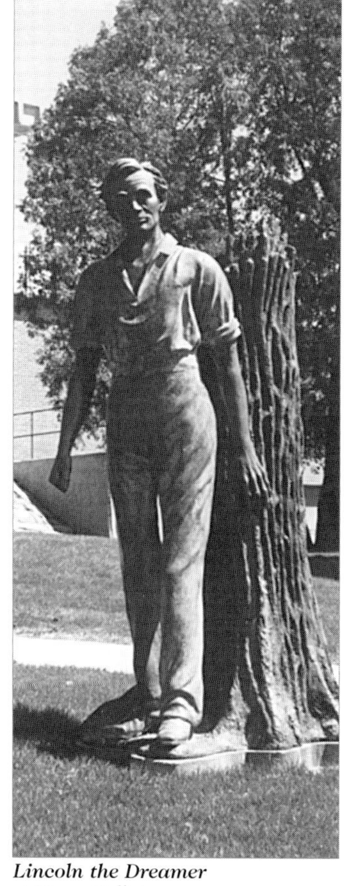

Lincoln the Dreamer
at Ripon College

The Voyageur
O.V. Shaffer
1968
Forged and welded brass

Untitled
Jon Humleker
Circa 1990
Painted red steel

Untitled Abstract
Jon Humleker
Circa 1990
Painted medium blue steel

Untitled Geometric Abstraction
Jon Humleker
Circa 1990
Painted steel

Untitled with Abstract Faces
Jon Humleker
Circa 1990
Painted red steel

Mount Calvary

St. Lawrence Seminary
Highway 149, important religious
site which contains many statues

Father Frey
Robert Udultsch
1966
Cast bronze

Father Haas
Robert Udultsch
1966
Cast bronze

Saint Joseph
Circa 1872
Carved limestone

14 Stations of the Cross
Painted plaster encased in glass

Ripon

Bird Haven (Memorial to Ross Spirgler)
Lester Schwartz
1994
Mixed media, metal, located at
615 W. Oshkosh Street

Untitled
Lester Schwartz
Seven metal sculptures, located at
615 W. Oshkosh Street

Ripon College

A Delicate Balancing Act
Robert Webster
1994
Welded steel, located on north lawn
of Rodman Center for the Arts

Being
Dennis Nechvatel
1993
Painted white metal and concrete,
located on east lawn of Rodman
Center for the Arts

Congruent Ribbons
Eugene Kain
1995
Stainless steel, located west of front
entrance, Rodman Center for the Arts

Genesis
Clarence Addison Shaler
1936
Bronze, located north of Seward
Street between Middle and West Hall

Gymnast II
Stephen J. Fischer
1987
Fabricated Corten steel, located on
south lawn of Rodman Center for the
Arts

Joy of Music
George Lundeen
1993
Bronze, located at the main entrance
of Rodman Center for the Arts

Lincoln the Dreamer
Clarence Addison Shaler
1939
Bronze, located north of Seward
Street, northwest of Farr Hall

Rosendale

Fishin' Buddies
Bear Holding up Roof
Bear and Two Cubs
Jim Kivela
Wood, chain saw art, located at
Tabbert's Restaurant, Highway 26

St. Cloud

Grotto to the Virgin Mary
Stone and concrete, located at
St. Cloud Catholic Church,
Highway 149

St. Peter Township

Grotto to Our Lady of Fatima
Circa 1940s
Concrete, stone, and painted statuary

FOREST

Crandon

Bear
Jim Tenant
1995
Wood, chain saw art, located three miles east of Crandon on Highway 8 and Bug Lake Road

Totem Pole
George F. Nemetz
Circa 1940s
Painted wood, located at Forest County Historical and Genealogical Society, 105 W. Jackson

WWI Veterans Memorial
Dedicated May 31, 1926
Wausau granite and bronze, located at Courthouse Square, 299 E. Madison Street

Sterling Heights

World Globe Veterans Memorial
Stephen E. Kanyusik with Northland Stainless Steel
Stainless steel, located at southwest corner of Courthouse Square, 200 E. Madison Street

Wabeno

Crucifix
Circa 1950
Metal, located north of Highway H on Cemetery Road

Larry the Logroller
Painted steel, cement, and plaster, located on Highway 32

KEWAUNEE

Algoma

Totem Pole
Painted wood, located on Highway 42
Removed from site

Kewaunee

Civil War Monument
Dedicated 1898
Granite, located at the Kewaunee County Courthouse

Kubule Memorial with Stations of the Cross
Painted concrete, located in the Holy Rosary Church Cemetery

Portrait of a Native American
Carved tree trunk

Virgin Mary with Star
White marble, located in front of Holy Rosary School

Pilsen

Crucifixion Grouping
Painted cast iron, located at St. Joseph Cemetery on Highway 29

LANGLADE

Antigo

Queen of Peace Cemetery
Aurora and 6th Avenue

Civil War Monument
Stone

Church Memorial
Cast Concrete

Dietl Memorial
Stone

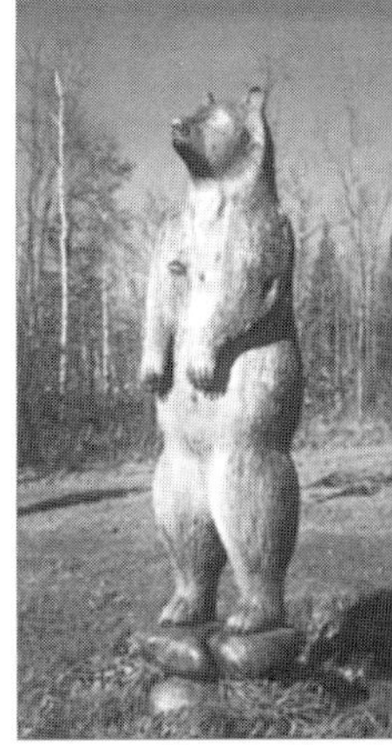

Bear in Crandon

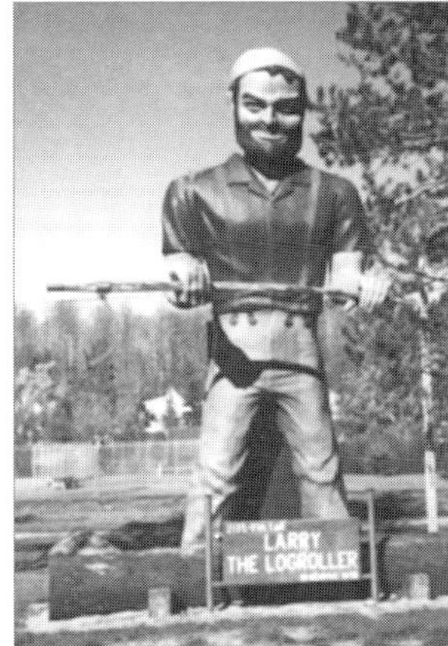

Larry the Log Roller in Wabeno

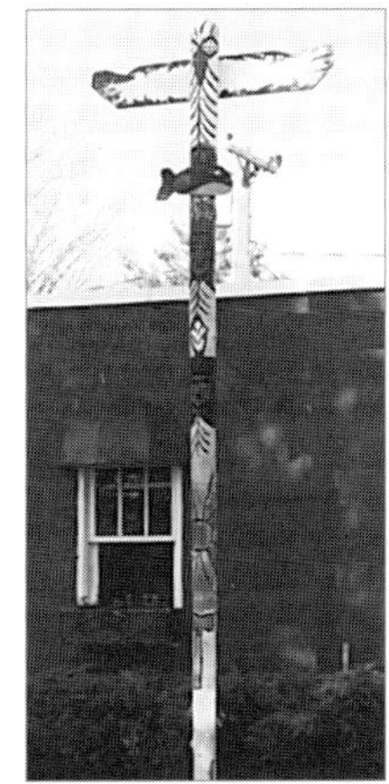

Totem Pole in Algoma

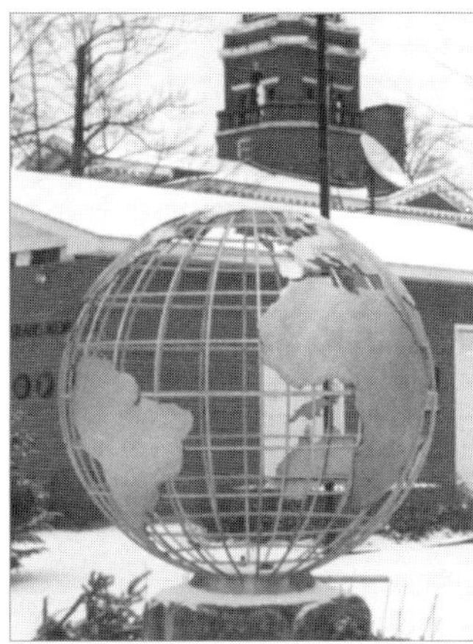

World Globe in Sterling Heights

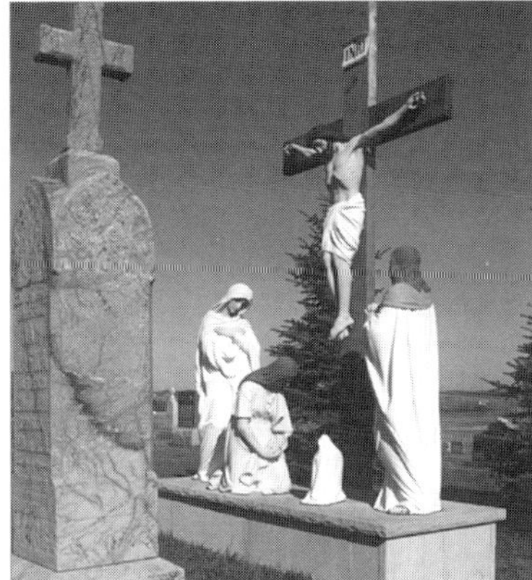

Crucifixion Group in Pilsen

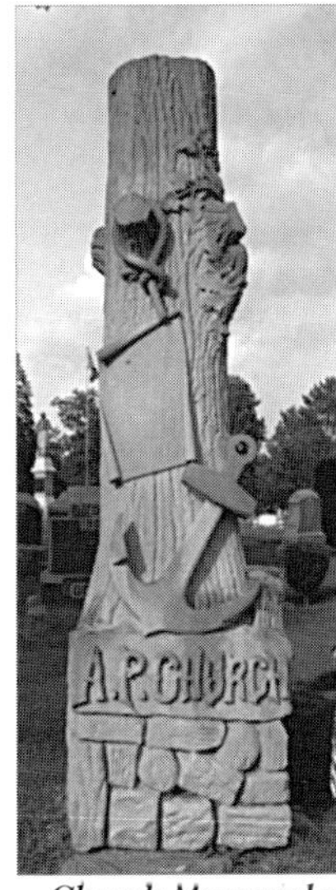

Church Memorial in Antigo

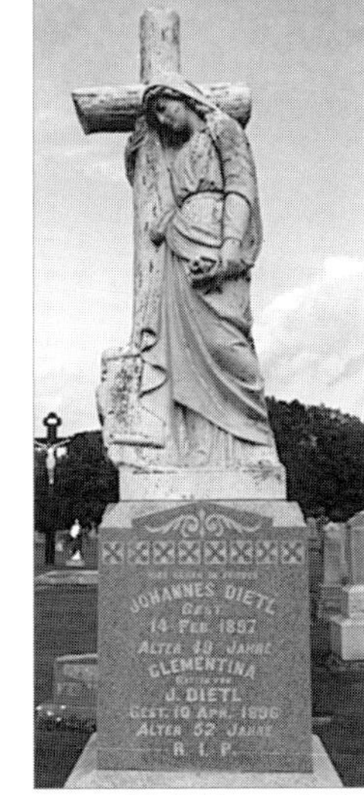

Dietl Memorial in Antigo

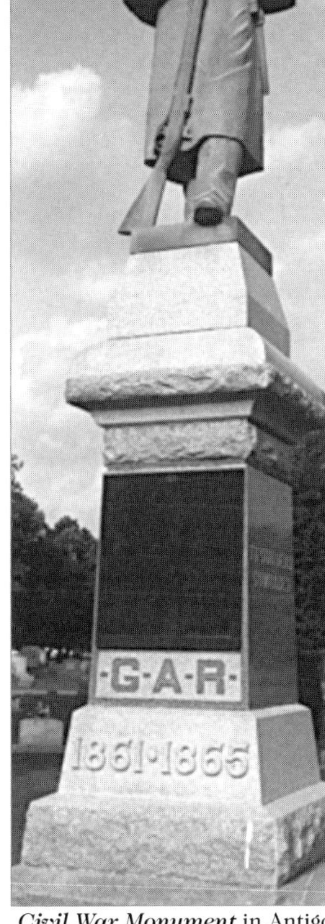

Civil War Monument in Antigo

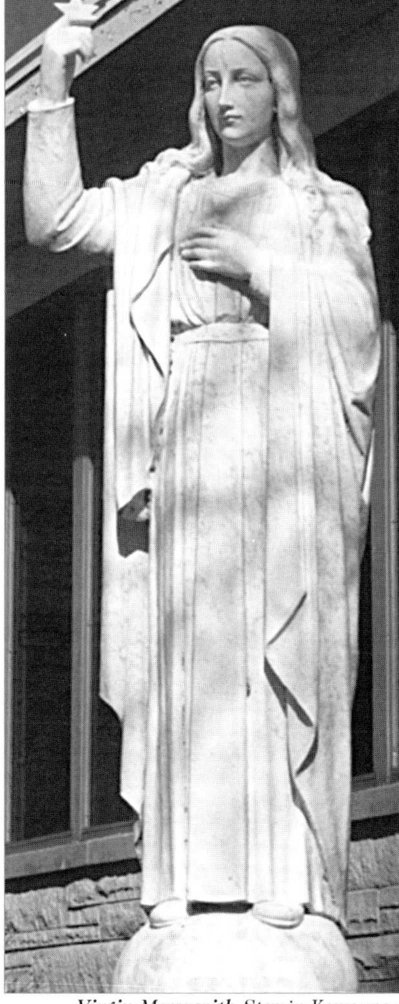

Virgin Mary with Star in Kewaunee

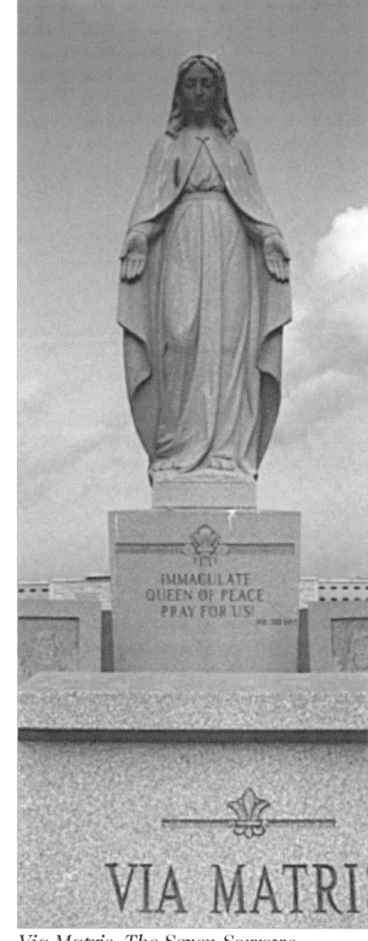

Via Matris, The Seven Sorrows of Mary in Antigo

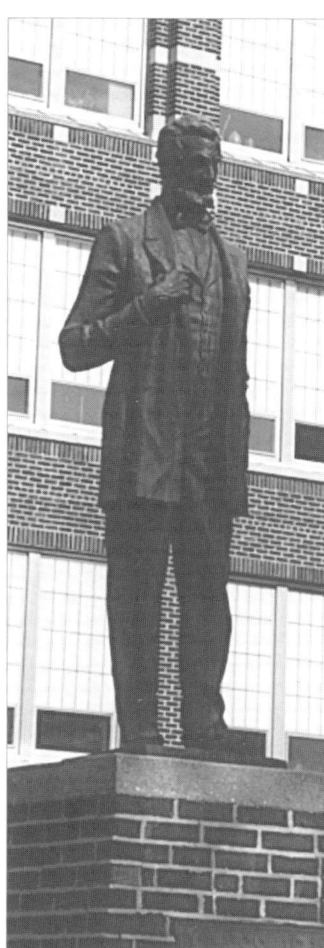

Abraham Lincoln in Manitowoc

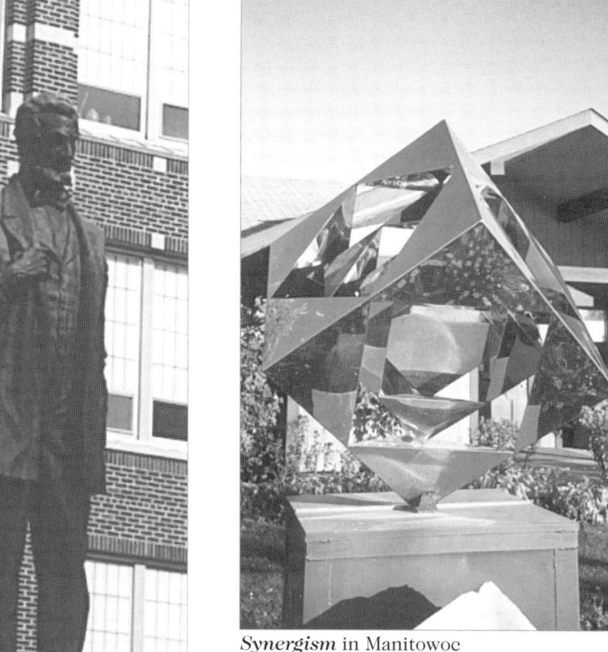

Synergism in Manitowoc

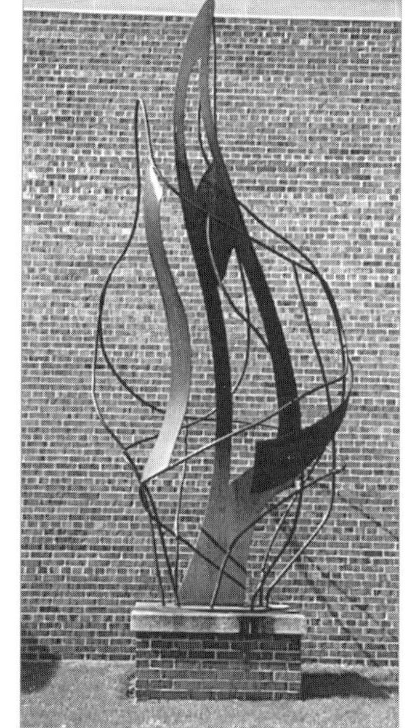

Flame of Knowledge in Manitowoc

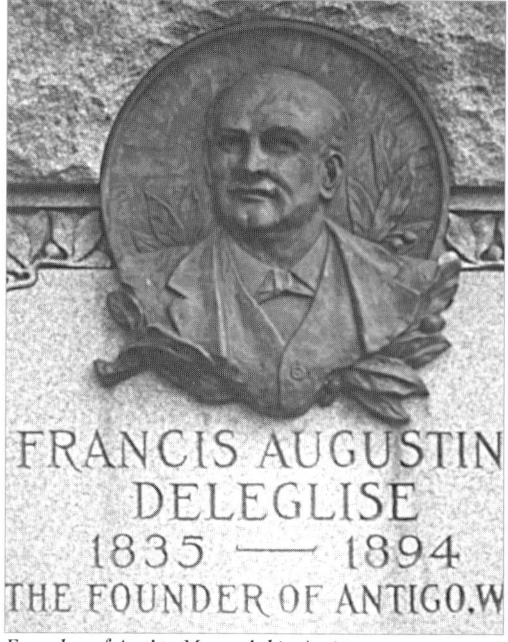

Founder of Antigo Memorial in Antigo

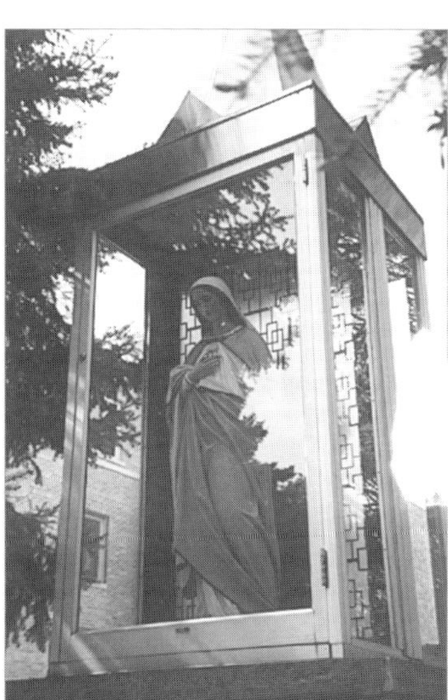

Blessed Virgin Mary in Manitowoc

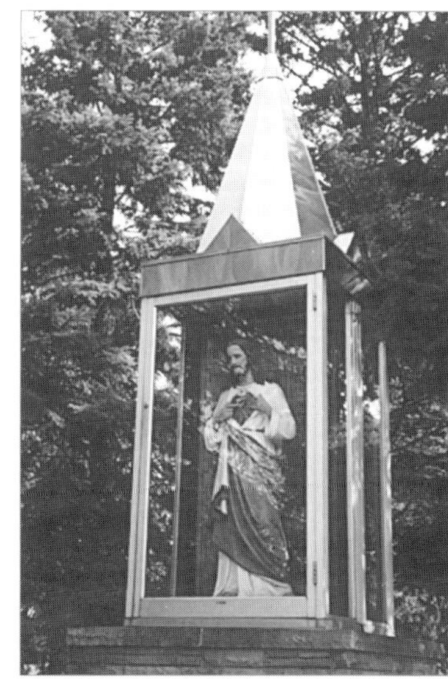

Sacred Heart of Jesus in Manitowoc

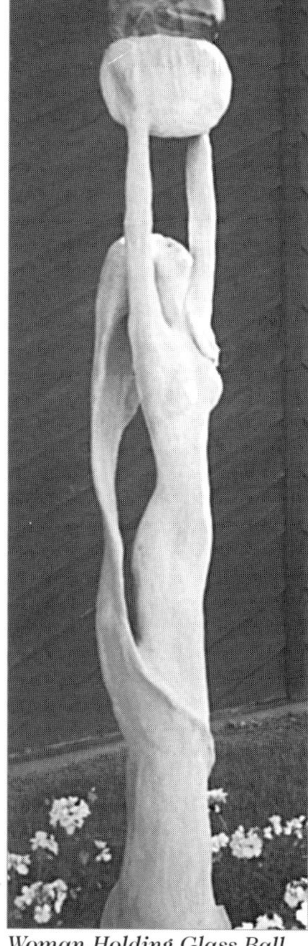

Woman Holding Glass Ball in Kiel

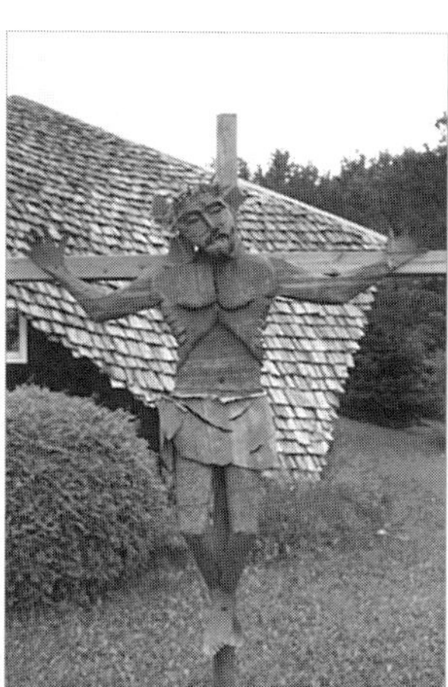

Art Environment (Christ) in Phlox

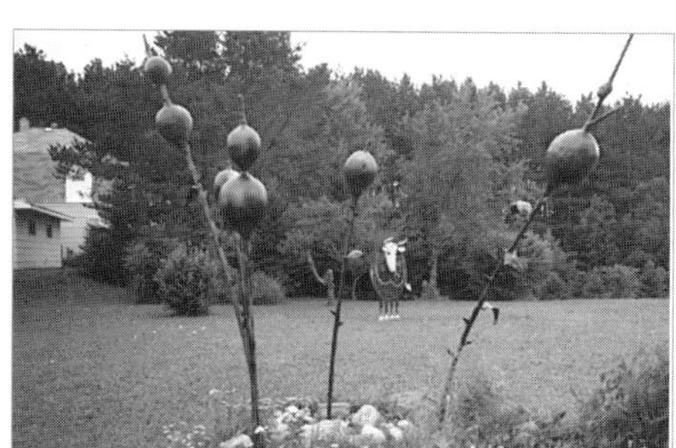

Art Environment (Seed Pods) in Phlox

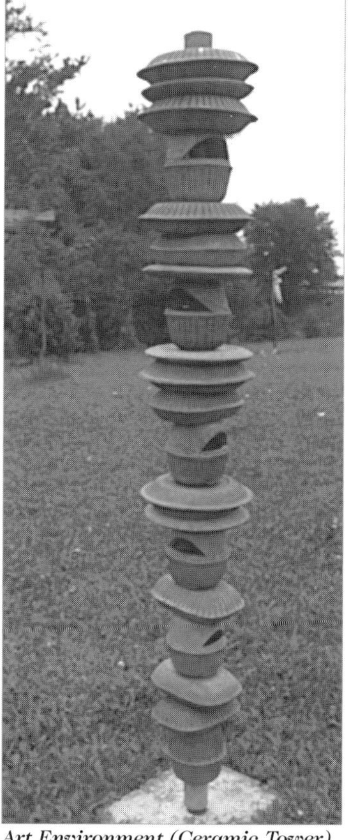

Art Environment (Ceramic Tower) in Phlox

Religious grouping
Painted metal

Via Matris, The Seven Sorrows of Mary
1957
Granite

Founder of Antigo, Francis Deleglise Memorial and Memory Mound
1979
Bronze and stone, located in front of Normal School building, corner of Milton and Superior streets

Vietnam Memorial
Granite, located in front of Langlade County Courthouse on Clairmont

Phlox

Art Environment
Mixed media collection of sculptures which include ceramic and wood towers, metal pod forms, metal cow form, and a mixed media Christ figure, located at W7429 Highway 47 on lawn of private residence, view from road

MANITOWOC

Kiel

Woman Holding Glass Ball
Jan Drees, sculpture &
John Abler, glass
Cement and glass, located at Abler Art Glass Gallery,
16205 Little Elkhart Lake Road

Manitowoc

Abraham Lincoln
Alice Schoenke
Given by class of 1961
Bronze cast by Americo Bastani Company, Italy, located at Lincoln High School, 1400 S. 8th

All Wars Veterans Monument Plaza
Circa 1995
Granite tablets and flag poles, located on Revere Drive near Michigan and 18th streets

Flame of Knowledge
Corroded steel, was located in front of the Manitowoc Public Library and moved to Silver Lake College.

Guernsey Cow
Fiberglass, located at Cedar Crest Ice Cream, 2000 S. 10th Street

Seated Woman
B. Lucchesi
1990
Cast bronze, located in the courtyard of the Rahr West Art Museum, North 8th Street

Soldiers and Sailors Monument
1923 colonnade with eternal flame
Granite, located on Revere Drive, at the corner of Michigan and 18th streets

Synergism
William Severson
1980
Stainless steel, located at Manitowoc Chamber of Commerce, 1515 Memorial Drive

St. Boniface
1985
White marble, located at St. Boniface Catholic Church, 10th and Marshall streets

The Apparition at Fatima
White Italian marble (Pietrasanta) grouping, located at Holy Innocents Catholic Church, 1500 block of Waldo Boulevard

Virgin Mary
Sacred Heart of Jesus
Painted plaster, located at St. Mary's Convent, 2200 Division Street

Virgin Mary with Christ Child
Concrete, located at St. Mary's Home for the Aged, 2200 Division Street

Knollwood Memorial Park
Highway 310 west of Manitowoc/Two Rivers

Christ
Christ in the Garden
Four Evangelists
Last Supper
The Praying Hands
All Pietrasanta, white Italian marble

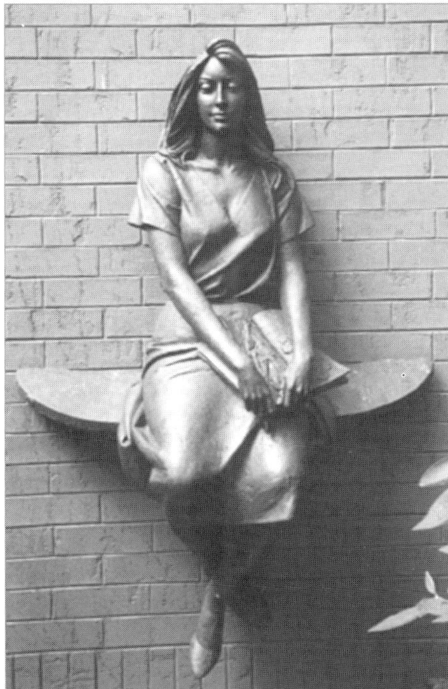

Seated Woman in Manitowoc

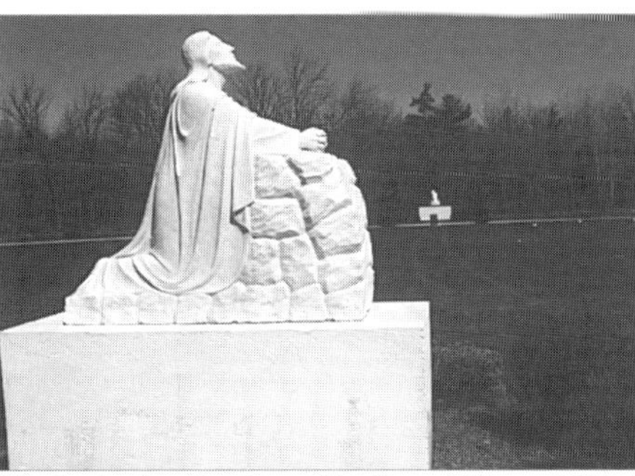

Christ in the Garden at Knollwood Memorial Park near Manitowoc

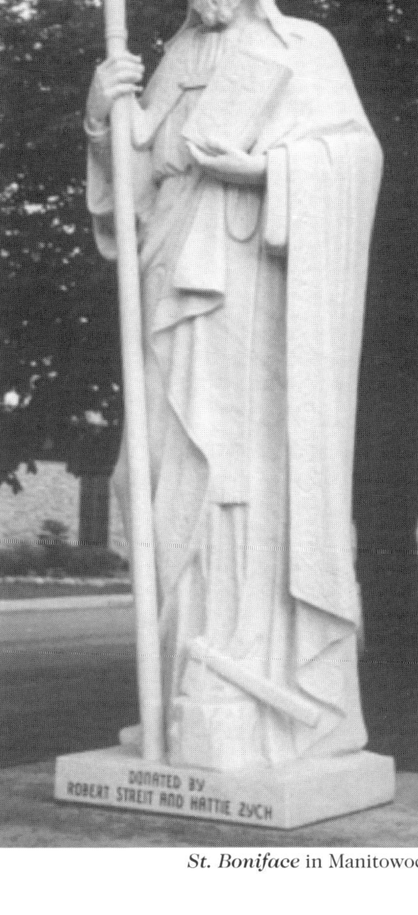

St. Boniface in Manitowoc

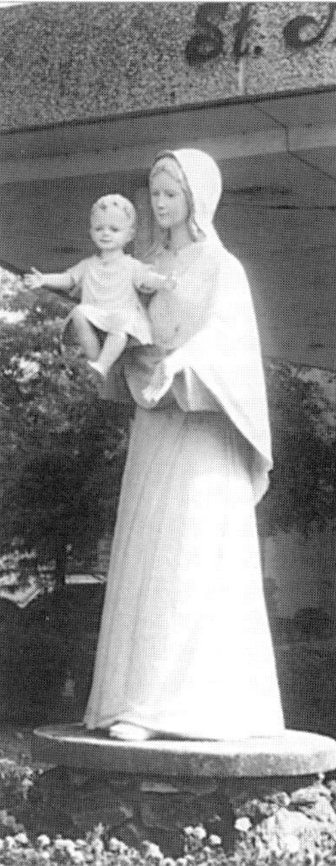

Virgin Mary with Christ Child in Manitowoc

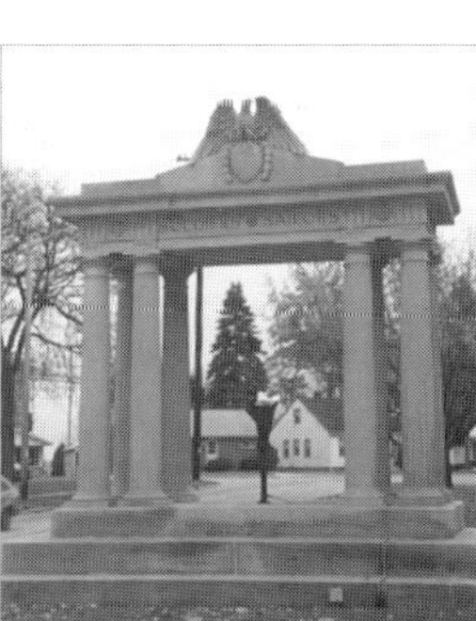

Soldiers and Sailors Monument in Manitowoc

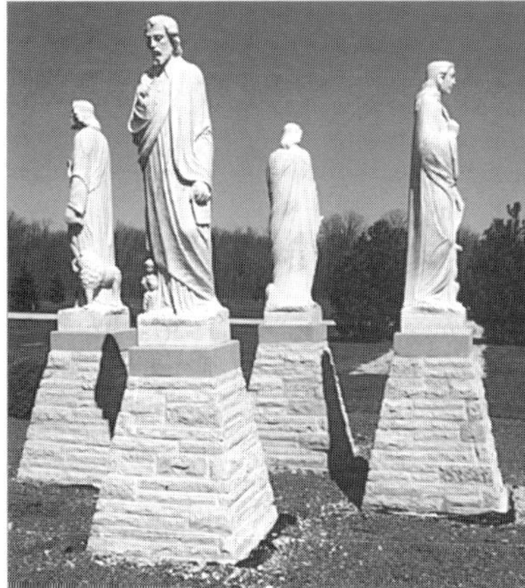

Four Evangelists at Knollwood Memorial Park near Manitowoc

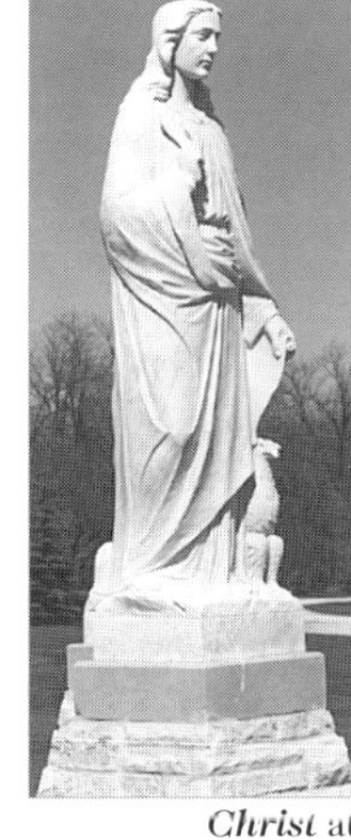

Christ at Knollwood Memorial Park

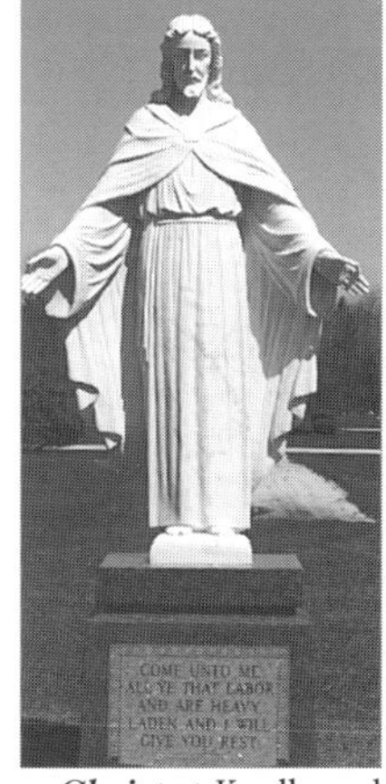

Christ at Knollwood Memorial Park near Manitowoc

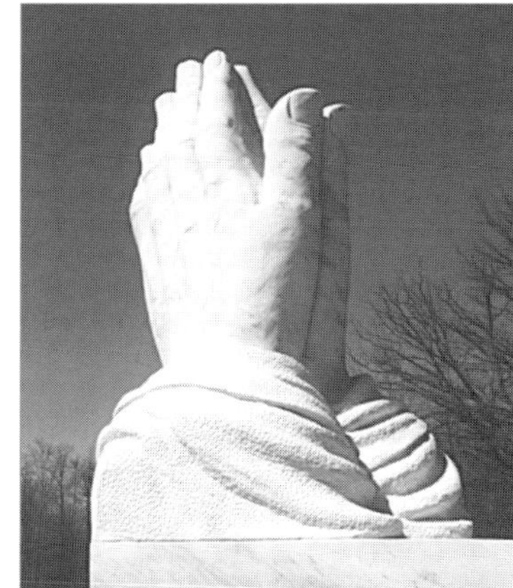

Praying Hands at Knollwood Memorial Park near Manitowoc

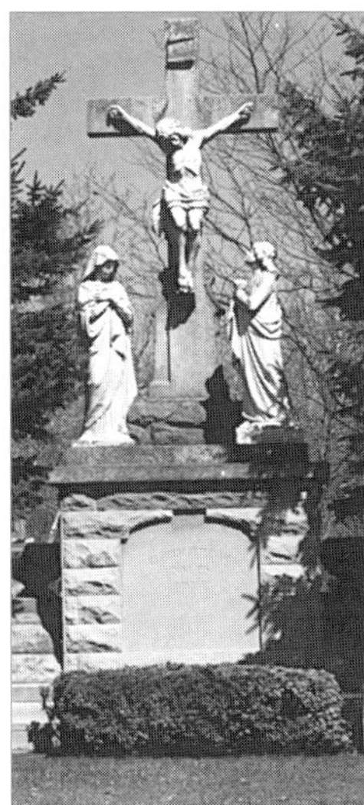

Christ at Calvary
in Whitelaw

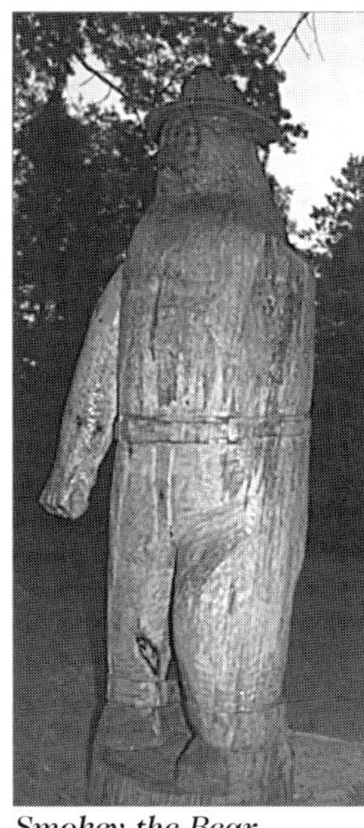

Smokey the Bear
in Keshena

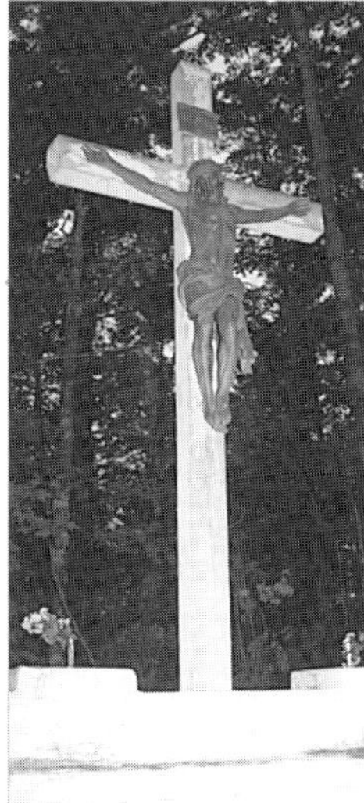

Christ on the Cross
in Neopit

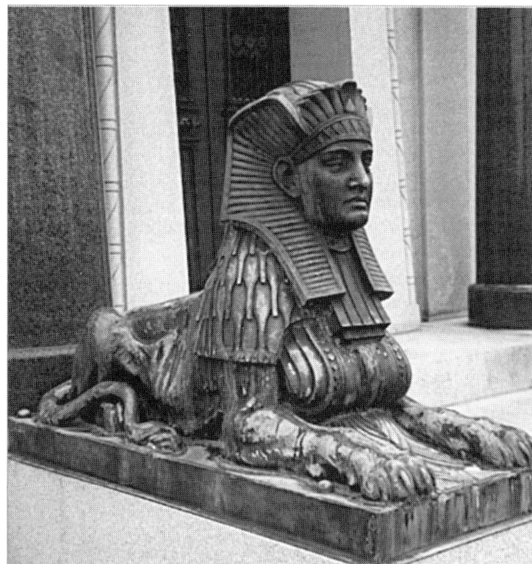

Sphinx in Two Rivers

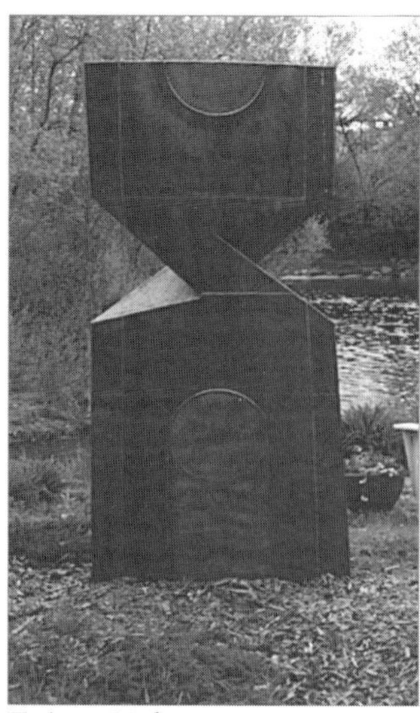

Twist in Mishicot

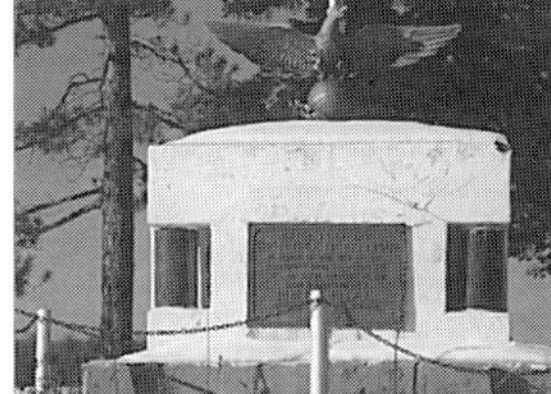

Goodman War Memorial
in Goodman

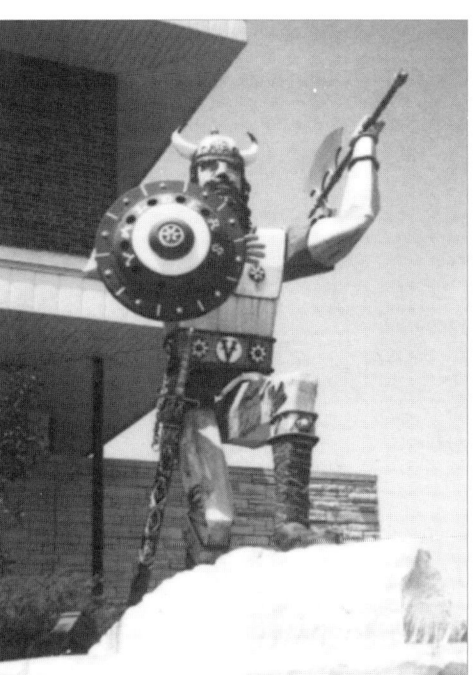

Valders Viking in Valders

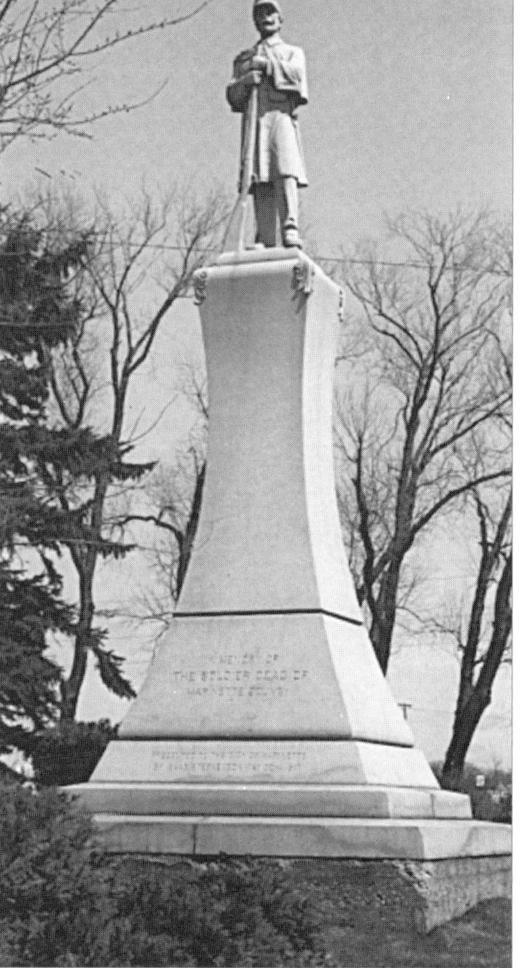

Civil War Monument in Marinette

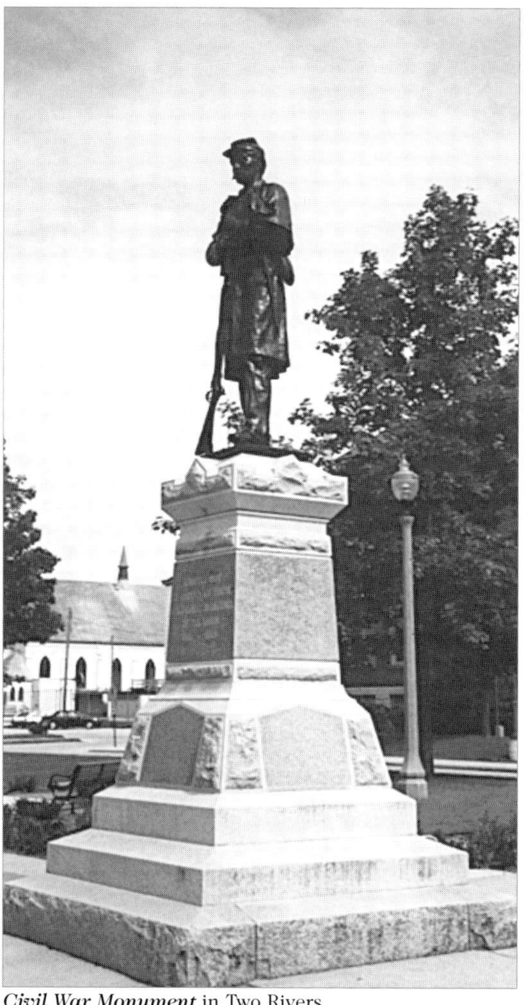

Civil War Monument in Two Rivers

Mishicot

Twist
> Narendra Patel
>
> Circa 1980
> Fabricated copper with surface colors achieved by heat treating, located at the River Edge Galleries Sculpture Garden

St. Nazianz

Several Religious Grottoes dedicated to St. Nazians, Christ, Virgin Mary, and Our Lady of Lourdes
> Mixed media, located at the former Catholic Seminary on County Trunk A, 206 Church. Statues Removed

Two Creeks

Untitled Door Relief
> 1971
> Oak relief, located at Two Creeks Nuclear Plant, Information and Education Building front door

Two Rivers

Civil War Monument
> 1900
> Copper sheeting, located at Central Park, Highway 42

Sphinxes
> Cast bronze, located at Pioneer Rest Cemetery, Forest Avenue, Vaghardt Mausoleum

Valders

Valders Viking
> F.A.S.T. Jerry Vetterus
> Painted fiberglass, located at Valders High School

Whitelaw

Christ at Calvary
> Stone, located at Street Michaels Cemetery on Highway 10

MARINETTE

Beaver

Veterans Memorial
Stone and concrete, located on Town Hall grounds

Goodman

Goodman War Memorial
1919
Concrete, granite, and bronze, located in Goodman Park across from the Town Hall

Marinette

Civil War Soldier Memorial
Granite, located on Stephanson Island

Soldiers Monument
Stone and metal, located in Forest Home Cemetery

Marinette County Veterans Memorial
Stone and brick, located downtown

Peshtigo

WW I Dough Boy
Copper, located at Peshtigo Riverside Cemetery

MENOMINEE

Keshena

Smokey the Bear
Wood, about 12 feet tall, located at Hilary J. Waukau Sr. Forestry and Environmental Resources Center, 1 mile west of town on Highway 47

Neopit

Christ on the Cross
Bronze, wood, concrete, located at St. Anthony Cemetery west of town on Highway 47

OCONTO

Oconto

Christ on the Cross
Metal and wood, located at cemetery

Nicolas Perrot Monument
R.W. Fries
Park completed in 1983
Large mound of field stone in shape of a cone, located in Donlevy Park on Main Street

O'Keef Child's Memorial
Circa 1921
Marble, located at St. Joseph and St. Peter Catholic Cemetery

Oconto Falls

Oconto County Veterans Monument
Mixed media, located at Oconto County Courthouse, 301 Washington Street

OUTAGAMIE

Appleton

Appleton Aurora
Dale Eldred
1989
Embossed aluminum sealed in glass solar sculpture, located atop the Appleton Center and best viewed driving north across the Skyline Bridge

Fox River Oracle
Dimitri Hadzi
Dedicated June 12, 1987
Dolomite and limestone monumental work, located on the north side of Appleton's Skyline Bridge near city center

Indian Statue
James Chadek
Circa 1930
Wood, located at Pierce Park

Metamorphosis
Richard C. Wolter
1985
Painted steel, located in Houdini Plaza, downtown and dedicated to artist/magician Harry Houdini

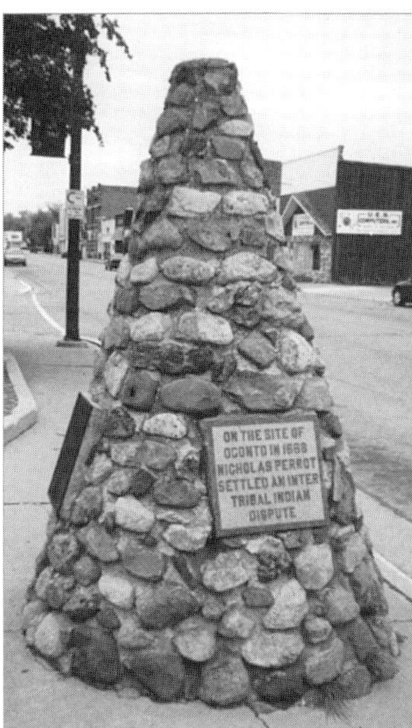
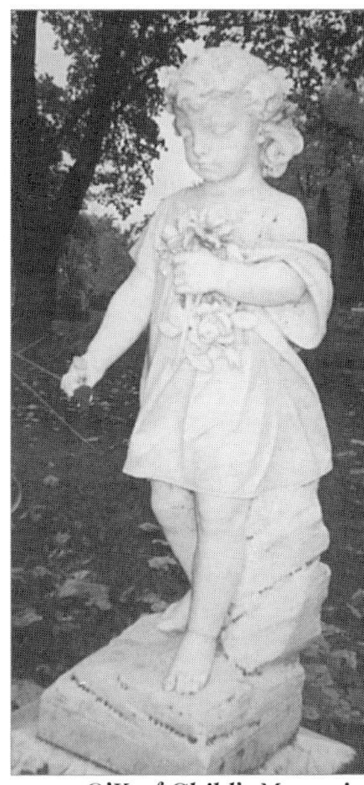
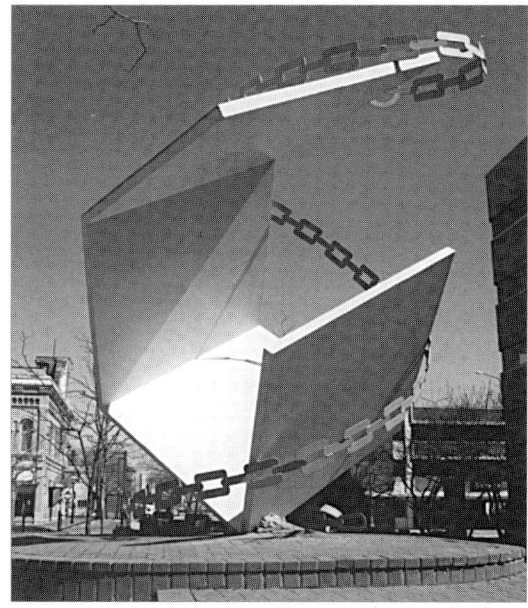

Nicolas Perrot Monument in Oconto

O'Keef Child's Memorial in Oconto

Metamorphosis in Appleton

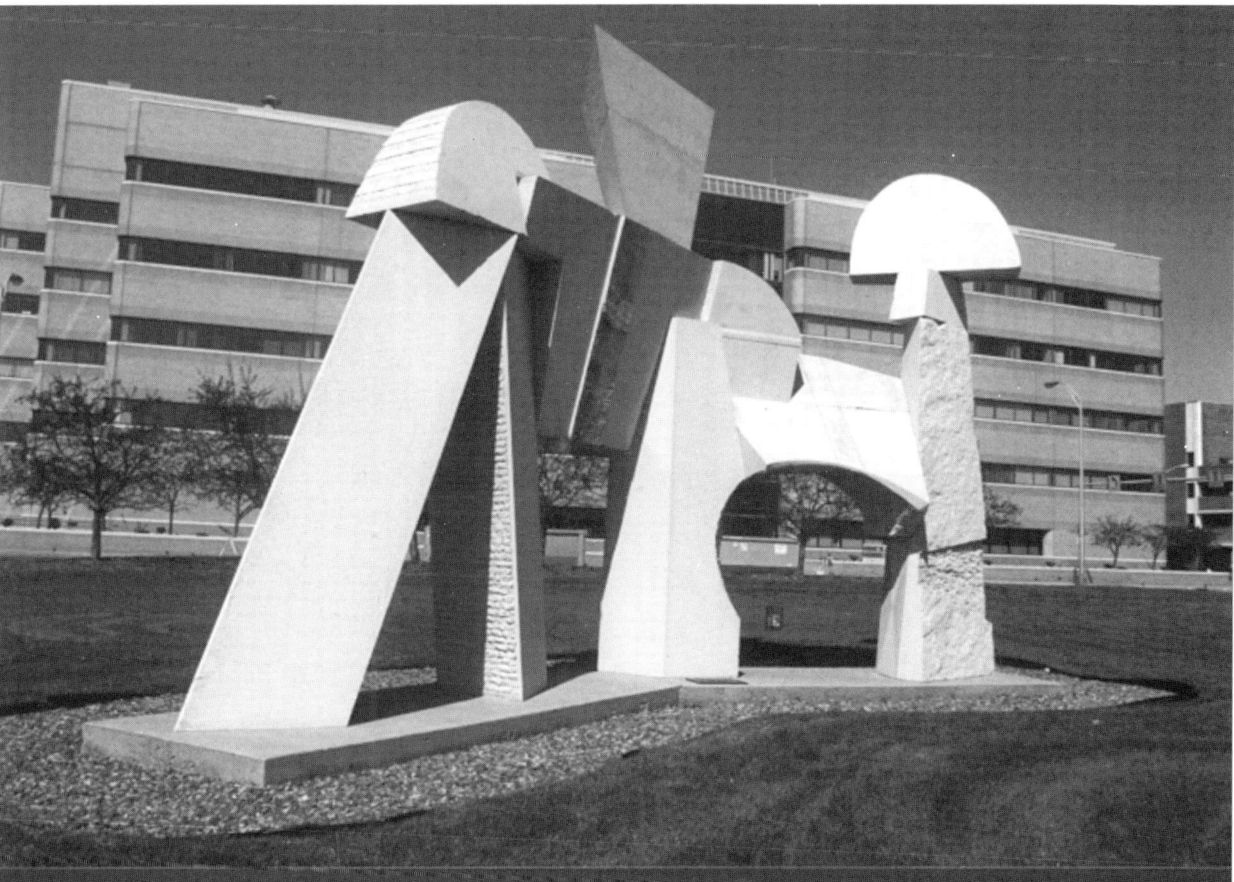

Fox River Oracle in Appleton

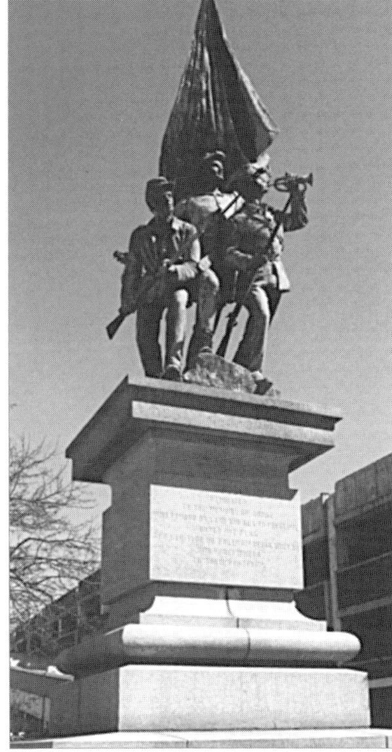

Soldiers' Square Monument in Appleton

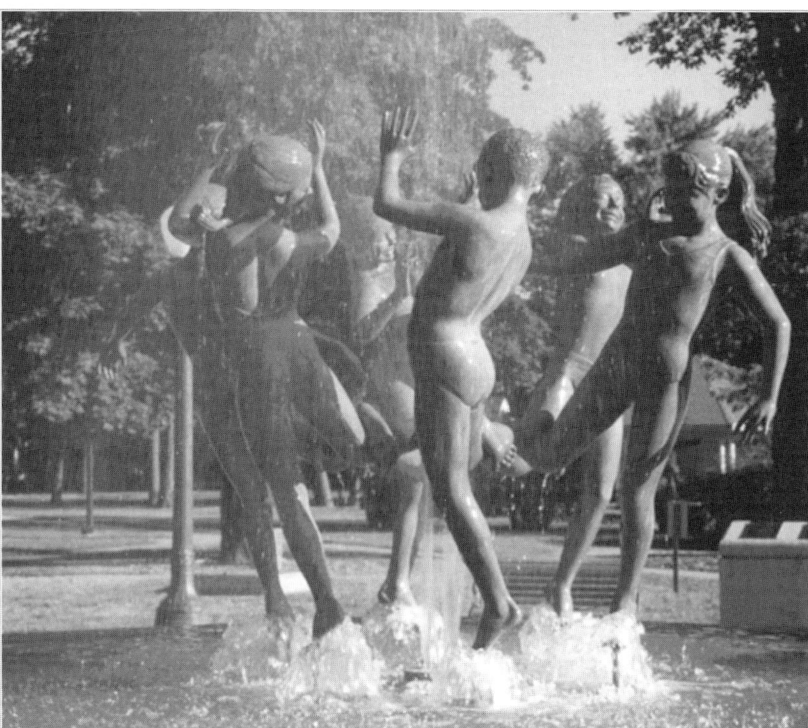

Ring Dance in Appleton

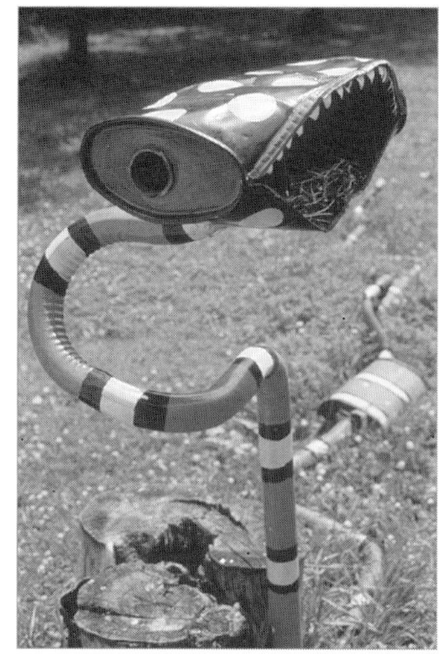

Look Out Jack in Appleton

Soldiers' Square Monument
Chevalier Gaerano Trentavone
Dedicated 1911
Bronze, commissioned by Post No. 133 of the Grand Army of the American Republic, located on the 100 block of North Oneida Street

Spirit of the American Doughboy
Dedicated 1934
Metal, located on Memorial Drive

Red and Black
Look Out Jack
Blue and Yellow
No Danger Fellow
Steve Ballard
1991 / 1994
Four assemblages of painted mufflers, tailpipes, and suspension springs, located at 915 E. Sunset Avenue

Ring Dance
Dallas Anderson
1993
Bronze figures in fountain, located at City Park

Totem Pole
Tim Britton
White oak, located at Peabody Park

Untitled Arches
Ted Sutheri
Three steel arches and six towers, located at Telulah Park

Lawrence University

Four Abstract Forms
Constantine Nivola
Concrete, made for McCormick Place, Chicago, Illinois, rescued and brought to Lawrence University after the January 16, 1967 fire

Self Portrait
Kimberly Clarke Robinson
1988
Bronze, located west past Ornsby Hall over the Drew Street walkway

Untitled Fountain
Rolf Westphal
Stainless steel and glass, located on the north side of the Wriston Art Center

Untitled Monumental Hockey Sticks
Painted steel, located at the entrance to the Union

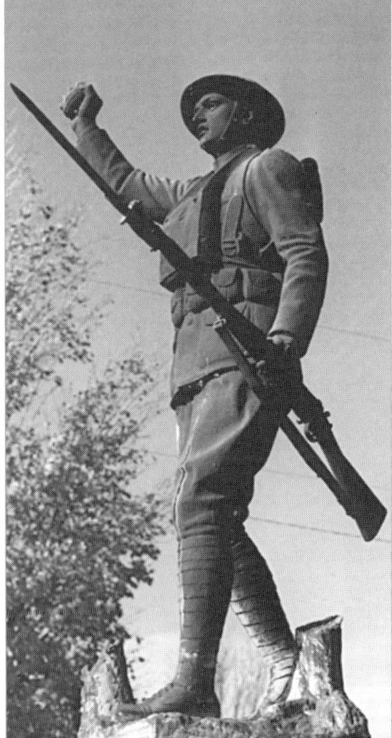

Spirit of the American Doughboy in Appleton

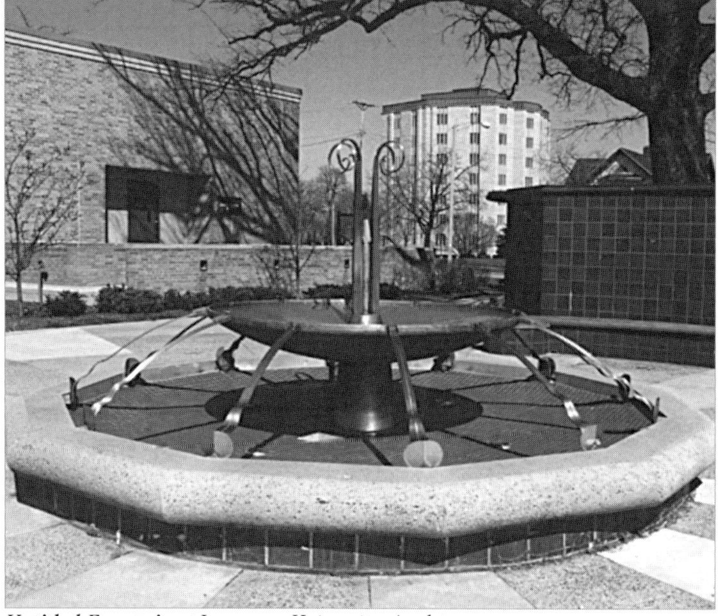

Untitled Fountain at Lawrence University, Appleton

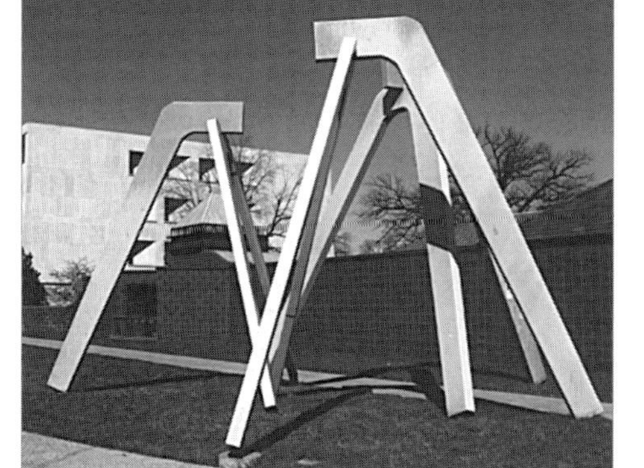

Four Abstract Forms at Lawrence University, Appleton

Untitled Monumental Hockey Sticks at Lawrence University, Appleton

UW-Fox Valley campus

Centerspan
Jeffrey Boshart
Wood, cement, and steel, located at edge of campus

Eyeman
Bob Pruchnofski
Welded steel

Kaukauna

Family and Friends
James Hupfensperger
Dedicated 1996
Bronze grouping of eight pieces, located at the trailhead for the Fox River Locks Trail off Wisconsin Avenue

Fessbender Crock
Stone, located across from the F&M Bank to commemorate the founder of Kaukauna Kulb Cheese

Soldier and Sailors Monument
Fox River Valley Marble and Granite Works
1918
Granite, located at Lawe Park, Lawe and Catherine streets

Kimberly

Kimberly Veterans Memorial
Granite, located at 515 W. Kimberly Avenue

Seymour

Justice and Scale
Carved wood tree stump, located at Factory Street and Main Street

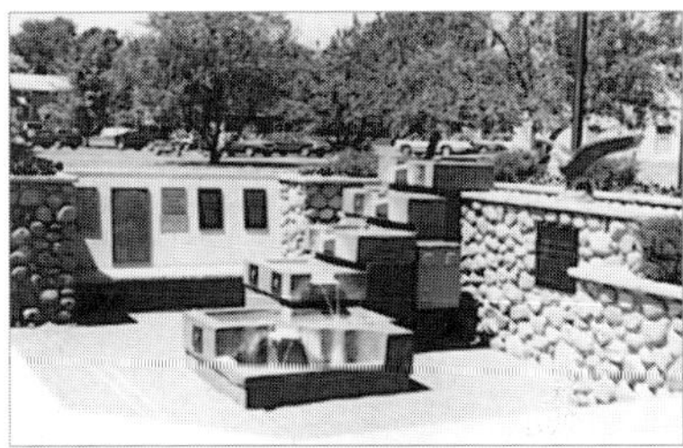
Kimberly Veterans Memorial
in Kimberly

SHAWANO

Birnamwood

Gigantic Badger Head
Gigantic Squirrel on Log
Painted concrete, located at the Badger Country Refuelling Station on Highway 45 north of town

Gigantic Chicken
Fiberglass, located on Highway 45 on top of sign

Bonduel

Angel of Deliverance
White marble, located at St. Paul's Lutheran Church Cemetery on Highway 29

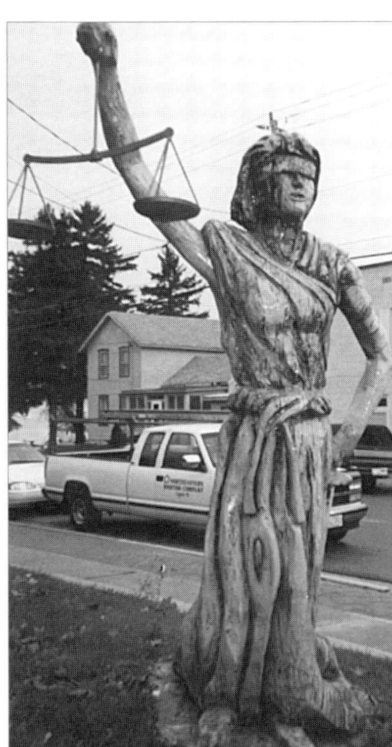
Justice and Scale in Seymour

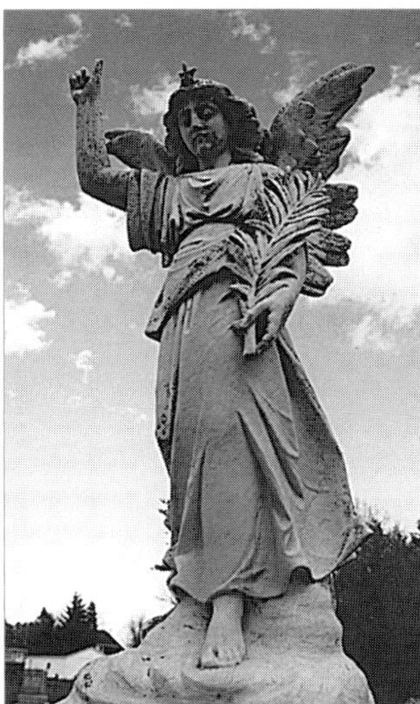
Angel of Deliverance in Bonduel

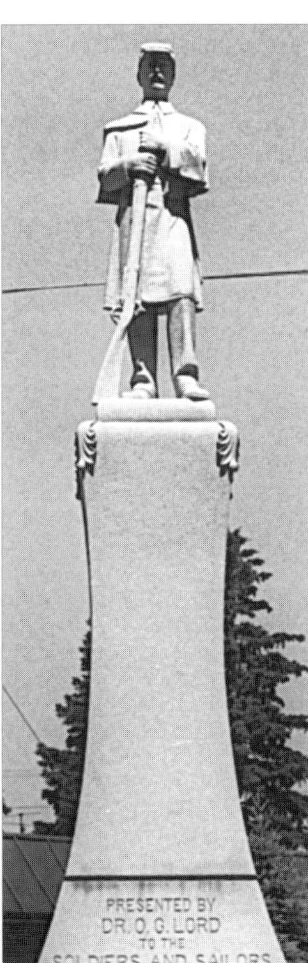

Soldier and Sailors Monument
in Kaukauna

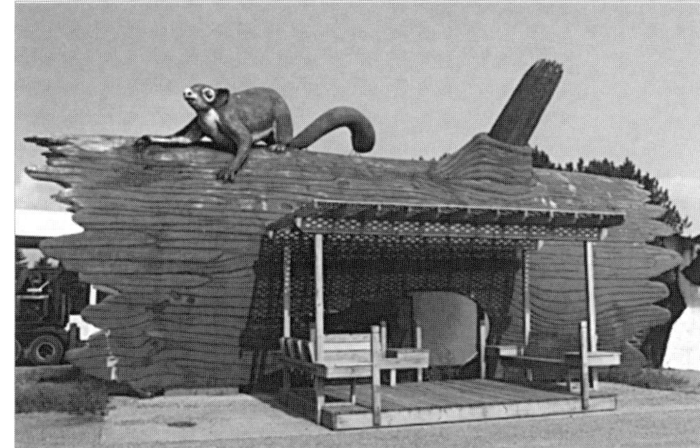
Gigantic Squirrel on Log in Birnamwood

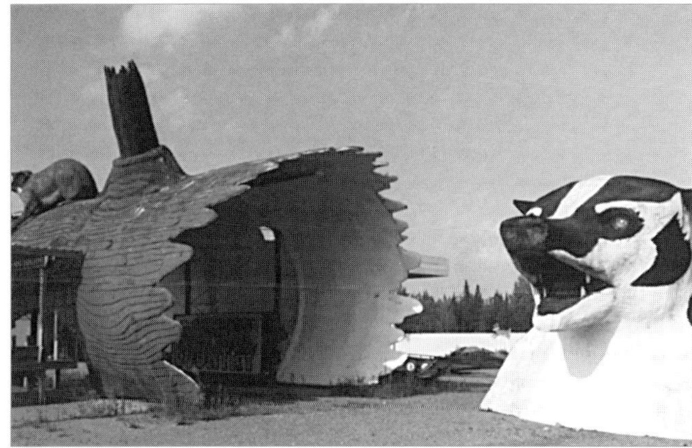
Gigantic Badger Head and Squirrel on Log in Birnamwood

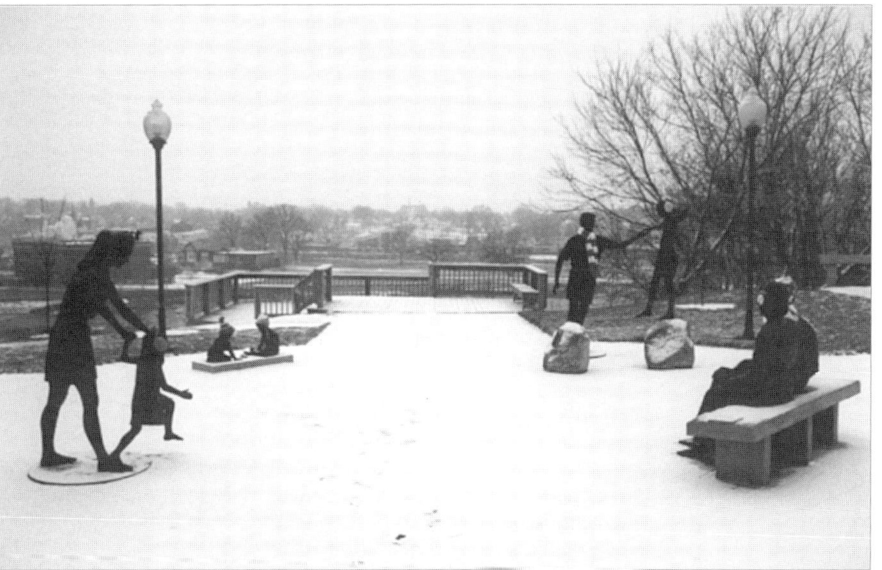
Family and Friends grouping of eight pieces in Kaukauna

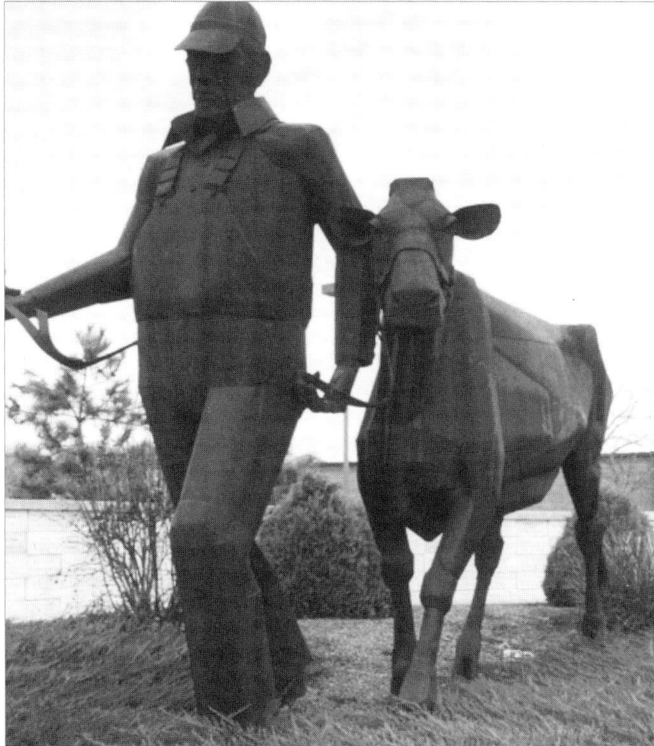

Man and Heifer in Shawano

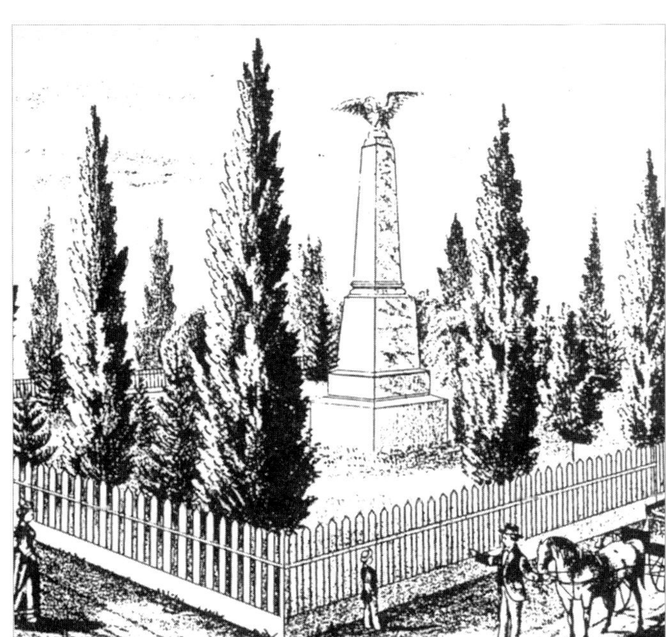

Civil War Soldiers Monument in Rhine Center, Sheboygan County

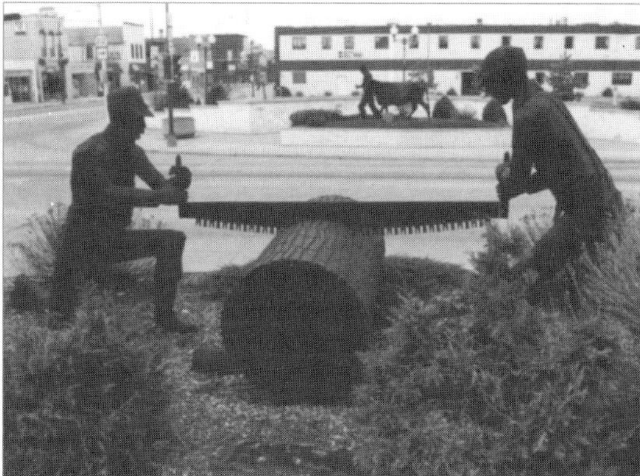

Log Sawing in Shawano

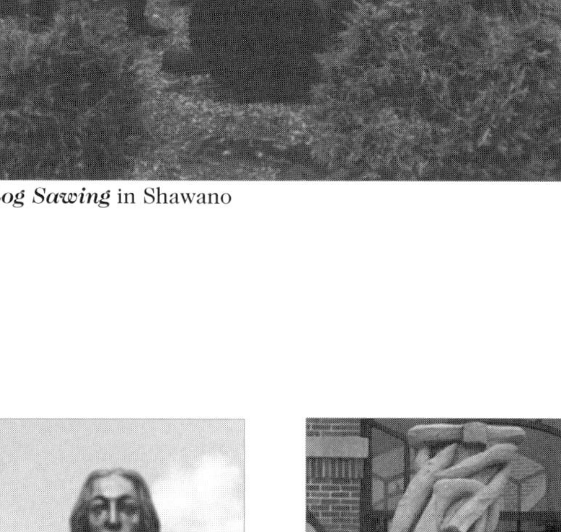

Shawano County Veterans Memorial in Shawano

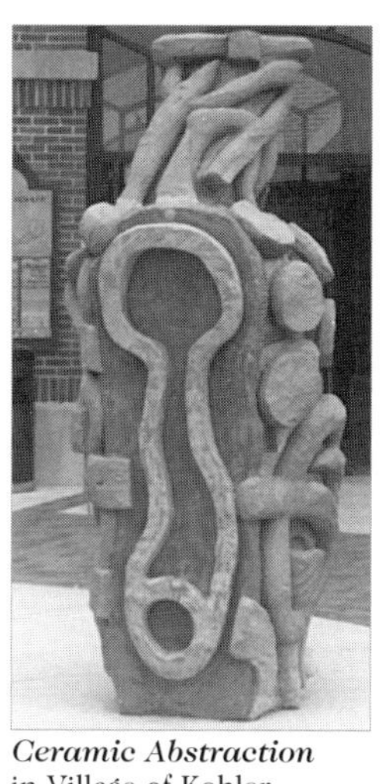
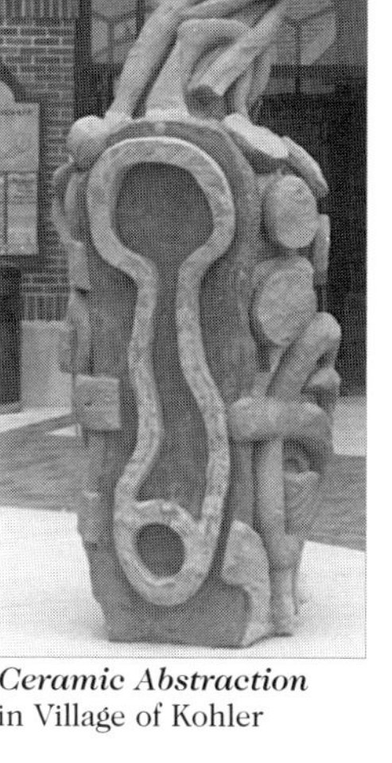

Sacred Heart of Jesus in Shawano

Ceramic Abstraction in Village of Kohler

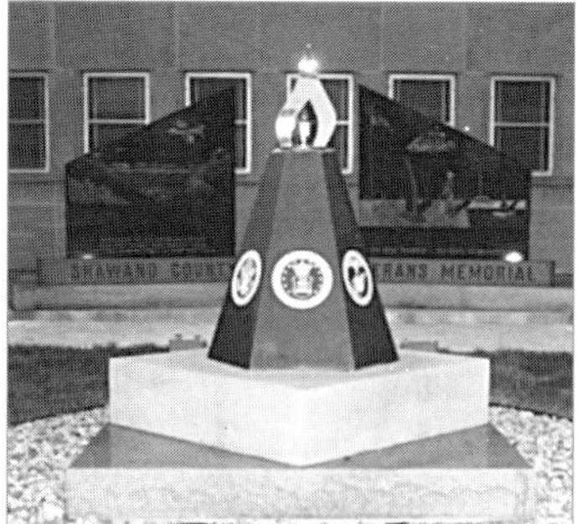
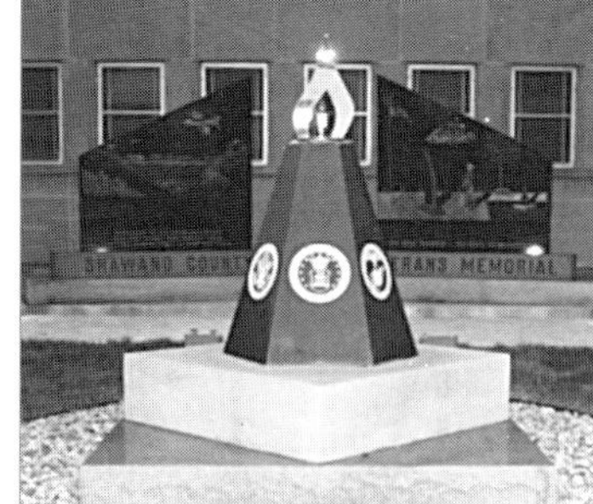

Civil War Monument in Sheboygan

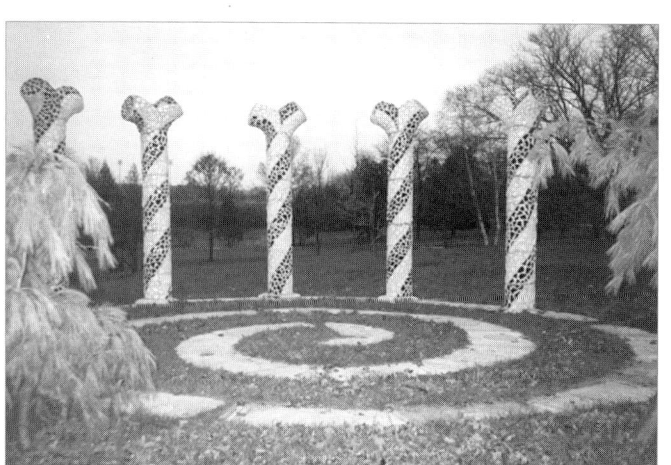

Cullumed Spiral in Village of Kohler

Shawano

Christ at Calvary
Painted concrete, located at Sacred Heart Cemetery east of town on Highway 29

Log Sawing
Fayne Pomeroy
Presented on September 29, 1990
Oxidized steel, located in Spirit of Shawano Park, corner of Green Bay and Main streets

Man and Heifer
Fayne Pomeroy
Presented on September, 29, 1990
Oxidized steel, located at Spirit of Shawano Park, corner of Green Bay and Main Street

Sacred Heart of Jesus
1997
Bronze, located at Sacred Heart Cemetery

Shawano County Veterans Memorial
Granite and stainless steel, located on Highway 55/47 at 4th Street

SHEBOYGAN

Elkhart Lake

Christ on the Cross
Circa 1970
Cast iron, located at St. George Catholic Church, 94 N. Lincoln Street. Removed

Sacred Heart of Jesus
Circa 1950
Stone, located at St. George Catholic Church, 94 N. Lincoln Street

Village of Kohler

Ceramic Abstraction
Arnold Zimmerman
1986
Ceramic, located at Wood Lake

Iron Man
Gerhard Hahn
1997
Cast ductile iron, located at Wood Lake

Rabbit
Todd McGrain
1995
Cast bronze, located at entrance to
Johnson Bank at Wood Lake

Cullumed Spiral
Robert Harrison
1989
Ceramic, concrete, stone, located at
Kohler Village Arboretum, Woodland
Road north of Highway C

Iron Bear
Marilyn Lysohir
1987
Concrete and bronze, located at
The Inn on Wood Lake

St. George and the Dragon
Murat Prierre
Haitian metal work, located at the
Kohler Fire Department,
Highland Road

Sundial
Kasper Albrecht
Circa 1930s
Metal, wood, located at Waelderhaus,
1100 W. Riverside Drive

American Club
Highland Drive

Deer Grill
Chris Weaver
1994
Bronze

Lady with a Scarf
Leonard Agathon
Circa 1900
Bronze

Plymouth

Antoinette the Cow
1977
Fiberglass, located south of
Highway 67 on Mill Street

Rhine Center

Civil War Soldiers Monument
Dedicated July 11, 1868
Marble, located at Junction of County
Trunks E and FF, one mile south of
Rhine Center. Bronze eagle is missing

Sheboygan

Abstraction
Circa 1970
Steel, located on the UW-Sheboygan
campus

Benediction
1974
Carrara marble, located at
St. Clements Parish, 522 New York
Avenue

Civil War Monument
1889
Bethel Vermont granite, located in
Fountain Park

Clocktower Bas Reliefs
Sharron Quasius (bas relief) and
Erik Jensen (clocktower)
1996
Four large cast bronze reliefs, located
at the north entrance to the
Mead Public Library

Farmer with Plow Horse
Mixed media, located at J. Circa
Goking farm at 5614 Superior Avenue

Folk Art Environment
James Tellen
1942-1957
19 concrete folk art sculptures with
various historical and religious subjects, located on Evergreen Drive, in
Black River area. Private property,
view from road

Folk Art Environment with Boat
Jim Schneider
1978, 1981-1985
Mixed media, it was located along the
Sheboygan River across from the
Harbor Lights Tavern on Pennsylvania
Avenue and has been demolished

Fountain Park Water Sculpture
Concrete, stone, brick, and water,
located at corner of 8th Street and
Erie Avenue

Gymnast III
Stephen Fischer
Corten steel, located at South High
School

Holy Angel
Stone, located at Saint Cyril and
Methodius Catholic Church

Hope
Circa 1886
Stone, located at the Mead Public
Library, 710 N. 8th Street—Sculpture
is missing, it was one of the first
public sculptures in Sheboygan and
it decorated the Scheele Monument
Company

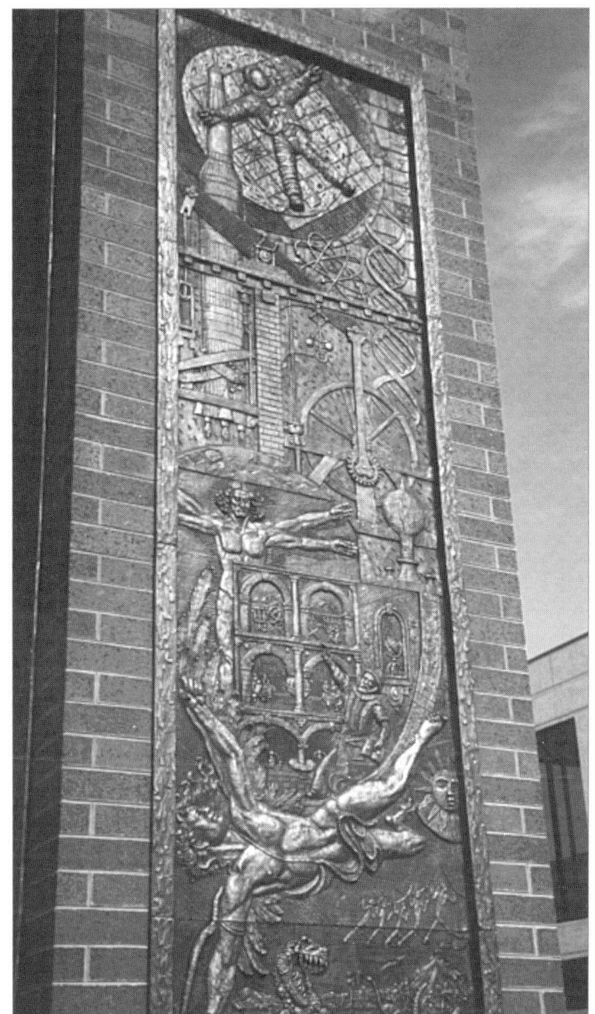

Clocktower (detail) in Sheboygan

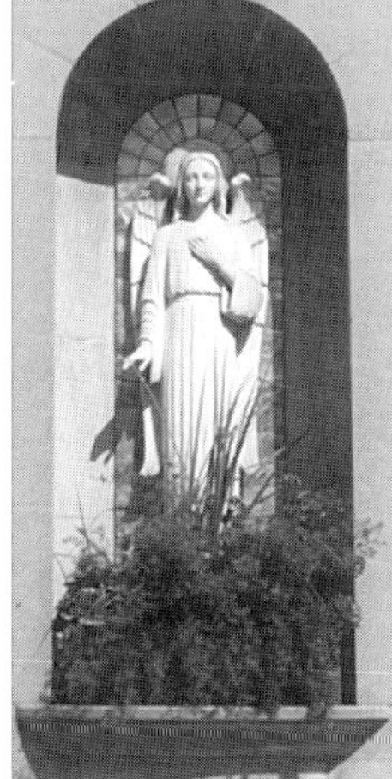

Holy Angel in Sheboygan

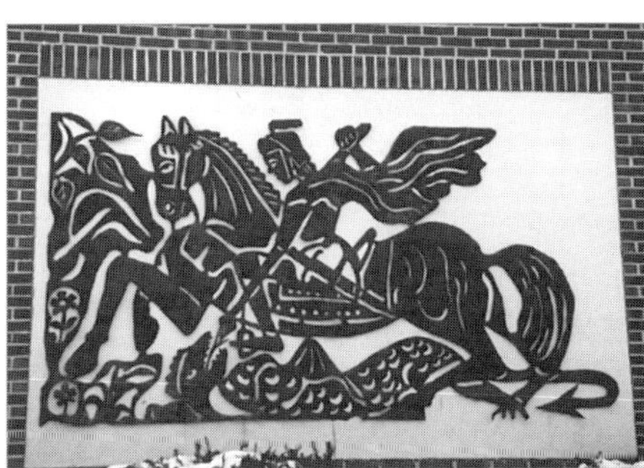

St. George and the Dragon in Village of Kohler

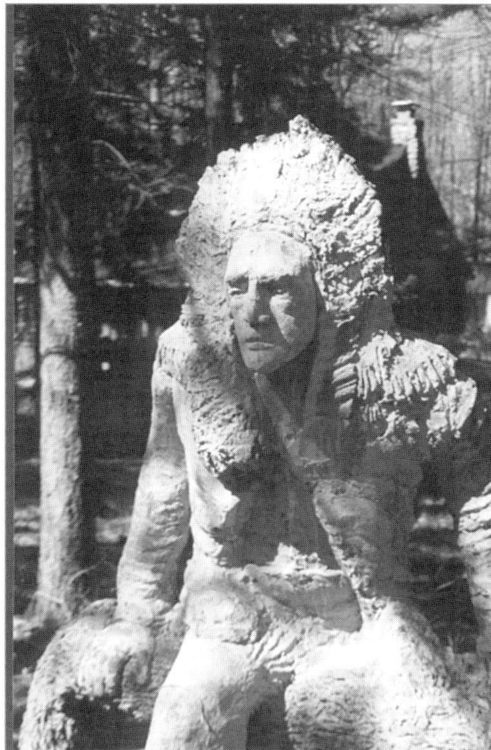

Folk Art Environment, Indian in Sheboygan

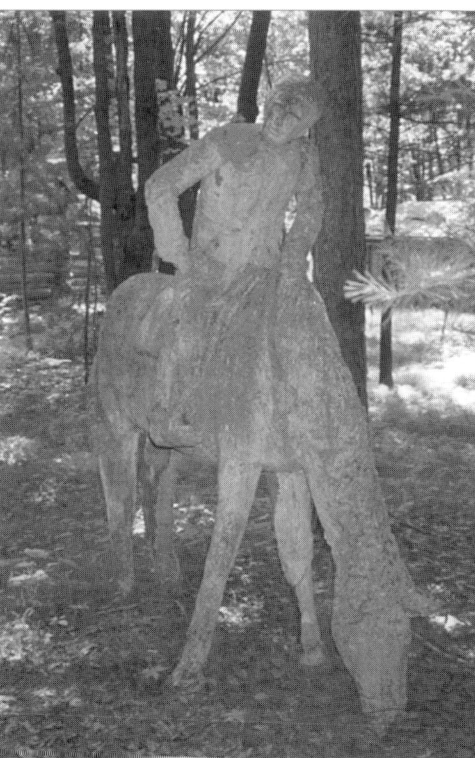

Folk Art Environment, Rider on Horse in Sheboygan

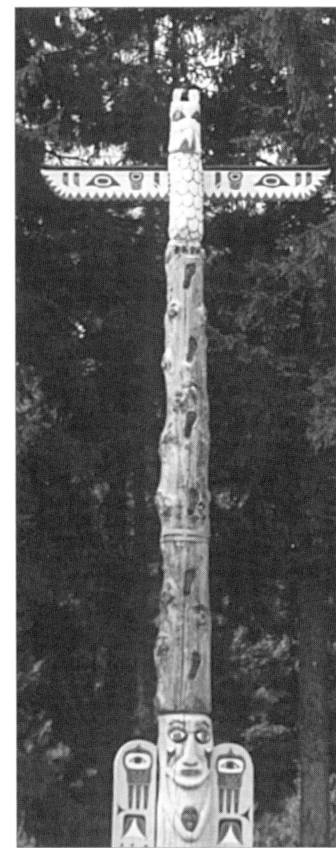

Totem Pole in Sheboygan

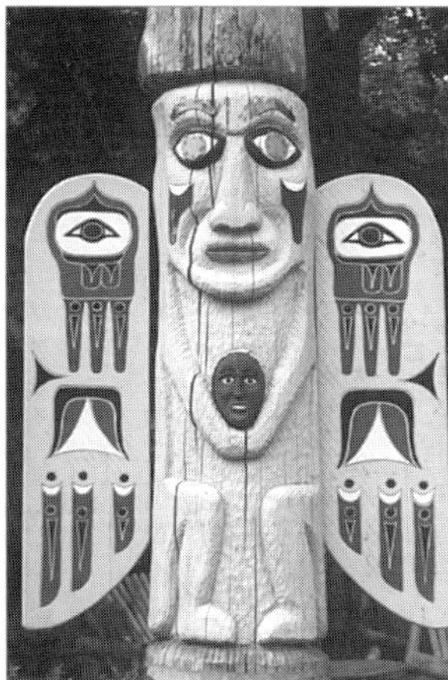

Totem Pole in Sheboygan
(detail)

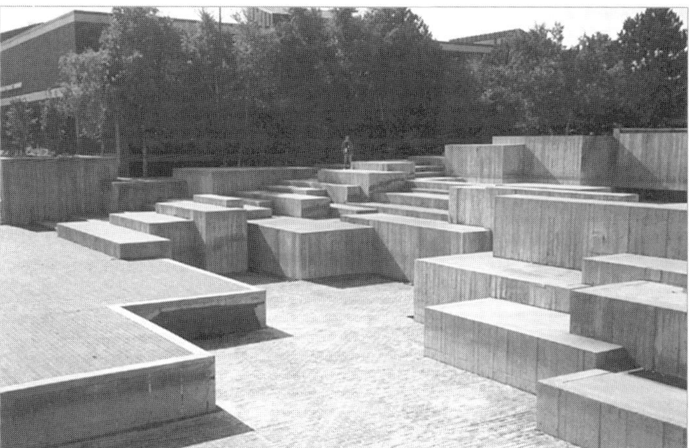

Plaza Eight, Water Feature in Sheboygan

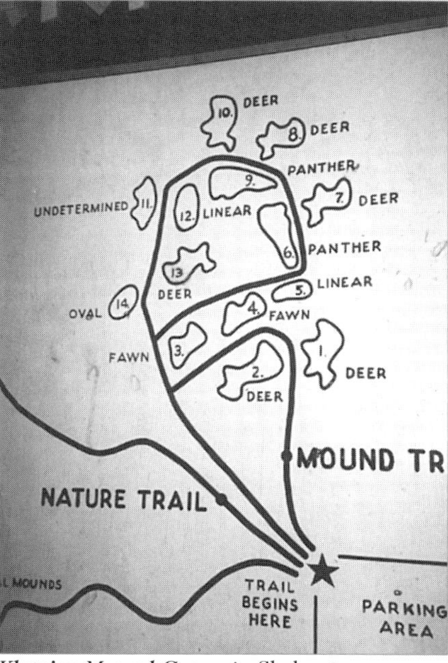

Kletzien Mound Group in Sheboygan

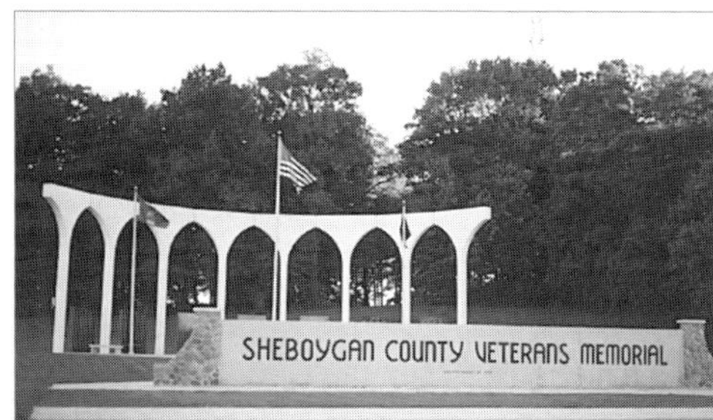

Sheboygan County Veterans Memorial
in Sheboygan

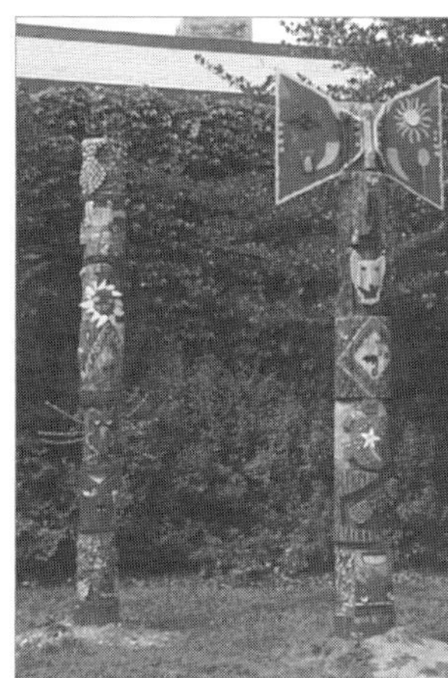

Two Modern Totem Poles
in Sheboygan

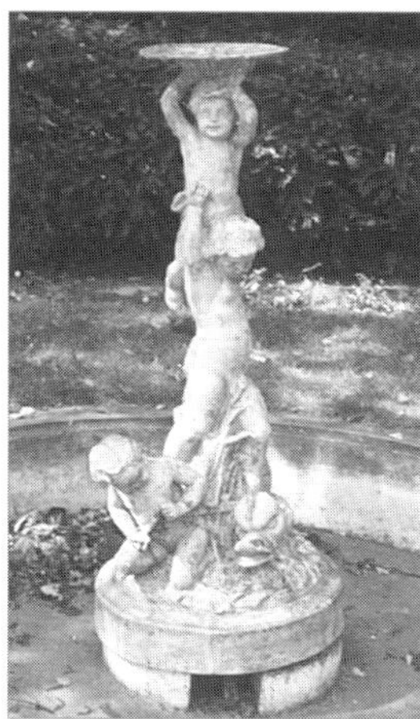

*Three Children with
Dolphin Fountain*
in Sheboygan

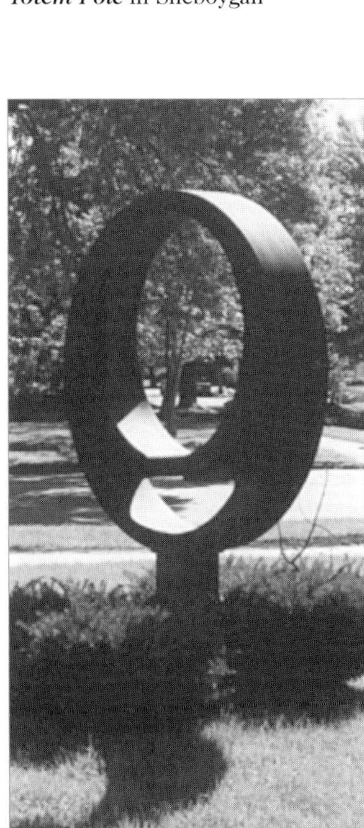

New Beginnings in Sheboygan

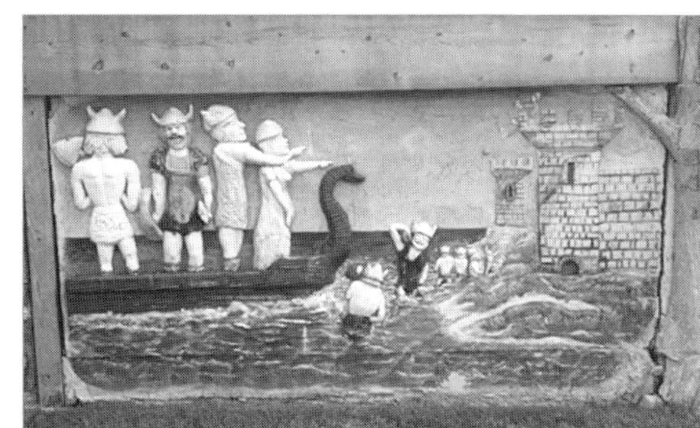

Painted Wall Relief Folk Art in Sheboygan

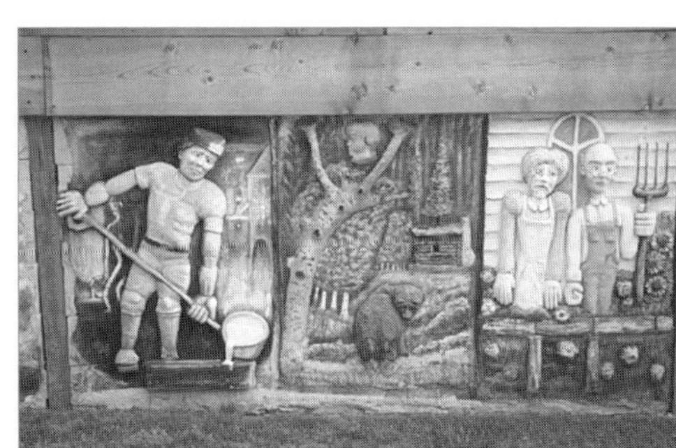

Painted Wall Relief Folk Art in Sheboygan

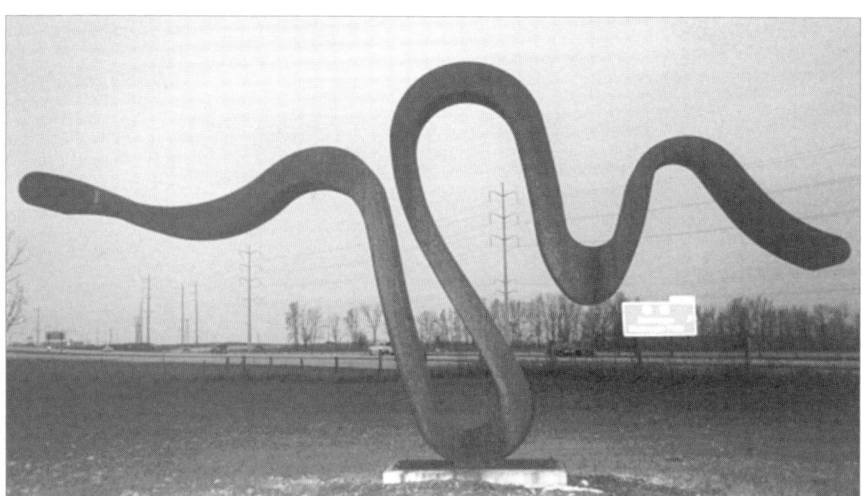

Ribbon III in Sheboygan

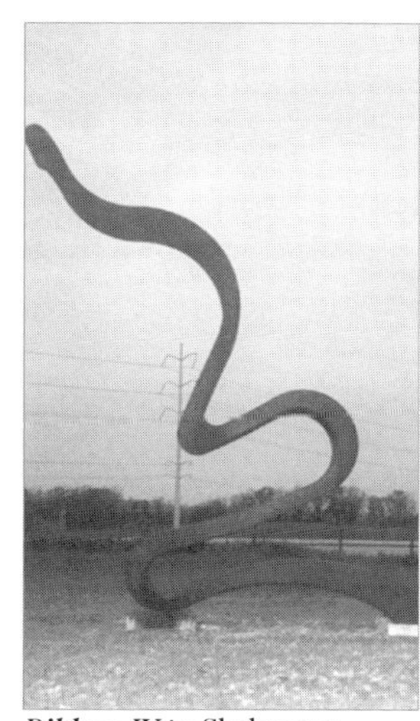

Ribbon IV in Sheboygan

↗ *Kletzien Mound Group*
18 effigy, oval and conical mounds in Sheboygan Indian Mound Park, located in Black River Township, near S. 12th Street

New Beginnings
Stephen Fischer
Dedicated 1980
Corten steel, located at 1720 N. 8th Street

Painted Wall Relief Folk Art
Dan Erbstoesser
1950s -1976
Themes include: *Viking Raid, European History, Norse and Russian History, Cossack Attack*, and *Keystone Cops.*
Concrete, stone, located at 548 Whitcomb Avenue

Plaza Eight Water Feature
Designed by Halpien & Associates
1974
Concrete and brick fountain, located at 8th and Wisconsin Avenue near the Mead Public Library

Ribbon III
Ribbon IV
Ribbon XVIII
Stephen Fischer
Corten steel, located at Heritage Insurance Corporate Headquarters, 2800 S. Taylor Drive

Sheboygan County Veterans Memorial
Norman Minster
1992
Concrete, granite, and stone, located at the north slope of Taylor Park on Highway 23

St. Francis
circa 1955
Carrara marble, located at St. Nicholas Hospital, 1601 N. Taylor Drive

St. Nicholas
Victor Moroder
1979
Bronze, located at St. Nicholas Hospital, 1601 N. Taylor Drive

St. Peter the Fisherman
James Tellen
1948
Concrete, located at 1202 Stahl Road

Three Children with Dolphin Fountain
Circa 1920-1930
White metal cast at Kohler Company, located at John Michael Kohler Arts Center, 608 New York Avenue

Totem Pole
Painted wood, located on 4422 S. 12th Street

Two Modern Totem Poles
Circa 1992
Painted wood, located at the Kohler Arts Center, 608 New York Avenue (in storage)

Woodlot Gallery site
5215 Evergreen Drive, Sheboygan
920-458-4798

Active Hybrid, Second Growth
Richard Hunt
Bronze

Balzac
David Anderson
Cast iron

Childhood Fountain
Jorge Ulisses
Cast bronze

Column Breakdown II
Joe Martell
Mild steel and bronze

Column Breakdown III
Joe Martell
Mild steel and bronze

Cuculidae
Narendra Patel
Painted steel

Double Split Time
John Hickman
Bronze, Corten, and stainless steel

Earth Form
Richard Hunt
Cast bronze

Epitaph to a Poet
Jorge Ulisses
Cast bronze

Espiritu de las Mesas
Jesus Moroles
Dakota granite

Female Torso
Jorge Ulisses
Portuguese marble

Fragmentary Bones
Robert Stackhouse
Cast bronze

Galaxy & Drape
David Anderson
Cast iron

Hammers
Joe Martell
Cast bronze and Swiss red granite

Homage to Garcia Lorca
Jorge Ulisses
Cast bronze

Hybrid
Richard Hunt
Cast bronze

Knot
Joe Martell
Armenian granite and Carrara marble

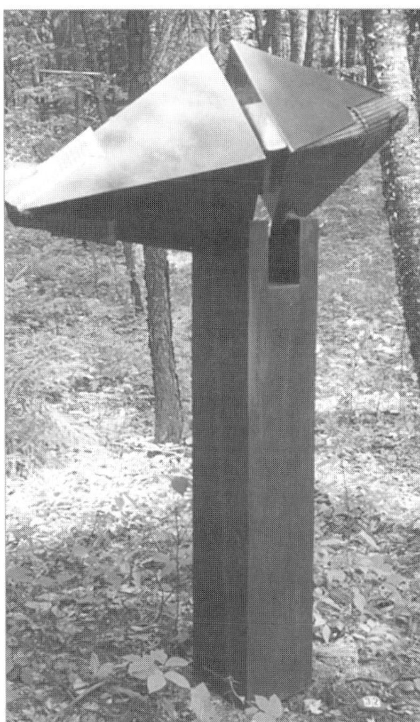

Double Split Time at Woodlot Gallery, Sheboygan

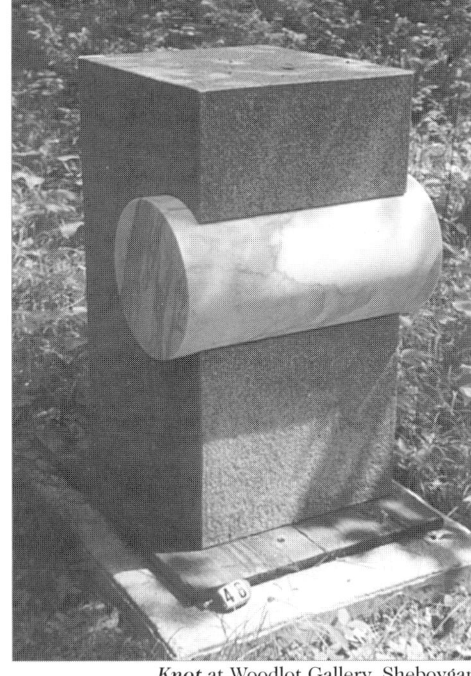

Knot at Woodlot Gallery, Sheboygan

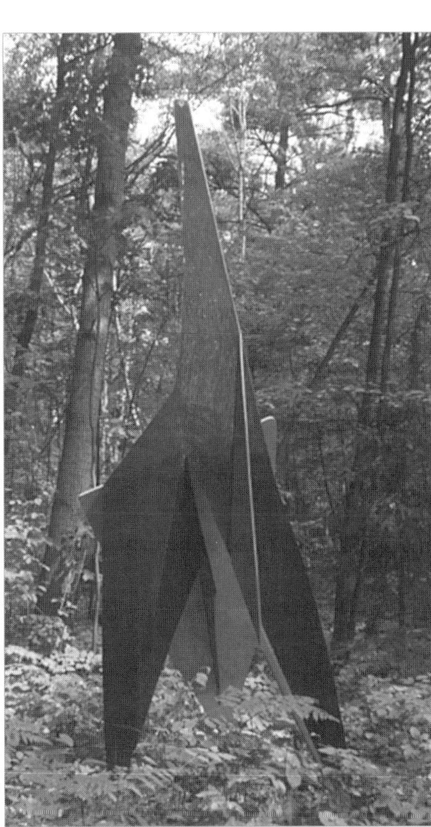

Cuculidae at Woodlot Gallery, Sheboygan

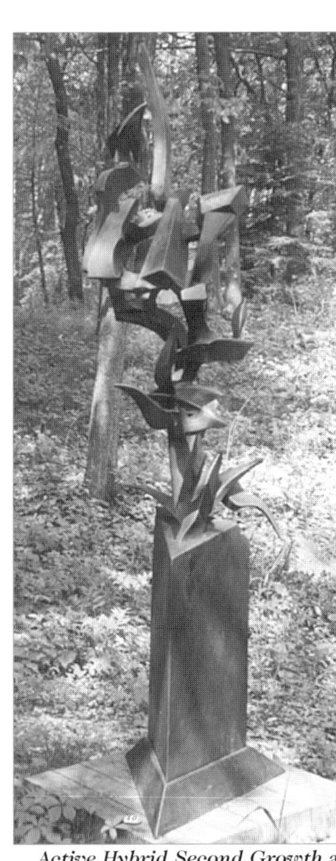

Active Hybrid Second Growth at Woodlot Gallery, Sheboygan

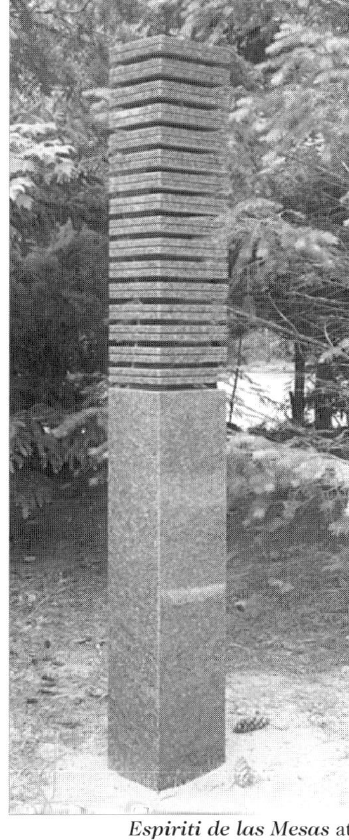

Espiriti de las Mesas at Woodlot Gallery, Sheboygan

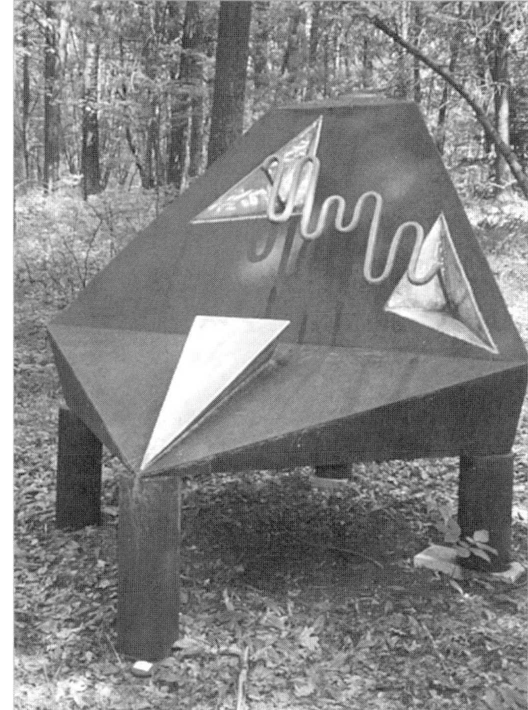

IV Prime Resonance at Woodlot Gallery, Sheboygan

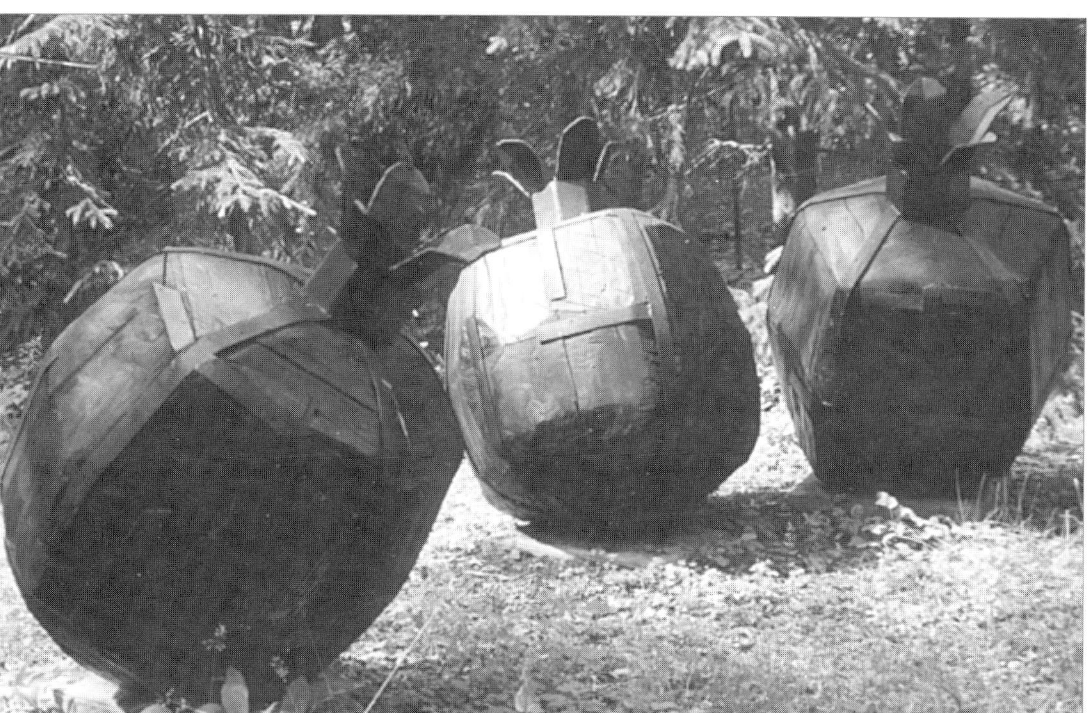

Pomegranates at Woodlot Gallery, Sheboygan

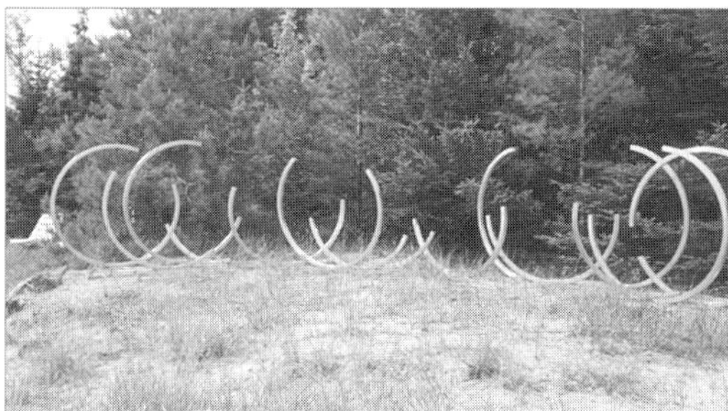

Tumbling Tumbleweed at Woodlot Gallery, Sheboygan

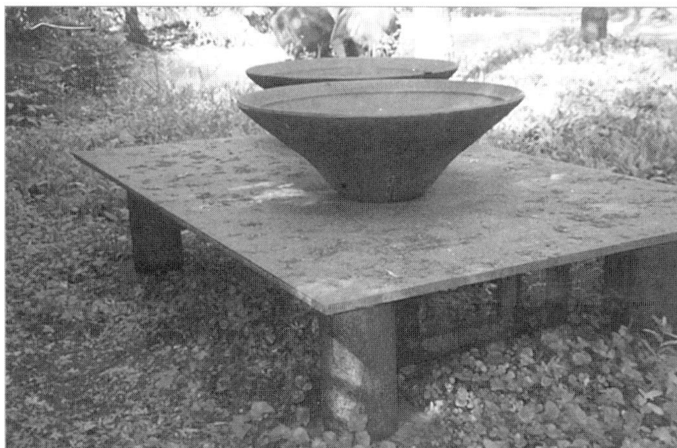

Tea Bowls at Woodlot Gallery, Sheboygan

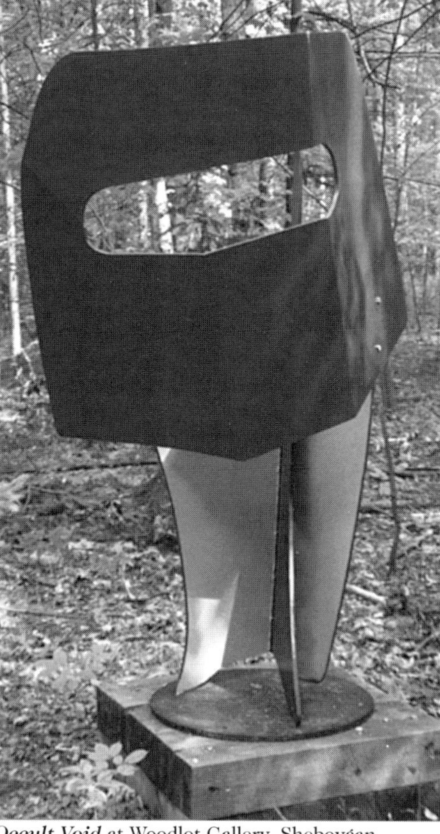

Occult Void at Woodlot Gallery, Sheboygan

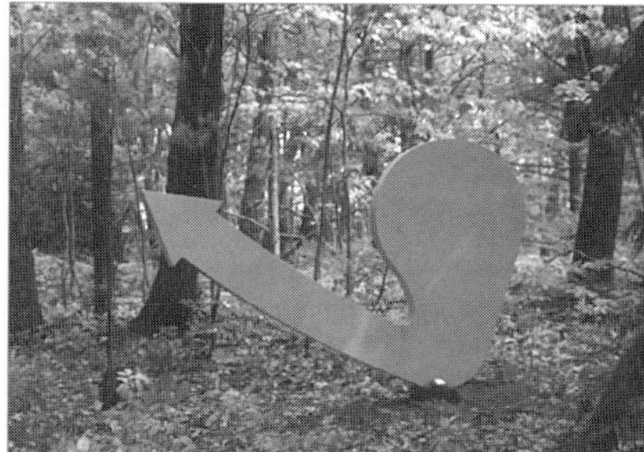

The Remains at Woodlot Gallery, Sheboygan

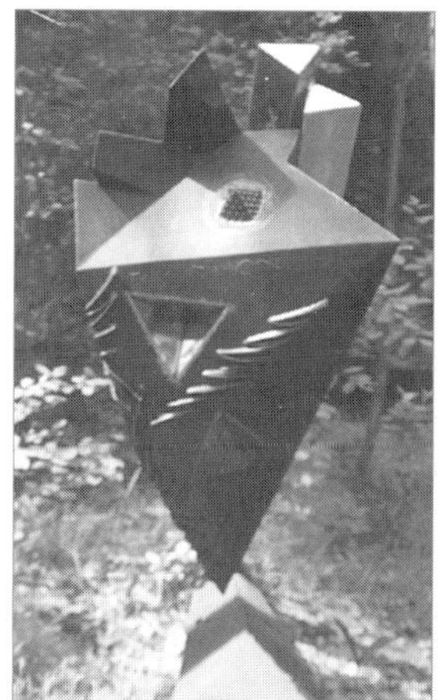

V Prime Resonance at
Woodlot Gallery, Sheboygan

Landscape
Mark Overs
Copper, bronze and stainless steel
wall piece

Male torso
Jorge Ulisses
Portuguese marble

Musical form
Jorge Ulisses
Cast bronze

Occult Void
Narendra Patel
Painted steel

Pas de Trois
Bill Weaver
Fabricated bronze

Pomegranates
Ilan Averbuch
Yellow pine and steel

IV Prime Resonance
John Hickman
Steel, bronze castings, and stainless
steel

V Prime Resonance
John Hickman
Bronze, Corten steel, and stainless
steel

Quadrangular Form
Jorge Ulisses
Cast bronze

Small Fountain
Jorge Ulisses
Cast bronze

Source
Jorge Ulisses
Cast bronze

Storm Rock
Stephen Fischer
Painted steel and stainless steel

Tea Bowls
David Anderson
Steel

The Remains
Stephan Fischer
Painted steel

Tumbling Tumbleweed
Virginio Ferrari
Stainless steel

Holy Name Catholic Church

807 Superior Avenue

Apparition of the Blessed Virgin at Lourdes

Circa 1925
Painted metal

Apparition of the Virgin at Fatima

1920s
Six marble sculptures

Pope Leo XIII

Painted cast iron from Union
Artistique, il Vaucouleurs, France

St. Joseph with Jesus

Acquired in 1950s
Metal

Christ and Blessed Virgin

Painted metal

St. Peter Claver Church

1444 S. 11th Street

St. Peter Claver

Carved stone

Virgin Mary

Boratti
Carrara marble (Pietrasanta)

Sheboygan Falls

Virgin Mary

Andrea Roffo
Carrara marble (Pietrasanta), located
at St. Mary's Parish Catholic Church,
327 Giddings Avenue

WINNEBAGO

Menasha

Golden Boy

Metal, located at Smith Park

➤ *Smith Park Mound Group*

Three panther mounds are still
visible in Smith Park. The panthers
measure 217 feet, 200 feet, and
125 feet in length and are 1.5 to
2 feet high

The Brain Station

Circa 1996
Painted wood, located at railroad
tracks on Clybourn Street

Veterans Memorial

Cast bronze and polished granite,
located at Memorial Park, corner of
2nd and Racine streets

Virgin Mary

Circa 1935
White marble, located at St Mary's
School and Church, 2nd and
Appleton streets off Highway 114

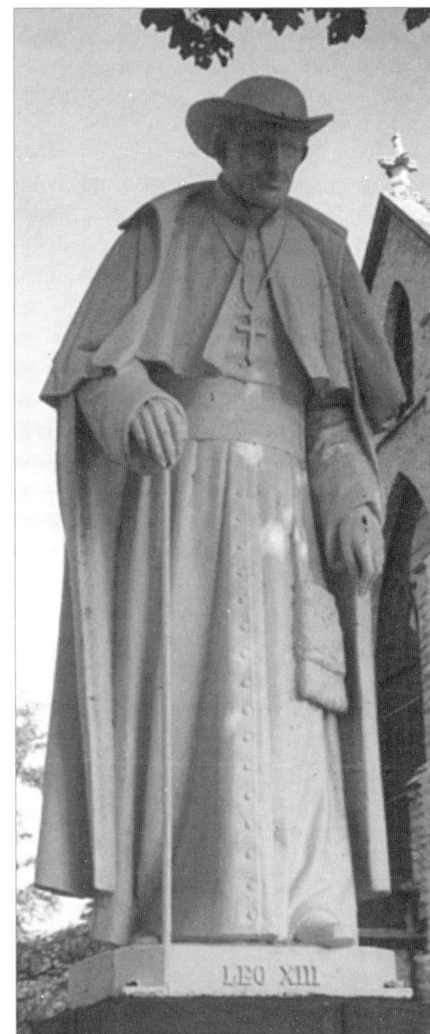

Pope Leo XIII at Holy Name Catholic Church,
Sheboygan

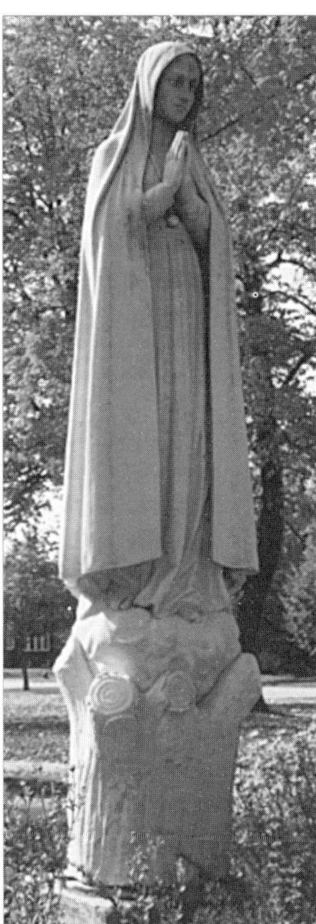

*Apparition of the Virgin at
Fatima* at Holy Name Catholic
Church, Sheboygan

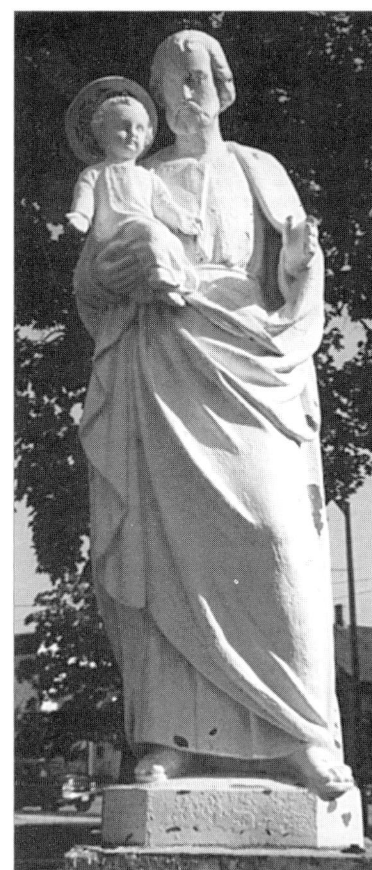

St. Joseph with Jesus at Holy Name
Catholic Church, Sheboygan

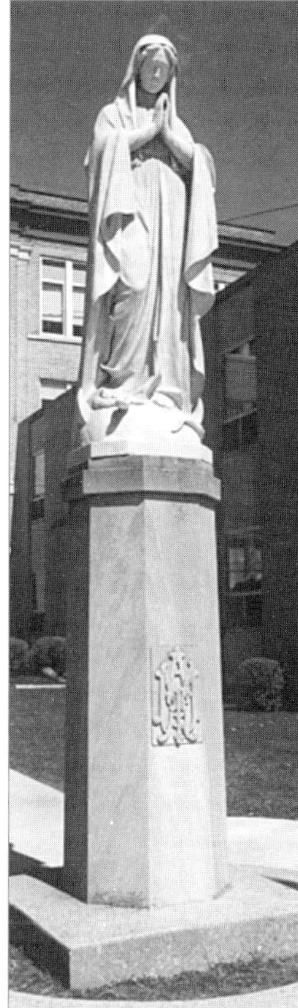

Virgin Mary in Menasha

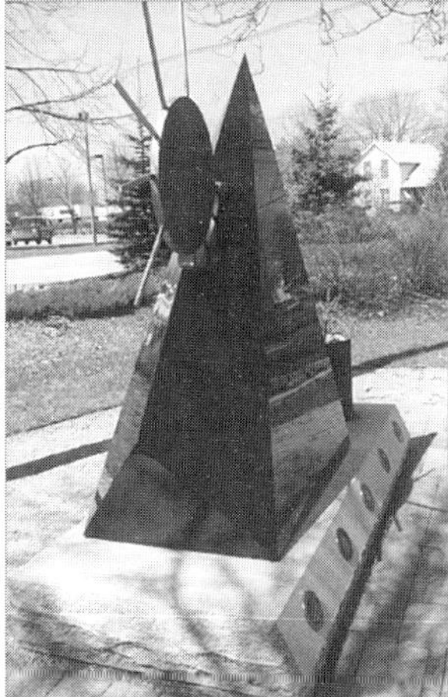

Veterans Memorial in Menasha

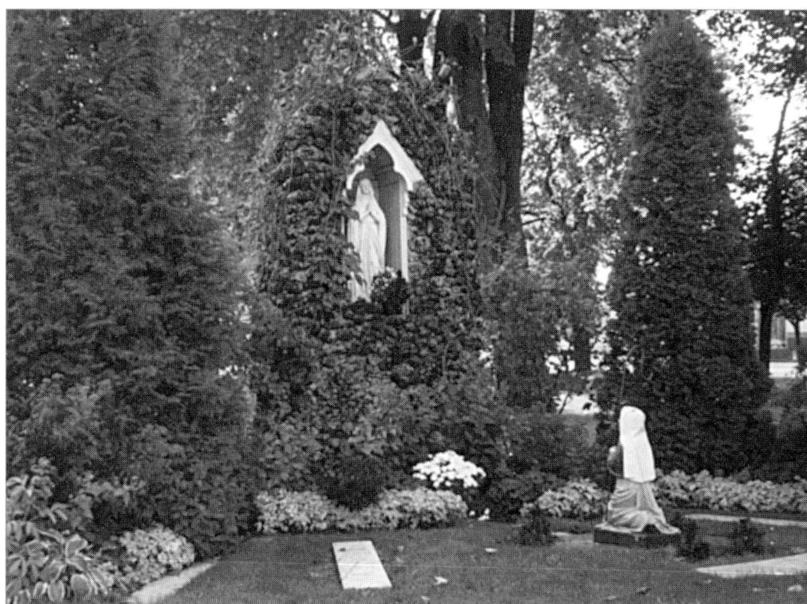

Apparition of Blessed Virgin at Lourdes at Holy Name Catholic Church, Sheboygan

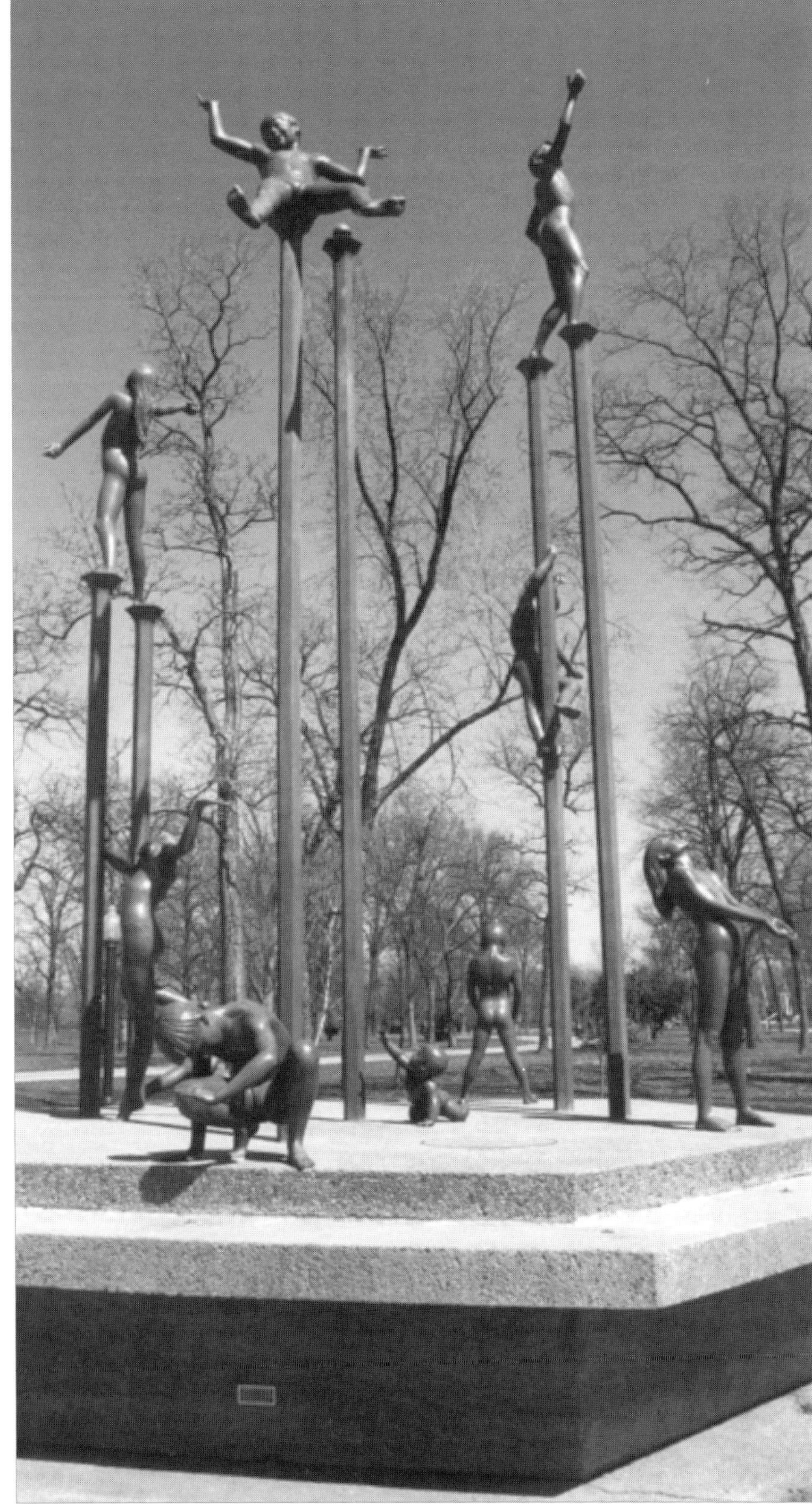

Playing in the Rain in Neenah

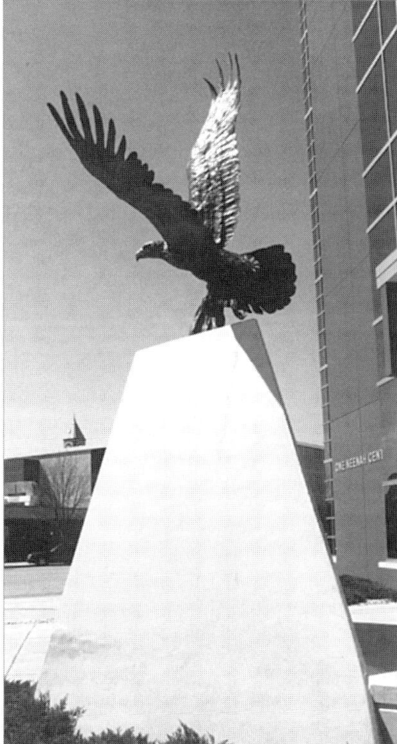

Eagle in Neenah

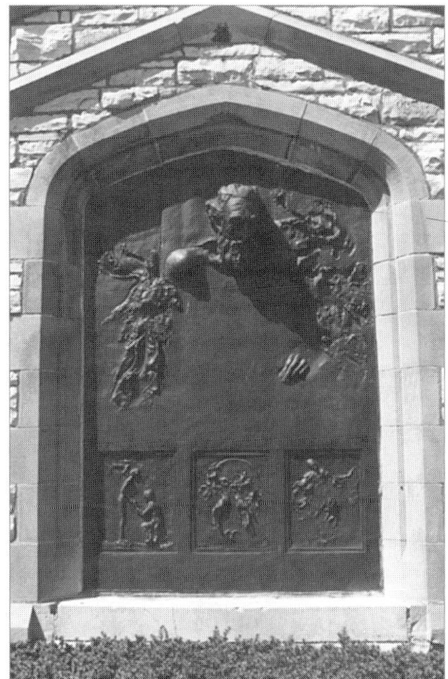

St. Thomas in Neenah

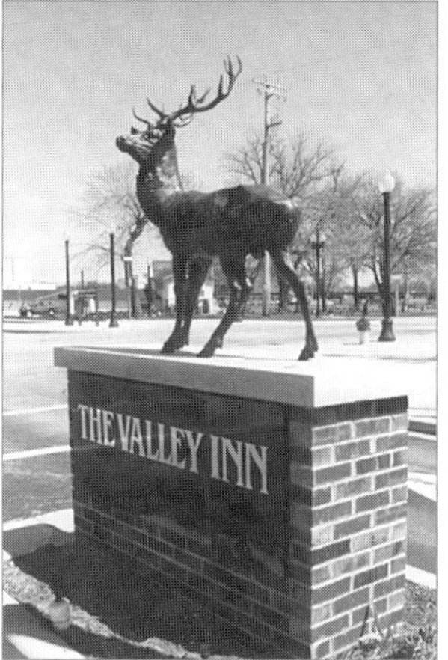

Buck (Deer) in Neenah

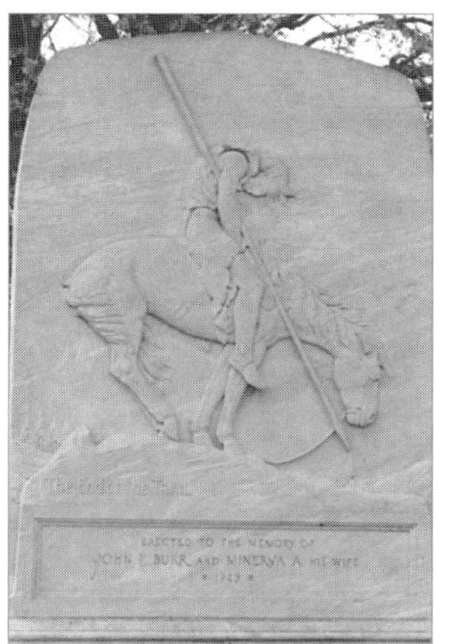

End of the Trail in Oshkosh

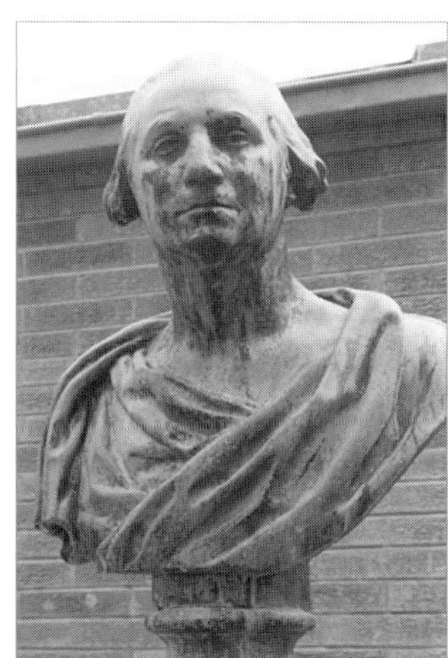

George Washington Portrait Bust in Oshkosh

Neenah

Buck (Deer)
Cast bronze, located at the entrance to The Valley Inn

Eagle
Cast bronze on granite pyramid, located in front of the Neenah Center

Memorial log marker
Concrete at Cemetery west of town

Playing in the Rain
Dallas Anderson
1991-1993
Bronze, located at Riverside Park, E. Wisconsin Avenue

St. Thomas
Bronze, located at St. Thomas Episcopal Church, corner of Nicolet Boulevard and Sanford Street

Oshkosh

Abraham Lincoln
Adolph Alexander Weinman
1909
Bronze, located at Lincoln School, 608 Algoma Boulevard

B. Franklin, after Houdon
1911
Bronze, located at Franklin School, 1401 W. 5th Avenue

Christ with St. Peter
Circa 1970
Limestone, located at St. Peter Church, 435 High Street

End of the Trail
James Earl Fraser
Circa 1928
Carved marble bas relief, located at Riverside Cemetery, 1901 Algoma Boulevard

George Washington Portrait Bust
Dedicated 1911
Bronze, located at Washington Elementary School, 929 Winnebago Avenue

Henry Longfellow
Thomas Broke
Donated 1915
Bronze, located at Longfellow School

Human Form in Abstract
Daithi Alice (a.k.a. David Kelley)
1996
Welded steel, located at 1109 Hazel Street

Monument to George Washington
Jean Antoine Houdon (copy)
1911
Bronze, located at intersection of
East New York, Menominee, and
Hazel streets

Odd Fellows Lodge Bas Relief
1884
Terra cotta, located near 103 Main
Street and 109 Algoma Boulevard

Passion Dance
Daithi Alice
1996
Welded steel, located at 1109 Hazel
Street

Red Arrow Monument
1971 by the Red Arrow Division
Granite, located in Red Arrow Park,
Westfield Street and Taft Avenue

Soldiers' Monument
Gaetano Trentanove
Dedicated 1907
Bronze, located at Soldiers Square,
High Avenue and Market Street

St. Francis of Assisi
Circa 1980
Painted aluminum, located at
Neuman Center on W. Irving Avenue

**The Children at Fatima with the
Madonna**
Circa 1920
Italian marble, located at St. Vincent's
School, 1225 Oregon Street and
Park Avenue

The Hiker Monument
Theo Alice Ruggles Kitson
Dedicated October 22, 1939
Bronze, located across from Oshkosh
Public Museum and the Paine Art
Center, Algoma Boulevard and
Highway 21

**The Library Lions, Sawyer and
Harris**
Gaetano Trentanove
1912
Bronze, located in front of the
Oshkosh Public Library on
Washington Avenue

Thomas Jefferson
Gorham Company Foundry
Circa 1910
Bronze, located at Jefferson
Elementary School, 244 W. 11th
Avenue

Winnebago Lady
Donald Hord
1967
Cast bronze, located at Paine Art
Center, Algoma Boulevard

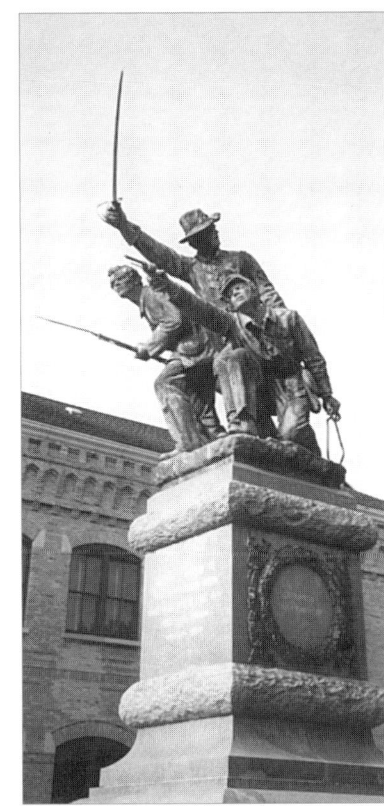

Soldiers' Monument in Oshkosh

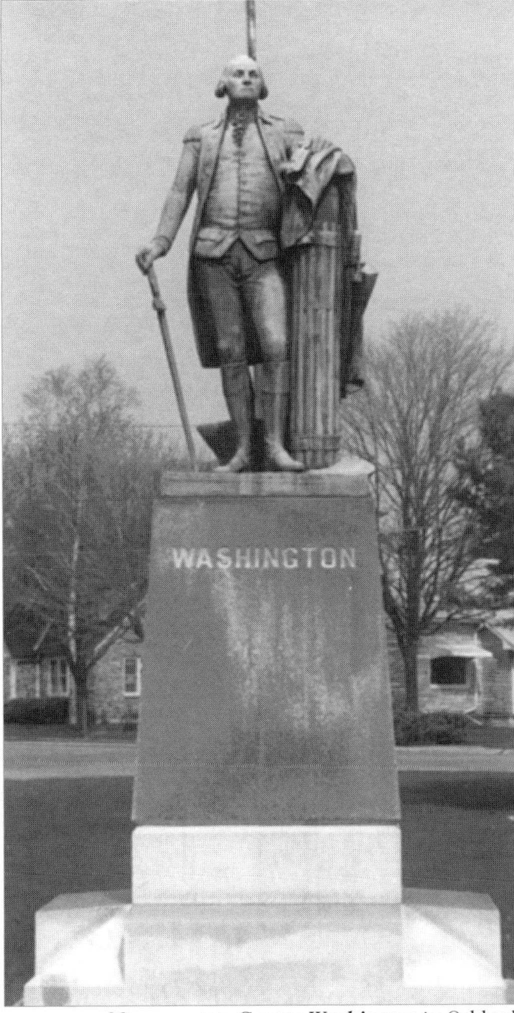

Monument to George Washington in Oshkosh

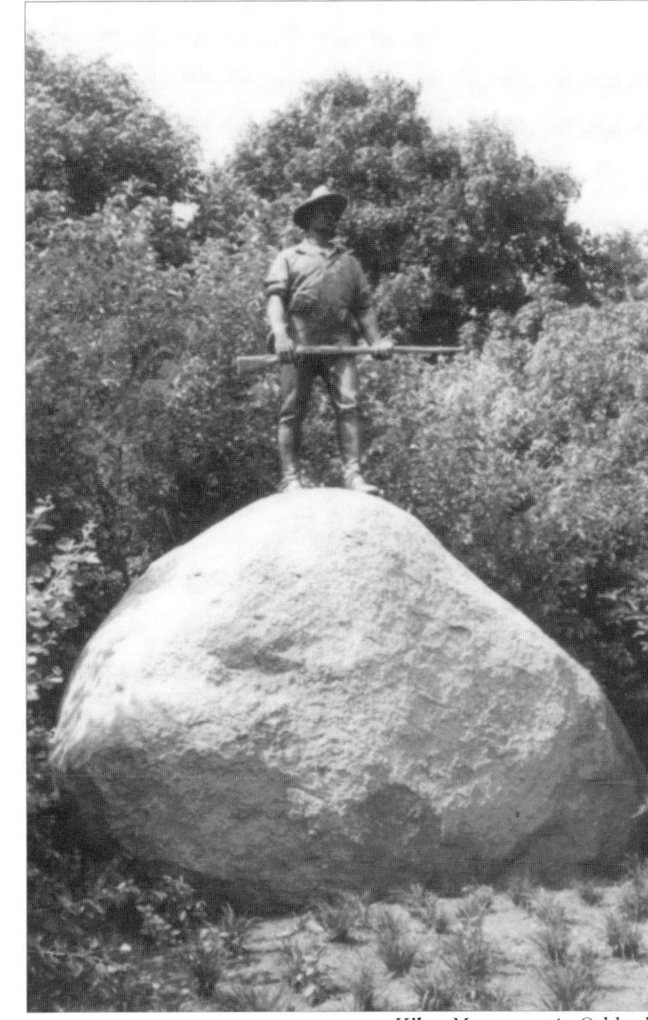

Hiker Monument in Oshkosh

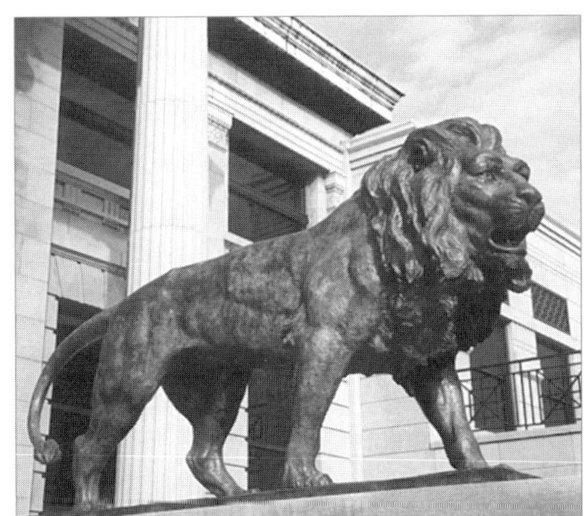

The Library Lions in Oshkosh

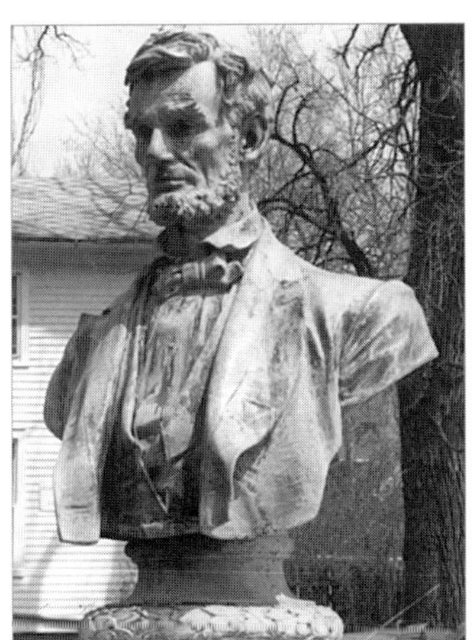

Abraham Lincoln in Oshkosh

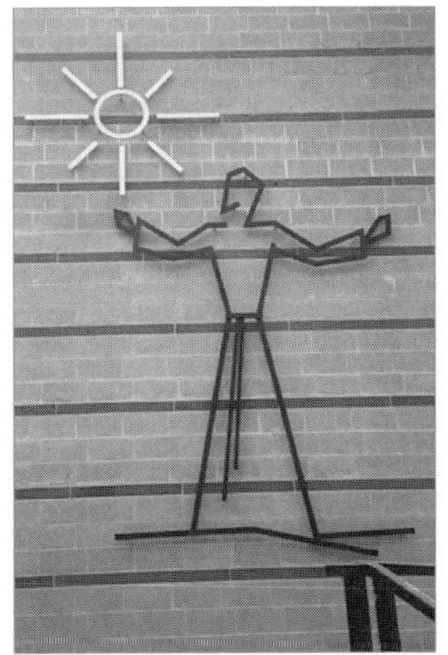

St. Francis of Assisi
in Oshkosh

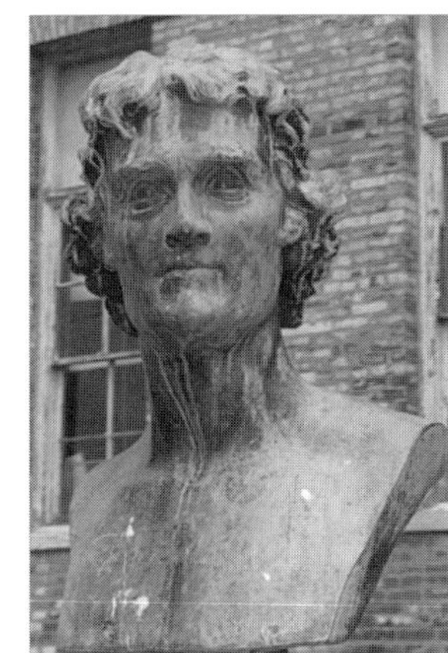

Thomas Jefferson in Oshkosh

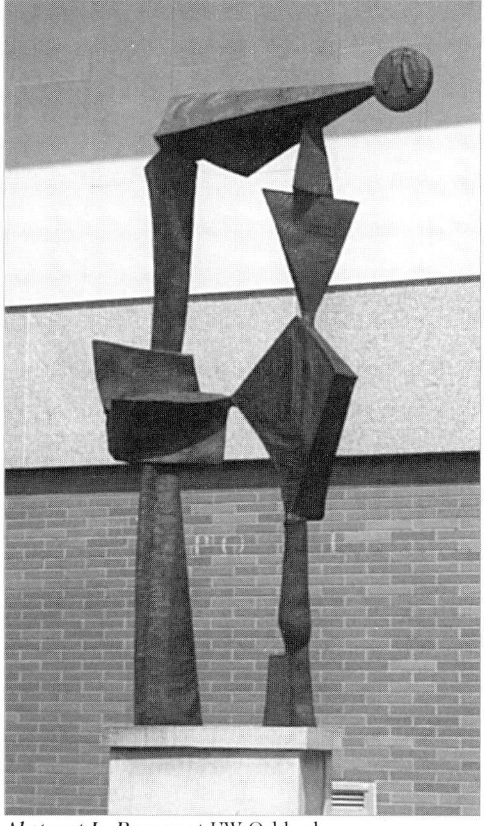

Abstract In Bronze at UW-Oshkosh

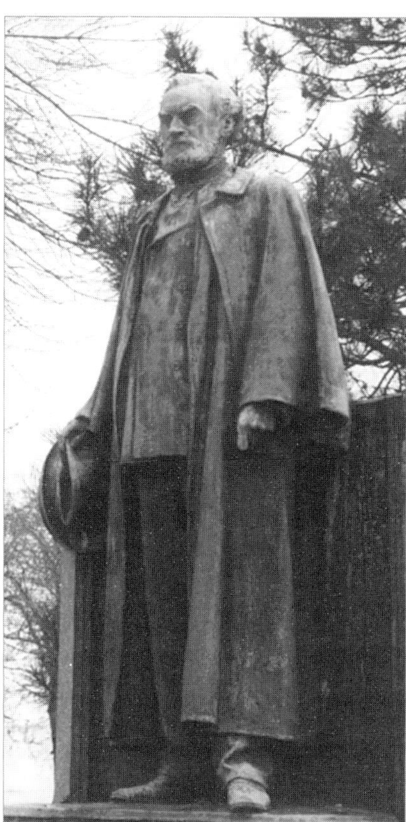

The Carl Schurz Monument at
Menominee Park, Oshkosh

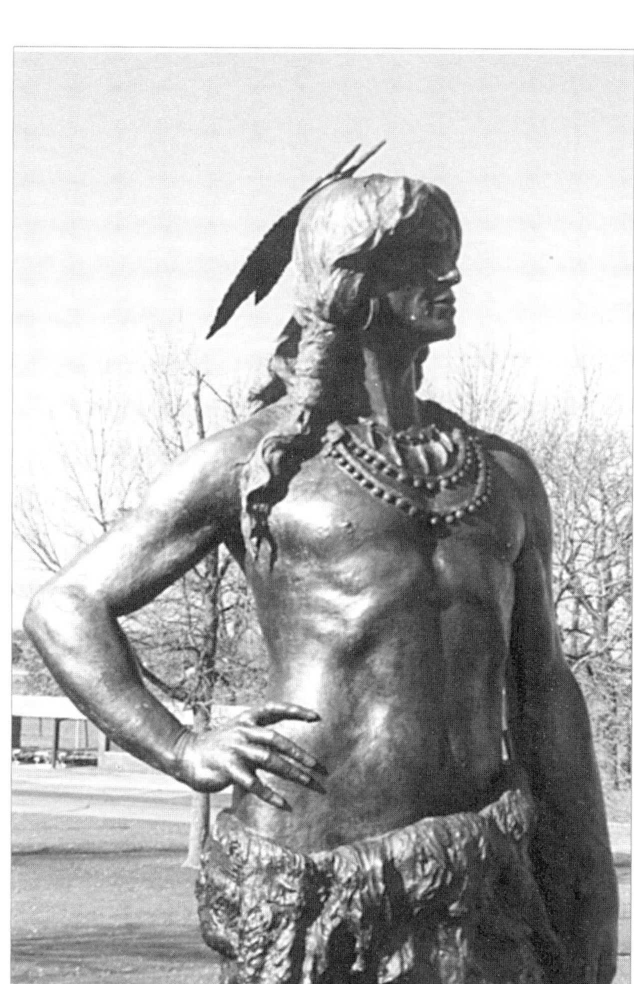

Monument to Chief Oshkosh in Menominee Park, Oshkosh

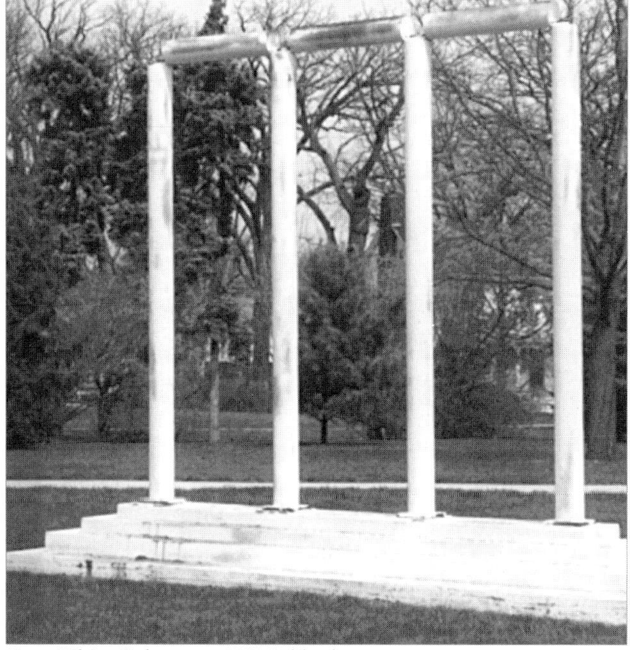

Four White Columns at UW-Oshkosh

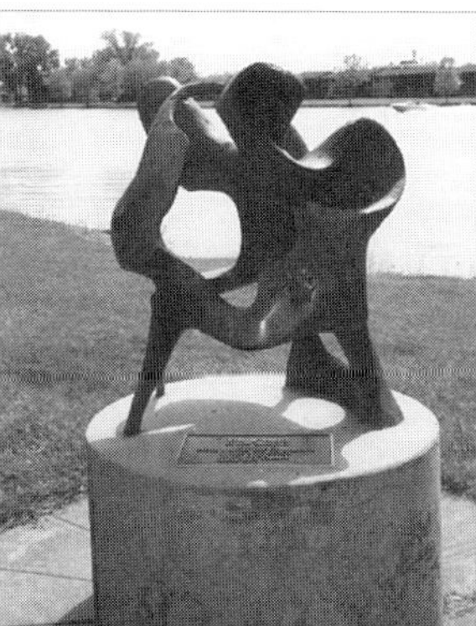

Yin and Yang at UW-Oshkosh

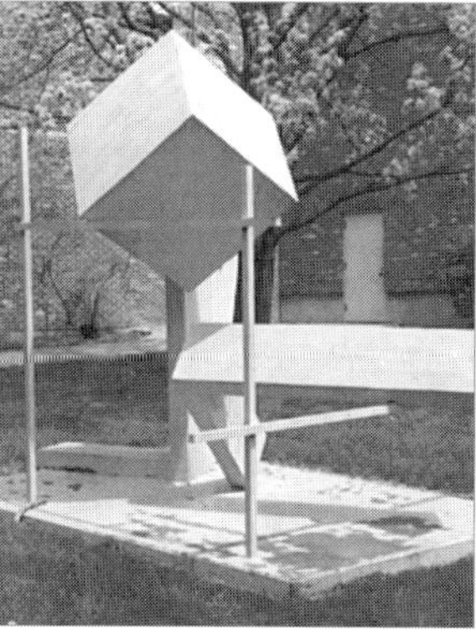

Abstract in Blue
at UW-Oshkosh

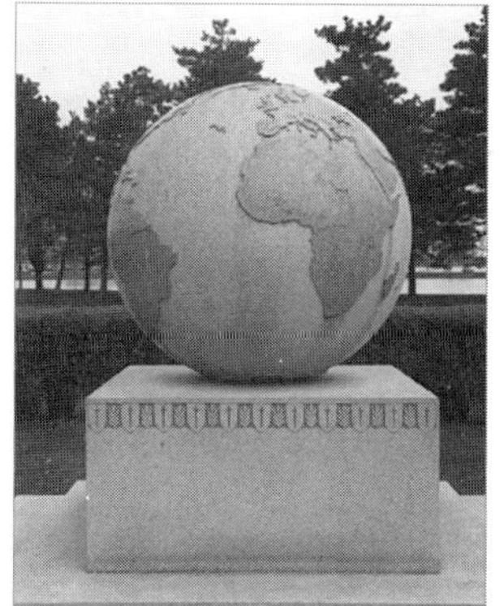

The Globe All-Wars Monument
at Menominee Park, Oshkosh

Menominee Park

Chief Oshkosh
Dave Watson
Wood, chain saw art, located near
playground

The Carl Schurz Monument
Karl Theodore Francis Bitter
Dedicated 1914
Bronze, located at the foot of
Washington Avenue

Monument to Chief Oshkosh
Chevalier Gaetano Trentanove
Dedicated June 21, 1911
Bronze

The Globe All-Wars Monument
1963
Grey granite

UW-Oshkosh
Algoma Boulevard

Abstract in Bronze
Leo Steppat
1962
Bronze, located at Forrest R. Polk
Library

Abstract in Blue
Richard Medlock
Circa 1975
Painted steel, located in front of the
Arts and Communications Building,
Algoma Boulevard and Woodland
Avenue

Four White Columns
Richard Medlock
Circa 1975
Painted steel, located on grounds of
the Arts and Communications
Building, Algoma Boulevard and
Woodland Avenue

Yin and Yang
Milt Gardener
Circa 1980
Bronze, located along the shore of
the Fox River

The Guardian
Leo Steppet
Corroded steel and iron, located at
the entrance to Polk Library

Central Wisconsin Counties

Adams
Green Lake
Juneau
Marathon
Marquette
Portage
Waupaca
Waushara
Wood

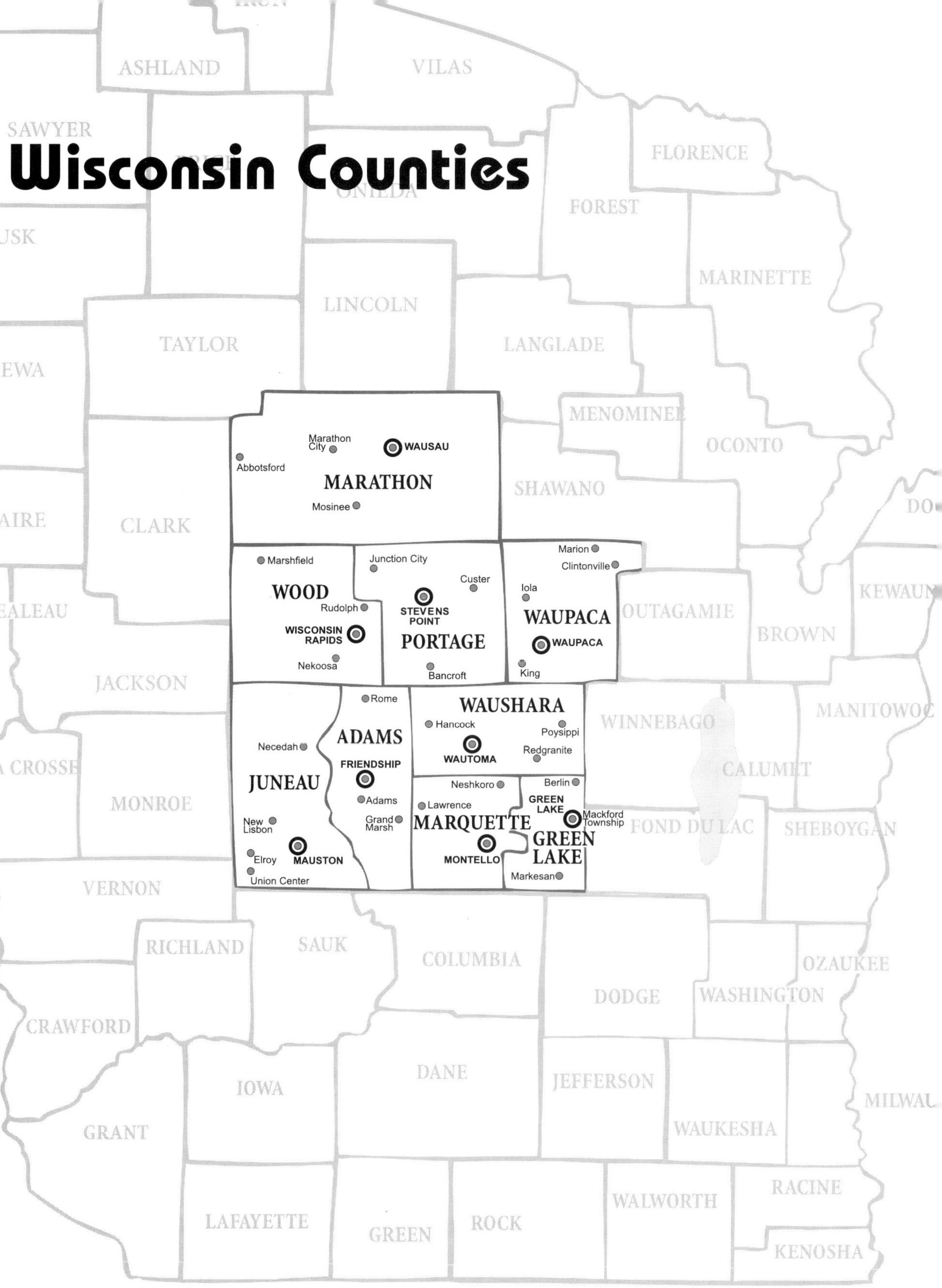

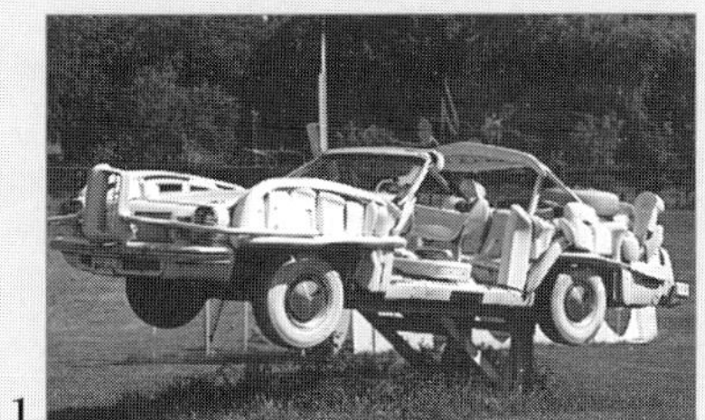

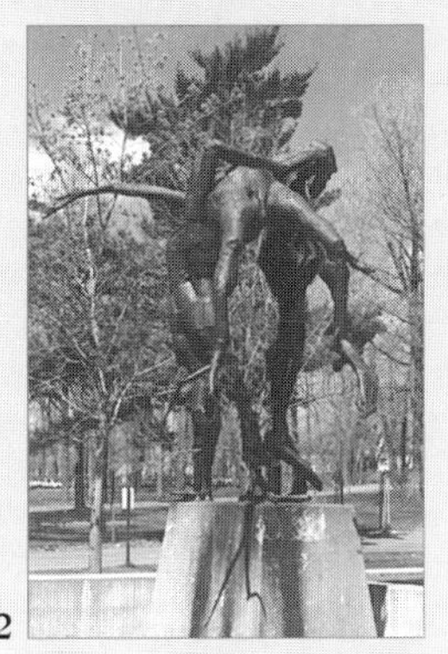

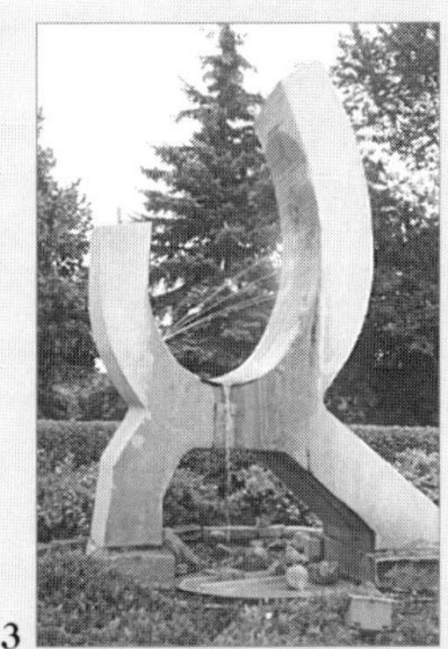

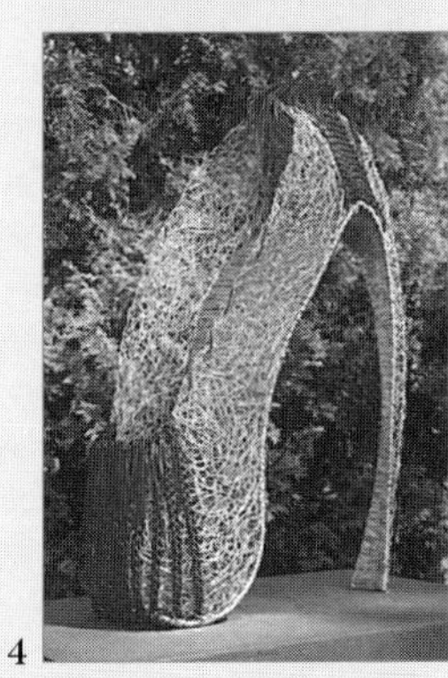

1 *Gloria Hills Car Assemblage*, Green Lake, Green Lake County

2 *Untitled (three figures)* with Fountain in Wausau, Marathon County

3 *Abstract Concrete* (currently in storage), Wausau, Marathon County

4 *The Height of Fashion* at Margaret Woodson Fisher Sculpture Gallery, Wausau, Marathon County

5 *Rudolph Grotto, Jesus Dies on the Cross* in Rudolph, Wood County

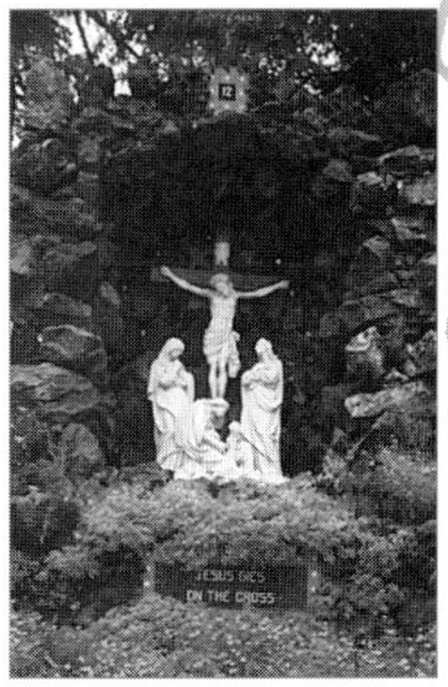

Central Wisconsin Counties

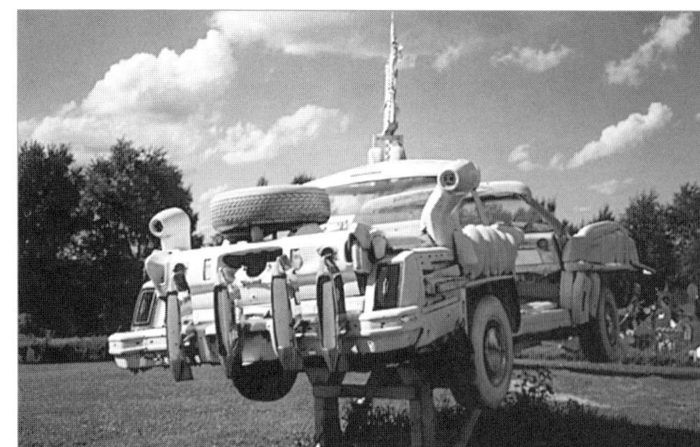
Gloria Hills Sculpture Garden in Green Lake

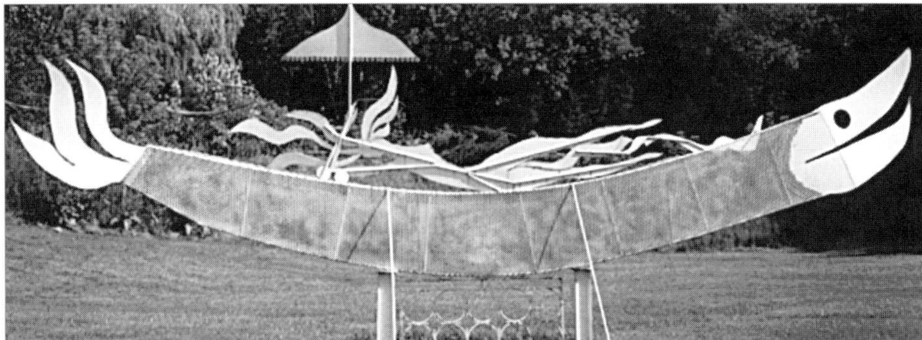
Gloria Hills Sculpture Garden in Green Lake

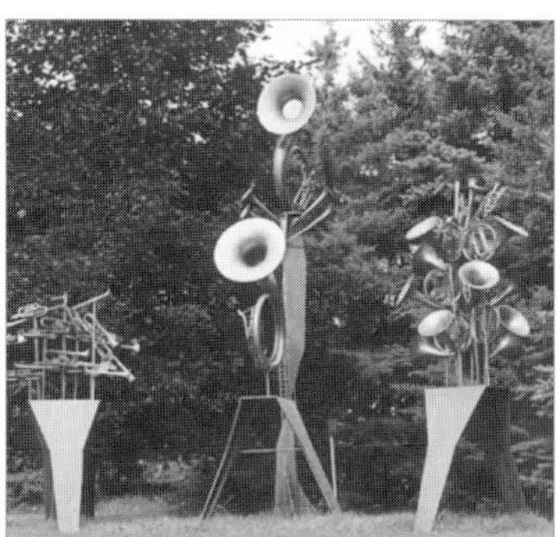
Gloria Hills Sculpture Garden in Green Lake

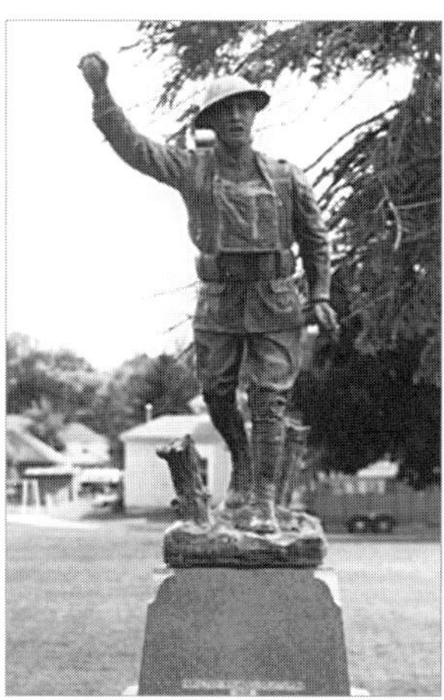
WWI Doughboy in Markesan

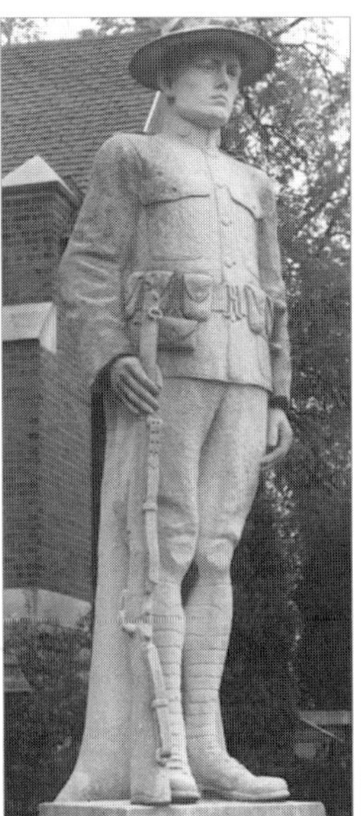
Veterans Monument in Elroy

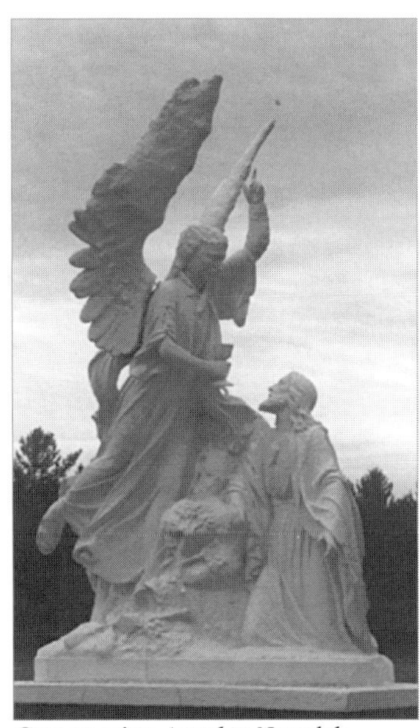
Communion Angel in Necedah

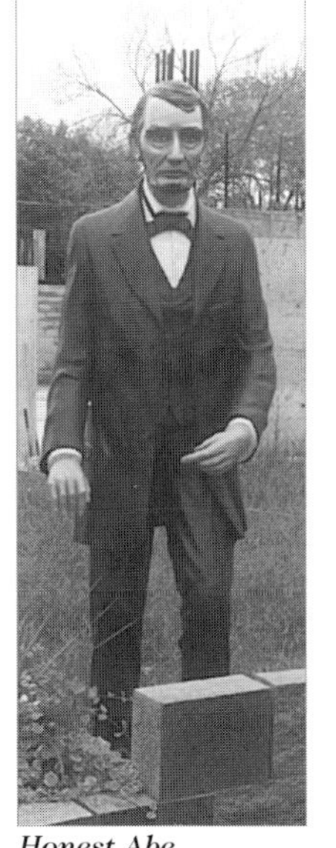
Honest Abe in Necedah

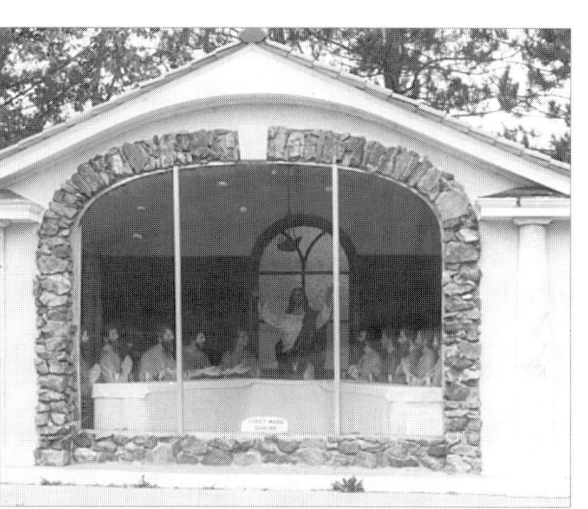
Last Supper Shrine in Necedah

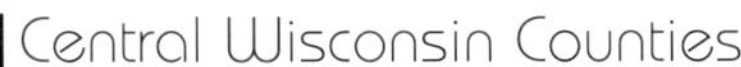
Williams Monument in Berlin

ADAMS

Adams

St. Joseph and the Christ Child
White marble, located at St. Joseph Catholic Church, Main and State streets, Highway 13

Friendship

Father/Son
Dave Watson
Wood, chain saw art, located on Highway 13

Sea Captain
Dave Watson
Wood, chain saw art, located on Highway 13

GREEN LAKE

Gloria Hills Sculpture Garden
W908 Scott Hill Road

Art Environment of over 50 large sculptures
Lester Schwartz
1980-1996
Mixed media and painted steel works including giant fish, embellished cars, instrument ensembles, fantasy forms, and more

Berlin

Soldiers and Sailors Monument
Bronze and marble, located in Nathan Strong Park on E. Huron Street

Williams Monument
Stone relief, located in cemetery

Mackford Township

The Morning of Life
Clarence Shaler
1936
Bronze, located at Mackford Union Cemetery on County Highway X, east of County Highway A

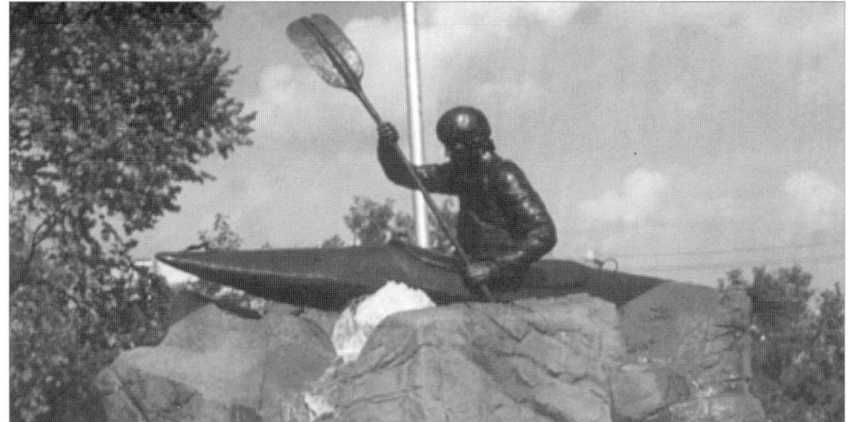

Challenge in Wausau

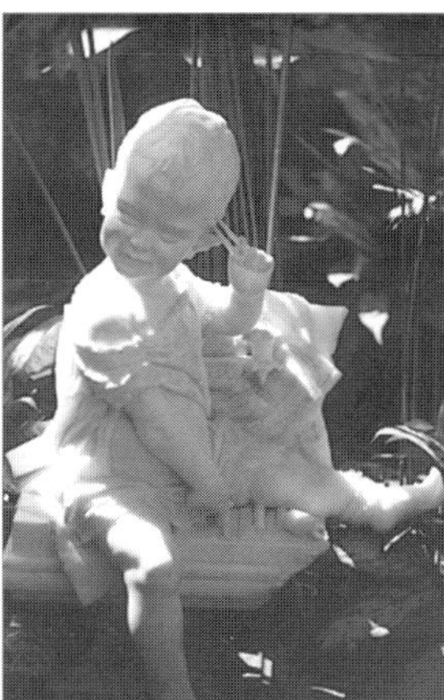

Cherub on Piano in Wausau

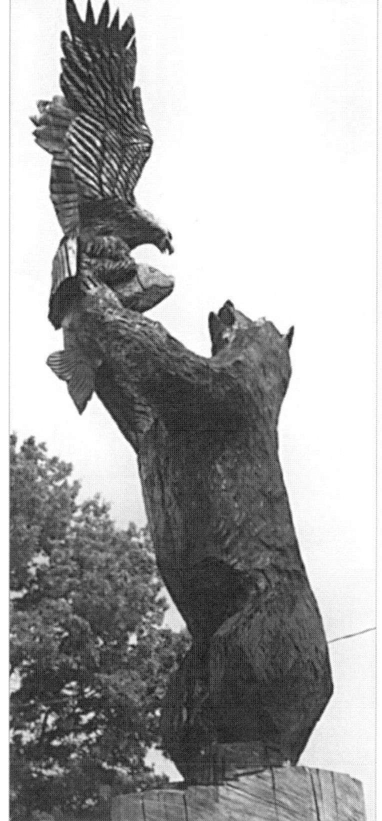

Bear, Fish, and Eagle in Mauston

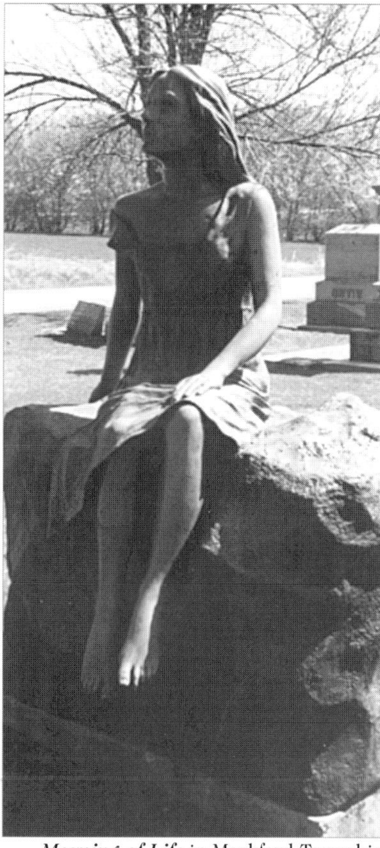

Morning of Life in Mackford Township

Markesan

Spirit of the American WWI Doughboy
E.M. Viquesney
Metal, located in August F. Hein Park

JUNEAU

Elroy

Veterans Monument
Dedicated May 30, 1924
Limestone, located at the Elroy
Public Library, 501 S. Main Street

Mauston

Bear, Fish and Eagle
Dave Watson
August 1990
Wood, chain saw art, located at
W5641 Highway 82

The Dragon and the Wizard
Dave Watson
Wood, chain saw art, located on
Highway 82 at Interstate 94

Necedah

The Grotto of the Blessed Virgin
With sculptures of Christ, Mary,
the Saints and dozens more
Variety of media, located on
Highway 21

MARATHON

Wausau

Boy With the Leaky Boot
J.L. Mott Iron Company
Circa 1923
Bronze, now located in Wausau
Center Mall

Challenge
Mike Capser
1998
Bronze, located on boulevard island
at west entrance to the downtown

Cherub on a Piano Keyboard
Italian marble, located at Wausau
Hospital Center, 333 Pine Ridge
Boulevard

Civil War Soldier
Alexander Robertson and
L.C. Cohn, commissioned by
Lysander Cutler, Post 55
Dedicated July 1886
Pink granite, located at Marathon
County Courthouse grounds, Forest
and 6th streets

Formal Gardens
Wood and concrete, located at
Woodson Park, corner of Stewart and
Washington streets

The Pinery
Edward Schoenberger
1980
Wood telephone poles, located at
Stewart Street, next to Wisconsin
River (temporarily in storage)

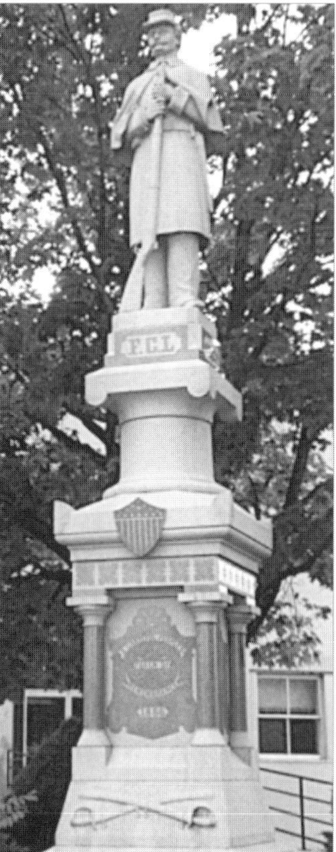

Civil War Soldier in Wausau

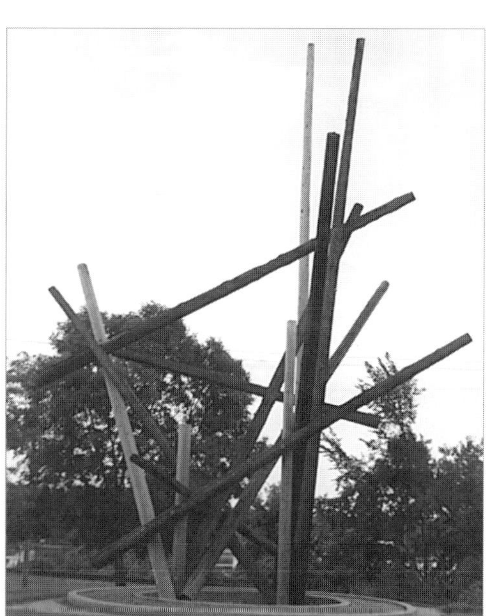

The Pinery in Wausau

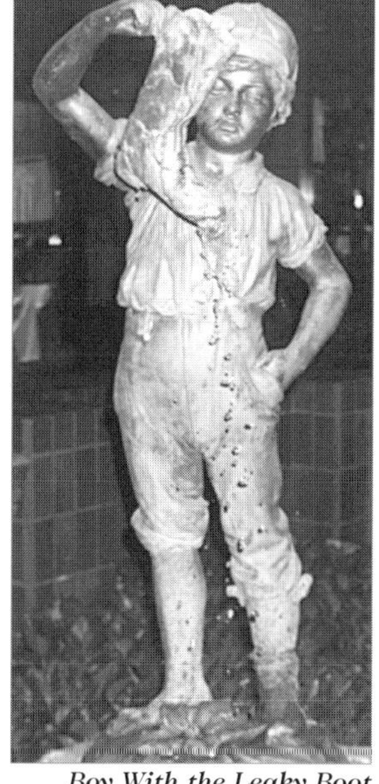

Boy With the Leaky Boot
in Wausau

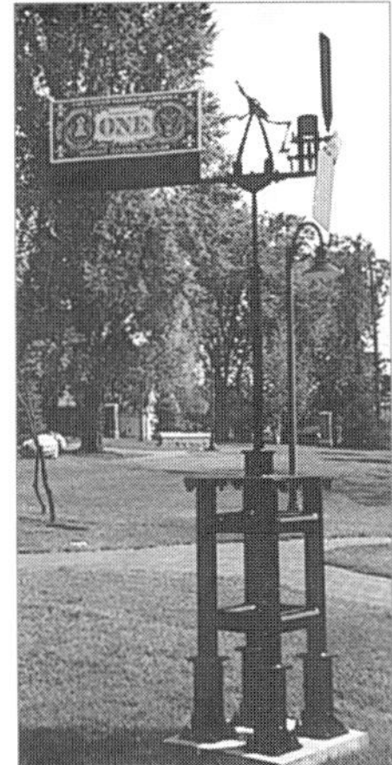

Uncle Sam Blessing the American Way in Margaret Woodson Fisher Sculpture Gallery, Wausau

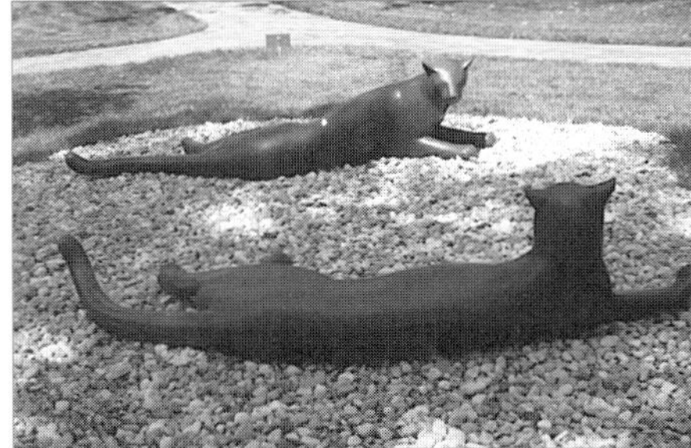

Cougar LA and Cougar LB in Margaret Woodson Fisher Sculpture Gallery, Wausau

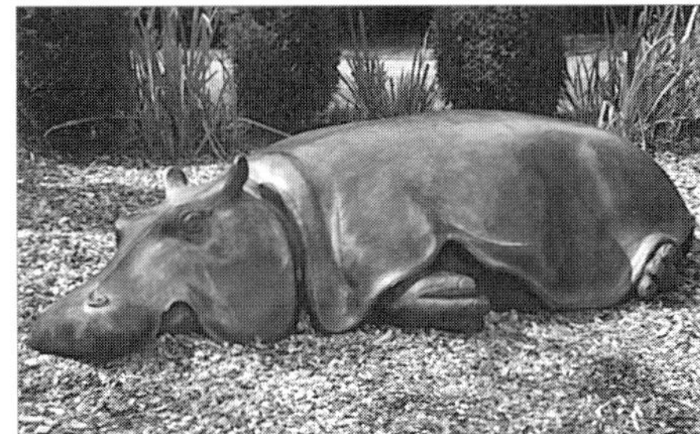

Bronze Hippo in Margaret Woodson Fisher Sculpture Gallery, Wausau

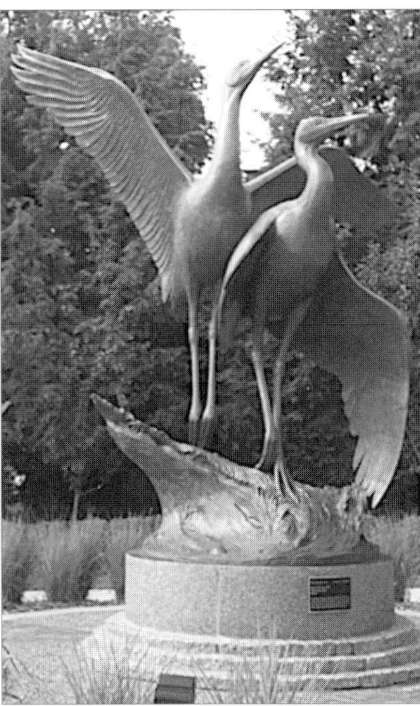

The Great Blue Heron at Leigh Yawkey Woodson Art Museum, Wausau

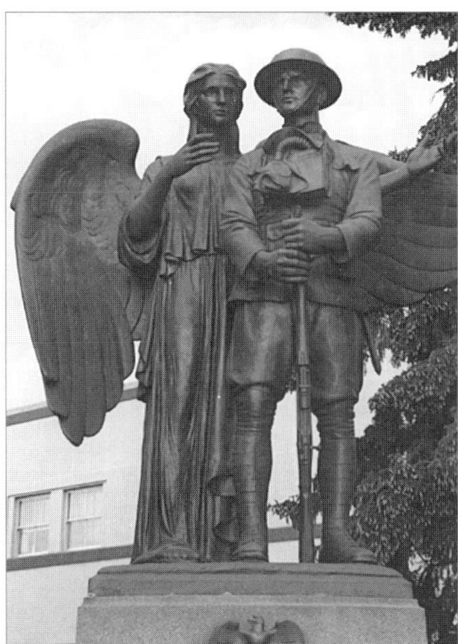

World War I Monument, Doughboy with Angel in Wausau

Untitled (three figures) with Fountain
Dennis Bauer
1971
Iron, located at the UW-Marathon County campus, student commons area

Wenebojo (Way-Na-Bow-Sho)
Edward Schoenberger
Copper, 22 foot tall sculpture, located downtown at the First American National Bank Plaza

Willie's Dilemma
Wausau Tile Company
1981
Concrete, located at Hammond Park, Grand Avenue and Thomas Street

World War I Monument, Doughboy with Angel
Carl A. Heber
Dedicated Memorial Day, 1923
Bronze, located at Marathon County Courthouse lawn, 500 Forest Street

Leigh Yawkey Woodson Art Museum & Margaret Woodson Fisher Sculpture Gallery

700 North Twelfth Street, Wausau

Cougar LA and Cougar LB
Gwynn Murrill
1993-1994
Bronze

Duck Baby
Edith Barretto Parsons
Donated 1922
Bronze

Eagle Rock
Kent Ullberg
1983
Bronze, located at the museum entrance

Folded Square Alphabet U
Fletcher Benton
1988-1994
Steel and paint

Harmony Ridge
Robert Lobe
1993
Heat-treated hammered aluminum

Kakheti
Barry Tinsley
1994
Granite and bronze

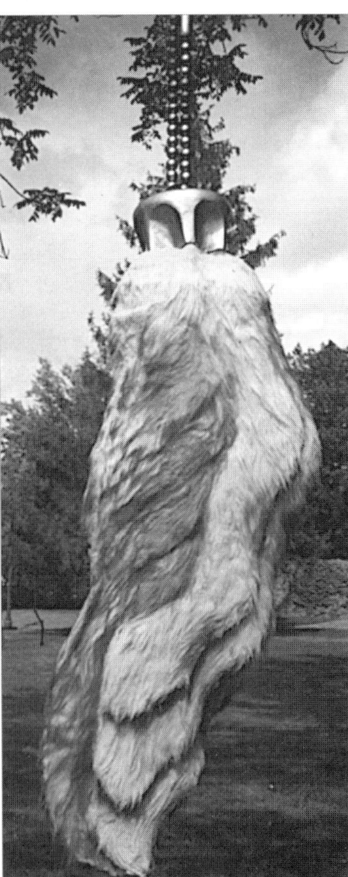

Bon Chance Bébé at Margaret Woodson Fisher Sculpture Gallery, Wausau

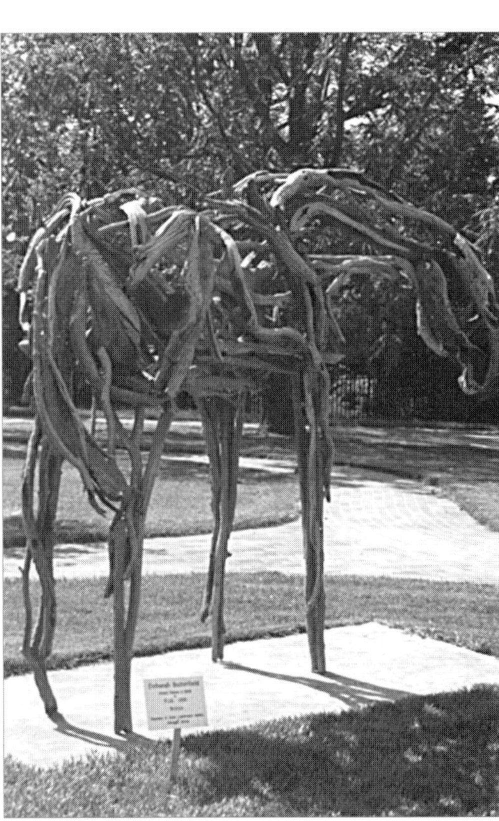

Kua in Margaret Woodson Fisher Sculpture Gallery, Wausau

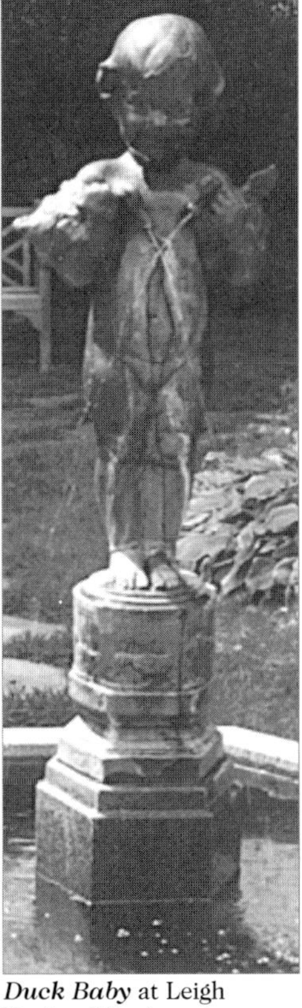

Duck Baby at Leigh Yawkey Woodson Art Museum, Wausau

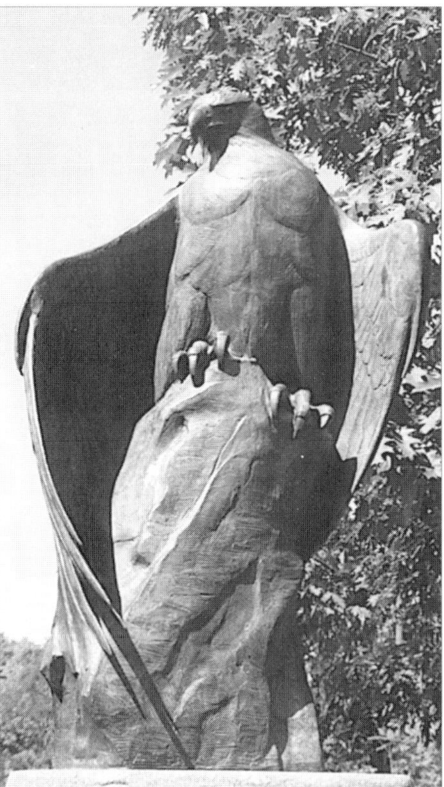

Eagle Rock at Leigh Yawkey Woodson Art Museum, Wausau

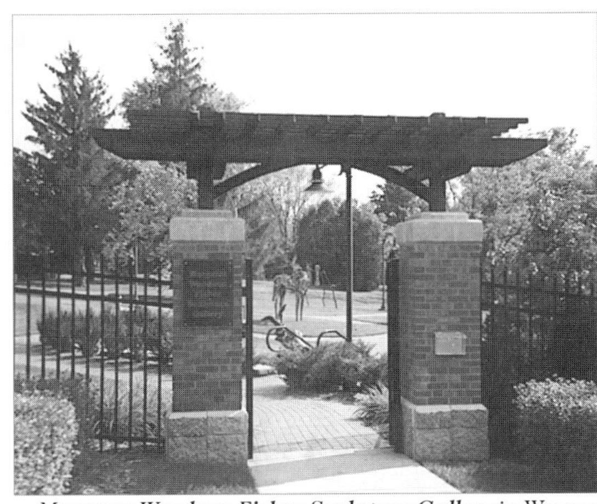

Margaret Woodson Fisher Sculpture Gallery in Wausau

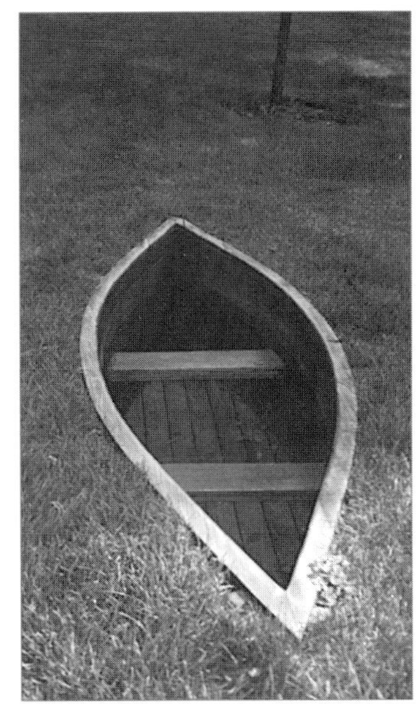

Untitled (Boat) in Margaret Woodson Fisher Sculpture Gallery, Wausau

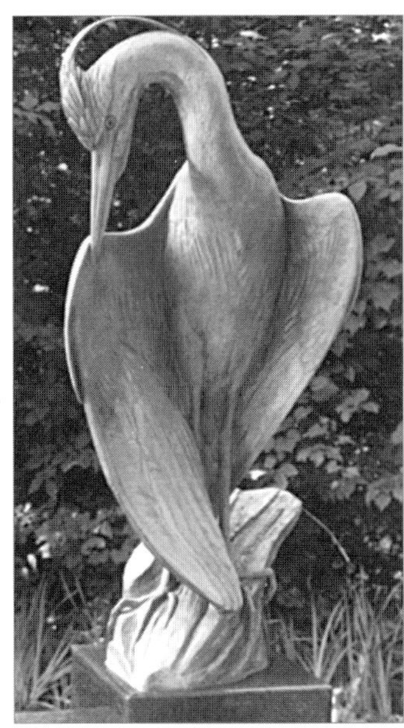

Great Blue Heron at Yawkey Woodson Art Museum, Wausau

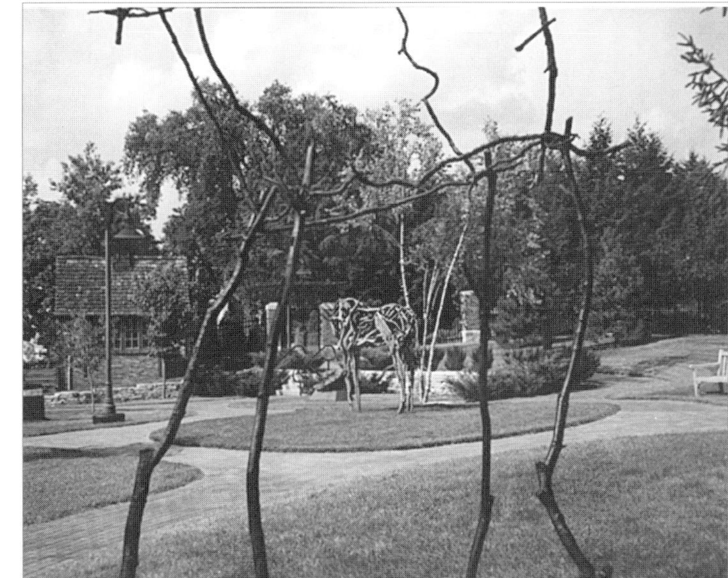

Overview of the Margaret Woodson Fisher Sculpture Gallery in Wausau

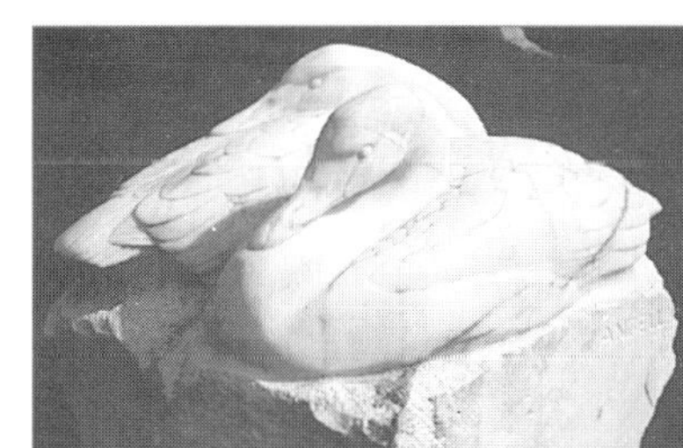

Trumpeter Swans at Leigh Yawkey Woodson Art Museum, Wausau

Margaret Woodson Fisher Sculpture Gallery

Temporary, 2 year exhibits, *Just the Thing, Contemporary Outdoor Sculpture and the Object*, 700 North Twelfth Street

Kua
Deborah Butterfield
1995
Bronze

Mia's Dance X
Michael Todd
1988
Bronze, brass, and paint

The Great Blue Heron
Walter Matia
1986
Bronze

The Great Blue Heron
Kent Ullberg
1988
Bronze

Trumpeter Swans
Tony Angell
1967
White marble

Bon Chance Bébé
Karin Giusti
1998
Polyfoam, synthetic fur, aluminum, two works

Dark Stance
Shaun Cassidy
1994
Painted steel

My Funny Valentine
Ruth Green
1998
Wood, gypsum cement, mason's pigment, metal foil, plastic letters

Pumpkin Series
John Ruppert
1996
Cast aluminum

Silent Head
Meredith Bergmann
1997-1998
Mixed media

Still Life
Christopher Frost
1998
Concrete, two works

The Height of Fashion
Niki Ketchman
1996
Metal and plastic wire

The Helper
Tony Stanzione
1990
Marble, shredded yucca

Treed Gowns
Leslie Wilcox
1998
Galvanized steel screen, lacquer and enamel paint

Uncle Sam Blessing the American Way
George Mossman Greenamyer
1990-1996
Forged and fabricated steel, painted with enamels

Untitled (Boat)
Jun Hoshino
1992
Pinewood boards, gravel

Vacancy
Ed Shay
1998
Cast bronze

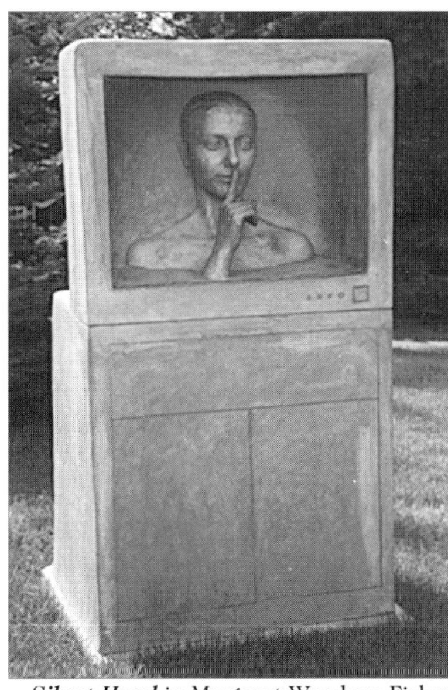

Silent Head in Margaret Woodson Fisher Sculpture Gallery, Wausau

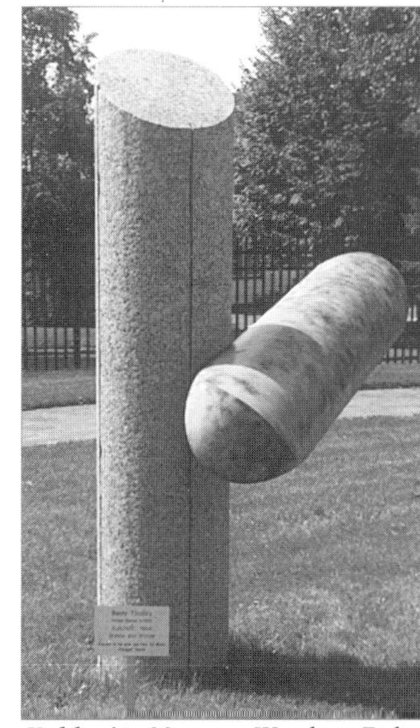

Kakheti in Margaret Woodson Fisher Sculpture Gallery, Wausau

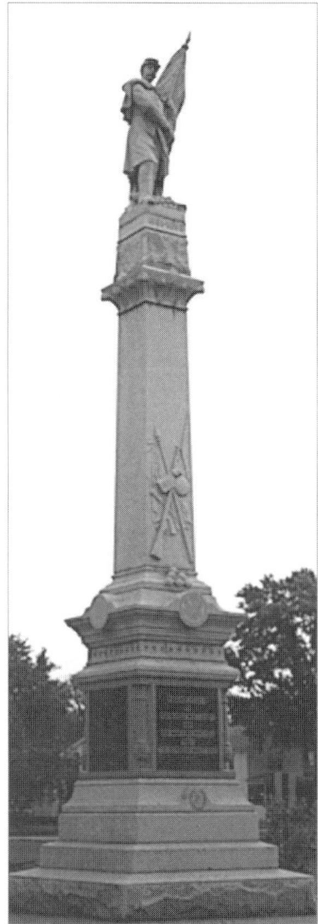

Civil War Monument
in Stevens Point

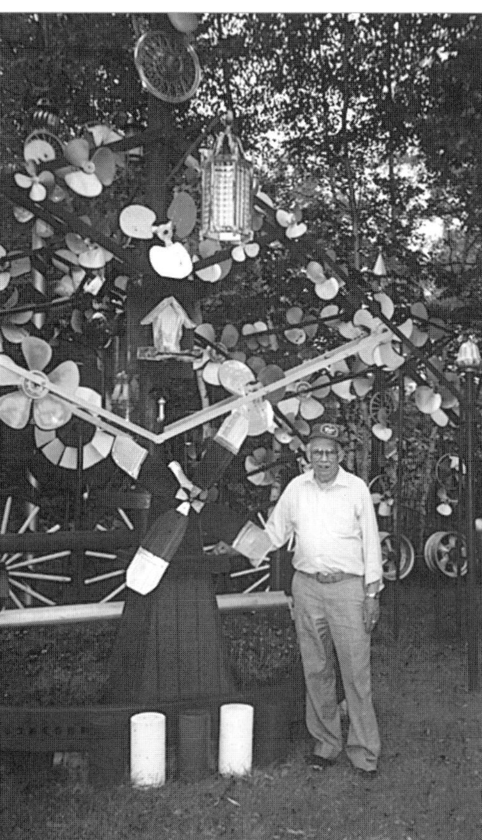

Folk Art Environment with Tony Flatoff, Stevens Point

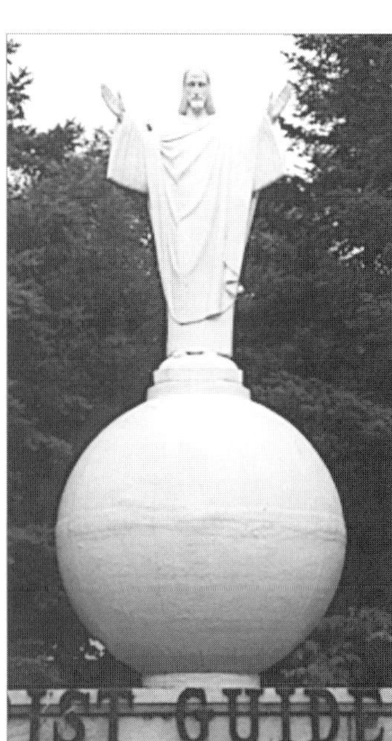

Christ Guide Us in Marshfield

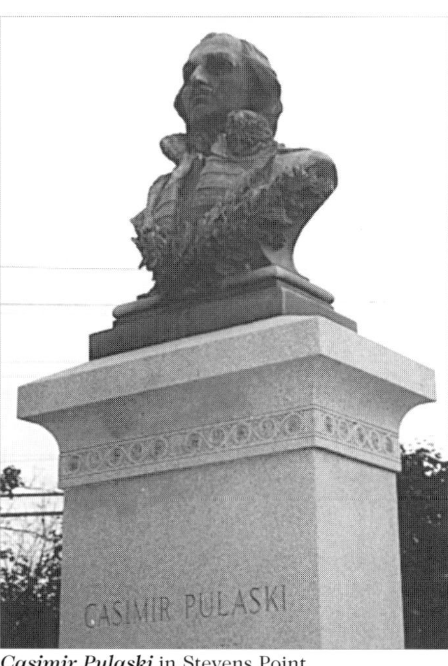

Casimir Pulaski in Stevens Point

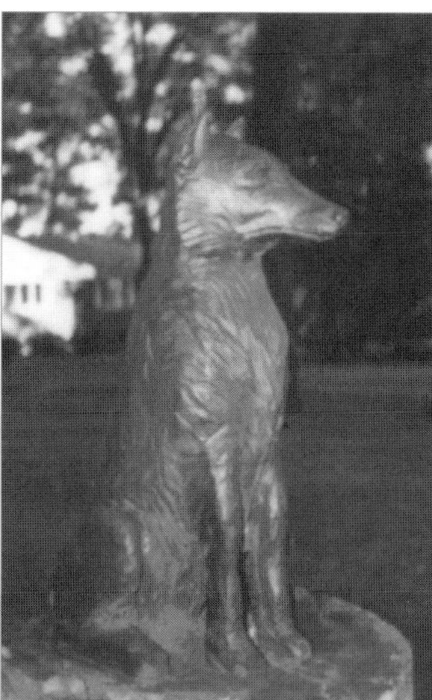

Red Fox in King

MARQUETTE

Neshkoro

Veterans Monument
Mixed media, located at Main and Wall streets

PORTAGE

Custer

The Virgin Mary
1950
Marble, located at St. Mary's Catholic Church, 7176 County Q

Stevens Point

Airborne Forces Monument
Granite and bronze, located at Memorial Park on the Wisconsin River

Blue Star Compass
Norman Keats
1983
Blue concrete and white steel tubing located at UW-Stevens Point, north of the library

Casimir Pulaski
John Paulding
1929
Bronze, located at Main Street (Highway 10), a few miles from intersection of Highways 51 and 10

Civil War Monument
Granite, located at 1516 Church Street

Folk Art Environment
Tony Flatoff
Mixed media, located at the corner of Highway 10 and 556 West Harding Avenue

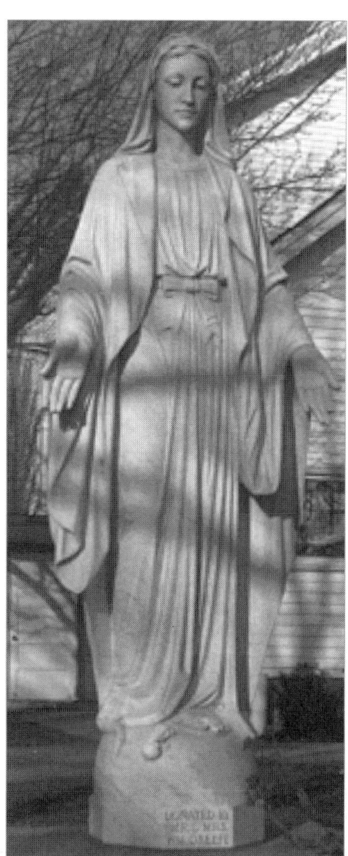

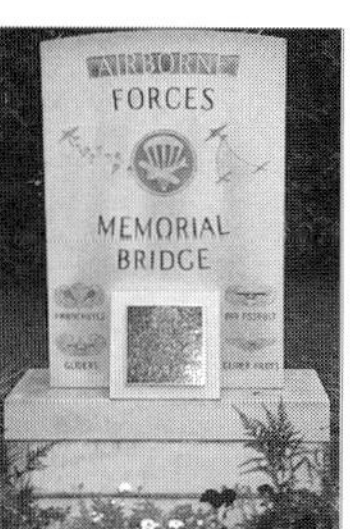

The Virgin Mary in Custer

Airborne Forces Memorial in Stevens Point

The Virgin Mary
Circa 1940
Concrete and stone, located at St. Peters Church, 808 4th Avenue

WAUPACA

Iola

Iola Scandinavia Veterans Memorial
Mixed media, located at Legion Park

King

Bear
Eagle
Red Fox
Kevin Meighan
1992
Wood, carved tree stump figures, located near Bank One building

Marion

In Memory of All Veterans
Mixed media, located at Main Street and Parkview Avenue

WWI Veterans Memorial
Mixed media, located at the Meyer Law Office

WAUSHARA

Poysippi

Veterans Memorial
Mixed media, located at Poysippi Community Park

Redgranite

Memorial to All Veterans
Mixed media, located at Foster Road Cemetery

Wautoma

WWI Doughboy Monument
Mixed media, located at Waushara County Courthouse

WOOD

Marshfield

Christ Guide Us
Mixed media, located at Praschak Wayside on Highway 13

Rudolph

Rudolph Grotto and Gardens

Religious Folk Art Environment
Father Wagner
1927-1983
Concrete and stone, includes *The Wonder Cave*, *The 14 Stations of the Cross*, *The Apparition of Fatima*, *Patriotism*, and other scenes of Christ and the Saints. Also includes gift shop, chapel, gardens and museum

Wisconsin Rapids

Cross Sculpture
William J. Karberg
1997
Corten steel, located at First Lutheran Church, 440 Garfield

Progression
Steve Johnson
1980
Steel, located at Lincoln High School, 1801 S. 16th Street south

Mermaid
Sea Captain
Two Shipmates
Dave Watson
Wood, chain saw art, located at Pirates Cove, 8th Street

Spire
William J. Karberg
1980
Corten steel, located at Lincoln High School, 1801 S. 16th Street

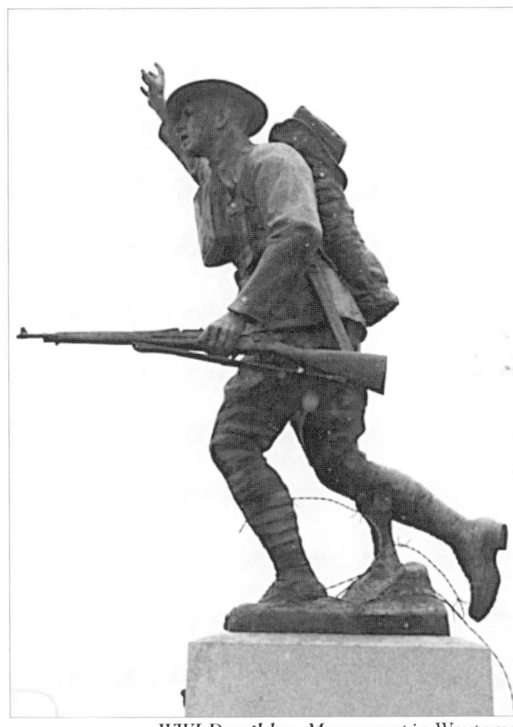

WWI Doughboy Monument in Wautoma

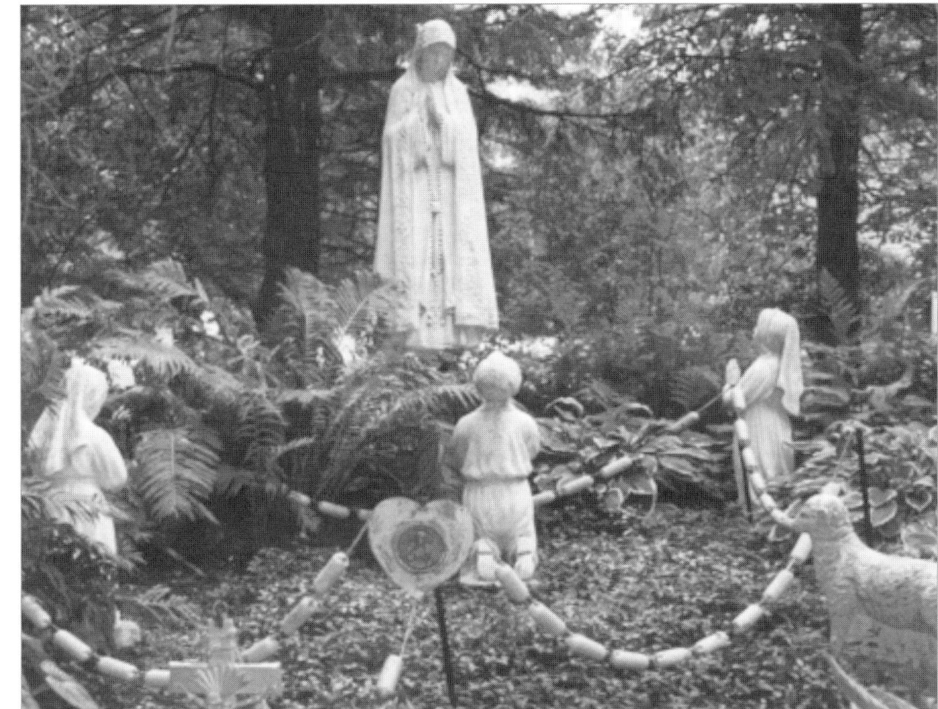

Rudolph Grotto, Virgin at Fatima in Rudolph

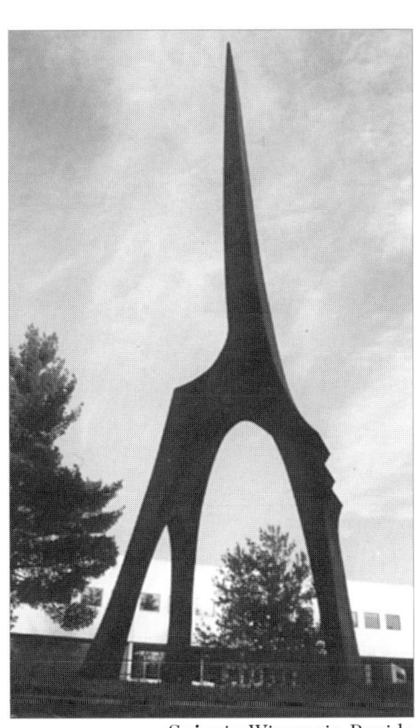

Spire in Wisconsin Rapids

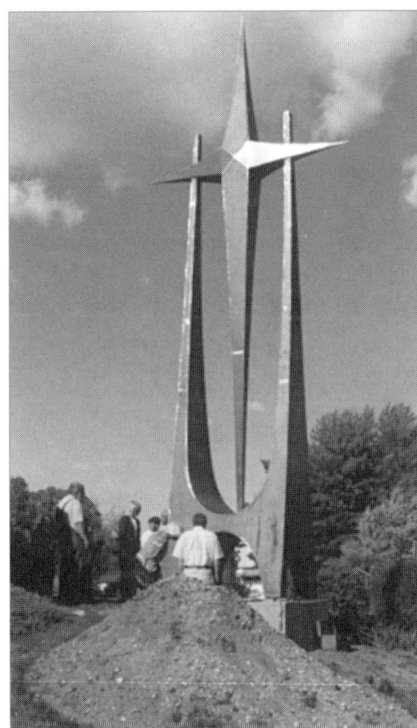

Cross Sculpture in Wisconsin Rapids

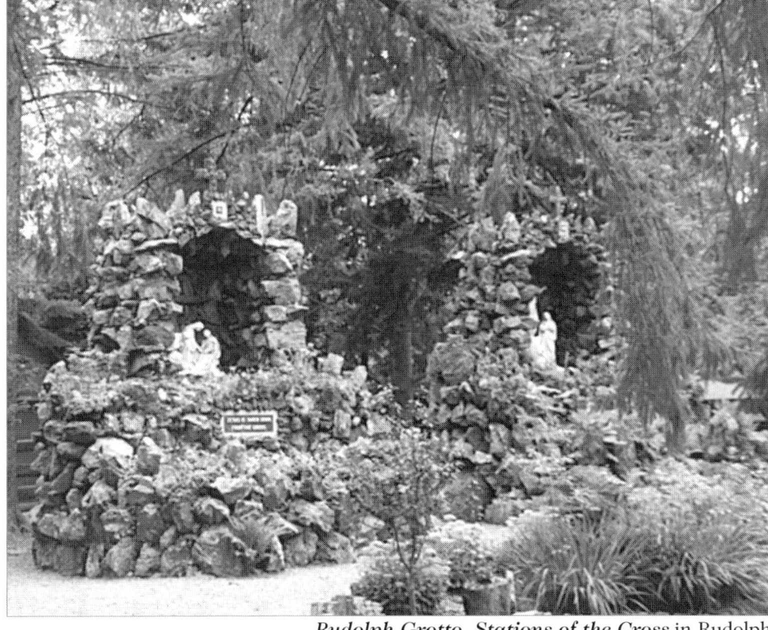

Rudolph Grotto, Stations of the Cross in Rudolph

Southwest Wisconsin Counties

Columbia
Crawford
Dane
Grant
Green
Iowa
LaCrosse
Lafayette
Monroe
Richland
Sauk
Vernon

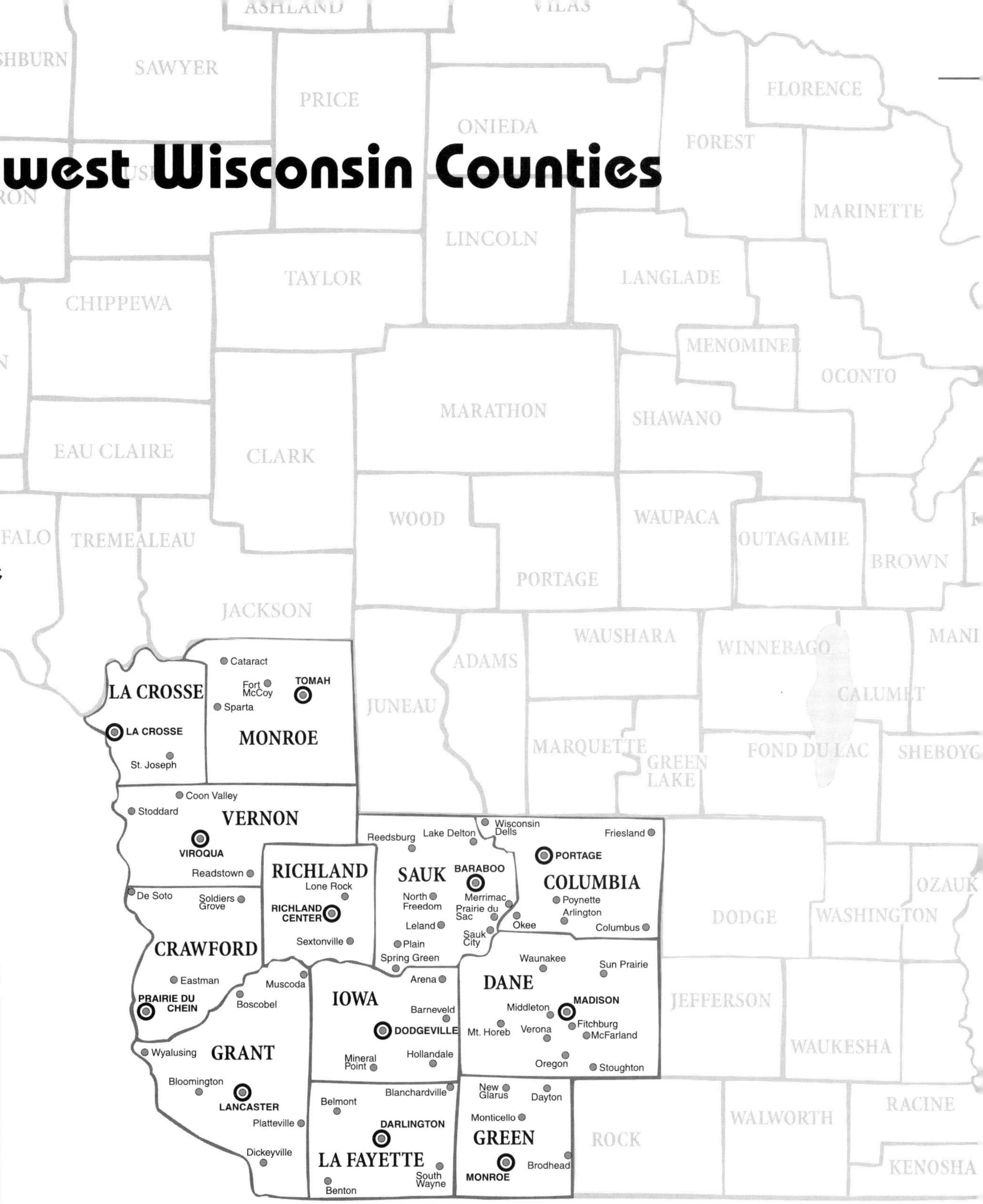

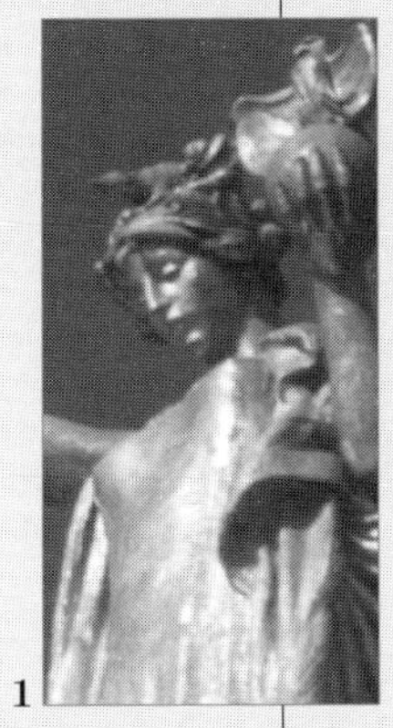

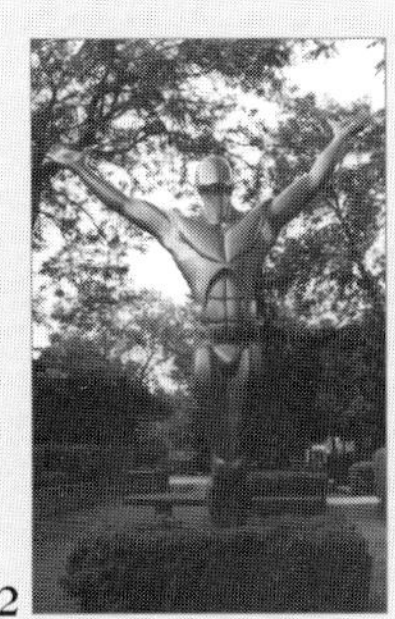

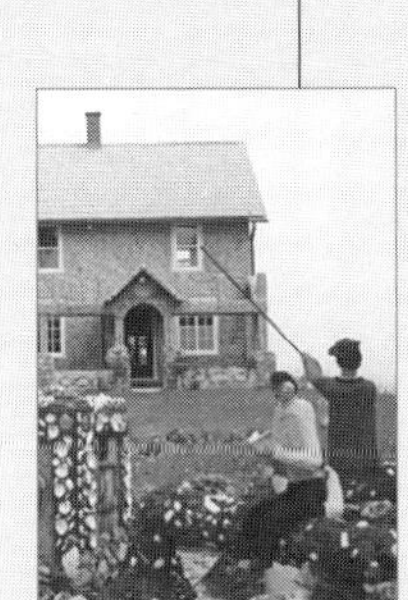

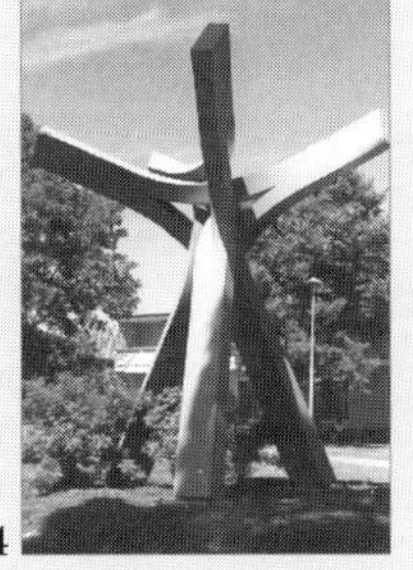

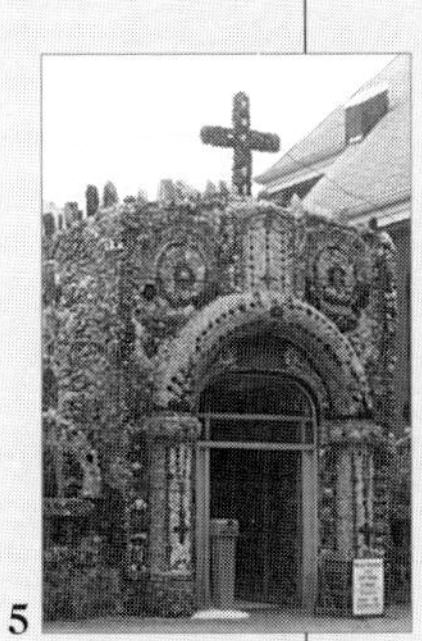

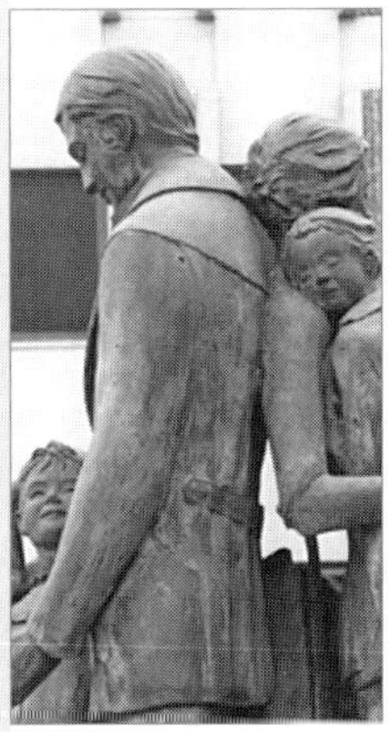

1 *Wisconsin* detail in Madison, Dane County

2 *Asclepius* in Madison, Dane County

3 *Grandview Folk Art Environment* in Hollandale, Iowa County

4 *Lyra* in LaCrosse, LaCrosse County

5 *Holy Ghost Grotto* in Dickeyville, Grant County

6 *Family* detail in LaCrosse, LaCrosse County

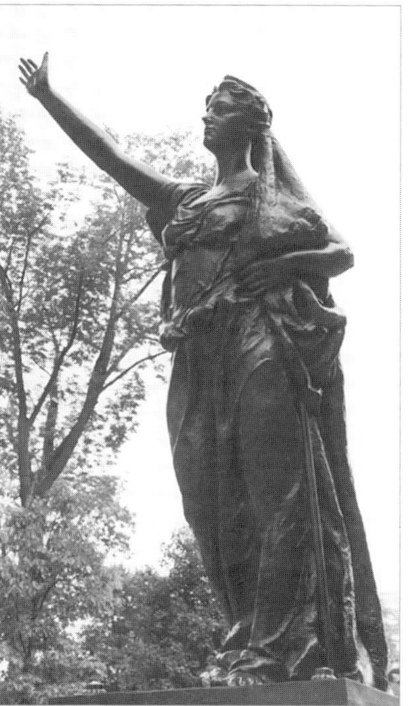
Amphitheater in the Plaza, the Forum of Origin in Madison

Trojan Horse in Wisconsin Dells

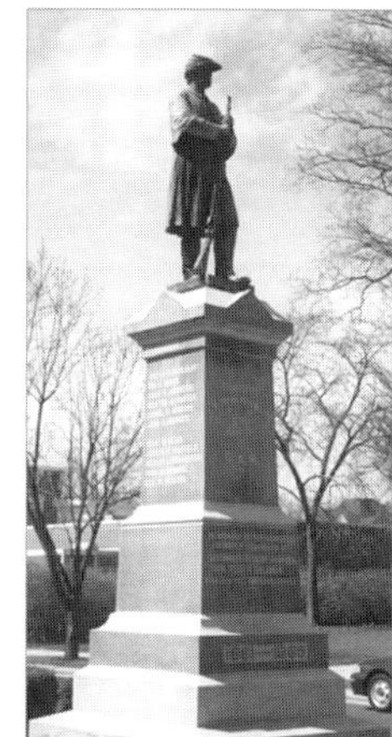
Civil War Soldier Monument in Columbus

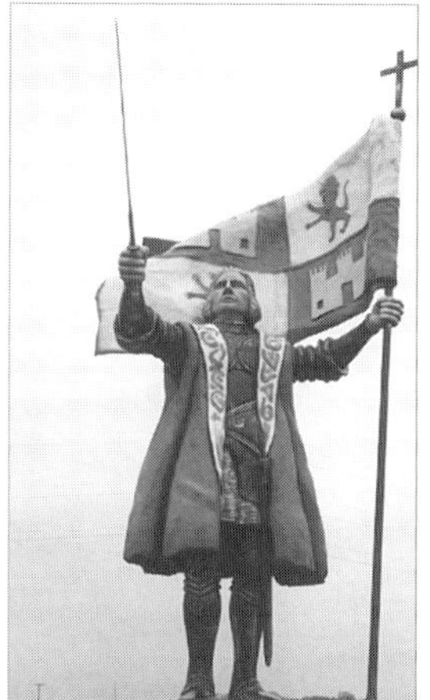
Christopher Columbus Monument in Columbus

Christ and the Children in Madison

Act in Madison

Forward in Madison

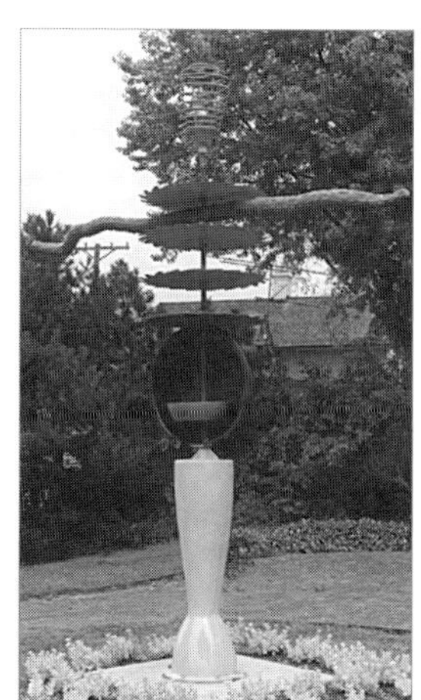

Annie C. Stewart Memorial in Madison

Alexa in Madison

COLUMBIA

Columbus

Christopher Columbus Monument
David W. Oswald
Dedicated Columbus Day, 1988
Painted fiberglass, located on Highway 151 and Highway 16

Civil War Monument
Circa 1900
Granite, located at the corner of West James Street and Dickinson Boulevard

Poynette

Fabricated Fish
Becky Chader
1992
Metal, located on County Highway B

Robert Kellner Memorial
Carol Yasko
July 14, 1984
Concrete, located at MacKenzie Environmental Center, W7303 County Highway CS

Wisconsin Dells

Trojan Horse
1998
Wood, located in Amusement Park on Highway 13

CRAWFORD

De Soto

The Temple, Folk Art Environment Structure
C. M. Powell
Active dates circa 1930
Now dismantled

Prairie du Chien

Veterans Memorial
Granite, located at 220 N. Beaumont Road

DANE

Black Earth

Folk Art Environment
Wally Keller
Circa 1990s
Painted welded steel including Pirate and imaginary creatures, located at 3931, Highway 78

Fitchburg

Weary Veteran
Harry Whitehorse
Circa 1960s
Aluminum, located at 2377 S. Fish Hatchery Road

Madison

Act
William King
1979
Aluminum plate, 26 feet tall, located in Olbrich Park on Atwood Aveune. Originally located behind the Madison Civic Center

Alexa
Susan Walsh
1992
Painted cast iron, steel and aluminum, located at Kerr-McGee Park, 728 Jennifer Street

Amphitheater in the Plaza, the Forum of Origin
L. Brower Hatcher
1993
Stone columns, stainless steel mesh, bronze, aluminum, and iron, 30 feet across and 23 feet high. Located at the intersection of North Carroll and West Mifflin streets

Annie C. Stewart Memorial
Frederic J. Clasgens
1924
White Italian Carrara marble fountain, located south of 632 Wingra Street, the old pedestrian entrance to Vilas Zoo

Asclepius - Greek God of Healing
Harry Whitehorse
Circa 1960s
Aluminum, 8 feet high, located at Monona Grove Clinic, 5001 Monona Drive

Christ and the Children
Mary Ann Lohman
Circa 1960s
Metal, located in front of Edgewood Elementary School, 2324 Edgewood Drive

Christ and the Children
Stone, located at Lutheran Church, Gorham and Wisconsin Avenue

Content: James A. Graaskamp
Michael A. Burns
1989
Quartzite, limestone, granite, bronze, and iron, located at 1953 E. Mifflin Street

County War Memorial Fountain
James Potter
1970
Concrete, located at 1881 Expo Mall E., off Highways 12 and 18

Entrance Arch
Cass Gilbert
1907
Stone, located at Madison Area Technical College, 211 N. Carroll Street. Formerly entrance to Madison Central High School which was torn down in 1987 leaving in place only this arch and its relief carved figures

Fiddleheads
Sylvia U. Beckman
Dedicated June 5, 1988
Dubuque limestone, 12 feet high, located at Olbrich Botanical Gardens, 3330 Atwood Avenue

Flight Column
O.V. Shaffer
1982
Welded stainless steel, located at Verex Building courtyard at the end of Butler Street

Forward
Jean Pond Miner Coburn
1893
Copper, located at the State Historical Society. This *Forward* was located at the State Capitol for a hundred years

Gateway Project
Edgar Jerome Jeter
Dedicated October 24, 1987
Bronze and fiberglass, 10 feet tall, located at 1401 S. Park Street.

Gay Liberation
George Segal
1980
Cast bronze of four figures, it was located in Orton Park and was donated to New York City in 1990

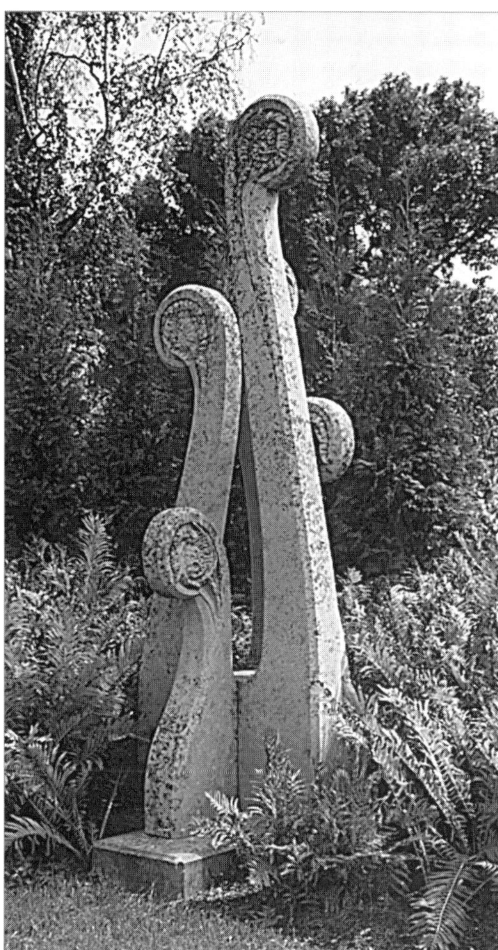

Fiddleheads in Madison

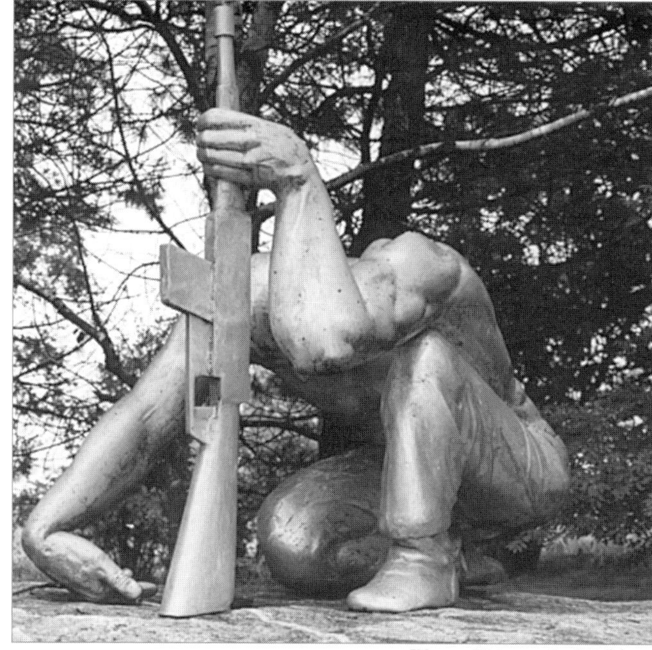

Weary Veteran in Fitchburg

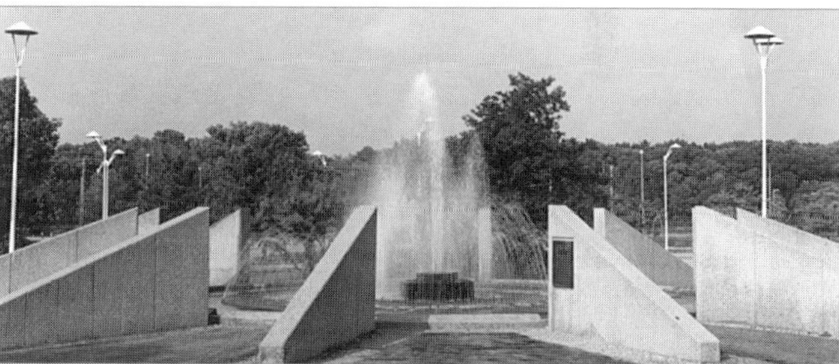

County War Memorial Fountain in Madison

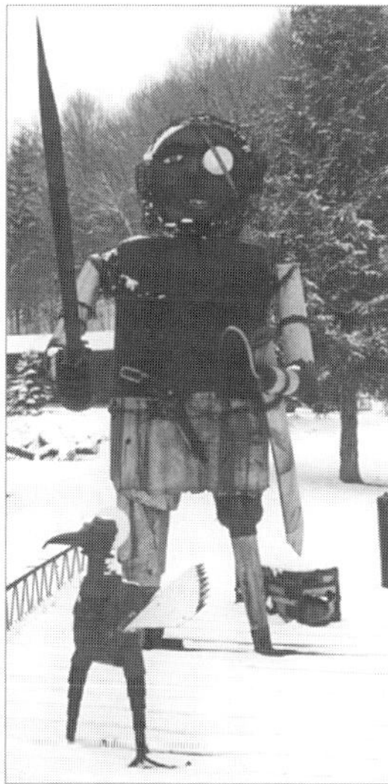

Folk Art Environment, Pirate in Black Earth

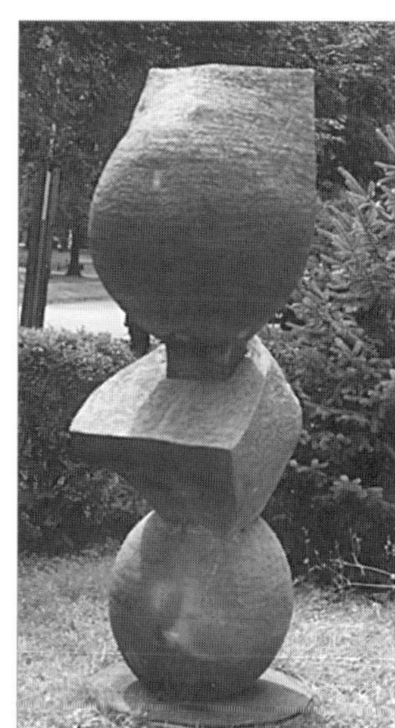

Homage to Brancusi in Madison

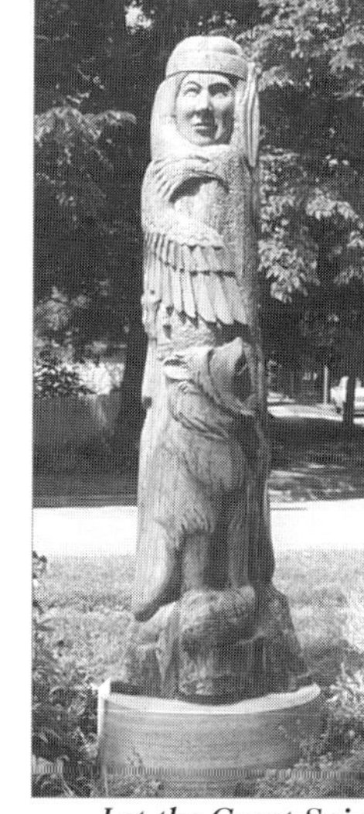

Let the Great Spirit Soar in Madison

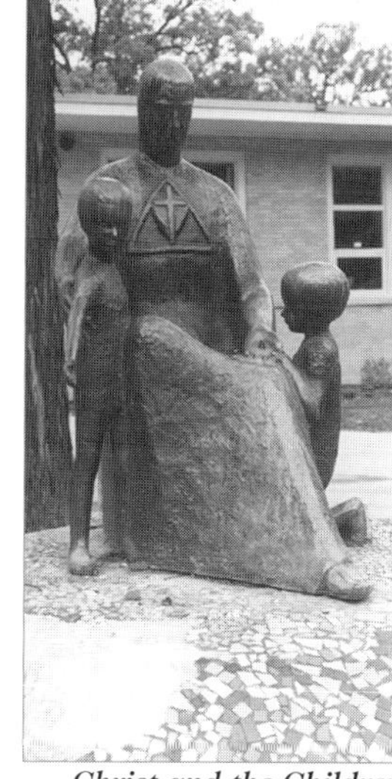

Christ and the Children in Madison

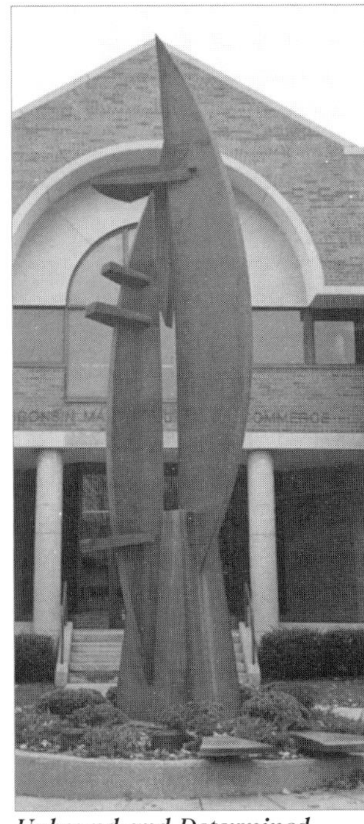

Unbound and Determined
in Madison

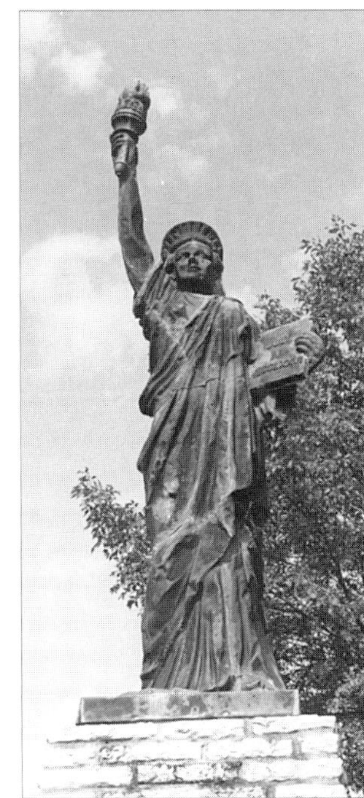

Statue of Liberty Replica
in Madison

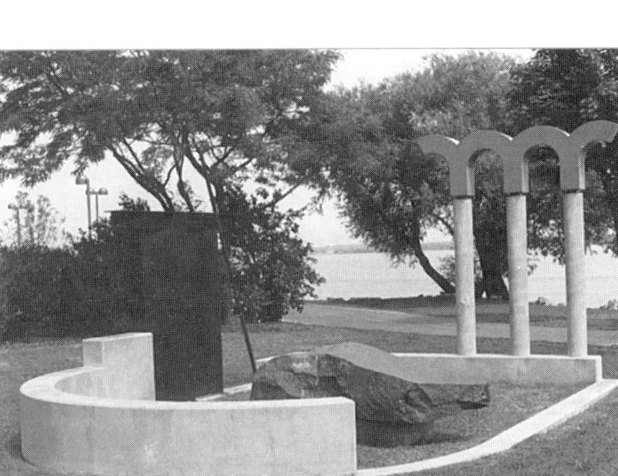

Timekeeper in Madison

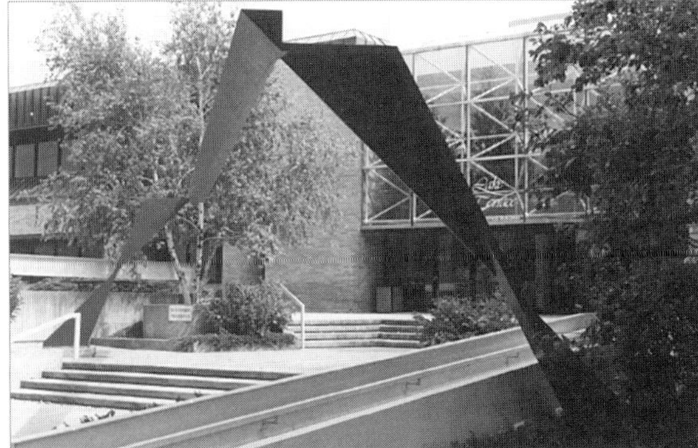

Levitation of the Enchanted Princess in Madison

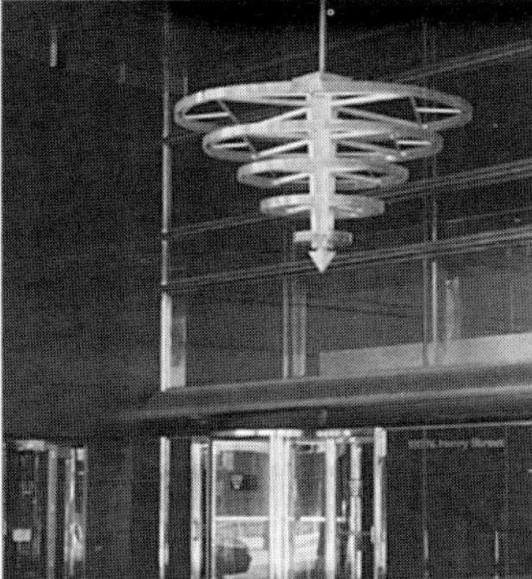

Madison at Federal Courthouse
in Madison

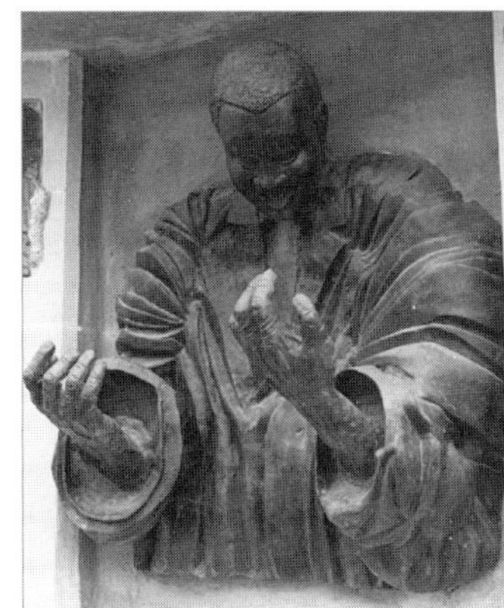

Living the Dream in Madison

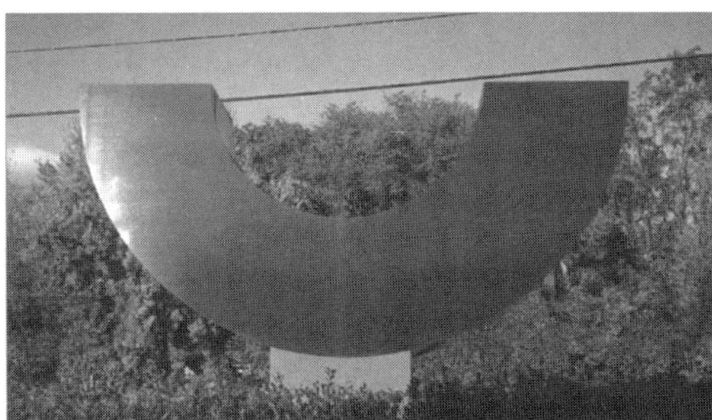

Up Reach in Madison

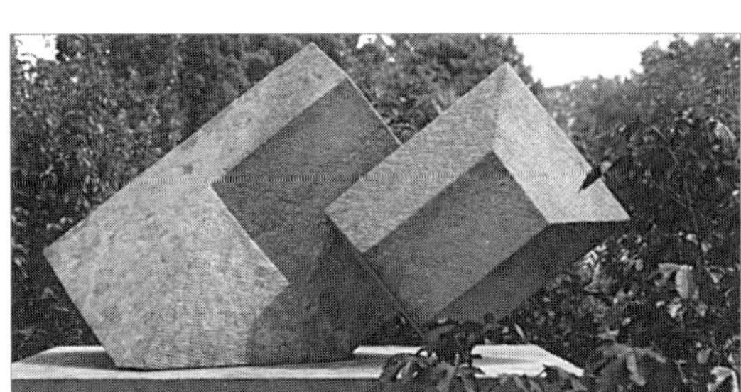

Untitled (Tollakson) in Madison

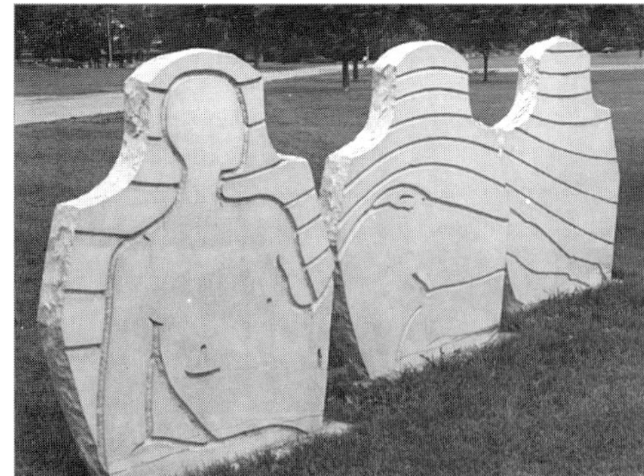

Sunbathers in Madison

Hieroglyph

O.V. Shaffer

1965

Forged and welded brass, 12 feet high, located in front of Madison Public Library, 201 W. Mifflin Street

Homage to Brancusi

Joan Gardy Artigas

1994

Ceramic, wood fired sculpture, located at 1150 Spaight Street

Justice

James Watrous

1951

Aluminum, located on the City County Building on the wall facing South Carroll Street

Let the Great Spirit Soar

Harry Whitehorse

1991

Carved hackberry tree trunk, located at 2930 Lakeland and Maple streets

Levitation of the Enchanted Princess

Tony DeLap

1984

Painted blue steel, 11 feet high by 42 feet long, located at the entrance of the Lake Terrace building, 121 E. Wilson Street

Living the Dream

Frank J. Brown

1993

Ceramic, stone, bronze, eight feet by eight feet, located at 210 Dr. Martin Luther King, Jr. Boulevard

Madison

Christopher Sproat

January 24, 1987

Metal, plastic, glass, and red neon light sculpture located in outer portico of Federal Courthouse, 120 N. Henry Street

Mona Webb Art Environment

Mona Webb

Circa 1970-1998

Mixed media, located at 1356 Williamson Street

Resolving

Michael A. Burns

Circa 1989

Brass, concrete, neon lights, and water, located in the courtyard of the Wiedenbach Industrial Warehouse Apartments, West Mifflin Street

Spare Time

John Martinson

Dedicated 1979

Painted steel, 11 feet high, located on the roof of 11 W. Main Street

Spiraling Tower

Wood, located at 5805 Hammersley Road

Statue of Liberty Replica

Replica of F. A. Bartholdi's Statue of Liberty

Dedicated June 14, 1951

Copper, Boy Scout Project, located at Warner Park, corner of Northport Drive and Sherman Avenue. One-nineteenth the size of the original statue on Bedloe's Island in New York City

Sunbathers

Mary Michie

1993

Limestone, located in Olbrich Park, on Atwood Avenue

Timekeeper

Robert Curtis

1983

Granite boulder, stone, Corten steel, 16 by 24 feet, located in Law Park, on the west side of Lake Monona

Unbound and Determined

Michael Anderson

Dedicated September 1998

Corten steel, 24 feet high, located at WMC, 501 E. Washington

Untitled
Points of Contact

Stephan Rekstad

1990

Welded steel, located at Center and Ohio (in storage)

Untitled

Alan Tollakson

1980

Indiana limestone, located at Olbrich Botanical Gardens, 3330 Atwood Avenue

Up Reach
Bo von Hohenlohe
1993
Painted steel, 14 feet high, located in front of Marshall Erdman and Associates, 5117 University Avenue

Verex Syzygy
O.V. Shaffer
1986
Stainless steel, two stories high, located at 150 E. Gilman Street, in front of the Verex Corporation

Wisconsiana
Lloyd Hamrol
1988 installation
Wausau red granite, Percent for Art funds, located at 101 South Webster Street

Art Environment
Sculptures by Sidney E. Boyum
237 Waubesa Street
Private property; art to be relocated

Untitled abstraction
Circa 1987
Concrete, plastic

Untitled, Bear Chair
Untitled, Japanese lantern
Untitled, Reclining female nude abstraction
Circa 1987
Concrete

The following Sid Boyum sculptures are to be relocated in the Atwood neighborhood on Madison's east side in the near future.

Blue Urn
Concrete, located at Atwood and Jackson

Geometric with Round Window
Concrete, located near First Street

Head with Owl Columns
Concrete, located at Atwood and Dunning streets

Lantern
Concrete, located at Schenk's Corners

Layered Pyramid
Lion Lantern
Concrete, located in Olbrich Park

Man Eating Mushroom
Concrete, located near bike path at Atwood

Man With Book
Concrete, located near bike path on Corry Street

Mushrooms
Concrete, located in Yahara Place Park

Polar Bear
Concrete, located in Elmside Circle Park

Three-Leg Lantern
Woman in Square
Concrete, located near the Blue Plate Diner Restaurant on Atwood

Tree-Limb Faces
Concrete, located Division Street and Atwood Avenue

Wisconsin State Capitol

Badger
Circa 1900
Cast bronze, now located inside near Governor's Office. Originally from the First *USS Wisconsin* Battleship

Wisconsin
Daniel Chester French
erected in 1914
Gilded bronze, 15 feet 5 inches high, on top of the Capitol dome in Capitol Square, one of the finest statues in Wisconsin

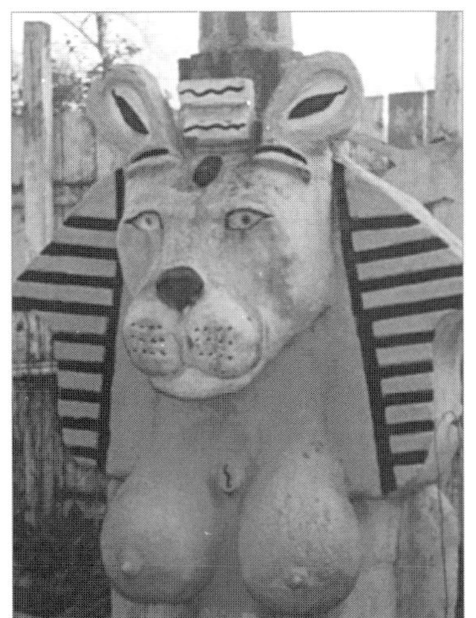

Sid Boyum Art Environment in Madison

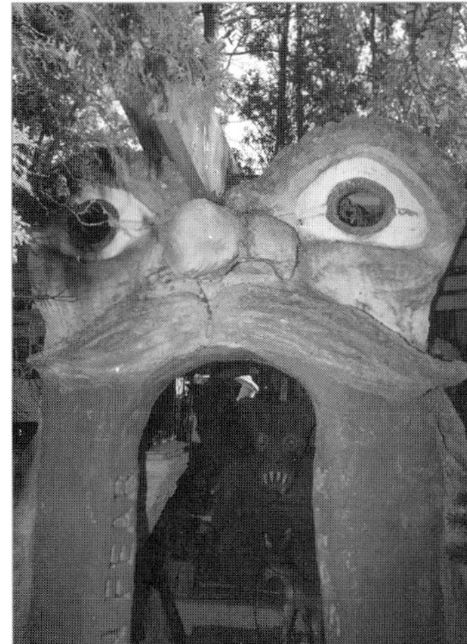

Sid Boyum Art Environment in Madison

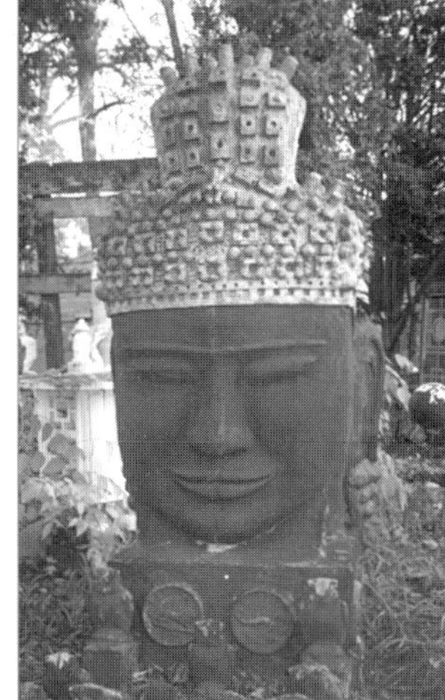

Sid Boyum Art Environment in Madison

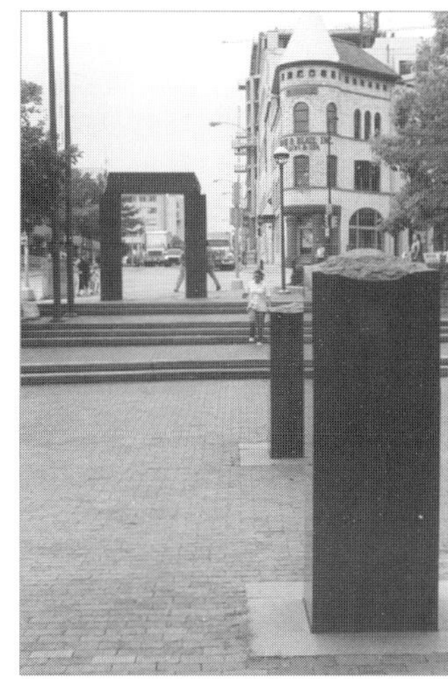

Wisconsiana in Madison

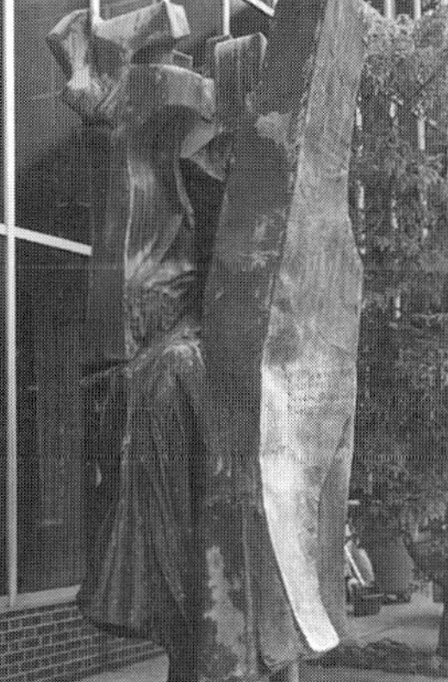
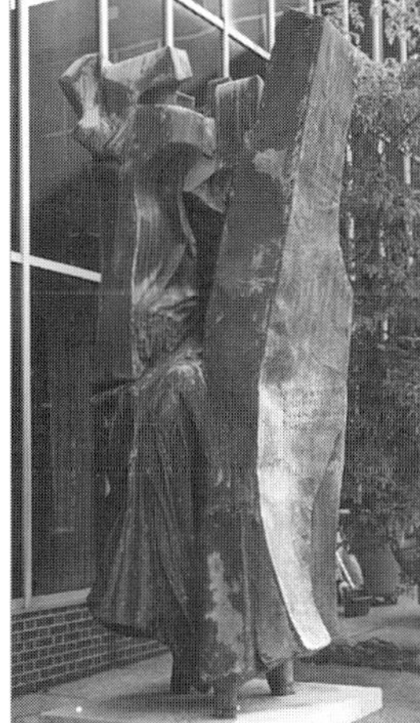

Hieroglyph in Madison

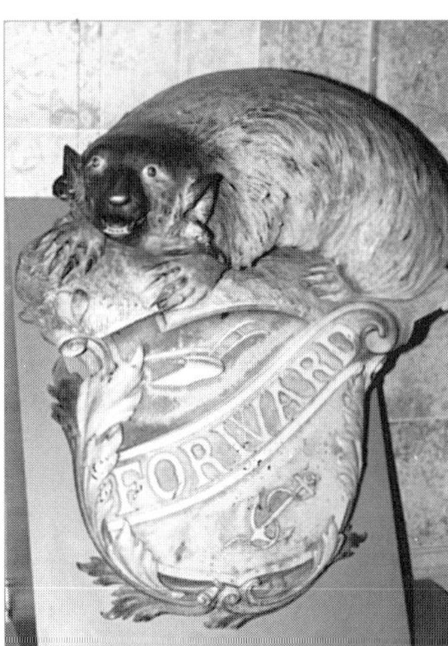

Badger at State Capitol in Madison

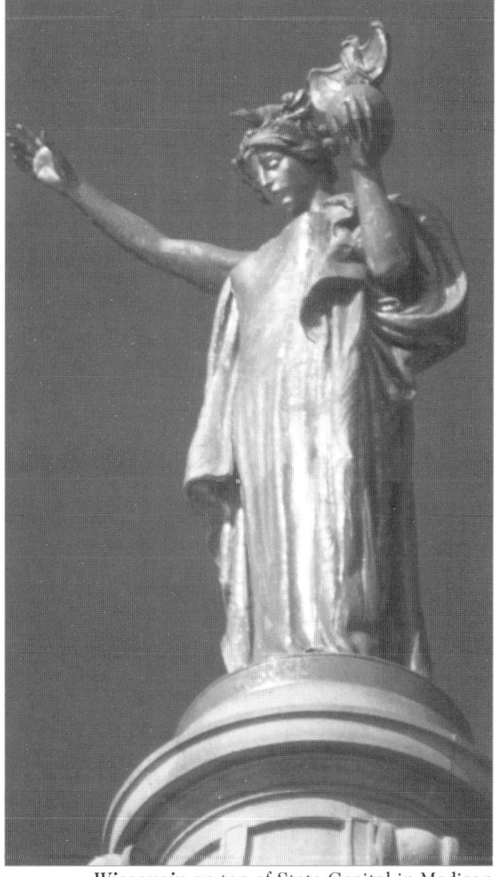

Wisconsin on top of State Capitol in Madison

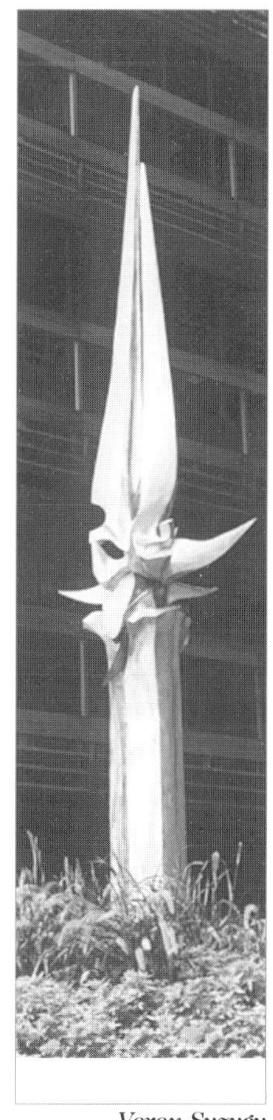

Verex Syzygy in Madison

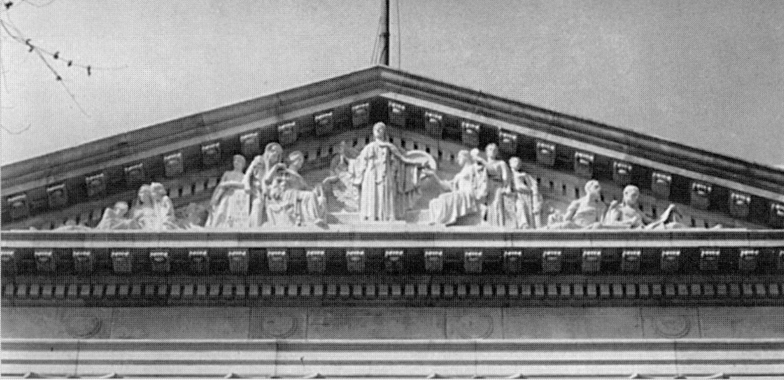

East Pediment at State Capitol in Madison WHi (W6) 6191

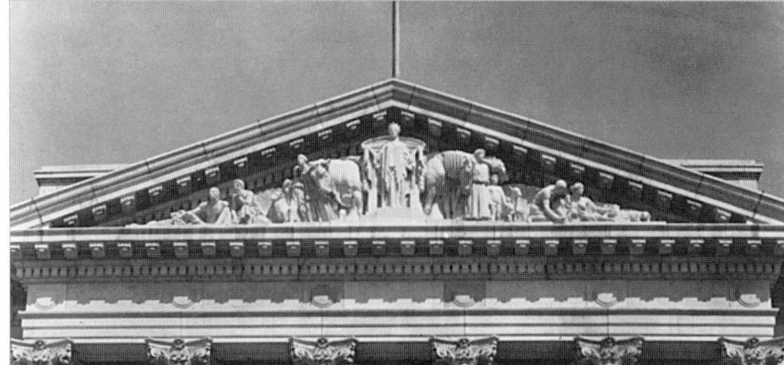

West Pediment at State Capitol in Madison WHi (W6) 6192

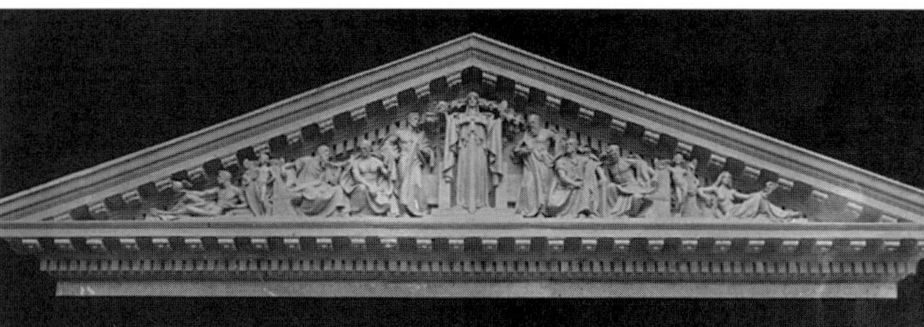

South Pediment at State Capitol in Madison WHi (W6) 6211

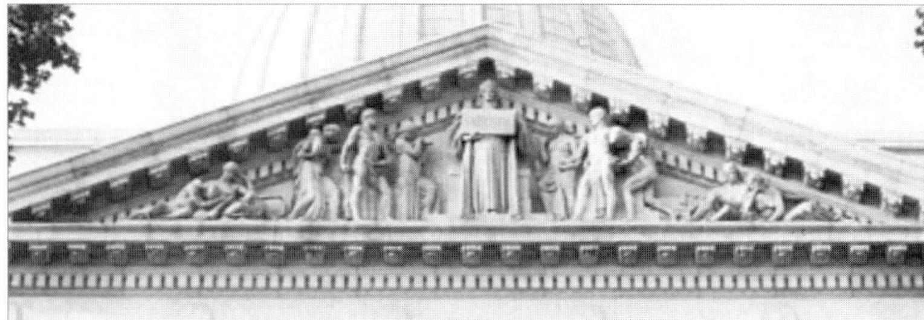

North Pediment at State Capitol in Madison

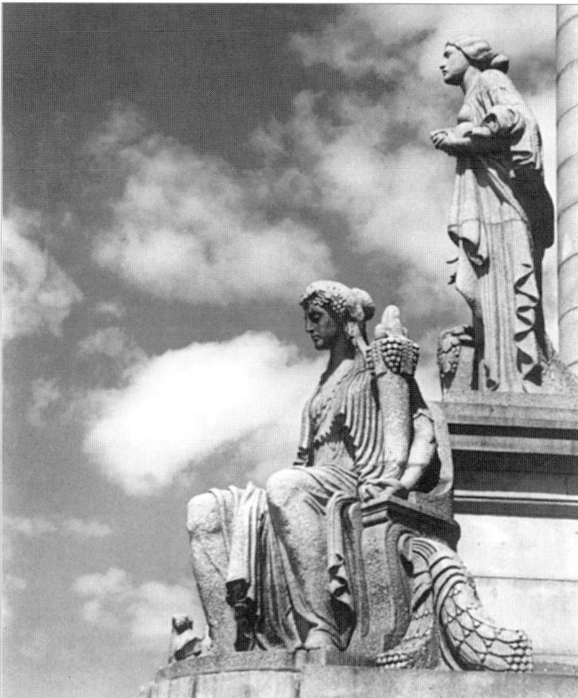

Prosperity and Abundance at State Capitol in Madison
WHi (X3) 12581

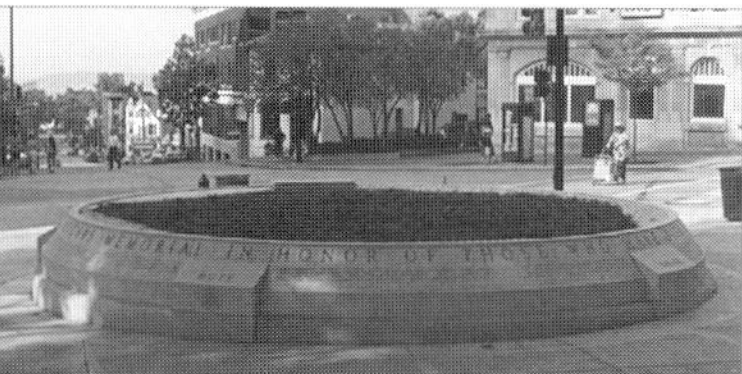

Law Enforcement Officers Memorial at
State Capitol in Madison

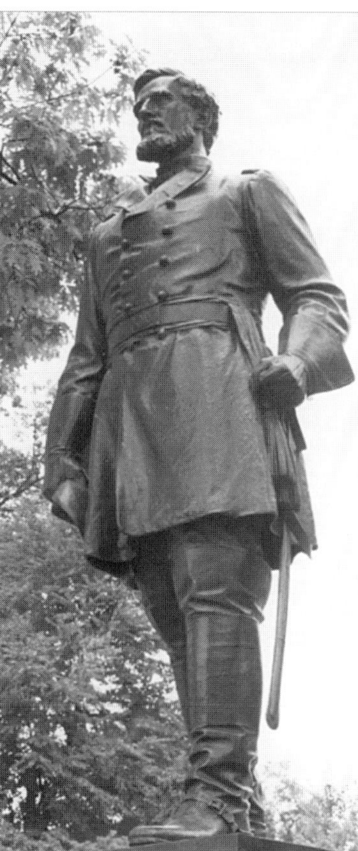

Hans Christian Heg at State Capitol in
Madison

State Capitol Pediment East
Karl Bitter
1910
Granite, located above the wing
facing King Street (Supreme Court
chambers and the Governor's Office).
The figures symbolize liberty, justice,
and truth.

State Capitol Pediment West
Karl Bitter
1909
Granite, located above the wing facing State Street (Assembly Chamber).
The figures symbolize resources of
the state: dairy industry, agriculture,
forest products, fishing, and hunting.

State Capitol Pediment South
Adolph A. Weinman
1913
Granite, above the Senate Chamber
with central figures symbolizing
virtues and traits of character

State Capitol Pediment North
Attilio Piccirilli
1917
Granite, with figures that express
attributes of civilization, wisdom,
and learning

Wisconsin State Capitol
State Capitol Park

Forward
Jean Pond Miner Coburn
1893, replica made in 1995
Bronze replica located at Capitol
State Street entrance. The original
copper statue is in the lobby of the
State Historical Society of Wisconsin
Headquarters

Hans Christian Heg
Paul Fjelde
1925, dedicated 1926
Bronze, 12 foot high, located at the
King Street entrance

Law Enforcement Officers Memorial
1998
Granite, located at N. Pinckney and
Mifflin streets

Wisconsin State Capitol
Statuary groups around base of dome

Faith
Karl Bitter
1910-1912
Vermont granite, located at the base
of dome facing Dr. Martin Luther
King Jr. Boulevard. Grouping of three
female figures.

Knowledge
Karl Bitter
1911-1915
Vermont granite, located at base of
dome facing East Washington Avenue.
Grouping of three male figures.

Prosperity and Abundance
Karl Bitter
1911-1915
Vermont granite, located at base of
dome facing Wisconsin Avenue.
Grouping of three female figures.

Strength
Karl Bitter
1911-1915
Vermont granite, located at base of
dome facing West Washington Avenue.
Grouping of three male figures.

University of Wisconsin-Madison

Boy Between Classes
Seward Johnson, Jr.
1996
Cast and painted bronze, located at the School of Engineering, 1415 Engineering Drive

Camp Randall Memorial Arch
Lew Porter
Dedicated June 19, 1912
Gray Vermont granite, located at Randall Avenue at W. Dayton Street. Includes Old Abe, the eagle mascot of the 8th Wisconsin Infantry Regiment and the 1861-65 young soldier and the 1912 veteran.

Earth Flight
Beth Sahagian
September 27, 1988
Indiana limestone, six feet high and 16 feet in diameter, located at Clinical Science Center, 600 Highland Avenue

Freedom of Communication
James Watrous
1971-1973
Brass, plywood, epoxy, and glass tesserae, located at Werner Journalism Court, 821 University Avenue

Generations
Richard Artschwager
1991
Plexiglass domes, and stainless steel posts with blue spruce trees (a site-specific work), located at 800 University Avenue at the entrance to the Elvehjem Museum of Art

Interspirit
James T. Russell
1983
Polished stainless steel, 13 feet high, located at the entrance to the SERF

building at 715 W. Dayton Street. Percent for Art Program commission

Lincoln
Adolph A. Weinman
1909
Bronze, located at 500 Lincoln Drive, in front of Bascom Hall. This is the only replica of the original sculpture which is located near Lincoln's birthplace in Hodgenville, Kentucky.

Máquina, The Descendant's Fountain
William Conrad Severson
1996
Concrete and stainless steel, located at the College of Engineering on Engineering Drive

Mother and Child
William Zorach
1957
Bronze, located at Elvehjem Museum of Art, 800 University Avenue, 50th anniversary gift of the University of Wisconsin Class of 1927

Rotational Shift
Andrea Blum
1987
Concrete, located at 1210 West Dayton Street, between UW Department of Computer Science and Union South

Territorial Sanctuary No. 11
Stanley Shafer
1986
Concrete, aluminum, wood, and earth, located west of 420 Henry Mall, removed for the new Bio Chemistry building

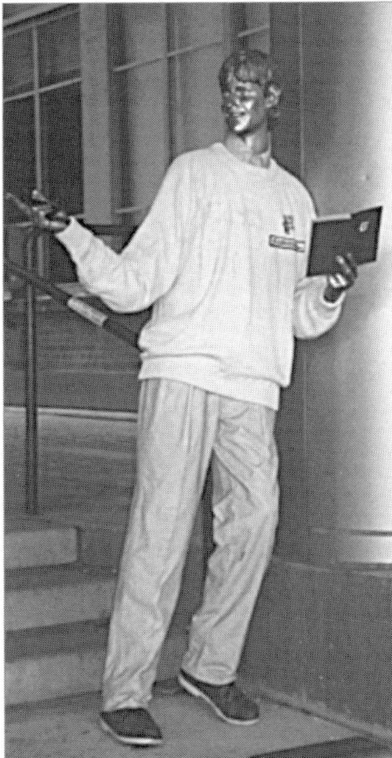

Boy Between Classes at UW-Madison

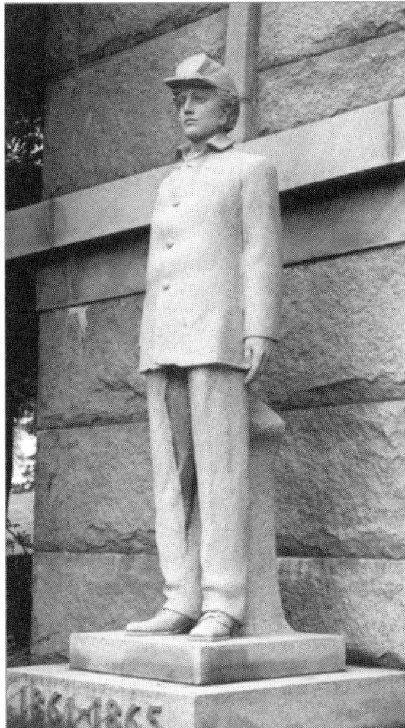

Camp Randall Memorial Arch (detail) at UW-Madison

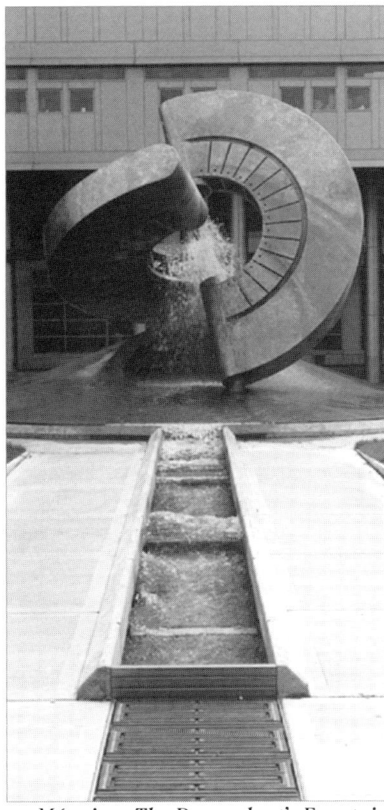

Máquina, The Descendant's Fountain at UW-Madison

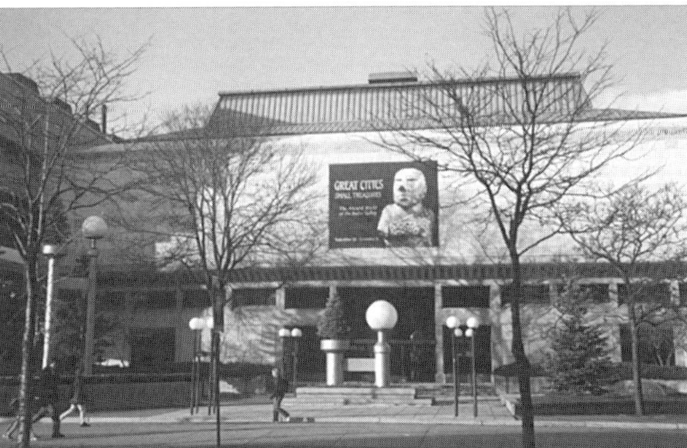

Generations at UW-Madison

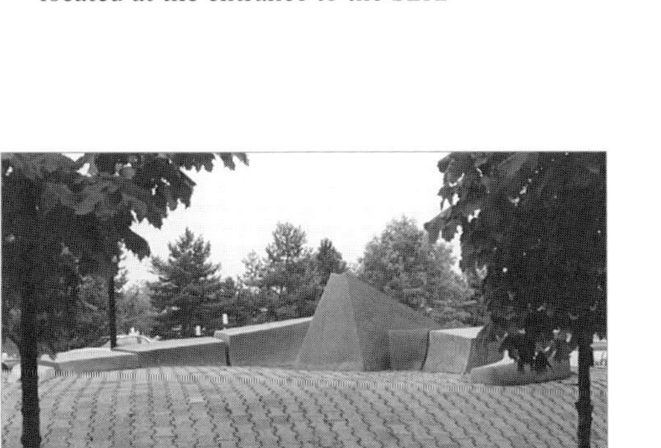

Earth Flight at UW-Madison

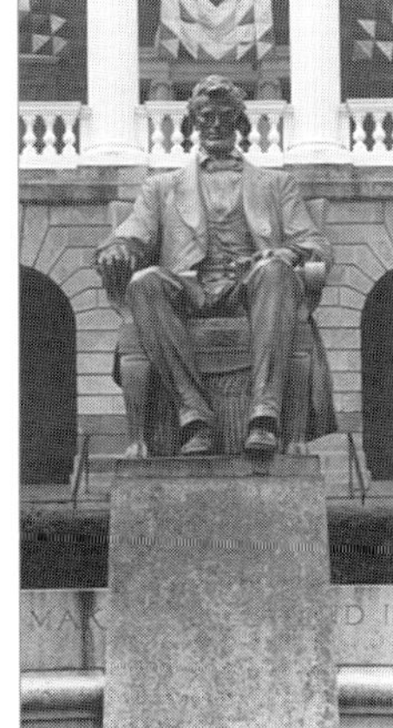

Lincoln at UW-Madison

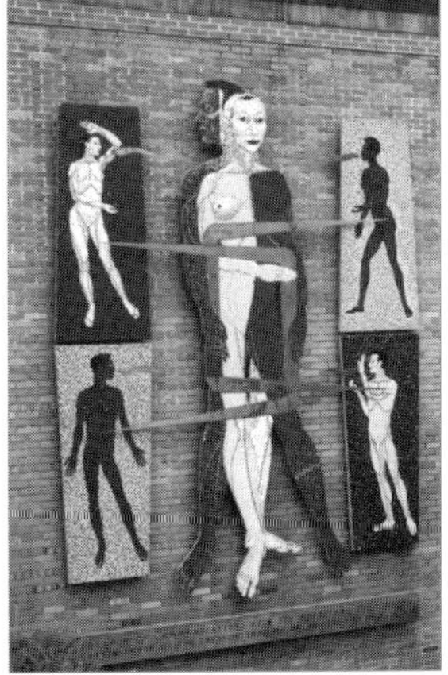

Freedom of Communication at UW-Madison

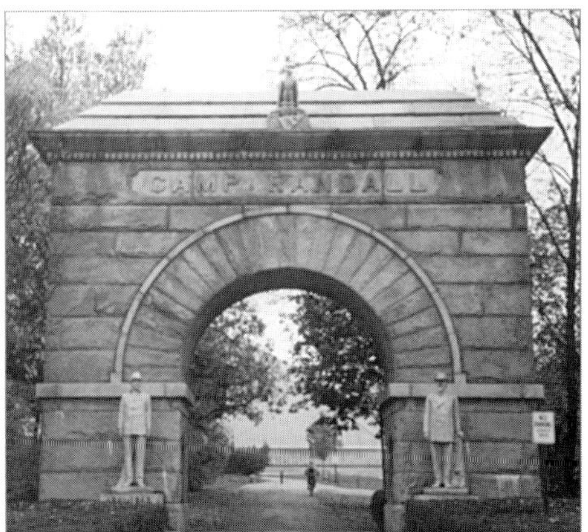

Camp Randall Memorial Arch at UW-Madison

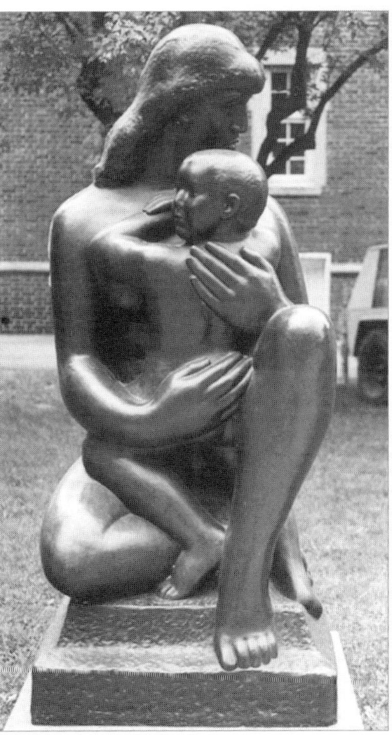

Mother and Child at UW-Madison

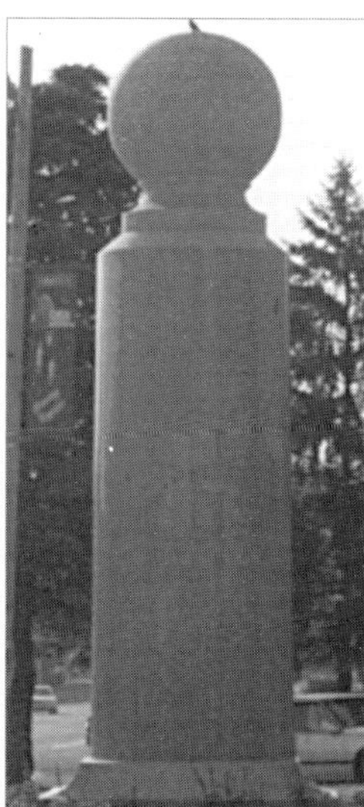

Veterans Memorial in Oregon

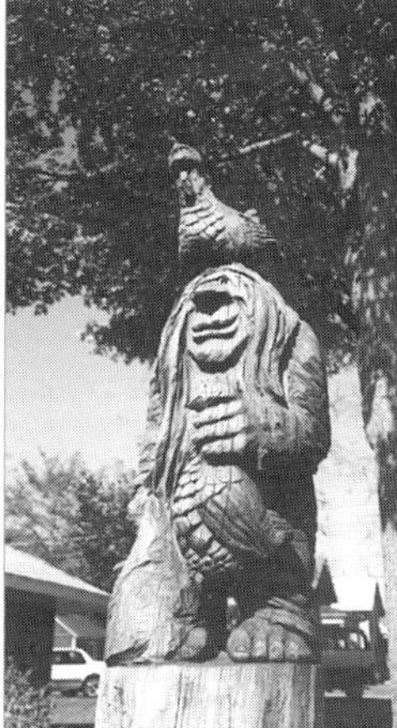

Troll in Mount Horeb

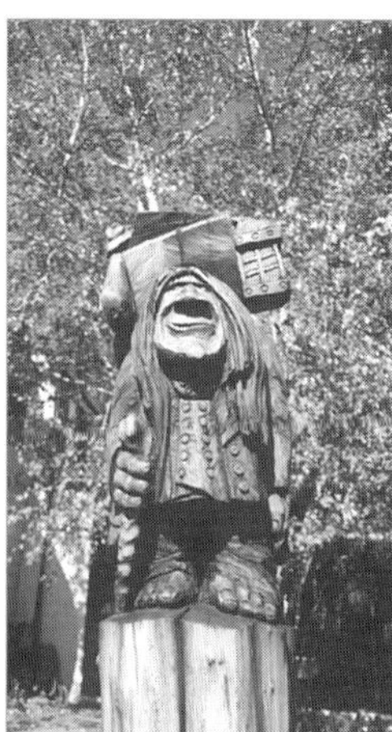

Troll in Mount Horeb

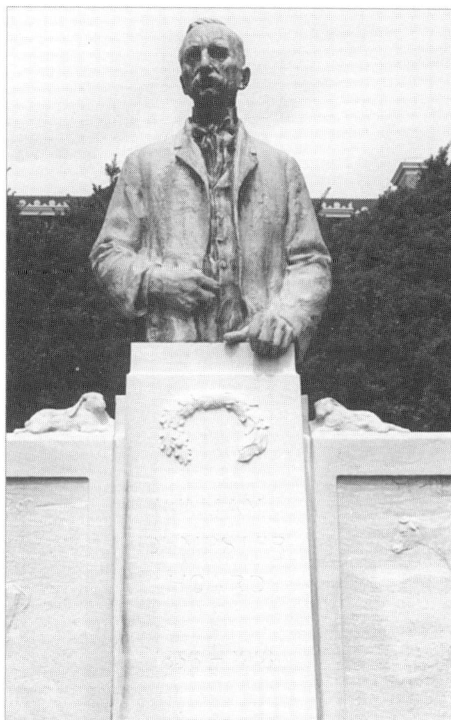

William D. Hoard at UW-Madison

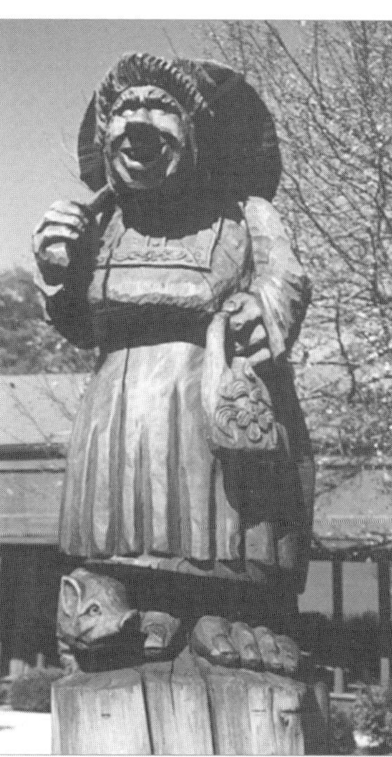

Troll in Mount Horeb

William D. Hoard

Gutzon Borglum
Dedicated February 3, 1922
Bronze bust, located on Henry Mall below Agriculture Hall between University Avenue and Linden Drive

Madison Area Effigy Mounds

Burrows Park Late Woodland Mound

Burrows Park on Lake Mendota contains a Late Woodland bird effigy mound

Edgewood College Mounds

Located on the Edgewood College campus, this site contains twelve mounds

Edna Taylor Conservancy Effigy Mound

This site contains six linear and one panther effigy mound

Elmside Park Effigies

Located at the intersection of Lakeland and Maple Avenue, this site contains two animal effigies referred to as a lynx and bear

Forest Hill Cemetery Late Woodland Effigy Mound Group

Forest Hill Cemetery contains a Late Woodland effigy mound group consisting of most of a goose effigy, two panther mounds, and one linear mound

Halverson Group

Yahara Heights County Park contains mounds referred to as the Halverson Group. Of the original group which had two panthers, one bear, one oval, and one linear, only the bear and panther remain

Hudson Park Late Woodland Animal Effigy Mound

Located in Hudson Park, at the intersection of Lakeland and Hudson Avenue, there is A long-tailed Late Woodland animal effigy mound

Late Woodland Bear Effigy Mound

Vilas Park Circle, situated between the 1400 and 1500 blocks of Vilas Avenue, contains a Late Woodland bear effigy mound

Late Woodland Effigy Mound Groups

UW-Madison Arboretum, on both sides of McCaffrey Road, contains two Late Woodland effigy mound groups.

Mendota State Hospital grounds contains portions of two large mound groups.

Farwell's Point Mound Group consist of a number of large conicals, a part of a linear and a bird effigy

Mendota State Hospital Mound Groups, located east of the group described above, contains some of the finest and largest effigy mounds preserved anywhere in the Upper Midwest

Morris Park Mound Group

Located in Governor Nelson State Park on the northern Shore of Lake Mendota, this site contains a group of six conicals and a large panther-shaped effigy mound

Observatory Hill Mounds

Located on the UW-Madison campus, directly to the west of the UW Observatory, this site contains a bird effigy and an unusual two-tailed effigy

Vilas Park Late Woodland Mound Group

Vilas Park contains a Late Woodland mound group which consists of a bird effigy, a linear mound, and six conical mounds. Part of a small conical mound is preserved in the Zoo near the Otter cage

Willow Drive Mounds

Located on the UW-Madison campus, on Willow Drive just behind the Natatorium. Mound contains an effigy mound and the remnants of three other Late Woodland mounds

McFarland

Indian Mound Park

Consists of two conicals, one oval, two linears, a bear effigy, and an unusual hook-shaped mound

Sjur Johnson Mound Group

Siggelkow Park contains the Sjur Johnson Mound Group which consists of five linears, two ovals and an earthen enclosure

Middleton

Hand, Bird, Fish

Martha Glowacki & Lynn Whitford
1991
Copper artifacts in the style of the ancient Native Americans of Wisconsin, Percent for Art Project, located at Governor Nelson State Park

Mount Horeb

Trolls
The Old Troll
The Peddler Troll
Sweet Swill Troll
The Chicken Thief
The Gardener
The Accordion Player
The Tourist
Tub Troll

Mike Feeney
Wood, chainsaw art, all located along Main Street

Oregon

Together We Stand

Nicole Noyce, Elizabeth Godschalx
1998
Painted steel, located at Oregon High School, 456 N. Perry Parkway

Veterans Memorial

Granite pillar, located on Main Street

Stoughton

Resurrection Gates

O.V. Shaffer
1986
Welded steel, located at Convent Lutheran Church courtyard

Dove

O.V. Shaffer
1986
Welded stainless steel, located at Convent Lutheran Church courtyard

Verona

Bear and Coyote

Wood, chainsaw art, located at 411 E. Verona Avenue

GRANT

Boscobel

Civil War Memorial to the Unknown Soldier

Mixed media, located at northwest corner of Courthouse lawn on Maple Street

Dickeyville

Holy Ghost Grotto (Dickeyville Grotto)

Father Wernerus

1918-1931

Mixed media, located at Holy Ghost Catholic Church, 305 W. Main Street. This is the largest Religious Folk Art Grotto in Wisconsin. Contains scenes of the life of Christ, the Blessed Virgin, Christopher Columbus, the Stations of the Cross, and a gift shop.

Effigy Mounds in Grant County

⌖ Dewey Mound Group

Two miles north of Cassville on County Highway VV

Nelson Dewey State Park contains *Dewey Mound Group #1*, which consists of more than 25 conicals, linears, and compound mounds that stretch out in a long line along the bluffs.

⌖ Riverside Park Mounds

Located in Riverside Park, the park contains a section of a linear mound, which is behind and parallel to a bird effigy.

⌖ Wyalusing State Park Mounds

Contains several mound groups

Wyalusing State Park Mound Group, located at the confluence of the Wisconsin and Mississippi rivers, contains some of Wisconsin's most spectacular Native American mound groups. Bear, deer, a turtle, conical, linear, and several compound mounds are remarkably intact in magnificent groups that stretch out along the bluff lines.

Council Ground or *Ball Field Mound Group* contains two bear effigy mounds which are visible from the road.

Sentinel Ridge Mound Group consists of conicals, linears, compounds and effigies and it extends for more than 200 feet along the bluff.

Rollway Point consists of three linear and three conical mounds which were built along the top of the ridge.

Homestead Mound Group contains effigies, linears, and compound mounds.

Lancaster

Civil War Monument

First Civil War Monument in the State

Dedicated 1867

Carved stone, located at Grant County Courthouse grounds

Civil War Soldiers' Fountain

1906

Cast iron, located at Grant County Courthouse lawn

Governor Nelson Dewey

Chevalier Gaetano Trentanove

1907

Bronze, located at Grant County Courthouse Square

GREEN

Brodhead

Bowen Monument

1857

Stone, located in Greenwood Cemetery

Civil War Monument

1914

Stone, located in Veterans City Park

New Glarus

Small Folk Art Environment

Fred G. Zimmerman

Circa 1920s

Concrete embellished garage, flag pole, and birdhouse, located at 1319 Second Street. Private property, view from road.

IOWA

Barnevald

Abstract Arched Sculpture

Painted steel, located on 7811 Highway 151 at Deer Valley Golf Course

Hollandale

Grand View Park Folk Art Environment

Nick Englebert

1937-1950s

Numerous sculptures at the site reopened to the public in 1997. Concrete, ceramic, glass, and paint, located on Highway 39, 1 mile west of Hollandale. Includes *Neptune's Fountain* and many others

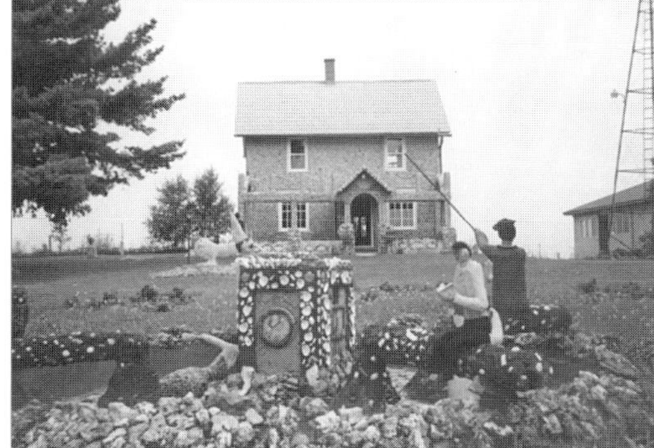

Grand View Park Folk Art Environment in Hollandale

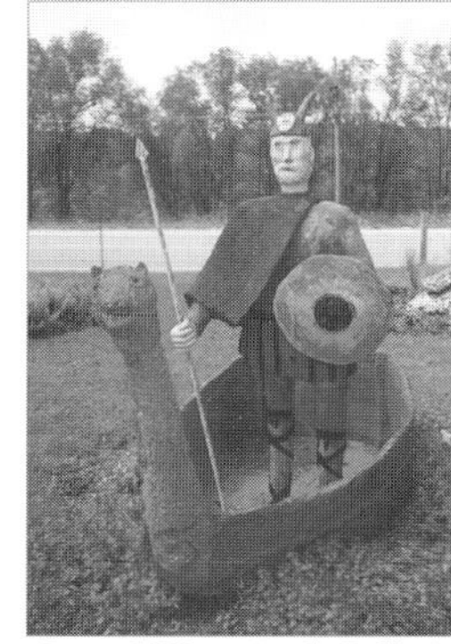

Grand View Park Folk Art Environment in Hollandale

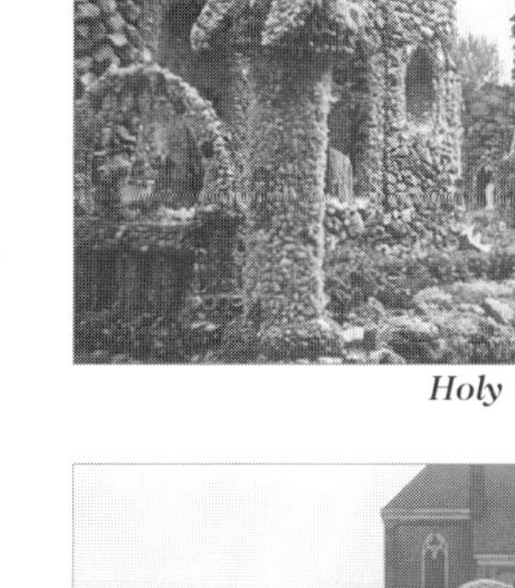

Holy Ghost Grotto in Dickeyville

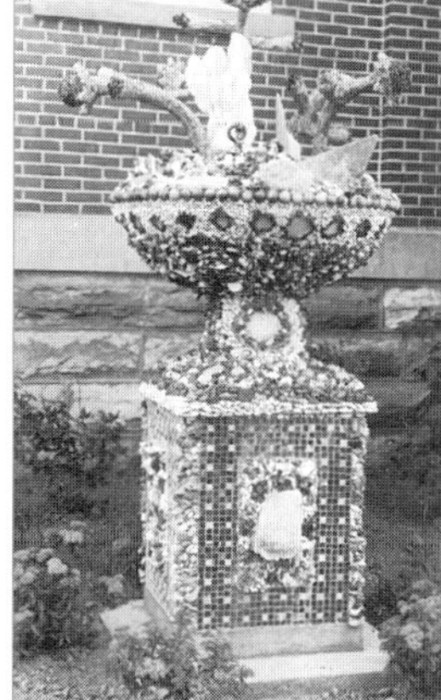

Holy Ghost Grotto in Dickeyville

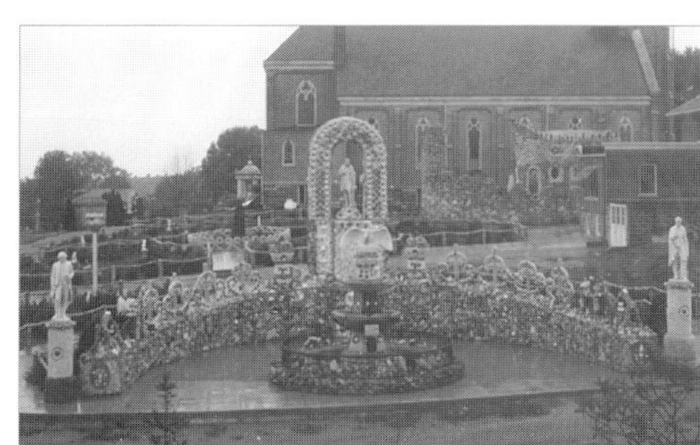

Holy Ghost Grotto in Dickeyville

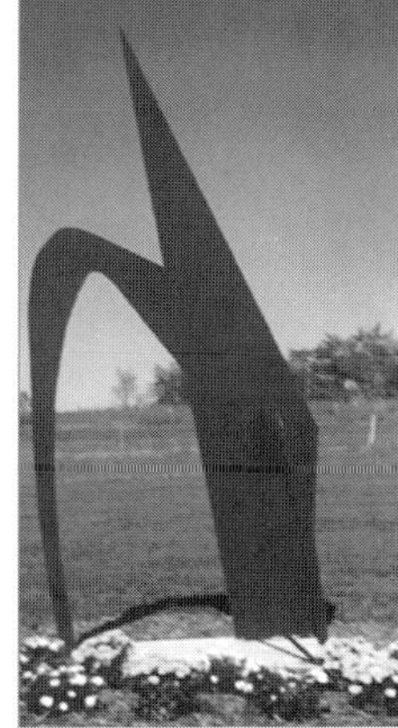

Abstract Arched Sculpture in Barneveld

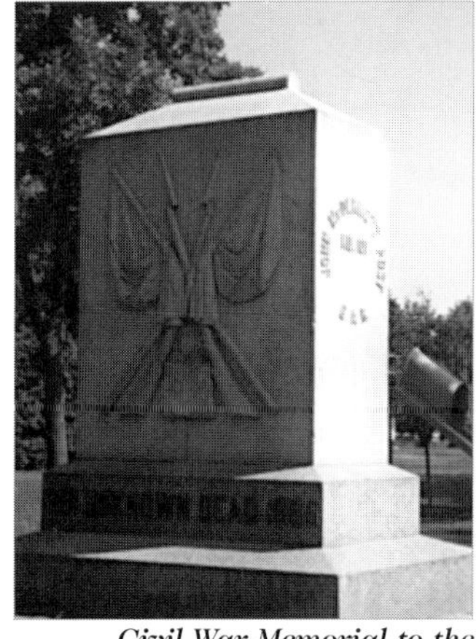

Civil War Memorial to the Unknown Soldier in Boscobel

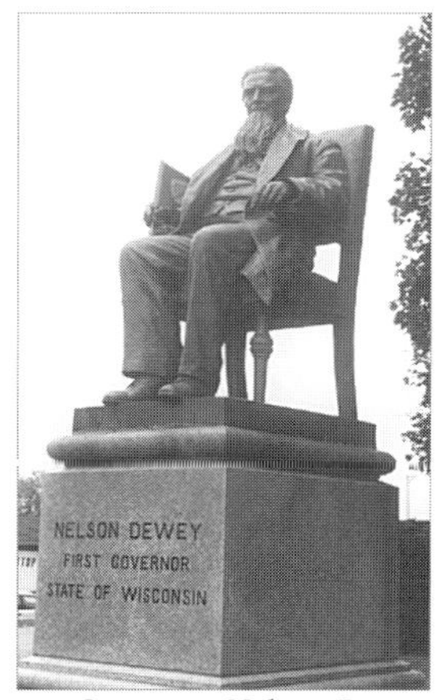

Governor Nelson Dewey in Lancaster

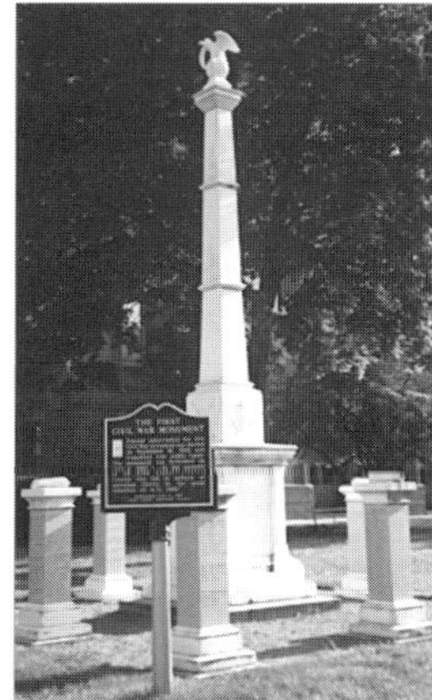

Civil War Monument in Lancaster

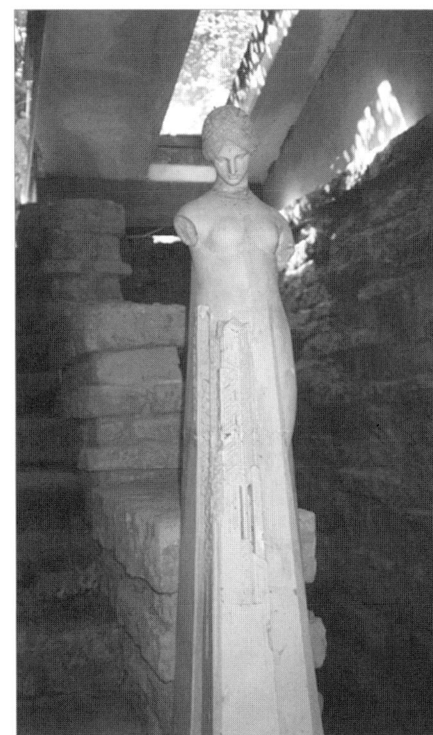

The Flower in the Crannied Wall at Taliesin, near Spring Green Area

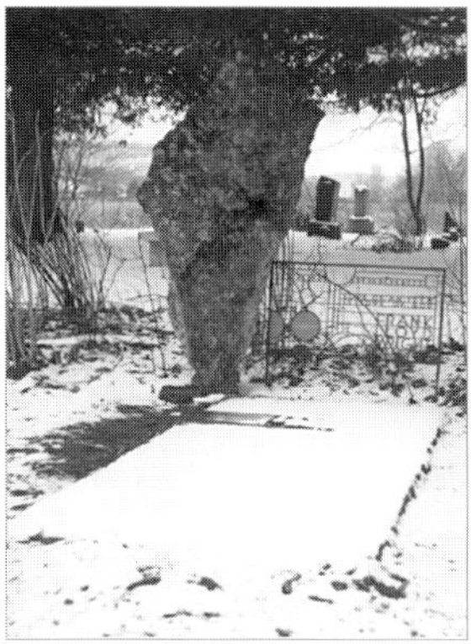

F. L. Wright Cenotaph, at Unity Chapel Cemetery near Spring Green Area

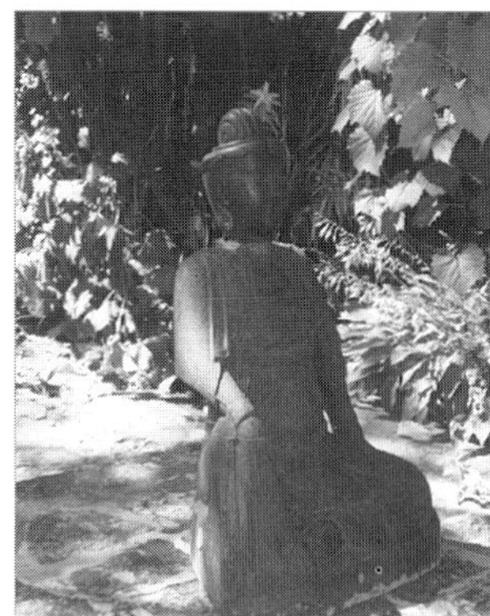

Taliesin Garden Sculptures near Spring Green Area

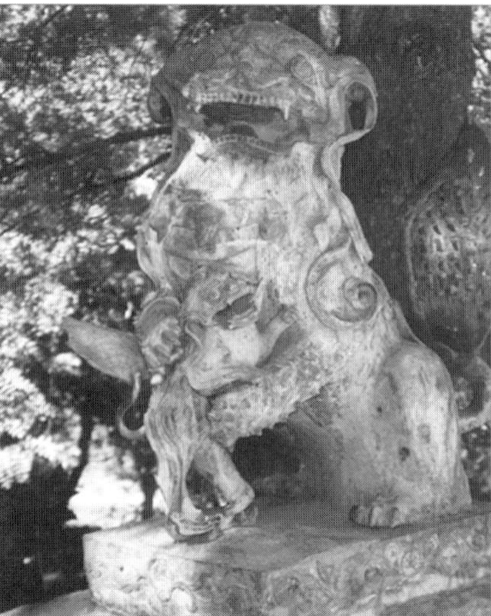

Taliesin Garden Sculptures near Spring Green Area

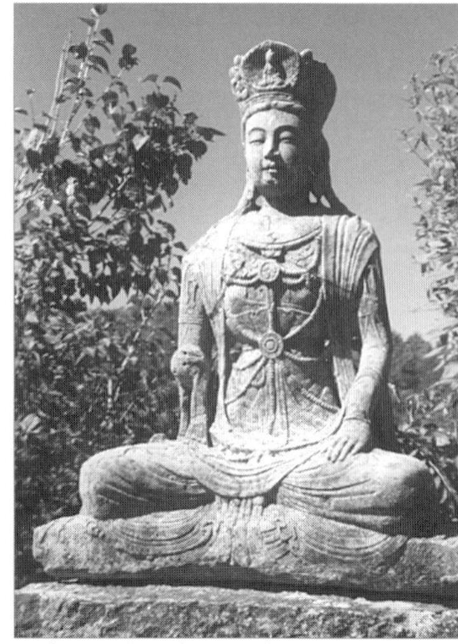

Taliesin Garden Sculptures near Spring Green Area

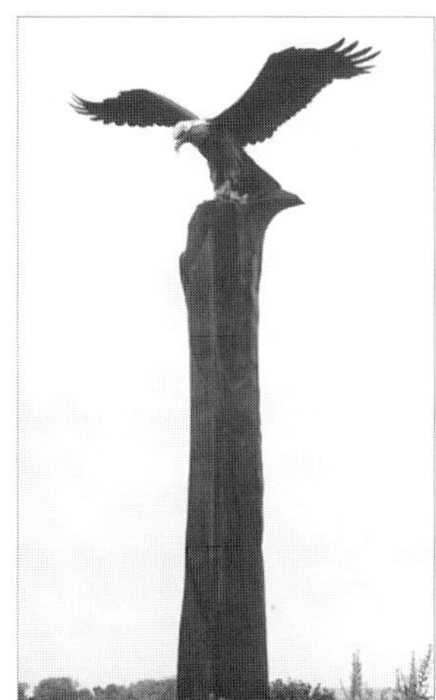

Eagle Landmark in LaCrosse

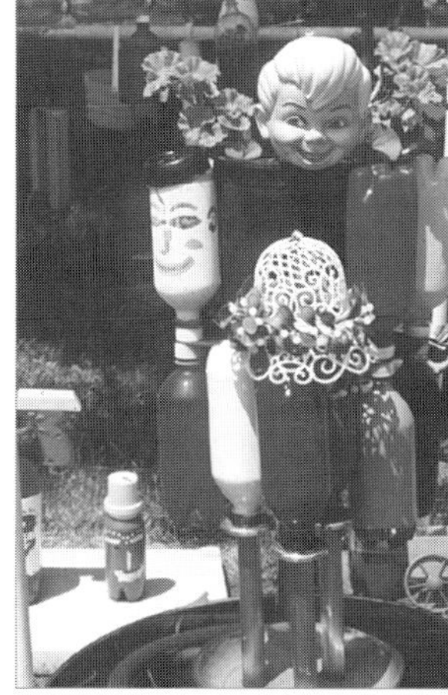

Art Environment, Paul Hefti, in LaCrosse

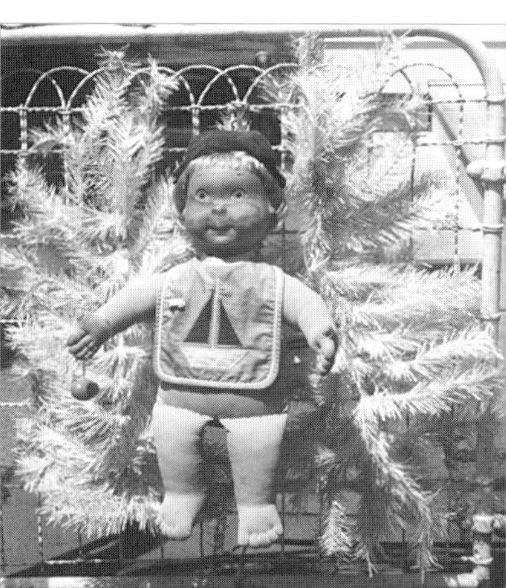

Art Environment by Paul Hefti, in LaCrosse

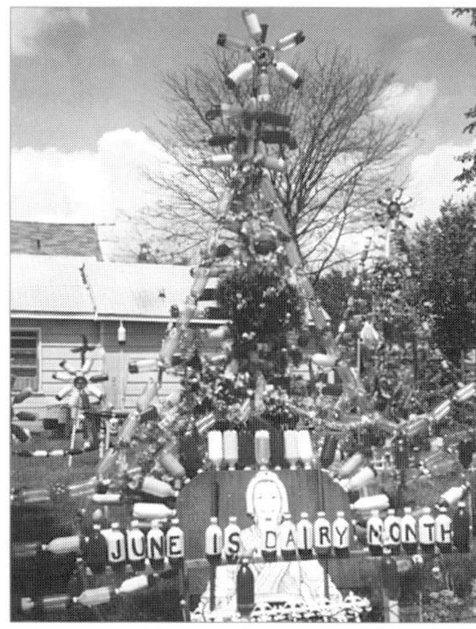

Art Environment, by Paul Hefti, in LaCrosse

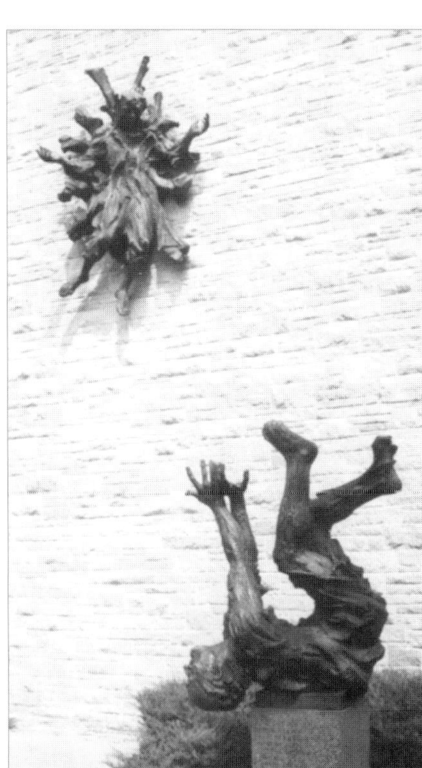

Damascus Illumination at St. Paul's Lutheran Church, LaCrosse

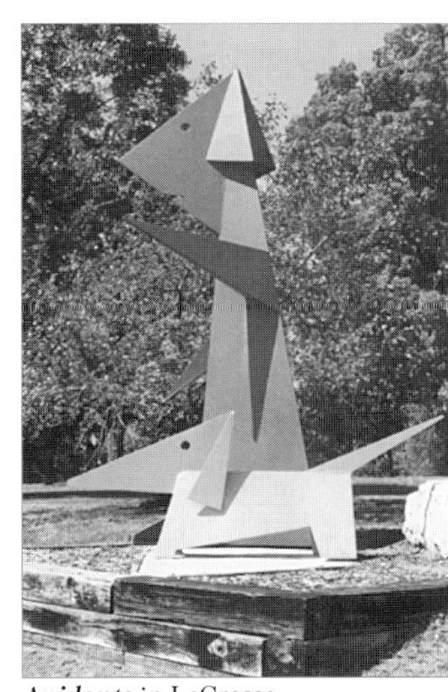

Anidonts in LaCrosse

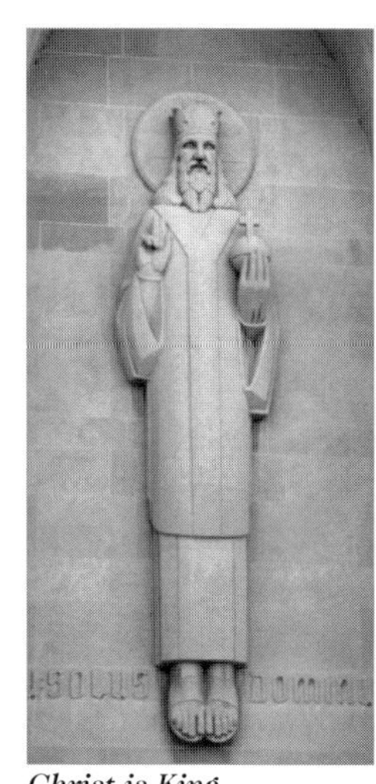

Christ is King in LaCrosse

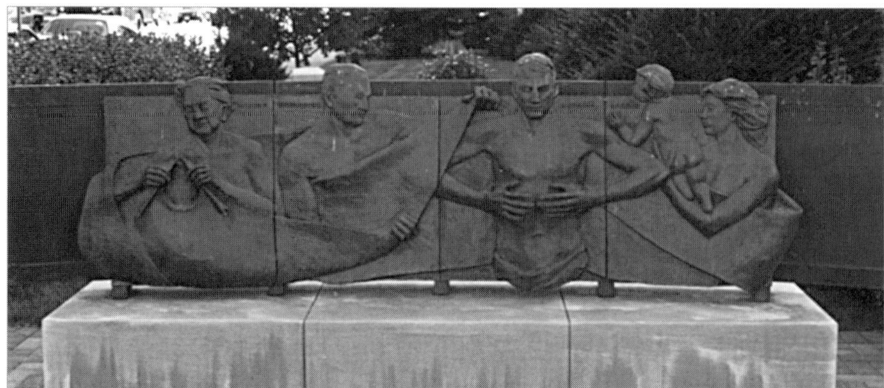

Common Cloth in LaCrosse

Spring Green Area

Taliesin Garden Sculptures
Numerous Japanese and Oriental sculptures in various media brought to Wisconsin by architect Frank Lloyd Wright, located on Highway 23

The Flower in the Crannied Wall
Richard Bock
1904
Painted plaster at Taliesin, and an identical statue is at the Dana-Thomas House in Springfield, Illinois.

Frank Lloyd Wright Cenotaph
1959
Stone, metal, and glass, located at Unity Chapel Cemetery, off Highway 23, near Taliesin

LaCrosse

LaCrosse

Anidonts
Luis Arata
Dedicated 1982
Aluminum, located at entrance to Myrick Park

Art Environment
Paul Hefti
Mixed media, located at 515 Adams Street. Entire house and yard is a sculptural environment. Private property, view from road

Christ is King
1957
Stone, located at 3710 East Avenue South

Common Cloth
R.T. Leverich
1993
Bronze, located at 6th and Main streets

Damascus Illumination
Paul T. Granlund
1967
Bronze, located at St. Paul's Lutheran Church, 420 West Avenue South

Eagle Landmark
Elmer P. Peterson
1986
Corten and stainless steel, located at west end of State Street in Riverside Park

Family
Elmer Peterson
1982
Bronze, located in the Gundersen Clinic courtyard, 1836 South Avenue

Fledgling
Michael Martino
1996
Metal, located at 400 N. 4th Street

Good Shepherd
Elmer Peterson
1984
Iron and slate, located at 4141 Mormon Coulee Road

Hiawatha
Anthony Zimmerhakl
1961
Concrete, located at north end of Riverside Park

Hope of Harvest
1957
Stone, located at 3710 East Avenue South

Kids Coulee—3 River Project
Community Effect
1994
Concrete, located at Myrick Park

King Gambrinus
Elmer P. Peterson
1980
Corten steel, located at G. Heileman Brewing Co., 100 Harborview Plaza, 2nd and State streets

King Gambrinus
Circa early 1990s
Painted metal and concrete, located at G. Heileman Brewing Co., 100 Harborview Plaza, 2nd and State streets

LaCrosse Players
Elmer Peterson
1981
Corten steel, located at Center Court between Radisson and Heilemann's

Lyra
Bruce White
1980
Aluminum, located at Burns Park, 8th and Main streets

➤ Myrick Park Effigy Mound
This consists of a conical mound about 25 feet in diameter, located in Myrick City Park on LaCrosse Street

Point of Origin
David Klahn
1980
Bronze, located at 700 West Avenue South

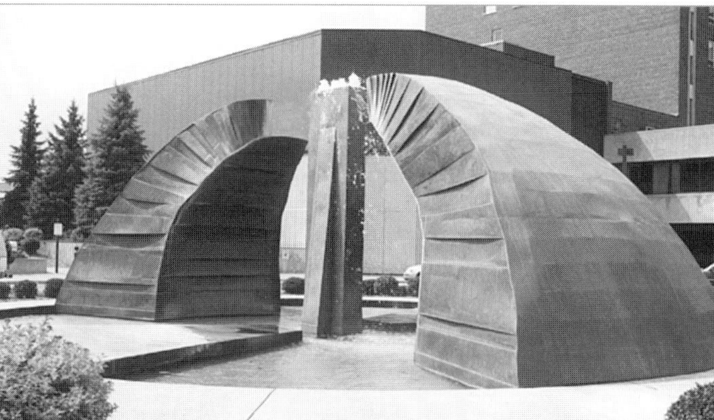

Point of Origin in LaCrosse

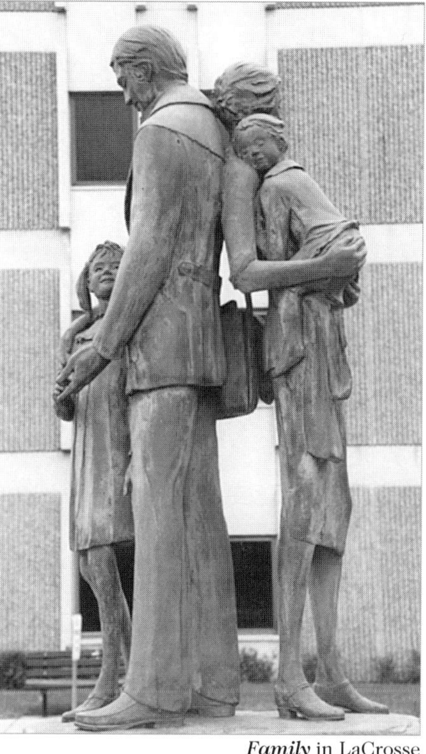

Family in LaCrosse

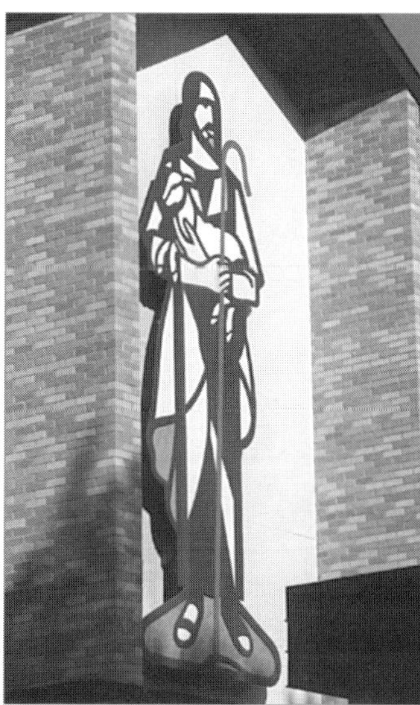

Good Shepherd in LaCrosse

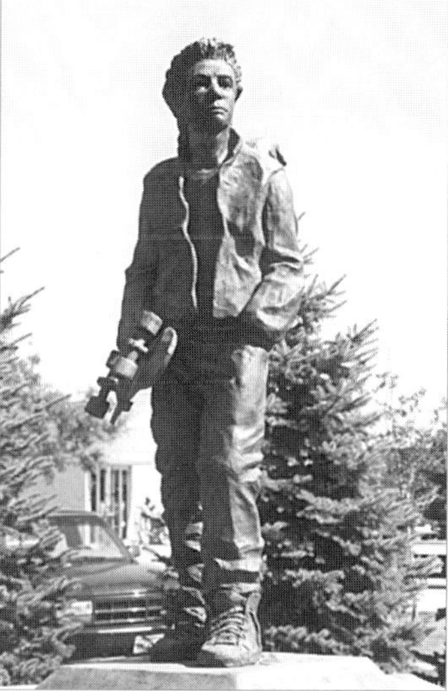

Fledgling in LaCrosse

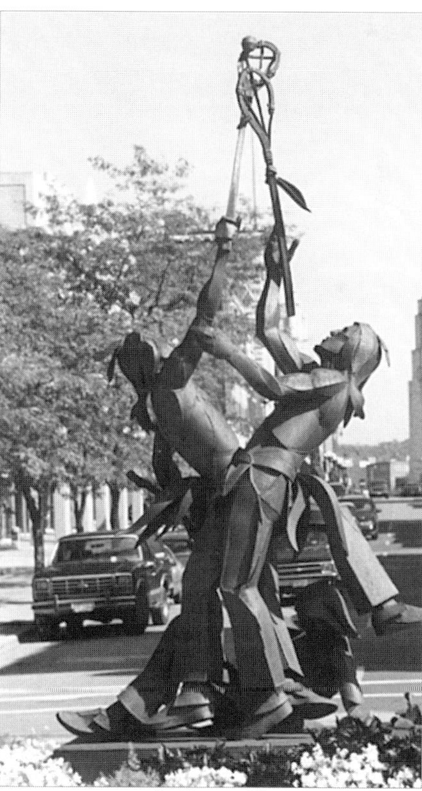

LaCrosse Players in LaCrosse

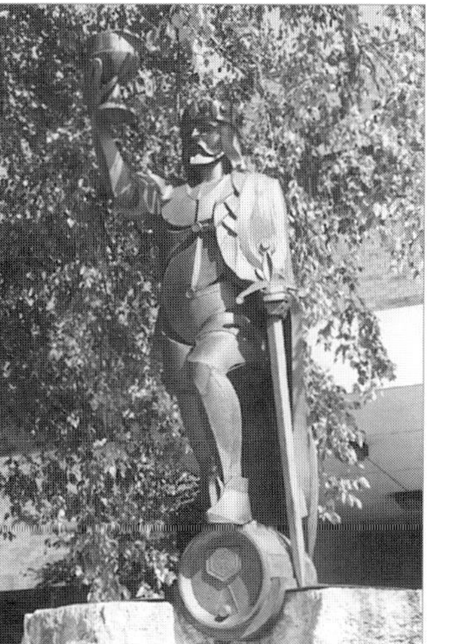

King Gambrinus (1980) in LaCrosse

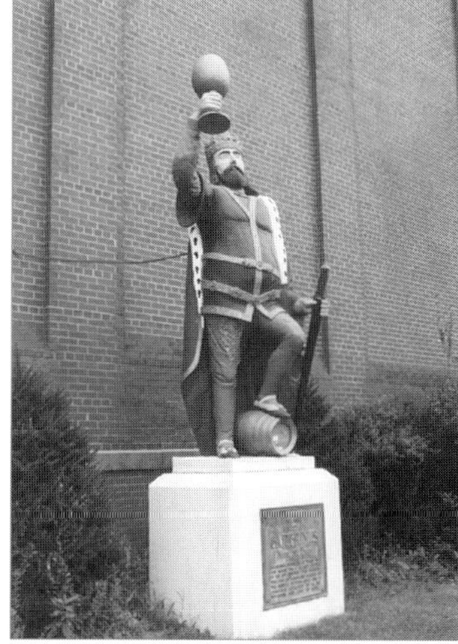

King Gambrinus in LaCrosse

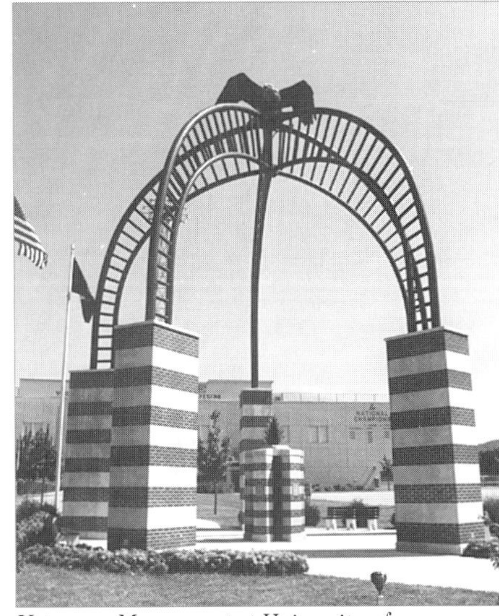

Veterans Monument at University of Wisconsin-LaCrosse

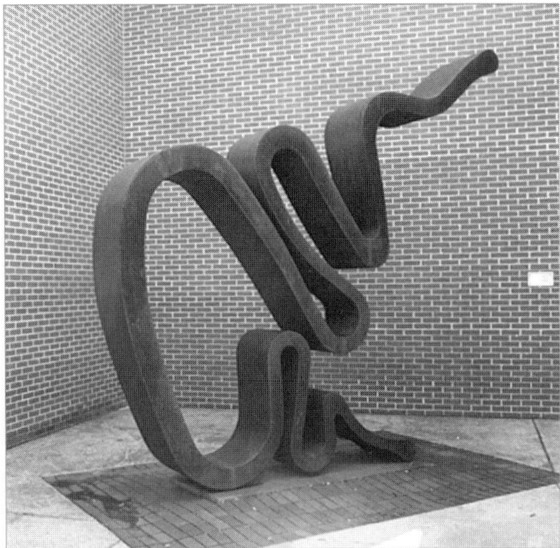

Ribbons V at University of Wisconsin-LaCrosse

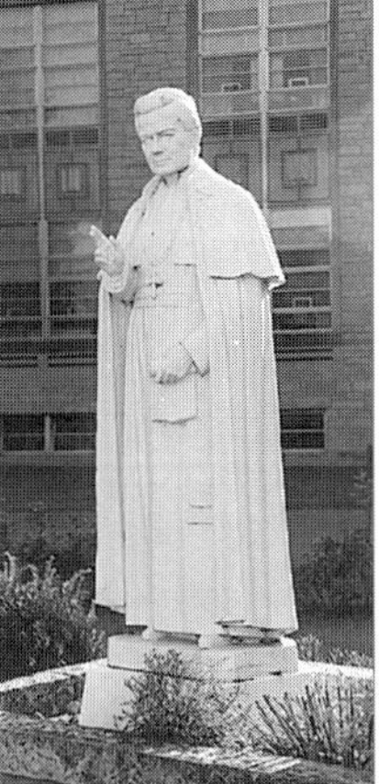

St. Thomas Moore in LaCrosse

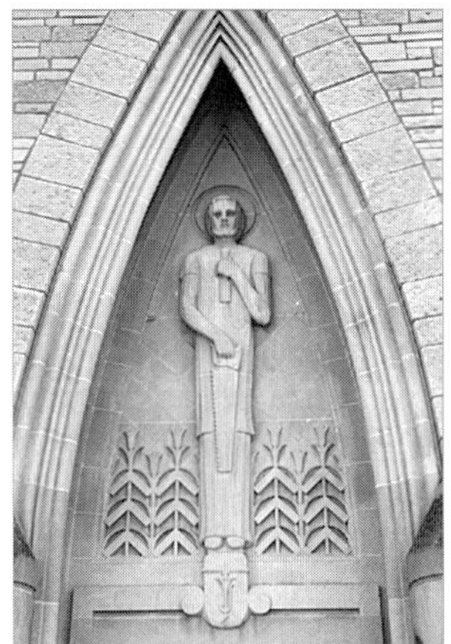

St. Joseph the Workman in LaCrosse

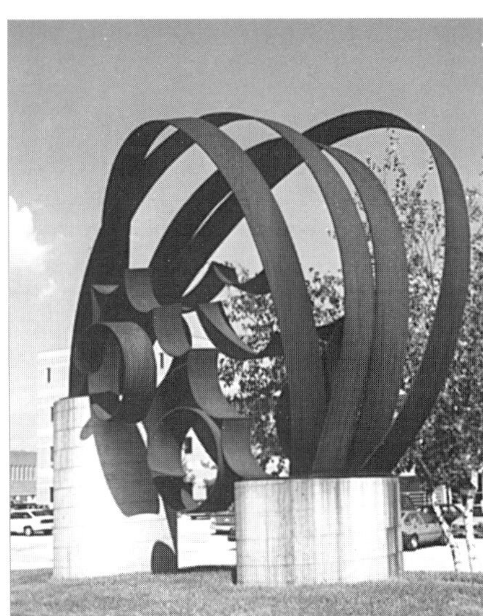

Water Over the Dam in LaCrosse

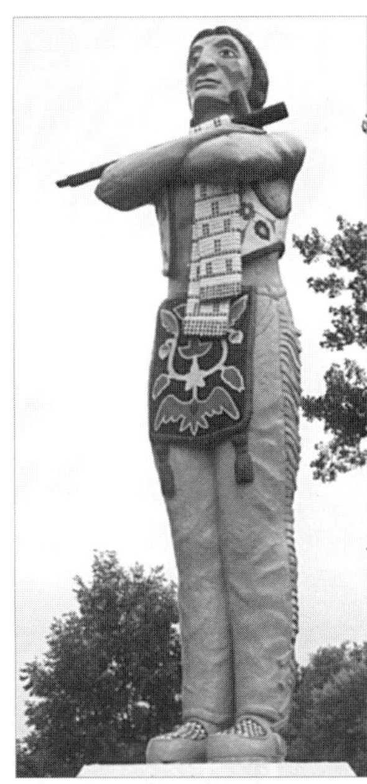

The Big Indian (Native American) in LaCrosse

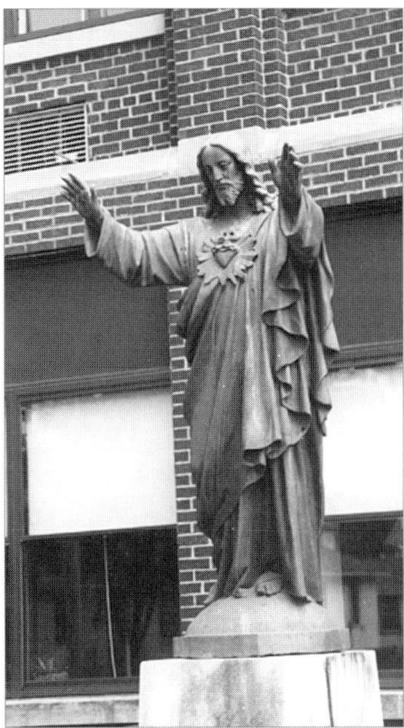

Sacred Heart of Jesus in LaCrosse

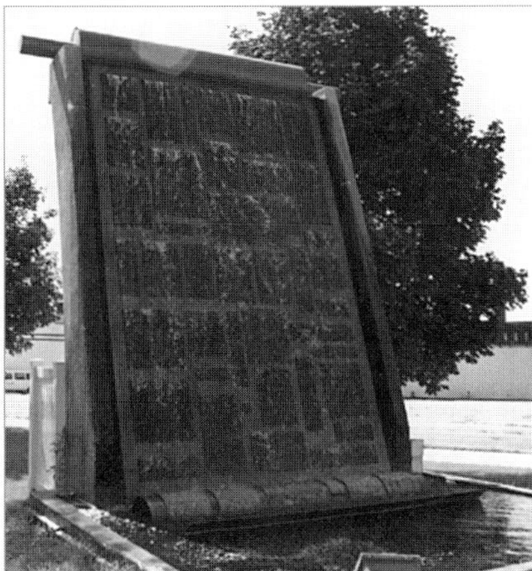

Scroll in LaCrosse

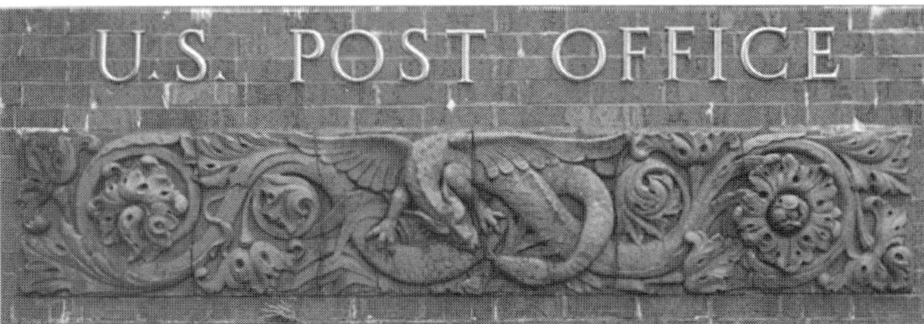

Post Office Dragon Panel in LaCrosse

Postal Union Panel in LaCrosse

LaCrosse continues

Post Office Reliefs
5th and State streets

Dragon Panel
1889
Terra-cotta

Beust
1889
Terra-cotta

Postal Union Panel
1889
Terra-cotta

Justice Panel
1889
Terra-cotta

LaCrosse continues

Queen of the Clergy
Located at south end of St. Pius School

Reclining Lion
Dedicated 1880
Terra-cotta, located at Swarthouse Museum Courtyard, 112 S. 9th Street

Reflections III
Paul T. Granlund
1979
Bronze, located at the LaCrosse Public Library, 800 Main Street

Sacred Heart of Jesus
Stone, located at Aquinas High School, 11th and Cass streets

Scroll
Dale Kenrick
1998
Bronze, located at 400 North 3rd Street

St. Joseph the Workman
1968
Stone, located at 6th and Main streets

St. Rose Grotto
Father Dobberstein
Circa 1940s
Mixed media, it was a large, embellished stone structure, demolished circa 1992. Was located at 715 South 9th Street

St. Thomas Moore
Granite, located at 2006 Weston Avenue

The Big Indian (Native American)
Anthony Zimmerhakl
1961
Painted concrete, located at north end of Riverside Park

Virgin Mary with Young Girl
Granite, located at Aquinas High School, 11th and Cass streets

Water Over the Dam
Jeff Weideman
Dedicated 1995
Steel, located at 4th and Vine streets

UW-LaCrosse

Female Figure (probably Italian)
Circa 1870
Marble, located at Research Center, now indoors

Ribbons V
Stephen Fischer
Dedicated 1985
Corten steel, located at 212 Cartwright Center

Veterans Monument
1994
Steel, brick, stone, and concrete

Viterbo College
815 9th Street South, LaCrosse

Dancing St. Francis
Paul T. Granlund
Dedicated October 4, 1985
Bronze, located in Assisi Courtyard

Harmony and Peace
Luis Arata
1985
Steel
Grassy knoll south of Murphy Center,
corner of Ninth and Mississippi

Catholic Cemetery-Mausoleum
519 Losey Boulevard, LaCrosse
established circa 1880s

Angel
Marble

Angel
Marble

Christ and St. Francis
Granite, in Nuns section

Holy Cross with Two Figures
Marble

Grottoes
Erhard Reisinger
1883-1916
Stone, three remain, along with the
14 Stations of the Cross

Hegenbart Monument
1930
Marble

Hennsler Monument
Marble

Kriz Monument
1924
Marble, Sect. 7

Noelke Monument
1922
Marble

Sikorski Monument
1916
Marble

St. Francis of Assisi
Marble

Oak Grove Cemetery
1407 LaCrosse Street, LaCrosse

Civil War Monument
Granite

Hixon Memorial
Leonard Crunelle
1913
Bronze

McMillan Monument
Marble

Smith Monument
1912
Marble, Sect. 30

Wood Monument
1912
Marble, Sect. 8-M

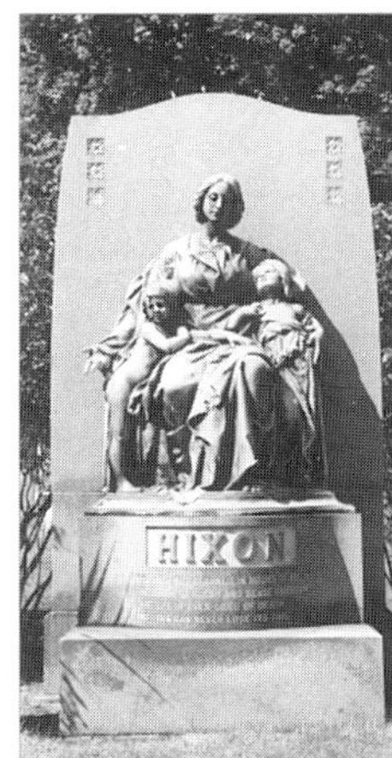

Hixon Memorial
at Oak Grove Cemetery,
LaCrosse

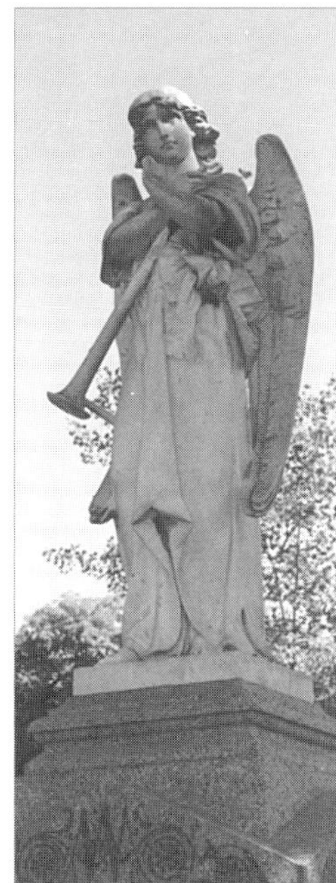

Wood Monument at Oak
Grove Cemetery, LaCrosse

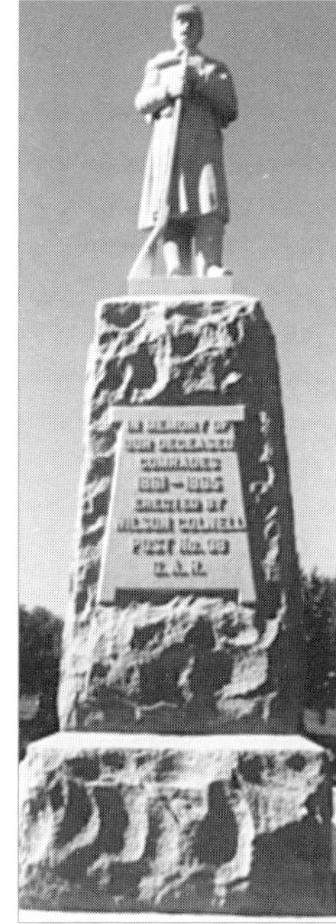

Civil War Monument
at Oak Grove Cemetery,
LaCrosse

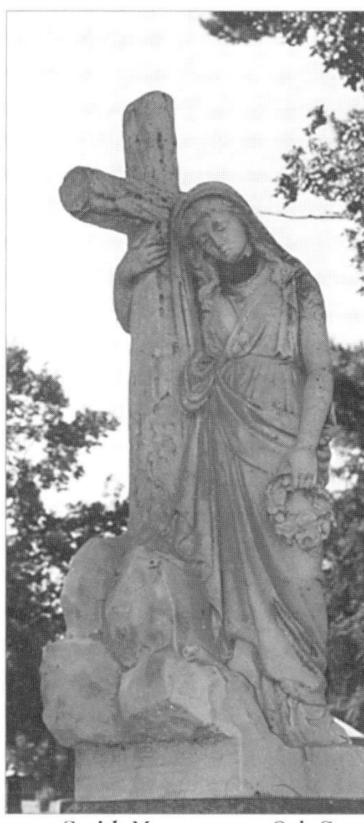

Smith Monument at Oak Grove
Cemetery, LaCrosse

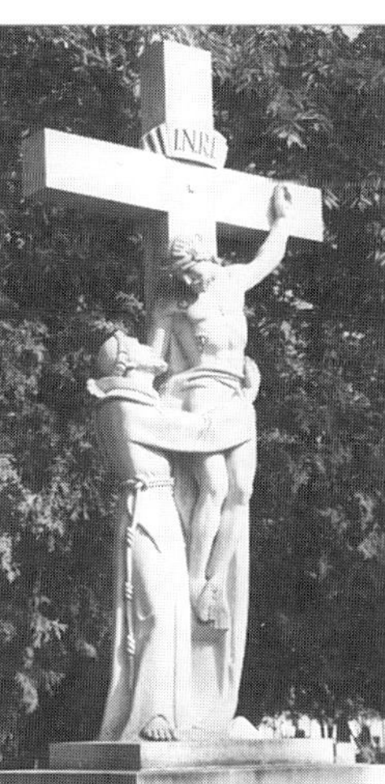

Christ and St Francis
at Catholic Cemetery-
Mausoleum, LaCrosse

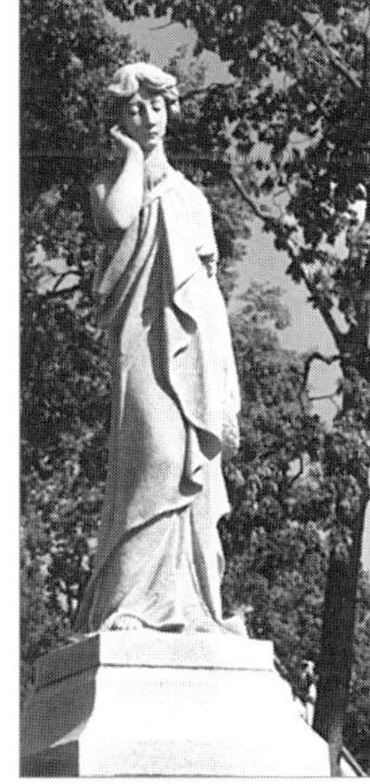

Hennsler Monument
at Catholic Cemetery-
Mausoleum, LaCrosse

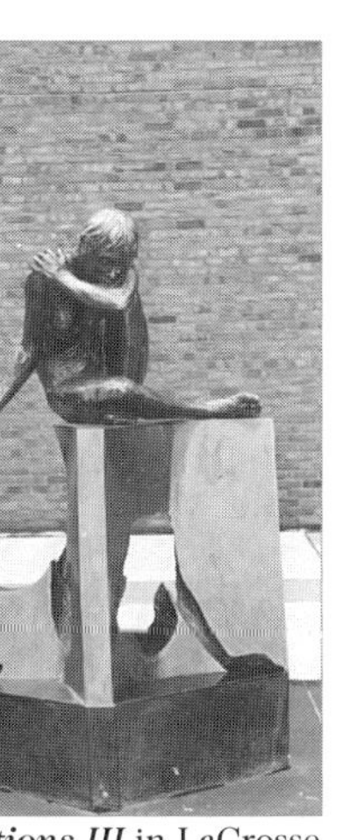

Reflections III in LaCrosse

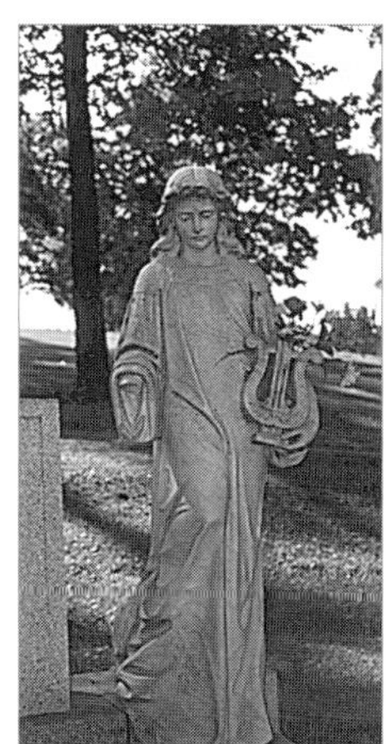

Kriz Monument
at Catholic Cemetery-
Mausoleum, LaCrosse

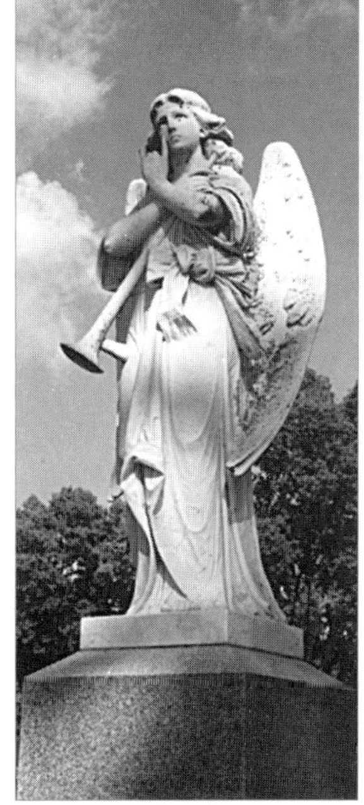

Sikorski Monument
at Catholic Cemetery-
Mausoleum, LaCrosse

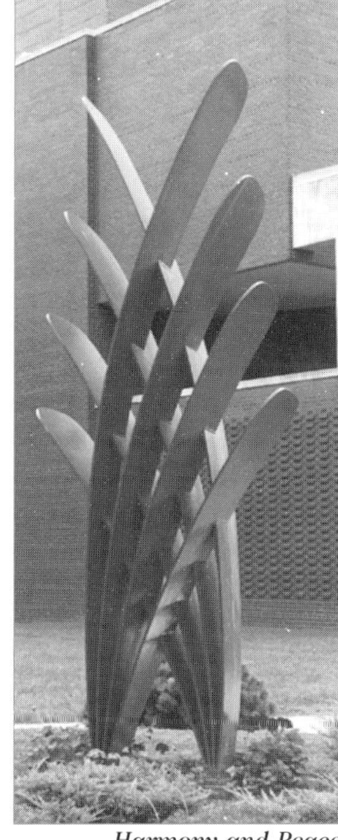

Harmony and Peace
at Viterbo College, LaCrosse

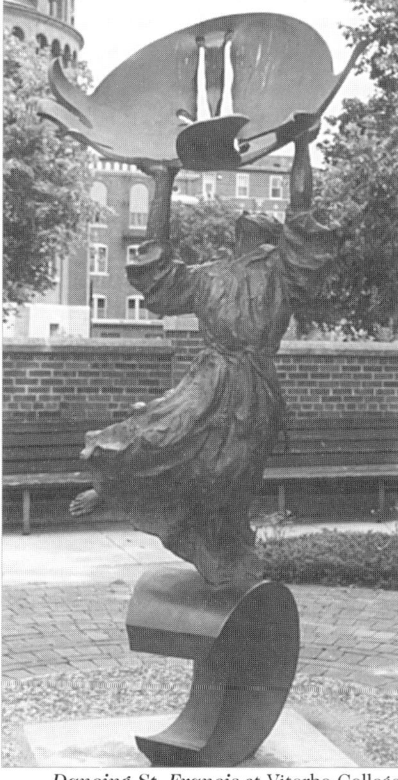

Dancing St. Francis at Viterbo College,
LaCrosse

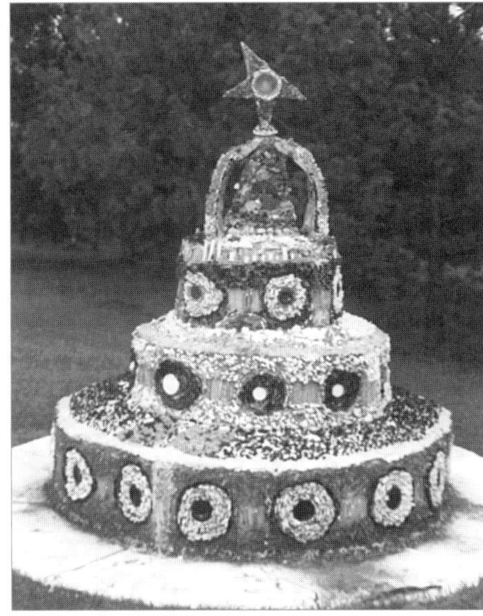

Wegner Grotto in Cataract

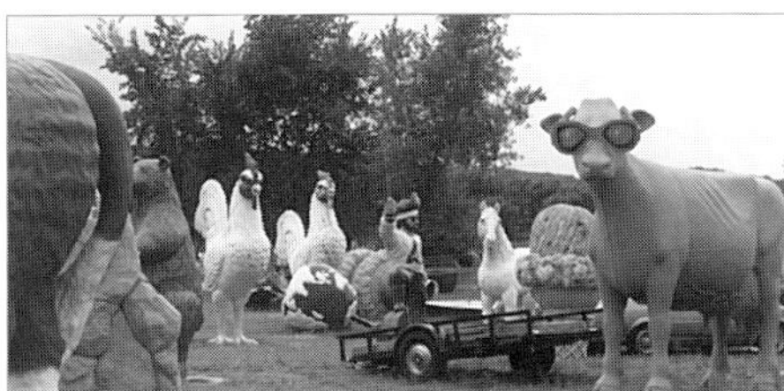

F.A.S.T. in Sparta

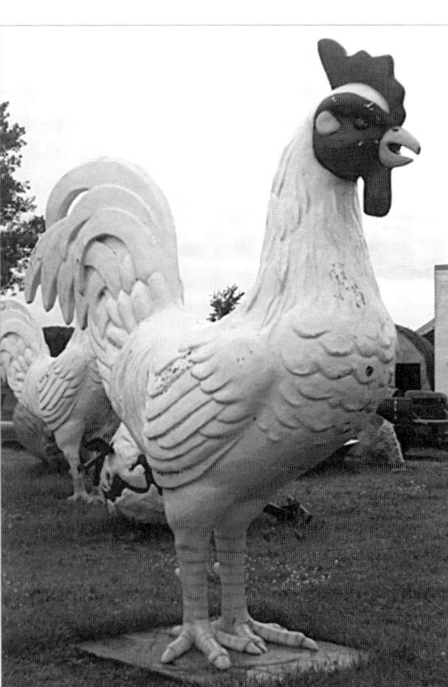

Chicken at F.A.S.T. in Sparta

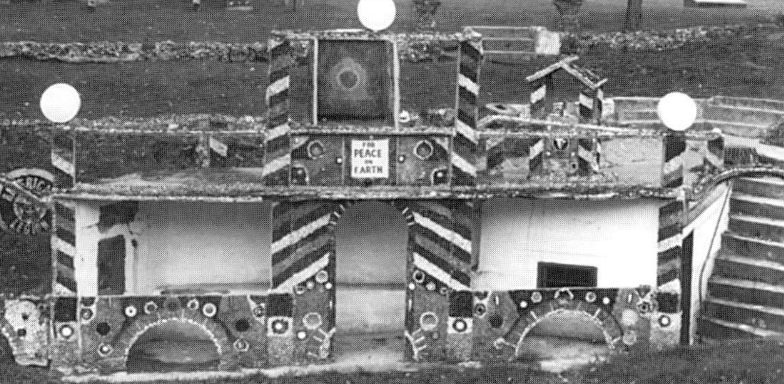

Wegner Grotto in Cataract

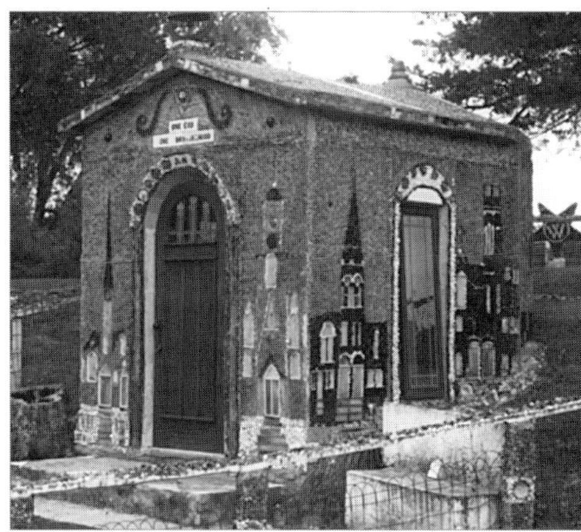

Wegner Grotto in Cataract

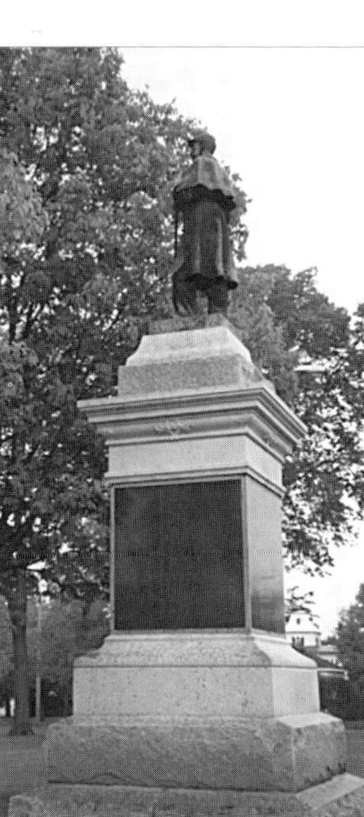

Civil War Soldier in Boyton Park
in Sparta

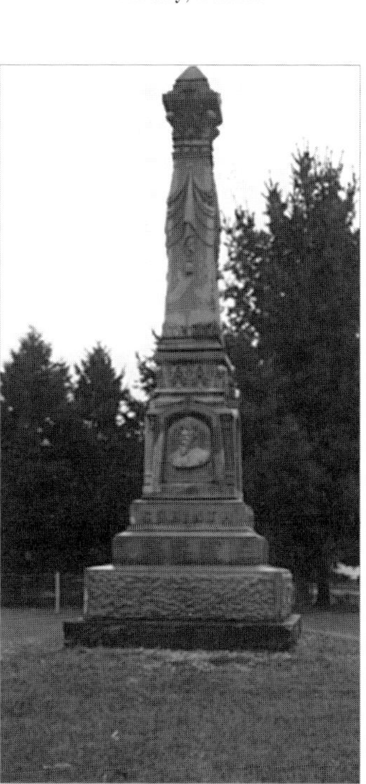

Civil War Monument in Lone Rock

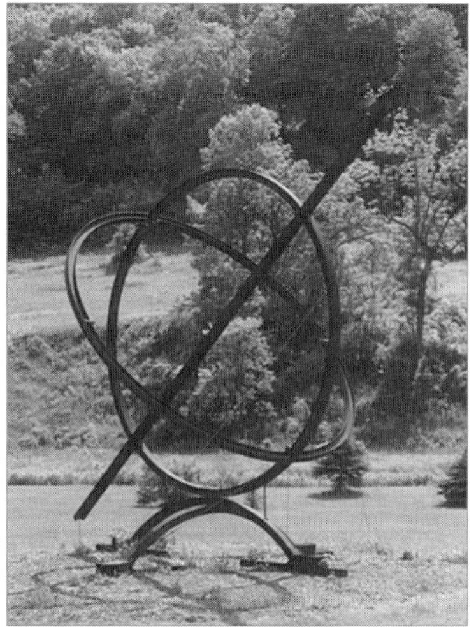

Atlas (Abstract of Sundial)
in Readstown

St. Joseph

Holy Family Grotto
Father Paul Dobberstein, Matt
Szerense, and Frank Donsky
1925-1930
Mixed media, concrete, and stone,
located at Franciscan Sisters of
St. Joseph's Ridge, Highway 33

LAFAYETTE

Darlington

Soldiers and Sailors Monument
Dedicated October 15, 1889
Vermont gray granite, located on
Boulevard, 400 block of Main Street

MONROE

Cataract

Wegner Grotto
Folk Art Environment
Paul and Matilda Wegner
1929-1942
Mixed media, approximately 16
sculptures at this site located at
Wegner Grotto County Park on
Highway 71. Includes: *Embellished
Wedding Cake, Peace Memorial,
Glass Chapel,* and *Steamship
Bremen*

Wegner Monuments
Paul and Matilda Wegner
Circa 1930s
Mixed media, located in cemetery
near *Wegner Grotto*

Fort McCoy, Tomah

Minuteman
Fiberglass, located near Fort McCoy,
on Highway 21

Sparta

Civil War Soldier (Boyton Park)
Bronze and stone, located inside
rotunda of library on both sides of
north entrance. It was in Blyton Park,
Highway 21 and Benton Street

Justice
Circa 1890
Copper, located at County
Courthouse (temporarily removed)

Spartacus
Jerry Vetterus
Fiberglass, located at Sparta High
School, Highway 71/27

F.A.S.T. (Fiberglass, Animals, Shapes, and Trademarks)
Jerry Vetterus
Located on Highway 21, this is one of
the largest fiberglass art factories in
the United States with dozens of subjects including the *Statue of Liberty,
Chickens, Cows, ET, Buffalo,* and
many more

RICHLAND

Lone Rock

Civil War Monument
1884
Metal, Detroit Bronze Company,
located in Battery Park on
Highway 131

SAUK

Baraboo

Tom Every Art Environment
Doctor Evermore

Extensive folk art environment made from recycled materials including *The Forevertron*, located on Highway 12 across from the old Badger Army Ammunition Plant, south of Baraboo

Christ with St. Joseph
Limestone, located at St. Joseph School, 310 2nd Street

Civil War Soldier Monument
Dedicated 1896

Granite, located at Sauk County Courthouse, 515 Oak Street

Drum People, 1991
Devil, 1992
Skier, 1993
Bruce Squires

Metal, located at S. 3901 Highway 12

Bear and Cub
Dave Watson

Wood, chain saw art, located on sign for Log Cabin Restaurant, Highway 23

➔ Man Mound Park

Contains the upper part of the legs and the body of a man-shaped mound. Human figures of this type usually represent shamans, priests or religious figures. Take Highway 33 east out of Baraboo about 1 mile and turn north on County Highway T for about 1 mile, turn east on Man Mound Road.

➔ Devil's Lake State Park

Contains Native American Mounds in several locations:

The Terminal Moraine Mound Group now only consists of two clusters of 11 mounds

The Devil's Lake Group was originally composed of five mounds, including a bear, two conicals and two large linears

The Devil's Lake Mound is a spectacular bird mound. The mound was described as a "bird of most unusual form, having a forked tail and wings that bent downward at their pointed tips."

Folk Art Environment
Bruce Squires

Welded steel humanoids and bug creatures, located at S3901 Highway 12

Lake Delton

Gargoyles
1955 erected

Carved stone, located at 469 County Highway A

Lost City of Newport

Totem Pole
Dave Watson

Wood, chain saw art, located on Fawn Lake

North Freedom

Civil War Monument
Dedicated 1896

Stone, located at North Freedom Cemetery, County Highway I

Prairie du Sac

Wind Breeze and Open Wind
Tom Nelson

1994

Painted metal, located at Harolow Acres, corner of Center Street and County PP

Reedsburg

Roots and Wings
O.V. Shaffer

1998

Stainless steel 25 feet high, located at Reedsburg High School

Timber Monument
Dedicated December 31, 1976

Metal and wood, located at Main Street, River Bridge

Town of Plain

Grotto to Saint Bernadette
Joseph Dischler

Circa 1920s

St. Luke Catholic Church, located on Highway 23

VERNON

Coon Valley

Zerogee II
Paul T. Granlund

1983

Bronze, located at Norskedalen

Readstown

Sundial
Royce Jones

Circa 1990

Welded steel, located in Arboretum, S7375 Highway 14

Viroqua

Bru
Kati Monson Casida

Dedication 1987

Stone, located at Viroqua City Park

Rockside Folk Art Environment
Rockside with numerous small folk art structures made of stone, glass and concrete, located near Viroqua

Tin Man
Danny Deaver

1993

Painted steel, located at 317 Main Street

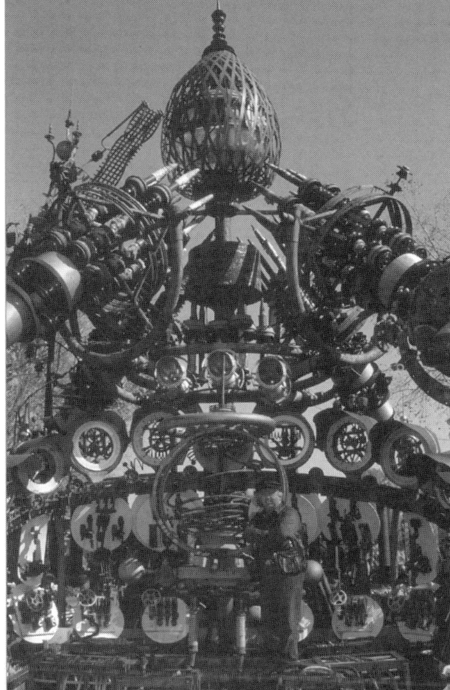

Tom Every Art Environment, The Forevertron
near Baraboo

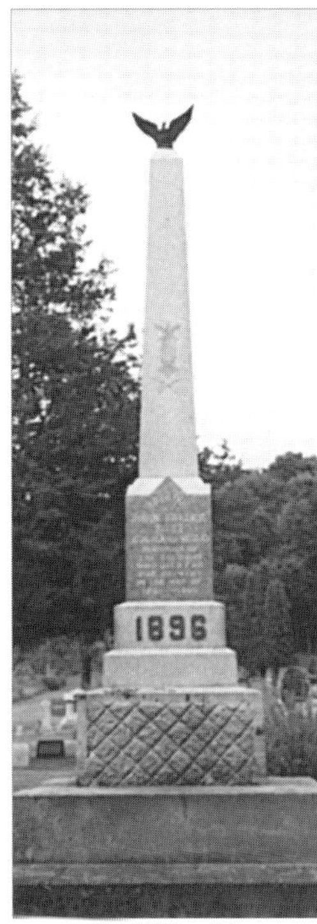

Civil War Monument
in North Freedom

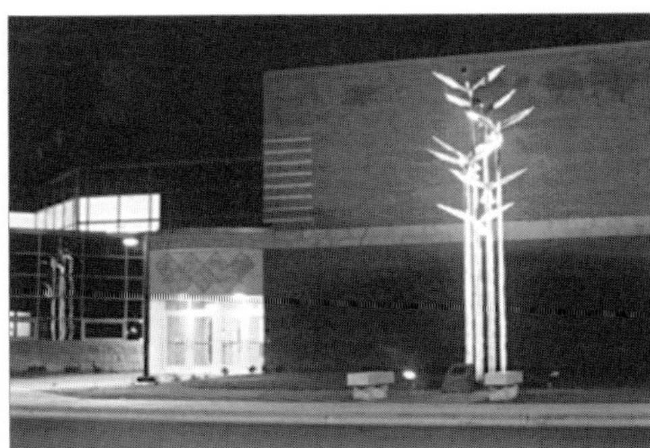

Roots and Wings in Reedsburg

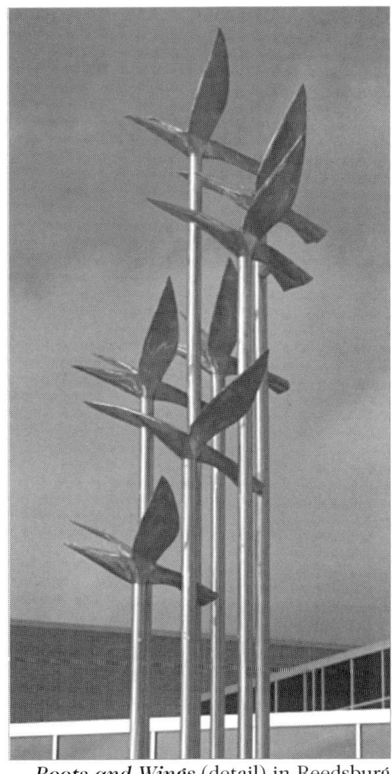

Roots and Wings (detail) in Reedsburg

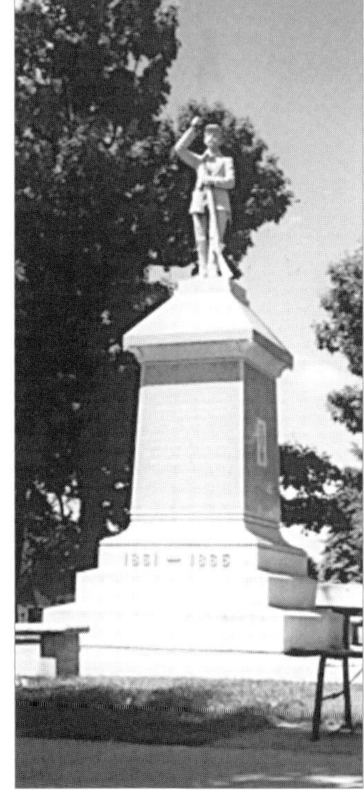

Civil War Soldier Monument
in Baraboo

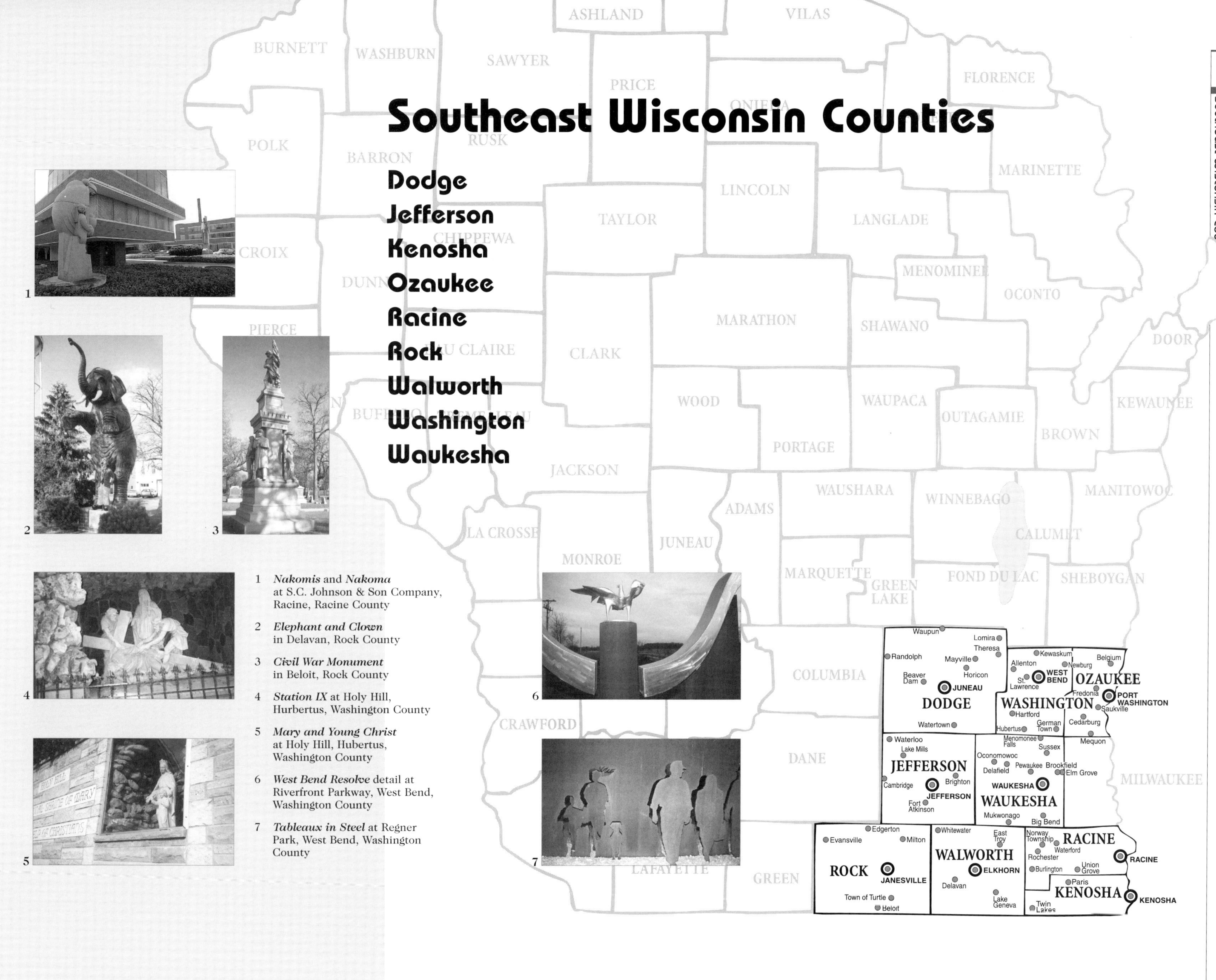

Southeast Wisconsin Counties

Dodge
Jefferson
Kenosha
Ozaukee
Racine
Rock
Walworth
Washington
Waukesha

1 *Nakomis* and *Nakoma* at S.C. Johnson & Son Company, Racine, Racine County

2 *Elephant and Clown* in Delavan, Rock County

3 *Civil War Monument* in Beloit, Rock County

4 *Station IX* at Holy Hill, Hurbertus, Washington County

5 *Mary and Young Christ* at Holy Hill, Hubertus, Washington County

6 *West Bend Resolve* detail at Riverfront Parkway, West Bend, Washington County

7 *Tableaux in Steel* at Regner Park, West Bend, Washington County

Southeast Wisconsin Counties

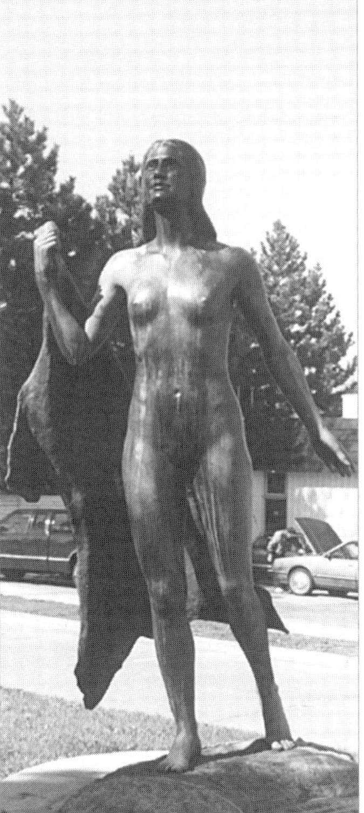

Dawn of Day in Waupun

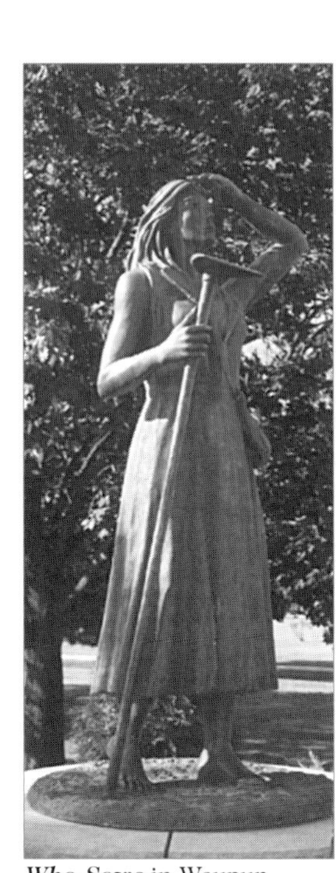

Who Sows in Waupun

The End of the Trail in Waupun

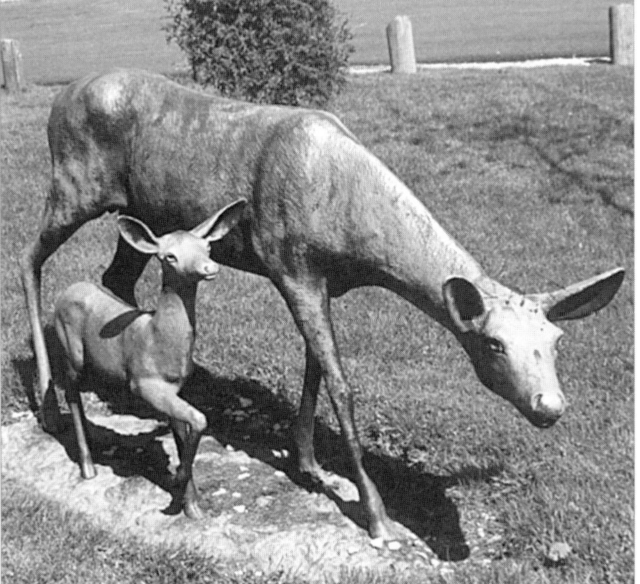

Group of Deer in Waupun

DODGE

Beaver Dam

Blessed Virgin
Four Evangelists
Christ
> White marble, located at Highlands Memorial Gardens, Highway 151

Mayville

Civil War Soldier
> Dedicated May 30, 1928
> Stone, located at north end of Foster Park, on N. Main Street

Crucifixion Scene With Mary and St. John
> Dedicated 1922
> Metal, located in St. Mary's Cemetery, St. John Street

Veterans Fountain Square
> Mixed media, located on N. Main Street

Rubicon

Christ with Urns
> Stone, located at Catholic church

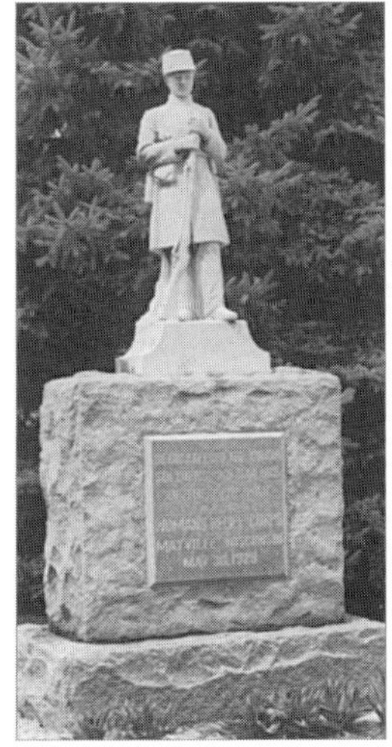

Civil War Soldier
in Mayville

Theresa

Bust of Virgillis Anninger
  Frank Anninger
  Concrete, located at Theresa
  Historical Society complex

Waupun

Dawn of Day
  Clarence Addison Shaler
  1931
  Bronze, located at Waupun City Hall,
  201 E. Main Street

End of the Trail
  James Earle Fraser
  Dedicated June 23, 1929
  Bronze, located at Shaler Park

Group of Deer
  Clarence Addison Shaler
  1932
  Bronze, located at Rock River
  Country Club, N375 County Trunk
  Highway MMM

The Citadel
  Clarence Addison Shaler
  1939
  Bronze, located at Historical Society

The Pioneers
  Clarence Addison Shaler
  1938
  Bronze, located at Wilcox Park,
  corner of Lincoln Street and
  Watertown Street

The Recording Angel
  Lorado Taft
  1923
  Bronze and marble, located in the
  Forest Mound Cemetery

Veterans Memorial, All Wars
  1994
  Granite with flagpoles, located in
  Shaler Park

Who Sows
  Clarence Addison Shaler
  1938
  Bronze, located in front of hospital on
  Highway 26. Also titled *He Who Sows
  Believes in God*

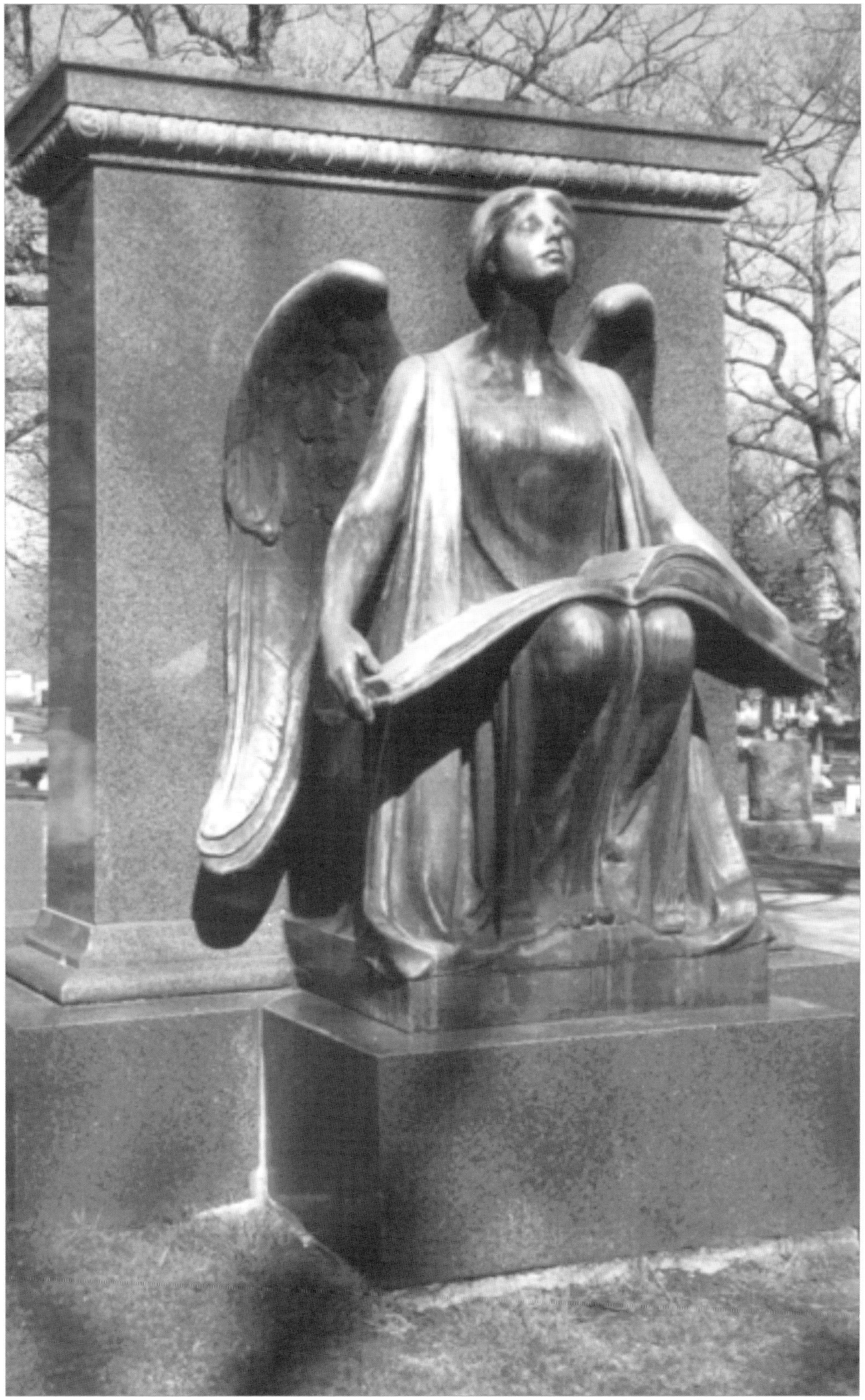

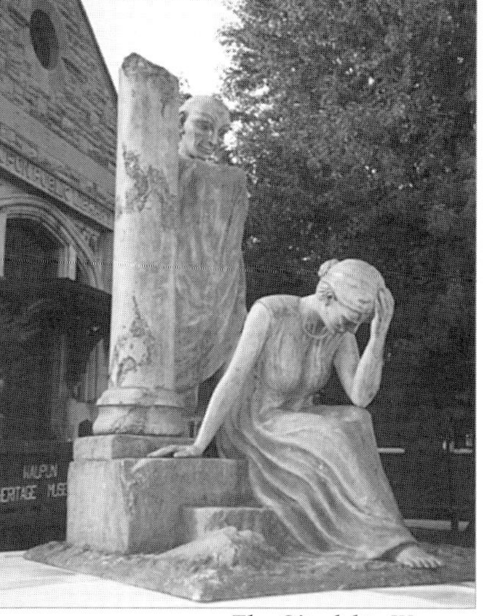

The Citadel in Waupun

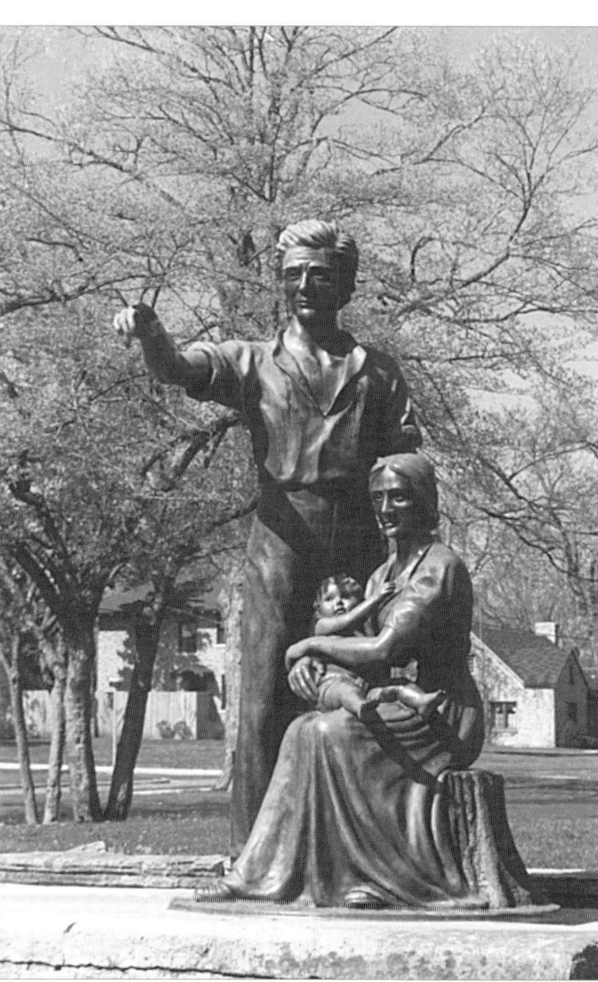

The Pioneers in Waupun

The Recording Angel in Waupun

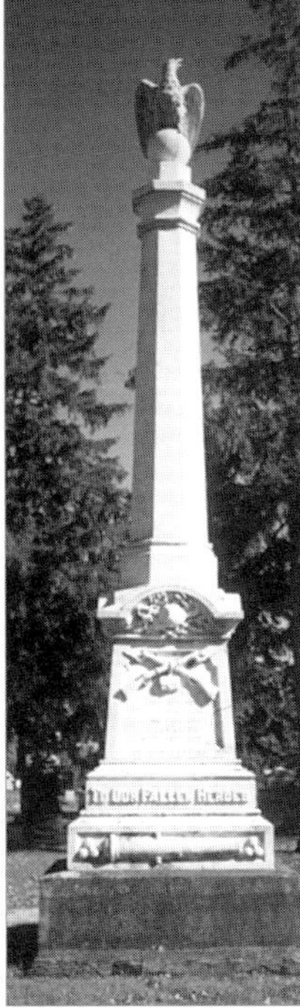

Veterans Eagle Monument in Brighton

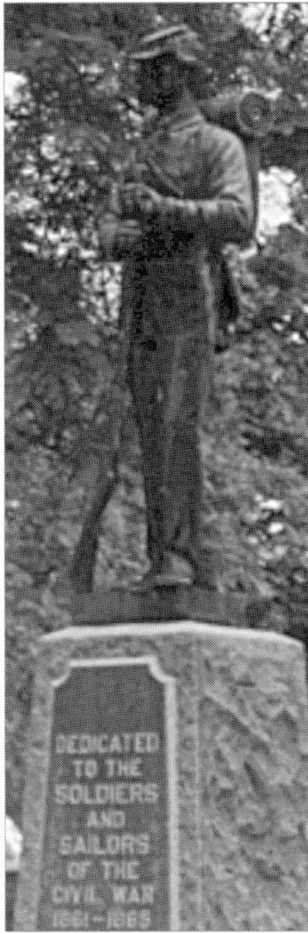

Civil War Soldier in Cambridge

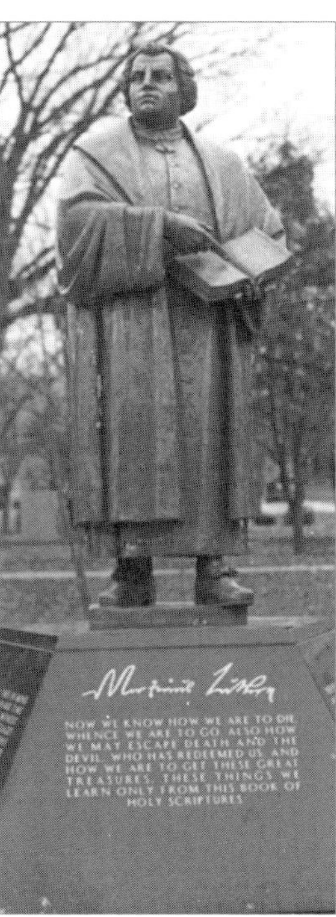

Martin Luther in Watertown

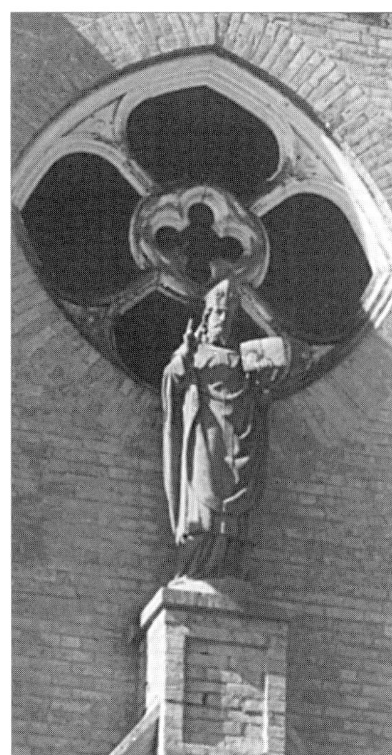

St. Henry in Watertown

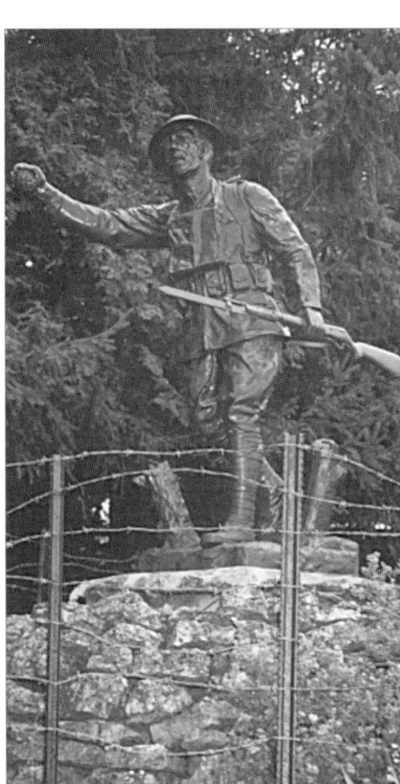

WWI Doughboy Memorial in Fort Atkinson

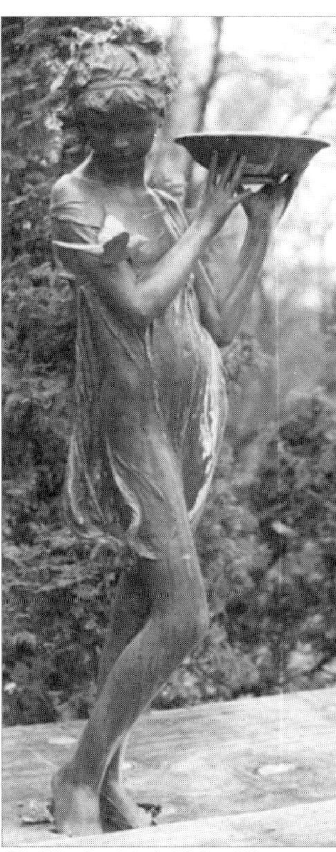

Phyllis the Bird Girl in Watertown

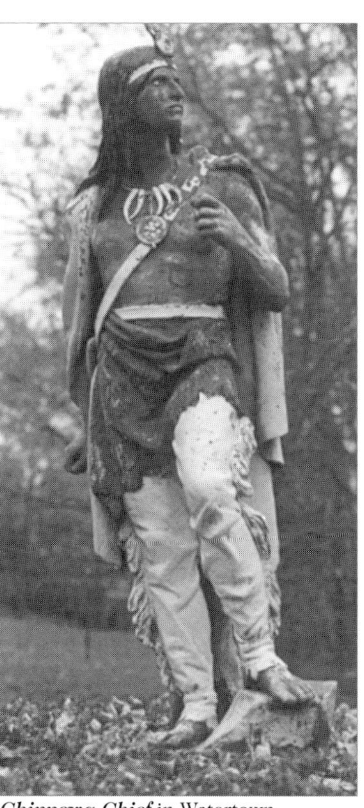

Chippewa Chief in Watertown

JEFFERSON

Brighton

Veterans Eagle Monument G.A.R.
Bronze and granite, located at 1702 240th Avenue

Cambridge

Civil War G.A.R. Soldier
Copper alloy, located on Highway 12/18

Fort Atkinson

Civil War Soldier
Dedicated 1914
Bronze and marble, located in Evergreen Cemetery, N. Main / Highway 12

Panther Intaglio Effigy
This intaglio effigy is a depression that has been dug, or sculpted, into the earth. It is a reverse of a mound. Located Highway 106, Riverside Drive.

WWI Doughboy
Painted metal, located at Wayside on Highway 12 west

Jefferson

Soldiers and Sailors Monument
Granite figures, located at Courthouse

Lake Mills

Aztalan State Park
Near Lake Mills, this is one of Wisconsin's most important archaeological sites

Jefferson County Indian Mounds and Trail Park
General Atkinson Mound Group was described in 1908 as containing 72 mounds. 40 of these were conical, 17 were linear, 13 were effigies, and 2 were somewhat amorphous in shape. Located at 320 S. Main Street

Veterans Memorial
Grey granite, located in Veterans Memorial Park, S. 3rd Street

Veterans Monument
Granite columns with pyramid, located in City Park

Watertown

Chippewa Indian (Indian Chieftain)
1893
Painted metal, located at the Octagon House Grounds (since 1964), 919 Charles Street. This was part of a public water fountain

Martin Luther
Circa 1928
Metal, located at Luther Preparatory School, 1300 Western Avenue

Phyllis the Bird Girl
Bessie Potter Vonnon
Circa 1930
Bronze, located on the Octagon House grounds (since 1970), 919 Charles Street, original in Central Park, New York City

Soldier and Sailors Monument
Jones Brothers
Circa 1899
Granite with bronze eagle, located at Memorial Park, 600 block between S. 3rd and S. 4th streets

St. Henry
Marble, located at St. Henry's Catholic Church, 412 N. 4th Street

KENOSHA

Kenosha

A Learning Moment
Michael Martino
1997
Bronze grouping of Abraham Lincoln teaching a student, located at Carthage College campus, David A. Straz Jr. Center

Abraham Lincoln
Charles Neihaus
Dedicated 1909
Bronze and granite, located in Simmons Library Park, 7th Avenue

Blessed Virgin
Stone, located at St. Mark Catholic Church, 73rd and Sheridan Avenue

Statue of Liberty
1950
Bronze, located at 57th and Sheridan Avenue

Veterans Memorial Fountain (Globe)

Dedicated November 1976
Metal, stone, colored lights, located at the east side of the Kenosha Municipal Building, 625 52nd Street

Winged Victory

Italian sculptor
1900
Bronze statue on grey Vermont granite, located in Gilbert M. Simmons Library Park, 711 59th Place. This 12-foot Civil War *Nike* (symbol of victory) interpretation stands on top of a 60-foot Corinthian column.

Greenridge Cemetery

66th and Sheridan Avenue

Captain Augustus Quarles Monument

Marble

Civil War Monument

Granite

Crucifixions

Stone

O'Neill Monument

1902
Stone

Zerk Monument

1996
Stone and metal

All Wars Monument

1955
Stone

Rotary Tot Park

3rd Avenue and 57th Street, northeast corner of Marina

Bowfin Ruin

Theresa Agnew
1991
Mixed media

Carved Boat

1991
Wood

Rainbow Trout Run

1991
Painted wood

UW-Parkside

A Game of War, Part I and Part II

John Zehren
1987
Welded metal, located at Wyllie Hall and Communications Arts Concourse

Dancing Figure

Concrete and iron, located at Wyllie Hall and Communication Arts Concourse

Self Inflicted

Daniel Leonhardt
1998
Steel and stainless steel, located near Communication Arts Building

Untitled

Jeff Shauhan
Painted steel, located at the Communications Arts Building. Removed

Paris

Veterans G.A.R. Memorial

1868
Stone shaft, 12 feet tall, located at the Paris Safety Building, 16607 Highway 14

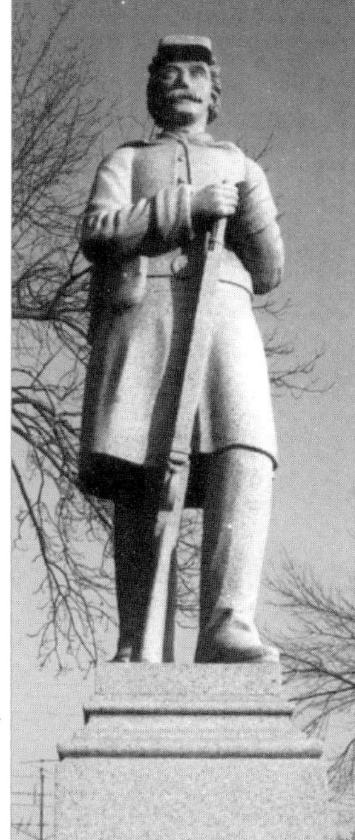

Civil War Monument at Greenridge Cemetery, Kenosha

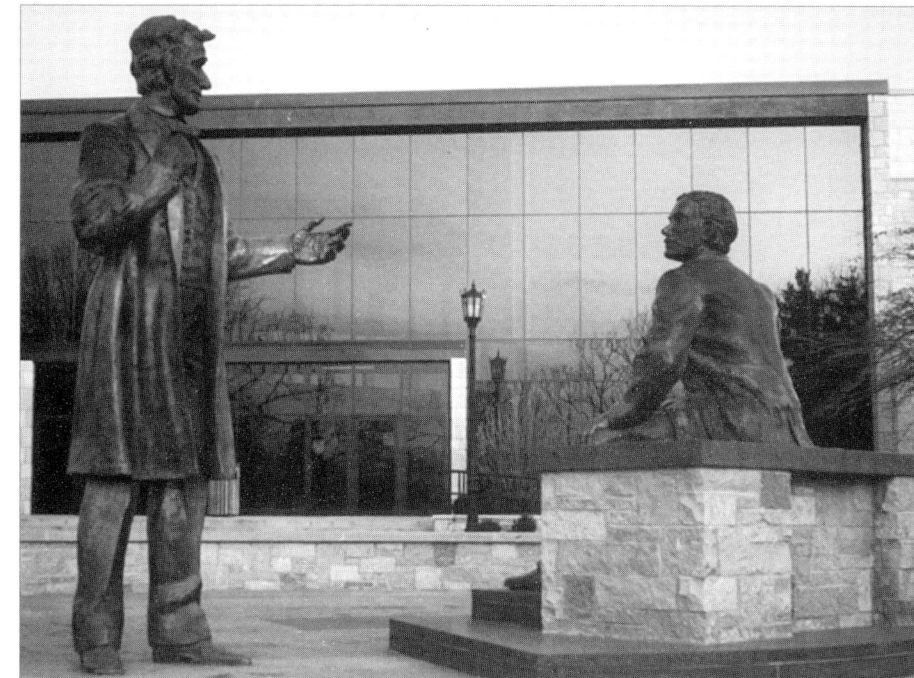

A Learning Moment in Kenosha

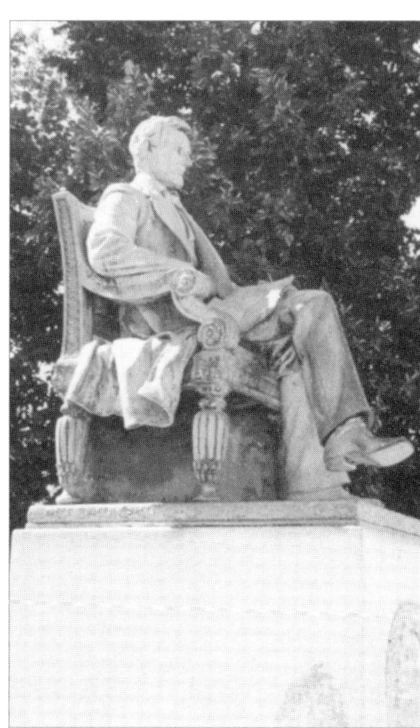

Abraham Lincoln in Kenosha

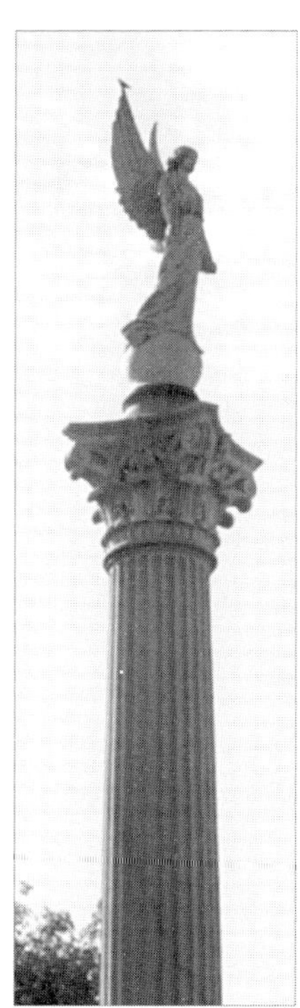

Civil War Monument in Racine

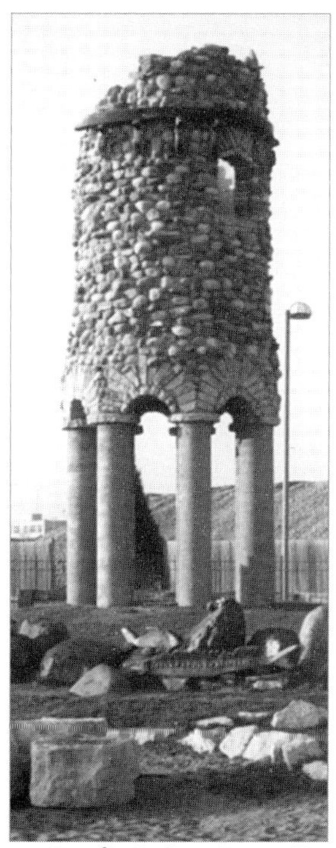

Bowfin Ruin at Rotary Tot Park, Kenosha

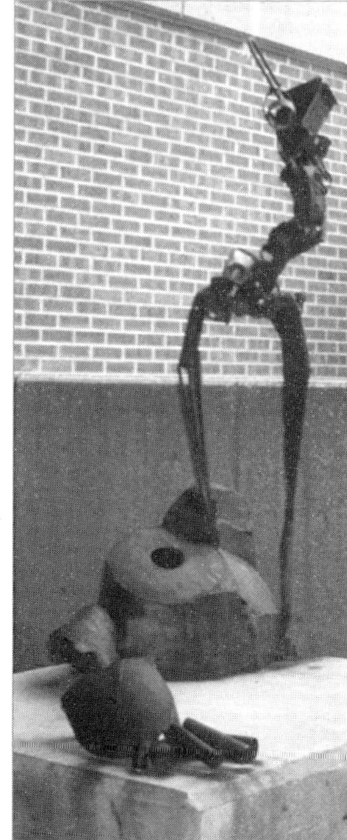

A Game of War at UW-Parkside, Kenosha

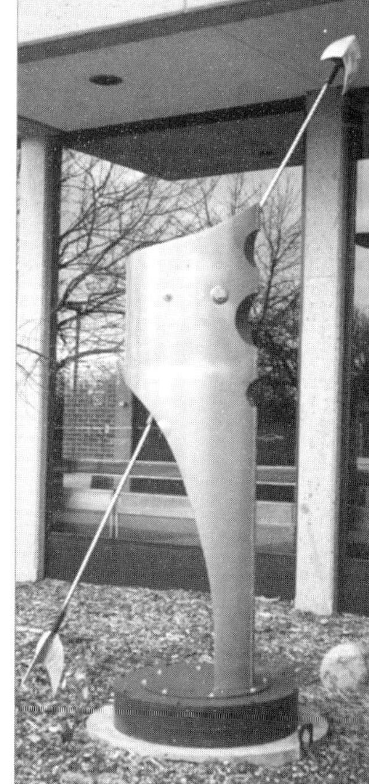

Self Inflicted at UW-Parkside, Kenosha

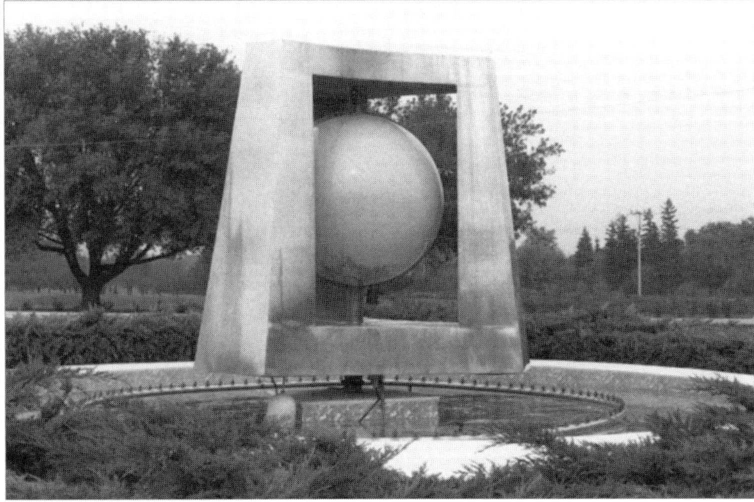

Ball Fountain in Cedarburg

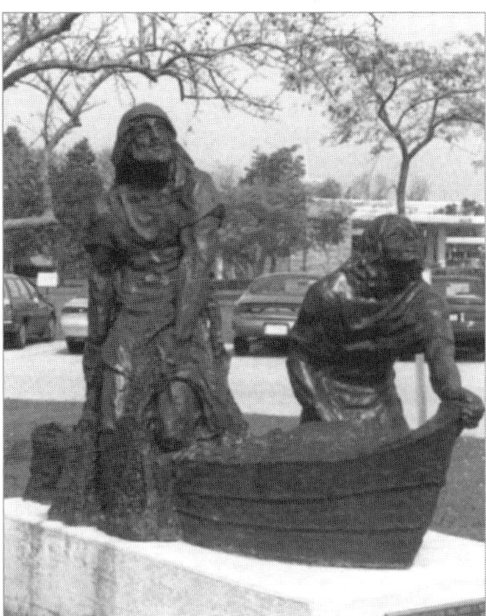

Come Follow Me and I Will Make You a Fisher of Men at Concordia College in Mequon

OZAUKEE

Cedarburg

Ball Fountain
Paul Yank
Circa 1995
Bronze and Corten steel, located at the Orion Corporation on Cedar Creek Road

Funny Faces
Ceramic, located at Studio Six on Washington Avenue

Paul Yank Studios
Paul Yank
Circa 1990
Mixed media metal, located downtown, includes *Free Form* (Corten steel rods), *White Fennel* (painted metal), and many more

Sun Burst
Metal, located at the Cedarburg Cultural Center on Washington Avenue

Vogenitz Memorial
Concrete tree form, located at Zur Ruhe Cemetery on Bridge Road

Fredonia

Totem Pole
Ivan House
Painted wood, located on Milwaukee River at 2009 Riverview Trail, view from road

Mequon

Chief Thomas E. Buntrock
Jeune Nowak-Wussow
1983
Bronze, located at the City of Mequon Safety Building, Buntrock Avenue and Mequon Road

Verticil Intercept Sequi I
Bilhenry Walker
1996
Painted aluminum, located at Softworks Development Corporation, 10202 N. Enterprise Drive

Concordia College
East of I-43 on Highland Road

Come Follow Me and I Will Make You a Fisher of Men
Igor Wasiljev of Latvia
Bronze

Port Washington

Billy Goat Hill, Folk Art Environment
Circa 1940s
Mixed media, located at Wisconsin Street and Franklin. Included *Miniature Ferris Wheel*, stone and concrete *Houses*, and *Lighthouse*. Demolished

Relief Doors
Bronze, located at St. Mary's Church

Saukville

Green Bay Packer
1997
Chainsaw art, located at Northwoods Road, off Highway 33

RACINE

Burlington

Abraham Lincoln
George Etienne Ganinie
Florentine Brotherhood Foundry
1913
Bronze, located at triangle of Kane and State

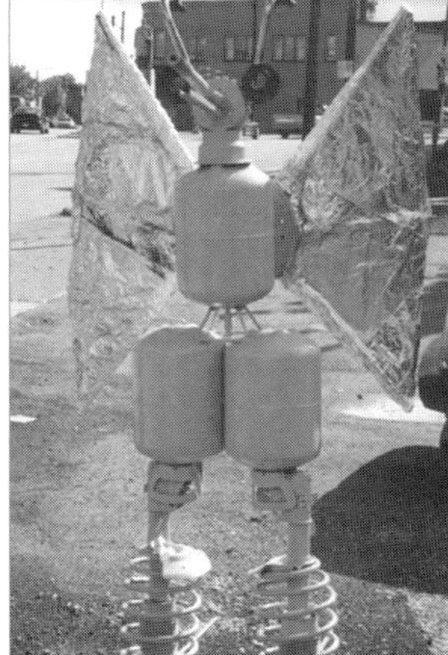

My Bird in Racine

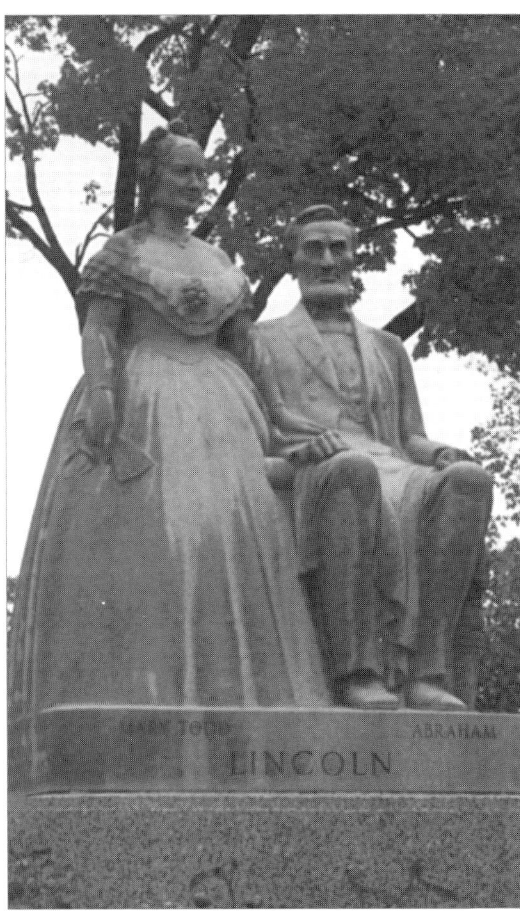

Abraham and Mary Todd Lincoln Monument in Racine

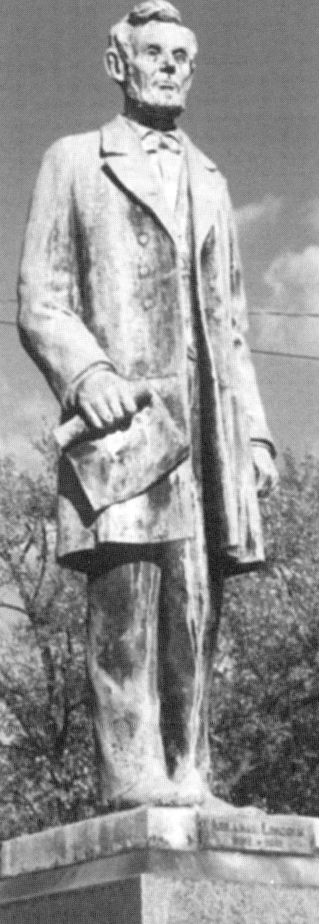

Abraham Lincoln in Racine

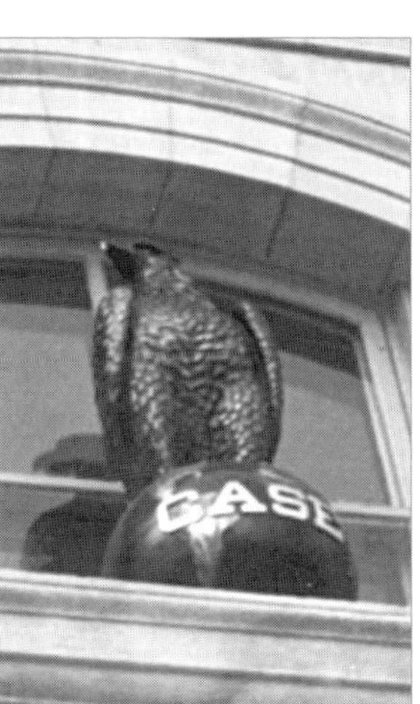

Case Eagle in Racine

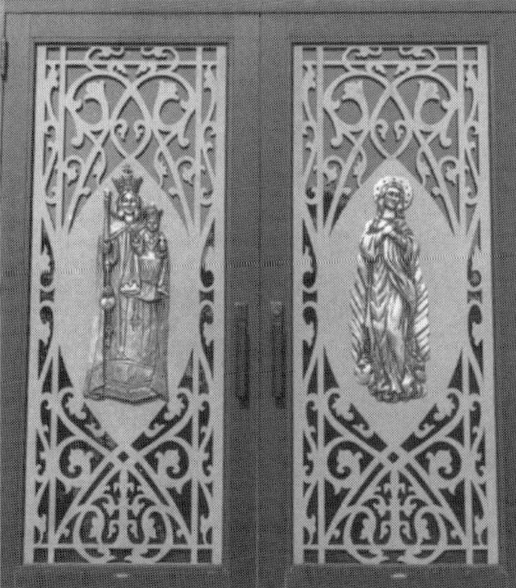

Relief Doors of St. Mary's in Port Washington

Calvary Grotto
Lourdes Grotto
Replica of Portinumcula Chapel
Shrine to Our Lady of
Czestochowa
Mixed media, located at St. Francis Friary and Retreat Center, 503 South Brown's Lake Drive

Soldiers Monument
Late 19th century
White marble, located at Burlington Cemetery

Norway Township
Near Waterford

Colonel Hans Christian Heg
Paul Fjelde
1926
Cast bronze, located in Heg Park, Highway 36, corner of Heg Park Road and S. Looming Road near Waterford. Identical statue at the Wisconsin State Capitol.

Racine

Abraham Lincoln
A.L. Van den Bergen
Installed 1923
Bronze, located at Lincoln School, State Street

Abraham and Mary Todd Lincoln Monument
Frederick C. Hibbard
July 6, 1943
Granite, located in East Park, S. Main Street between 10th and 11th streets, in front of Gateway Technical College

Ants
Mosquito
Shark Fins
Weld-a-Saurus
1998
Steel, located at Jensen Metal Products, 7800 Northwestern Avenue

Art Environment
Bill Reid
Mixed media collection of sculpture, located at 240 Windridge Drive. Private, view from road.

Barney
Men in Black
My Bird
David Schultz
1997-1998
Welded car parts, located at 1720 Douglas

Case Eagle
Bronze, located at 700 State Street

Civil War Soldiers Monument, G.A.R.
C. Allen Campbell
Dedicated July 4, 1884
Granite, located at Monument Square, 521 Main Street at 5th and 6th streets

Doughboy
Dedicated Memorial Day, 1926
Bronze, located in Graceland Cemetery, Osborne Boulevard

Dr. Martin Luther King, Jr.
Frank Colicki
Dedicated 1995
Bronze, located in Plaza at intersection of State Street and Marquette Street and Martin Luther King Drive

Eagle Bench
Bill Reid
Painted metal, located at Samuel C. Johnson Upper School, 4025 3-Mile Road

Freeing the Animals
Bill Reid
June 1994
Painted metal, located in front of the primates building at the Racine County Zoo

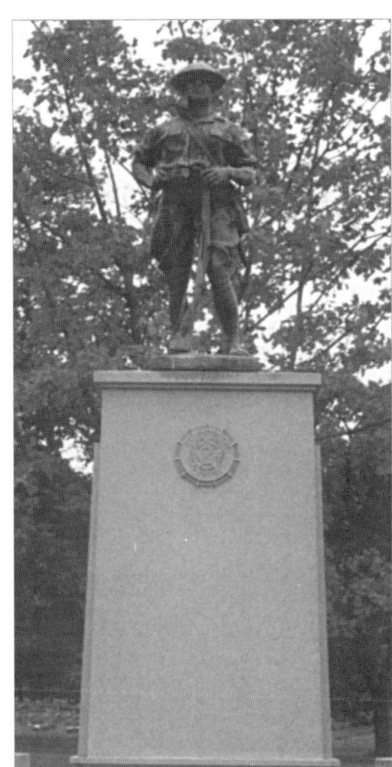
Doughboy in Racine

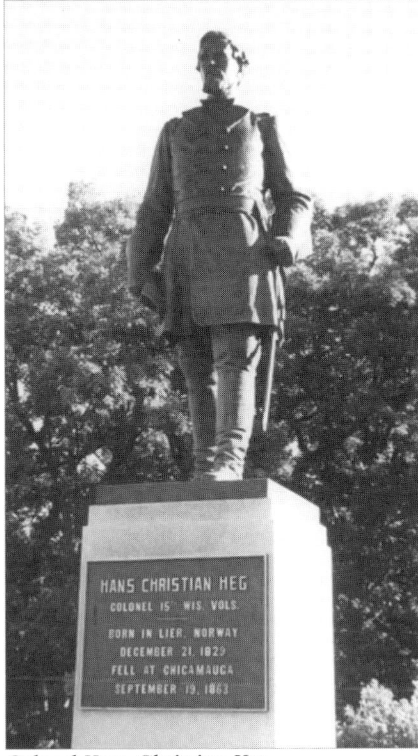
Colonel Hans Christian Heg in Norway Township

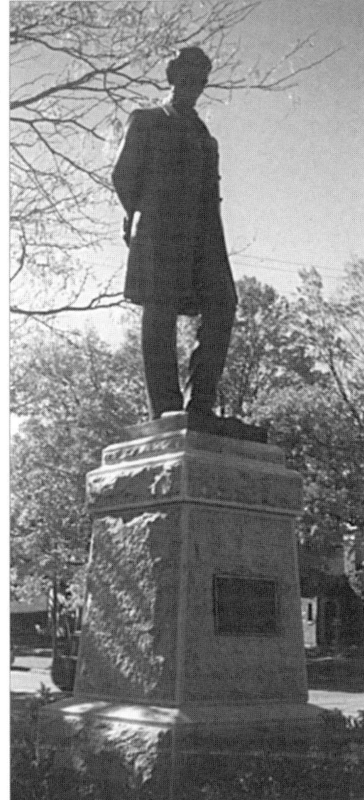
Abraham Lincoln in Burlington

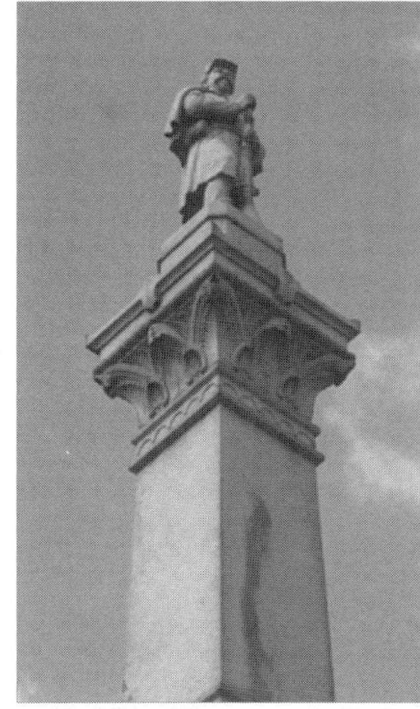
Civil War Monument in Racine

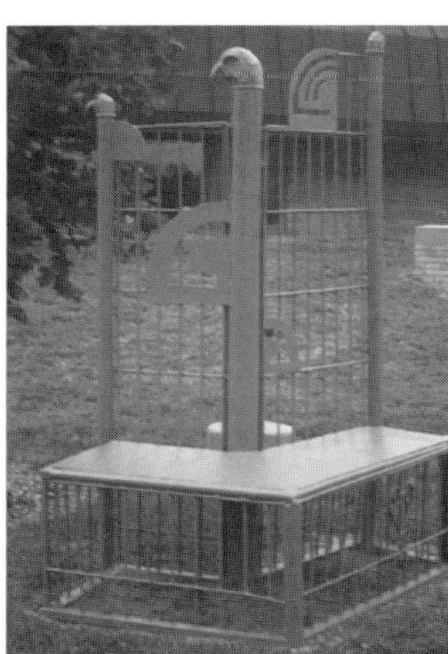
Eagle Bench in Racine

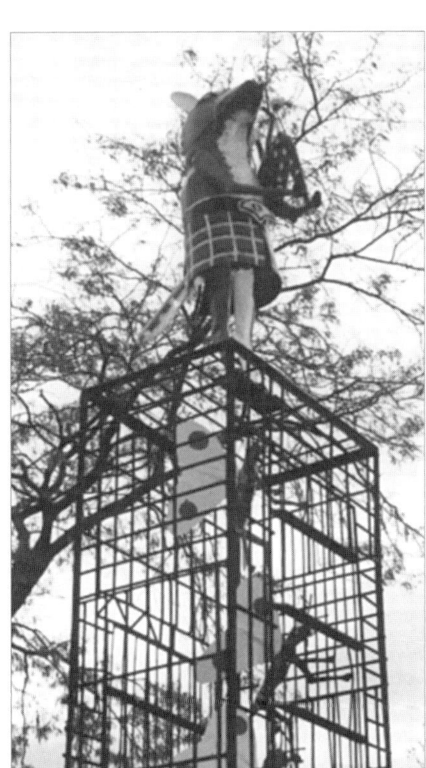
Freeing the Animals in Racine

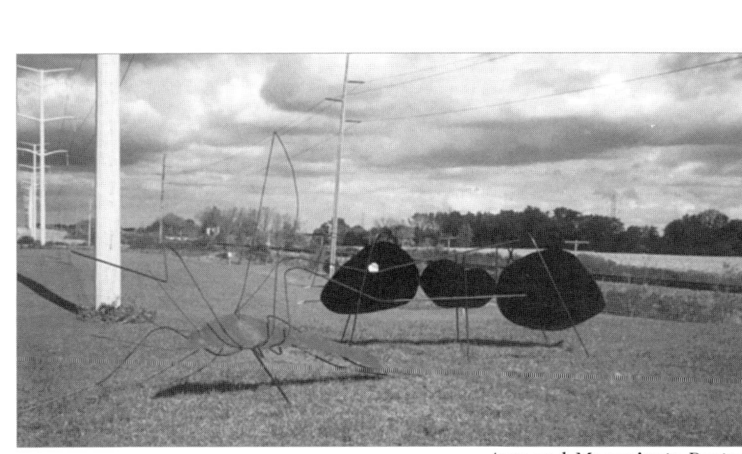
Ants and *Mosquito* in Racine

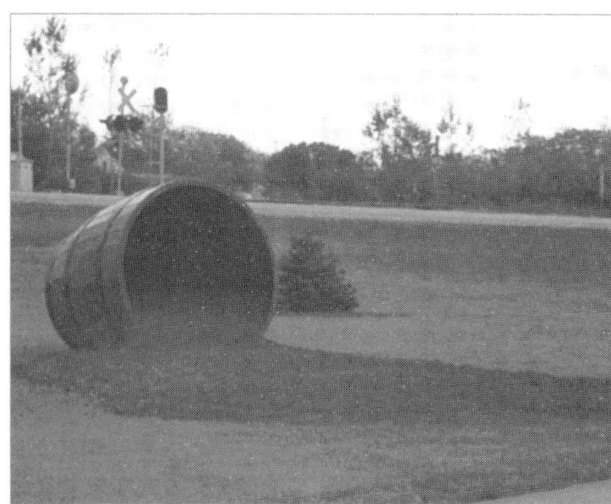

Random and Senseless Acts of Vandalism in Racine

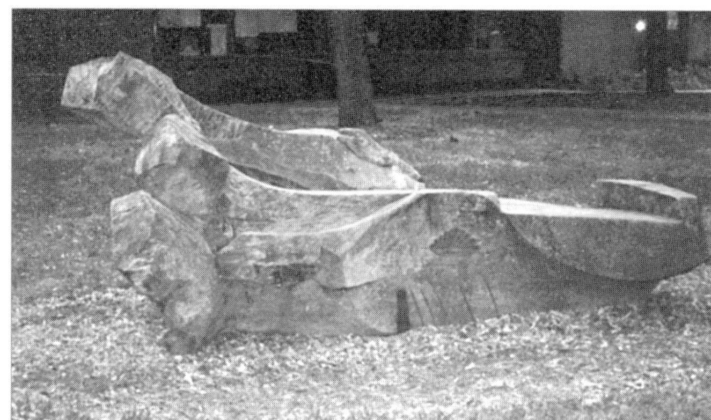

Shell Bench in Racine

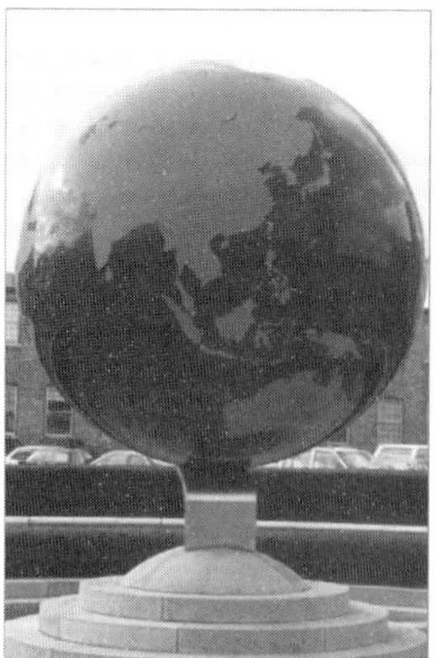

World Globe in Racine

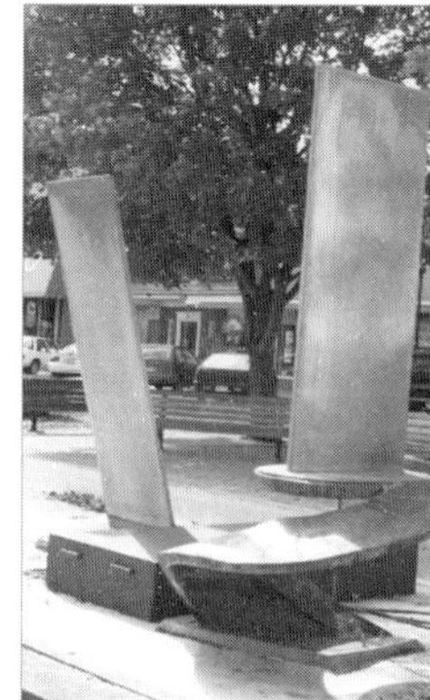

Water Sculpture in Racine

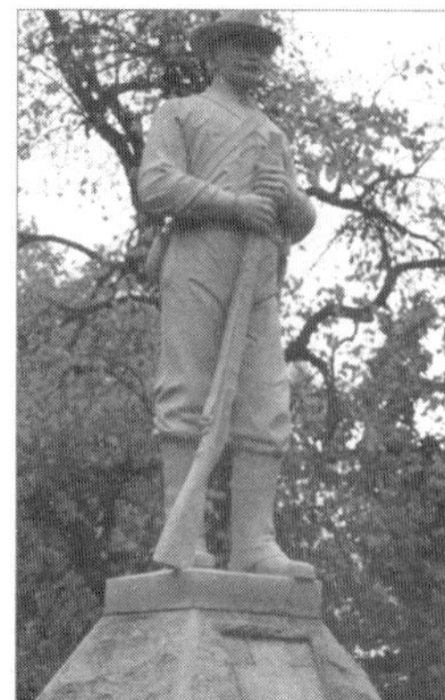

Spanish American War Memorial in Racine

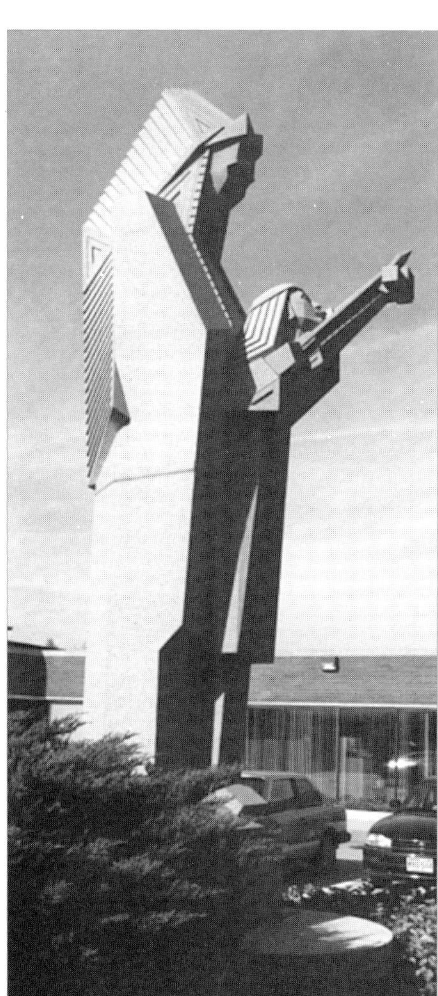

Nakoma at S.C. Johnson & Son Company, Racine

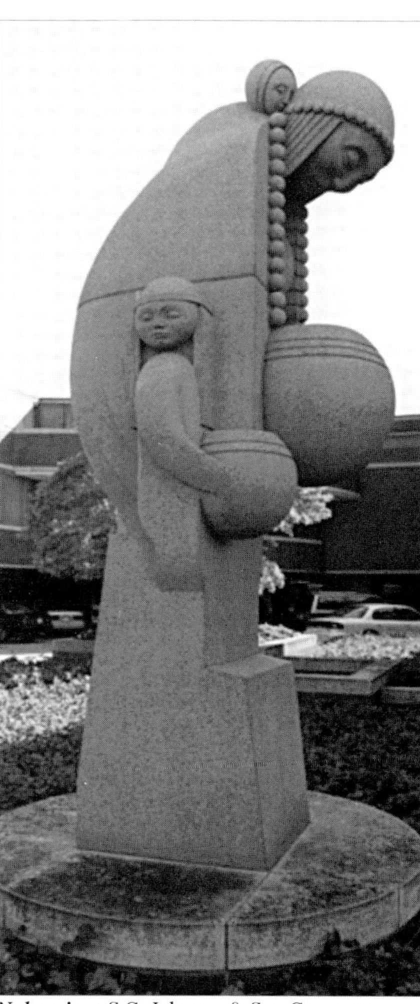

Nakomis at S.C. Johnson & Son Company, Racine

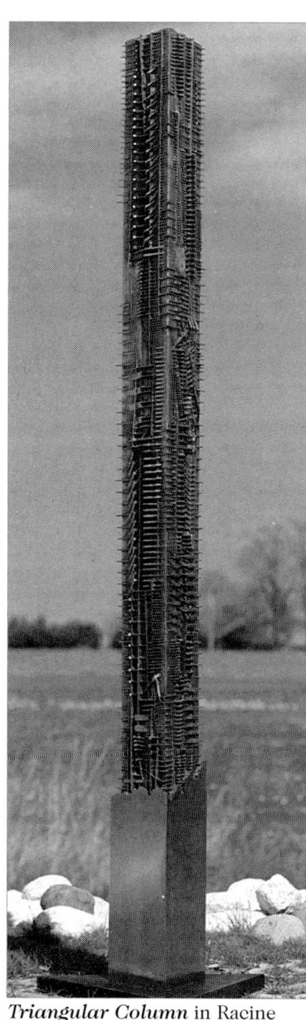

Triangular Column in Racine

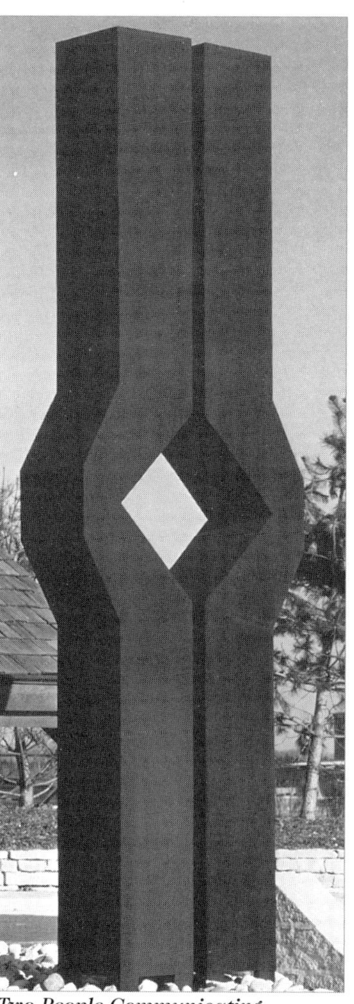

Two People Communicating in Racine

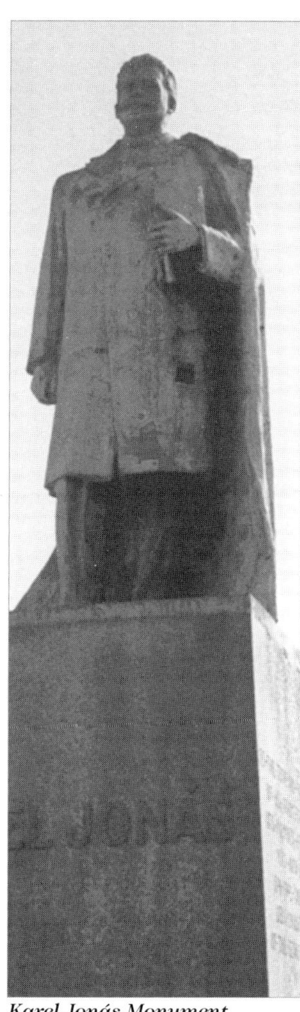

Karel Jonás Monument in Racine

George W. Slauson Monument

1882
Marble, located at Mounds Cemetery

Karel Jonás

Mario Korbel
Dedicated 1913
Bronze, located at triangle of High Street, Douglas, and Martin Luther King Drive

Lincoln Memorial

Leonard Volk
1923
Stone, located at Summit Street and Northwestern Street

Random and Senseless Acts of Vandalism

1997
Barrels with dirt, located at Jensen Metal Products, 7800 Northwestern Avenue

Shell Bench

Carved wood, located at Prairie School, Fine Arts building

Spanish American Veterans Memorial

Dedicated Memorial Day, 1909
Granite, Mound Cemetery, 1100 West Boulevard and Kinzie

Statue of Liberty

P.J. Kamin
1952
Bronze replica, located in Plaza, Sheridan and 57th Street

Triangular Column

Arnoldo Pomodoro
1978
Bronze, located at Council House, 222 3-Mile Road

Two People Communicating

Billy Omabegho
Corten steel, located at Council House, 222 3-Mile Road

Water Sculpture

Oliver Andrews
Dedicated June 1972
Metal, located at 500 block Main Street

S.C. Johnson & Son Company

Howe and 14th Street, 1525 Howe Street, Racine

Nakoma

Frank Lloyd Wright
Granite warrior figure, Conceived 1924 and executed by sculptors Flaviano Cenderelli and Bruno Borgioli

Nakomis

Frank Lloyd Wright
Granite female figure conceived in 1924 and executed by sculptors Flaviano Cenderelli and Bruno Borgioli

World Globe

1986
Metal and stone

Charles A. Wustum Museum of Fine Arts

2519 Northwestern Avenue, Racine

Birdbath Fountain

Gerhard Kroll
1975
Bronze and copper abstract sculpture that serves as a birdbath with running water with slight suggestion of bird face

Fighting Stallions

Anna Hyatt Huntington
1948
Cast aluminum, located in garden

Hummer

Amy Podmore
1989
Painted cement, steel, gypsum and copper, located in garden

School Scenes

Cherry Barr Jerry
1959
Mosaic sculpture, located on east wall on front porch

St. Francis

Cherry Barr Jerry
1959
Mosaic sculpture, located on south wall

The Great Fortune

Milton Elting Hebald
1967
Cast bronze, located in fountain in front yard

Waterford

Saint Thomas Aquinas

Circa 1970
Limestone, located at St. Thomas Aquinas Catholic Church, corner of St. Thomas Street and 1st Street

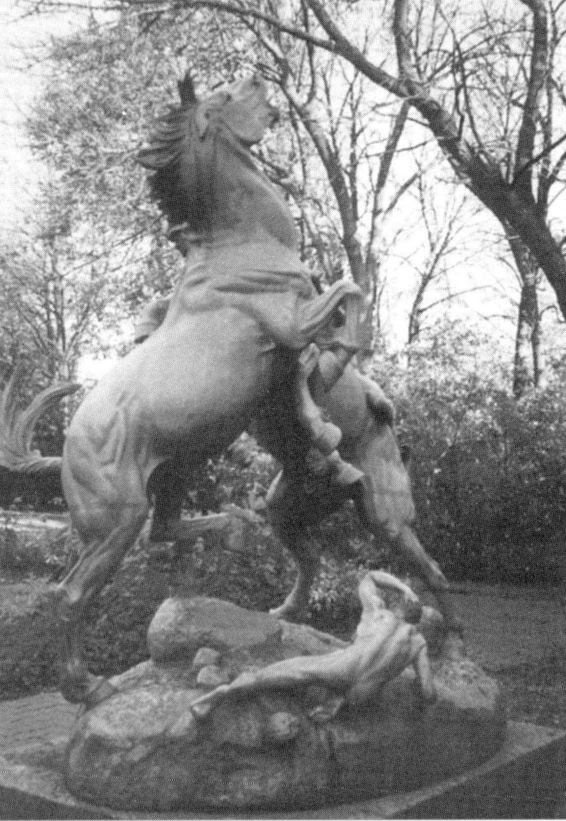

Fighting Stallions at Charles A. Wustum Museum of Fine Arts, Racine

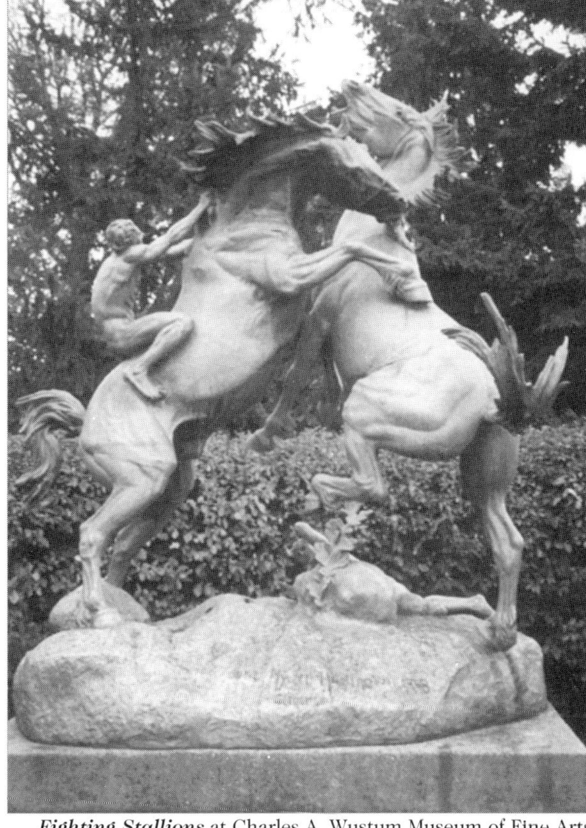

Fighting Stallions at Charles A. Wustum Museum of Fine Arts, Racine

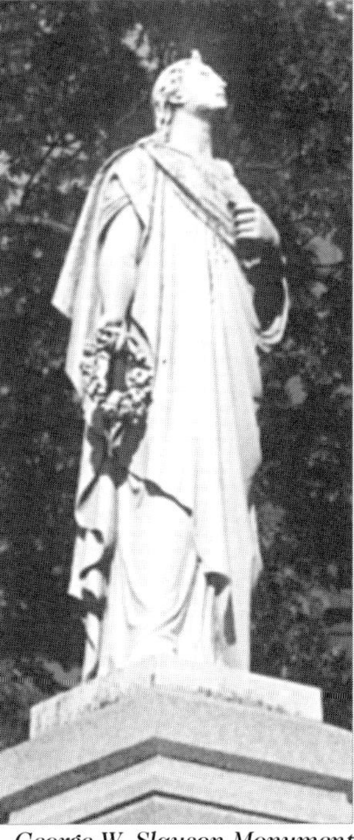

George W. Slauson Monument in Racine

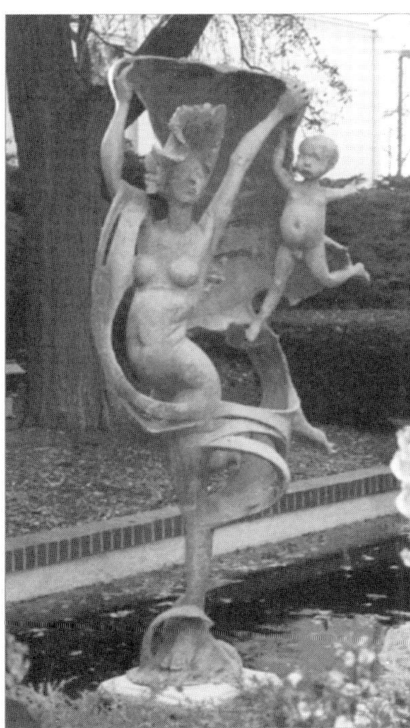

The Great Fortune at Charles A. Wustum Museum of Fine Arts, Racine

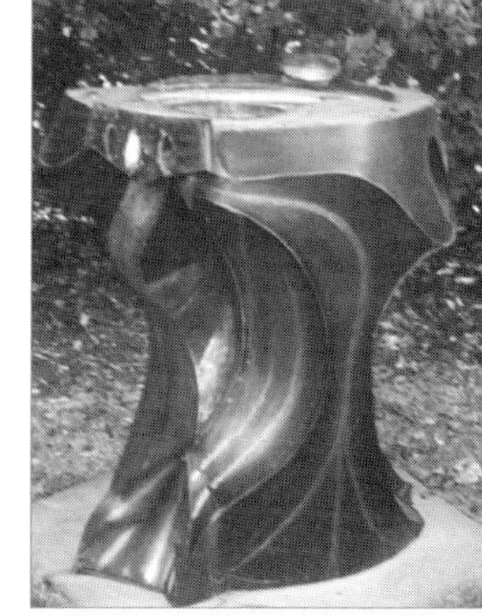

Birdbath Fountain at Charles A. Wustum Museum of Fine Arts, Racine

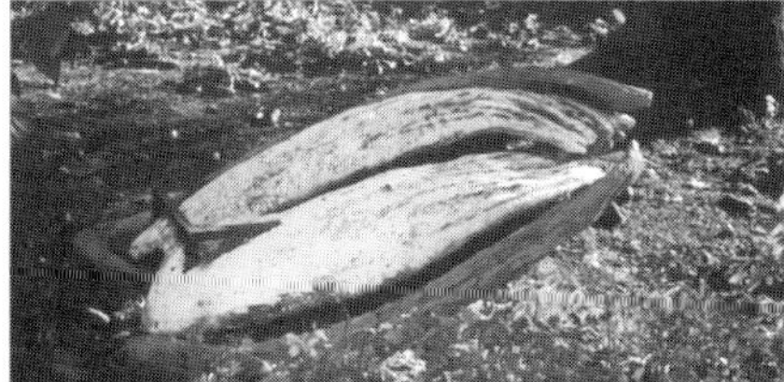

Hummer at Charles A. Wustum Museum of Fine Arts, Racine

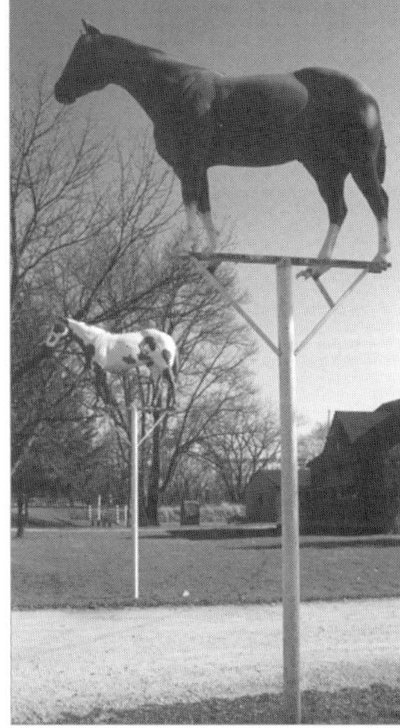

Two Horses in Beloit

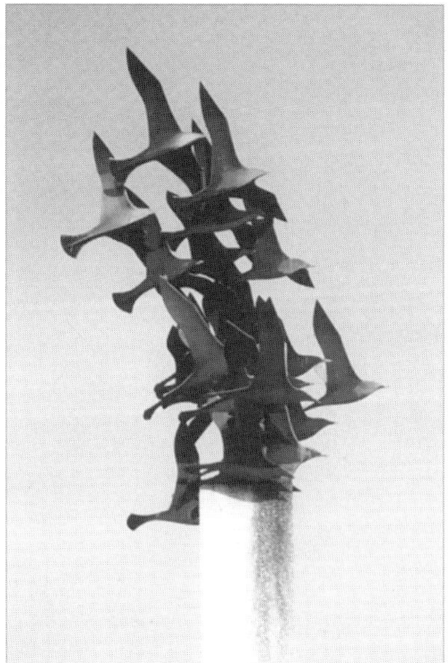

In Flight in Beloit

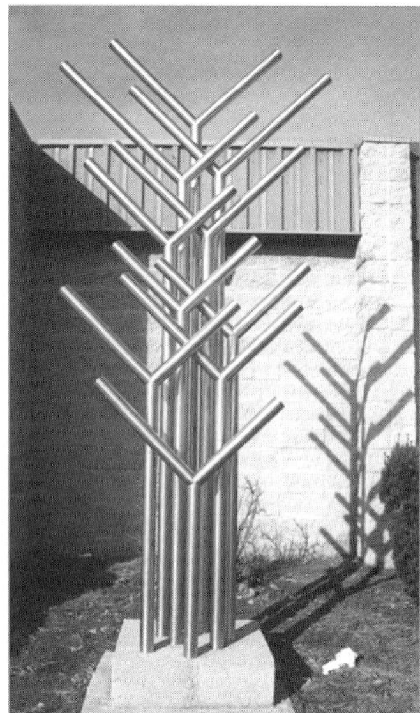

Hometown Crowd in Beloit

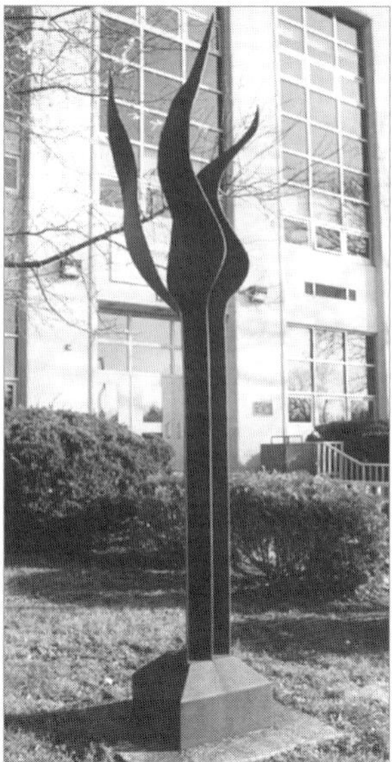

Flame in Beloit

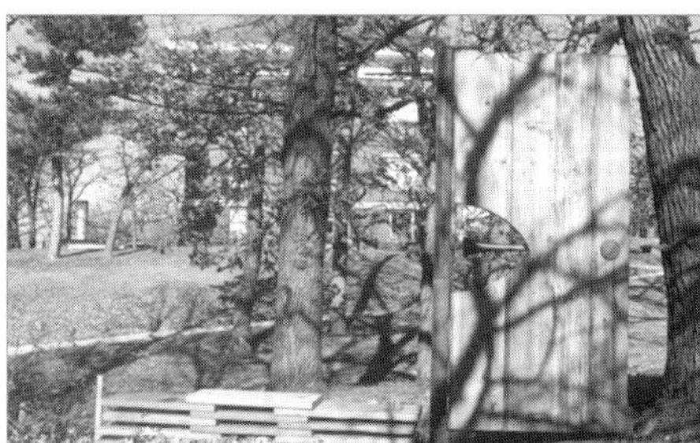

Construction Gate at Beloit College, Beloit

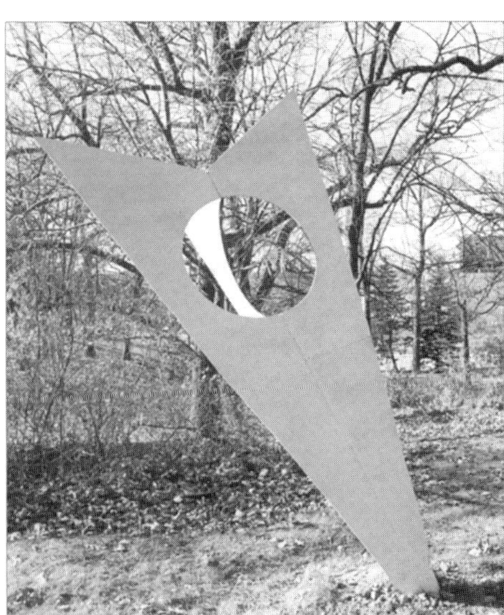

Tipped Triangle at Beloit College, Beloit

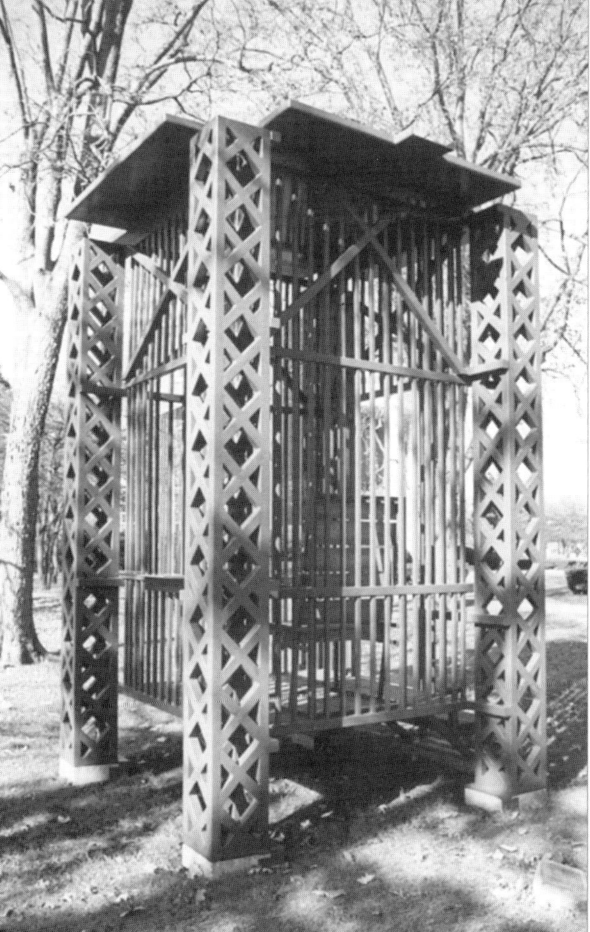

Gazebo for One Anarchist at Beloit College, Beloit

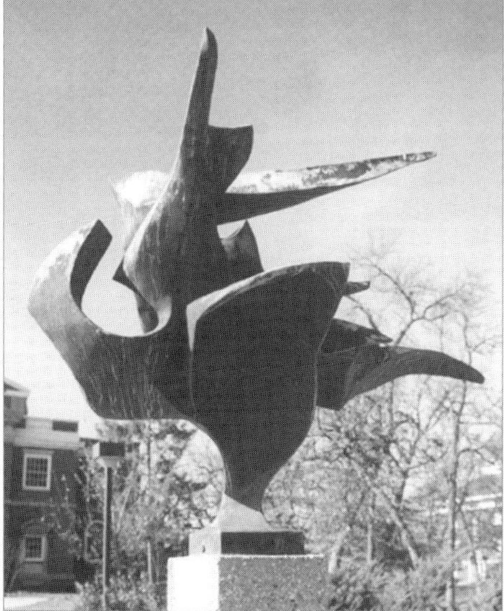

Winds of Change at Beloit College, Beloit

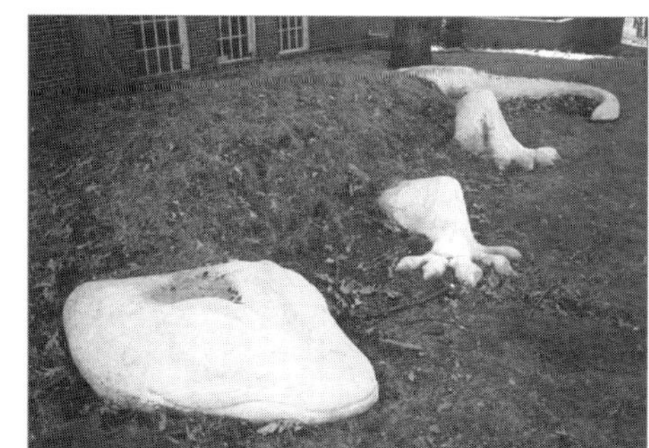

Emerging Lizard at Beloit College, Beloit

ROCK

Beloit

Flame
O.V. Shaffer
Circa 1978
Corten steel, located at Beloit Memorial Senior High School, 1225 4th Street

Hometown Crowd
O.V. Shaffer
1985
Welded stainless steel, located at Telfer Park, Edwards Activity and Sports Center, Cranston Road

In Flight
O.V. Shaffer
1961
Cast bronze, located at Aldrich Middle School, 1859 Northgate Drive

Menorah
O.V. Shaffer
Corten steel, located at Congregation B'nai Abraham, 2400 Oxford Lane

Monument to Horace White
Tohetti
1918
Bronze relief, located in Horace White Park, Public Avenue and College Street

Saint Jude
Dedicated Trinity Sunday, 1950
Concrete, located at rear of St. Jude Catholic Church, 747 Hackett Street

Two Horses
Painted fiberglass, located at 1114 East Colley Road

Beloit College
700 College Street

↗ Beloit College Effigy Mound Group
This site contains a total of 19 mounds which represent a turtle, 13 conicals, and 5 linears

Construction Gate
Wood and metal, located north of Wright Art Museum

Eagle
Concrete, located at Chamberlain Hall

Emerging Lizard
Concrete and glass in earth, located north of Wright Art Museum

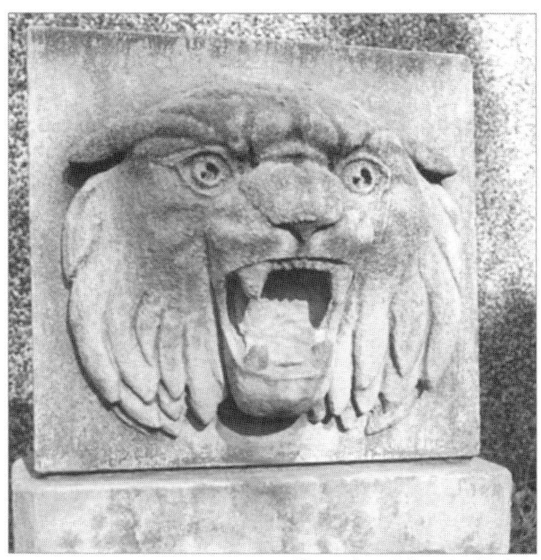

Roaring Lion in Beloit

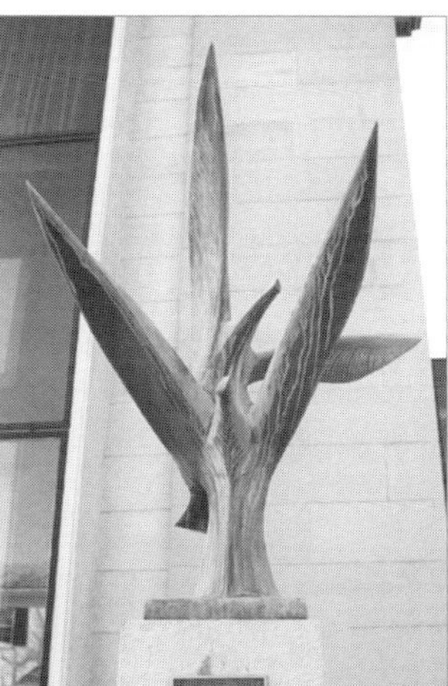

Condor Two in Beloit

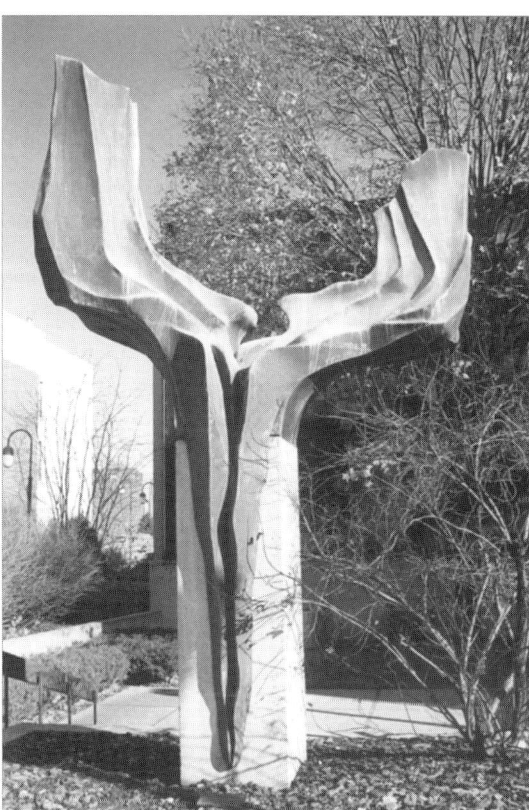

Confluence in Beloit

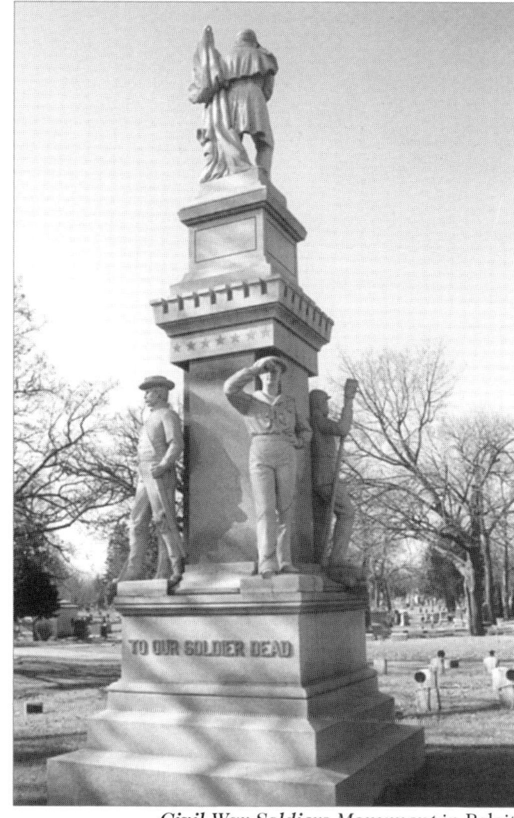

Civil War Soldiers Monument in Beloit

Freedom

Welded metal, located at the Smith Building

Gazebo for One Anarchist, Emma Goldman

Siah Armajani
Steel, located at the center of campus

Pod Abstraction

Arnold Popinsky
1968
Aluminum, located in front of Chamberlain Hall

Reach

O.V. Shaffer
1965
Brass, located at Middle College

Tipped Triangle

Painted metal, located north of Wright Art Museum

Winds of Change

O.V. Shaffer
1950
Welded brass, located in front of Wright Art Museum

Beloit Public Library

409 Pleasant Street

Condor Two

O.V. Shaffer
Dedicated 1982
Welded brass

Confluence

O.V. Shaffer
1979
Brass

Roaring Lion

Concrete, located in front of library. The Lion was originally part of the Beloit Daily News building

Oakwood Cemetery

1221 Clary Street and Milwaukee Road

Broder Mausoleum

Circa 1867-1881
Marble

Civil War Soldiers Monument

Dedicated 1905
Marble and granite, four figures surrounding base with a single figure on top of the obelisk

Crout Memorial

1884
Cast cement

The Hiker, Spanish American War Monument

American Art Bronze Foundry, Chicago
Dedicated June 13, 1926
Cast bronze

Edgerton

Soldiers, Sailors, Marines Memorial

W. Woodruff
Stone, located in Fassett Cemetery

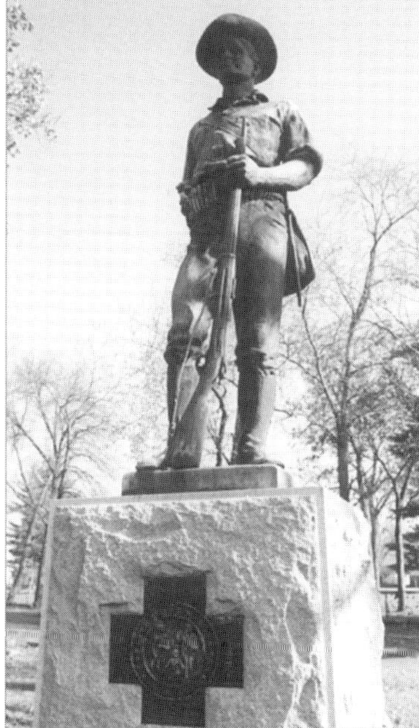

The Hiker, Spanish American War Monument in Beloit

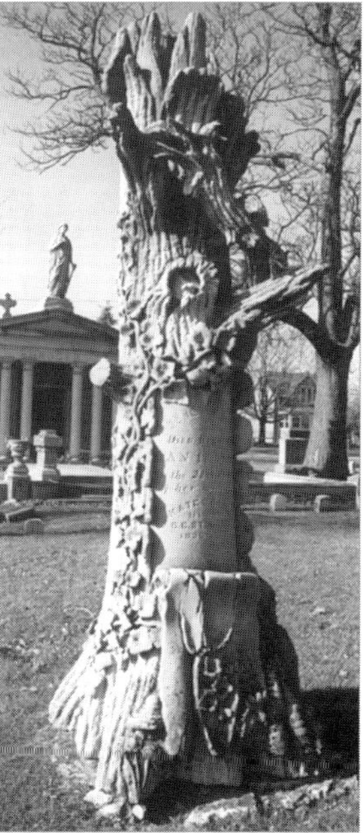

Crout Memorial in Beloit

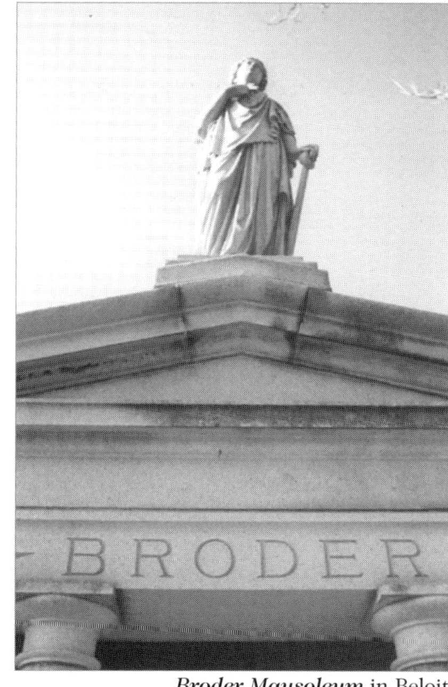

Broder Mausoleum in Beloit

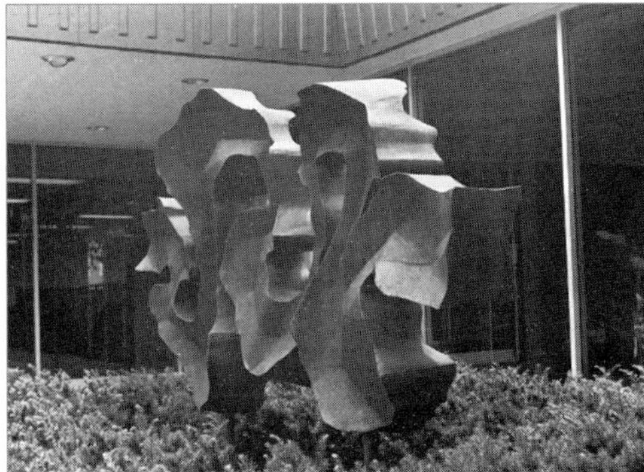

The Rock River in Janesville

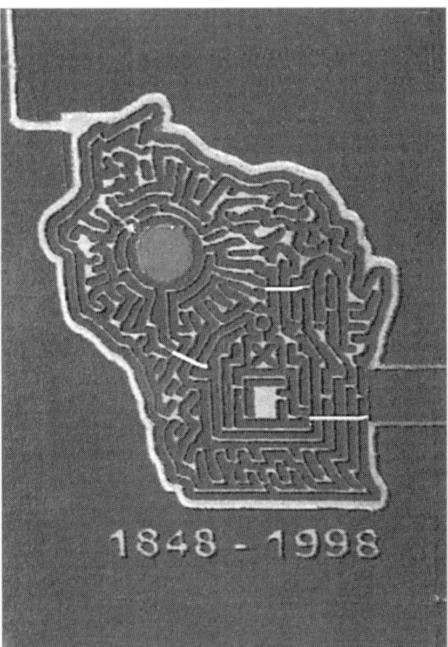

1848 - 1998

Corn Maze in near Janesville

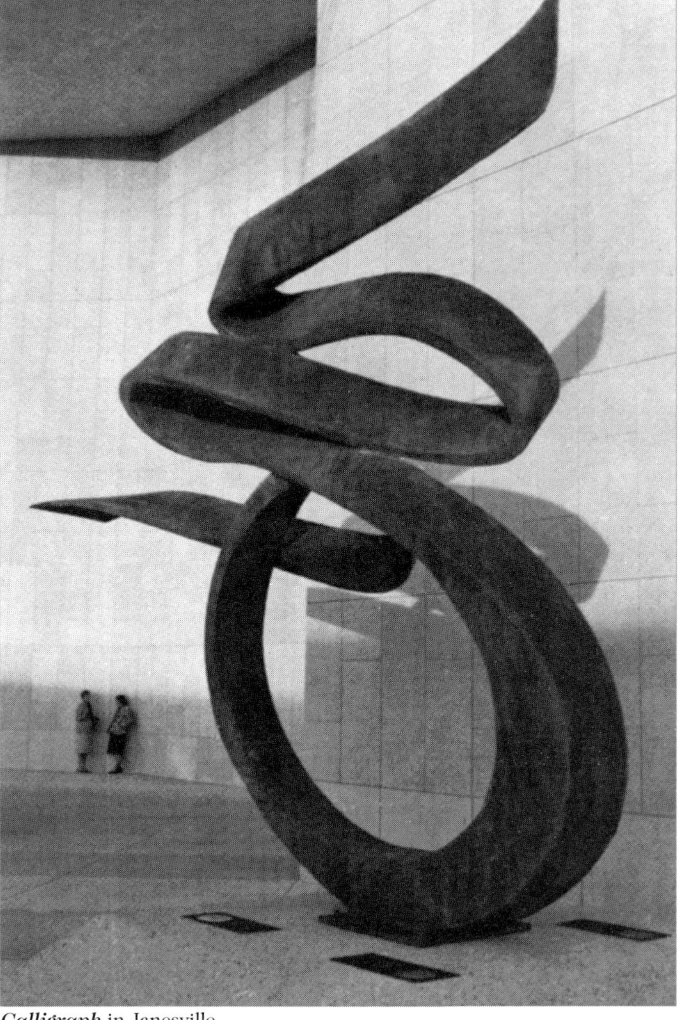

Calligraph in Janesville

Janesville

Calligraph
O.V. Shaffer
1980
Welded brass, 16 feet high, located at Parker Pen Company, 1 Parker Place

Civil War Monument, G.A.R.
Designed by Hutchins and Rundle Co. erected by A.S. Jackson
Dedicated 1901
Granite, located at 51 S. Parker Drive

Corn Maze
Wildren Hughes Family
1998 only
Corn field cut in a maze pattern, July 25 - October 31, 1998, located at the Wildren Hughes Farm. Largest Sesquicentennial outdoor sculpture.

Cycle
O.V. Shaffer
1980
Steel, located at M&I Bank, 100 N. Main Street

Dialogue: World Peace Through Friendship
O.V. Shaffer
Dedicated September 6, 1991
Sheet brass, located in Rotary Gardens, 1455 Palmer Drive

Doughboy
E. M. Viquesney
Dedicated 1926
Metal, located in Corn Exchange Park, corner of W. Milwaukee Street and N. Franklin Street

The Arts of Communication
Constantine Nivola
Reinforced concrete, located at Janesville Gazette, 1 S. Parker Drive

The Rock River
O.V. Shaffer
1969
Corten steel, located at Janesville Public Library, 316 S. Main Street

Untitled
Jackie Graham and Richard Thomas
Aluminum, located in courtyard next to 27 S. Main Street

Untitled
O.V. Shaffer
Steel, located at the Rath Company, 2505 Foster Avenue

Wings of Change
O.V. Shaffer
Donated 1979
Welded brass, located at 108 S. Jackson Street

Wooden Totem Poles
Joseph Kinnebrew IV
Dedicated October 1, 1981
Wood, located in River's Edge Park, N. Main Street. Sculpture was removed in 1995 and is in storage until it can be repaired and relocated.

Town of Turtle

Lester F. Butler Memorial
Circa 1925
Metal, located at the southwest corner of County Trunk Highway S and Butterfly Road

WALWORTH

Delavan

Giraffe
Elephant with Clown
Lion Drinking Fountain
F.A.S.T. Corporation
1990
Painted fiberglass, located on Main Street and Walworth Avenue

Civil War Eagle Monument
1870
Stone, located in Spring Grove Cemetery, 7th Street

East Troy

Bas Relief of Christ
Circa 1970
Limestone, located at St. Paul Evangelical Lutheran Church, 2665 Highway 20

Lake Geneva

Agony Grotto
Lourdes Grotto, and others
Brother Paul Tanner and Brother Anton Fridolin
Circa 1925- 1930
Mixed media, located at Divine Word Seminary

Phoenix Chi Rho
O.V. Shaffer
Circa 1975
Forged and welded brass, located at side entrance wall of the Episcopal Church

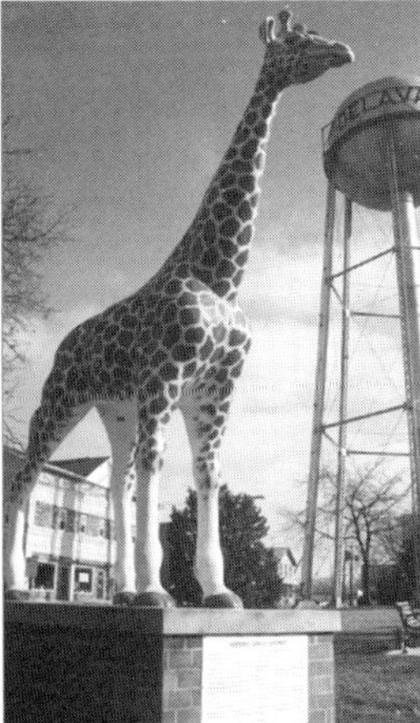

Giraffe in Delavan

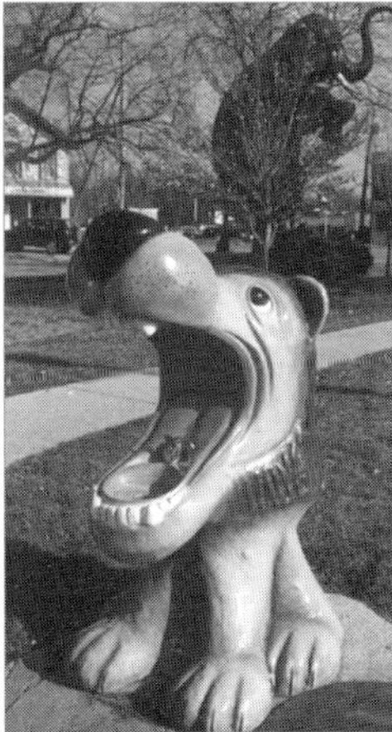

Lion Drinking Fountain in Delavan

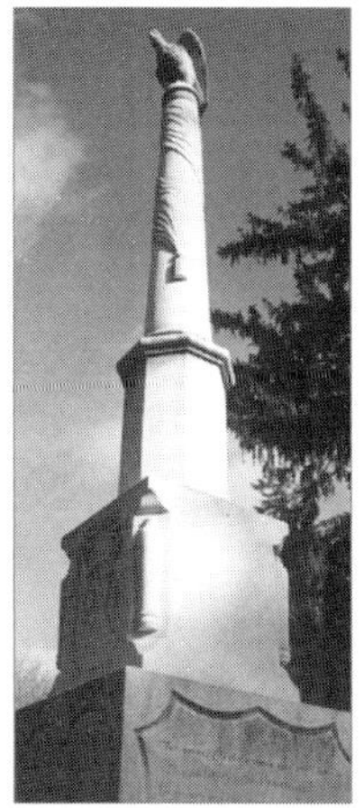

Civil War Eagle in Delavan

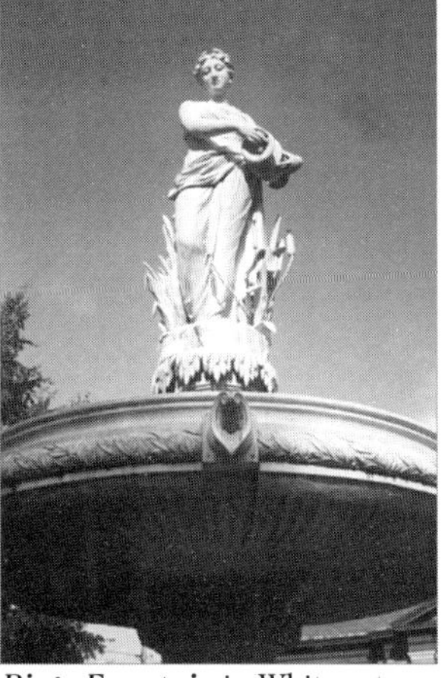

Birge Fountain in Whitewater

Whitewater

Abstract Figures With Hands
Guido Brink
Steel, located at UW-Whitewater
Auditorium

American Eagle
Circa 1920
Cast bronze, located at corner of Main
Street and W. North Street

Birge Fountain
Late 19th century
Painted cast iron, located on
Highway 12

✈ Maples Effigy Mound Group
This group is located in Whitewater
Effigy Mounds Park and contains a
panther, a mink, a turtle, a bird, a
conical, a linear, and several oval
mound shapes

Standing Christ
Circa 1990
Limestone, located at St. Patrick's
Catholic Church, corner of Main
Street and S. Elizabeth

WASHINGTON

Allenton

Sacred Heart of Jesus
Circa 1930
White marble, located at Sacred Heart
Catholic Church, Highway 33

Hartford

Animals in Motion
Bruce Howdle
Ceramic tiles on concrete, located off
Highway 60

Lions Club Fountain
Red granite and field stone, located in
front of Lions Club, Highway 60

Hubertus

Holy Hill
The 14 Stations of the Cross
Shrine and pilgrimage destination
since 1858

St. Rose
Mary and Young Christ
Madonna and Child
Stone

Station I
Jesus Is Condemned to Death
1922-8
Marble, stone, cement, wrought iron,
wood

Station II
Jesus Carries His Cross
1922-8
Marble, stone, cement, wrought iron,
wood

Station III
Jesus Falls the First Time
1922-8
Marble, stone, cement, wrought iron,
wood

Station IV
Jesus Meets His Mother
1922-8
Marble, stone, cement, wrought iron,
wood

Station V
Simon Helps Christ Carry His Cross
Joseph Aszklar
1922-8
Marble, stone, cement, wrought iron,
wood

Station VI
Veronica Wipes the Face of Jesus
Joseph Aszklar
1922-8
Marble, stone, cement, wrought iron,
wood

Station VII
Jesus Falls the Second Time
Joseph Aszklar
1922-8
Marble, stone, cement, wrought iron,
wood

Station VIII
Jesus Speaks to the Weeping Daughters of Jerusalem
Joseph Aszklar
1922-8
Marble, stone, cement, wrought iron,
wood

Station IX
Jesus Falls the Third Time
Joseph Aszklar
1922-8
Marble, stone, cement, wrought iron,
wood

Station X
Jesus is Stripped of His Garment
Joseph Aszklar
1922-8
Marble, stone, cement, wrought iron,
wood

Station XI
Jesus is Nailed to the Cross
Joseph Aszklar
1922-8
Marble, stone, cement, wrought iron,
wood

Station XII
Jesus Dies on the Cross
Joseph Aszklar
1922-8
Marble, stone, cement, wrought iron,
wood

Station XIII
Descent from the Cross

Station XIV
Christ is Laid in Tomb

Kewaskum

Kewaskum War Memorial
Bronze and stone

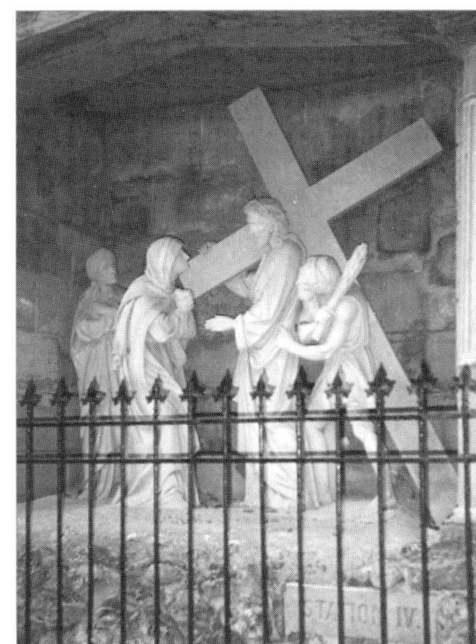

Station IV at Holy Hill, Hurbertus

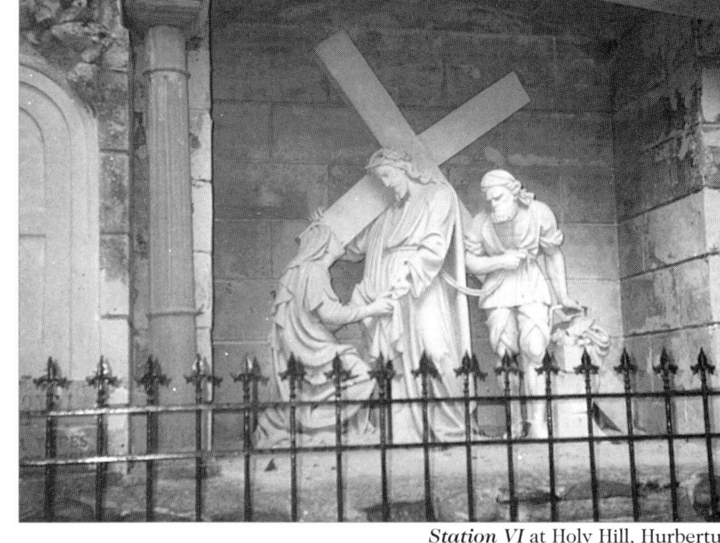

Station VI at Holy Hill, Hurbertus

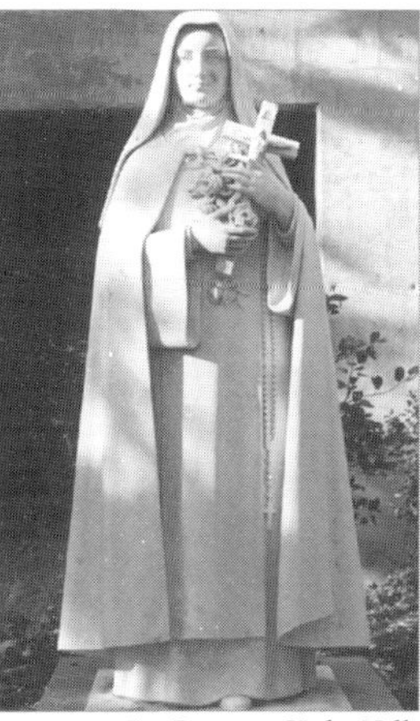

St. Rose at Holy Hill,
Hubertus

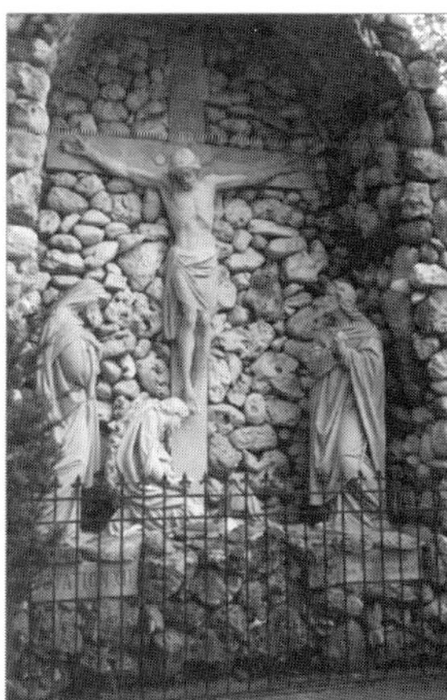

Station XII at Holy Hill,
Hurbertus

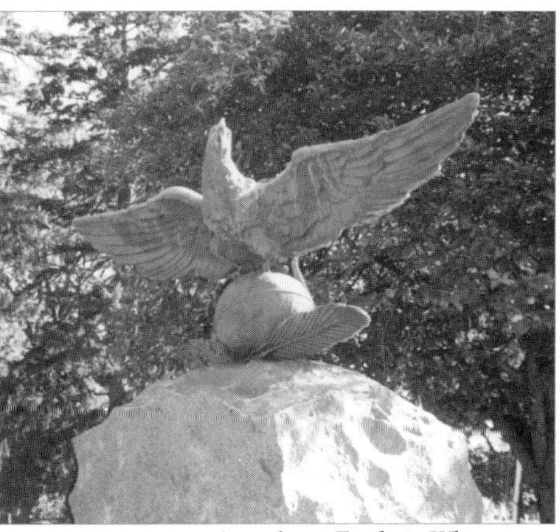

American Eagle in Whitewater

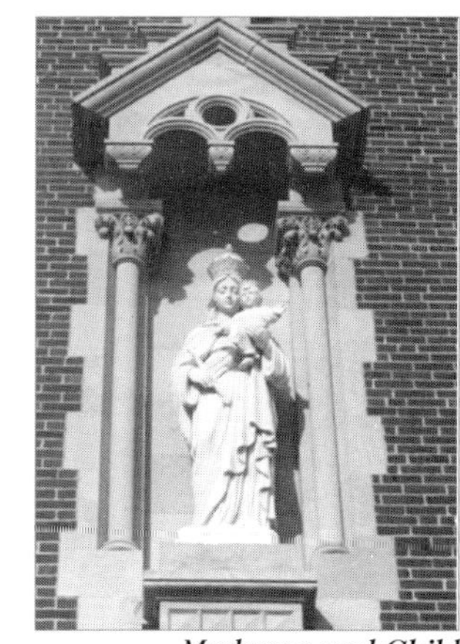

Madonna and Child
at Holy Hill, Hurbertus

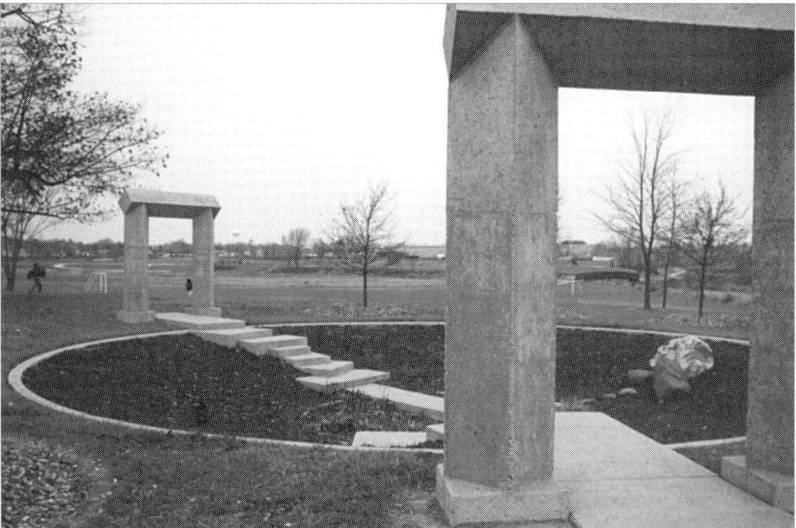

Ajuga Daydream at Riverfront Parkway, West Bend

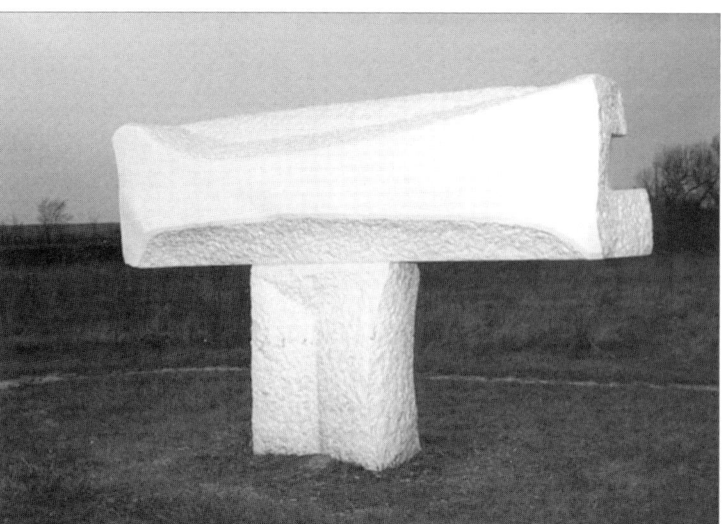

Fluvio at Riverfront Parkway, West Bend

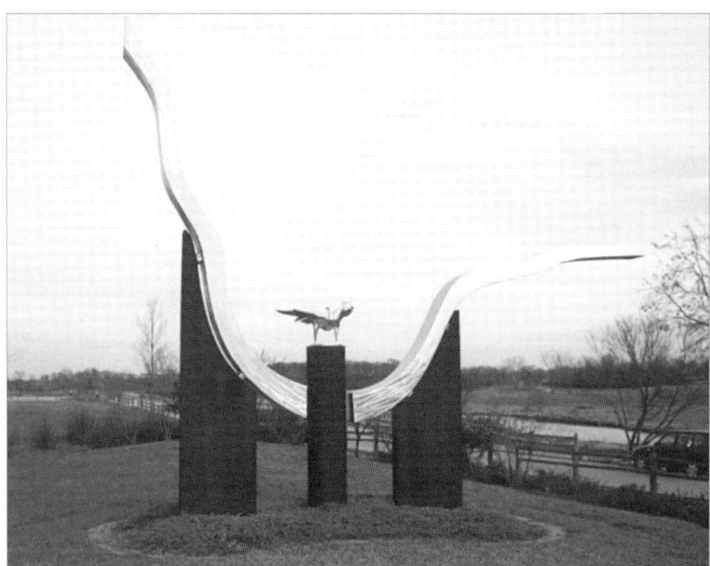

West Band Resolve at Riverfront Parkway, West Bend

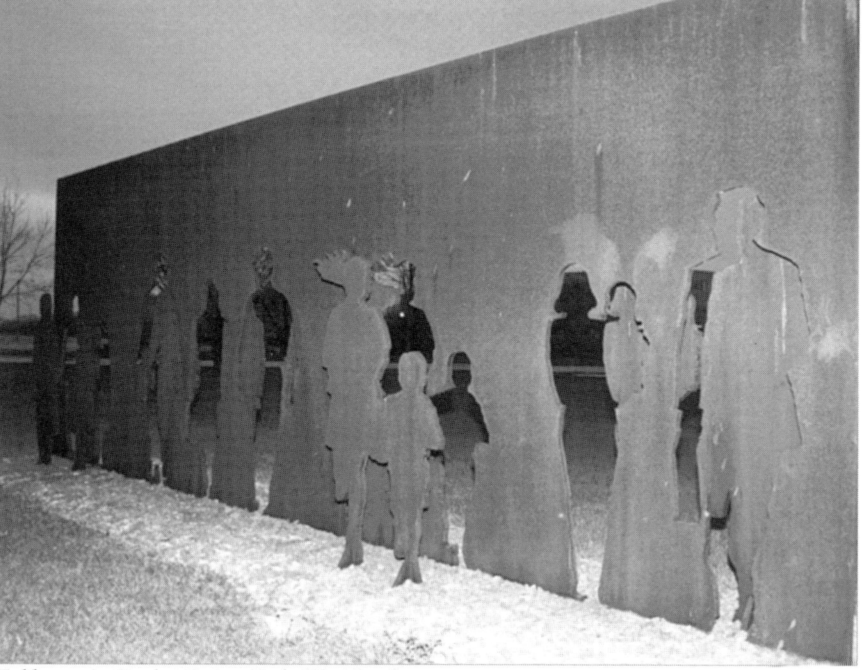

Tableaux in Steel at Regner Park, West Bend

Newburg

Weiss Memorial

1940
White marble, located at Holy Trinity
Catholic Cemetery, Highway 33 and
Franklin Street

Christ with Outstretched Arms

Marble, located at Holy Trinity
Catholic Church, Highway 33 and
Franklin Street

St. Lawrence

Mr. Sun

David P. Griesbach
1988
Painted wood, located at
6091 St. Anthony Road

West Bend

All Wars Veterans Monument

1998
Cast bronze and stone, located at
Washington County Historical
Museum grounds, formerly the
Washington County Courthouse

Columns

P.M. Goulding
Stone, located downtown off Island
Avenue, next to the river

Doughboy War Memorial

Dedicated November 16, 1927
Stone and metal (painted copper
color), located at the Washington
County Historical Society Museum,
formerly the Washington County
Courthouse

➤ Lizard Effigy Mounds

This site with 28 effigy mounds is
located in Lizard Mound County
Park. There are 6 conical mounds, 1
oval mound, 8 linear mounds (one
of which is partially destroyed), 2
tapering linears, and 11 panther effigies. The
panthers make this one of the most
unusual mound groups in the Upper
Midwest

Rust in Peace

Tom Gross
Circa 1970-1979
Steel and old farm machinery parts,
located at 459 N. 9th Avenue

The Goddess of Justice

1889
Terra-cotta relief, located at Washington County Historical Society, formerly the Washington County Courthouse

Veterans Memorial

Black granite, located at Veterans Memorial Plaza, Main Street and Island Avenue

Regner Park

Main Street and Barton Avenue north of Highway 33

Nice Spirit

Narendra Patel
Concrete and fly ash

Ornithopod

Narendra Patel
Mixed media

Single Heart

John K. Lee
Steel bands

Tableau in Steel

David Genszler
1993
Corten steel

Riverfront Parkway

Indiana Avenue, south of Highway 33
Sculpture walk along the river's edge

Ajuga Daydream

Thomas D. Lidtke
1995
Concrete, earth, Siberian iris, ajuga, and snowdrift crabapple trees

Fluvio

Paul Trappe
August 29, 1993
Valders Wisconsin limestone

Outside History

Preston Jackson
1997
Steel, stainless steel, bronze, and resin, will be placed on the Riverfront Parkway, just east of the Water Street Bridge when site is ready

Paradisedae

Narendra Patel
Painted steel

West Bend Resolve

O.V. Shaffer
1995
Corten steel, stainless steel and gold leaf over bronze

WAUKESHA

Brookfield

Armed Forces Monument

Stone obelisk, located in Wisconsin Memorial Park

Marines Monument

Stone, located in Wisconsin Memorial Park

Wisconsin Vietnam MIA Memorial

Mixed media, located in Wisconsin Memorial Park

Delafield

Cushing Brothers Memorial

Bronze relief busts, located in Cushing Park

Menabin Fountain

Circa 1885
Bedford limestone, located at the old Wisconsin State Fish Hatchery, 400 block Main Street. Relocated to this site in 1998

Totem Pole

Painted wood, located Chamber of Commerce, 400 block Main Street

Unknown Soldier Memorial

Concrete, located in Cushing Park

Elm Grove

Lourdes Grotto

Mixed media, located at Notre Dame of Elm Grove, 13105 Watertown Plank Road

Menomonee Falls

Keeper of the Gift

Charles A. Kraus
August 12, 1992
Bronze, located in front of the Village Municipal Building, off the Joe and Ann Esser Parkway, W156 N8480 Pilgrim Road

Mukwonago

Growling Bear

Dedicated 1993
Painted wood, located at Mukwonago Village Hall 625, Highway 83, south of town

Ursa

Dave Watson
1993
White pine, located at the Mukwonago Museum, Main and Atkinson streets

New Berlin

Sylvan Amphora

William Taylor
1998
Concrete and broken tile, located at 5150 S. Balboa Drive

Oconomowoc

Griffins

Metal, located in 1983 in front of Oconomowoc Public Library. Originally part of the 1893 Chicago World's Fair

Pewaukee

Abstract Figures

Guido Brink
1972
Painted steel, located at Waukesha County Technical College, County T, near Student Commons

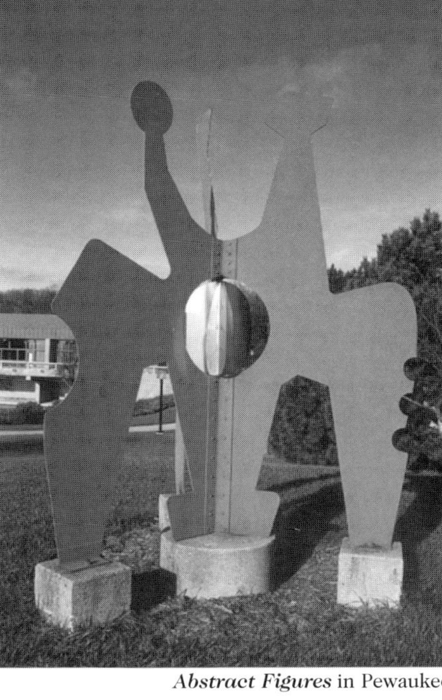

Abstract Figures in Pewaukee

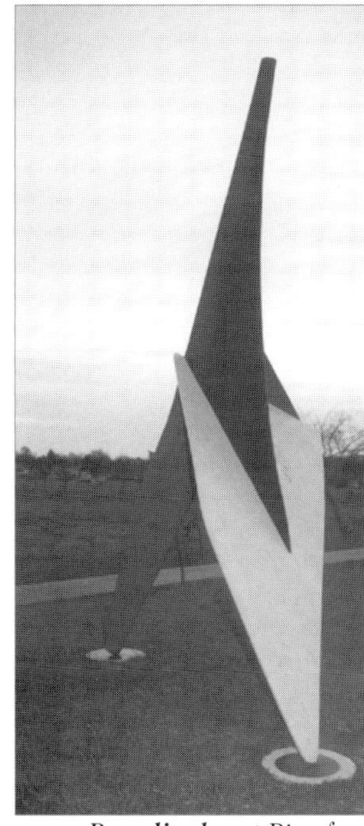

Paradisedae at Riverfront Parkway, West Bend

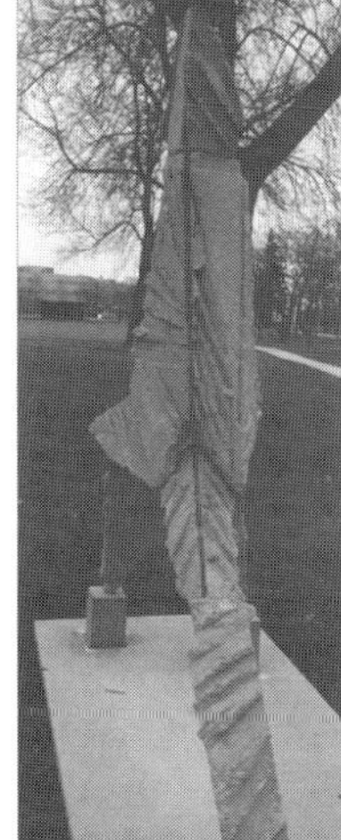

Ornithopod at Regner Park, West Bend

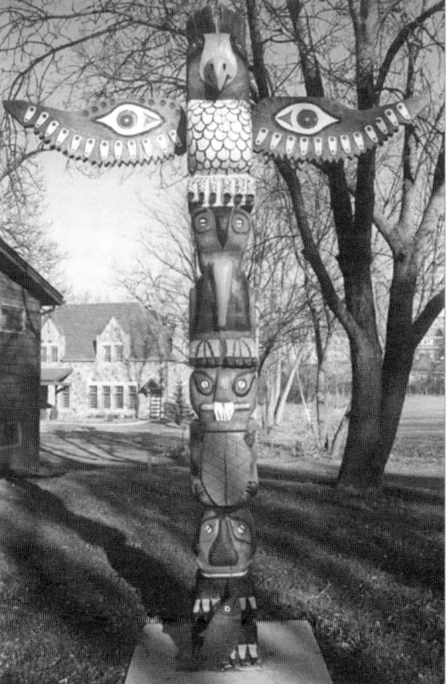

Totem Pole in Delafield

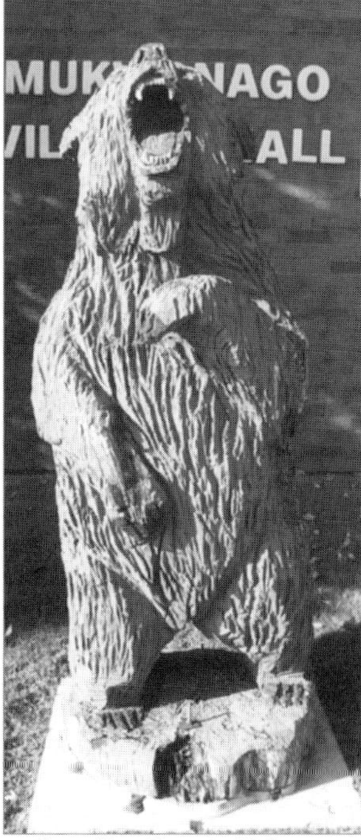

Growling Bear in Mukwonago

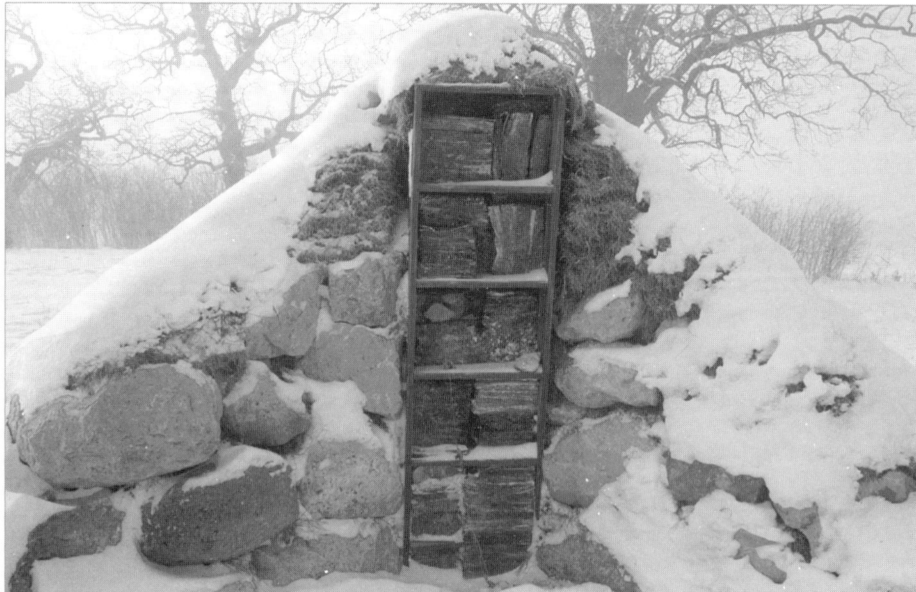

Embedded Bookcase in Waukesha

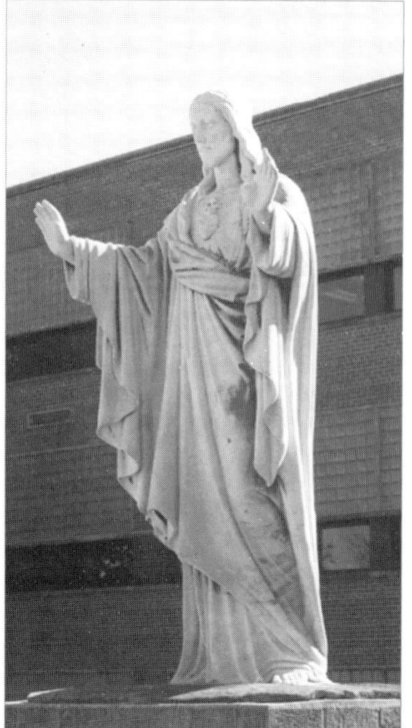

Sacred Heart of Jesus in Waukesha

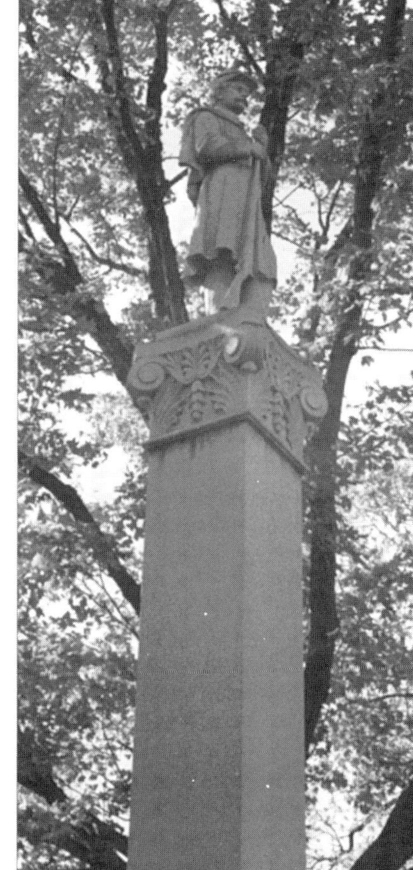

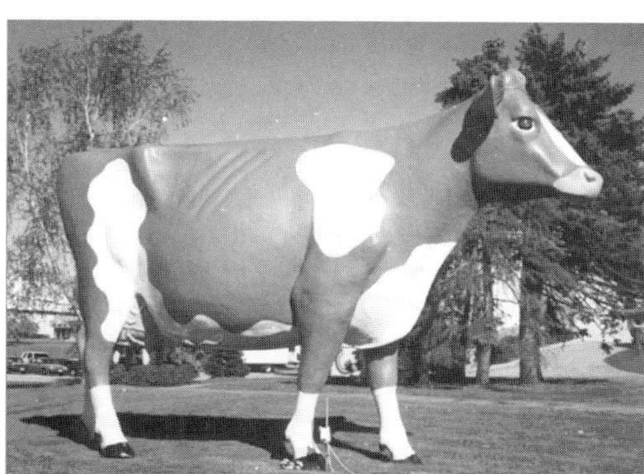

Bessie in Waukesha

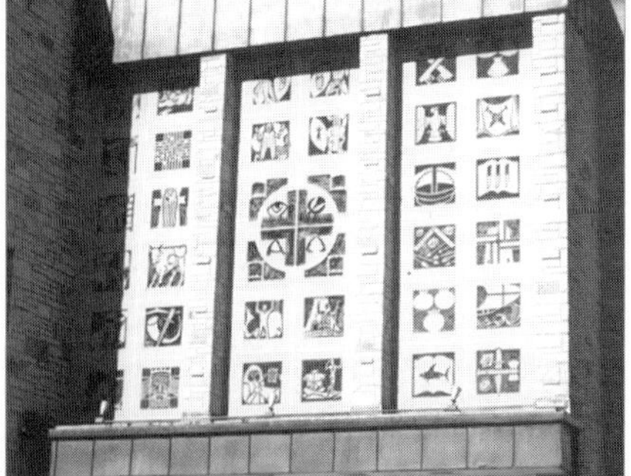

Religious Relief in Waukesha

Civil War Monument in Waukesha

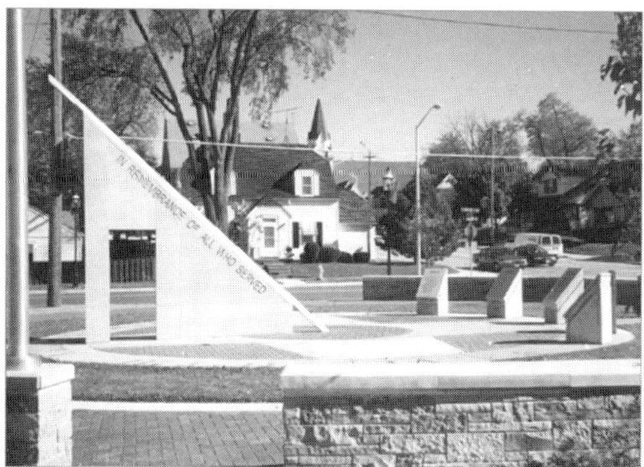

In Remembrance in Waukesha

Inate
> Bill Bedford
> Bronze, located in front of Port Shell Molding Inc., 604 Hickory Street, Pewaukee

Waukesha

Bessie
> Sculptured Advertising
> Fiberglass, located at Golden Guernsey Dairy Company, County FT and Delafield Street

Blessed Virgin
> Marble, located at St. Mary's Catholic Church, 500 E. Newhall Street

Civil War Monument
> Stone, located in Cutler Park, 321 Wisconsin Avenue

Easter Island Head
> Concrete, located at 15400 Cleveland

Embedded Bookcase
> Amy Cropper
> 1997
> Wooden bookcase, books and paper in an earth mound, located at UW-Waukesha at Waterville Field Station

In Remembrance
> Stone, located at corner of West Main Street, Wisconsin, and North West Avenue

Religious Relief
> Stone, located at St. Luke's Lutheran Church, Grand and Carroll streets

Sacred Heart of Jesus
> Marble, located at Catholic Memorial High School, College Avenue

Spanish American War Memorial
> 1949
> Stone, located at Cutler Park, 321 Wisconsin Avenue

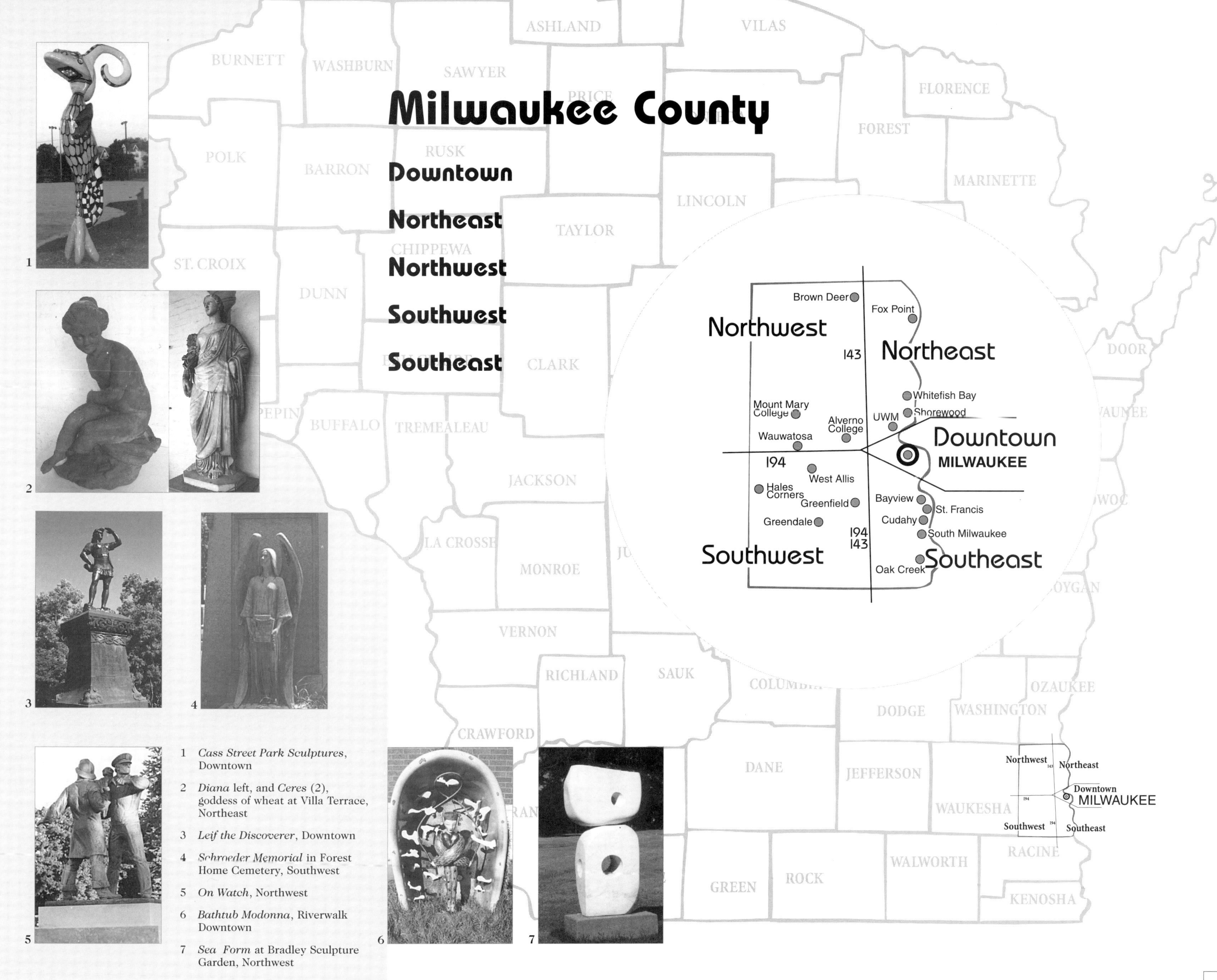

1   *Cass Street Park Sculptures*, Downtown

2   *Diana* left, and *Ceres* (2), goddess of wheat at Villa Terrace, Northeast

3   *Leif the Discoverer*, Downtown

4   *Schroeder Memorial* in Forest Home Cemetery, Southwest

5   *On Watch*, Northwest

6   *Bathtub Modonna*, Riverwalk Downtown

7   *Sea Form* at Bradley Sculpture Garden, Northwest

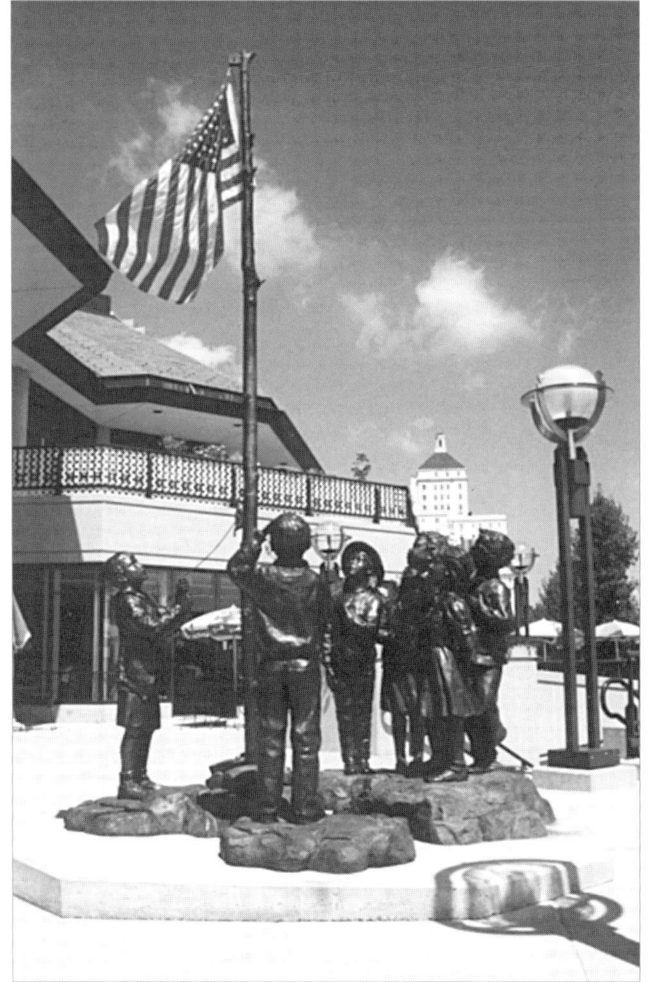

Children Putting Up Flag, Downtown

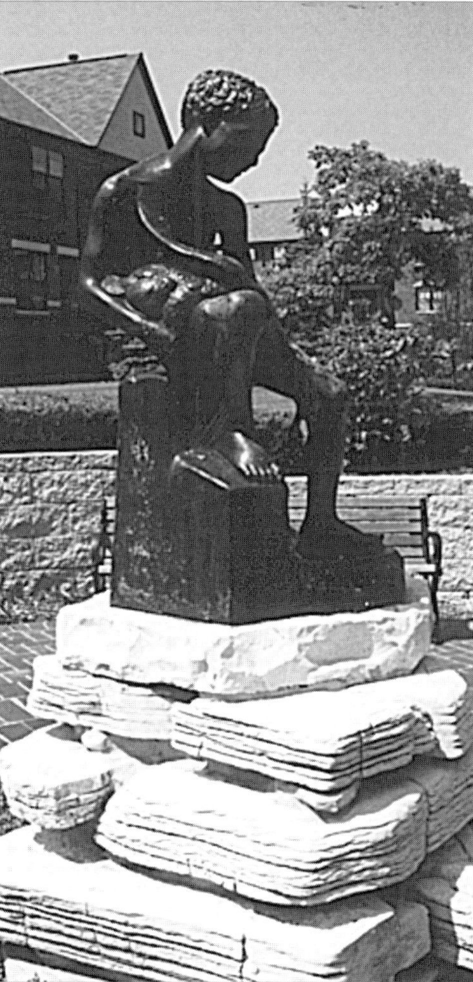

Boy With Goose, Downtown

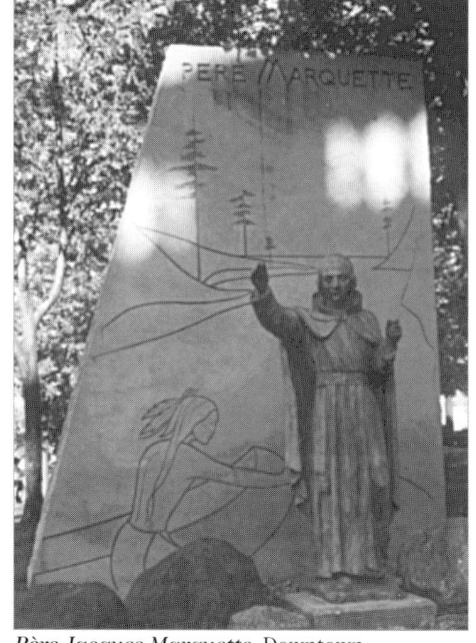

Père Jacques Marquette, Downtown

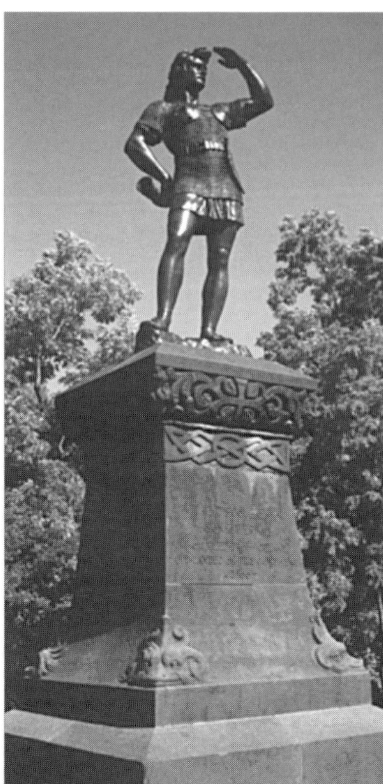

Leif the Discoverer, Downtown

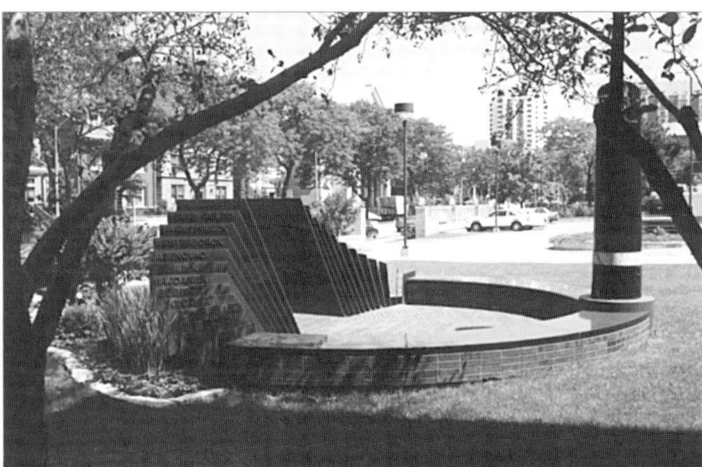

Holocaust Memorial, Downtown

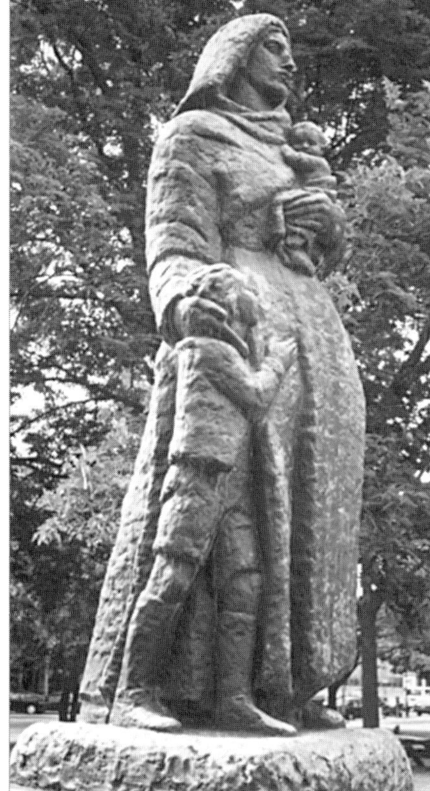

Cass Street Park Entrance Arch, Downtown

Immigrant Mother, Downtown

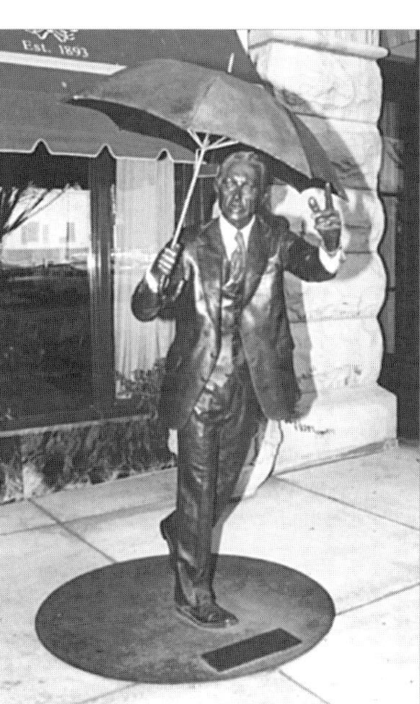

Allow Me, Downtown

Downtown Milwaukee

Additional public sculpture information is found in *Outdoor Sculpture in Milwaukee* by Diane Buck and Virginia Palmer, published by The State Historical Society of Wisconsin, 1995.

Allow Me
Bronze, located at the Pfister Hotel, Wisconsin Avenue

Boy With Goose
Girolamo Piccoli
1926
Bronze, located in the 800 block of E. Lyon Street between N. Marshall and N. Cass streets

Cass Street Park Sculptures
Painted fiberglass, located around the park

Children Putting Up Flag
Bronze, located at Betty Brin Children's Museum

Diana
Dick Wiken
1954
Bedford limestone, located at the Milwaukee Athletic Club, 758 N. Broadway

Dr. Martin Luther King, Jr.
Bronze, located at the corner of Dr. Martin Luther King Jr. and Brown streets

Erastus Bradley Wolcott Statue
Francis Herman Packer
1920
Bronze, located at Lake Park northwest from the north end of the Lion Bridge

Family
Helaine Blumenfeld
1938
Norwegian blue granite, located at Reuss Federal Plaza, 310 W. Wisconsin Avenue

Fountain of Communication
Dick Wiken
1979
Bronze, located at northwest corner of 3rd Street and Highland Avenue. Fountain removed, only the spritz figures on wall remain.

General Douglas MacArthur
Robert L. Dean
1979
Bronze, located in MacArthur Square, Civic Center Plaza, N. 7th Street, between W. Wells and W. State streets

George Washington
Richard H. Park
1885
Bronze, located on median of W. Wisconsin Avenue between N. 8th and N. 9th streets

Holocaust Memorial
Claire Lieberman
1983
Stone, metal, and wood, located at the Helfaer Community Service Building, 1360 N. Prospect Avenue

Immigrant Mother
Ivan Mestrovic
1960
Bronze, located at Cathedral Square, E. Wells and N. Jefferson Street

King Gambrinus, Legendary Patron of Brewing
Carl Kuehns
1967 copy of the original wood version made in 1872
Painted cast aluminum, located in Gate Courtyard of old Pabst Brewery, at 915 W. Juneau Avenue.

Last Alarm
Bronze, located at Fire Engine No. 2, 711 W. Wells

Leif the Discoverer
Anne Whitney
1887
Bronze, located in Juneau Park, on Lake Michigan bluff

Letter Carriers' Sculpture
Elliot Offner
1989
Bronze, located at intersection of N. 2nd Street, W. Wells Street and 820 N. Plankinton Avenue

Midsummer Carnival Shaft
Alfred C. Clas
1900
Bedford limestone, located at the Court of Honor, W. Wisconsin Avenue between N. 9th and N. 19th streets

Mutual Fountain
Concrete, located at Mutual Life Building

PAC Fountain
Mixed media, located at Performing Arts Center, Water and State streets

Père Jacques Marquette
Restored by Thomas Queoff
1987
Bronze with granite backdrop, located at the Milwaukee County Historical Society, 910 N. 3rd Street

Peter John
John Raimondi
1978
Corten steel, located at Blue Cross & Blue Shield United of Wisconsin, 401 W. Michigan Street

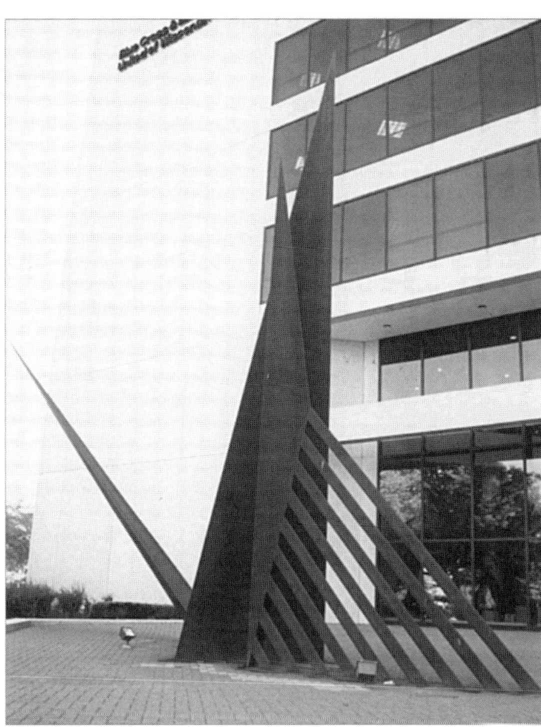

Peter John, Downtown

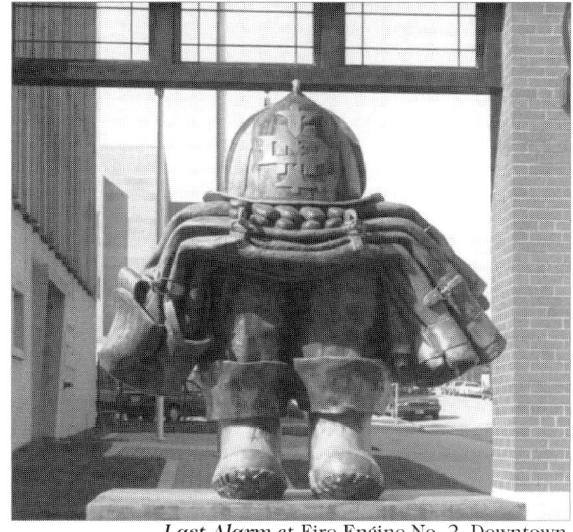

Last Alarm at Fire Engine No. 2, Downtown

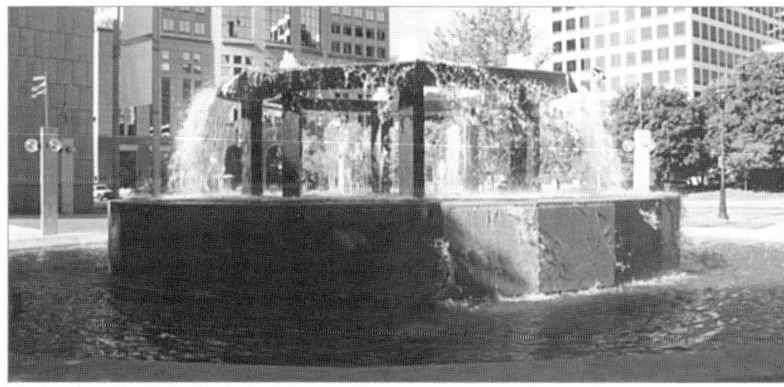

PAC Fountain, Downtown

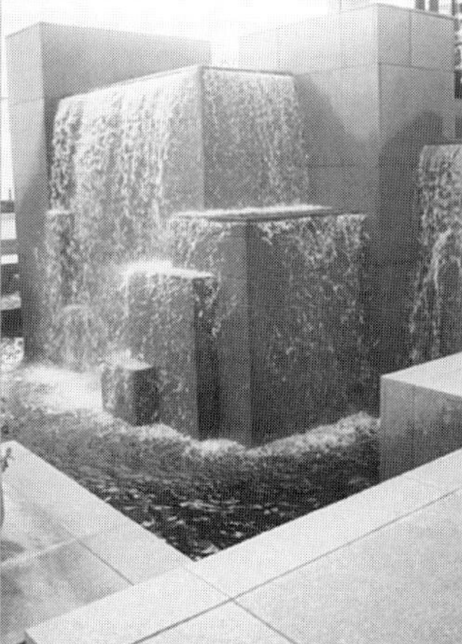

Mutual Fountain, Downtown

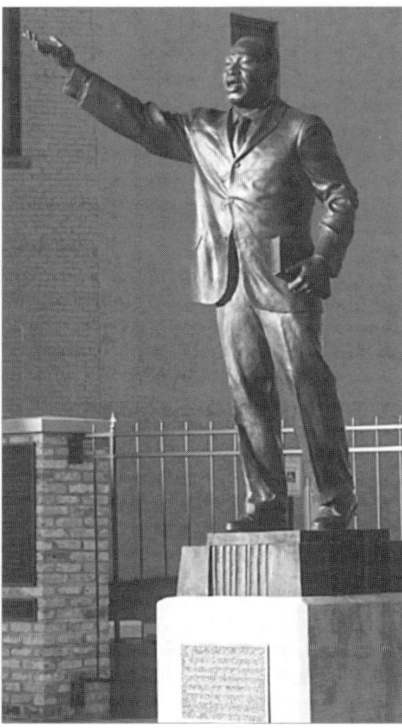

Dr. Martin Luther King, Jr., Downtown

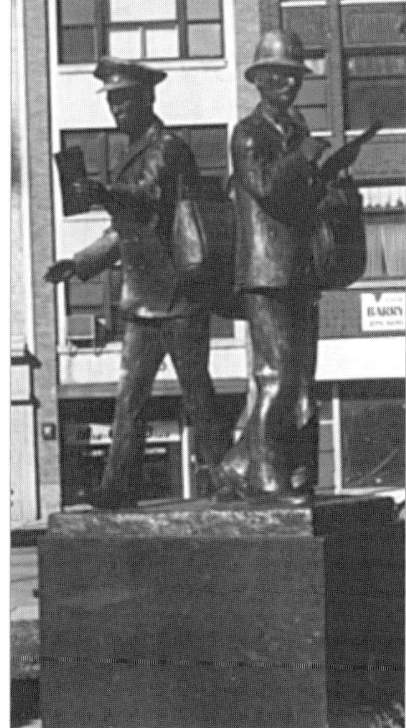

Letter Carriers' Sculpture, Downtown

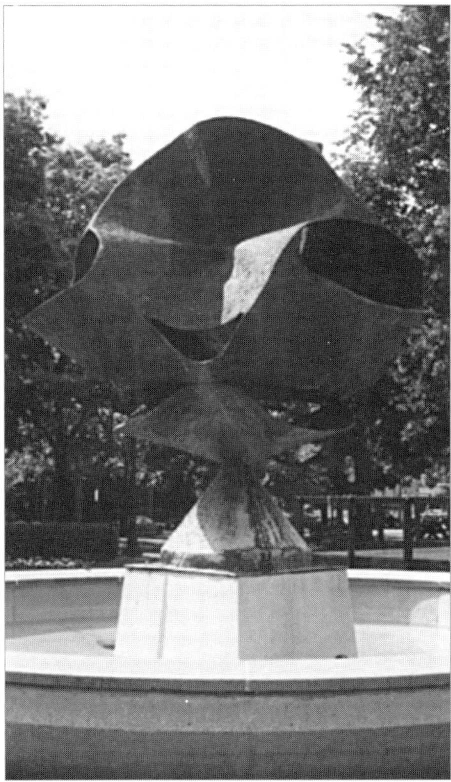

Tulip Fountain, Downtown

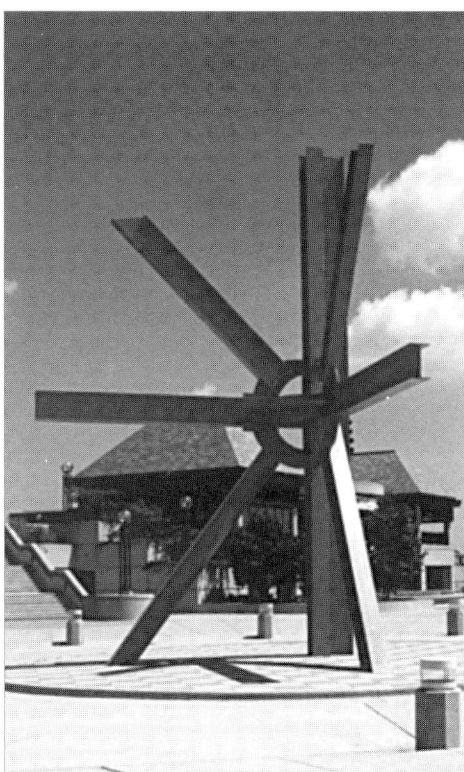

The Calling, Downtown

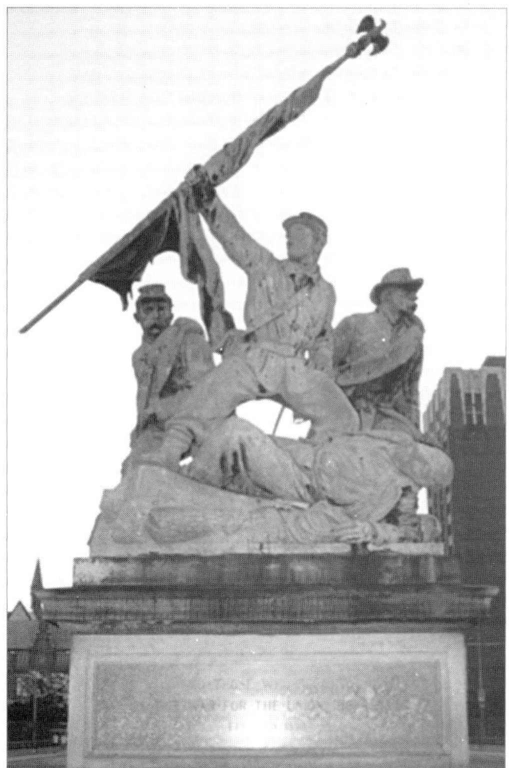

The Victorious Charge, Downtown

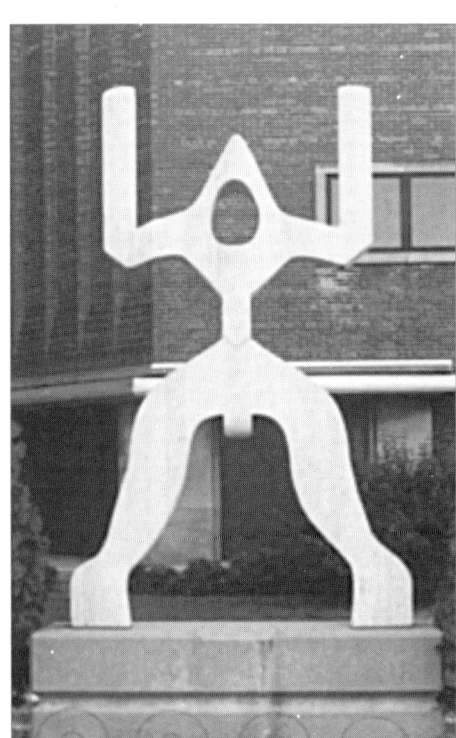

Referee, Downtown

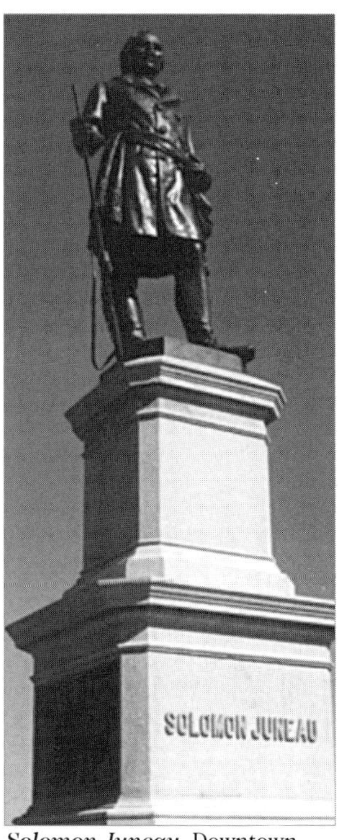

Solomon Juneau, Downtown

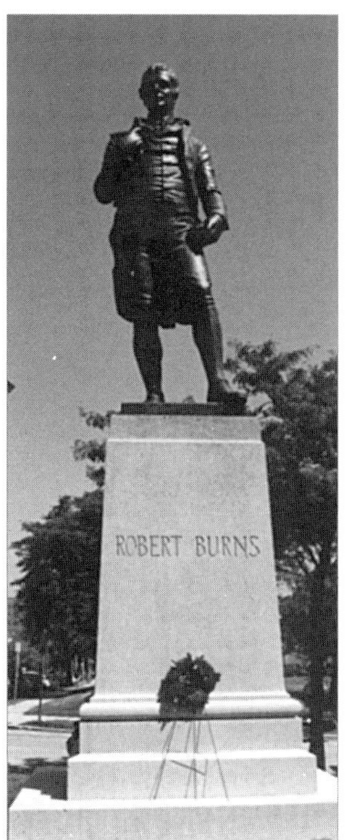

Robert Burns, Downtown

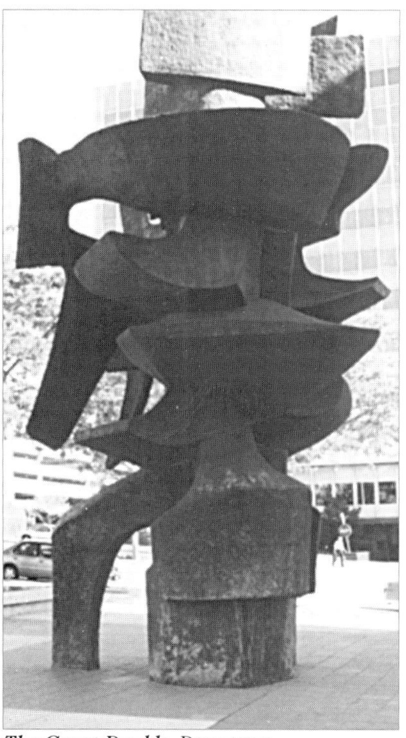

The Great Double, Downtown

Red Arrow 22nd Division
Granite, located on Water between Kilbourn and State streets

Referee
Tom Queoff
1978
Stone, laminated travertine marble, located at 500 W. Kilbourn Avenue, south entrance to Arena. A CETA (Comprehensive Employment & Training Act) project

Robert Burns
William Grant Stevenson
1909
Bronze, located at intersection of E. Knapp, N. Prospect and N. Franklin Place

Robert J. Jendusa Memorial Fountain
Paul J. Yank
1974
Bronze, located at MECCA, southwest corner of W. Kilbourn Avenue and N. 4th Street

Solomon Juneau
Richard H. Park
1887
Bronze, located in Juneau Park at E. Kilbourn and Prospect

Spanish-American War Soldier
Ferdinand Koenig, attributed
1932
Bronze, located on Wisconsin Avenue median between N. 9th and N. 10th streets

Spirit of Polonia (Solidarity)
Edmund D. Lewandowski
1969
Stainless steel and brass, located at Clas Park, Milwaukee County Courthouse on W. Wells between N. 9th and N. 10th streets

The Boy and Sea Gull
Joseph McDonnell
1964
Bronze, located in front of the Milwaukee Public Museum, 800 W. Wells

The Calling
Mark DiSuvero
1981-1982
Painted steel, located at O'Donnell Park, at the end of E. Wisconsin Avenue, Milwaukee Art Museum Collection

The Great Double
Alicia Penalba
1972
Bronze, located at 250 E. Kilbourn Avenue between N. Water and N. Broadway streets

The Victorious Charge / The Soldiers Monument
John Severino Conway
1898
Bronze, located at Court of Honor, W. Wisconsin Avenue between N. 9th and N. 10th streets

Trigon
Allen Ditson
1970
Stainless steel, located at the Performing Arts Center, 929 N. Water Street, E. Kilbourn Avenue side

Tulip Fountain
Paul J. Yank
1969
Cold cast bronze-reinforced polyester with anodized aluminum chipped into the surface, 18 feet high, located at Cathedral Square, E. Wells Street and N. Jefferson Street

Wisconsin Scottish Rite Cathedral Relief Sculptures
Adolph Roegner
1936
Bedford limestone, located at the Masonic Wisconsin Consistory Scottish Rite Cathedral, 790 N. Van Buren Street

Woodland Indian and the Whistling Swans
Marshall M. Fredericks
1963
Bronze, located on wall above entrance to Milwaukee Public Museum, 800 W. Wells Street

World War I Memorial Flagpole
Benjamin Franklin Hawkins
1932
Bronze, located at northeast corner of N. Prospect and Mason Street

Haggerty Art Museum
North 13th and West Clybourn

Ruins X
Ernest Carl Shaw
1978
Painted metal

Sculpture Table and Benches
Ernest Carl Shaw
Circa 1980
Stone and metal

Marquette University

Ex-Stasis
Richard Lippold
1988
Stainless steel, anodized aluminum and gold plated cables, located at the Marquette University Union Courtyard, 15th and Wisconsin Avenue

Teaching Sculpture
1998
Painted steel, located behind Science Building

Milwaukee Art Museum
Milwaukee War Memorial
Lakefront Sculpture Park
750 North Lincoln Memorial Drive

Abraham Lincoln
Gaetano Cecere
1934
Bronze, located at War Memorial on Lincoln Memorial Bridge, east end of Mason Street

Argo
Alexander Liberman
1974
Painted steel, temporarily removed

Bullfinch
Lyman Kipp
1968
Mild steel, temporarily removed

Calipers (Four Corners)
Forrest Myers
1967
Painted steel, temporarily removed

Delicate Balance
Tal Streeter
1968
Painted steel, temporarily removed

Milwaukee War Memorial
Granite, located north of museum

Minerva
Reuben Nakian
1963-1966
Bronze from the *Judgement of Paris* series, located in the Sculpture Court

Monumental Holistic III
Betty Gold
1978
Steel, temporarily removed

Sculpture in the Form of a Trowel Stuck in the Ground
Claes Oldenburg
1970
Aluminum, located in Sculpture Court

The Walking Man
Auguste Rodin
1905, cast in 1907
Bronze figure 63 inches tall, located in the Sculpture Court

Untitled 1 (107 inches)
Untitled 2 (94 inches)
Arnold Zimmerman
1987
Ceramic, located in Sculpture Court

War Memorial Mosaic
Edmund Lewandowski
1954
Ceramic, located on west wall of War Memorial

Wiggins Fork
Kenneth Snelson
1967
Stainless steel and wire, located in Sculpture Court

Riverwalk Sculptures
Permanent and temporary sculpture displays along the Milwaukee River, 929 N. Water Street

Bathtub Madonna
Tom Uebelherr
Mixed media, located at Riverwalk, Mason and Water streets (removed). Kohler Art Center, Arts and Industry program

Cuculide
Narendra Patel
1992
Painted steel, located at Riverwalk

Epiphanic Recurve, Redux
Bilhenry Walker
1995
Aluminum, located at Riverwalk

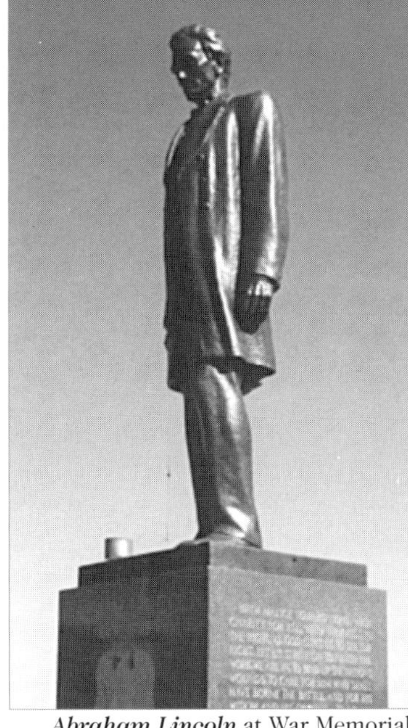

Abraham Lincoln at War Memorial, Downtown

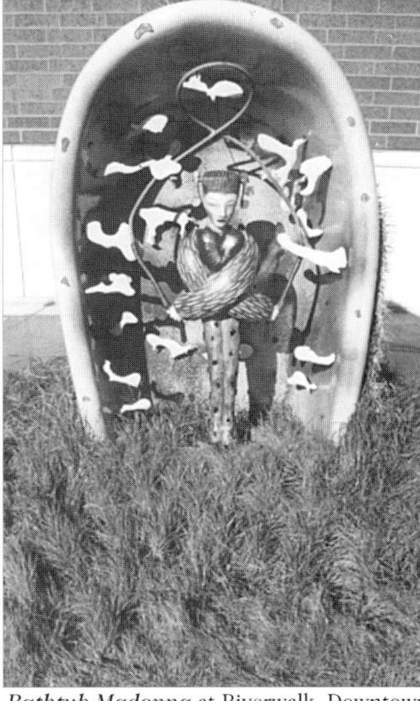

Bathtub Madonna at Riverwalk, Downtown

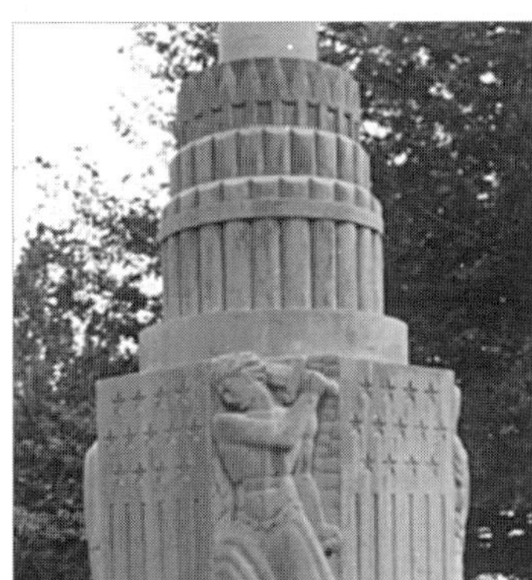

World War I Memorial Flagpole, Downtown

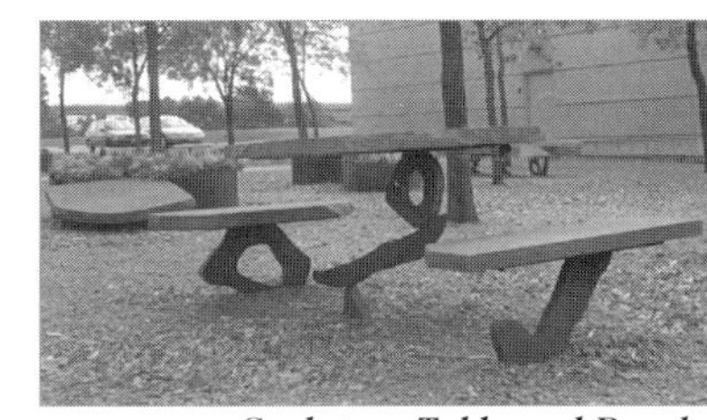

Sculpture Table and Benches at the Haggerty Art Museum

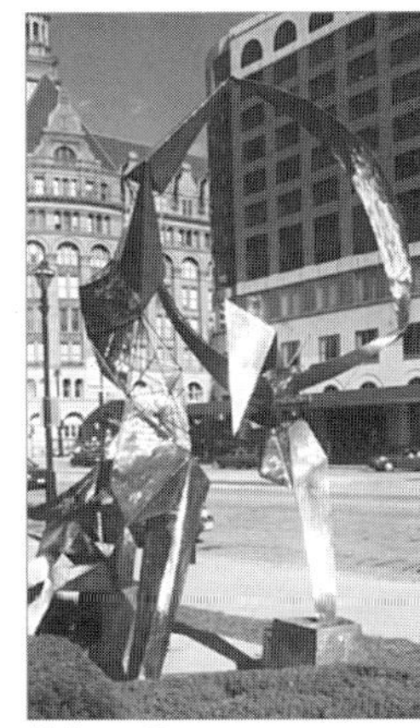

Trigon, Downtown

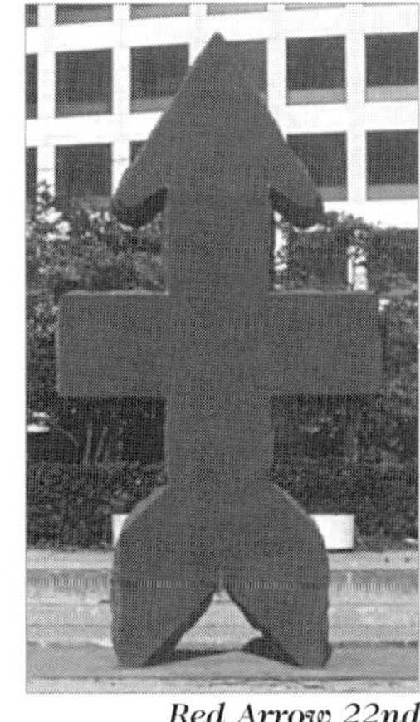

Red Arrow 22nd Division, Downtown

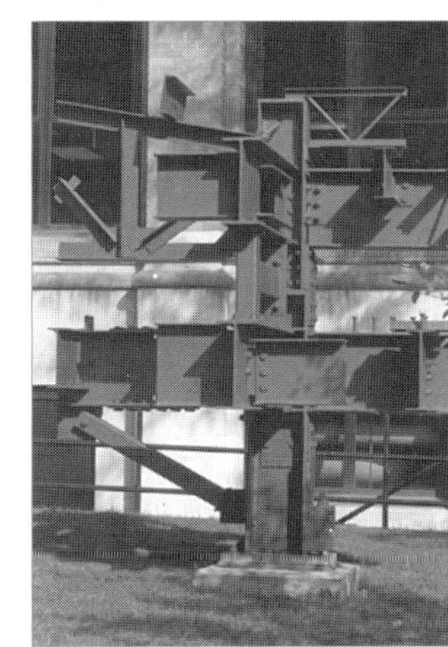

Teaching Sculpture at Marquette University

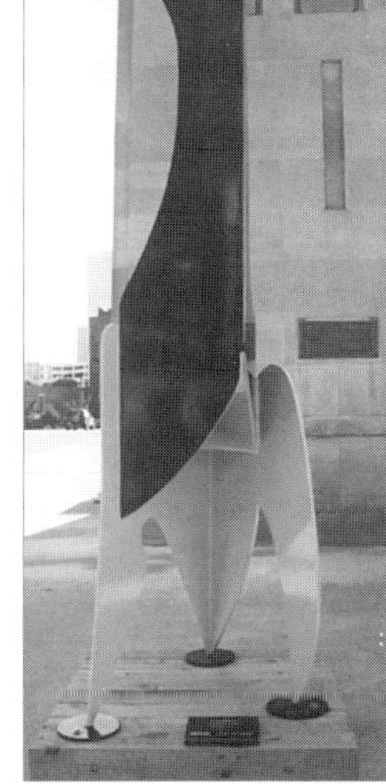

Cuculide at Riverwalk, Downtown

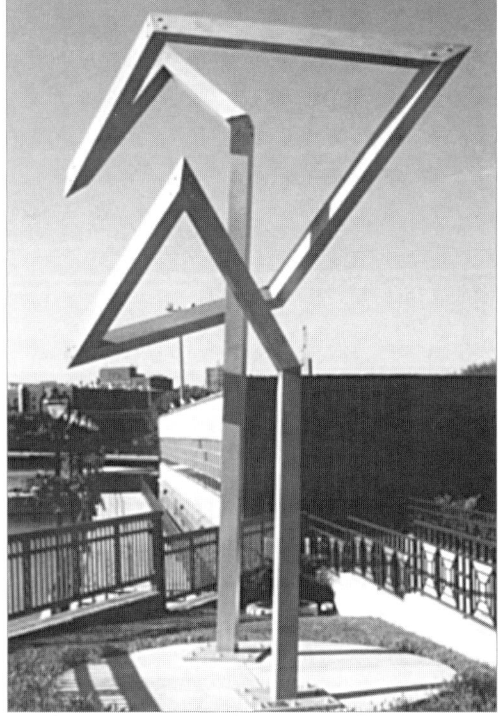

Epiphanic Recurve, Redux at Riverwalk, Downtown

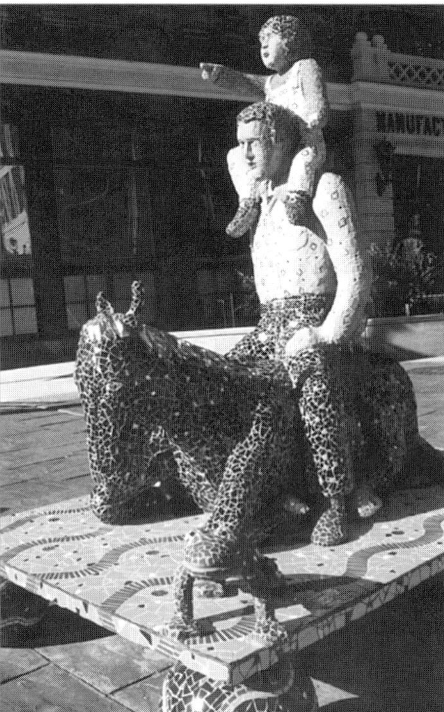

OK Ready for Zora at Riverwalk, Downtown

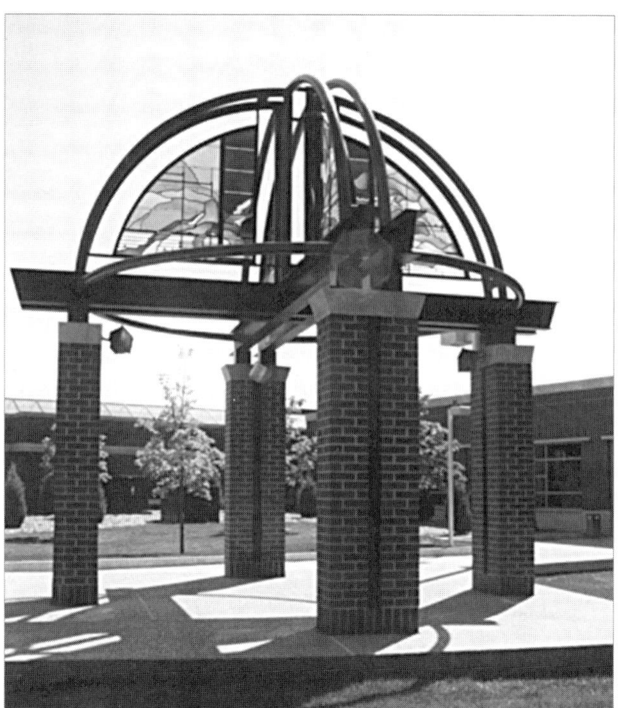

Double Crossed Arch at UW-Milwaukee, Northeast

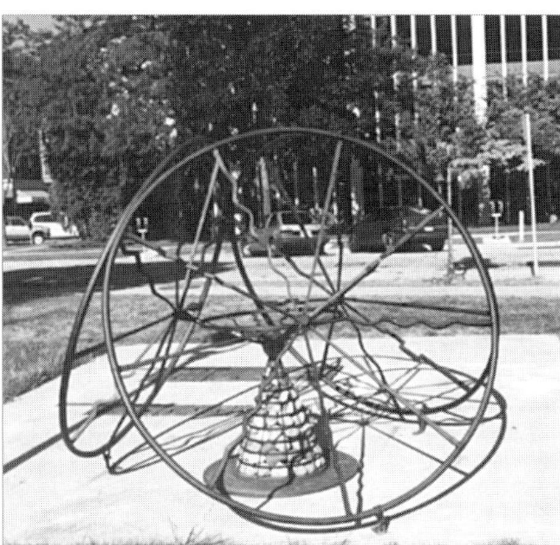

Island at Riverwalk, Downtown

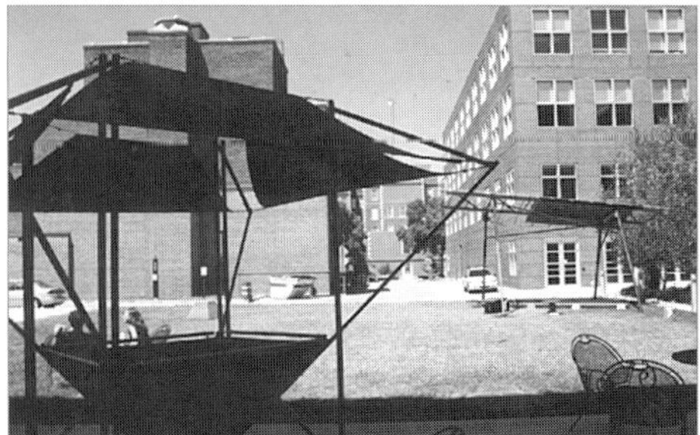

Grill (foreground) and *Gazebo* (far right)
at UW-Milwaukee, Northeast

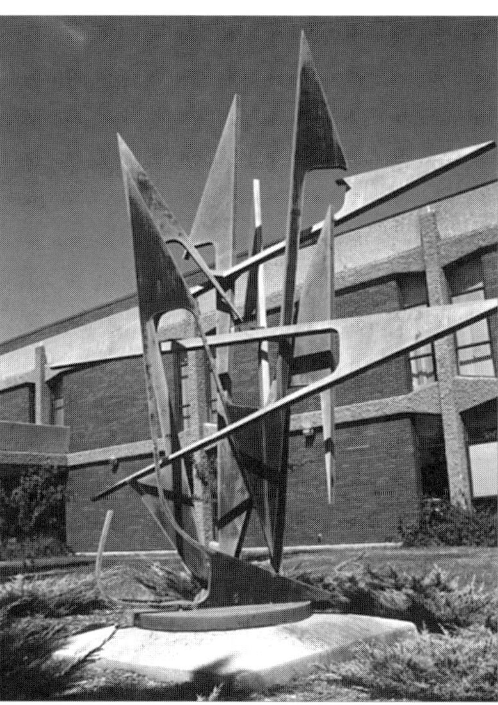

Polyphony at UW-Milwaukee, Northeast

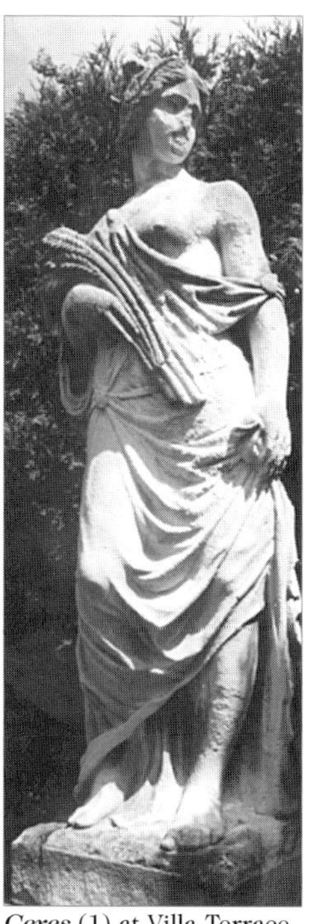

Ceres (1) at Villa Terrace,
Northeast

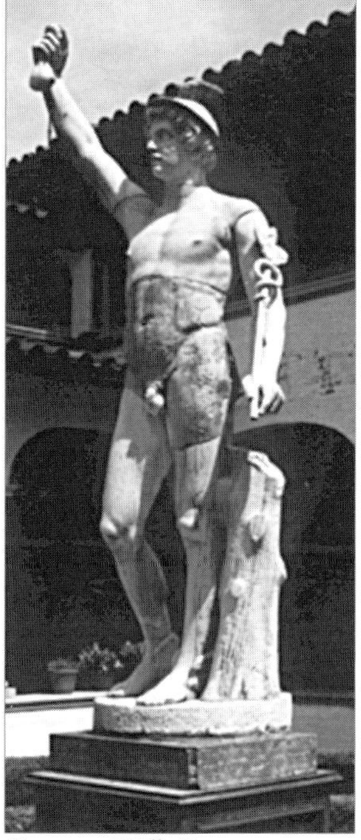

Hermes at Villa Terrace,
Northeast

Island
Peter Flanary
1995-1997
Steel, located at Riverwalk

Laureate
Seymour Lipton
1969
Nickel silver on Monel metal, located
behind the Performing Arts Center

OK Ready for Zora
Steve Feren
1988
Ceramic and concrete (removed)

Northeast Milwaukee

Celebrating the Arts
Narendra Patel
1989
Painted steel, located at Roosevelt
Middle School of the Arts, 800
W. Walnut Street

Flight (Atwater Park Fountain)
Paul J. Yank
1969
Steel, bronze and copper, located
at Atwater Beach Village Park,
Shorewood, 4000 N. Lake Drive

Henry Bergh
John H. Mahoney
1891
Bronze, located at the Wisconsin
Humane Society, 4151 N. Humboldt
Boulevard

In Celebration of the Arts
Narendra Patel
1989
Painted steel, located at Roosevelt
Middle School of the Arts, 800
W. Walnut Street

Sharing the Load
Daniel Leonhardt
Metal and stone, located across from
Woodland Pattern Book Center,
Locust Street

Three Dolphins and a Fountain
Franci Schoenfield
1965
Bronze, located at the Shorewood
Library, 2030 E. Shorewood
Boulevard in Shorewood

Lake Park NE

3233 E. Kenwood Boulevard

Eight Stone Lions
Paul Kupper
1897
Bedford limestone, located on Lake Park Walkway

General Erastus B. Wolcott
Francis Herman Packer
1919
Bronze, located near Lion Bridge, 3233 Elkenwood

Villa Terrace Museum of Decorative Arts NE

2220 North Terrace Avenue

Diana
Terra-cotta

Ceres (1) Goddess of Wheat
Stone, goddess of wheat in lower garden

Ceres (2) Goddess of Wheat
Stone, goddess of wheat in courtyard

Hermes
Marble, 1st century AD torso /rebuilt 17th century, located in the courtyard

UW-Milwaukee NE

Double Crossed Arch
Mixed media

Gazebo
Circa 1998
Mixed media, located behind the Architecture and Urban Planning Building, Maryland and Hartford

Grill
Circa 1998
Mixed media, located behind the Architecture and Urban Planning Building, Maryland and Hartford

Increase A. Lapham Memorial Tablet
Albert Henry Atkins
MCMXIV (1914)
Bronze set into boulder, located near UW-M at 3209 N. Maryland Avenue. Plaque has been removed from rock.

Milwaukee
George Mossman Greenamyer
1989
Painted steel, located at the Golda Meir Library, 2311 East Hartford Avenue

Mneme XXXI: Dwelling in the Plan
Carol Emmons and Paul Emmons
1993-1995
Cast iron part of larger work, located at the School of Architecture and Urban Planning, southwest corner of Hartford and Maryland. The primary location of the work is the building's interior four story central glassed corridor. Percent for Art commission.

Polyphony
Egon Weiner
1963
Bronze, located at the southwest corner of Maryland and Kenwood Boulevard

Tanto Mantor
Narendra Patel
Concrete

Three Bronze Disks
James Wines
1967
Bronze, located at the Golda Meir Library, 2311 E. Hartford Avenue

The Happy-Go-Luckies of Nature and Technology
Guido Brink
Dedicated October 23, 1992
Stainless Steel, located behind Lapham Hall, 3209 N. Maryland Avenue

Union Relief
O.V. Shaffer
1962 & 1970
Two poured-in-place concrete relief murals, located on side of Student Union

City of Fox Point NE

Folk Art Environment
Mary Nohl
1968-present
Embellished home with fantastic concrete sculptures, located at 7328 N. Beach Drive. Private, view from road only.

Whitefish Bay NE

Fallow Field
Kirsten Christianson
1980
Stone and wood, removed from original site at University School of Milwaukee to be rebuilt at new site in River Hills

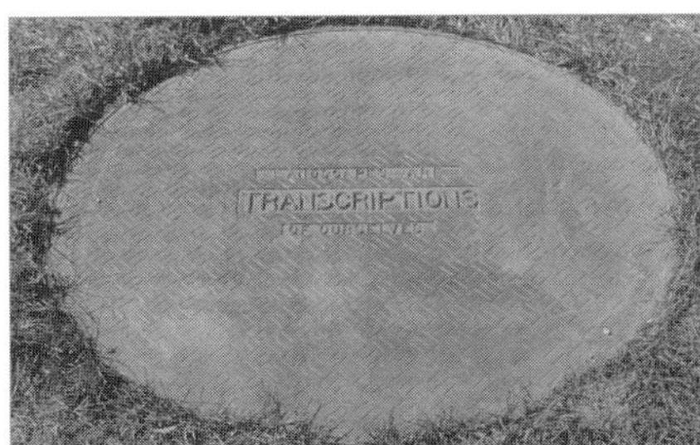

Mneme XXXI: Dwelling in the Plan (detail) at UW-Milwaukee, Northeast

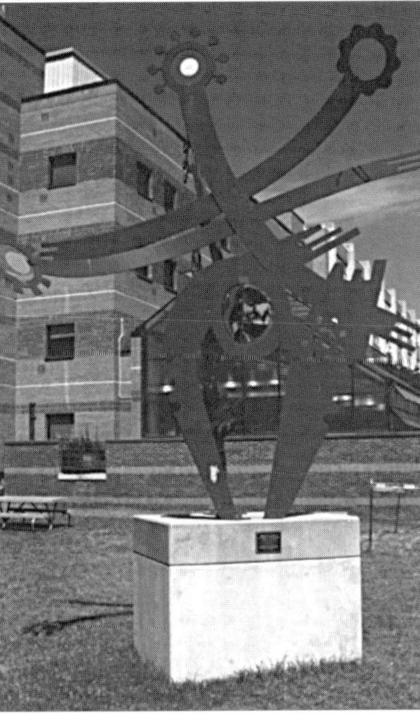

The Happy-Go-Luckies of Nature and Technology at UW-Milwaukee, Northeast

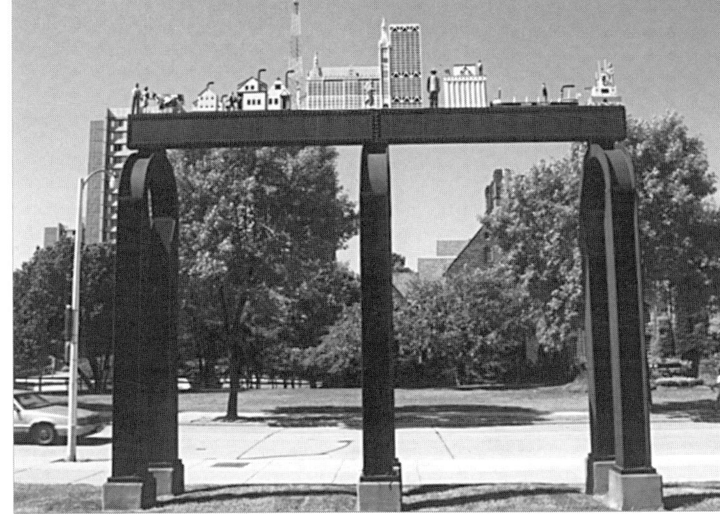

Milwaukee at UW-Milwaukee, Northeast

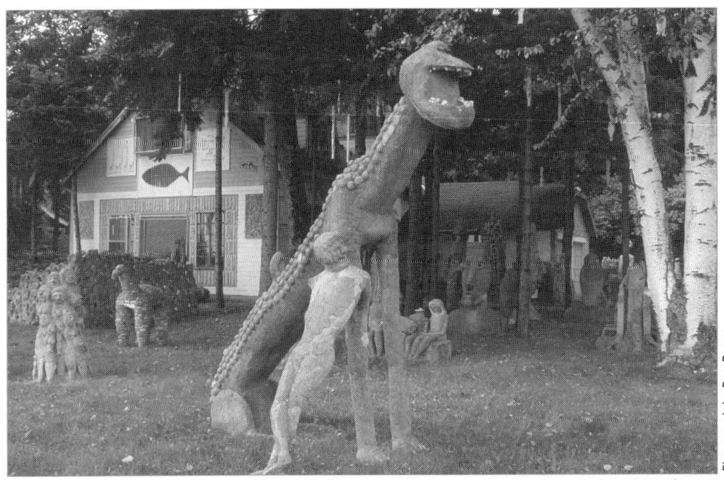

Photograph by Ron Byers

Folk Art Environment at Fox Point, Northeast

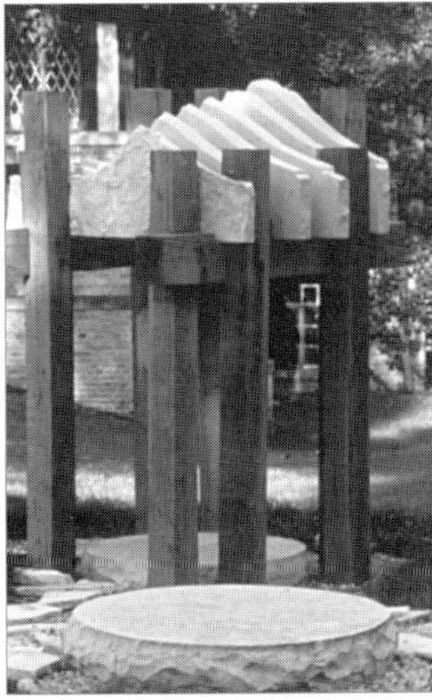

Fallow Field in Whitefish Bay, Northeast

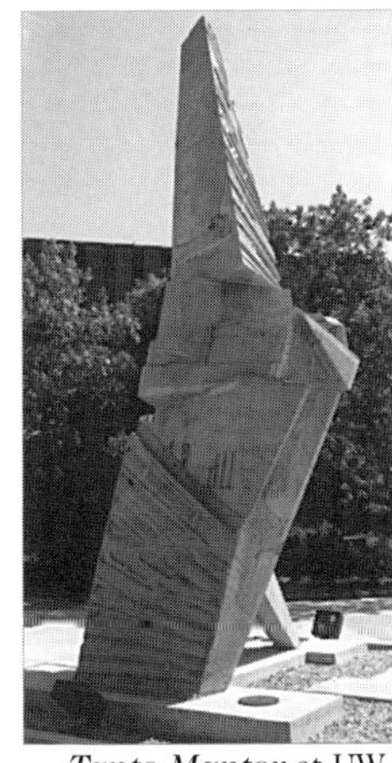

Tanto Mantor at UW-Milwaukee, Northeast

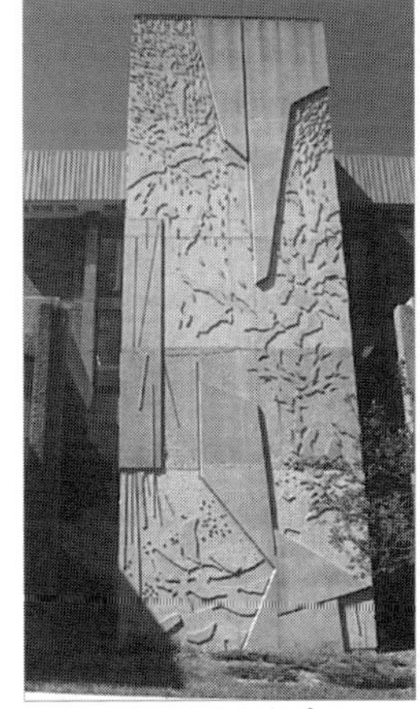

Union Relief at UW-Milwaukee, Northeast

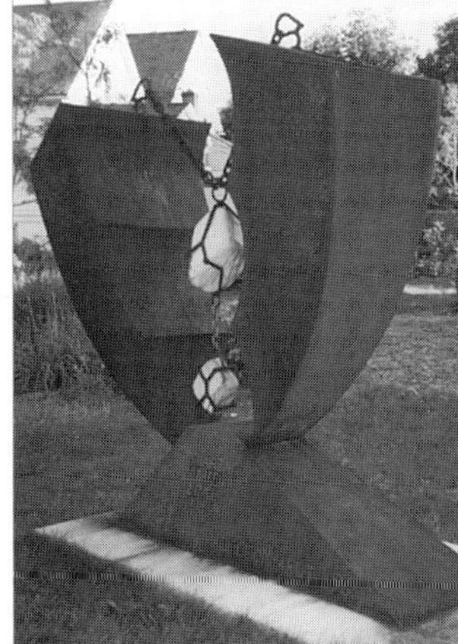

Sharing the Load, Northeast

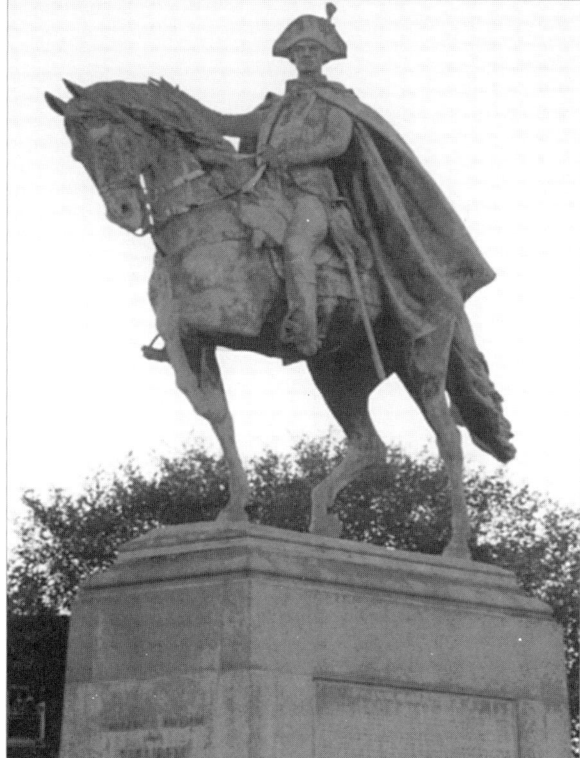

Baron Frederick Wilhelm von Steuben, Northwest

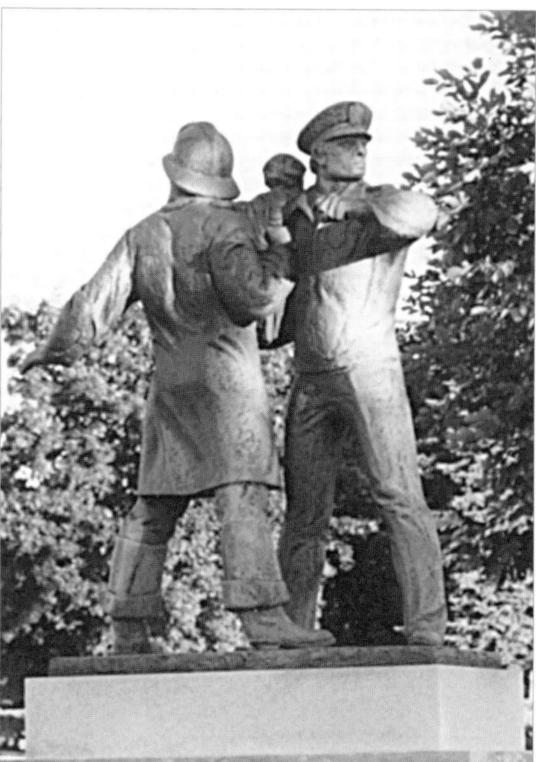

On Watch, Northwest

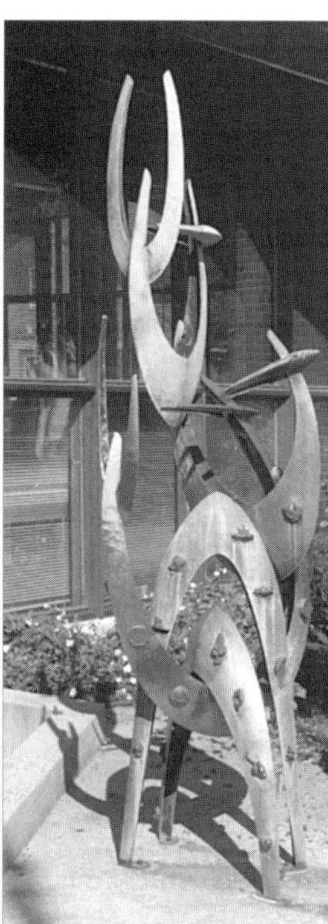

Four Freedoms, Northwest

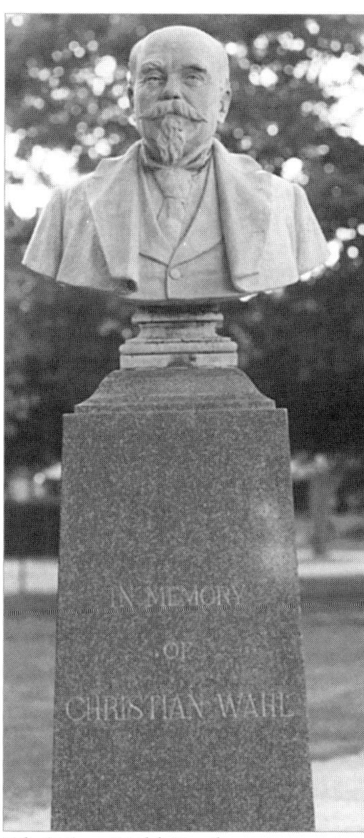

Christian Wahl, Northwest

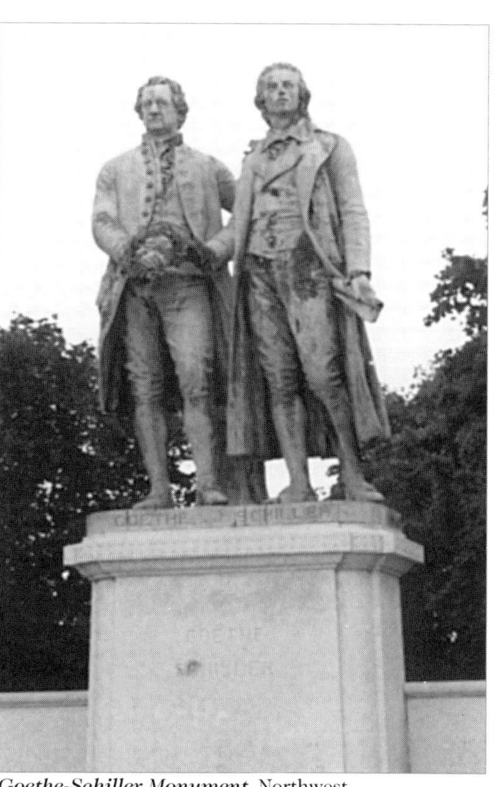

Goethe-Schiller Monument, Northwest

Northwest Milwaukee

Baron Frederick Wilhelm von Steuben
Jacob Otto Schweizer
1921
Bronze, located facing Washington Park on Sherman Boulevard and Lloyd Street

Brown Deer
James Gehr, attributed
Originally in stone, re-cast in bronze, located at Brown Deer Park, 7835 N. Green Bay Road north end of park

Buildings 1992
Susan Walsh
1992
Steel, located at Fire Engine No. 16 at 103rd and Fond du Lac streets

Christian Wahl
Gaetano Trentanove
1903
Bronze, located at Wahl Park, 4750 N. 47th Street and W. Hampton Avenue

Chrysalis
Beth Sahagian
1990
Limestone and bronze, located at the Marion Chester Read Girl Scout Center, 131 S. 69th Street

Dancers
Marceil Pultorak
1969
Bronze, located at the Mayfair Plaza, 2421 N. Mayfair Road

Dauntless Guardian
Jeune Nowak Wussow
1984
Bronze, located at Fire Engine No. 9, 4141 W. Mill Road

Elk
Paul Kupper, attributed
July 23, 1901
Zinc and natural antlers, located at Benevolent Protective Order of Elks, Milwaukee Lodge No. 46, 5555 W. Good Hope Road

Fish Eating Banquet Urn
V.J. Kocowrek
1908
Stone, located at Ronald McDonald House, 8948 Watertown Plank Road

Four Freedoms
Dick Wiken
1961
Bronze, located at the Atkinson Branch Library, 1960 W. Atkinson Avenue

Gear, 23
Steven Feren
1992
Concrete and ceramic mosaic, located at Fire Engine No. 4, 9511 W. Appleton

Goethe-Schiller Monument
Ernest Friedrich August Rietschel
1908 (original model 1847)
Bronze, located in Washington Park, 1859 N. 40th Street

Milwaukee, *Spirit of the Firefighter*
Mark Jeffries
1983
Bronze, located at Fire Engine No. 37, 5335 N. Teutonia Avenue

New Twist
Mark Overs
1978
Welded aluminum, located at the Finney Library, 4243 W. North Avenue

On Watch
David M. Wanner
1990
Bronze, located at Fire & Police Safety Academy, 6680 N. Teutonia Avenue

The Impossible Dream
Elmer L. Winter
1981
Welded automobile bumpers, 20 feet high, located at Manpower Temporary Services, 5301 N. Ironwood Road

United We Stand
Thomas Queoff
1991
Stainless steel, located at Froedtert Memorial Hospital, 9200 W. Wisconsin Avenue

City of Brookfield   NW

Ribbons
Stephen Fischer
1988
Painted steel, located at 3825 W. Burleigh

Unfolding Red
Guido Brink
1973
Metal, located at Brookfield Library, 1900 N. Calhoun Road

The Bradley Family Foundation Sculpture Garden NW

2145 W. Brown Deer Road, Milwaukee 53217, call for tour information 414-276-6840

Ancestor
Masayuki Nagare
1965
Black granite

Arch
Ernest C. Shaw
1976
Steel

Axletree
Alexander Liberman
1967
Steel-painted red

Bench-Stone
Masayuki Nagare
1964-65
Granite

Bremen Town Musicians
Gerhard Marcks
1951
Bronze

Campond Junior
Beverly Pepper
1970
Stainless steel

III Columns
Earnest C. Shaw
1976
Steel

Curve VI
Ellsworth Kelly
1974
Aluminum

Double Up
Clement Meadmore
1970
Corten steel

Embrace
Sorel Etrog
1966-67
Bronze

Epicenter I
Ernest C. Shaw
1976
Steel

Epicenter II
Ernest C. Shaw
1976
Steel

Flight
Arlie Sinaiko
1966
Bronze

Floating Sculpture No. 3
Marta Pan
1972
Red polyester

Knife Tree
Heinz Mack
1966
Chrome plated steel

Kumo
Isaac Witkin
1972
Corten Steel

Large Torso: Arch
Henry Moore
1962-63
Bronze

Lodgepole
Lyman Kipp
1968
Steel - painted red

Lover
Mark di Suvero
1971-73
Steel - painted red

Magic Stone 3, of Conversations with Magic Stones
Barbara Hepworth
1973
Bronze

Mo, Ni, Que
Samuel Buri
1971-76
Polyester/fiberglass

Olympus
Charles Ginnever
1976
Corten steel

Orbits
Alexander Liberman
1967
Steel - painted red

Orizzontale
Aldo Calo
1964
Bronze

Peristyle - Three Lines
George Rickey
1963-64
Stainless steel

Pin Oak I
John Henry
1976
Aluminum - painted yellow

Poland
Mark di Suvero
1966
Steel and wire

Queen of Sheba
Alexander Archipenko
1961
Bronze

Rainbow
Duayne Hatchett
1970
Aluminum and deep blue enamel

Rhythm in Space
Max Bill
1967
Black diorite

Ritual II
Alexander Liberman
1966
Steel - painted black

Round About
Linda Howard
1976
Aluminum

Salem N. 7
Antoni Milkowski
1967
Corten steel

Sara
Barney Bright
1967
Bronze

Sea Form (Atlantic)
Barbara Hepworth
1964
Marble

Sinai
Isamu Noguchi
1966
Iron

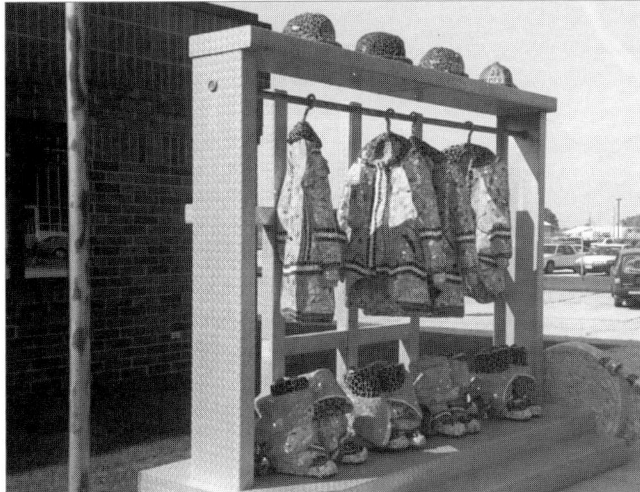

Gear, 23 at Engine No. 4, Northwest

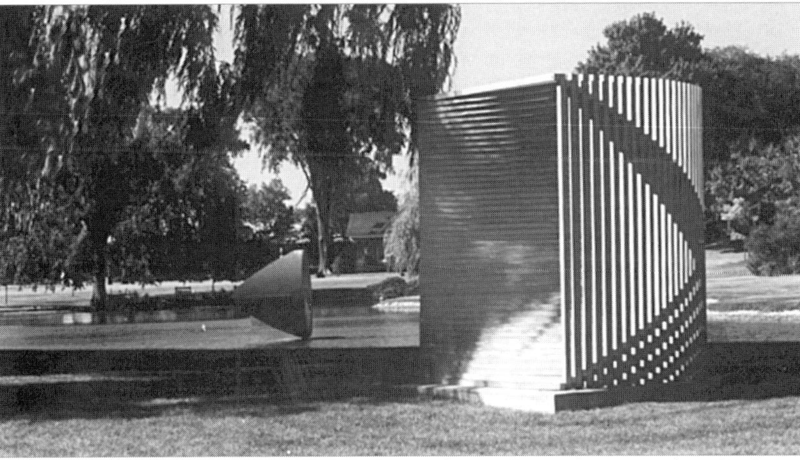

Round About at The Bradley Sculpture Garden, Northwest

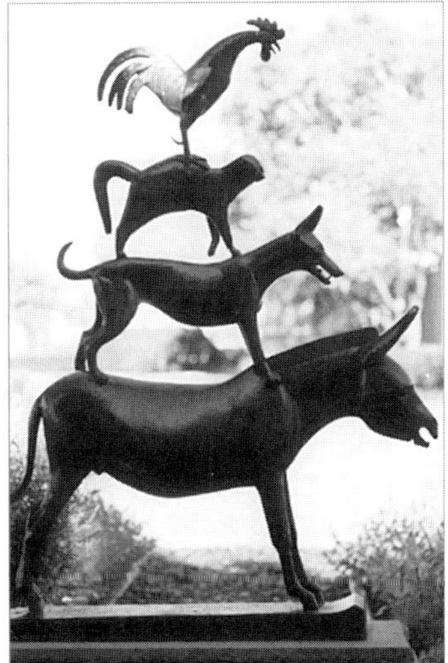

Bremen Town Musicians at The Bradley Sculpture Garden, Northwest

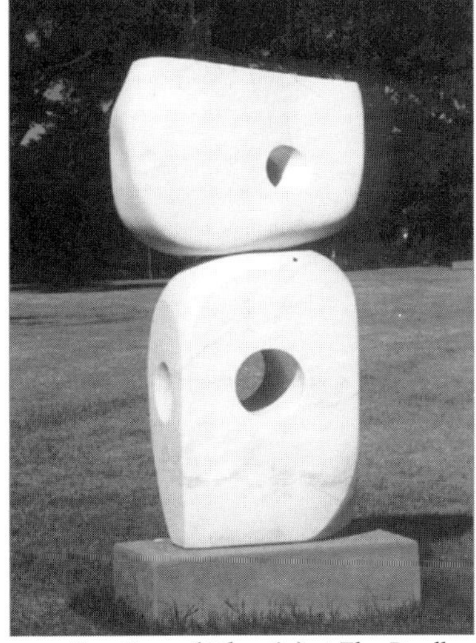

Sea Form (Atlantic) at The Bradley Sculpture Garden, Northwest

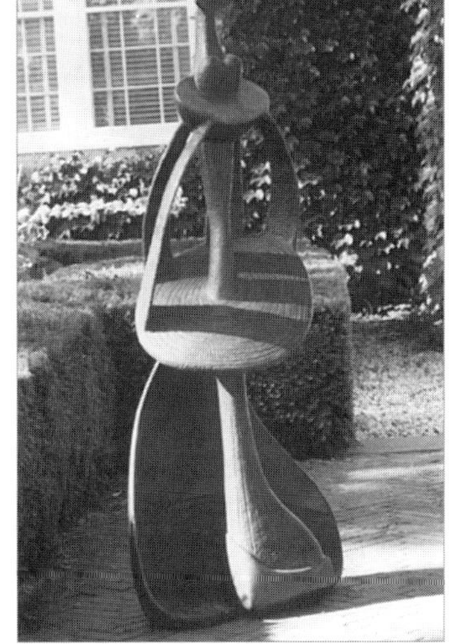

Queen of Sheba at The Bradley Sculpture Garden, Northwest

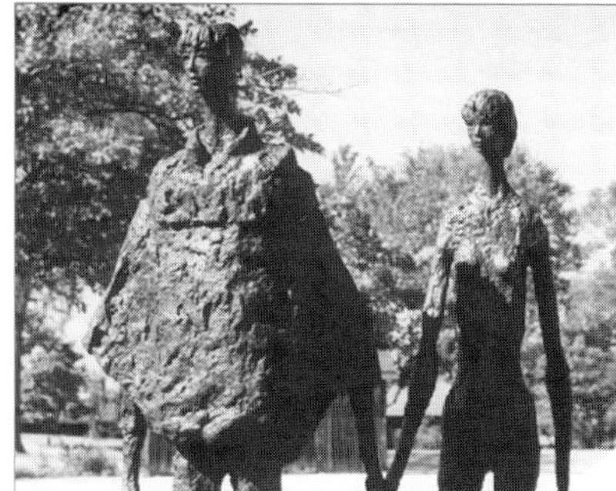

The Lovers at The Bradley Sculpture Garden, Northwest

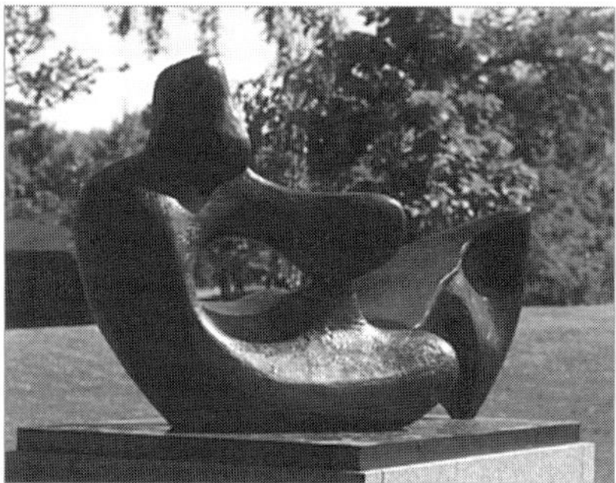

Two Piece Reclining Figure Number 9 at The Bradley Sculpture Garden, Northwest

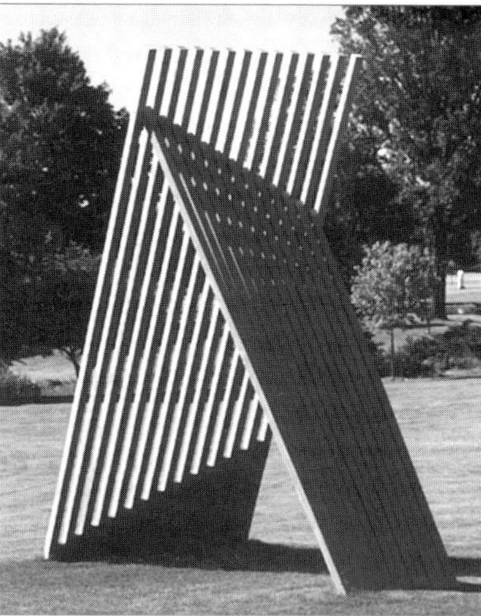

Sky Fence at The Bradley Sculpture Garden, Northwest

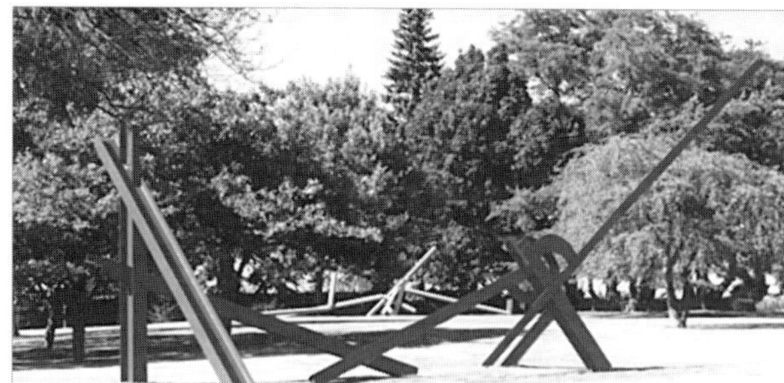

Windfall at The Bradley Sculpture Garden, Northwest

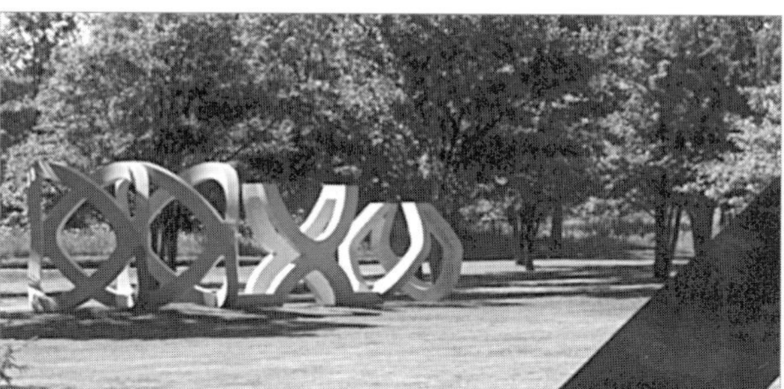

Trio at The Bradley Sculpture Garden, Northwest

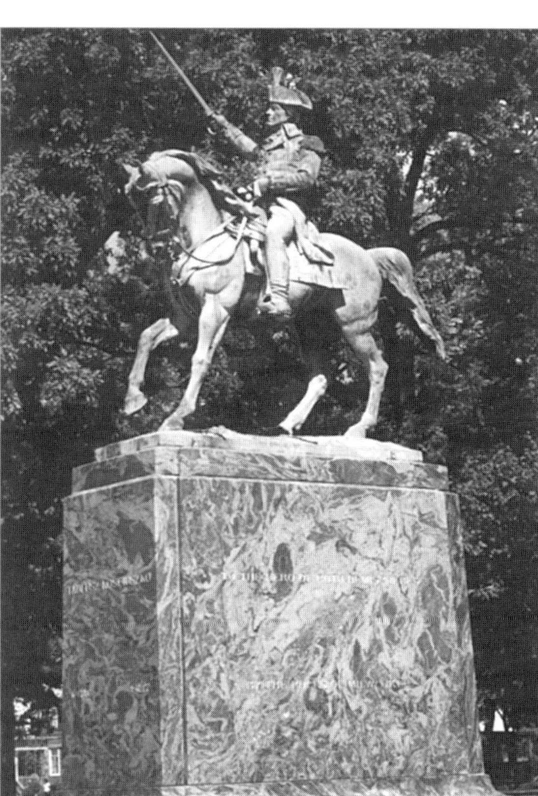

Thaddeus Kosciuszko, Southwest

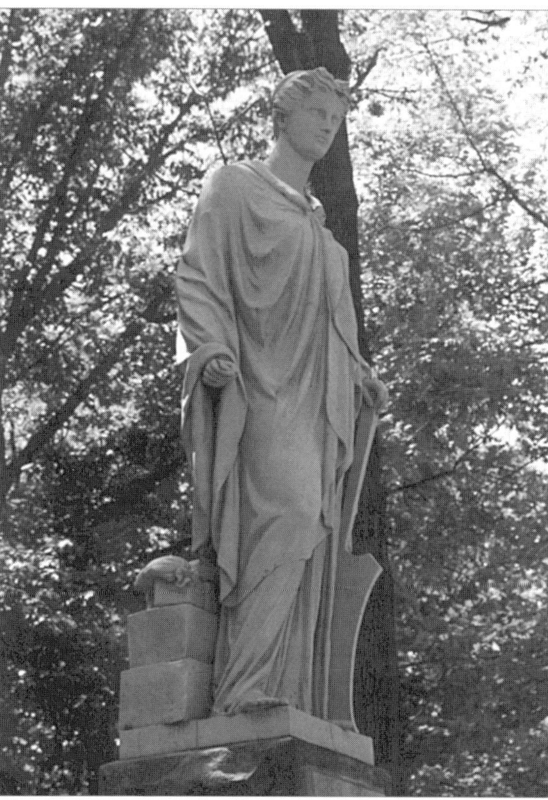

Spirit of Commerce, Southwest

Sky Fence
Linda Howard
1976
Aluminum

Tensione
Aldo Calo
1962
Bronze

The Lovers
Lindsey Daen
1964
Bronze

The Source
Sorel Etrog
1964
Bronze

The Three Graces: Thalia, Aglaia, and Euphrosyne
Heinz Mack
1965
Polished stainless steel

The Wandering Rocks: Crocus, Dud, Shaft, and Smohawk
Tony Smith
1969
Mild steel

Two Piece Reclining Figure No. 9
Henry Moore
1967
Bronze

Twist for Max
Bernard Kirschenbaum
1974
Anodized aluminum

Trio
George Sugarman
1972-73
Aluminum - painted yellow

Ursa Major
William Underhill
1966
Corten steel

Upstart
Clement Meadmore
1967
Corten steel

Untitled
James Rosati
1975-76
Corten steel

Unfolding
Bernhard Heiliger
1968
Bronze

Vegetative Sculpture I
Bernhard Heiliger
1959
Bronze

Way Four
Bernard Kirschenbaum
1976
Stainless steel

Windfall
Robert Murray
1966
Aluminum - painted red

City of Wauwatosa NW

Hippocrates
Menelaos Katafiglotis
Dedicated 1991
Pentelino marble, located at Medical College of Wisconsin, 8701 N. 87th Street

Ideal Boy Scout
Robert Tait McKenzie
1937 original, copy in 1985
Bronze, located at the Walter and Olive Steimke Boy Scout Service Center, 330 S. 84th Street

Joy
Marciel V. Pultorak
1968
Welded sheet bronze, located at Mayfair Plaza Building, 2421 N. Mayfair Road

Herman's Dilemma
Mark Overs
1979
Forged and welded steel, located in front of Gammex building, 9722 Watertown Plank Road

Southwest Milwaukee

History of Malting and Brewing Reliefs
Dick Wiken
1951
Bedford limestone, located at Froedtert Malt Corporation, 3830 W. Grant Street

Spirit of Commerce
Gustav Haug
1881 executed - 1901 dedicated
Cast zinc, located at Jackson Park, W. Forest Home Avenue at S. 38th Street
One of the first pieces of public sculpture in Wisconsin

The Hiker Monument
Ferdinand Koenig
Dedicated 1941
Bronze, (a copy of the Spanish-American War Soldier), located at Clement J. Zablocki Medical Center, intersection of Mitchell and Hines streets

The Sower
The Reaper
Bird and Fish
Gustav Bohland
1952
Bronze, three pieces located together at Froedtert Malt Corporation, 3830 W. Grant Street

Thaddeus Kosciuszko
Gaetano Trentanove
1905
Bronze, located at S. 9th Place and W. Lincoln Avenue

Two Opposites Reaching Up Toward the Peak of Progress
Tom Queoff
1977
Wausau ruby red granite, located on the median of S. Layton Boulevard, between Greenfield Avenue and Orchard Street

'Untitled' Red and Blue Abstraction
Narendra Patel
1992
Painted steel pair of sculptures, located at the 6th District Police Station, 3006 S. 27th Street

Walls of Flame
John Luthropp
1988
Brick, plexiglass, neon, located at Fire Engine No. 25, 300 S. 84th Street

Emmpak Foods Inc.   SW
Division of Peck Foods
1515 W. Canal Street

Angel in a Cage
Richard Pflieger
1987
Metal, polyester resin and fiberglass

Menomonee
Hilary Goldblatt
1985
Corten steel

Opps, Missed!
Bernard Peck
1987
Stainless steel lightning rod and brick wall

Space Game
Joseph Mendla
1971
Painted and welded steel

Stone Monolith
Stone

Untitled
Gene Galazan
1980
Corten steel, removed from the site

City of Greendale   SW

Greendale Flagpole Base
Alonzo Hauser
1938
Carved limestone, located at 6600 block of Schoolway and Parking Street

West Allis   SW

Deflected Jets
Guido Brink
1988
Stainless steel, located at Fire Engine No. 29, 3529 S. 84th Street

Man Truly Unchained and Unshackled
George Adams Deitrich
1963
Metal, located at the Zablocki Library, 3501 W. Oklahoma Avenue

The Family (Abstract)
Joseph Puccetti
1982
Stainless steel, located at the West Allis City Hall, 7225 W. Greenfield

The Pieta
Dedicated circa 1958
Painted stone, located at St. Joseph's Home for the Aged, 5301 W. Lincoln Avenue

Two Dogs
Salvatore Albano
Dedicated 1878
Austrian marble, located at 6301 W. Lincoln Avenue

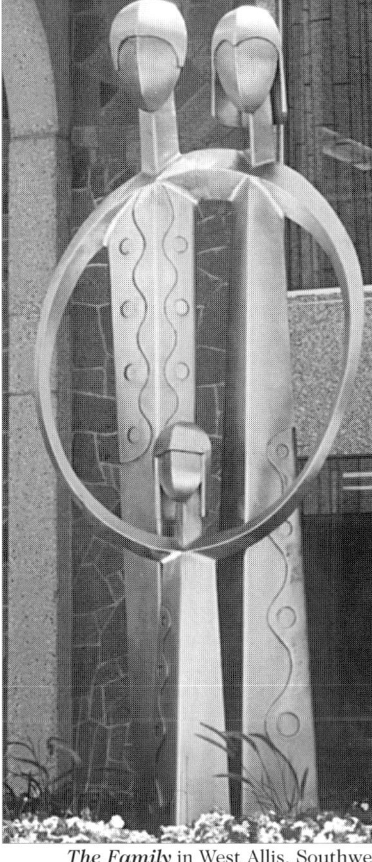

The Family in West Allis, Southwest

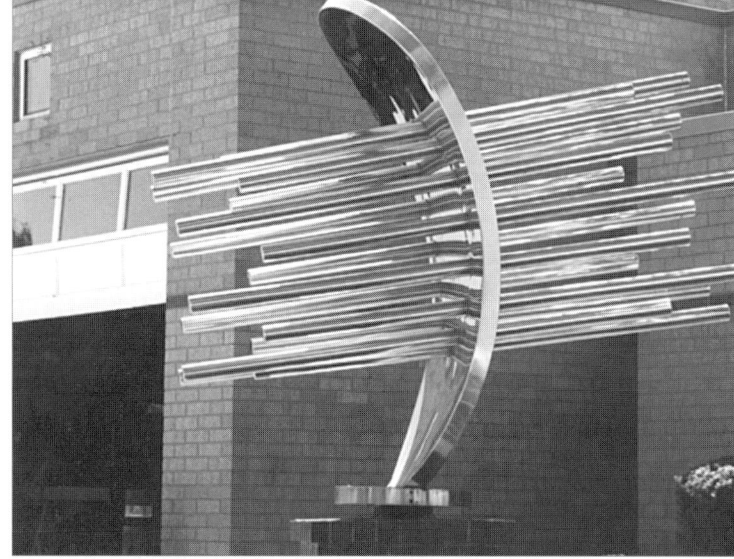

Deflected Jets in West Allis, Southwest

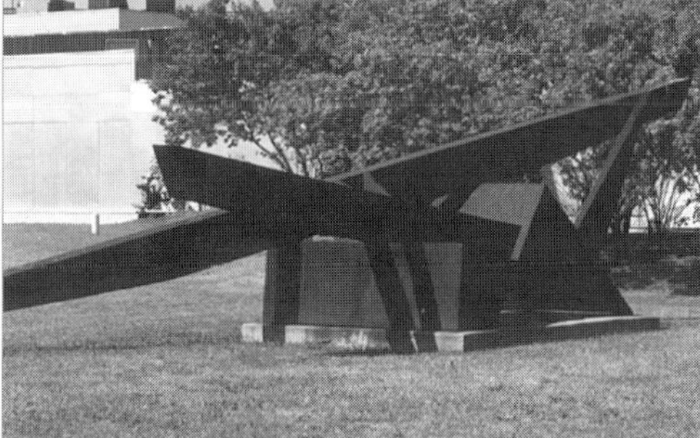

Menomonee at Emmpak, Southwest

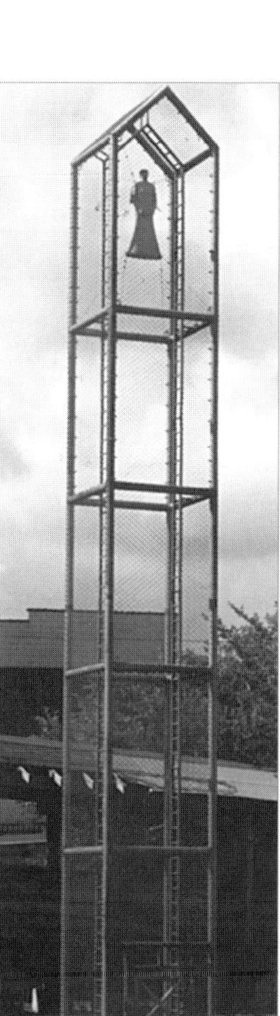

Angel in a Cage at Emmpak, Southwest

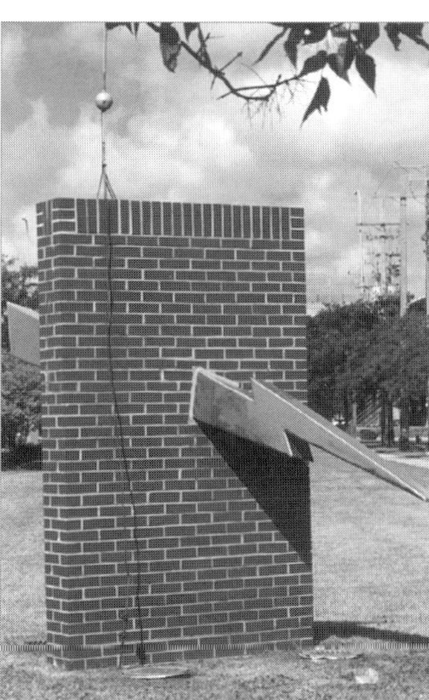

Opps, Missed at Emmpak, Southwest

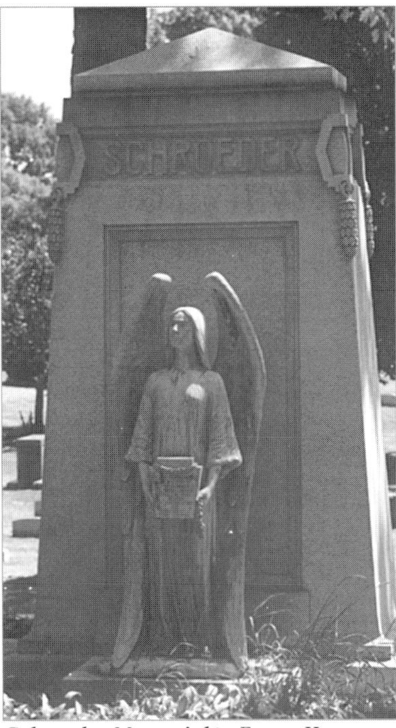

Schoreder Memorial in Forest Home, Southwest

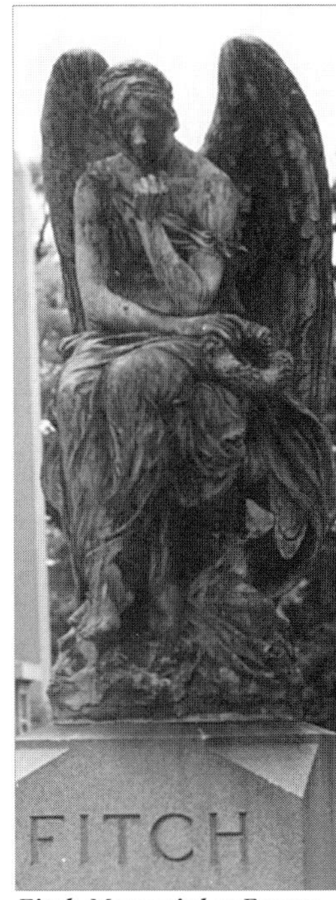

Fitch Memorial at Forest Home, Southwest

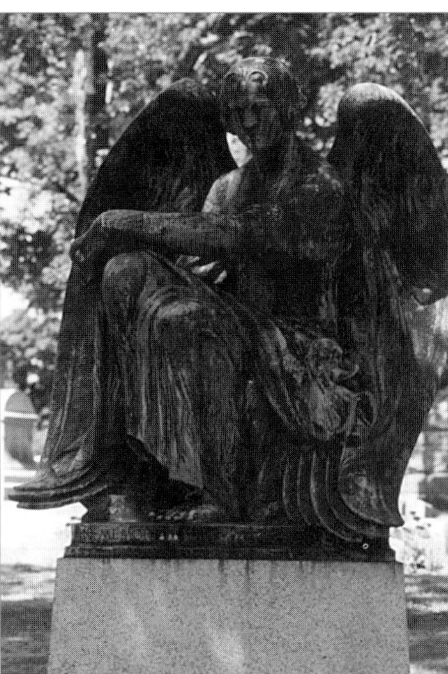

William A. Starke Memorial in Forest Home, Southwest

Forest Home Cemetery   SW

2405 W. Forest Home Avenue and Lincoln Street

Fitch Memorial
Bronze

Schoreder Memorial
Bronze and stone

T. A. Chapman Memorial
Daniel Chester French
1896
Bronze, Section No. 33

William A. Starke Memorial
Robert Ingersoll Aitken
1921
Bronze seated angel, Section No. 33

Hales Corners   SW
Boerner Botanical Gardens

5879 S. 92 Street, sculptures were created as part of Wisconsin's WPA projects, 1930s. For further information call 414-425-1130.

Boy
Girl
Jefferson Greer
1936-1937
Stone, *Garden Statuary*

Mother and Two Sons
George Adams Dietrich
1936
Stone, *Reflecting Pool Statuary*

Pelican
Stone

Sundial Base
Stone

Wooden Animals
Karl Kahlich

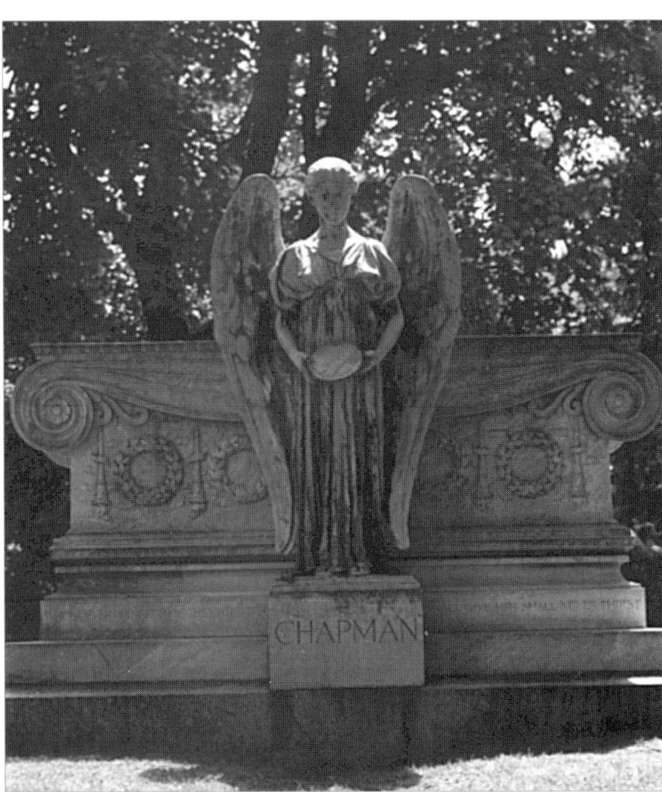

T. A. Chapman Memorial in Forest Home, Southwest

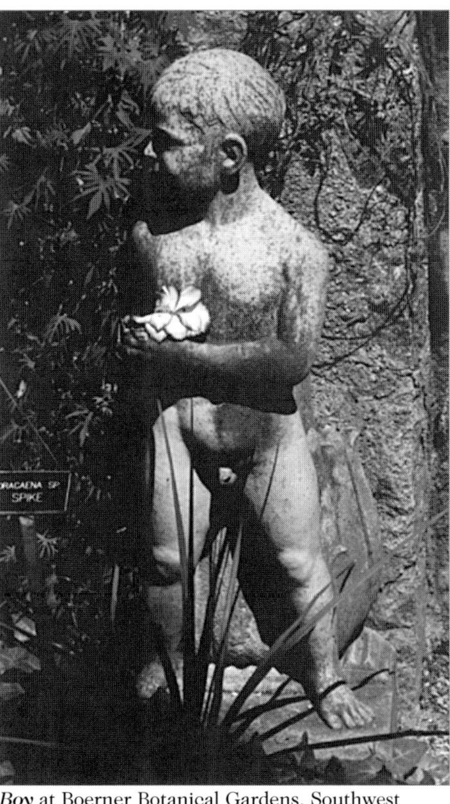

Boy at Boerner Botanical Gardens, Southwest

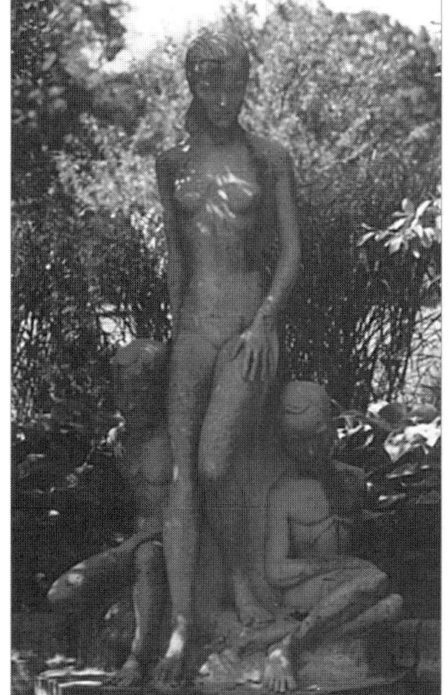

Mother and Two Sons at Boerner Botanical Gardens, Southwest

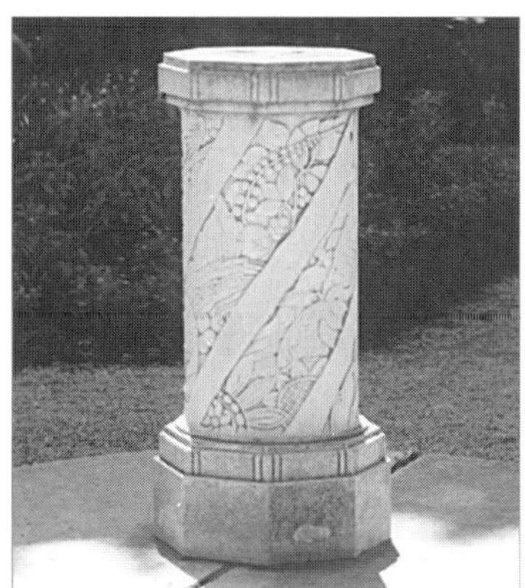

Sundial Base at Boerner Botanical Gardens, Southwest

Southeast Milwaukee

Bay View War Veterans of WWII
Stone with bronze eagle, located at triangle intersection of Kinnikinnic, Russell Avenue and Logan Avenue

Count Casimir Pulaski
Joseph Kisielewski
1931
Bronze, located at intersection of S. 16th, W. Harrison and W. Windlake Avenue

Engine No. 10
Bronze, located at the old Fire Engine No. 10 on Broadway between Chicago and Menomonee

Lourdes Grotto
Father Dobberstein (attributed)
Mixed media, located at St. Francis Seminary, 3257 S. Lake Drive

Man Helping Man
P. Richard Szeitz
1975
Copper, located at DePaul Hospital, 4143 S. 13th Street

Memorial for Belle Austin Jacobs (Girl with Squirrel)
Sylvia Shaw Judson
1931
Bronze, previously located in Kosciusko Park, S. 9th and W. Lincoln, it was stolen in 1980

Milwaukee World Festivals Fountain

Jeune Nowak Wussow

1982

Three bronze panels in a fountain, located at main entrance to Summerfest grounds, 200 N. Harbor Drive

Bay View Series

Peter Flanary

1993

Iron ore, boulders, and trees (all with inscribed text), located around the Bayview Public Library, 2566 Kinnickinnic Avenue

Steel Reborn

Charles Toman

1965

Welded steel ball atop a 30 foot steel pillar, located at Miller Compressing Company, 1000 E. Bay Street at Harbor Drive

R.D. Whitehead Monument

Whitehead Animal Friends Memorial Fountain

Sigvald Asbjornsen

1910

Grey granite and bronze relief, located at the triangle of S. 16th, W. Bow and S. Pearl streets

Tera

Kristine N. Rippel

1998

Metal and dirt, located at Catalono Square, corner of Erie and Milwaukee streets. Temporary exhibit area used by Milwaukee Institute of Art and Design (MIAD).

City of Cudahy   SE

Bust of Casimir Pulaski

Joseph Aszklar

Dedicated 1932

Metal, located facing east towards corner of S. Swift Avenue and Mallory Avenue

Patrick Cudahy

Felix George Weihs de Weldon

1965

Bronze, located at Sheridan Park on E. Layton Ave at S. Lake Drive

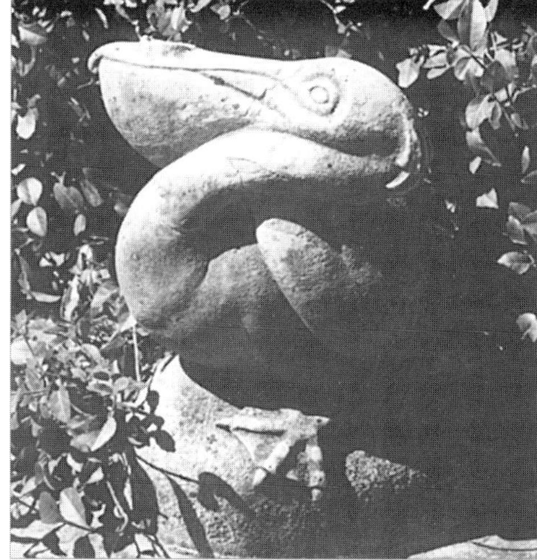

Pelican at Boerner Botanical Gardens, Southwest

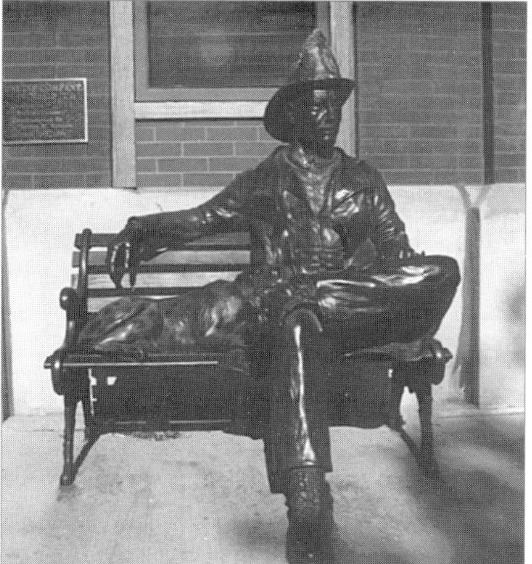

Engine No. 10, Southeast

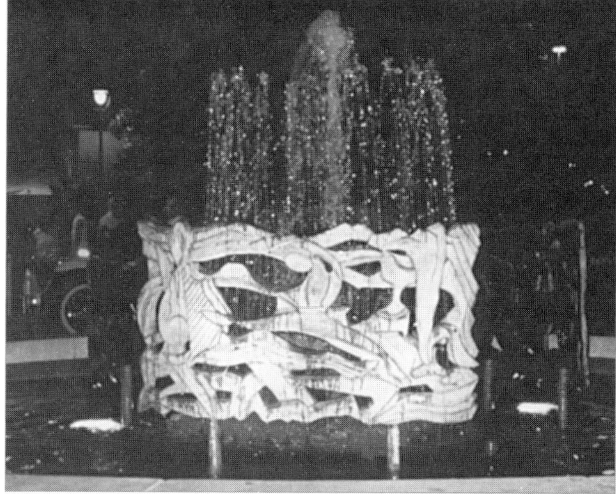

Milwaukee World Festivals Fountain, Southeast

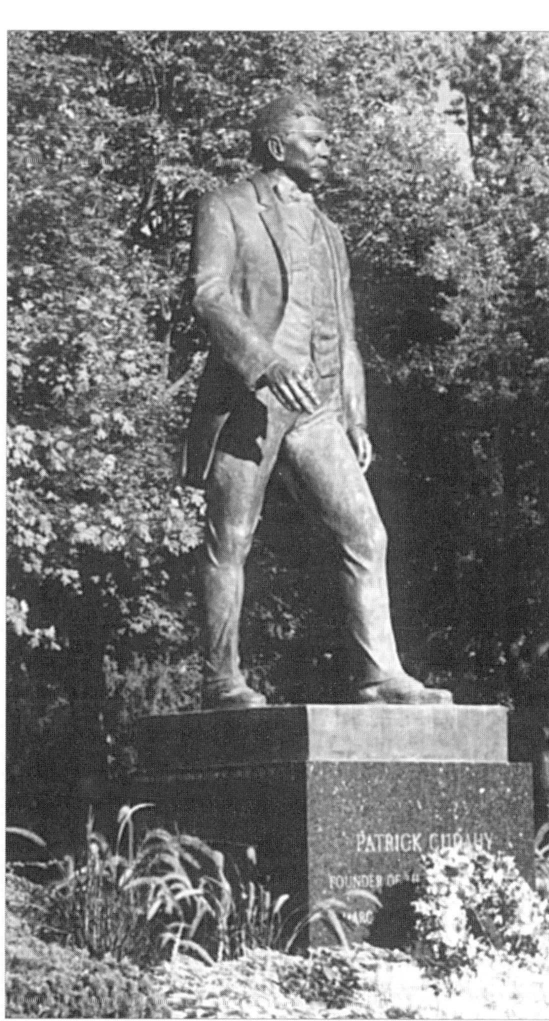

Patrick Cudahy in Cudahy, Southeast

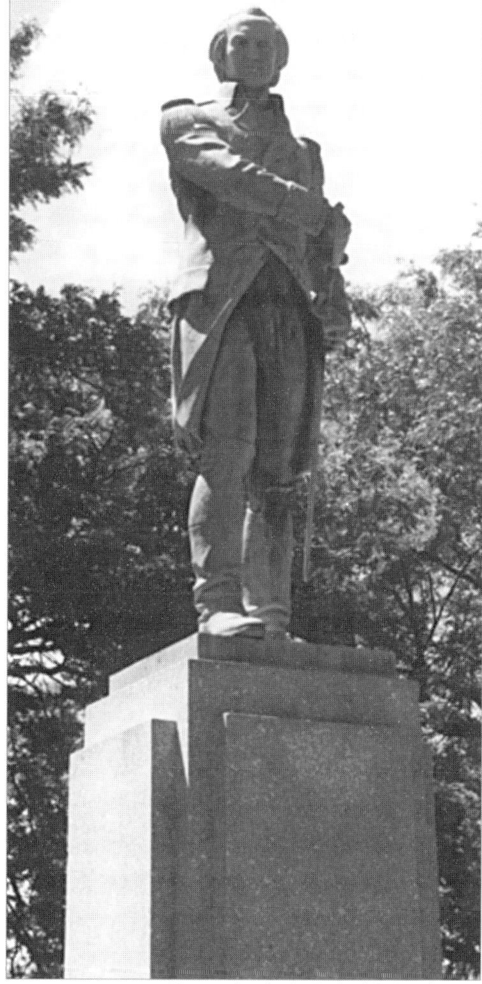

Count Casimir Pulaski, Southeast

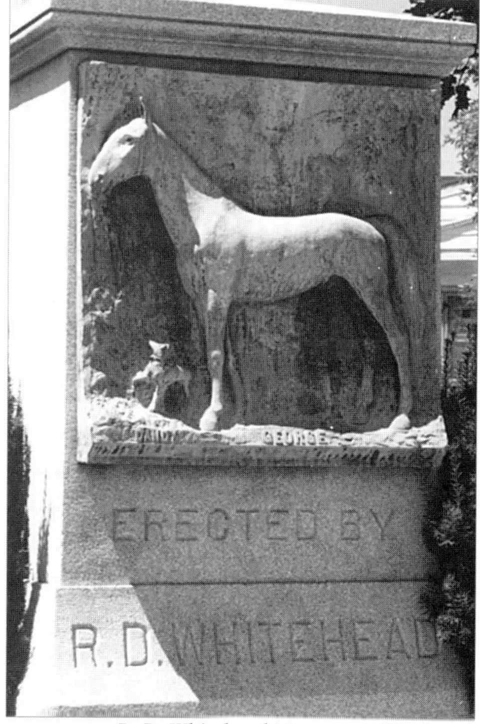

R. D. Whitehead Monument, Southeast

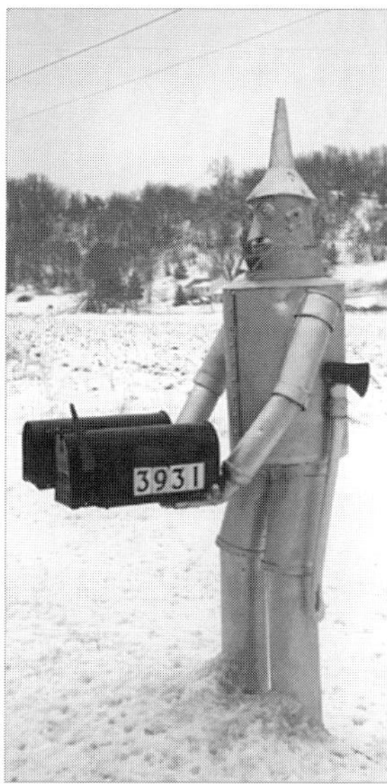

Tin Man by Wally Keller in Black Earth, Dane County

Veterans Memorials and Monuments are numerous and located throughout the state making a full index listing difficult. They will best be located by looking in the inventory or by city name in Index A.

Fire Enginehouse Sculptures in Milwaukee:

Engine #2	*Last Alarm* bronze at 711 W. Wells, 45, 139	
Engine #4	*Gear, 23* by Steve Feren at 9511 W. Appleton, 45, 144	
Engine #9	*Dauntless Guardian* by Jeune Nowak Wussow at 4141 W. Mill Road, 144	
Engine #16	*Buildings 1992*, by Susan Walsh at 103rd and Fond du Lac, 144	
Engine #25	*Walls of Flame* by John Luthropp on 84th Street, 147	
Engine #29	*Deflected Jets* by Guido Brink, 1988, at 3529 S. 84th Street, 147	
Engine #37	*Milwaukee, Sprirt of the Firefighter* by Mark Jeffries at 5335 N. Teutonia Avenue, 144	
Fire & Police Acedemy	*On Watch* by David Wanner at 6680 N. Teutonia Aveune, 144	
Old Engine # 10	*Engine #10*, bronze on Broadway between Chicago and Memomonee, 148	

Authors' Biographies

Anton (Tony) Rajer is a native of Sheboygan, Wisconsin where he worked at the Kohler Arts Center for years. Academically, he completed his undergraduate work in art history at the University of Wisconsin-Milwaukee with additional studies at the Sorbonne in Paris, France. He completed graduate work in art conservation at Harvard University, Straus Center for Art Conservation and as a UNESCO fellow at Centro Churubusco in Mexico City and the University of London. He received additional training at ICCROM-Rome under the auspices of the Kress Foundation. He has taught extensively in the field as a Fulbright scholar throughout Latin America, specializing in collections care, documentation of cultural property, and folk art. He was State Capitol conservator in Madison for five years and for the past seven years has been associated with SOS! Save Outdoor Sculpture a joint project of the Smithsonian Institution and Heritage Preservation. He teaches part time at the University of Wisconsin-Madison and works as a museum consultant.

Christine Style is Assistant Professor in Communication Arts at the University of Wisconsin-Green Bay. She received her Bachelors of Science degree in art from the University of Wisconsin-Madison in 1974, and her Masters in Fine Arts degree in printmaking from the University of Wisconsin-Milwaukee in 1986. From 1987-93 she was assistant to the Curator of Art at the University of Wisconsin-Green Bay and in addition taught printmaking, drawing, design, graphics and arts management. She has taught printmaking for eight years during the summer at the Peninsula Art School in Door County, Wisconsin. She is president of the Milwaukee Art Museum Print Forum and has an extensive exhibition record and graphic design experience. Style has worked in collaboration with Rajer on SOS! and this project as well as the Rudy Rotter Spirit-Driven Art book (1998) and they co-teach the Arts Italy travel course through the University of Wisconsin-Green Bay.

SPANISH SUMMARY

Spanish Abstract For Public Sculpture in Wisconsin
MONUMENTOS DE ARTE PUBLICO EN EL ESTADO DE WISCONSIN

Este libro es un documento que contiene la recopilación de mas de 700 obras de arte de escultura exhibidos en espacios publicos del estado de Wisconsin. Esta recopilación se realizó bajo una beca de investigación de la Institución Smithsonian, y Heritage Preservation a traves de vareis organizaciones del estado de Wisconsin como el Arts Board, Veterans Museum, y University of Wisconsin durante 7 años. La intención de este proyecto es dar a conocer el patrimonio cultural de monumentos de arte en el estado y fomentar un programa de restauración de estos monumentos, trabajando con el pueblo para revalorizar este patrimonio. El libro contiene varios capitulos, teniendo como puntos importantes: la história de monumentos de la guerra en el estado, proyectos gobernmentales de arte, obras patrocinado por entes privados. El arte folklorico de la iglesia, gente auto-didactico y sobre todo el como mantener escultura en el clima de Wisconsin. Este libro fue escrito para el aniversario del estado, 150 años de unión con el Estados Unidos. (1848-1998)